Reports on
India's Tax Reforms

Published in 2003 by

ACADEMIC FOUNDATION
4772-73 / 23 Bharat Ram Road,
(23 Ansari Road), Darya Ganj,
New Delhi - 110 002.

Phones : 23245001, 02, 03, 04.

Fax : 011-23245005

e-mail : academic@vsnl.com

www : academicfoundation.com

Reports on India's Tax Reforms
(Book + CD-ROM)
ISBN 81-7188-294-3

Laser-Typeset at AF's DTP Division.
Printed at Jeetendra Art Press, Delhi.

Contents

From the Publisher. 7

Using the CD-ROM. 11

- ***Report of the Task Force on Direct Taxes*** *(The Complete Report)*
  Chairman : Vijay L. Kelkar
  (Ministry of Finance and Company Affairs, Govt. of India)
  DECEMBER 27, 2002 13

- ***Report of the Task Force on Indirect Taxes*** *(The Complete Report)*
  Chairman : Vijay L. Kelkar
  (Ministry of Finance and Company Affairs, Govt. of India)
  DECEMBER 26, 2002 255

- ***Report of the Advisory Group on Tax Planning and Tax Administration for the Tenth Plan*** *(The Complete Report)*
  Chairman : Parthasarathy Shome
  (Planning Commission, Govt. of India)
  MAY, 2001 523

- *Report of the Tax Reforms Committee-I*
  (1992) ; Summary
  Chairman : Raja J. Chelliah *561*

- *Report of the Tax Reforms Committee-II*
  (1993) ; Summary
  Chairman : Raja J. Chelliah *587*

- *Consultation Papers :*
  Task Force on Direct Taxes and
  Indirect Taxes *(Full Text on CD-ROM)*
  Chairman : Vijay L. Kelkar
  (Ministry of Finance and Company Affairs, Govt. of India)
  NOVEMBER 2, 2002 .... *CD-ROM*

- *Indian Public Finance Statistics :*
  2001-02 *(Complete on CD-ROM)*
  (Ministry of Finance, Govt. of India)
  JUNE, 2002 .... *CD-ROM*

From the Publisher...

THE process of fiscal reforms was initiated alongwith the programme of economic reforms and liberalization in 1991. A committee on India's Tax Reforms was set up under the Chairmanship of Raja J. Chelliah. The Committee submitted its reports in 1992 and 1993 and made some bold recommendations. Accordingly, beginning with 1992-93, various reforms were introduced in successive budgets by different finance ministers : Manmohan Singh, P. Chidambaram and Yashwant Sinha.

It would not be wrong to say that India is currently facing a mix of complex fiscal problems pertaining to central government as well as state governments. In July 2000, the Planning Commission set up an Advisory Group under the chairmanship of Parthasarathy Shome to study Tax Policy and Tax Administration and make appropriate recommendations for generating adequate resources for the Tenth Five Year Pan. The advisory group submitted its report in May 2001 and made recommendations for tax reforms also.

On September 3, 2002, the Ministry of Finance & Company Affairs set up a Task Force on Indirect Taxes (under the Chairmanship of Vijay L. Kelkar) with the objective of bringing the indirect tax systems and procedures at par with the best international practices, and thus encourage compliance and reduce transaction cost, taking the advantage of Information Technology. Another Task Force for Direct Taxes was constituted on September 6, 2002 with the objective of rationalising and simplifying the Direct Tax Laws and re-design the procedures to bring them at par with best international practices so as to encourage voluntary compliance and reduce cost.

The Consultation Papers on Direct and Indirect Taxes were presented to the government on November 2, 2002, and generated an intense public debate. The Task Force – in finalising their reports and reformulating their proposals – have accepted the principle that no vulnerable class of tax payers shall be worse off because of their proposals. Keeping this principle in view the Task Force has modified its consultation paper proposals. The final reports on Direct and Indirect Taxes were submitted on December 27, 2002.

Quoting from the Report: "The report of the Task Force is a continuation of the Fiscal Reforms initiated by the path-breaking work of the Tax Reforms Committee under the chairmanship of Raja J. Chelliah, in 1991. We also benefited from the outstanding work done by the Advisory Group on Tax Policy and Tax Administration for the Tenth Plan under the chairmanship of Parthasarathy Shome in 2001"

The present publication includes all the said reports and papers on Tax Reforms viz : (i) Report of the Task Force on Direct Taxes; (ii) Report of the Task Force on Indirect Taxes (also including the consultation papers); (iii) Report of the Advisory Group on Tax Reforms (chairman Parthasarathy Shome) 2001 and the Chelliah Committee Reports, 1992 and 1993. The document on Indian Public Finance Statistics of the Ministry of Finance, Government of India (June 2002) is also included, to provide the statistical data relating to India's Public Finance from 1950-51 to 2001-02.

It is hoped that these important reports and statistical data, put together at one place, will prove handy to all those interested in the subject.

Using the CD-ROM...

This book is accompanied by a CD-ROM which comprises the voluminous/supplementary portion of some of the Reports comprising this publication. Also privided along with the CD-ROM is a 3½ inch floppy disk (copy protection device) which acts as a "key disk" to run the CD. This CD-ROM is accessible on any computer operating under **Windows 98** environment (or higher). Installating and using the CD involves a simple user-friendly process given below.

Installation :

1. Click on 'Start' icon (on the lower left corner of Windows initial screen). A pop-up menu appears.
2. Click 'Run.' A dialogue box appears.
3. In the white space within the dialogue box type the following command :

   D:\setup

   NOTE : This command presumes that the CD drive in your computer is designated 'D'. If any other, then replace the letter **D** in the above command by the appropriate one which stands for your CD drive. Also make sure you have used the backslash (\ ) and not (/).
4. Click 'OK'
5. From here on, simply respond to the instructions and prompts that appear on your screen and it takes few minutes for the CD to be installed on your system.

contd...

Viewing the Contents on CD :

Once installation is complete, you are ready to view the contents stored on the CD from the shortcut **"TAX"** created automaticaly on your computer's desktop.

Please make sure that all through the process of viewing the contents on the CD, your system requires the presence of the CD in the CD-drive and **Key-Disk** (the $3^{1/2"}$floppy provided with the CD") in the floppy drive. Otherwise it prompts an error message.

Well-preserving the CD and the key-disk, is therefore, very important.

Report of the Task Force on Direct Taxes

2002

Report of the Task Force on Direct Taxes

CONTENTS

Preface. ....

1. **Chapter 1 – Reaction to the Consultation Paper: Response of the Task Force** 19

Approach for Reformulation
Benefits for Salaried and Non-salaried Taxpayer
Treatment of Housing
Tax Incentive for Saving
Enlarging the Tax Base
Tax as a tool of Developmental Policy
Going Back on Promises?
Towards Strengthening the Financial System
Implementation Options for Corporate Tax Reforms
Charitable Organisations
Taxpayer Services and Tax Administration
Combating Tax Evasion through More Effective Enforcement
Concluding Remarks

2. **Chapter 2 – Approach to Tax Reform** 40

3. **Chapter 3 – Reform of Tax Administration** 47

Role of the Tax Administration
Taxpayer Service
Taxpayer Identification and Registration
Collection of Information
Search and Seizure
Survey Operations
Verification of Tax Returns
Computerisation of the Tax Administration
Collection of Taxes and their Accounting
Refund
Income Tax Clearance Certificates
Dispute Resolution
Accountability
Delegation of Financial Powers
Human Resource Management
Infrastructure

4. **Chapter 4 – Personal Income Tax Reform** 84

Ramification of Tax Policy for Tax Administration
Personal Income Tax Rates
Personal Income Tax Base
Exemption Based on Residential Status
Standard Deduction for Employees

Treatment of Imputed Income from Owner Occupied House Property
Tax Treatment of Agricultural Income
Rationalising Income Tax Exemptions on Saving Instruments
Treatment of Educational Expenses
Treatment of Medical Expenses
Treatment of Senior Citizens
Other Personal Deductions
Personal Tax Reforms : Implementation Strategy

5. **Chapter 5 – Corporate Tax Reform** **136**

Case for levy of Corporate Tax
Case for Integration
Case for "Classical" System
The Case Against the Classical (Nonintegrated) System
The Case for Retaining a Classical System
The Meaning of "Integration"
Economic of Tax Incentive
Widening the Corporate Tax Base
Exemption for Exports (section 10A and 10B)
Depreciation
Tax incentive for Shipping Industry
Tax incentive for Scientific Research and Development
Deduction for payment of interest on Borrowed Capital
Tax Treatment of Non-performing Assets of the Financial Sector
Tax Treatment of Statutory Liabilities
The Treatment of Corporate Tax Losses
Tax incentives under section 80IA and 80IB
Promissory Estoppel
Corporate Tax Reforms : Implementation Strategy

6. **Chapter 6 – Taxation of Capital Gains**
Treatment of Capital Gains **186**

7. **Chapter 7 – Treatment of Other Entities** **190**

Taxation of Investment Funds
Tax Treatment of Partnership Firms
Tax Treatment of Charitable Trusts
Tax Treatment of Cooperative Societies
Tax Treatment of Non-Residents

8. **Chapter 8 – Other Taxes** **199**

Wealth Tax
Expenditure Tax

9. **Chapter 9 – Impact of the Recommendations** **202**

On Equity
On Revenues
On Savings
On Financial Sector
On Transaction Costs
Conclusion

10. **Chapter 10 – Summary and Recommendations** **218**

Annexure **251**

Preface

The Task Force presented the Consultation Paper to the Government on 2nd November, 2002 with the request that the paper may be made available to all concerned for discussion and debate. The response received has been overwhelming and there has been universal appreciation of the Minister of Finance & Company Affairs for bringing in transparency in the formulation of tax policies.

An intense public debate was generated and tax professionals, tax officials and academicians, trade and industry associations and invididuals from all walks of life contributed to the debate by sending hundreds of emails, letters and through articles in the media. On its part, the Task Force interacted with a large number of trade and industry associations and individuals at Pune, Ahmedabad, Ludhiana, Chennai, Bangalore, Mumbai and Delhi. The Task Force has immensely benefited from these comments and suggestions and we thank them all. These consultations and discussions have also convinced the Task Force that the launching of growth promoting tax reforms is one idea whose time has come.

The Task Force would like to express its gratitude to the Chairman and Members of the Central Board of Direct Taxes and the officers of the Department of Revenue for their full cooperation and support. The Task Force is also grateful to the Ministries and Departments of the Government of India which commented on the Consultation Paper and made valuable suggestions, many of which have been included in the Report.

In many ways, the report of the Task Force is a continuation of the fiscal reforms initiated by the path breaking work of the Tax Reforms Committee under the chairmanship of Dr. Raja J. Chelliah in 1991. We also benefited from the outstanding work done by the Advisory Group on Tax Policy and Tax Administration for the

Tenth Plan under the chairmanship of Dr. Parthasarathi Shome in 2001 and the Expert Committee to Review the system of Administered Interest Rates and Other Related Issues under the chairmanship of Dr. Y.V. Reddy in September, 2001. Our report aims to meet the country's strategic needs of accelerating growth and the reduction of poverty.

The Task Force wishes to also place on record their deep appreciation of the outstanding contribution of Shri Arbind Modi, IRS in the preparation of the Report. But for his efforts, presentation of this rcport would not have been possible in such a short time. We also wish to thank Shri Rahul Naveen, Under Secretary, Department of Revenue for painstakingly estimating the revenue impact of the various recommendations, Ms. Vibha Bhalla, Deputy Director of Income Tax, Shri Bharatendu Dobriyal, Asstt. Director of Income Tax, Shri Om Prakash, Programmer, Directorate of Income Tax (Systems), Shri S. Ravi, Private Secretary to Chairman of the Task Force and Shri Santosh Kumar Gupta who assisted Shri Modi, for their valuable support.

The Task Force also wishes to thank CMIE for allowing the use of their database and ASSOCHAM, CII, FICCI and their affiliates for making excellent arrangements for the meetings of the Task Force in Delhi and other parts of the country.

(Vijay L. Kelkar)

Advisor to Minister of Finance &
Company Affairs & Chairman of the
Task Force on Direct Taxes

New Delhi,
27th December, 2002

1

Reactions to the Consultation Paper

Response of the Task Force

The Consultation Paper of the Task Force on Direct Taxes was made available on the web site of the Ministry of Finance & Company Affairs (http://finmin.nic.in) on 2nd November 2002, inviting comments and suggestions of all concerned. The Task Force was overwhelmed by the response.

1.2 We received 1500 emails. There were more than 200 op-ed and other articles in English newspapers, and even more in regional newspapers. Almost 100 memoranda were received from various organisations. The Task Force visited major centres of trade and industry – Pune, Ludhiana, Ahmedabad, Chennai, Bangalore, New Delhi and Mumbai, thus supplementing the discussions in Mumbai, New Delhi and Kolkata which had taken place earlier.

1.3 There has been universal appreciation of the initiative by the Union Minister of Finance & Company Affairs for bringing transparency in the formulation of tax policy. The breadth and intensity of the responses clearly brought out the all-round desire to contribute to the country's Fiscal Policies.

1.4 Each one of the responses was constructive. Our discussions with trade and industry, tax professionals, income tax officials and scholars indicated considerable support to our basic proposals leading to simplification, reduction in tax burden of the salaried and non-salaried tax payers as well as of equity (risk) capital, greater usage of information technology in tax administration, outsourcing of non-core functions of the tax administration, improving services to tax payers and fundamental change in incentives and disincentives for tax compliance and against tax evasion. For instance, in a Web poll conducted by *India Today*, a majority of those who polled supported the implementation of our proposals. The support for establishing the Tax Information Network (TIN) – which will facilitate secure and seamless logistics of tax collection – was particularly enthusiastic. We also observed an interesting correlation: younger taxpayers were more likely to support our proposals. Of course, there have been critical comments as well. Many of the reactions received contradicted each other since they offered conflicting suggestions, particularly regarding tax rates and tax exemptions. In this Chapter, we have attempted to distill the major themes that emerged from the reactions to the Consultation Paper. In addition, there are a number of individual proposals that have been addressed in the respective chapters. The Task Force wishes to express its appreciation to everyone who took time to prepare and send her or his responses and documents. We thank them all.

Approach for Reformulation

1.5 One of the most perceptive reactions received by the Task Force is that while appreciating the thrust of our tax reforms proposals, the advice is that it must have a "human face". In other words, it must especially address the concerns of the vulnerable sections such as senior citizens. It was felt that the Consultation Paper was not sufficiently sensitive to the problems and requirements (such as housing and old age income security) of senior citizens and low-income groups. The Task Force accepts this thoughtful advice[1].

1.6 Hence, in reformulating our proposals, while maintaining their essential thrust and approach, we have accepted the principle that no vulnerable class of taxpayer shall be worse off because of our proposals. Keeping this principle in view, the Task Force has modified its Consultation Paper proposals so as to, *inter alia*, (i) provide additional tax reliefs to senior citizens, (ii) maintain fiscal support to the housing needs of low income groups, and (iii) strengthen old age income security by encouraging long term savings. We would however also like to add that, in addition to the proposed tax measures, the Government will need to formulate sooner rather than later a well functioning pension system based on contributions by individuals into personal pension accounts.

Benefits for salaried and non-salaried tax payers

1.7 A major underlying theme in the comments received was that the Task Force proposals are pro-corporate sector rather than pro-individual taxpayers. Fortunately, this perception is easy to rebut since it couldn't be further from the truth.

1.8 With the proposed personal tax rates, disposable income will be higher for every class of taxpayer, that is, the tax burden is lower for each income group as well as for senior citizens (Table-1.1). This table is based on the actual taxpayer profile, computed on the basis of average for each income group using CBDT database of 9.25 lakh taxpayers spread over assessment years 1998-99 to 2001-02. This also means that the entire "middle class" will benefit from our proposals. It is estimated that the personal tax burden for the existing taxpayers will be reduced by as much as Rs.7,900 crores per annum.

1.9 Our proposals achieve overall revenue neutrality, and enhance buoyancy by widening the personal and corporate income tax bases. This is sought to be done by reducing tax rates, pruning tax exemptions, aligning taxable profits with book profits and improving compliance. Our proposals completely eliminate the dividend tax, and long term capital gains tax on listed equities in the hands of the investors. These have been recommended with the express purpose of reducing the exorbitant cost of equity capital in our country. These gains or benefits accrue entirely to individual shareholders.

1.10 Further, we have recommended that all individuals with an annual income below Rs.1 lakh will be fully exempted from income tax. This also helps reduce the tax burden on individuals, and particularly low-income groups. Currently, with per capita income in the country at about Rs.25,000 per year, our proposal implies that an "average" family of four would not pay any income tax and thus meet their needs better.

1.11 The proposed tax reforms leave the choice of deploying a taxpayer's income to the individual. In other words, choice regarding how much to save and in which asset is left to the individual rather than being "directed" by the tax code. Effectively, by moving away from a paternalistic tax system, the Task Force has sought to empower the individual taxpayer.

1.12 Our analysis of the existing tax framework shows that thanks to myriad, often contradictory tax exemptions, the system has become increasingly complex. In tax policy and tax administration, such complexity is inherently regressive and therefore favours the rich and the powerful[2]. Our proposals to simplify and enhance transparency of the tax system would thus in fact help individual taxpayers, by reducing their compliance costs, which have been estimated to be as high as 48 per cent of taxes paid[3].

1.13 Thus, our tax proposals aimed at reducing the tax burden, lowering transaction costs and promoting transparency, are individual taxpayer-friendly proposals. With the consequent downward reduction in the compliance costs by even 10 percent, individual taxpayers will have further gains of Rs.4,000 crores per annum.

1.14 In addition, we would like to emphasise that our tax proposals will make the tax system the most equitable in the last two decades as is seen in the graph below.

1.15 This feature of enhanced equity or progressivity of our proposals is important to be recognised as some analysts have mentioned that our proposals are pro-rich because we have proposed removal of dividend and long-term capital gains tax. As we have argued, with the withdrawal of exemption and alignment of taxable profits with the book profits, the corporations will bear the full burden of the corporate taxation. Richer individuals generally own corporations and therefore our proposals will effectively increase the burden of such individuals. This means that our proposals are even more progressive than what is suggested in the graph since it does not "factor in" the incidence of the corporate tax liability. We may note that we have also recognised the need to maintain the dividend tax in Option – II where the elimination of tax exemptions is spread over a three-year period.

Table – 1.1

Impact on Tax Incidence Across Income Groups

Income Range (in Rs)	Salaried Taxpayers			Non-Salaried Taxpayers			Senior Citizens		
	Existing Tax Liability	Proposed Tax Liability	Tax Relief (in Rs)	Existing Tax Liability	Proposed Tax Liability	Tax Relief (in Rs)	Existing Tax Liability	Proposed Tax Liability	Tax Relief (in Rs)
0-40,000	0	0	0	0	0	0	0	0	0
40,000-50,000	0	0	0	0	0	0	0	0	0
50,000-60,000	0	0	0	382	0	382	0	0	0
60,000-80,000	0	0	0	2196	0	2196	0	0	0
80,000-1,00,000	1587	363	1224	5452	0	5452	0	0	0
1,00,000-1,50,000	8901	6334	2567	10697	4057	6640	0	0	0
1,50,000-2,00,000	22897	15746	7151	23522	14369	9152	7772	4369	3402
2,00,000-3,00,000	43353	29058	14295	44830	30872	13959	29080	20872	8209
3,00,000-4,00,000	75600	49335	26265	76855	52576	24279	61105	42576	18529
4,00,000-5,00,000	106643	76662	29980	108923	82590	26334	93173	72590	20584
5,00,000-10,00,000	185415	140886	44528	188671	154168	34503	172921	144168	28753
Above 10,00,000	733666	664070	69597	1177511	1094566	82946	1161761	1084566	77196

Note: This table is based on the actual taxpayer profile, computed on the basis of average for each income group using CBDT database of 9.25 lakh taxpayers spread over assessment years 1998-99 to 2001-02.

Trend of Progressivity of Tax Schedule

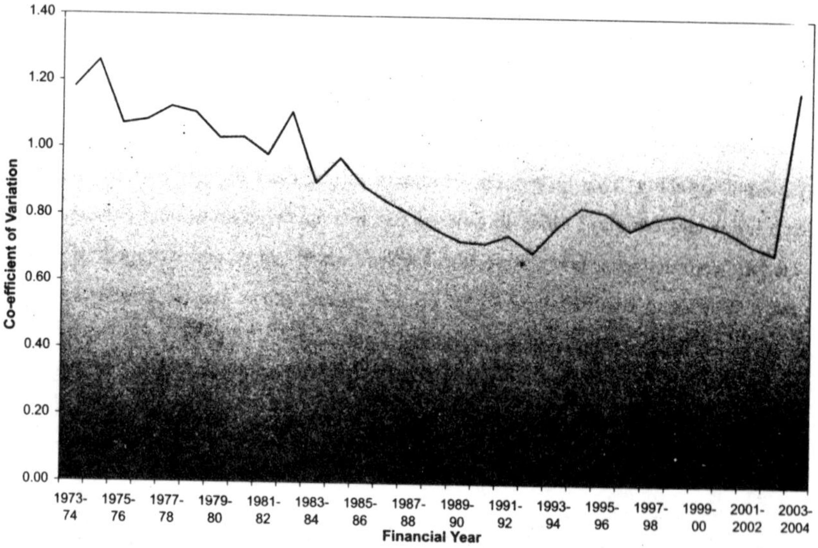

Treatment of housing

1.16 The Task Force received a very large number of comments with regard to our proposal for withdrawal of tax exemptions on interest payment on loans for self-occupied houses. The Task Force accepts the view that the housing sector is one of the key sectors of the Indian economy in terms of providing growth and employment and it is indeed a leading sector. However, our proposal was based essentially on the consideration of horizontal equity (equity between sectors) and vertical equity (equity amongst various income groups)[4].

1.17 The extant treatment also generates a tax distortion in the investments of a household among different classes of assets. For instance, a family that invests in the professional education of its children is putting resources into building human capital which can cost as much as many a small dwelling. This investment in human capital does not get tax benefits, while buying a house and living in it does. In other words, if a family wants to send a daughter/son to a medical, engineering or other professional college which can be an investment of around Rs.5 lakhs-Rs.6 lakhs, this investment gets no tax benefit, unlike the tax benefit given for owner occupied houses. This violates horizontal equity.

1.18 Currently, up to Rs.1,50,000 of interest payments are allowed as deductibles in taxable income, which implies a subsidy of Rs.45,000 per year for individuals who are living in their own house costing Rs.20 lakhs or more. This violates vertical equity. The richer sections of society are being "subsidised" to purchase their own dwellings, which can hardly be justified by a fiscally constrained economy, which is aiming to reduce subsidies on food and fuel. If a housing subsidy ought to be given, then it should be directed only to low-income households. Presently, a power loom worker whose taxable income is less than Rs.80,000 receives no tax subsidy for loan repayment for his own dwelling for the simple reason that he is not a tax payer.

1.19 It is for these reasons that the Task Force had initially recommended the elimination of this tax benefit. However, we have received almost universal reaction that this facility should not be eliminated for a number of reasons. In order to protect low-income groups, we suggest an interest subsidy of 2% for housing loans up to Rs.5,00,000 to all borrowers. This will help prospective homebuilders whose income is less than Rs.1 lakh. Until such time this proposal is adopted, we also recommend the continuation of interest deduction of up to Rs.50,000. According to the data provided by the National Housing Bank this would cover about 85 percent of total borrowers and all borrowers from low income groups (Table–1.2).

Table – 1.2

Number of Loanees and Amount Dispersed by Housing Finance Companies during 2001-02

Size of the Housing Loan (in Rs.)	No. of Loanees	Amount Disbursed (Rs. in crores)	Percentage		Average size of the loan (in Rs.)
			Loanees	Amount	
Up-to Rs. 5 lakh	376556	8761	85%	59%	232661
Rs. 5 lakhs to Rs. 10 lakh	48145	3442	11%	23%	714923
Above Rs. 10 lakh	16442	2608	4%	18%	1586182
Total	441143	14811	100%	100%	335741

Source : National Housing Bank.

Tax incentives for saving

1.20 As far as support to savings is concerned, the view of the Task Force is that the implicit costs of the present structure of tax incentives outweighs the benefits.

1.21 Firstly, the incentives are for gross savings, which has led to "round-tripping" of savings and, as pointed out by the Y.V. Reddy Committee, leads to very high implicit cost of borrowing for the exchequer. This has also been an important factor in reducing public savings. Consequently, the tax incentives for savings while changing the composition of household savings have perhaps led to a decline in total savings of the national economy.

1.22 A recent paper published in *Economic & Political Weekly* has shown how tax incentives for small savings increases the overall interest rate structure, including medium and long term rates[5]. In our view, this has been one of the factors that has led to a reduction in the investment, employment and growth momentum, thereby hurting the economy in the macro economic sense. In other words, showing that what may be "micro rational" for individuals has become "macro irrational" for the economy.

1.23 Our proposals will lead to lower tax outgo for all assessees and consequently set off any perceived increase in tax liability arising from the elimination of "directed" savings in specific instruments. It is noteworthy that there is no unambiguous international evidence that the overall savings rate of an economy is influenced by tax breaks on specific savings instruments.[6]

1.24 Furthermore, savings incentives are available to only certain savings instruments. This implies that presently the choice to taxpayers to deploy their savings is perforce circumscribed, e.g., there is an implicit disincentive for deploying savings into the equity market. It is for this reason that the Task Force has recommended removal of exemptions. However, the (social) objective of promoting genuine long-term savings for increasing old age economic security is undoubtedly important. To promote this, in Chapter 4 we have proposed doubling of the ceiling on contributions to the pension plan under section 80CCC to Rs. 20,000/- that will be eligible for tax relief. These pension plan schemes are presently operated by Life Insurance Corporation of India and other insurance companies.

Enlarging the tax base

1.25 A concern has also been voiced in the comments on the Consultation Paper that by increasing the limit to Rs.1 lakh, a large number of taxpayers will escape from the tax net. These apprehensions are misplaced. For the wider goal of increasing the tax revenue-to-GDP ratio, the key question should be the total income that is being brought into the tax net, and not the number of taxpayers. Surely, a simple toll tax would bring more tax payers, but that would not give buoyancy to the tax-GDP ratio. Also, most taxpayers with incomes of up to Rs.1 lakh will continue to file returns on account of the one-by-six scheme and therefore the concern that they "drop out" of the tax net is misplaced.

1.26 Now we move to the implications of our proposals. First, by removal of the various exemptions, we are in fact enhancing transparency as well as increasing the quantum of income – corporate and personal – that will attract taxes, albeit at lower rates. Second, by reversing the trend over the last two decades of an increasing burden upon the income group between Rs.2 lakhs to Rs.5 lakhs, we would be bringing more income into the tax net due to improved compliance.

1.27 A recent study by Surjit Bhalla has shown how over time, due to increased tax rates, the tax compliance by tax payers with an income between Rs.2 lakhs-Rs.5 lakhs has steadily declined and is currently the lowest among all income groups[7] (in fact, the estimated compliance rate (in percentage terms) is in the single digit for this particular class) as shown in Table-1.3 below. His study also shows that, congruent with international experience, tax compliance in India is tax rate responsive. Hence our proposals, by reducing the tax burden will capture this "missing middle" into the tax net due to greater compliance, which enlarges the tax base.

Table – 1.3

Compliance Ratios

Year	Range of Returned Income (in '000s of Rupees)							
	0-50	50-100	100-200	200-300	300-400	400-500	500-1000	above 1000
1988	1.2	13.2	11.1	21.6	112.6	10.2	24.1	42.9
1989	1.3	11.1	8.3	21.7	32.5	110.2	5.9	15.5
1990	1.1	17.9	4.8	10.0	39.4	136.5	5.0	22.6
1991	1.2	16.5	3.5	8.9	19.2	36.9	5.2	22.4
1992	1.3	13.1	4.8	9.2	26.9	55.5	9.2	28.4
1993	1.7	16.4	10.3	4.4	10.7	28.6	12.9	44.6
1994	1.7	12.9	9.0	3.8	7.9	20.7	26.9	17.7
1995	1.9	13.1	7.3	3.5	5.5	7.8	19.7	18.0
1996	1.7	17.2	12.0	4.5	7.0	10.2	27.2	33.4
1997	2.1	21.6	12.3	3.8	7.6	8.9	41.8	42.7
1998	2.9	28.0	14.6	4.2	5.5	8.4	32.9	35.7
1999	3.3	40.3	15.1	4.0	4.7	8.3	27.3	41.4
2000	4.4	41.4	23.2	3.7	6.7	9.0	23.7	33.6
2001	4.7	42.9	23.1	3.4	5.4	7.6	21.1	32.9

Source: Surjit Bhalla, Tax Compliance in India, January 2002 (mimeo).

1.28 Since the continuation of the one-by-six scheme is recommended, there would be a steady accretion to the number of tax returns filed, and with an improved tax information system, the tax base would be further enlarged.

1.29 We should also note that international comparisons regarding the minimum level of taxable income, against our proposed Rs.1 lakh, are not fair. This is because unlike other countries, Indian families with less than Rs.1 lakh in annual income pay much higher quantum of indirect taxes on the goods and services that they consume. In other words, the comparison of total tax burdens should incorporate direct and indirect taxes.

1.30 Regarding our proposals to tax agricultural income, there was considerable support as it promotes horizontal equity and captures agricultural income of non-agriculturists. However, a number of observers have made a point that it could result in considerable administrative difficulties and increase transaction costs for agriculturists. Given the proposed exemption level of Rs.1 lakh and other systemic reforms that have been recommended, the Task Force believes that administrative problems may not be insurmountable. However, it is entirely for State governments to consider our proposals in this area given the Constitutional provisions.

Tax as a tool of developmental policy

1.31 One of the important points made by some commentators is that our proposals imply a reduction in the developmental role of the State. According to them, tax exemptions are aimed to meet certain development objectives, and a policy of abstaining from tax exemption is synonymous with vitiating these objectives.

1.32 Our proposals in no way dilute the role of the State. The approach of the Task Force regarding the removal of tax incentives is no different from that proposed in the Tenth Five Year Plan – which embodies the development aspirations of the State – that was recently approved by the National Development Council[8]. Our approach seeks to improve the role of the State by making it more efficient, transparent, better targeted and more accountable.

1.33 Tax exemptions are opaque since their incidence as well as implicit cost is nontransparent. Further, the present "exemptions raj" promotes rent-seeking behaviour, and contributes to the complexity in tax laws. In terms of administration, exemptions more often than not lead to tax leakage and tax abuse thus increasingly making the system counter productive and dysfunctional. Consequently, it has increased tax rates for tax complying sectors, thereby leading to an all-round increase in the ex-ante costs of "risk" (equity) capital in the economy. This adversely affects investment, growth dynamics and employment generation. Today, full tax paying corporations, including small and medium enterprises pay almost 50 per cent tax ex ante on risk (equity) capital since they can avail of only few, if any, tax exemptions; on the other hand, certain classes of corporations that are privileged to "access" these exemptions pay much lower taxes. Clearly, there is cross-subsidisation. Moreover, such exemptions mean greater complexity, which burdens the tax authorities further and leads to an increasingly antagonistic relationship between the Revenue official and the taxpayer. This complexity is one of the major reasons for tax leakage and tax abuse.

1.34 Hence, the Task Force is of the view that this is not an efficient way of achieving the developmental objectives and that there are better and more efficient alternatives to achieve these goals. For instance, if we want to promote investment in economically backward regions, the government should give an up-front capital subsidy to a project in place of tax exemptions. Such an expenditure-based instrument will make the policy transparent and directly accountable – through the CAG audit – to Parliamentary oversight. More examples can be given. If the State wishes to encourage use of renewable energy, it can pay a direct subsidy of, say, 25% of the purchase price of a windmill instead of tax incentives.

1.35 One of the important objectives of our proposals is to increase the tax revenue-to-GDP ratio through better compliance, and a larger tax base. As a consequence, additional resources will become available to the State, which can be used to increase expenditures for producing public goods, particularly in the areas of health, education and other social infrastructure.

Going back on promises?

1.36 Yet another important set of comments received, particularly from the corporate sector, related to the need to observe the doctrine of promissory estoppel. According to this doctrine, a Government should maintain the promises that it has given even if these are not contractual. This doctrine was particularly referred to in the context of tax exemptions relating to 80IA & 80IB and 10A & 10B. We would like to make several observations in this regard:

1. It is important to recognise that it is individuals or citizens who pay taxes, and not "corporate buildings or plant & equipment". Promises can only be made to individuals and our proposals do not lead to any diminution of the promises made to individual shareholders who own corporations.

   In fact, our proposals improve the lot of the shareholders as for them we are eliminating not only dividend tax, but also capital gains tax. Consider what is being proposed: Currently, there are firms which pay no tax on profit, while their shareholders pay dividend tax at 30 percent and capital gains tax at 10 per cent, which are (indirectly) taxes on profits. Our proposal is to charge 30 percent tax on all corporations, and remove the dividend tax and capital gains tax (on listed equity). After all, corporations are only "vehicles" or instruments that are owned by shareholders. Therefore, there is no reduction in benefits enjoyed by shareholders if our proposals are implemented, and consequently all promises are being observed.

2. In important infrastructure sectors such as power generation and distribution, basic telephoning, major ports, toll roads etc the rate of return is regulated. This means that the tax incidence is effectively a pass through. Further, in our proposals, we have made provisions regarding the indefinite carry over of losses. This removes the financial constraints faced by the infrastructure sector, and obviates the need for complex rules relating to various sections in Chapter VIA.

3. There is also a legal perspective. A number of judgements of the Supreme Court have upheld that in the realm of tax policy, the principle of promissory estoppel does not hold and the State can change tax policies in the public interest.

4. An argument has been made that although our proposals imply equivalence for their shareholders, profit making firms may have transitional cash flow concerns regarding financing their investments. There are three comments in this regard: Firstly, such profit making firms will have

little difficulty in financing investment as currently banks and financial institutions are looking for such opportunities. Secondly, there is adequate liquidity available to finance profit making firms and that too at declining interest rates. Hence, there shall be little transitional problems for profit making firms. Thirdly, reducing the cash flow problems of firms may aggravate the cash flow problems of shareholders as they currently have to pay dividend tax, i.e., what is really involved is the "shifting" of cash flow problems.

1.37 Regarding tax benefits available to computer software exports under section 10A, domestic as well as foreign firms with investments in India in this sector had made a detailed presentation pointing out the peculiar taxation problems faced by Indian firms on their onsite revenues and how section 10A is helpful. In light of the complexity of tax treatment for software exports, the Task Force would like to briefly flag some issues pertinent to compensating Indian software companies that provide services on-site in foreign countries (often involving the stationing of Indian employees abroad).

1.38 Exemption under sections 10A and 10B for software off-site exports (services provided from India to clients abroad) has implications for allocative efficiency and equity. From the point of view of the sector itself, the exemption is a "tax cross-subsidy" between on-site and off-site exports (the foreign tax burden on the former being mitigated by exempting from corporate-tax profits from the latter). Therefore, the exemption results in a distortion in the "relative value" signals of different activities. Equity is impacted on two grounds. First, it differentiates between service providers within the software sector: those that cater for the domestic segment and those that export. Secondly, inasmuch as the sector is treated differentially from other productive sectors of the Indian economy (including, but not limited to, exporters of both goods and non-software services). Exempting incomes of companies providing on-site software services from tax on considerations of avoiding double incidence is analogous to correcting the (price) disadvantage faced by exporters of goods arising from the imposition of customs duties by the importing country's government. Furthermore, the need for continuing monitoring of exemptions has adverse consequences for the effectiveness of the tax administration as well. Finally, the Indian treasury loses revenue to the foreign exchequer – a case of "transfer of resources" from a developing country to a developed country.

1.39 Since the Task Force could not reach unanimity regarding the treatment of profits of computer software exports, even after discussing these issues in depth, it has suggested two possible alternatives to mitigate the tax problems faced by the software sector. The first is the elimination of exemptions under sections 10A & 10B together with retention of an amended Section 91 (to partially offset the burden). The second is retention of these exemptions until a totalisation agreement is ratified with trading partners, simultaneously with taxes being levied on dividend distribution and long-term capital gains.

Towards strengthening the financial system

1.40 There is one relatively unnoticed but important positive aspect of our proposals and this relates to the strengthening of India's financial system.

1.41 Our proposals on corporate taxes are based on real income[9]. This implies that with our proposals, banks that meet RBI prudential standards for NPA provisioning will get full tax credit for the same. This would encourage banks to clean their Balance Sheets, achieve improved capital adequacy ratio, and help us move towards a sound and robust banking system. Since Banks do not avail of any capital allowances the benefit from lower tax rates will increase retained profits of the financial sector, which will facilitate an increased supply of commercial credit.

1.42 There is another more profound relationship between the proposed tax rationalisation and modernisation of the financial sector, and this is from improved allocative efficiency. The decision to incur capital expenditure will now depend on return considerations rather than tax considerations. The recommendations of the report are aimed at greatly simplifying and rationalising the tax system. This will better focus investment decisions of households upon an evaluation of the underlying risk and return of alternative investment avenues, without distortions induced by tax considerations. It will hence help us obtain a system of financial market prices that reflect risk and return, as should prevail in a dynamic market economy.

Implementation options for corporate tax reforms

1.43 In the Consultation Paper, we proposed two options regarding changes in Corporate Income Tax. Option I is to implement the proposals at "one go". Option II suggests a phased implementation. Some commentators have argued that the second option of staggered implementation appears to be superior.

1.44 Our preference is clearly for Option I. It was unanimously agreed that it is rather difficult for any government to give a credible *ex-ante* time commitment. Such commitments are rarely sustainable. Past experience shows while tax rates were reduced, successive governments failed to implement measures for strengthening the tax base eg. phased withdrawal of incentives. As a result, we have reached a point where the corporate tax rates are close to their resting points and yet the statute continues to be riddled with exemptions and deductions. Any attempt to sequence the reduction in the corporate taxes and the withdrawal of exemptions and deductions could lead to disastrous impact on revenue flows, particularly taking into account the proposed reduction in the personal income tax rates. The two must necessarily be implemented simultaneously. Phasing also gives rise to uncertainty and "hope" that reforms could be reversed. There is an additional factor in favour of Option I. Given the present weak state of the international economy, the proposed package has the potential to impart a strong counter-cyclical boost to the Indian economy by promoting domestic demand – both consumer demand as well as investment demand. A number of influential economic analysts in India have argued that our industrial economy is facing a cyclical slow down and our package would meet this challenge. In other words, the timing for the immediate launching of the proposed fiscal reforms is most opportune.

Charitable organisations

1.45 There were also concerns expressed by a number of NGOs and charitable organisations. The concerns were regarding our proposal for the use of rating agencies. While NGOs accept the principle, they suggested that the details should be fully worked out before implementing it. We have modified our proposals in this regard, giving more time to all concerned to adapt to the new procedures.

1.46 Also, a number of organisations have argued in favour of setting up a National Charities Commission along the lines of the National Charities Commission, U.K., a body which both regulates and also helps in developing the sector. A number of States in India have the office of Charities Commissioner which regulates charity organizations. Hence, it may be more appropriate to have, at the national level, a National Charities Board which will be an advisory and promotional organization. The Task Force recommends that the Ministry of Finance & Company Affairs may explore this in consultation with the Ministries concerned.

1.47 The Task Force fully recognises the important role played by charitable organisations and NGOs in our country in strengthening civil society. Our proposals are in fact aimed at strengthening these institutions through the provision of more efficient services by the tax authorities.

Taxpayer services and tax administration

1.48 On the subject of tax administration, the Report has sought to encourage rapid improvements in both administration and accountability, in the firm belief that tax policy is only as good as its administration. The responses the Task Force received during consultations has only served to validate these concerns. The four main areas of complaints consistently perceived by taxpayers regarding tax administration related to delays in refunds, high-pitched assessments, harassment and inordinate delays in the interface process and widespread corruption. The Task Force would like to reiterate here that the measures it has recommended will help address these concerns and will put *samman* for taxpayers back into the spotlight.

1.49 A general emphasis on computerisation of the entire tax system, the cornerstone of which is the recommended Tax Information Network (TIN), is designed to streamline tax administration. A particular benefit is felt to be a reduction in the personal interface. Process improvements, such as outsourcing the non-core functions of the administration, will mitigate the high pitch of assessments by freeing up administration time for making assessments more accurate. The recommendation to route refund and tax payment transactions through banks based on PAN will both cut delays and enforce compliance, a double benefit for a move to a wide-based and efficient tax administration. Our proposals in their entirety reduce the avenues for rent seeking behavior, which *ipso facto* mitigates scope for corruption.

1.50 Accountability and oversight of the tax administration have been relentlessly emphasised in the Report. The establishment of a tax Ombudsman, on the lines of a similar body for the banking sector, has been recommended. Tax information will have to be routinely and periodically supplied by each Commissioner, enabling evaluation of the deviations of the tax administration from a set of explicit performance parameters (that have been laid out in Chapter 3).

Combating tax evasion through more effective enforcement

1.51 A number of individuals have pointed out in their responses that the Consultation Paper has failed to evolve a comprehensive strategy for enforcement against tax evaders. This is far from reality.

1.52 The Task Force at the outset recognised the importance of evolving a strategy, which would considerably enhance the ability of the tax administration to detect and penalise non-compliance. We decided to first address various issues that impact on the effectiveness of tax administration. Tax policy issues, dealt in the later chapters, are essentially addressed to improve the core functions of the tax administration, i.e., to improve taxpayer services and to enhance deterrence against tax evasion.

1.53 The underlying philosophy of the report is to substantially alter the economics of tax evasion. The cost of compliance is proposed to be drastically reduced by simplifying the tax laws and reducing the tax rates. The emphasis on taxpayer service through extensive use of information technology will enable the department to promote voluntary compliance amongst the general class of taxpayers and identify the "hard core" tax evaders. Similarly, the cost of non-compliance is intended to be increased substantially by establishing the Tax Information Network (TIN) which will enhance the probability of identification of tax evaders as well as help in the detection of income evaded. It will also substantially improve the quality of evidence against tax evaders and enable successful prosecution. As a corollary, the current tendency of high pitched assessment based on presumptions and conjectures will be a thing of the past. In effect, the present Block Assessment policy operates as an "Amnesty Scheme" for tax evaders detected as a result of search. The proposal of the Task Force to do away with Block Assessment in cases of search and seizure will provide further deterrence against tax evasion by levy of interest, penalty and prosecution of persons found guilty of tax evasion.

Concluding Remarks

1.54 A number of commentators have made the point that although the thrust of the Consultation Paper was broadly acceptable, the Paper could be criticised on two grounds:

1. There were drafting issues. For instance, the Consultation Paper should have made it clear that while deleting section 36(iii) all the relevant benefits would continue under section 37 and this fully takes into account the borrowing costs of the entrepreneur in determining the tax liability.
2. The Consultation Paper did not present adequate data. Consequently, commentators made their own assumptions and, in some cases, this led to incorrect conclusions.

1.55 We accept these shortcomings and, in this Report, we have endeavored to make our proposals as clear as possible and to provide necessary tables to support the recommendations. Further, we recommend that the Central Board of Direct Taxes should regularly make available data on CD-ROMs to scholars and analysts. This will help in encouraging in-depth research and analysis of the tax data and other economic trends. Such research will be of vital importance for improving our tax policies.

1.56 Penultimately, we would like to point out that our proposals should be seen as a continuum of the reform process which began in 1991. Various eminent committees, viz., the Chelliah Committee, the Y.V. Reddy Committee and the

Parthasarathi Shome Committee have recommended an open, transparent tax system with low tax rates, minimal exemptions and effective tax administration. Since 1991, our fiscal policy has substantially reduced the corporate tax rate, from 51.75 per cent in 1991-92 to 36.75 per cent in 2002-03 and now proposed to be further reduced to 30 per cent in 2003-04. Similarly, the maximum income tax rates have also been substantially reduced from 56 per cent to 31.5 per cent in 2002-03 and now proposed to be further reduced to 30 per cent in 2003-04. However, such reductions have been effected without reducing (indeed, enhancing) exemptions. This has adversely impacted potential tax revenues, and failed to impart the necessary buoyancy. In turn, this has constrained the ability of the economy to invest in the social sector and in physical infrastructure. Our proposals are aimed to correct this distortion by increasing the buoyancy of taxes and enhancing resources for investment and, hopefully, play a role in boosting economic growth to 8%, the target growth rate of the Tenth Five Year Plan.

1.57 Finally, our proposals should be seen as an integral part of the second generation of reforms, aimed to meet India's strategic needs, i.e., to accelerate the growth rate while meeting the challenges of globalisation. To achieve this, our fiscal policy should promote transparency, reward efficiency, provide economic security to employees, protect economic rights of shareholders and discourage rent seeking and crony capitalism. We believe that the proposals laid out in this Report will enable our country to reach this worthy objective.

Notes

1 On a personal note, this was also the unanimous advice of the spouses of the Task Force members.

2 This is due to the presence of information asymmetries, and the fixed costs of reorganising economic activities in a way that avoids taxes.

3 These estimates are from a NIPFP Study (2002) prepared for the Planning Commission

4 There is a basic inconsistency in the traditional tax treatment of housing, which recognises rental income as taxable income in the hands of a homeowner who does not live in a house, while ignoring the notional rental income in the hands of a homeowner who lives in his house.

5 Lal, Deepak, S. Bhide and D. Vasudevan, (2001), Financial Exuberance: Savings Deposits, Fiscal Deficits and Interest Rates in India, Economic and Political Weekly, Vol. XXXVI, No. 44, pp. 4196-4203, November 3, 2001

6 See Report of the Expert Group to Review Existing Fiscal Incentives for Savings (Chairman: P. Shome) for a review of evidence in this regard.

7 Surjit Bhalla, Tax Compliance in India, January 2002 (mimeo).

8 Planning Commission : Tenth Five Year Plan 2002-2007, December 2002, see Box 3.1

9 Real Income here refers to commercial profit.

2

Approach to Tax Reform

The Government of India is emphasising, inter alia, enhanced fiscal transparency to improve budgetary management, which the impending passage of the Fiscal Responsibility and Budget Management Act will further reinforce. In this regard, the Government is convinced that rationalising and simplifying direct tax laws and redesigning procedures to bring them at par with practices of other dynamic economies is *sine qua non*. Accordingly, the Task Force was assigned the following Terms of Reference: (i) Rationalisation and simplification of the direct taxes with a view to minimising exemptions, removing anomalies and improving equity; (ii) Improvement in tax-payer services so as to reduce compliance cost, impart transparency and facilitate voluntary compliance; (iii) Redesigning procedures for strengthening enforcement so as to improve compliance of direct tax laws; and (iv) Any other matter related to the above points.

2.2 The Task Force was intended as the forum to deliberate upon and correct many of the existing anomalies in the Indian direct tax system. Towards fulfilling this mandate, an attempt has been made to outline steps required for initiating and expediting a requisite change in the *fiscal paradigm* of the country by way of a *process transformation* on the direct tax side. The Task Force deliberated on ways to reduce costs of tax administration, examined best tax practices in the world and extensively debated means of empowering Central Board of Direct Taxes (CBDT) to fulfill its function effectively. The approach of the Task Force has been influenced by the recognition that in the recent past, economies have increased their tax revenue-to-GDP ratio not by increasing tax rates but by simplifying tax structures, widening the tax base and improving tax administration. This Report contains the Task Force's considered judgement, melded from views culled from a diverse section of stakeholders. In conjunction with the reduction in the incidence of commodity taxes – which are by definition regressive – recommended by the Task Force on Indirect Taxes, the tax structure of the Indian fiscal system is sought to be made more progressive and to improve the functioning of markets.

2.3 Hitherto, tax policy, including exemptions, has been used in instances where other instruments at the disposal of the government are *prima facie* more suited to achieve stated objectives. There is a widespread perception that (frequent) changes in the tax code in the last decade or so have (unintentionally) been akin to substituting the erstwhile "license raj" with an "exemptions raj". Confusion in assigning instruments to objectives result in an inefficient allocation of resources and often defeat stated aims. Clearly demarcated distinctions among objectives to be achieved and increasing transparency in the use of expenditure and tax instruments for these objectives can be expected to yield better results. Old-age social security and pensions, for instance, can be better provided through transfers funded by explicit social security taxes (as is done elsewhere). A definitive separation of the two broad classes of instruments will have the secondary effect of reducing ambiguities in justification of expenditures and also impart greater effectiveness to parliamentary oversight of the government's fiscal decisions.

2.4 The Task Force has endeavored to ensure that the recommendations pertaining to the direct tax codes are congruent with generally accepted principles of taxation. The three principles relate to efficiency (minimising distortions in resource allocation), equity (which *inter alia* includes progressiveness of effective tax rates) and effectiveness (of tax administration). The Task Force recognized that the best means of advancing the three principles – thereby being one of the principal outcomes that was set of this Report – is an alignment of the objectives of the tax authorities with obligations of taxpayers; in other words, enhance the incentive compatibility of the two groups. The effects of most changes overlap all three principles; it is impossible (and artificial) to ascribe any particular desired principle as the sole motivator of a recommended change.

2.5 The design of tax policies has emerged as a concern of critical importance. The tax policy must be outcome oriented rather than input specific; for instance, many tax incentives reward higher usage of particular factors of production (inputs) or provide tax breaks for specific savings instruments. These incentives need to be re-engineered so that desired outcomes – viz., higher productivity of income taxpayers and increased returns to shareholders – are encouraged. This is the case with the most dynamic countries among the emerging markets. Additionally, in conformity with recent initiatives in other parts of the world, transparency & corporate governance has sought to be enhanced (by, among other things, aligning book and taxable profits).

2.6 An equitable treatment of tax incidence is critical to the acceptability – and thereby the success – of any tax structure. Equity – both horizontal (similar tax treatment for similar classes of taxpayers) and vertical (progressive nature of tax incidence) – is consciously sought to be enhanced. The regime of a multitude of exemptions has been detrimental not only to tax efficiency but also equity by enabling a vocal (often rich and powerful) minority to enjoy rents arising from the resultant distortions (complexity) in the system, consequently undermining the postulate of equitable incidence (and thereby foster a regressive tax structure).

2.7 Optimal tax policy should be pursued in the general interest of the economy rather than for catering to sectional interests. Every exemption has a constituency and democratic systems tend to respond to constituencies – a tax break to one constituency inevitably spawns similar demand by others. The dynamic nature of economic activity in India, with changes in the relative share of industry, services and agriculture-value added, is moreover sure to continually shift the taxpayer profile. The recommendations of the Report are embedded in a forward-looking approach to taxation by imparting a sector-neutral flavour (including fiscal impartiality between those who produce for the domestic market and those catering to external markets). Therefore, it is recommended that income from all sources and asset classes – skilled and unskilled labour, human capital, physical capital and financial (risk) capital – should have equal tax incidence.

2.8 Often, the exemptions looked to be rational at the micro level, but were irrational at the macro level. For instance, tax breaks on specific savings/investment products did help in resource mobilisation of particular financial instruments with associated high rates of return to subscribers of these instruments. Selective exemptions did not only engender dichotomy of real returns on various instruments, they also helped to increase the cost of borrowing for everyone with debilitating consequences for investment and growth for the whole economy – in other words, the strategy was harmful at the macro level. If this wasn't bad enough, to make investments in specific assets affordable – given the high cost of borrowing brought about, in part, by the aforementioned tax breaks – tax incentives were conferred! Removal of tax breaks on specific savings vehicles will impart downward flexibility to the (implicit) floor on rates of return on these instruments and contribute towards further lowering the cost of debt capital. Furthermore, by the elimination of taxation on dividend and capital gains (on equity of listed companies), shareholders are taxed only once, and therefore the cost of (equity) risk capital also comes down. A *systemic* beneficial outcome will be a reduction in the cost of capital, thereby helping to boost investment and growth.

2.9 As a macroeconomic coda to these arguments, it should also be pointed out that that cross-section and inter-temporal evidence points overwhelmingly towards *simultaneity* in savings and growth behaviour of economies rather than causality from the former to the latter[10]. In other words, there is little evidence that high savings have actually caused high growth; the two normally move together. Encouraging savings as an objective *per se*, with little regard for the damage it might cause by raising the cost of funds, is likely to defeat the purpose of growth. The Task Force does recognize, though, that long-term savings might need to be encouraged and explicitly does this by rewarding the fruits of such savings, at the time they mature.

2.10 In addition to enhancing horizontal equity, vertical equity will, moreover, also be served. The specific tax proposals outlined in subsequent chapters – if accepted as an integrated package – will constitute the most progressive tax changes in India in the last two decades.

2.11 The Task Force would like to explicitly point out that elimination of various (corporate level) tax holidays, concomitantly with removal of dividend and capital gains tax (on listed equity), will bring down a shareholder's *ex ante* tax liability from about 50 percent at present to 30 percent. On that account, viewed from the unexceptionable perspective of a shareholder, the government is not going back on its moral commitment regarding corporate level tax breaks that have already been granted (and availed of).

2.12 The series of *ad hoc* exemptions and other tinkering, in addition to distorting economic incentives, has also served to clutter the culture of compliance. Tax policy and tax administration is inter-linked: complex tax policy leads to complex tax legislation, which inevitably leads to cumbersome administration through a cascading effect on filings, compliance procedures and enforcement measures. Unsurprisingly, a weak and porous system has evolved, which by increasing transaction costs of participation dissuades potential taxpayers. Over the years, a number of perverse incentives have crept in: taxpaying is often punished (by harassment) and tax evasion is not sufficiently deterred. The recommendations are designed to change the economics of tax compliance, viz., reduce transaction costs of tax paying and increase the price of evasion. One of the tax department's biggest challenges will be to bring the "missing middle". mainly urban, self-employed service sector professionals who, advertently or unwittingly, have dropped out of the tax base – into compliance, through the right mix of communication, education and enforcement. Presently, the compliance rate in percentage terms of this category of taxpayer is in the single digit. It is noteworthy that this undesirable outcome has occurred against the backdrop of considerable efforts in recent years by the tax authorities to fulfil its functions.

2.13 Just as the Task Force recommends that greater effort be expended on enlarging the taxpayer base, so must it emphasise that the quality of services extended to the taxpayer be improved. The tax department is no different than most businesses: world-class customer service is critical. Communication about taxes and tax policies is extremely important – taxpayer rights and obligations need to be clearly specified. The best tax systems in the world deal with taxpayers in a professional customer-relationship environment, which requires the system to be transparent, responsive and non-discriminatory. Furthermore, by increasing accountability of tax authorities, a durable welfare-improving social contract is established between taxpayers and tax administration.

2.14 A change in attitudes has distinctly and perceptibly emerged in a previously largely adversarial relationship between the tax collector and taxpayer, when neither was inclined to believe the other's integrity. Younger taxpayers are more willing to pay their dues to society. This bracket of young taxpayers, in line with global trends, constitutes the most dynamic and productive segment of India's population. Not only will they be the engine for higher growth, their contribution to the tax coffers will increase. At the same time, this willingness is conditional; based on their experience as customers for commercial services, they have come to expect a professional interaction with service providers. Leveraging this segment for both higher growth and tax revenues will consequently have to tread the fine line between incentivising effort and enterprise while simultaneously co-opting them into the tax base. The Task Force reiterates that all possible measures are instituted to prevent an alienation of this increasingly important demographic segment and an attendant reversion to the tax cynicism of earlier generations.

2.15 The Task Force cannot over-emphasise that effective tax reform must harness Information Technology (IT). The CBDT has to be commended for the effort it has expended and the actions it has initiated for computerisation of taxpayer records. However, business processes, systems and facilities have not kept pace with the growing demands on tax administration. Simple and transparent business processes are at the core of any service organisation and this is also true for a tax administration. Raising the resources required for the targets envisaged by the Tenth Plan involves much more than adjusting rates and rationalizing exemptions – a fundamental process change which empowers the tax department in more effectively fulfilling its functions is needed. Apart from facilitating increased efficiency, IT can contribute to aligning the incentive compatibility of the department and taxpayers by its potential of enhancing transparency thereby contributing to mitigating rent seeking. The mandatory web-based logging of details & parameters of taxpayer complaints and action taken on these complaints is an example of the use of IT facilitation in this context.

2.16 Availability of IT expertise and the presence of world class (common carrier) network systems developed by the National Stock Depository Limited (NSDL) can be relatively quickly deployed to make a systemic improvement in processes to reduce transaction costs (for both CBDT and the taxpayer). Establishment of a Tax Information Network (TIN) can facilitate transactions, akin to securities markets, and establish *secure and seamless logistics of tax collection* through integration of primary information, record keeping, retrieval and enforcement. Centralised processing of TDS certificates, for example, has the potential to increase compliance and reduce fraud – false certificates result in increased costs of cross-checking and verification. Reciprocally, not only is there reduced potential for discretion and concomitant harassment, but it can also help to expedite refunds. Some of these activities, as well as systems for process automation, can be out-sourced in conformity with procedures adopted by the best international tax administrations, thereby permitting the CBDT to pursue more effectively its core functions.

2.17 These broad recommendations are elaborated in subsequent chapters. In closing, however, the Task Force would like to strongly urge that these recommendations be adopted as a package. Deep organisational reform in the private sector occurs following the failure of discrete changes from preventing a threat to the viability of the enterprise; the same is true of the framework for direct taxes. The efficacy of the recommendations is likely to be seriously vitiated if individual components are selectively accepted or rejected and reforms continue in a piece-meal manner; success of tax reform efforts depends on their implementation as an integrated package.

Note

10 See Report of the Expert Group to Review Existing Fiscal Incentives for Savings (Chairman: P. Shome) for a review of evidence in this regard.

3

Reform of Tax Administration

It is widely accepted that a significant portion of potential tax revenue is not collected because of poor tax administration and high tax evasion in India. The question is whether the complexity of the tax structure or high tax rates have led to a high incidence of tax evasion, or if lax tax administration by itself has been unable to fulfill the revenue objectives implied by the tax structure. In practice, it is likely that both tax policy and tax administration have mutually affected each other.

3.2 It is widely recognized that tax policy and tax administrations are intrinsically linked. In this interrelationship, however, tax policy formulation is generally seen to precede tax administration. This is because only when a tax structure is legislated does tax administration come to play its role in the implementation of the law. In developing countries, however, the direction of the link may not be quite so apparent. Indeed, it is said that in developing countries tax administration is tax policy[11]. This would imply that, however fine the design of the tax structure might be in a representative developing country, it is the interpretation and implementation of the law that counts. These elements reflect the need for adequate capacity of the tax administration in place to implement the law[12].

3.3 At the same time, experience reveals that a particular tax administration mechanism could alter the original intention of tax policy and structure. Possible modes include large taxpayer units that continue to be emphasized in the long run at the cost of the overall universe of taxpayers, tax deduction at source used as a final withholding, purely financial, as opposed to physical, control as an administrative device in a rudimentary environment, and the use of distortionary or simplistic taxes purely on grounds of easy administration.

3.4 In many developing countries, tax laws may be quite well designed and detailed. But unless the accompanying tax administration is able to handle those laws in terms of having the appropriate staff to interpret and implement them, the field-level reality of the actual incidence of the tax system may be quite different from the original objectives[13]. The taxes may be passed on to those on whom they are not meant to fall, and the distribution of the burden may turn out to be indiscriminate. Lawyers find it easy to litigate tax matters because of the difficulties in interpreting complex tax laws and, accountants, ploughing through a myriad pages of the tax code, successfully advise clients in careful tax planning such that their tax burden is minimized. This implies that, in the long run, it has to be ensured that tax administration instruments facilitate, rather than ignore or hinder, the implementation of tax policy goals.

Role of the Tax Administration

3.5 If "tax administration is tax policy", as is widely recognised, it is imperative to identify the role of the tax administration, so that responsibility and accountability is clearly established. The existence of a tax administration is a necessity, even in the most law-abiding society. Where there is full compliance, the role of the tax administration would be restricted to the provision of facilities for citizen to discharge their responsibility. In case there is non-compliance, it will have to play the role of a policeman. Since it cannot play the role of a policeman to all taxpayers, its action must provide sufficient deterrence so as to induce voluntary compliance.

3.6 Collection of taxes are merely transfer of resources from the large masses of taxpayers to the Government. The resources used in the collection of taxes are a dead-weight loss[14] unless the benefit flowing from the expenditure policy exceeds the dead-weight loss. Hence, it is necessary to use minimum resources in the collection of taxes. Therefore, the fundamental role of tax administration is, in order of priority:

1. To render quality taxpayer services to encourage voluntary compliance of tax laws; and

2. To detect and penalise non-compliance.

The extent of success of the tax administration in its role would be reflected in higher revenue growth.

3.7 These functions of the tax administration comprise the following separable component activities:

1. Taxpayers' education and services
2. Collection of information
3. Collation of information
4. Dissemination of information
5. Storage and retrieval of information
6. Verification (appraisal/assessment of information)
7. Collection of taxes
8. Taxpayers' grievances redressal system
9. Accountability

Taxpayer Service

3.8 Traditionally, the role of the tax administration has been to enforce the tax laws and provide at least minimal taxpayer service. This was understandable in the context of a small potential taxpayer base and the then prevalent practice of administrative assessment. Over time, as the taxpayer base expanded and the scheme of self-assessment introduced, it became necessary for the tax administration to also facilitate compliance through the provision of quality taxpayer service. In most developing countries this shift in role focus is suspiciously viewed as abandonment of its traditional role of enforcement and softening of the tax administration. Most employees unable to reconcile to their new role continue to resist this shift in the role perception from an enforcement officer to a facilitator.

3.9 Tax evaders in most countries, particularly developing countries, can be classified into two categories. The first category relates to those who fail to comply because of information asymmetry (lack of information) and the tax administration's failure to provide this information. Recourse to private sources (tax practitioners) for information entails a relatively high compliance burden. These evaders are sitting ducks for the tax administration and entail a high administrative burden if pursued individually. The second category relates to those who refuse to comply because of deficiencies in the taxpayers' information system and supporting institutional setup. Therefore, the latter, in effect, is also because of information asymmetry (lack of information with taxpayers). The compliance burden in this category is relatively low. The first category constitutes the majority of tax evaders but account for a relatively small proportion of taxes evaded. The existence of the first category of evaders creates a general climate of non-compliance. Tax evasion being contagious, spreads widely! Since the second category is hard to nab and the first category is a sitting duck, the tax administration tends to prey on the first category for easy success. The second category continues to thrive under the umbrella of the first category. It is, therefore, efficient for the tax administration to provide quality taxpayer service and reduce the size of the first category. The limited resources hitherto deployed in the pursuit of the first category could be substantially released and redeployed to the task of tackling the second category. Hence, taxpayer service must be seen as complimentary to enforcement and not a substitute as is commonly understood in most developing countries – the mind set amidst tax officials in India is no different. Provision of quality taxpayer service is an integral part of the enforcement strategy of any tax administration.

3.10 Taxpayer service typically refers to the provision of information and material by the tax administration to the general mass of taxpayers so as to facilitate compliance with the tax law. A cross-country survey of taxpayer service indicates that the relatively more successful tax administrations provide relatively high levels of taxpayer service. Inspite of the mindset in favour of enforcement, the Income Tax Department indeed provides a range of services to facilitate compliance. These services include pamphlets, brochures, booklets, web-based information and return forms. In some Metropolitan centres, an Interactive Voice Response System is operational. The recently introduced scheme of Suvidha and Sampark are all extensions of the taxpayer service programme. However, these are just beginnings and are clearly not enough. The present scope of taxpayer service in India is too narrow compared to the range of services offered by other tax administrations across countries (Table - 3.1 below). The evolution of the package of taxpayer services in India is accidental – the entire programme seems to have evolved in an ad hoc manner rather then as a strategy to promote voluntary compliance. The Task Force was informed that this was primarily due to inadequate financial resources for taxpayer service. The expenditure set aside for taxpayer service is woefully small (less than 2 per cent of its annual budget). The existing taxpayer service programme is also handicapped by the absence of professionals trained for planning and executing focused media campaigns.

3.11 Given the best international practice in the area of taxpayer service and the future programme for widening the tax base through voluntary compliance, the Task Force recommends the following measures to expand the present scope of the taxpayer service programme:

(i) The income tax department must expand, qualitatively and quantitatively, the present scope of taxpayer service. These should cover the range of taxpayer services indicated in Table-1 above and, inter alia, include the introduction of a telephonic system (by voice message) to remind taxpayers of important dates and the provision of preformatted programmed floppy diskettes through retail outlets.

(ii) The expenditure on taxpayer service must be increased from the present level of about one percent of the total expenditure on tax administration to at least five percent. In this regard, an important start should be made by the establishment of taxpayers' clinic in different parts of the country to enable taxpayers to walk in for assistance. The Task Force feels that better treatment of existing taxpayers has an important role in encouraging those outside the tax net to become taxpaying citizens.

(iii) The department should provide easy access to taxpayers through Internet and e-mail and extend facilities such as tele-filing and telerefunds. It should design special programmes for retired people, low income taxpayers and other such groups with special needs who cannot afford expensive services of tax consultants.

Table – 3.1

Taxpayer Information Programs in Selected Countries

	Argentina	Canada	Chile	Colombia	Jamaica	Mexico	Trinidad	USA	India
A. Publications									
1 Tax guides (instructions)	x	x	x	x	x	x	x	x	x
2 Pamphlets and bulletins	x	x		x	x	x	x	x	x
3 Technical publications		x		x	x	x	x	x	x
4 Audio cassettes for visually impaired		x							
5 Newspaper tax supplements			x	x	x		x	x	x
6 Reminders in press			x			x			
B. Media									
1 Radio or television commercials	x	x	x	x	x	x	x	x	
2 Special television programs		x		x	x		x	x	
3 Video cassettes		x				x		x	
4 Press conferences			x			x		x	
C. Telephone contact									
1 Telephone assistance	x	x	x	x	x	x	x	x	
2 Tele-refund		x				x		x	
3 Tele-info		x						x	
D. Personal contacts									
1 Walk-in service		x	x	x	x	x	x	x	x
E. Correspondence									
1 Individually drafted letters		x	x		x		x	x	
2 Standardized letters		x	x		x		x	x	
F. Other programs									
1 Volunteers		x					x	x	
2 High school program	x	x	x		x	x	x	x	
3 Rural tax scene kits		x						x	
4 Native outreach		x						x	
5 Training for new business							x	x	
6 Participation in seminar and conferences		x		x		x		x	

Taxpayer Identification and Registration

3.12 The process of tax enforcement begins with the identification of taxpayers. This is truly a formidable task particularly in an economy where the unorganized sector predominates. Only an effective taxpayer information system and monitoring can help to achieve this task. The establishment of an effective taxpayer information system is crucially dependent upon a unique identification numbering system such that the information relating to various indicators of wealth, expenditure and financial transactions can be collected and collated.

3.13 The Income tax Act[15] provides for allotment of a Permanent Account Number (having ten alphanumeric characters). Every person who fulfils any of the following conditions has to compulsorily apply to the Assessing Officer for the allotment of a Permanent Account Number (PAN):

1) If his total income or the total income of any other person in respect of which he is assessable under this Act during any previous year exceeded the maximum amount which is not chargeable to income-tax; or
2) Carrying on any business or profession whose total sales, turnover or gross receipts are or is likely to exceed five lakh rupees in any previous year; or
3) A charitable trust or institution;
4) Any other person desiring to own a PAN; and
5) Any other person by whom tax is payable.

3.14 The PAN is required to be quoted by a person:

(a) In all his return to, or correspondence with any income tax authority.

(b) In all challans for the payment of any sum due under the income tax act

(c) In all documents pertaining to foreign transactions ;

(d) Sale or purchase of any immovable property valued at five lakh rupees or more ;

(e) Sale or purchase of motor vehicle or vehicle (does not

include two-wheeled vehicles);

(f) A time deposit exceeding fifty thousand rupees with a banking company;

(g) A deposit exceeding fifty thousand rupees in any account with post office savings bank;

(h) A contract of a value exceeding one lakh rupees for sale or purchase of securities;

(i) Opening an account with the bank;

(j) Making an application for a telephone connection including for a cellular (mobile) telephone;

(k) Payment of hotels and restaurants for an amount exceeding twenty five thousand at any one time;

(l) Payment in cash for purchase of bank drafts or pay orders or bankers cheque from a bank for an amount aggregating fifty thousand rupees or more during any one day;

(m) Deposit in cash aggregating fifty thousand Rupees or more with a bank during any one day; and

(n) Payment in connection with travel to any foreign country for an amount exceeding twenty five thousand rupees at any one time.

3.15 Given the ongoing and new initiatives by the Ministry of Home Affairs for issuing a Citizen Identification Number and by the Ministry of Labour for issuing a Social Security Number, the Task Force feels that the use of PAN can effectively integrate, on the lines of the US Social Security Number system, multiple tasks of tax and commercial enforcement, targeting government subvention, improving governance and enhance national security, both at the Central and State level. We recommend that:

(i) The PAN should be extended to cover all citizens and therefore serve as a Citizen identification number. This will obviate the need for the Home and Labour Ministries to issue new numbers.

(ii) Given the manifold increase in the coverage of PAN, the responsibility for issuing should be transferred to an independent agency outside the income tax department.

However, the income tax department should have online access to the database for tax enforcement like any other agency.

(iii) The requirement of quoting PAN may be expanded to cover most financial transactions.

Collection of Information

3.16 For administrative purposes, information for taxpayer for identification can be grouped broadly in three heads :

(i) Taxpayer's Declaration,

(ii) Information Returns and

(iii) Field Survey

(i) Taxpayer's Declaration : Under the system of self-assessment, the taxpayer forms the basic source of information. The taxpayer provides information to the tax administration through returns and accompanying documents. These returns contain valuable information on the taxpayer and his activities. All this information can potentially be used to help gauge the taxes due from the taxpayer. However, the Task Force was apprised that tax administration was unable to digitize the information since the staff in the income tax department, despite training in computer skills, is at the lower end of the learning curve. More than 2.5 crores of tax returns were pending for processing for lack of adequate skilled manpower.

(ii) Information Returns: This is a more widely used device to collect information. Information returns are declarations filed with a tax administration by persons required to report details of their financial dealings with other taxpayers. Information returns often require listing of all transactions of a certain kind, e.g., payments of corporate dividends or transactions of other kinds beyond a level with other taxpayers during a certain period. A wide variety of sources of information can be imagined which could be garnered by the tax administration through the device of information returns. Such returns also include information returns relating to tax deduction at source.

Under the extant procedure, the Central Information Branch (CIB) functioning under the Director-General (Investigation) within the Directorate of Income Tax (Investigation), spread all over the country, collects from predetermined sources information relating to financial transactions from various external and internal sources. Sources of information to be tapped in a financial year, are laid down by CBDT in its instruction No. 1943 dated August 22, 1997. The Director-General of Income Tax (Investigation) is empowered to revise the ceilings of the monetary limits fixed by the Board for collection of information. Currently, about 37 broad categories of external and internal sources are listed in the long-term action plan for information collection, formulated by CBDT. Section 133B (power to call for information) and 131 (power regarding discovery, production of evidence, etc.) constitute the main legal base for the process. Under Section 133(6) of the Income Tax Act, firms, companies, dealers, brokers, agents, banks, etc., can be called upon to provide the name and address of persons engaged in transactions with them. The information so collected is collated and then disseminated by the CIB to the assessing officers for verification in the respective cases.

The process starts with the collection of information, mainly from external sources. However, there are several hurdles in this area. First, the flow of information is not automatic in the sense that the CIB first issues letters to various agencies, calling for information under sub-section (6) of Section 133 of the Income Tax Act. Although the instruction identifies the broad sources of information to be tapped during the year, the specific identity of these sources, viz., the specific firms, dealers, brokers, banks, companies, etc., required to be tapped for this purpose are left to the discretion of the officer in the field formation, with the result that the coverage of sources is usually incomplete. Secondly, even where information is called for under Section 133(6), not all agencies respond promptly. In such cases summons under Section 131 are issued. Even then, many agencies try to stall or even resist communication of information. Refusal to part with information by banks and some other financial institutions is a case in point. This strains CIB's resources and delays verification and dissemination of information. Thirdly, because of limited manpower and infrastructure – including, importantly, the lack of automation and also the long delays in furnishing information, the CIB is not able to collect information from even the major external sources every year. The inability to collect annually comprehensive information from all or at least the major sources dilutes the efficacy of CIB verifications.

Under the Income tax Act, deduction at source is required to be made from specified categories of payment like salaries, interest, commission etc. The deductor is required to file with the TDS circle in the Department annual returns relating to deduction of tax at source. These information returns are also an important source of information.

(iii) Information and evidence collected by the Department during the course of investigation : In addition to information from taxpayer's return and other information returns, a large volume of information also gets collected during assessment, searches and seizures and survey operations.

3.17 In view of the extant method of collection of information and constraints in digitising the volume of information received by the tax administration, the Task Force recommends:

1. Income Tax Act should be amended to provide for submission of 'annual information return' by third parties in respect of various transactions as may be prescribed. For this purpose, a proper format of the return also needs to be prescribed. Consequently, the flow of information will be continuous and the discretionary power with the CIB to collect information will be eliminated.
2. Such annual return of information (including returns relating to tax deducted at source) should be mandatorily required to be submitted on electronic format.
3. Many of the Departments involved in transactions specified in Rule 114B do not have any mechanism for obtaining the PAN of the concerned person. It is, therefore, necessary that the pro forma used by them for their departmental purposes, e.g., the application form for transfer of motor license, should have the necessary column requiring the applicant to disclose his Permanent Account Number (PAN).
4. The Department should set up a structure for Electronic Data Interchange (EDI) with some of the major departments and organisations involved in the transactions

specified in Rule 114B, such as, Banks, Stock Exchanges, Telephone Companies, Regional Transport Authority etc.

Search and Seizure

3.18 In the public perception, the Income tax department is identified with "raids". That is its identity. That is its most visible enforcement activity. Raids are conducted with the help and in the presence of the police force. The search and seizure activity is immediately reported in the press, highlighting "big names" and large amounts of undisclosed income. It also provides publicity to the concerned officer.

3.19 The objective of the search is to ascertain facts and collect evidence of concealed income and to give a message that tax evasion will not go undetected or unpunished. But, in the course of the search as they are conducted, the main objective of the search team is to obtain a declaration of undisclosed income from the person searched. It confirms success of the raid. Further investigations are slowed down or abandoned. Often such declarations are obtained under pressure. They are retracted in subsequent proceedings. After the raid, the officers of the investigation in charge of the raid, call to their office the persons searched to understand from them the seized accounts and documents. They record further statements.

3.20 The officer, in charge of the raid, prepares a report on the seized material in about 60 days, giving an (own) appraisal of the search and seizure, without any accountability for what he discloses (or omits) to put down in the report. This report is the basis for assessment in the searched case. The assessing officer does not independently investigate the case. He neither has time nor inclination to do so. The assessment is one sided, high pitched, completed in a hurry when it is close to getting barred by limitation, ignoring the contentions of the assessee. About half the arrears are accounted for by Search & Seizure assessments. When the case goes through first and second appeal, the additions are deleted.

3.21 In a search case, there is no "real" investigation. As a result, the assessment does not stand the test of judicial scrutiny in appeals. There is nominal revenue gain from the searched case. Overall, the contribution of searched cases to total revenue collection is less than one per cent.

3.22 In view of the scheme of block assessment and settlement by Settlement Commission, the person searched is not required to pay any interest or penalty and is never subjected to prosecution in respect of the income he had concealed and which was detected as a result of search and seizure action by the department. He gets away by paying tax at the rate of 60 per cent as against normal rate of 30 per cent or 35 per cent. As a result, the deterrence effect of a search is also doubtful.

3.23 Today, in the income tax department the most sought after posting for most of the officers in any grade is to the search and seizure wing (officers deploy all sorts of "strategies" to obtain a posting to the search and seizure wing). The reason is not that the search and seizure work provides high visibility with a sense of being in power without accountability for acts or omissions, but the main reason is that it is profitable. The department gives handsome rewards to members of search team based on seizures and revenue realisations. A substantial proportion of the rewards have been received only by officers posted to search and seizure wing. This practice has contributed to obtaining forced confessions of undisclosed income and seizure of money, jewellery, stock or other assets recorded in accounts or acquired from disclosed sources of income.

3.24 To sum up, income tax raids in India are the most visible activity of the department. In public perception, the identity of the Income tax department is "raids". Search and seizure has become a substitute for all investigations and an end in itself. Search and seizure does not serve as deterrence against tax evasion. It has become a routine exercise. There is no meaningful investigation prior to, during, or after the search. The concealed income declared as a result of search is widely publicized, but in judicial proceedings the additions made on that basis are not sustained. Search and seizure cases contribute less than one per cent to total revenue realizations and search and seizure cases do not suffer interest, penalty or prosecution. Nevertheless, the social and economic cost of search and seizure activity is very high.

3.25 Search and seizure has a limited role, in the income tax proceedings. Search and seizure is not a substitute for investigation. It is only a tool for investigation. It is not an end in itself. Search and seizure cannot be a way of life for any civilized society.

Search and seizure should be used in rarest of rare cases, when it is a must and where alternative measures of investigation have failed. And once it is used, it should have its full impact as a deterrent. The tax evader should suffer the penal consequences of interest, penalty and prosecution in respect of the concealed income detected as a result of the search.

3.26 Based on the aforesaid considerations, the Task Force recommends the following :–

a) Special procedure for assessment of search cases in chapter XIV B (Block Assessment) which provides for tax at the rate of 60 per cent, be omitted. As and when concealment is detected and established, it should suffer full penal consequences of interest, penalty and prosecution.

b) Power of Settlement Commission to grant immunity from interest, penalty and prosecution may be restricted to cases other than those where the assessee admits of tax evasion consequent to search and seizure action taken by the department in his case.

c) The scheme of rewarding officers engaged in search and seizure activity be abolished.

d) Often in the course of search and seizure, stocks are either seized, deemed seized or put under order of attachment or prohibition. This hampers business, without any gain to revenue. Commerce Ministry has unveiled new export-Import Policy (2002-2007). At para 2.42.1 it states "No seizure of stock shall be made by any agency so as to disrupt the manufacturing activity and delivery schedule of export goods. In exception cases, the concerned agency may seize the stock on the basis of prima facie evidence. However, such seizure should be lifted within 7 days.". In line with this policy of the government, the stocks found during the course of search and seizure operation under the Income Tax Act may only be inventorised but not seized. This can be done by issuing administrative instruction.

3.27 A cross section of people cutting across trade and industry complained of a high handed behaviour of raiding parties particularly while recording a statement. It was pointed out that over enthusiastic raiding parties would often coerce a "surrender". As a result all follow up investigations are distracted and generally brought to a stand still. Since, the surrender is not backed by adequate evidence, the tax evader invariably retracts from the statement of surrender, by which time it is too late for the department to resume investigations. Similarly, where adequate evidence is indeed found, a surrender is not necessary to establish tax evasion. Therefore, the Task Force recommends that the Central Board of Direct Taxes must issue immediate instructions to the effect that no raiding party should obtain any surrender whatsoever. Where, a taxpayer desires to voluntarily make a disclosure, he should be advised to make so after the search. As a result, the taxpayer will not be able to allege coercion and successfully distract investigations. All cases where surrender is obtained during the course of the search in violation of the instructions of the CBDT, the leader of the raiding party should be subjected to vigilance enquiry. Further, the Task Force also recommends that all statements recorded during the search should be video recorded. This will, indeed, add to the confidence of the taxpayer in the impartiality of the system.

Survey Operations

3.28 Section 133A empowers an Income Tax Authority to enter any business premises to inspect books of accounts, stocks or other valuable articles or seek information. The income tax authority is also empowered to place marks of identification on the books of accounts or documents inspected by him or take extracts or copies therefrom, make inventory of cash, stock or other valuable articles verified by him or record statement of any person present at the business premises. The Finance Act, 2002 has now empowered the income tax authority to also impound and retain in custody the books of accounts or documents after recording the reasons for so doing. Furthermore, she/he is also required to obtain the approval of the Chief Commissioner or Director General or Commissioner or Director to retain such books after a period of fifteen days. It was represented before the Task Force that consequent to the amendment by the Finance Act, 2002 the survey, which was a routine field verification exercise, has been upgraded to that of a search and seizure. Further, unlike the search and seizure where reasons for conducting the search must be recorded in writing and the warrant issued by a senior officer in the rank of Commissioner, there is no such requirement in the case of a survey. A junior officer at the assessing officer level can authorise a survey without assigning any reason. The public at large was very apprehensive about the possible misuse of such unbridled power. Accordingly, we recommend the following:–

1. A survey should be authorised after recording the reasons in writing and the power of authorization should not be vested in any officer below the rank of a Joint Commissioner of Income Tax.

2. The books of accounts impounded by the survey team should not be retained beyond a period of seven days since it has the potential of disrupting the business of a taxpayer. Where it is felt that the books need to be retained beyond the period of seven days, the department may obtain photocopies duly attested by the taxpayer for further investigation.

Verification of Tax Returns

3.29 The Income tax assessment system in India comprises of 'Intimation' of tax/refund on returned income (Section 143(1)(a)); 'limited scrutiny' (Section 143) introduced by the Finance Act, 2002 with effect from 1st June, 2002 to disallow inadmissible loss, exemption, deduction, allowance, or relief claimed in the turn; and 'full scrutiny' (section 143).

3.30 'Intimation' of tax or refund on the basis of returned income is to be routinely generated and sent to the taxpayer once computerisation is in place. Processing of the return of income by the integrated computerised system will ensure that the refund generated is after adjustment of the outstanding arrears if any against the assessee. Till then, manual verification and adjustment of the outstanding demand against the assessee will be necessary before the refund is issued to him. Unfortunately, despite training in computer skills, the staff in the income tax department is at the lower end of the learning curve and in-house clearing of the backlog in a short period is not possible. As a result, more than 2.5 crores of tax returns remain unprocessed. A large number of these would be refund cases contributing to the grievance against non-issue of refunds. Against this background, the Task Force recommends that:-

1. In line with our view that the tax department should concentrate on its core functions, the department should be allowed to outsource data entry work and clear the backlog of returns (which number 2.8 crores as on 30th September, 2002) by end February 2003.

2. All returns must be processed within four months of receipt. For this purpose, it would be necessary for the department to either hire additional personnel on a temporary basis during the peak period for filing returns, or, outsource data entry work, as is done routinely by national tax administrations all over the world. Further, we must emphasis that outsourcing of such data entry work relating to processing of returns should be done only to supplement the efforts of the departmental staff and officers and not as a substitute.

The cost of hiring additional personnel or outsourcing data entry work would be far less in comparison to the benefit from reduced interest burden on refunds and taxpayer satisfaction.

3.31 The audit (scrutiny) programme is the most important element of the enforcement strategy of any tax administration. The overriding aim of such a programme is to provide a credible deterrence to protect the tax yield[16]. Such deterrence is established through the process of selective verification of the volume of information received by the tax administration. The success of this process is greatly influenced by the method used for selecting the returns.

3.32 The Task Force was appraised about the negative aspects of the existing discretion based system of selection of returns. We also received large-scale complaints about rent seeking by officials engaged in this discretion-based system of selection of returns. Therefore, we recommend the immediate abolition of the existing discretion based system of selection of returns. The department should progressively develop an audit selection system for risk analysis and assessment, which forms a scientific (and, therefore, objective) basis for identifying cases of potential tax evasion for in-depth scrutiny.

3.33 Risk Analysis is by definition the process carried out by a computer program using data where there are proven statistical relationships, whereas risk assessment is a cognitive process. However, before an audit selection system can be driven by risk analysis good quality data has to be obtained over a number of years. Risk analysis will help to rank taxpayers and any local knowledge and intelligence must be factored to make a risk assessment. This will provide the most efficient and effective means of targeting tax officials to arrears of greatest risk. It is important that cases for audit are selected on the basis of perceived risk and not simply by intelligence or speculation since intelligence would be available for only a few taxpayers. Further, selection of cases based on risk analysis and assessment must be combined with a certain small percentage of random audit, and carrying out issue-specific audits, such as refund audits.

3.34 In the interim, we recommend the identification of cases through a random non-discretionary centralised method deploying the PAN database. The current practice of issuing guidelines for selection of cases for scrutiny, which eventually finds its way to the public, must be given up.

3.35 Once a case is selected for scrutiny, it should be fully investigated, covering investments, accretion to assets, expenses incurred, savings, transactions entered and profits made, turnover etc. The scrutiny assessment will then serve its purpose of deterrence against tax evasion and contribute to revenue realisation. The present practice in scrutiny assessments is mostly to make statutory disallowances of exemptions, deductions and other claims made in the return to achieve zero error assessments from the point of audit objections. 100 per cent policing is not possible. Therefore, the number of cases selected for effective scrutiny should be on the basis of available manpower, their number and capability.

3.36 Penalty proceedings for concealment of income are required to be initiated in the course of assessment proceedings (Section 271(1) of the IT Act). The order imposing the penalty can be passed within six months from the end of the month in which the order of the Appellate Tribunal against the order of the assessment is received. It takes about seven years on an average before the order of the second appellate authority against the order of assessment is received. Therefore, the order of penalty for concealment of income is passed only after seven years and thereafter it goes through the process of appeals, which takes another five to seven years. Hence, given the judicial process, any order that imposes penalty for concealment takes more than a decade to fructify. Consequently, the deterrence effect is considerably diluted. This is so, because penalty proceedings are treated as separate from assessment proceedings, though the same material is considered in both the proceedings. One possible solution is to pass the order of penalty for concealment along with the order of assessment. This would indeed have positive impact on the deterrence of scrutiny assessment and penalty on tax evasion. It would also reduce multiple proceedings and litigation.

3.37 However, during the process of consultation it was pointed out that the simultaneous passing of both assessment and penalty orders would result in very high tax demands from the taxpayers who would then be pressed for payment. This will result in considerable harassment. In the alternative, if the demand is stayed, the department would invite severe criticism for lack of performance. The Task Force was also informed that with the increase in the number of first appellate authorities, the pendency of appeals at this level has reduced substantially and decisions would now be forthcoming within one year. This being so, we recommend that Section 275 of the Income Tax Act should be suitably amended to provide that the penalty order should be passed within one year from the end of the financial year in which the first appellate order is received. Consequently, the delay in passing the order-levying penalty for concealment would be considerably reduced to about two years.

Computerisation of the Tax Administration

3.38 The assessment of most modern taxes requires the ability to marshal the numerous pieces of information needed to determine the base of the tax and the rate to be applied. With many taxpayers, the level of information that needs to be processed and – for tasks that need centralised coordination – the magnitude of the coordination problem increase rapidly and possibly faster than the number of taxpayers. Either taxes requiring less information must be adopted or the information processing and coordination capacity of the tax administration must be improved.

3.39 Radical improvement in tax administration calls for a transformation of organisation and methods. Modern information technology greatly facilitates such transformation. The availability, cost, and accessibility of modern computers make them ideal for the large-scale information processing and coordination problems facing tax administrations. Benefits to taxpayers from computerisation, through such systems as electronic filing, electronic data interchange and computerised taxpayer assistance can also be immense in terms of lower compliance costs and time saving. Nonetheless, it is critical to have a clear strategy and to consider a number of important aspects of the problem when considering the introduction of technology to upgrade the information handling capacity of any tax administration.

3.40 The Task Force cannot over emphasise that effective tax reform must harness Information Technology (IT). The tax department is no different from most businesses. World-class customer service is critical when "all of India is its customer and Parliament its Board of Directors". While the CBDT has to be commended for the effort it has expended and the action it has initiated for computerisation of taxpayer records, the business processes, systems and facilities have not kept pace with the growing demand on tax administration. The Task Force firmly believes that the tax department should be allowed to concentrate on its core functions – an increasing emphasis on assessment and enforcement duties, rather than logistics and support services – which will surely lead to increased effectiveness of the tax administration. In this context, rapid and progressive outsourcing of many tasks of the tax department is not only feasible, given the significant pool of talent in the Indian software industry, but it is also desirable. In order to make IT infrastructure commensurate with the requisite processing tasks, the Task Force would like to explicitly put on record that implementation of this enhanced integration-software requires considerable investment in upgrading associated IT hardware and sufficient access to high-capacity bandwidth for implementing the network.

3.41 The process of systemic modernisation of tax administration cannot be further delayed. To empower the tax administration in executing its core function, the Task Force studied the existing depository system of the National Stock Depository Limited (NSDL) and concluded that it offered a scalable system to meet the requirements stated above. As this proven and tested infrastructure already exists, it can readily be adapted to offer a world-class, state-of-the-art IT architecture to rapidly empower the tax administration. Our study suggests that the system could be operational and available on-line by the beginning of the 2003-04 fiscal year.

3.42 To speed up the process of modernisation, the Task Force therefore recommends the following:

(a) The Government should establish a national Tax Information Network (TIN) on a build, operate and transfer basis. This will comprise of a world class (common carrier) network system and have access to state-of-the-art IT infrastructure. A requisite in-built feature of the system is that it should be scalable to offer ease of access across tax administration and taxpayers. The network that is envisaged will facilitate transactions, akin to securities markets, and establish secure and seamless logistics of tax collection through integration of primary information, record keeping, dissemination and retrieval. It should be a repository of information, with a database of all tax payments and refunds. Data mining software associated with such relational databases will allow a quick and systematic identification of non-compliance and abuses, thereby helping to improve compliance. The existing facilities of the National Securities Depository Ltd. (NSDL) can be relatively quickly deployed to make a systemic improvement in processes and reduce transaction cost.

(b) TIN will receive, on behalf of the tax administration, all TDS returns and other information returns for digitisation. The information would be received either online, or through magnetic media or in printed format. The digitised information will be downloaded by the National Computer Centre / Regional Computer Centres of the income tax department for further processing.

(c) TIN will also receive online information about collection of taxes from the banks. The information could be downloaded by the income tax department as and when required.

(d) The taxpayer will have the facility of accessing the TIN system through a secure and confidential Permanent Account Number (PAN)-based identification to ascertain tax payments credited to his/her account and the status of returns and refunds.

The TIN will therefore serve as a gateway to the National Computer Centre of the Income Tax Department. It will help overcome the paucity of technical manpower and inadequate technical infrastructure.

Collection of Taxes and their Accounting

3.43 The Income tax Act provides for collection of taxes on a pay-as-you-earn basis. Some form/sources of income are subjected to withholding tax (known as "tax deduction at source" in the Income Tax Act and commonly referred to as TDS). To the extent, the tax liability is in excess of the amount of TDS, the same is required to be paid as advance tax in installments during the financial year. The shortfall, if any, is required to be paid at the time of filing the tax return.

3.44 The system of collection of taxes through TDS is justified on the ground that it helps identify those who are liable to pay taxes and once identified, a taxpayer is induced to even declare incomes which he would not have otherwise declared. It is also perceived as a "costless" method of collection of taxes. Therefore, the coverage of TDS has been expanded over time; a significantly large proportion of the direct tax revenues is collected through this mechanism.

3.45 Our interaction with trade, industry and a cross-section of taxpayers across the country revealed considerable resistance to TDS. Their complaint was essentially against the high private cost to discharge what was essentially a government function. In a recent study on compliance cost estimates of income tax commissioned by the Planning Commission, such private compliance costs (for TDS) have been estimated to be as high as 11.8 percent of revenues. Generally, compliance costs are regressive; smaller the payer, larger is the compliance cost of TDS. Such costs essentially relate to issuing of TDS certificates to the payee, payment of TDS to the Government account and filing of TDS returns (information returns) with the tax authorities. If there are compliance deficiencies, there is an additional cost of compliance. Given the relatively high levels of compliance cost estimates, the Task Force recommends that firms and individuals whose total sales, gross receipts or turnover from the business or profession carried on by it is less than the monetary limits specified under clause (a) or clause (b) of section 44AB should continue to be exempted from the liability of deducting tax at source.[16a] However, once the TIN, which has been recommended by this Task Force, is fully operationalised, the requirement to issue TDS certificates to the payee can be dispensed and the scheme can be extended to the smaller taxpayers.

3.46 As indicated above, TDS serves as a mechanism to counteract tax evasion through third party matching of information. However, such matching is constrained in the absence of PAN of the payee. Since we have recommended in the earlier section of this report the decentralisation of allotment of PAN, we also recommend that where a payee receiving salary fails to furnish his PAN, tax should be deducted at a flat rate of 30 percent. In all other cases of such failure, tax should be deducted at twice the normal rate or 30 percent, which ever is lower.

3.47 Under the existing system payee can claim exemption from TDS:

1. She/he can apply to an assessing officer u/s 197, for a certificate for deduction of income tax at a lower rate or no deduction of income tax. If the assessing officer is satisfied she/he shall issue a certificate as may be appropriate.
2. She/he can make a self-declaration (u/s 197A) to the effect that the tax on her/his estimated total income in which income is to be included will be NIL.
3. Where the income received by the payee is below a specified limit, no tax is required to be deducted at source irrespective of the level of income of the payee.

4. All interest payments by cooperative banks and other cooperative societies must be subjected to TDS so that the cooperatives do not develop into institutions for parking of black money. This will also ensure that there is a level playing field for all agencies competing for deposits.

3.48 However, various options are not available in respect of all categories of payments; in most cases, only the first and third options are available. Given the procedure for issue of certificates for exemption from TDS, the Task Force observed considerable dissatisfaction amongst a large number of taxpayers, particularly those at relatively low income levels and senior citizens, about the efficiency of the procedure. Most complained about having to visit the tax office repeatedly and also being subjected to fishing and roving inquiries. Some taxpayers also complained of unethical behaviour in this regard. If the tax administration has to take recourse to TDS as an efficient system of tax collection, it must necessarily design procedures where non-taxpayers do not have to shoulder the same burden of compliance cost as other taxpayers. Concerned with the lack of such procedures, the Task Force recommends the following:-

1. Tax should be required to be deducted at source irrespective of the amount of payment.
2. A payee should be allowed to claim exemption from TDS if she/he furnishes a self declaration to the payer that the tax on her/his estimated total income in which the income is to be included will be NIL and quotes her/his Permanent Account Number (PAN) on such.
3. The present system of obtaining a certificate from the assessing officer for deduction at lower rate should be abolished so as to minimize the interface between the taxpayer and tax authorities.

3.49 Currently, payment of taxes can be made only at the specified branches of designated public sector banks in a given city. The taxpayer is required to fill up the right challan depending upon the major and minor head of the payment, i.e., whether it is a payment against Corporation-tax or Income-tax and whether it is by way of self assessment tax, advance tax, regular tax or TDS etc. The challan together with the corresponding amount of cash or cheque is presented before the authorised branch of the designated bank. In case of a cheque payment, the banks give the receipted copy of challan only after the cheque is cleared, which usually takes 2-3 days. Branches of designated banks send the challans of their various branches in a city/region to a Nodal branch from where these come together with a scroll to the Computer Centre/Central Treasury Units (CTUs) while another set goes to concerned Zonal Account Office (ZAO). The banks are entitled to a service charge of 11.18 paise per hundred rupees of tax deposited with them. Besides, they enjoy a float period of 15 days after which they transfer the tax deposited with them to the Reserve Bank of India (RBI). The procedure of reconciliation of taxes paid between Banks, Department's Computer Centres, Central Treasury Units and the Zonal Account Office is, entirely manual-based on paper copies of the challans and scrolls.

3.50 Since only a limited number of public sector banks are designated for collection of taxes and these, in turn, have authorised only a few of their branches for giving this facility, the choice before a taxpayer is very limited. In a very large number of cases, the taxpayers have to deposit taxes in a bank/branch in which they do not have their own bank account. This entails an extra period of 2-3 days for clearance of the cheques and thus the taxpayer has to visit the bank again (after 2-3 days) for collecting the paid copy of the challan.

3.51 The service charge of 11.18 paise per hundred rupees is not related to the cost of service or the cost of transaction but is related to the amount of tax paid in one challan. This is a historical legacy and, entirely, illogical. In addition, since the banks are simply collecting together the counterfoils of challans under a daily/weekly scroll and forwarding them to the Central Treasury Unit (CTU) / Zonal Account Office (ZAO) via their nodal banks, there is hardly any value added to justify the service charges of 11.18 paise per hundred rupees, in addition to the benefit of retaining the tax money for 15 days.

3.52 There are numerous instances of mistakes in challans and scrolls. There are even cases where the name of the taxpayer is not mentioned on the challan!

3.53 Since the Tax Accounting System in the Department has been fully computerised, it becomes necessary to transcribe the data on the challans after they are received in the Department. This involves huge (and increasing) data work. A delay in this affects reporting of tax collection and makes forecasting of the budget revenue collection to the Government more difficult.

3.54 In view of our recommendation for the establishment of TIN, we recommend a revised procedure for collection of taxes and their accounting. The new procedure will be as follows:

(a) A taxpayer will be required to fill up only one copy of the challan while making payment of taxes in the bank. The present requirement of filling up four copies of challan for payment of any tax will be given up.

(b) The banks will be networked to the TIN and receive payments online. The banks will be required to issue a computerised receipt to the taxpayer instantaneously. The date of presentation of a cheque will be treated as the date of payment. If a cheque bounces, the bank will reverse the receipt online, and the department would then be expected to prosecute the delinquent taxpayer.

(c) With instant accounting of tax collection, the requirement of enclosing a copy of the challan as evidence of tax payment, along with the annual return of income could be done away.

(d) Since the TIN will digitise all TDS returns, the requirement to file TDS certificates along with the return of income will also be dispensed with.

(e) At present, taxes are collected through approximately 10,500 bank branches. Since the proposed procedure requires banks to receive online payment, those banks that do not have adequate infrastructure for establishing online connectivity will be debarred from collecting taxes. Accordingly, the Government, in consultation with the Reserve Bank of India, should also consider paying higher charges for services rendered by banks.

The process outlined above will facilitate real-time accounting of TDS, Advance Tax and Self-Assessment Tax, and help the tax administration to swiftly identify noncompliance. Furthermore, the new procedure of tax accounting will facilitate electronic filing of tax returns.

Refund

3.55 The failure of the tax administration to issue refunds continues to be a major source of public grievance. This is partly due to its inability to promptly process the returns, whose numbers have increased substantially in the last three years, and partly due to the cumbersome process for issuing of refunds[17]. Therefore, we recommend the following:

(a) The existing cumbersome and manually-operated procedures for issue of refunds must be replaced by a more efficient IT-based system. Under the new system the department will prepare a separate file of all refunds daily which will be downloaded by a payment intermediary, i.e., a designated bank.

(b) The designated bank will be authorised to issue computerised refunds as is the current practice for issuing dividend and interest warrants by companies.

(c) The designated bank will be required to transmit the information relating to the issue of refunds to the TIN, which will also allow a taxpayer to verify the status of his/her refund claim.

Income tax Clearance Certificates

3.56 A person leaving India by land, sea or air is required to obtain from the Competent Authority a certificate that he has no liabilities under the direct tax laws or that he has made satisfactory arrangement for payment of his existing liabilities as also for payment of the tax that may become payable by him. The persons requiring income tax clearance are those:

(i) not domiciled in India provided they have stayed in India over a period of 120 days. Generally, a person holding a foreign passport is considered as not domiciled in India;

(ii) domiciled in India at the time of departure but-

(a) intends to leave India as an Emigrant; or

(b) intends to leave India on a work permit for employment or occupation abroad; or

(c) in respect of whom income tax authority considers that a clearance is necessary.

3.57 Case 1 was intended to facilitate collection of taxes from foreigners in respect of income that they may have earned during their stay in India. Case 2 was also intended to ensure that residents do not leave India without discharging their tax liabilities. However, over time the machinery for issuing such clearances has degenerated often leading to complaints of harassment and unethical behavior. In fact, international travel guides advice foreign tourist to budget for a certain sum to obtain such clearances. This is indeed an inhibiting factor for foreign tourists to visit India and stay long periods. It is also learnt from a cross section of officers and staff in the Department that they have yet to come across any case where such a clearance has facilitated recovery of taxes.

3.58 India has a network of treaties for avoidance of double taxation. These treaties do not provide for any bilateral arrangement for assistance in tax recovery by one country from the residents of another country. It is now learnt that OECD has proposed the incorporation of such an arrangement in all treaties and therefore India will have to renegotiate for this purpose.

3.59 The Group on Tax Policy and Tax Administration set up by the Planning Commission under the chairmanship of Dr. Parthasarathi Shome has recommended that the requirement to obtain tax clearance by foreign tourists must be dispensed with immediately. The Task Force also discussed this issue and endorsed the view of the Group.

3.60 It is therefore recommended that the present requirement of obtaining a tax clearance certificate before leaving the country must be abolished. However in order to protect the interest of revenue, we can continue to allow the income tax authorities to notify the immigration/custom authorities to prevent any particular person from leaving the country if such person is considered to be a proclaimed offender. As a result only a handful of notified persons will be subjected to the process of tax clearance as against the present practice of requiring all and sundry to comply with the requirement of obtaining tax clearance before leaving the country.

3.61 In terms of the policy of the Government of India, patronage in the form of grant of license, government contracts, permits, etc should be extended only to honest taxpayers. All the Ministries, their attached and subordinate offices, public sector undertakings, ordinance factories, Directorate-General of Supplies and Disposals and Central Public Works Department strictly ensure that those who fail to discharge their tax obligations do not get any patronage from them. The concerned Department/Agencies, before granting the contract insist on the production of Income Tax clearance certificate from the Assessing officer to the effect that the concerned person has paid his taxes unless stayed by the competent authority; he has cooperated with the department in the completion of assessments by filing return of income and complying with the notices and in the past three years, she/he has not been penalized or prosecuted for tax defaults. It is also learnt that some banks have also been insisting on income tax clearance certificate before granting loans.

3.62 Application for the tax clearance is required to be made to the Assessing officer having jurisdiction over his case in a specific form. This form brings out the state of tax compliance by the concerned person. On receipt of the form, the Assessing Officer verifies from his records the facts stated therein. He looks into the position regarding payment of taxes, assessee's cooperation in completing assessment and whether he was penalised or prosecuted. Thereafter, the certificate of tax clearance is recorded by the Assessing Officer on the Application form.

3.63 The certificate is valid for one year. Application for fresh certificate can be made one month prior to the date on which the validity of the previous certificate is due to expire. Those firms of repute who have clean tax records are by Government notification exempted from the production of income tax clearance certificate. Such exemption certificate is issued on the recommendation of the Commissioner.

3.64 The existing system of issuing income tax clearance certificate has become a source of harassment and encourages rent-seeking behavior. A taxpayer is required to visit the income tax office a number of times, thereby increasing the interface with the department, which must be avoided to the extent possible. It is not necessary that we should enforce compliance with the tax laws by denying "patronage". The tax laws provide for adequate penalties and prosecution for this purpose.

3.65 In view of the above, it is recommended that the system of issuing Income Tax Clearance Certificates to contractors and others should be eliminated forthwith. However, to help in enhancing effective tax enforcement, all government agencies should be required to obtain the PAN of entities participating in tenders, being designated as vendors to the government, etc., and periodically submit (pre-specified) relevant information to the tax administration.

Dispute Resolution

3.66 Under the current scheme of dispute resolution, the taxpayer has the option to either seek administrative redressal or judicial remedy. The Income tax Act specifies the categories of orders in respect of which a judicial remedy can be availed. There are several orders for which there is no judicial remedy and the administrative redressal mechanism is ineffective. This results in considerable dissatisfaction amongst taxpayers. The Task Force therefore recommends that the Income tax Act should be amended to provide that all orders/intimation imposing any additional burden should be made appealable.

3.67 A cross section of taxpayers lamented the absence of administrative response to their grievances particularly to those relating to issue of refunds (mostly women and senior citizens), rectification appeal effects etc. It was suggested that the office of Ombudsman along the lines in the banking sector may be setup which will help redress taxpayer grievances. Accordingly, the Task Force recommends creating the institution of Ombudsman in the top ten-taxpaying cities and all state capitals along the lines of that in the banking sector. This institution will provide an independent system to assure that tax problems, which have not been resolved through normal channels, are promptly and fairly handled. It will also identify issues that increase burden or create problem for taxpayers, and bring those issues to the attention of the Central Board of Direct Taxes (CBDT). The Ombudsman will also enquire into, should a complaint be filed, the practices and performance of all classes of tax professionals. Where necessary, it will also make appropriate legislative proposals. This institution will be independent of the local tax office. Its goal will be to protect individual taxpayer rights and to reduce taxpayer burden. A consolidated annual report of the Ombudsman system will be tabled in Parliament.

Accountability

3.68 The ability of the tax administration to perform its role effectively and efficiently is in turn determined by its ability to coordinate and adapt over time the organisational structure and its resources. The organisational structure should follow from the organisations' objectives and conditions prevailing in the country. Until recently, the organisational structures of many tax administrations were not based on any overarching rationale, but instead had either emerged as a result of historical accident & bureaucratic inertia or had evolved in an ad-hoc manner. In the last few years, however, there has been a worldwide interest in reforming the organisational structure of tax departments.

3.69 One of the important general organisational issues relate to the placement of the tax administration in relation to the Ministry of Finance. While traditionally the tax administration has been placed within the Ministry of Finance, tax administrations are increasingly attracted to the Canadian model where the tax administration is placed outside the Ministry of Finance with full autonomy. Since the Finance Ministry is responsible for the preparation and execution of the government budget, it must necessarily continue to have authority over both revenue collection and expenditure to fulfill that responsibility. Analogously, CBDT, which is responsible for administering the direct tax laws, should be given the requisite autonomy so that it is made more accountable.

3.70 Deeply concerned about the lack of any meaningful accountability of the tax administration, the Task Force recommends the following:

(a) The control of the Central Government over the tax administration be exercised through a Memorandum of Understanding (MOU) between the Central Board of Direct

Taxes and the Central Government (we understand that there is already a Cabinet decision to this effect). The Central Board of Revenue Act provides that the two boards (CBDT and CBEC) must function subject to the control of the Central Government, but the mechanism and the extent of control still remains unspecified.

(b) The MOU should, inter alia, specify the financial commitment of the Central Government for tax administration.

(c) The MOU to provide for full financial autonomy and control over deployment of human resources to the CBDT. The Central Government should only specify the general guidelines for financial expenditure and deployment of human resources.

(d) The MoU should be for a period of five years specifying observable performance indicators for CBDT and the financial resources that would be made available to CBDT on a year-to-year basis.

(e) The CBDT should have exclusive power for designing the enforcement strategy, subject to the condition that it is non-discriminatory and transparent.

3.71 The Task Force also observed that the turnover of Members and Chairman of the Board was too high. The Task Force recommends that the rules for appointment of Members should provide for selection on criteria of merit-cum-seniority from amongst those who have a minimum period of two years of service before retirement as on the date on which the vacancy arises. Further, an officer once appointed as member of the Board should be debarred from any appointment either in the ITAT or Settlement Commission. Similarly, the Chairman, CBDT should be selected on criterion of merit cum seniority and once appointed should have a minimum tenure of two years.

3.72 The Task Force also noted that the standards of accountability at the field formation level were considerably diluted since, inter alia, the performance targets, particularly those related to revenue collection, were unrealistic and thrust upon them. The field formations were either resigned to the failure of the targets or resorted to questionable practices to meet revenue targets divorced from underlying economic trends. The Task Force was informed that very often officers were (informally) directed to hold back refunds to boost revenue collection. Accordingly, it is strongly recommended that the revenue targets should be based on underlying economic trends.

3.73 Regrettably, the Task Force received large number of complaints from taxpayers across the country about lack of accountability of any tax administrator for actions that were sometimes malafide. While our recommendations on systemic improvement and policy changes would certainly enhance transparency and reduce discretion, thereby reducing opportunities for rent seeking, nevertheless it is necessary for the tax administration to be even handed both with the taxpayers and its officials and staff. We are informed that a set of Conduct Rules exists to regulate the conduct of officers and staff. Inspite of this we consider it necessary to reiterate the direction by the Honorable Supreme Court[18] that disciplinary action must be taken in the following cases:

1. Where the officer had acted in a manner as would reflect on his reputation for integrity or good faith or devotion to duty;
2. If there is prima facie material to show recklessness or misconduct in the discharge of his duty;
3. If the officer has acted in a manner which is unbecoming of a Government servant;
4. If the officer has acted negligently or that he omitted the prescribed conditions which are essential for the exercise of the statutory powers;
5. If the officer has acted in order to unduly favour a party;
6. If the officer has been actuated by corrupt motive, however small the bribe may be because Lord Coke said long ago 'through the bribe may be small, yet the fault is great'.

3.74 Further, as a confidence building measure, the Task Force recommends that the Central Board of Direct Taxes should release annual information (giving Chief Commissioner-wise break-up) of number of complaints received from the public or acts of omission or commission identified through internal mechanism or by external agencies and the result of official enquiry into such complaints. The information must be provided separately for officers and staff. Such information may relate to tax payer profiles, returns received, headwise breakup of income, number of appeals filed and disposed of, penalty orders, rectification applications, reopening of assessment, refund orders, refunds issued, returns selected for scrutiny assessment and their results, break up of collection, etc.

3.75 The ultimate accountability of the tax administration is to the citizens. With a view to enhancing accountability of (and transparency in) tax administration, it is important that the CBDT publishes an annual report of its own, along the lines of the UPSC/CVC, that is tabled in Parliament and put on its web site. The annual report must separately provide for performance achievements of each Chief Commissioner/Commissioner. In addition, the quarterly progress of achievement must be displayed on the web site, so that taxpayers have an opportunity to respond. While defining a stricter accountability structure, however, care must be taken to eschew an excessive and regimented accountability system which over-burdens AOs with onerous and fragmented oversight that ultimately only serves to reduce its overall effectiveness.

Delegation of Financial Powers

3.76 The Central Board of Direct Taxes was created out of the Central Board of Revenue in the early Sixties. Ever since it has functioned as a part of the Department of Revenue.

3.77 In those days, the Income tax department had only a few offices and not a very large number of employees. Decision making was relatively less complicated and the tax laws were simple and remained unchanged for long periods of time. This situation continued for almost three decades, with only incremental changes.

3.78 Things, however, began to change very rapidly in early nineties. The number of taxpayers increased sharply. Induction of technology was no longer a choice but a necessity.

3.79 Decision making has now ceased to be simple since speedy decisions are necessary on all issues of tax policy as well as management. Most decisions today have to be in hard real time as even soft real time may be late. Delays in decision making impose a great burden on the effectiveness of the tax administration.

3.80 In the context of the rapidly changing environment, CBDT has to attend to several functions critical to efficient functioning of Income Tax Department. It has to get ready about 55,000 personnel for induction of technology and provide world class services to more than 2 crore taxpayers. The technology induction initiative involves reorientation of the entire staff and also training them in new skills, extensive communication with taxpayers and public at large and constant review and updating of technology. It is only appropriate that at this critical juncture the CBDT is given necessary and sufficient authority to manage the affairs of the Income Tax department. Powers over the use of resources (both financial and human) must be commensurate with responsibility. A comprehensive technology induction initiative requires comprehensive authority for its implementation.

3.81 In this backdrop, it will not be out of place to mention that it is a declared policy of the Government to encourage Ministries to delegate powers to subordinate offices. As a matter of fact, Government of India decision number 7 under Rule 13 of Delegation of Financial Rules, 1978 mentions not only suitable delegation to match requirements of subordinate offices, it also stipulates a three-yearly review of the delegated powers. Unfortunately, CBDT has continued to function without any financial authority to guide and control affairs of Income Tax offices across the country. The Task Force is of the view that the position should be immediately rectified through adequate delegation of powers to bring in synergy and effectiveness in management functions.

Human Resource Management

3.82 The absence of control over human resources has further undermined accountability. Therefore, we recommend that the Central Government should delegate to CBDT full authority and responsibility regarding staff of the income tax department and its secretariat. The CBDT should, however, exercise such delegated powers in a transparent manner within the framework of rules and guidelines framed for this purpose. Such rules and guidelines should be framed with the approval of the government.

Infrastructure

3.83 The Task Force was aghast at the physical environment prevailing in most tax offices. We were also told by professionals that office space, work conditions and basic conveniences for staff, as well as storage facilities for tax records, are grossly inadequate. Facilities for taxpayers are even worse. The existing office layout is inimical to modernisation and induction of information technology. To institute these changes, the Task Force recommends the following:

(a) Based on the report of the Task Force set up by the CBDT in pursuant to our recommendation in the Consultation Paper, the CBDT should request Chief Commissioners to identify the shortcomings in their offices by 1st April 2003 and send forward a proposal to CBDT.

(b) By 1st August 2003 a model Commissionerate including the offices at the range, circle and ward levels should be established in each zone.

(c) CBDT should seek the requisite financial sanction to replicate the model offices by either upgrading existing offices or, where necessary, by purchasing new premises, etc. The entire exercise should be time bound so that by January 2005 modern offices are in place in all Commissionerates.

Notes

11 Bird, Richard M. and Milka Casanegra (1992), Improving Tax Reform in Developing Countries, International Monetary Fund, Washington D.C.

12 Faria, Angelo and Zutu Yucelik (1995), 'The Interrelationship between Tax Policy and Tax Administration' in Parthasarathi Shome (ed.), Tax Policy Handbook, International Monetary Fund, Washington D.C.

13 Faria, Angelo and Zutu Yucelik (1995), 'The Interrelationship between Tax Policy and Tax Administration' in Parthasarathi Shome (ed.), Tax Policy Handbook, International Monetary Fund, Washington D.C.

14 This is exclusive of the dead-weight loss on account of distortionary impact of taxes.

15 Section 139A

16 The other objectives of an audit programme are to (i) protect the expected yield from the tax; (ii) identify the true amount of tax, and bring errors to account; (iii) seek value for money in the deployment of audit resources; and (iv) maintain social acceptance of the tax.

16a. A suggestion was made that companies with a turnover of less than Rs.40 lakhs should also be exempted from the requirement to deduct tax at source. Since such incorporated bodies are organized institutions with adequate infrastructural facilities, we are not inclined to accept this suggestion.

17 For detail procedure for Issue of Refund, reference may be made to DOMS Circular No.:54, dated 16/ 12/87 and Circular No.: 58, dated 08/ 02/98.

18 Union of India and Others Vs. Upendra Singh (207ITR-782, SC)

4

Personal Income Tax Reform

Ramifications of Tax Policy for Tax Administration[19]

By the late 1960s and early 1970s, Scandinavia, the United Kingdom and other developed countries, as well as many developing nations, had legislated multiple and high individual income tax rates. Among the highest was India's, where it was well over 95 per cent. Such high and multiple rates not only made tax administration very difficult, but also led to a state, especially in developed countries, where income tax evasion became widely accepted as standard behaviour. During this era, corporate income tax rates were also very high — with most countries legislating rates between 50 per cent and 60 per cent.

4.2 The expected negative ramification of such high marginal tax rates was that income tax became replete with exemptions, allowances, deductions and incentives. What started as sectoral and specific reliefs from high taxes were soon extended to facilitate and accommodate social or development goals. It was rarely analysed whether such tax exemptions actually achieved the desired objectives. But these developed lives of their own and, in most countries, inevitably multiplied over time — driven by interests of specific power groups at different points of time. India was no exception.

4.3 Thus, over and above the personal exemption or threshold, the individual income tax base became eroded by explicit deductions for household size (which has been used both as an allowance in some countries and as a disincentive in others), education expenses and loans (as social objective), life insurance (both for social security and saving objectives), and particular saving instruments such as government securities or small banks such as post-office saving banks. It also excluded implicit income from owner occupied housing, sometimes pecuniary income from second homes, agriculture income and so on, across the world. In some Asian and Latin American countries, certain sources of income such as interest, dividends, and gains from capital were exempted altogether. Understandably, in not a few countries including some developed ones, individual income tax came to be popularly known as a 'voluntary tax'.

4.4 The corporate income tax base also became analogously eroded. Accelerated depreciation for select activities, tax incentives for employment generation or capital equipment, tax holidays for export-oriented industry, breaks for backward region development, small-scale industry and environmental investment, and the like — all these became a part of the fiscal landscape of India. Often, these exemptions led to inequitable taxation. For example, the jewellery industry produced very large incomes, but contributed to little revenue. In other instances, it led to excessive imports of unused accessories such as windmills or solar energy panels. Such examples can be multiplied.

4.5 While some countries attempted to narrow the scope of incentives over time, many failed to carry out comprehensive reform in tax policy and concomitant tax administration. In most part, this reflected the power of lobbies and political economy constraints associated with removing a vast spectrum of incentives in one go. However, the incremental approach to reform is also fraught with dangers. The electoral cycle of democracies make it very difficult for even reformist governments to credibly pre-commit to a time-table and schedule of reforms. More often than not, this has resulted in the original objectives being diluted — only to recreate new opacity in the 'reformed' tax system.

4.6 A few facts need to be stated at this stage — facts that are common knowledge to most experts in fiscal policy.

- First, there is hardly any evidence to prove that tax incentives have, per se, increased investment or saving — for which these incentives were devised.
- Second, the corollary has been proven very often — namely, that scaling back of tax incentives and exemptions

have almost always had a positive effect on tax policy, tax revenue, tax compliance and tax administration.

- Third, decreasing the intensity of tax incentives automatically translates to a tax expenditure. Thus, even if gross tax revenues remained the same, the net tax revenue would necessarily be higher.
- Fourth, the other important implication of "exemption raj" tax regime is the loss of effective parliamentary oversight as the resultant "tax expenditure" are not transparent and not amenable to the C&AG audit; a clear loss to democratic governance.
- Fifth, the tax incentives create antagonistic tension between the tax administrator and the taxpayer as the tax system is being asked to meet multiple objectives such as support to R&D, development of backward area etc. This becomes a source of litigation.
- Sixth, fewer the tax incentives, the less is the discretionary space available to tax administrators to interpret the law or executive statutes. It has been repeatedly emphasised to this Task Force that the 'control over the provision of tax incentives to a particular investor' by 'government officials' is a 'major instrument that makes corruption possible' — which often results in unwarranted discretion in the hands of officials, and militates against arm's length transactions.

4.7 The results of the income tax laws due to the "exemption raj", comprising of complex, allowance and exemption, are two-fold. For honest taxpayers, on the one hand, filing the income tax return continues to be an annual exercise in complexity, and an uncomfortable fear of the assessment by the tax administrator that is to follow. On the other, a direct result of the complexity in the tax structure is the difficulty faced by tax administrators in carrying out initial assessments, as well as to execute selective audit functions.

4.8 By the beginning of the 1980s, things had begun to change — starting with developed countries and then spreading to globalising developing nations. By the mid-1990s, the structure, design and enforcement of both individual and corporate income taxes underwent major changes. Earlier ideological objectives were substituted by considerations of incentive compatibility, reasonableness, administrative feasibility, stability and the credibility of fair enforcement.

4.9 The first step in reforming the income tax structure was reducing the number of as well as the level of rates. By the mid-1990s, many developing countries had emerged from the reform process having legislated individual income tax structures with significantly lower and fewer rates — typically 15-25-35 per cent. Even India legislated comparable rates in 1997. Similarly the corporate income tax rates were slashed — sometimes halved from the prevailing rate — driven by the twin objectives of administrative feasibility and better tax compliance.

4.10 Forces of globalisation also played a major role in the international convergence of tax rates and structures. In a world on increasingly mobile and frictionless international flow of capital, outward looking national governments soon realised that getting a share of competitive global capital necessitated keeping the tax rates low and tax rules simple — in line with global trends.

4.11 The global experience is with lower tax rates and fewer opaque exemptions, the administration of income tax became much simpler. The administration's resources was better spent on alternative investments — such as modernising the tax administration through widespread computerisation, including electronic filing, better data processing and mining, and production of far better statistical output. These resources and inputs, in turn, were more usefully employed both in formulating future tax policy, as well as in better enforcement, through more transparent and finer tax audit selection.

4.12 At the beginning of the 21st century, some truths about taxation have become self-evident. Even so, they bear repetition.

- First, the design of tax policy is of paramount importance for tax administration.
- Second, if the objective is to have a transparent, efficient and feasible tax administration, then the structure of all taxes should comprise common elements. These are low rates, few nominal rates, a broad base, few exemptions, few incentives, few surcharges, few temporary measures.

And in the rare instances where there are exceptions, there should be clear guidelines.

4.13 The Task Force is unanimously in favour of these overarching fiscal principles. And the recommendations that follow in this chapter and the next derive from these objectives.

Personal Income Tax Rates

4.14 It is well recognised that the rates of tax affect economic behaviour of taxpayers i.e. choice between work and leisure, the choice between consumption and savings, and also the compliance behaviour of taxpayers. The design of a personal income tax rate schedule must therefore be equitable and efficient — which are potentially conflicting objectives. A highly progressive tax rate schedule, while meeting the ends of vertical equity, causes higher distortion in the economic behaviour of taxpayers and therefore promotes inefficiency. Further, high rates of taxes induce tax evasion, thereby undermining the effective impact on equity. The Report of the Advisory Group on Tax Policy and Tax Administration for the Tenth Plan has enumerated the following principles for designing the rate schedule:

- The basic exemption limit must be at a moderate level — an appropriate balance between the tax liability at the lowest levels, administrative cost of collection and compliance burden of the smallest taxpayers. The ability of the tax administration to render quality services to taxpayers will also significantly affect the choice of the exemption limit.
- The number of tax slabs should be few and their ranges fairly large to minimise distortions arising out of bracket creep.
- The maximum marginal rate of tax should be moderate, so that the distortions in the economic behaviour of taxpayers and incentive to evade tax payment are minimised.

This Task Force endorses these principles.

4.15 Personal income tax rates in India were at their peak in 1973-74 — with the exemption limit at Rs.5,000, the minimum marginal rates of tax at 10 per cent, and the maximum marginal rate of tax rising to 85 per cent spread over eleven tax slabs. Additionally, there was also a surcharge of 10 per cent where the total income was below Rs.15,000, and a rate of 15 per cent in other cases. Therefore the "effective" maximum marginal statutory rate was 97.75 per cent. The progressivity of the tax system was very high.[20] The large number of tax slabs, also distorted the progressivity of the tax system due to bracket creep. The design of the tax rate schedule was neither economically efficient nor equitable, nor amenable to voluntary compliance.

4.16 Since those days, there has been a steady increase in the exemption limit, decrease in the maximum marginal rate of tax, and reduction in the number of tax slabs. As a result, the design of the tax rate schedule has been made relatively more efficient. Since the number of tax slabs has been reduced substantially, the distortion in the equity of the schedule arising due to bracket creep has also been considerably minimised. However, there has been a steady decline in the progressivity due to the sharp reduction in the maximum marginal rate of tax and failure to adjust the tax slabs to inflation.

4.17 The exemption limit of Rs.5,000 in 1973-74 is equivalent to Rs.50,000 at current prices in 2001-2002. However, the exemption limit was increased to Rs.50,000 in 1998-99 itself i.e. 3 years in advance. Therefore, the increase in the exemption limit has outpaced inflation. Further, a survey of the effective exemption levels across countries indicate that the exemption level in India is relatively high — thereby keeping out a relatively larger number of people outside the tax net. If the share of direct taxes to GDP has to be increased to internationally prevalent levels, it is equally necessary that the tax system is as broad based as in other countries.

4.18 At present, there are three tax slabs. Most countries have three to five slabs. As mentioned, greater the number of tax slabs, larger is the distortion due to bracket creep. The fairest (in terms of horizontal equity in the broadest sense), the simplest and the most easily administrable form of income tax is a moderately progressive flat, or single marginal rate, income tax levied on a comprehensive base[21]. With a flat rate income tax, most of the defects in, and the problems caused by, an income tax with a progressive rate schedule virtually disappears[22] . With a moderate single rate, almost all the deductions and tax preferences could be eliminated making the task of administration easy. All those with taxable incomes can opt for tax deduction at source to the maximum extent possible — thus making tax deduction at source can become an important way of collecting tax.

4.19 Full integration of personal and corporate income taxes can be achieved by applying the same single rate to both incomes and exempting dividends in the hands of the shareholders. With a single rate, the inequality in the treatment between steady and fluctuating incomes as well as between incomes that are concentrated during a short period in life and those that are spread over a long period will be greatly reduced. All capital gains can be taxed as ordinary income, with long-term gains being suitably indexed for inflation. With a single rate, "bunching" does not cause any serious problem. There will be need only for the indexation of the exemption level; there will be no bracket creep. Inflation will still create problems, but the interaction of inflation and income taxation will produce much less iniquitous effects than under a progressive schedule.

4.20 However, a single rate cannot be pitched at a high level. Therefore, the rate of progression that can be achieved will inevitably be moderate. By many, this is considered to be the single most significant demerit of the system. In the Indian context, since a single rate would have to be around 30 per cent, the exemption level would also have to be fairly high. That, in turn, would leave out some people who could reasonably be brought within the income tax net with a lower tax rate.

4.21 The Task Force, therefore, decided to reject the imposition of a single individual income tax rate, and instead opt for a reformed system of personal income tax with more than one rate. The Task Force believes that the alternative lies in a multiple rate schedule, but with very little spread.

4.22 An opinion was expressed in some quarters that the entry tax rate in personal income tax should be relatively low so that it does not frighten potential taxpayers from being in the tax net. However, with a low entry rate, the number of rates inevitably multiplies, and the tax administration ends up at square one — all the problems associated with a progressive rate schedule.

4.23 The Task Force's aim is precisely to minimise these problems. Our perception is that potential taxpayers at the lower end of the scale are frightened not by the entry rate of tax (since the average tax continues to be very low) but more by the compliance and enforcement procedures. The Task Force, therefore, believes that it is not necessary to lower the entry rate of tax. Further, in view of the distortionary impact of multiple slabs, the Task Force recommends a two rate schedule for personal income tax.[23] But before outlining the slabs and their rates, it is necessary to explain the empirical reasons for arriving at such a conclusion.

4.24 In 1973-74, the tax rates of 10 per cent and 20 per cent were applicable for incomes up to Rs.10,000 and Rs.20,000 respectively. The corresponding inflation adjusted income levels are Rs.1,00,000 and Rs.2,00,000 in 2001-2002. Thus, the existing corresponding income levels of Rs.60,000 and Rs.1,50,000 are substantially lower than the inflationindexed levels — thereby resulting in an increase in the real tax liability. Historically, while the top marginal rates of tax have been reduced, the tax liability at the middle has indeed increased. This has, not surprisingly though, has given rise to the problem of "the missing middle". If the full effect of lower tax rates has to be realised, it is not only necessary to have an optimal enforcement strategy but also ensure that the benefits of a tax cut apply to all class of taxpayers — rather than be restricted to a handful of taxpayers at the top end. This is possibly achieved by broad basing the tax slabs and we recommend accordingly.

4.25 In view of the above, we had recommended in the Consultation Paper for public debate that the personal income tax rate schedule should be revised along the lines indicated in Table 4.1.

Table – 4.1

Proposed Personal Income Tax Structure

Income level	Tax rates
Below Rs. 1,00,000	Nil
Rs. 1,00,000-4,00,000	20 percent of the Income in excess of Rs. 1,00,000/-
Above Rs. 4,00,000	Rs.60,000/- plus 30 percent of the Income in excess of Rs. 4,00,000\-

4.26 Further, the revenue gain from levy of surcharge is generally illusory since such a levy has the effect of increasing the marginal rate of tax, which adversely affect compliance. Therefore, we had also recommended that the present surcharge of 5 per cent on taxpayers with incomes above Rs. 60,000/- must be eliminated.

4.27 Reacting to the rate schedule proposed in Table 4.1, some section of the public (including tax administrators) have expressed apprehension at the possibility of a large number of taxpayers dropping out of the tax net consequent to the sharp increase in the exemption limit. It was felt that if indeed this happened, the programme for widening the tax base would suffer a serious set back. However, given the package of administrative and policy reforms and empirical evidence, the apprehension is misplaced.

4.28 A substantial part of the proposed increase in the exemption limit will be neutralized by our recommendations in the subsequent sections for the withdrawal/elimination of standard deduction, saving incentives u/s 80-L, and conversion of income based deduction into rebates. Therefore, the effective increase in the exemption limit is substantially less.

4.29 The recent sharp increase in the number of taxpayers is attributed to the one by six scheme, which provides for filing of returns by any person who owns the specified assets or has incurred specified expenditure. This scheme has had a direct effect on increase in the number of non-taxpayer filers. However, it appears that this scheme has also had a deterrent effect[24]; taxpayers who would not have otherwise filed their tax returns and disclose their income, have been induced to file their return for fear of identification through the one by six scheme. Since there is no recommendation by us to abolish this scheme, we believe that it would not be possible for existing filers to escape their filing liability.

4.30 We recognise that there could be filers who are not covered by the one by six scheme but have taxable income in the range of Rs. 50,000/- to Rs. 1,00,000/-. Consequent to the increase in the exemption limit, such filers would drop out of the tax net. This is possible only in a static condition. With annual increase in taxpayers income, such filers would be pushed back into the tax net. Empirical evidence suggests that increase in exemption limits have never resulted in the fall in the number of taxpayers (Table 4.2).

Table – 4.2

Trend of Exemption Limit for Personal Income Tax and the Growth of Taxpayers Base

Financial year	Number of taxpayers (as on 1st April of the year)	Exemption limit (at current prices)	Financial year	Number of taxpayers (as on 1st April of the year)	Exemption limit (at current prices)
1965-66	2126398	3000	1984-85	4932094	15000
1966-67	NA	3500	1985-86	4937657	18000
1967-68	2696407	3500	1986-87	5502142	18000
1968-69	2708464	3500	1987-88	6261465	18000
1969-70	NA	3500	1988-89	7883247	18000
1970-71	3230000	5000	1989-90	8583690	18000
1971-72	3012570	5000	1990-91	8934442	22000
1972-73	3208516	5000	1991-92	9391172	22000
1973-74	3388259	5000	1992-93	9671289	28000
1974-75	3460843	6000	1993-94	10450677	30000
1975-76	3637434	6000	1994-95	11668075	35000
1976-77	3796258	8000	1995-96	13208781	40000
1977-78	3778724	10000	1996-97	14094644	40000
1978-79	3955244	10000	1997-98	15979205	40000
1979-80	3969965	10000	1998-99	17578326	50000
1980-81	4175615	12000	1999-2000	21744508	50000
1981-82	4594425	15000	2000-01	25052380	50000
1982-83	4660865	15000	2001-02	28681380	50000
1983-84	4797260	15000	2002-03	34407380	50000

Sources :
1. Annual Reports of the Ministry of Finance (different years)
2. Comptroller and Auditor General of India, reports for various years.
3. Performance Statistics of the Income Tax Department (different years).
4. CAP statement of Income Tax Department(different years)

Note : The number of taxpayers as on 1st April, 2002 indicated is based on the above sources. The CBDT has informed that the number of taxpayers as on 1st April, 2002 is 300.02 lakhs. This needs to be reconciled. However, this difference does not in any way effect the point that the Task Force intends to make.

4.31 Our recommendation relating to broad basing of the tax slabs will reduce the marginal rate of tax for most taxpayers. This in turn, at existing enforcement levels, will induce a large number of taxpayers (particularly businessman / professionals) to disclose higher incomes. Increase in voluntary compliance will therefore contain the potential damage to the tax base.

4.32 The creation of the Tax Information Network (TIN), would enable the department to continue to keep a watch on non-taxpayers at the margin and also identify non-filers. This will, in-fact, provide an impetus to the ongoing programme for widening of tax base. Further, we are also guided by the consideration that an average family[25] need not necessarily be subjected to a progressivity tax in the form of income tax and its compliance burden. Their contribution to the national exchequer through consumption tax should be adequate.

4.33 A large number of individuals file their returns to claim refund because their income has been subjected to TDS even though their aggregate income is below the exemption limit. Since income will continue to be subject to TDS, such returns will continue to be filed. In the light of the above, the Task Force is of the view that the current initiatives to widen the tax base would not be jeopardised in anyway.

4.34 A section of the public (including some in the government) expressed a view that a two rate structure is not progressive enough. It was also argued that as in most other countries, we should continue to have a three rate structure with a lower entry point of tax.

4.35 The Task Force has estimated the progressivity of the tax schedule as measured by the coefficient of variation of tax liability at assumed levels of taxable income (Table – 4.3 and Chart – 1). The progressivity of the tax schedule has registered a steady decline since 1973-74 from a high of 1.18 to 0.7 in 2002-03[26]. The progressivity will increase from 0.7 to 1.04 consequent to the reduction in the number of slabs. The intuitive logic for this increase in progressivity is simple. Under the existing three slab rate schedule, the maximum marginal rate of 30 per-cent is applicable to incomes above Rs. 1,50,000/-. Therefore, most taxpayers are subjected to tax at the same higher rate. Under the

Table – 4.3

Progressivity of the Personal Income Tax Schedule

Fin. Year	Average tax Liability for Assumed Level of taxable Income at 2003-2004 prices												Coefficient
	Income Levels 50000	60000	75000	100000	120000	150000	175000	200000	300000	500000	1000000	2000000	of Variation
1973-74	0.00	1.47	3.37	5.28	7.26	9.55	12.10	13.89	22.08	37.91	58.51	75.26	1.18
1974-75	0.00	1.96	4.21	6.95	8.54	10.95	12.83	15.35	26.07	0.00	57.08	67.04	1.26
1975-76	0.00	0.00	2.15	6.29	8.36	10.99	20.95	22.46	34.28	61.78	70.33	73.66	1.07
1976-77	0.00	0.00	1.90	5.55	7.37	9.76	11.59	13.58	21.79	32.55	47.02	56.51	1.08
1977-78	0.00	0.00	0.00	6.54	6.19	9.09	11.66	13.96	23.38	35.00	50.16	59.58	1.12
1978-79	0.00	0.00	0.00	6.89	6.66	9.47	12.22	14.63	24.12	35.73	50.78	59.89	1.10
1979-80	0.00	0.00	4.63	7.97	8.02	11.34	14.03	16.78	26.83	39.09	54.37	63.18	1.03
1980-81	0.00	0.00	5.54	4.38	6.95	10.83	13.82	16.94	25.96	38.03	51.34	58.67	1.03
1981-82	0.00	0.00	0.00	5.45	10.05	14.96	18.47	21.66	29.90	41.16	53.27	59.63	0.98
1982-83	0.00	0.00	0.00	7.49	11.74	16.62	20.36	23.31	31.76	0.00	54.56	60.28	1.11
1983-84	0.00	0.00	1.85	8.79	13.10	18.72	22.48	25.29	34.54	46.09	56.79	62.15	0.90
1984-85	0.00	0.00	3.06	8.69	12.49	17.51	9.59	14.02	32.40	42.68	52.28	57.08	0.97
1985-86	0.00	0.00	0.78	6.83	10.65	14.52	16.73	18.39	25.53	33.24	41.62	45.81	0.89
1986-87	0.00	0.00	2.46	8.40	12.00	15.60	17.66	19.81	26.54	34.41	42.21	46.10	0.84
1987-88	0.00	0.00	4.43	10.29	13.57	16.86	19.89	22.65	29.10	37.56	45.03	48.77	0.80
1988-89	0.00	1.18	5.94	11.74	14.78	17.82	21.51	24.07	30.05	38.66	45.58	49.04	0.76
1989-90	0.00	2.66	7.16	12.87	15.72	20.14	23.43	25.91	31.74	40.65	47.32	50.66	0.73
1990-91	0.68	3.90	8.18	13.63	16.36	20.14	22.98	25.11	34.86	43.32	49.66	52.83	0.72
1991-92	0.00	2.69	6.71	12.53	15.61	20.49	23.27	28.41	36.26	44.16	50.08	53.04	0.74
1992-93	1.18	4.32	8.90	14.17	17.90	22.32	24.85	26.74	38.12	45.27	50.63	53.32	0.69
1993-94	0.00	1.33	5.07	8.80	12.33	15.87	17.89	21.73	29.42	35.57	40.19	42.49	0.77
1994-95	0.00	0.00	2.62	6.97	9.83	13.86	16.17	17.90	29.45	33.67	36.83	38.42	0.83
1995-96	0.00	0.00	2.21	6.66	10.54	14.43	16.66	18.32	25.54	31.33	35.66	37.83	0.81
1996-97	0.00	0.00	3.72	8.63	12.19	15.75	17.79	20.16	26.77	32.06	36.03	38.02	0.76
1997-98	0.00	0.46	2.37	5.70	8.08	10.46	11.83	12.85	18.08	22.85	26.42	28.21	0.80
1998-99	0.00	0.00	1.45	5.90	8.25	10.60	11.94	13.34	18.89	23.33	26.67	28.33	0.81
1999-00	0.00	0.00	2.20	7.15	9.63	12.10	13.51	15.45	21.30	25.98	29.49	31.25	0.79
2000-2001	0.00	0.30	3.21	7.91	10.26	12.61	14.61	17.09	22.89	27.54	31.02	32.76	0.77
2001-2002	0.00	0.77	3.83	7.97	10.04	12.11	13.81	15.91	20.81	24.72	27.66	29.13	0.72
2002-2003	0.00	1.22	4.77	8.83	10.86	12.89	15.06	17.12	21.91	25.75	28.62	30.06	0.70
2003-2004	0.00	0.00	0.00	0.00	3.33	6.67	8.57	10.00	13.33	18.00	24.00	27.00	1.04

Chart – 1

Trend of Progressivity of Tax Schedule

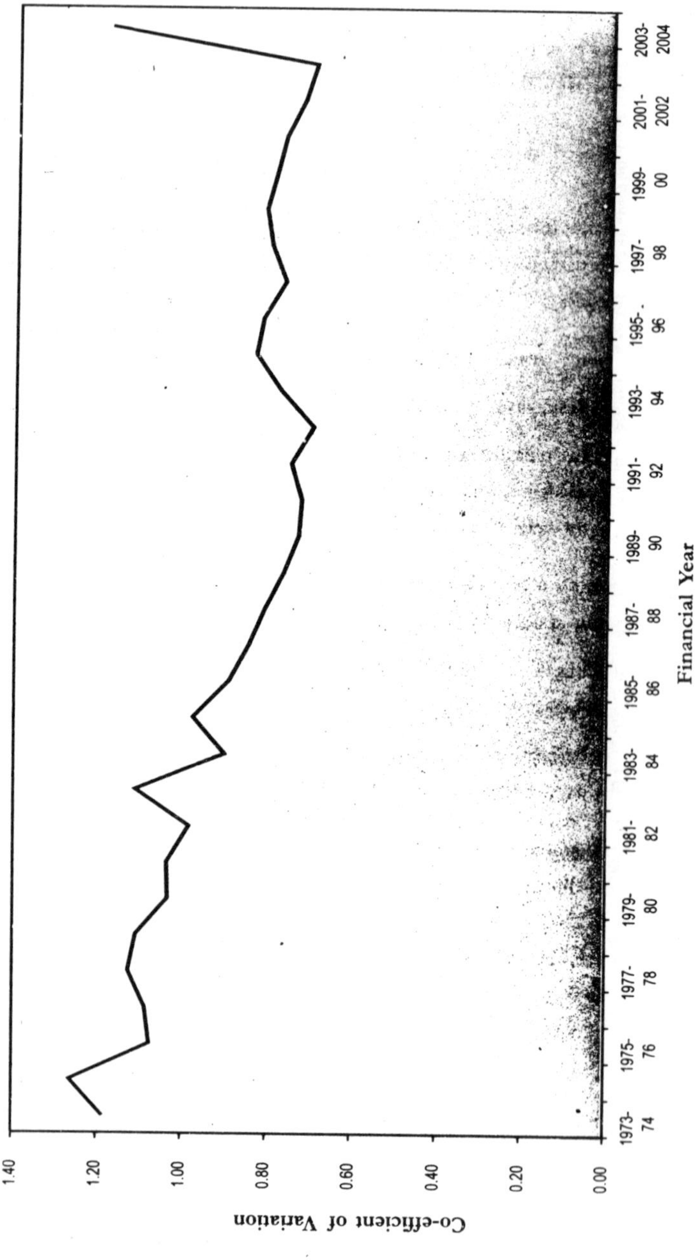

rate schedule proposed by us, most taxpayers would be taxable at the lower rate of 20 per cent and about 2 per cent of the taxpayers at the upper end only will be liable to tax at 30 per cent.

4.36 Most countries across the world have three to five rates, not because of the virtues, if any, of a multiple rates structure. Infact, multiple rate structures enhance problems of bracket creep and income smoothening. These countries have such a structure because of a low exemption limit with virtually no other exemptions/incentives. As a result, it is necessary to have low rates at the entry point to maintain the average rates at reasonable levels. If you have a low entry point of tax, then it becomes necessary to have multiple rates to reach a specified maximum rate. In India, the general exemption limit is at a moderate level coupled with large number of tax exemptions. Reform of such a system is possible only by substituting specific incentives by a generalized deduction in the form of an increase in exemption limit[27]. If the general exemption limit has to be raised, the rate of tax at the entry point cannot be relatively low since it will result in significant revenue loss without any design improvement.

4.37 In view of the above, we do not consider necessary to alter the personal income tax rate schedule contained in Table-4.1 and accordingly endorse the same.

Personal Income Tax Base

4.38 A negative effect of the early high marginal tax rates was that the income tax became replete with exemptions, allowances, deductions and incentives. Various exemptions and deductions still continue — in spite of significant reduction in personal income tax rates. As a result, the personal income tax law remains riddled with complexity, which inhibits voluntary compliance. Further, these benefit only a class of privileged taxpayers[28] and to the extent base is eroded, the large mass of general taxpayers have to bear the entire burden of a target revenue mobilisation effort. The consequential effect is the increase in marginal rates of tax — which in turn distorts economic efficiency and incentivises tax evasion. The very objective of reduction in tax rates is, therefore, only partially achieved. If compliance is to be fostered and nurtured and economic incentive sustained, it is necessary to review the various exemptions, deductions and rebates.

Exemption Based on Residential Status

4.39 Under the Income Tax Law in India, the tax base of a taxpayer is effected by the residential status enjoyed by him. A taxpayer could have one of the following three residential status:-

- *Resident :* A taxpayer is treated as a resident if he is:
  - (a) Resident in India for 182 days or more during the financial year;
  - (b) In India for a period of 60 days or more during the financial year and resident in India for at least 365 days in aggregate during the preceding four financial years.
- *Resident but Not Ordinarily Resident :* A taxpayer is treated as resident but nor ordinarily resident if he is:
  - (a) Resident in India for less then 9 years out of the preceding 10 financial years; or
  - (b) Resident in India for a period or periods amounting in all to less then 730 days during the preceding 7 financial years.
- *Non Resident :* A taxpayer is treated as non resident if he is neither a resident or resident but not ordinarily resident.

4.40 Residents are subject to tax on their world-wide income. Persons who are resident but not ordinarily resident are taxed only on Indian-sourced income[29], Non-residents are taxed only on Indian-sourced income and on income received, accruing or arising in India[30].

4.41 Persons who are resident but not ordinarily resident, enjoy exemption in respect of their foreign sourced income, even though in qualitative terms they are no different from residents. To the extent that most double taxation avoidance agreements provide for taxation of interest income in the country of residence, persons who are residents but not ordinarily residents enjoy exemption from foreign tax by claiming to be residents in India for the purpose of a treaty. Thanks to this peculiar category, therefore, a large number of such taxpayers end up paying no tax on their foreign sourced income, either in India or in any other part of the world. Further, most countries across the world provide for only two status: Residents and Non-residents.

4.42 Accordingly, the Task Force recommends that residents but not ordinarily residents must be subjected to tax on their global/ world-wide income at par with residents. To do so, this unusual category of resident but not ordinarily resident taxpayers must be deleted.

4.43 This will not only enhance the income tax base, but also remove an antiquated anomaly and simplify the law.

Standard Deduction for Employees

4.44 Under the Income Tax Act, a taxpayer is allowed a deduction of a certain percentage of his salary income subject to a maximum amount as standard deduction in the computation of his salary income chargeable to income tax. At present standard deduction is allowed from the gross salary of the taxpayer, according to the following schedule:-

1. For gross salary below Rs.1.5 Lakh the amount is restricted to 1/3rd of the gross salary or Rs.30,000, whichever is less.
2. For gross salary between Rs.1.5 Lakh and Rs.3 Lakh, the amount is restricted to Rs.25,000.
3. For gross salary between Rs.3 Lakh and Rs.5 Lakh, the amount is restricted to Rs.20,000.
4. For gross salary above Rs.5 Lakh, no standard deduction is allowed. In addition to the above, salaried employees are also eligible for a deduction up-to a maximum of Rs.9,600 towards conveyance allowance received from their employer.

4.45 The standard deduction allowed against salaried income is ostensibly to compensate, on an estimated basis, for the expenditure incidental to the employment of the taxpayer. The existing high level is often justified on the ground that unlike in the case of a selfemployed taxpayer, a salaried employee does not have opportunities to evade taxes[31]. As a result, the effective tax burden on salaried employee is greater then those deriving income from self-employment/business and that the bulk of the personal income tax revenues flow from salaried employees. Therefore, the standard deduction should be seen as compensating for loss of such 'privilege' and mitigating the effective tax burden.

4.46 It is indeed true that a self-employed taxpayer has greater opportunities to evade taxes by lumping there personal expense with other expenses which are tax deductible. However, such lumping is often investigated and in most cases disallowed. Further, it is not uncommon amongst salaried employees both in the private and public sector to evade taxes (like self-employed taxpayers) on their illegitimate incomes through rent seeking and voucher payments.

4.47 Similarly, the perception that the effective tax burden on salaried employee is greater than those deriving income from self-employment/business is also not borne by the tax treatment of perquisites received by a salaried employee. The tax treatment of various forms of income in the hands of a salaried employee and a self-employed is summarised in Table 4.4. A large number of perquisites which are available to salaried employees is either concessionally treated or fully exempt, thereby substantially reducing the effective tax burden on a salaried employee. In the case of a self-employed all such benefits have to be paid for out of the post tax income. Hence, the justification of standard deduction on the count that the effective tax burden on salaried taxpayers is relatively higher then selfemployed taxpayers is extremely weak.

4.48 The argument that the bulk of the income tax revenues are contributed by the salaried taxpayers is driven by perception rather than facts. On estimate, salaried taxpayers contribute only about 35 per cent of the personal tax revenues; the balance 65 per cent is contributed by the self-employed.

4.49 The levels of standard deduction have increased substantially over the years both in terms of the percentage and the overall ceiling — almost out of sync with the actual employment related expenses. The level of Rs.500 in 1974-75 allowable as standard deduction would now be equivalent to approximately Rs.5,000 in current terms. Once conveyance expenditure is separately exempted from taxation, it is difficult to visualise any other employment related expenditure other than personal in nature. This is particularly so when most employers provide for books and periodicals in the work place[32].

Table – 4.4

Treatment of benefits/expenditures across salaried and self-employed taxpayers.

Nature of benefit/ expenditure	Treatment in the hands of the salaried employee	Treatment in the hands of the self-employed	Remarks
Expenditure on travelling from home to work place.	Almost, all salaried employees in the organised sector are granted a conveyance allowance, which is exempt from tax, subject to a ceiling of Rs. 9,600/-.	No deduction available.	
Expenditure incidental to the employment of the taxpayer.	A standard deduction restricted to 1/3rd of the gross salary or Rs. 30,000/- whichever is less for taxpayers with gross salary below Rs. 1.5 lakh. However, the standard deduction is restricted to Rs. 25,000/- and Rs. 20,000/- for taxpayer with gross salary between Rs. 1.5 lakh to 3 lakh and between Rs. 3 lakh to 5 lakh respectively. No standard deduction is available to a taxpayer whose gross salary exceeds Rs. 5 lakh.	No such deduction is allowed.	Lumping of any such personnel expenses with business expenses is disallowable.
Valuation of residential accommodation provided by the employer	Concessional tax treatment.	No such perquisite is available.	A self-employed can avail of the benefits of a residential accommodation can only be availed from post tax income.

(Contd...)

Table – 4.4 (Contd..)

Treatment of benefits/expenditures across salaried and self-employed taxpayers.

Nature of benefit/ expenditure	Treatment in the hands of the salaried employee	Treatment in the hands of the self-employed	Remarks
Value of furnished accommodation.	Concessional tax treatment.	No such perquisite is available.	A self-employed can avail of the benefits of a residential accommodation can only be availed from post tax income.
Perquisite value of motor car used for personnel purposes.	Concessional tax treatment.	Fully taxed.	
Provision of medical facilities (proviso to Sec. 17(2).	• Fully exempt, if the medical treatment is in specified hospitals • Medical reimbursement other than above is exempt up-to Rs. 15,000/-	Fully taxed	
Interest free/concessional loans for medical treatment of specified diseases	Fully exempt	Fully taxed	
Expenses on employee's telephone including mobile phone	Fully exempt	Fully taxed	
House rent allowance	Concessional tax treatment	Fully taxed	
Leave travel allowance	Fully exempt	Fully taxed	

4.50 Unfortunately over the years, the increase in the standard deduction is an outcome of periodic demand for increase in the exemption limit by the salaried employees. Further the provision of a standard deduction to salaried taxpayers over and above the basic exemption limit is iniquitous in as much as it discriminates against self-employment. The Advisory Group on Tax Policy and Tax Administration for the Tenth Plan strongly recommended downward adjustment of this benefit.

4.51 Since then, the Task Force has also collected information across countries on the allowability of employment related expenses (Table 4.5). In most countries, no deduction is allowed for employee related expenses. Where such expenses are allowed, these are either based on actuals supported by documentation or on a presumptive basis with a cap at a very low level both in percentage and absolute terms (except Thailand). Therefore, the scale of the deduction for employee related expenses in the form of standard deduction is not in line with the best international practice.

4.52 The loss in revenue on account of standard deduction is substantial — more so because conveyance allowance is exempt from tax. Also, standard deduction of this relative scale are not in line with the best international practice and our recommendation on enhancing the general exemption limit.

4.53 The Task Force, therefore, recommends that standard deduction under Section 16(1) of the Income Tax Act should be eliminated. However, the exemption of conveyance allowance subject to a ceiling of Rs. 9,600/- should be continued. This should serve as a reasonable deduction for employment related expenses. The additional liability of a taxpayer on this account will be more than met by the reduction in rates of personal income tax proposed by the Task Force.

Treatment of Imputed Income from Owner Occupied House Property

4.54 Up to assessment year 1986-87, a notional annual value subject to a maximum of 10 per cent of the adjusted total income was imputed to the benefit flowing from the selfoccupation of the house property. Accordingly full allowance by way of deduction was made for ground rent, repair and maintenance, interest on borrowed capital and similar other items of expenditure.

Table – 4.5

Tax treatment of Employee related expenses@

Country	Whether any deduction is allowed for employee related expenses@?	Remarks
Bangladesh	No	
Singapore	No	
Italy	No	
New Zealand	No	
Sri Lanka	No	
Malaysia	Yes	Actuals supported by documentation.
Indonesia	Yes	5 per cent up-to a limit of Rp 1296 a year.
Philippines	No	
Germany	Yes	A lump-sum amount of Euro 1044 is deductible.
Netherlands	No	
Argentina	No	
Peru	No	
United Kingdom	Yes	Actuals
Japan	Yes	Standard deduction
Australia	No	
France	Yes	10 per cent of the salary subject to a limit of Euro 12229.
Thailand	Yes	40 per cent subject to a limit of Baht 60000.
United States	No	
Canada	No	
India	Yes	Standard deduction of 33.3 per cent subject to a limit of Rs. 30000.

@ Employee related expenses are those, which are equivalent to the expenses, represented by the standard deduction u/s 16(1) of the Income Tax Act 1961 of India. Such expenses are wholly and exclusively incurred by the employee in the performance of the duty of employment, otherwise than those, which are reimbursed by the employer.

4.55 However, from assessment year 1987-88, the notional annual value imputed to the benefit flowing from self-occupation of the house property was deemed to be nil. Accordingly, it was provided that no deduction for the various items of expenditure would be allowed except a small amount of Rs.5,000 towards interest on borrowed capital. While non-deductibility of the various items of expenditure is consistent with the matching principle that expenditure relating to a particular item/source of income should be allowed only if the income is liable to tax in the economic/ accounting sense, the allowability of interest expenditure up-to Rs.5,000/- is a deviation from this principle. The problem has been further compounded by increasing the ceiling from Rs.5,000 to 1,00,000 in assessment year 2001-02, and further to Rs.1,50,000 for assessment year 2002-03 and subsequent years. The increase far exceeds the inflation during this period.

4.56 This incentive is in the nature of tax subsidy. Such a tax subsidy is both iniquitous and inefficient. To the extent income from owner occupied dwelling is not imputed for tax purposes, it encourages owners to keep the dwelling premises vacant rather than rent. Similarly, the incentive is inequitous between non-taxpayer owners and taxpayer owners — a housing subsidy for owners with higher income. Even amongst taxpayer owners, it confers relatively higher tax relief to those with higher income since they are subjected to a higher marginal rate of tax.

4.57 Table-4.6 below indicates that during 2001-02, an amount of Rs. 14,811 crores was disbursed by all the housing finance companies to 4,41,143 loanees[33]. Of this, there were 3,76,556 new loanees who availed of loans below Rs. 5 lakhs constituting 85 per cent of the new loanees. The share of this category of loanees in the total amount disbursed is only 59 per cent. The average size of the loan to these 85 per cent of the loanees is Rs. 2,32,661/-. The annual interest burden on such average loans would be around Rs. 25,000/-[34]. A large number of the new loanees in this category are likely to be nontaxpayers and therefore do not enjoy any kind of subsidy. Equally large number would be those who would be taxpayer owners, of which a significant proportion would have rented out their houses while a small proportion would be under owner occupation. Hence, a very small proportion of this category of loanees benefit from the tax treatment of mortgage interest on owner occupied dwelling.

4.58 Similarly, there were 48,145 and 16,442 new loanees during 2001-02 who availed of loans between Rs. 5 lakhs to Rs. 10 lakhs and above Rs. 10 lakhs, respectively. They constitute 11 per cent and 4 per cent of the new loanees, respectively. There share in the total amount disbursed is 23 per cent and 18 per cent respectively. The annual interest burden on the average loan in the two categories is estimated to be Rs.75,000/- and Rs. 1,60,000/- respectively. Given the size of the EMI payment for loanees in these two categories, it would be reasonable to assume that the average income of such loanees would be above Rs. 3 lakhs per year. Loanees in these categories will benefit substantially from our proposal to reduce tax rates and broaden the tax slabs. Additional relief by continuing with the tax subsidy for owner occupied dwelling for taxpayers with such high levels of income only helps to undermine vertical equity.

4.59 A conventional case for continuing housing incentive is based on the argument that it will adversely affect housing activities which has a multiplier affect on many other industries. It is also argued that the housing sector has been the engine of growth in the last two years driven mostly by the tax incentive for mortgage interest for owner occupied dwelling.

Table – 4.6

Number of Loanees and Amount Dispersed by Housing Finance Companies during 2001-02.

Size of the Housing Loan	No. of Loanees (Rs. in crs.)	Amount Disbursed loan	Percentage		Average size of the
			Loanees	Amount	
Up-to Rs. 5 lakhs	376556	8761	85%	59%	232661
Rs. 5 lakhs to Rs. 10 lakhs	48145	3442	11%	23%	714923
Above Rs. 10 lakhs	16442	2608	4%	18%	1586182
Total	441143	14811	100%	100%	335741

Source : National Housing Bank.

4.60 During the last two years the financial markets have witnessed instability due to scams etc. resulting in the erosion of investor confidence. This has compelled people to look for alternative forms of investment in the real sector like housing. Simultaneously during this period, the cost of housing has plummeted to its lowest; hence an attractive opportunity for people disillusioned with the performance in the financial market to invest in a house. While the opportunity is available, one of the factors affecting the decision to invest in a house would obviously be the effective cost of borrowing. Since this is, in turn, determined by the tax treatment of the nominal cost of borrowing, the tax incentive induces investment in housing. The prevailing nominal cost of borrowing was 12.5 per cent on housing loans for a period of 11 to 15 years[35]. The effective cost of borrowing for a taxpayer with a 20 and 30 per cent marginal rate of tax was 10 per cent and 8.75 per cent, respectively. The nominal cost of borrowing for similar loans have since reduced to 10.25 per cent. *Prima facie*, all the developments enumerated above are expected to have a positive effect on investment in housing. As yet, there is no study, which has disagreegated the impact of the various factors on the housing sector. It is therefore fallacious to argue that the withdrawal of the limited tax incentive will have any serious impact on housing. In any case, with the expected reduction in the interest rate for housing loans in the immediate future, the increased burden on account of withdrawal of the incentive would be substantially neutralised, if not eliminated.

4.61 Further, incentives for savings in financial instruments are proposed to be eliminated across the board. The relative attractiveness of investment in housing will therefore continue. Since most taxpayers with capacity to pay annual interest of Rs. 1,50,000 will benefit substantially[36] from reduction in tax rates due to broad basing of the tax slabs, they will have relatively larger amount of equity fund to invest in a house. The weighted average effective cost of borrowing will in most cases remain unchanged. It will also enable the taxpayer to accelerate the repayment thereby benefiting from reduced interest outgo[37]. Such investors in house will also benefit from our proposal to abolish wealth tax.

4.62 The proposal to reduce corporate tax rates in the subsequent sections of this report will substantially benefit the housing finance companies since they would be unaffected by the simultaneous withdrawal of a large number of tax preferences[38]. These companies should be expected to shift this benefit forward to the borrowers by way of reduced interest.

4.63 Our recommendations on capital gains restricting the exemption for rollover of capital gains, to investments in housing and the bonds of the National Highway Authority should divert more than Rs.1,000 crores to housing. This in itself should spur housing and other allied activities.

4.64 Further the deduction for mortgage interest for owner occupied dwelling is also inconsistent with international practice. In most countries, the mortgage interest in respect of loans for acquiring owner occupied dwelling is not deductible, as Table 4.7 shows.

4.65 It was argued before the Task Force that many of the smaller taxpayers, particularly in the working class, if left to them to fend for their old age, would end up requiring state support due to their individual myopia and destitution. Thus what is optimal at individual level may be socially sub-optimal. The aggregate of individual savings for old age income security, old age medical security and housing may not be adequate to generate socially optimal levels of such social security assets[39]. Therefore, such individuals should either be coerced or given adequate incentives to overcome their myopia. The Task Force recognises the potency of this argument even though there may not be any empirical evidence in support of the existence of individual myopia to the detriment of social needs.

4.66 In view of the aforesaid considerations, the Task Force recommends continued support to loanees of home loans. Since the existing scheme of tax treatment of mortgage interest for owner occupied dwelling is targeted to taxpayers alone, the problem of individual myopia may not be fully resolved. Infact, individual myopia is most likely to exist only amongst the lower category of taxpayers and non-taxpayers. Therefore, the first best policy option would be to incentivise borrowings for housing by providing 2 per cent interest subsidy on all loans below Rs. 5 lakhs. This subsidy should be granted by the Government through the National Housing Bank. This will indeed target such loanees who suffer from individual myopia. The second best policy measure for this purpose would be to continue with the tax treatment of mortgage interest for owner occupied houses. However, given the average size of the home loan (around Rs. 3.5 lakhs), we recommend that the ceiling on the amount of mortgage interest deductible for taxable income purposes should be reduced from the existing level of Rs. 1,50,000/- to Rs. 50,000/- only.

Table – 4.7

Tax Treatment of Mortgage Interest for Owner Occupied Dwelling

Country	Is the Imputed Income from Owner Occupied dwelling subjected to personal income tax?	Is Mortgage Interest Deductible for Tax Purposes?
Bangladesh	No	No
Singapore	Yes	Yes
Italy	Yes	Yes, A credit up to 19% of the interest paid, up to a maximum credit Italian 392.51 is granted to the loan drawn up before the year 1993.
New Zealand	No	No
Sri Lanka	No	Yes, No limit
Malaysia	No	No
Indonesia	No	No
Philippines	Not Available	No
Germany	No	No
Netherlands	Yes	Yes
Argentina	No	Yes, limited to ARS 20000
Peru	No	No
United Kingdom	No	No
Japan	No	Yes, subject to limit of Yen 5,00,000/-.
Australia	No	No
France	Not Available	No
Thailand	No	Yes, limited to Baht 50000
United States	No	Yes, subject to limits
Canada	Not Available	No
Sweden	Not Available	Yes
India	No	Yes, up to a maximum of Rs.1,50,000/-

Tax Treatment of Agricultural Income

4.67 The continued exemption of agricultural income from the scope of income tax continues to be a sore point with all taxpayers. For the sake of brevity, this Task Force does not consider it necessary to repeat/reproduce the various arguments advanced by experts. Briefly, the arguments in support of an income tax on agriculture are the following:

1. It distorts both horizontal and vertical equity;
2. It encourages laundering of non-agricultural income as agricultural income i.e. it has become a conduit for tax evasion.

Both the arguments are empirically verifiable. A close look at the tax returns of a large number of taxpayers in Mumbai by the Task Force revealed the following:

- A number of taxpayers had claimed large amount of income from agricultural operations. Since such income enjoyed exemption from the central income tax and there was no such tax effectively in place in the States, such taxpayers enjoyed favourable treatment vis-a-vis those earning equivalent level of income from nonagricultural activities. To this extent horizontal equity was distorted. Similarly, the favourable treatment of agricultural income also adversely affected vertical equity.
- *Prima facie* the claims for income from agricultural operations appeared to be doubtful to most officers since the agricultural operations are claimed to have been carried out in areas which are known to be infertile. Large-scale investigations against such claims are under progress. The department is expecting that most of these claims are likely to be withdrawn by the taxpayers.

4.68 Based on the sample in Mumbai, the revenue loss from laundering of nonagricultural income as agricultural income is estimated to be Rs.1,000 crores. Given the distortionary impact of continued exemption of agricultural income and the tax assignment under the Constitution, the Task Force recommends the following:-

(a) A tax rental arrangement should be designed whereby

States should pass a resolution under Article 252 of the Constitution authorising the Central Government to impose income tax on agricultural income. The taxes collected by the Centre would however be assigned to the States.

(b) Tax from agricultural income for the purposes of allocation between States will be the difference between the tax on total income (including agricultural income) and the tax on total income net of agricultural income.

(c) Where a taxpayer derives agricultural income from different States, the revenues attributable to a State will be in the ratio of the income derived from a particular State to the total agricultural income.

(d) A separate tax return form should be prescribed for taxpayers deriving income from agriculture.

These recommendations will help mobilise additional resources for the States without the attendant problem of administering the agricultural income tax. Further, given our recommendations on increasing the exemption limit to Rs.1,00,000 per individual, most agricultural farmers would continue to remain out of the tax net. The proposed rental arrangement with the States could be packaged with the rental arrangement for taxation of services.

Rationalising income tax exemptions on savings instruments

4.69 Tax exemptions for savings instruments have earlier been extensively analysed by various committees and expert groups in the course of their deliberations relating to other fiscal and financial issues. The most comprehensive of these reports have been those of the Committees chaired by Dr. Raja J Chelliah, Dr. Parthasarathi Shome[40] and Dr. Y.V. Reddy[41]. Given their sensible and comprehensive treatment of tax exemptions relating to savings, this Committee is of the view that the best way to proceed is a judicious adoption of the best recommendations culled from these Reports, with only some slight modifications designed to enhance consistency and ease of implementation, rather than an elaborate "re-invention of the wheel", as it were.

4.70 Consumption expenditure rather than income serves as the most efficient form of tax base under an ideal tax system.

Inspite of this, no country in the world has been able to successfully implement expenditure tax due to serious administrative problems. Almost all countries have relied upon income as a tax base. However, a tax on income is inherently biased against savings. There are two alternative ways of devising an income tax which neutralises this bias and therefore effectively uses consumption as a tax base :-

(a) Exempt Exempt Taxed (EET) Method : Under this method, the contributions to a saving plan/scheme are deductible from the gross income, the income (accumulations) of the plan/scheme is exempt from tax and the withdrawal of the contribution along with benefits in the form of interest, dividend etc. is subjected to tax.

(b) Taxed Exempt Exempt (TEE) Method : Under this method, the contribution to a saving plan /scheme are out of post tax income (i.e. contributions are taxable), the income accumulation is exempt from tax and the withdrawal of the contribution along with benefits in the form of interest, dividend etc. is exempt from tax.

4.71 In order to neutralise the bias against savings, most countries design their income tax structure, so as to provide for exemption/concessional tax treatment of the various savings instruments by following one of the two methods[42]. Some experts are also of the view that the distortion arising out of the inherent bias against savings could be tolerated by adopting a simple income tax structure with reasonable rates and a comprehensive base.

4.72 The theory of tax incidence on financial instruments indicates no reasons for differential treatment for those of long-term maturity from those of short and medium term maturity, taking the view that the term structure of interest rates would ensure efficient allocation of savings. In particular, the demands of fiscal neutrality that imposition of tax should not distort the choice between (a) different forms of saving, and (b) between consumption and saving are ensured under a non-discriminating tax treatment of savings irrespective of the maturity period. No strong empirical evidence exists, moreover, to support a hypothesis that tax incentives facilitate increased financial savings (by the private sector) at a macro level[43]. There is, therefore, a strong justification for taking an integrated view of fiscal concessions for financial instruments of all maturities.

Box – 4.1

Tax Treatment of Savings in Select Countries

In the USA, a section 401(k) plan is a type of deferred compensation plan in which an employee can elect to have his employer contribute a portion of his wages to the plan on a pre-tax basis. These deferred wages are not included in the taxable wages but they are subject to social security, Medicare, and federal unemployment taxes. The amount that an employee may elect to defer to a 401(k) plan is limited. During 2001, an employee cannot elect to defer more than $10,500 for all 401(k) plans in which the employee participates. But if the employee participates in a SIMPLE 401(k) plan, the limit for 2001 is $6,500. Both of these limits are indexed for inflation. Generally, all deferred compensation plans in which the employee participates must be considered to determine if the $10,500 limit is exceeded. All contributions to retirement plans (including deferred compensation plans) are subject to additional limits.

Housing, pensions and Individual Savings Accounts (ISAs) now cover the saving activity of the bulk of the population in the UK. Over the last two decades the UK has moved from an incoherent tax regime for savings to a seemingly more satisfactory one[44]. The four main schemes designed to encourage savings, keeping in mind an ageing population, had been the Business Expansion Scheme (BES), Private Personal Pensions (PPP), Personal Equity Plans (PEP) and Tax Exempt Special Savings Accounts (TESSA)[45]. Personal Equity Plans were announced in the 1986 Budget, implemented in 1987 but substantially reformed in later years. TESSA was announced in the budget of March 1990 and became available from January 1991. PEPs were a vehicle for investment in equities, with tax-free income. Contributions to PEPs were not tax deductible, but any income or capital gains accrued within a PEP are tax free, and there is no tax on withdrawals. TESSAs gave the same tax treatment as a PEP for funds in designated schemes with annual contribution limits; saving were out of taxed income but interest earned is tax free and there is no tax on withdrawals. This led to a situation of disparate tax treatment of different instruments used for similar purposes as well as for short- and long-term savings instruments. For example, for housing, equities and cash saving, saving was out of taxed income and there was no tax on returns and no tax on withdrawals, while, for pensions, saving is out of untaxed income, their fund income is untaxed but withdrawals are taxed. These two regimes produced the same effective tax rate of zero on the real return to saving. The one obvious exception is the existence of the tax-free lump sum in pensions, which makes the effective tax rate on the return to pensions saving negative.

In a bid to encourage personal saving, reforms introduced in November 2001 in Chile[46] allow new tax incentives to both salaried workers and the self-employed to encourage voluntary contributions to private pension funds. These will allow voluntary contributions to be deducted from an individual's taxable income. In order to qualify as deductible, they must, however, be invested in certain assets, such as mutual and other investment funds and life insurance, duly authorized by the appropriate regulatory authority. In addition, the new regulations allow individuals to withdraw part or all of their voluntary pension savings before reaching retirement age. However, in order to guard against excessive use of this prerogative, an exit tax will be levied on withdrawals, which will be treated as taxable income. Before the reform, only the AFPs (pension fund administrators) were allowed to offer taxdeductible savings schemes.

The Supplemental Retirement Scheme (SRS)[47] in Singapore, effective April 2001, is designed to encourage working employees to save for retirement, over and above their contributions to the Central Provident Fund (CPF). Contributions to the SRS by residents (up to an overall limit of S$15,000) are tax deductible the following year. The savings corpus, including interest, are to be taxed only upon withdrawal. Claims for deductions from taxable income are made automatically by the SRS operator to an individual's taxable income the following year. A penalty of 5 percent is imposed on premature withdrawal before retirement. The taxable base of the SRS corpus for an individual is 50 percent of his corpus, at a tax rate based on the individual's graduated tax rate of 0-26 percent.

4.73 The Indian tax system (emanating from the Income Tax Act, 1961) provides broadly the following types of tax incentives for financial savings:

(a) Deduction under section 80CCC for contribution to pension funds of Life Insurance Corporation of India or any other insurer, subject to a ceiling of Rs. 10,000/-. The pension/annuity under the scheme is, however, taxable.

(b) Deductions, provided in Section 80L allow for exemption

of income up to Rs.12,000/- from income tax on specified financial instruments (including bank deposits, NSC, post office deposits, Government securities, etc. with an additional and exclusive sub-ceiling of Rs.3,000 for interest income arising from Government securities).

(c) Exemption under Section 10(10D) in respect any sum received under a life insurance policy, including the sum allocated by way of bonus on such policy [other than any sum received under sub-section (3) of section 80DDA] [or under a Keyman insurance policy]

(d) Unlimited exemption under Section 10(11) and Section 10(12) in respect of any payment from a provident fund set up by the Central Government or set up under the Provident Fund Act 1925 or a recognised provident fund.

(e) Unlimited exemption under Section 10(13) in respect of any payment from a Superannuation Fund.

(f) Unlimited exemption under Section 10(15)(i) in respect of income by way of interest, premium on redemption or other payment on notified securities, bonds, annuity certificates, savings certificates, other certificates and deposits issued by the Central Government.

(g) Unlimited exemption under Section 10(15)(iib) in respect of interest on notified Capital Investment Bonds. However, no bonds can be notified after first day of June 2002.

(h) Unlimited exemption under Section 10(15)(iic) in respect of interest on Relief Bonds.

(i) Unlimited exemption under Section 10(15)(iid) in respect of interest on notified Bonds. However, no bonds can be notified after first day of June 2002.

(j) Unlimited exemption under Section 10(15)(iv)(h) in respect of interest on notified public sector bonds.

(k) Unlimited exemption under Section 10(15)(iv)(i) in respect of interest on deposits out of moneys received by an employee on retirement.

(l) Tax rebate, provided in Section 88, in respect of investment in specified assets (such as NSC, NSS, EPF and PPF, tax saving units of mutual funds, premium paid on life insurance, repayment of housing loans, and infrastructure bonds of IDBI and ICICI). In the financial year 2002-03, the rebates are provided at the following rates:

(i) The rebate shall not be available in case of persons having gross total income (before deduction under Chapter-VIA) more than Rs.5 lakhs.

(ii) For persons having gross total income (before deduction under Chapter-VIA) above Rs.1,50,000 but not more than Rs.5 lakhs, the rate of rebate shall be 15%

(iii) The rebate 20% shall continue for taxpayers having gross total income, (before deduction under Chapter-VIA) not exceeding Rs.1,50,000.

(iv) The rebate shall be higher @ 30% for salaried taxpayers having gross salary income not exceeding Rs.1 lakh (before allowing deduction under Section 16) and where gross salary income is not less than 90% of the gross total income from all other sources.

4.74 The limit of qualifying investment is Rs.1 lakh with exclusive limit of Rs.30,000 for subscription to equity shares or debentures of infrastructure companies, public financial institution and mutual funds.

4.75 The tax treatment of various financial instruments under the tax statue is summarised in Table 4.8.

Table – 4.8

Tax Treatment Of Financial Savings

Sl. No.	Nature of Instrument	Treatment of Contribution	Treatment of Accumulation	Treatment of Withdrawal	Method
1	Gratuity	Exempt[a]	Exempt	Exempt[2]	EEE
2	Pension/Deferred Annuity Plans	Exempt[b]	Exempt	Exempt[3]	EEE
3	Life Insurance Policy	Exempt[b]	Taxable	Exempt[2]	ETE
4	Provident Fund	Exempt[b]	Exempt	Exempt[2]	EEE
5	Superannuation Fund	Exempt[c]	Exempt	Exempt[2]	EEE
6	Notified Securities, Bonds, Annuity Certificates, Saving Certificates, and Other Certificates	Exempt[b]	Exempt	Exempt[2]	EEE
7	9% Relief Bonds	Taxable	Exempt	Exempt[2]	TEE
8	Public Sector Bonds/Debentures	Taxable	Exempt	Exempt[2]	TEE
9	Deposit Schemes for Retiring Employees	Exempt[d]	Exempt	Exempt[2]	EEE
10	Certain Pension Funds of LIC (Section 80 CCC)	Exempt[e]	Exempt	Taxable	EET
11	Medical Insurance (Section 80 D)	Exempt[e]	Taxable	Exempt[2]	ETE
12	Any Security of the Central Govt. or State Govt.	Exempt[b]	Exempt	Exempt[4]	EEE
13	National Saving Certificates (6th, 7th & 8th Issue)	Exempt[b]	Exempt	Exempt[4]	EEE
14	Debentures of any Institution, Authority, Public Sector Company or Co-operative Society Notified by the Govt.	Taxable	Exempt	Exempt[4]	TEE
15	National Deposit Scheme	Taxable	Exempt	Exempt[4]	TEE
16	Any Other Deposit Scheme Framed by the Central Govt. and Notified	Taxable	Exempt	Exempt[4]	TEE

(Contd...)

...contd...

17	Post Office (Monthly Income Account)	Taxable	Exempt	Exempt[4]	TEE
18	Units of Mutual Fund	Exempt[b]	Exempt	Exempt[4]	EEE
19	Units of UTI	Exempt[b]	Exempt	Exempt[4]	EEE
20	Deposits in Bank or Banking Co-operative Societies	Taxable	Exempt	Exempt[4]	TEE
21	Deposits in any other Bank	Taxable	Exempt	Exempt[4]	TEE
22	Deposits with Industrial Financial Corporations	Taxable	Exempt	Exempt[4]	TEE
23	Deposits with Local Development Authorities	Taxable	Exempt	Exempt[4]	TEE
24	Deposits by a member of a Co-operative Societies	Taxable	Exempt	Exempt[4]	TEE
25	Deposits with Housing Finance Companies	Exempt[b]	Exempt	Exempt[4]	EEE
26	Deposit Scheme of NHB	Exempt[b]	Exempt	Exempt[4]	EEE
27	ULIP	Exempt[b]	Exempt	Exempt[4]	EEE
28	10y.Rs. or 15 yrs Account Post Office Savings Bank (Cumulative Time Deposits) Rules 1959	Exempt[b]	Exempt	Exempt[5]	EEE
29	Purchase of House Property	Exempt[b]	–	Exempt[6]	E-E

Note :

a : Employees are not required to contribute and the employers contribution to the Fund are deductible.

b : Eligible for tax rebate under Section 88.

c : Contribution by the employee is eligible for tax rebate under Section 88. Contribution by the employer to the superannuation Fund is deductible.

d : Contributions are from retirement benefits which are exempt from tax.

e : Contributions are deductible under Section 80D.

2 : Withdrawal of both the contribution and benefits are exempt.

3 : Commutation of pension is exempt but the monthly pension is taxable.

4 : Withdrawal of contribution is exempt. The withdrawals of benefit is partially exempt under Section 80L.

5 : Withdrawal of contribution is exempt but the withdrawal of benefit is taxable.

6 : Cost of the property is exempt. Capital gain is treated concessionally. Imputed Rent is exempt. Rent received is taxable.

4.76 Under the existing income tax provisions, therefore, financial savings of households is generally exempted from taxation at all the three stages of savings, viz., contribution, accumulation and withdrawals[48]. This liberalized treatment has impacted economic efficiency, equity and revenue efforts.

4.77 Saving instruments with similar maturity but different tax concessions result in different effective yields, which involve a distortion of signals for investment decisions. While investment (or saving) under Section 88 is rewarded, disinvestment (dis-saving) is not brought under charge. The incentives encourage not necessarily just savings but also diversion of funds, from one form of investment to another and that too for mere locking up these funds (i.e., surrendering the purchasing power to the government) only for a specified period of time. The netting principle is not applicable and dis-savings remain untaxed. Therefore, there is a bias in favour of investment in short-term instruments, thereby creating serious distortions in the allocation of savings. The tax rebate, for repayment of instalments of housing loans made by taxpayers to specified institutions encourages debt as against "equity" financing.

4.78 In any scheme of incentives for savings, it is desirable that the investments to be encouraged have broadly similar rates of return. Any variation in these rates should only be due to differences in the holding period, underlying risk or some other overriding consideration of priority for a particular sector.

4.79 Deduction of net investment and allowing deduction of income from such investment are broadly equivalent in that each is sufficient to achieve treatment of savings as under a proportional expenditure tax. Yet, assets such as National Savings Certificates and provident funds enjoy both deductibility in investment (under Section 88) and of interest earning (under Section 80L and 10(11) or 10(12) respectively). This leads to inordinately high effective rates of return on these assets (see Table 4.9). In turn, these serve as a benchmark for rates of return (discount rate) and therefore lead to high cost of borrowing across all sectors in the economy and to dampening of investment.

4.80 The special limits of Section 80L deductions applicable to government securities create legally induced distortions in the allocation of savings as between these and other assets covered by Section 80L, irrespective of the intrinsic rates of return. While the major consideration behind the current incentive schemes seems to have been to encourage investment in financial assets so as to direct savings to the public sector, there are arbitrary variations in rates of return even among such assets. The rates of return bear no systematic relation to the length of the holding period of assets. In effect, by de-linking rates of return from holding periods, the public sector crowds out the private sector through offers of quick and perceptibly safer returns.

4.81 Exemptions from income tax for income from capital (as under Section 80L or Section 10) is equivalent to the expenditure tax principle but a progressive expenditure tax cannot be introduced through this route. Further, if exemption for capital income is given without limit under a progressive income tax, it amounts to having a progressive income tax only on work income. Hence, the introduction of public sector bonds and other instruments and exemption on these from income tax without any limit, as is the case under Section 10, leads to unjustified distortion.

4.82 A differential treatment of income from dividend/interest and capital gains introduces opportunities for distorted arbitrage arising between different maturities and different coupons and also leads to window dressing opportunities for tax purposes. Ideally, total return should form the basis for taxation. Moreover, certain savings instruments are more liquid than others. The resulting mis-alignment of the term structure of small saving instruments with market rates makes benchmarking more complex.

4.83 The existing tax treatment of saving schemes have also adversely effected the equity of the tax system. One consequence of the present scheme is that where the concessions take the form of deduction from income as in the case of Section 10, Section 80L and the provisions relating to rollover of capital gains tax, these favour upper bracket taxpayers disproportionately. The post-incentive rates of return vary substantially across taxpayers with different marginal tax rates. In general, the post incentive rate of return increases with the marginal tax rate of the saver. These provisions are therefore, regressive.

4.84 To the extent exemption is allowed for roll over of capital gains, the scheme is biased in favour of taxpayers with income on capital gains. Therefore, the scheme distorts horizontal equity. Further, since the large taxpayers generally have a larger proportion of their incomes from capital gains, the rollover provisions are biased in favour of the rich thereby distorting the vertical equity of the tax structure.

4.85 Inequity also arises from asymmetric information about the various tax concessions for savings. To the extent information is available with a taxpayer, he is able to avail of the tax concession. This problem is particularly aggravated in the absence of adequate taxpayer education and assistance program by the tax administration.

4.86 Table 4.9 provides an illustration of the "excess returns" to selected small savings instruments that underlie these costs. It shows that a major portion of the excess returns arise due to Section 88. For instance, the excess return to NSC VIII, solely on account of the benefit under Sections 80L and 88, is 0.97 - 2.92 per cent and 6.06 per cent, respectively, over the tax adjusted nominal administered rate. In order to accommodate the total effective yield of NSC VIII adjusted for all three benefits (i.e., 10, 80L and 88) together, the issuer of a taxable bond had to incur a cost of 16.2 to 17.1 per cent, depending upon the income tax bracket of the investor. Similarly, the excess returns from PPF turn out to be very high due to its eligibility in Section 10. This will be in addition to return attributable to Section 88. Consequently, a taxable bond without any tax exemption would have had to incur a cost of 25.8 per cent to accommodate the return accruable from PPF (with all permissible withdrawals) to investors falling in the tax bracket of 30 per cent in 2000-01.

4.87 The existing tax system on financial instruments is quite complex, distorting the information efficiency of capital and debt markets and providing arbitrage opportunities resulting in misallocation of financial resources. The provision of various tax exemptions for savings instruments not only increases the costs of compliance but also serves to distort economic incentives and actually hinder economic growth in the long run.

Table – 4.9

Total effective returns adjusted for all tax concessions

	Excess Return Arising u/s 10/80L			Excess Return Arising u/s 88			Total Tax Benefit Adjusted Effective Return to Investor			Cost to Issuer of Taxable Bonds to Accommodate Total Effective Return		
Tax Brackets	10%	20%	30%	10%	20%	30%	10%	20%	30%	10%	20%	30%
NSC VIII												
Sep, 1993	1.18	2.37	3.55	6.55	6.55	6.55	18.38	18.38	18.38	18.84	19.36	19.97
Jan, 2000	1.13	2.26	3.39	6.43	6.43	6.43	17.73	17.73	17.73	18.17	18.66	19.24
Mar, 2001	0.97	3.39	2.92	6.06	6.06	6.06	15.78	15.78	15.78	16.16	16.59	17.09
PPF												
Sep, 1993	1.18	2.37	3.55	2.48	2.48	2.48	14.74	14.74	14.74	13.45	14.64	15.82
Jan, 2000	1.08	2.17	3.25	2.49	2.49	2.49	13.78	13.78	13.78	12.38	13.46	14.55
Mar, 2001	0.94	1.87	2.80	2.51	2.51	2.51	16.89	16.89	16.89	10.77	11.71	12.64
PPF with All Permissible Withdrawals												
Sep, 1993	2.17	4.24	6.22	6.45	6.45	6.45	19.02	19.02	19.02	21.80	24.88	28.35
Jan, 2000	2.16	4.22	6.22	6.49	6.49	6.49	18.16	18.16	18.16	20.90	23.93	27.32
Mar, 2001	2.15	4.21		6.54	6.54		16.89	16.89	16.89	19.57	22.51	25.78

Source: Annexure 1, Report of Expert Committee to Review the System of Administered Interest Rates and Other Related Issues, 2001.

4.88 An ideal income tax design entails full exemption for savings either on a TEE or EET method. However, this may not fully meet the ends of vertical equity and revenue loss would also be considerable. In order to overcome these problems, the incentives are generally capped. As a result, the income tax system is not fully neutral to savings. Hence, so long as income remains the tax base, the bias against savings is inevitable. Further, the empirical evidence on the success of tax incentives for promoting savings is also extremely weak. Therefore, a comprehensive income tax packaged with a sufficiently high level of exemption limit and a two tier broad based rate schedule is preferred to income tax riddled with exemptions (including those relating to savings) with multiple rates on grounds of efficiency equity administrative simplicity and relatively low compliance burden. The bias against savings, if any is also minimised. The Task Force also recognizes the transitional administrative problems associated with the shift from the existing EEE method to EET method. Therefore, given the current imperatives of revenue and demographic profile of taxpayers, the preferred option is the TEE method.

4.89 A case for retention of the savings incentives is built around the argument that elimination of the saving incentives will adversely affect individual's savings behaviour and therefore national savings and social security. This is based on the consideration that the decision to save is affected, amongst other factors, by the return on savings (net of tax). Given the pre-tax return on savings, the post-tax return depends on the marginal rate of tax on personal income. In effect, the decision to save is also determined by the marginal rate of personal income tax. An exemption/deduction for savings has the effect of increasing the post tax return on savings. While, *a priori,* this may be true, the impact depends on the relative strengths of the income and the substitution effects, which in turn depends upon the individual's preferences for present consumption over future consumption. Empirical evidence indicates that given the pre-tax rate of return, taxation or exemptions from taxation have no significant effects on savings[49]. Considering the population as a whole, the income and substitution effects more or less cancel each other out. In fact, in recent years, the Kisan Vikas Patra mobilizes the maximum net savings in comparison to other instruments even though it does not enjoy any tax benefit. Therefore, the tax exemptions for savings do not in anyway enhance national savings. The impact on individual's savings behaviour and national savings is, at best, uncertain.

4.90 Further, consider the case of a person who is a "target saver". His only goal is to have a given amount of consumption in the future - no more and no less. For such "target saver", saving and the after-tax interest rate move in opposite directions. If the exemptions for savings are eliminated, then the only way for him to reach his target is to increase savings, and vice versa.

4.91 It has been repeatedly pointed out that providing tax incentive to the "gross" savings in small saving instruments will encourage consumption and not savings. Because the exemptions are not designed to penalise dissavings, people can roll over their savings, avail tax credit and with higher disposable income (due to tax credit) increase consumption. Therefore, the elimination of the incentives could potentially have a positive impact on national savings.

4.92 The elimination of saving incentives will in turn lead to the elimination of forced savings and forced pre-emption of savings for certain sectors. It will now enable savings to flow into the most productive channel in a competitive manner. The current provisions relating to tax rebates for savings essentially act as SLR on individuals. There is no justification for pre-empting individual savings. A taxpayer can be freed to make his savings and investment decisions. The options for him are much wider with capital market reforms both in the debt and equity segments and the entry of many new intermediaries such as mutual funds and private sector banks.

4.93 Apart from the costs to the economy through the adverse impacts on efficiencies and equity outlined above, tax concessions involve various economic costs to the government — in terms of interest payment and forgone revenue. below. Given the relatively short recycling period of the savings instruments, the marginal contribution to national savings of the elaborate tax exemption system is negligible, and the transaction costs it entails are considerable. Such costs are estimated to be around 40 per cent. Details of costs investment in the economy and therefore economic growth. What appears to be micro rational is, in fact, macro irrational.

4.94 Tax incentives for savings, particularly for government guaranteed instruments, have the effect of increasing the floor interest rates across the economy. As a result, investment is adversely affected which in turn slows down the economic growth and employment creation[50]. Further, such incentives result in revenue loss thereby increasing the borrowings by government to meet its current expenditure. This further raises interest rates thereby crowding out private investment. Consequently, there is a slow down of incurred by the Government in mobilizing small savings in FY 1999-2000 are tabulated in Table 4.10.

Table – 4.10

Cost of Small Saving Schemes incurred by Government (as at end-March 2000)

	Absolute cost (Rs.Crores)	% to gross collection of the year	% to outstanding balance at the beginning year
A. Interest Payment	20,198	32.5%	11.5%
B. Cost of Management	1,767	2.8%	1.0%
i. Remuneration to Department of Post	1,055	1.7%	0.6%
ii. Payment to Bank and Agent	691	1.1%	0.4%
iii. Promotion (NSO) and other Cost	21	1.0%	0.0%
C. Foregone Income Tax Revenue	5358	8.6%	3.0%
TOTAL COST	**27,323**	**46.8%**	**16.5%**

Source : Ministry of Finance, Government of India (Taken from Annexure 1 of the Report of Expert Committee to Review the System of Administered Interest Rates and Other Related Issues).

Note : Foregone income tax revenue is calculated in the table above by deducting 20 per cent of gross mobilisation during the year for the schemes eligible for tax deduction under Section 88, e.g , NSS 1992, NSS (VIII Issue) and PPF. Another 20 per cent of interest income is added to cost for schemes that enjoy tax free interest income under Section 10 or 80L. The 20 per cent tax rate on interest income is considered based on the assumption that all investors uniformly fall in this income tax bracket and they actually reap the tax benefit on interest income. The estimates of income tax revenue foregone are at best under-reported since the actual revenue loss on account of these incentives is estimated to be around Rs.12,000 crores based on typical tax payer profile.

4.95 The important variable for growth is social saving, defined as the sum of government and private saving. If the government were to save a proportion of tax receipt by eliminating the savings incentives, social saving could indeed increase even if private saving decreased.

4.96 Further, the tax exemptions are generally restricted to the small savings. A significant proportion of these small savings is indeed by individuals whose income is below the exemption limit and are therefore non-taxpayers. Such incentives do not benefit this category of savers. The amount of small savings attributable to taxpayers is indeed a very small proportion of the total savings in the economy. Even if, one were to assume that their saving behaviour will be adversely affected by the elimination of the saving incentives, the impact would be far too negligible[51].

4.97 Another argument extended in support of tax incentives for savings relates to the apprehension about its adverse impact on social security. It is also argued that in the absence of a social security system in the country, the government must incentivise longterm savings by individuals. The Task Force recognises that smaller taxpayers may not save enough for old-age security because of individual myopia, thereby imposing a social burden. Such individuals must necessarily be encouraged to overcome their myopia by providing incentive for contribution to saving plans[52].

4.98 The wide range of tax incentives for savings is inefficient and inequitous. The apprehension about the adverse effect of the elimination of these incentives on national savings is also misplaced. Therefore, the Task Force recommends the elimination of the tax incentives for savings under Section 88, Section 80L, Section 10(15)(i), Section 10(15)(iib), Section 10(15)(iic), Section 10(15)(iid), Section 10(15)(iv)(h) and Section 10(15)(iv)(i) of the Income Tax Act. These benefits must be withdrawn with immediate effect and not through a sunset clause.

4.99 Further, with a view to overcoming the problem thrown up by individual myopia, we also recommend the continuation of the deduction under section 80CCC for contribution to the pension fund of LIC or any other insurance company. The ceiling on the deduction should, however, be increased from the existing levels of Rs. 10,000/- to Rs. 20,000/-. This income-based deduction u/s

80CCC be converted to a tax rebate at the minimum marginal rate of 20 per cent[53]. Consequently, the ceiling on tax rebate for contribution to the pension fund should be Rs. 4,000/-. The new ceiling has been proposed keeping in view the needs of the smaller taxpayers with income below Rs. 2 lakhs. The scope of section 80CCC may also be extended to a larger number of pension/annuity schemes within the overall ceiling of Rs. 20,000/-. Since savings in these pension funds will be taxable at the withdrawal stage, the tax benefit for such savings will be consistent with the EET method of tax treatment.

4.100 However, any sum received under a life insurance policy (including bonus) will continue to enjoy tax exemption under section 10(10D) of the Income Tax Act. Similarly, any withdrawal (including interest) from the provident fund will continue to enjoy tax exemption under sections 10(11) and 10(12) of the Income Tax Act. As a result, the tax treatment of savings in these schemes will confirm to the TEE method as against the existing EEE method. To this extent, the change will be economically efficient. Our recommendations for not modifying the tax treatment of other saving plans u/s 88 or u/s 80L or u/s 10(15) either along the EET method or TEE method is primarily based on the consideration that the rates of return are considerably higher, or the maturity period is not long enough to discourage "round tripping".

Treatment of Educational Expenses

4.101 The income tax law provides for deduction of Rs.40,000 in respect of repayment of loan taken by any taxpayer for higher education (Section 80E).

4.102 In view of the International practice (Table 4.11) and the fact that education is one of the basic amenities of life, generating positive externalities, the Task Force considers it necessary to provide continued support under the tax law. However, on grounds of equity, we also recommend that the income based deduction under Section 80E should be converted to a tax rebate at the minimum marginal rate of personal income tax. The maximum amount of tax rebate should be restricted to Rs.4,000.

Treatment of Medical Expenses

4.103 The income tax law provides for deduction of Rs.15,000 in respect of payment of medical insurance premium (Section 80D) and Rs.40,000 for medical treatment (Section 80DDB). Since health is one of the basic amenities in life, the Task Force considers it necessary to provide continued support under the tax law.

4.104 However, the provisions of Section 80DDB relating to deduction for actual expenses incurred on medical treatment are liable to be considerably misused, in the absence of a strong verification system. Even if, the tax administration were to successfully put in place a strong verification system, it would impose considerable administrative and compliance burden. A survey across countries on the tax treatment of medical expenses (Table 4.11) indicate that while most countries do not provide any form of deduction, some exempt subject to a ceiling while some others exempt the perquisite value of medical expenses. Therefore, on balance of consideration, the Task Force recommends the immediate withdrawal of the tax benefit under Section 80DDB. However, consistent with international practice and in view of the special health circumstances of senior citizens[54], deduction for medical expenses may continue to be allowed in the form of a tax rebate at the rate of 20 per cent of the medical expenses, subject to a maximum of Rs.4,000. Further, on grounds of equity, we also recommend that the income based deduction under Section 80D should be converted to a tax rebate at the minimum marginal rate of personal income tax (i.e. 20 per cent). The maximum about of tax rebate should be restricted to Rs. 3,000.

Treatment of Senior Citizens

4.105 Section 88B of the Income Tax Act provides for a tax rebate of Rs. 15,000/- to a senior citizen. A taxpayer is considered as a senior citizen if he is of the age of 65 years or more on the last day of the previous year. In view of the recommendation for increase in the exemption limit to Rs. 1 lakh and deduction of medical expenses for senior citizens, the Consultation Paper submitted by the Task Force had proposed the deletion of the provisions of Section 88B of the Income Tax Act.

Table – 4.11

Tax Treatment of Medical and Educational Expenses Across Countries.

Country	Whether Medical Expenses are deductible?	Whether Educational Expenses are deductible?
Canada	No	No
France	No	Yes, only school fees of children is deductible from tax
Germany	No	Yes, if education is necessary for current profession
Italy	Yes, tax credit at the rate of 19 per cent.	Yes, tax credit at the rate of 19 per cent.
Japan	Yes, expenditure in excess of Yen 100,000 up to a maximum of Yen 2 million	Yes, expense exceeding Yen 10,000 up to a maximum of 25 per cent of adjusted total income
Netherlands	Yes, maximum of Euro 718 or 11.2 per cent of income, which ever is lower	Yes, only expenses above Euro 500/- but below EUR 15,000/-
United Kingdom	No	No
United States	Yes, if medical expenses exceed 7.5 per cent of adjusted gross income	No, except for higher education
Thailand	No	No
New Zealand	No	No
Malaysia	Yes, maximum tax credit of RM 7,000/-	Yes, maximum of RM 5,000/- of income
Indonesia	No	No
Philippines	No	No
Argentina	No	No
Peru	No	No
Australia	No	No
Singapore	No	Yes, maximum of $ 2,500 if the course is related to employment or profession.

4.106 The Task Force received a large number of representations through e-mails and post pointing out the sharp increase in tax liability of senior citizens because of the cumulative impact of the withdrawal of tax incentives on interest income, reduction in interest rates and the elimination of the tax rebate of Rs. 15,000/-. Even though part of the impact would be neutralised by the exemption of dividend income and long-term capital gains on equity, this would hold good only for a limited number of senior citizens. Most senior citizens are risk averse and therefore have a choice for debt instruments. Such senior citizens face the prospect of a double jeopardy: reduction in interest rates and withdrawal of incentives. Their problem is further compounded by their inability to recoup the loss of income through employment in view of their advancing age and physical condition. With a view to providing a human face to the tax reform proposals, we recommend that the basic exemption limit for senior citizens should be Rs. 50,000/- more then the exemption limit for the general class of individual taxpayers. In other words, the exemption limit for senior citizens should be Rs. 1,50,000/- as against Rs. 1,00,000/- for the general category of individual taxpayers recommended by us in Table-4.1. The exemption limit for senior citizens should be revised as and when the exemption limit for the general category of individual taxpayers is revised. We also recommend that this benefit of higher exemption limit should also be extended to widows.

Other Personal Deductions

4.107 The Income Tax Act provides for the following other personal deductions:

1. An income based deduction of Rs.40,000/- in respect of maintenance[55] including medical treatment of handicapped dependent (Section 80DD). This deduction is conditional to expenditure on maintenance being actually incurred.
2. An income based deduction of Rs.40,000 in case the taxpayer suffers from permanent physical disability (including blindness). (Section 80U)
3. A tax rebate of Rs.5,000 to women taxpayers below 65 years of age. (Section 88C)

4.108 Given the personal circumstances of handicapped, the Task Force recommends the continuation of the personal deductions under Sections 80DD and Section 80U. However, on grounds of equity, we also recommend that the income-based deduction under these provisions should be converted to a tax rebate at the minimum marginal rate of personal income tax.

4.109 Further, in view of our recommendations for increase in the exemption limit to Rs.1,00,000/- and deduction of medical expenses for senior citizens, we recommend that the personal deductions in the form of tax rebate for senior citizens (Section 88B) and women (Section 88C) should be deleted.

Personal Tax Reforms : Implementation Strategy

4.110 The policy measures for the reform of personal income tax therefore comprises of the following elements:-

(a) Increase in the generalised exemption limit from Rs.50,000/- to Rs.1,00,000/- for all individual and HUF taxpayers. The exemption limit for senior citizens and widows would, however, be at an enhanced level of Rs. 1,50,000/-.

(b) The existing three slabs in the personal income tax rate schedule will be replaced by two slabs. Incomes between Rs.1,00,000/- and Rs.4,00,000 will be subjected to tax at the marginal rate of 20 per cent. All incomes above Rs.4,00,000/- will be subjected to tax at the marginal rate of 30 per cent.

(c) Dividends received from Indian companies will be fully exempt.

(d) Long term capital gains on listed equity will be fully exempt.

(e) The standard deduction for salaried taxpayers will be reduced to NIL. However, exemption for conveyance allowance subject to a ceiling of Rs. 9,600/- will continue.

(f) The income based deduction under Section 80D subject to a ceiling of Rs. 15,000/- in respect of payment of medical insurance premium will be converted to a tax rebate at the rate of 20 per cent subject to a maximum of Rs.3,000.

(g) The benefit of deduction under Section 80DDB will be withdrawn in so far as it relates to the general category of taxpayers. However, consistent with international practice and in view of the special circumstances of senior citizens, deduction for medical expenses may continue to be allowed in the form of a tax rebate at the rate of 20 per cent of the medical expenses, subject to a maximum rebate of Rs.4,000.

(h) The income based deduction under Section 80E for repayment of educational expenses will continue to be allowed. However, on grounds of equity, the same should be allowed as a tax rebate at the rate of 20 per cent subject to maximum of Rs.4,000.

(i) The tax rebate schemes under Sections 88 for savings will be eliminated.

(j) The rebate under Section 88B for senior citizens will be eliminated in view of the enhanced exemption limit for them.

(k) The rebate under Section 88C for women taxpayers below the age of 65 years, will be eliminated.

(l) The income based deduction for handicapped under Section 80DD and 80U will however continue.

(m) The income based deduction under Section 80L for interest income and dividends will be eliminated.

(n) The exemption under Section 10 in respect of interest income from bonds, securities, debentures etc. will be eliminated.

(o) The deduction for mortgage interest in respect of loans for acquiring a owner occupied dwelling will be reduced to Rs. 50,000/-.

(p) The residential status of "Resident but Not Ordinarily Resident" will be eliminated.

4.111 The Task Force would like to place on record that the various recommendations relating to personal income tax in this report are interwoven and therefore indivisible. The recommendations must be seen as a package and piecemeal implementation must be avoided at all cost.

Notes

19 This section is heavily drawn from Parthasarathi Shome, India's Fiscal Matters, Oxford University Press, New Delhi (2002).

20 The Advisory Group on Tax Policy and Tax Administration for the Tenth Plan has measured the variation of tax liability for different levels of taxable income and estimated the coefficient of variation in 1973-74 was then at a high of 1.06. Since then the progressivity of the tax rate schedule has declined substantially to 0.64.

21 Government of India,(December 1991), Interim Report of the Tax Reforms Committee.

22 Ibid.

23 This is consistent with the recommendations in the Interim Report of The Tax Reforms Committee (Chairman : Professor Raja J. Chelliah)

24 However, this needs to be proved empirically.

25 Given the per-capita income of Rs. 18,000/- in 2001-02, the average family income in most cases would be Rs. 1 lakh in 2003-04.

26 It increased to 1.26 in 1974-75 before beginning to decline steadily.

27 The tax reform proposals are generally designed to be arithmetically revenue neutral and therefore withdrawal of incentives must necessarily be compensated by increase in the general exemption limit and/ or reduction/rationalisation in tax rates.

28 This is further restricted due to information asymmetry.

29 This includes income deemed to accrue or arise in India, income received in India or income received outside India arising from either a business controlled, or a profession established, in India.

30 Nonresidents may also be taxed on income deemed to accrue or arise in India through a business connection, through or from any asset or source of income in India, or through the transfer of a capital asset situated in India (including a share in a company incorporated in India).

31 Self-employed taxpayers have the opportunity of lumping their personal expenses with other business expenses which are tax deductible.

32 In fact in the government, the expenditure by senior officers on newspapers is reimbursed. In the case of the corporate sector, the expenditure on newspapers and periodicals is an allowable business deduction without being treated as a perquisite in the hands of the employee.

33 National Housing Bank has also informed that an equal amount with similar loan profiles can be estimated to have been disbursed as housing loans by the various commercial banks.

34 This would be so for a repayment period of 10 to 15 years.

35 This was so when the incentive was increased to Rs. 1,50,000 in the Union Budget 2001.

36 We estimate tax savings of more than Rs. 35,000.

37 The interest on home loans with shorter maturity period are relatively less than those with longer maturity period.

38 There post tax profit can be expected to increase by as much as 10 per cent.

39 Our decision to retain section 80CCC of the Income Tax Act which provides for tax relief for contributions to a pension scheme is primarily intended to provide old age income security. Similarly, our decisions to retain 80D of the Income Tax Act which provides tax reliefs for contribution to a medical insurance policy (mediclaim) and modify section 80DD to provide tax relief for medical expenses incurred by senior citizens, are intended to provide old age health security.

40 Advisory Group on Tax Policy and Tax Administration for the Tenth Plan, Planning Commission, May 2001.

41 Expert Committee to Review the System of Administered Interest Rates and Other Related Issues, September 2001.

42 The psychological impact of EET, however, providing tax benefits at the contribution stage, would be greater in promoting financial accumulation (Reddy Committee, 2001). *It may be noted that approximately two thirds of OECD countries follow the EET system, with some variations, for taxation of savings.*

43 Report of the Expert Group to Review Existing Fiscal Incentives for Savings (Chairman: P. Shome), May 1997.

44 Individual Savings Accounts (ISAs) have superseded PEP and TESSA (see text) since April 2001. ISAs are similar to the older schemes in most important respects and are designed to integrate the tax treatments for savings of disparate schemes. Existing subscribers to PEPs and TESSAs can continue with the schemes or migrate to ISAs.

45 The Institute for Fiscal Studies, UK, Briefing Note No. 9, "A Survey of the UK Tax System", November 2001.

46 "Capital Markets in Chile", Investment Review, Foreign Investment Committee, Chile, February 2002.

47 Internal Revenue Authority of Singapore, SRS Brochure, 2001.

48 except instruments listed at serials number 7, 8, 10, 14 to 17 & 20 to 24 of Table – 3. 101

49 Report of the Advisory Group on Tax Policy and Tax Administration for the Tenth Plan.

50 Infact a slowdown in the employment creation results in greater unemployment and therefore a tax at 100 per cent. Clearly the effect is regressive.

51 It will be fiscally prudent for the government to swap the high cost borrowing from taxpayers by the relatively low cost government securities.

52 Such individuals tend to apply whole of their current income for consumption and prefer to depend on the society for their future consumption.

53 In the case of a taxpayer whose marginal rate of tax is 20 per cent, and income based deduction of Rs. 100, confers a tax relief of Rs. 20 (Rs.

100*0.2). Similarly, a taxpayer whose marginal rate of tax is 30 per cent enjoys a tax benefit of Rs. 30 (that is, Rs. 100 * 0.3). Therefore, a taxpayer in the higher income bracket enjoys a relatively higher tax benefit and hence iniquitous. However, under the proposed scheme of tax rebate, all taxpayers irrespective of their personal marginal rate of tax, will enjoy a tax relief of Rs. 20 (Rs. 100*0.2).

54 Senior citizens should be defined as taxpayers who are more than 65 years. in age on the 1st day of the financial year.

55 Maintenance included payment to a scheme framed by the LIC and any other insurance agency for the maintenance of the handicapped.

5

Corporate Tax Reform

In most countries with income taxation, corporate entities are subject to tax on their profits and, in addition, dividends are taxed in the hands of shareholders (subject to exemption up to a point). The base of the corporate income tax, however, is commonly the accounting profits derived with reference to historical costs. Certain modifications are also often made by law to accounting profits to provide incentives for activities considered important for social and economic policies or to provide relief from inflation as well as to curb misuse of the corporate form to reduce personal tax liability. From an economic point of view, the main issue of substance in this area, however, is not the legal form of the tax on the incomes of different entities but rather the extent to which provisions are made under the corporate income tax, the personal income tax, or both, to reduce or eliminate "double taxation" of income which is earned by a corporation but accrues in one form or another to the individuals who are its ultimate owners.

Case for Levy of Corporate Tax

5.2 Under a system of general income taxation, whether companies should be taxed independently as separate entitles has been the subject matter of prolonged debate among tax economists. One view is that since corporations are not persons, strictly speaking, there is no case in equity for taxing the profits of companies as such. The tax should be levied only on the owners, that is, the equity holders, by attributing the profits of the companies to the shareholders. Such a system, however, can operate smoothly only if all profits are distributed every year among the shareholders. Where part of the profits is retained, the gain to the shareholders accruing from appreciation in the value of equities escapes taxation unless there is an effective tax on realised capital gains or unless the undistributed profits are attributed notionally to the shareholders. This is not simple in the case of large corporations in which the shares undergo sale or transfer all the time.

5.3 Since capital gains are usually treated preferentially, even where the income tax is levied on capital gains, exclusion of retained profits of companies from taxation provides an easy way of avoiding taxation by accumulating profits under the corporate cover. Taxation on the basis of attribution also encounters problems in the determination of capital gains when the shares are transferred, as the cost basis has to be adjusted annually to take account of the notional distribution of accumulated profits underlying the capital gain. Besides, taxation on notional basis gives rise to liquidity problems and hence does not seem equitable or feasible. It is therefore generally accepted that some tax has to be levied on the profits of companies so long as individuals and unincorporated enterprises are subjected to tax on their profits.

5.4 Taxation of companies as separate entities is also justified as a withholding tax, which may be a useful means of ensuring that income flowing through the conduit is taxed in a comprehensive and timely manner and that the base of the individual income tax is protected. Many economists, including some who have not advocated full integration, have argued that this withholding function is indeed the main argument for the imposition of a tax on corporate income.

5.5 A separate tax on the profits of companies is considered reasonable also on the ground that incorporation confers substantial benefits such as limited liability of shareholders, right to sue and be sued and so on. What is more, corporate taxation is an administratively simple device for taxing an important type of income from capital.

Case for Integration

5.6 Tax should be levied, as a matter of fiscal equity, according to "ability to pay" — as measured by income. Further, corporate entities do not have an ability to pay taxes, in the relevant sense;

they are simply a "conduit" through which income flows to individuals who are their ultimate owners. Combined, these propositions appear to suggest that corporate income should only be taxed in the hands of the individuals to whom it accrues. Hence, there is a case for integrating individual and corporate income taxes.

Case for the "Classical" system

5.7 Under a "classical" corporate tax system, income tax is levied separately, both on company income and on dividends received by shareholders. The defense of this system is based on denying one of the propositions on which the integrationist case rests, or both. First, the case against integration or in favour of the "classical" system rests on the issue of legal form; it is asserted that companies are "separate entities", legally distinct from the individuals who own them. Second, it has been argued that the case for integration is based on a concept of "ability to pay", which now seems narrow and out-moded. The principle of taxation according to ability to pay can be interpreted more broadly, as requiring taxes to be levied on income — and indeed on other tax bases such as consumption and wealth in such a way as to minimize loss of social welfare. A third defense of the principle of a classical corporate tax system rests on the "benefit" principle that taxes should be levied according to the benefit provided by the taxing authorities. It has been argued that corporations enjoy benefits in the form of limited liability, and from government services that are provided more directly, and that some form of taxation of those benefits is appropriate[56].

The case against the classical (Nonintegrated) system

5.8 Compared with a fully integrated system, a classical corporation tax which taxes the equity income of companies at a positive rate may distort incentives in four main ways.

5.9 First and most obviously, it acts to discourage businesses from incorporating, and hence from taking advantage of benefits which are associated with the corporate form of organization – such as the benefit of limited liability, which reduces the cost to companies of raising outside capital for expansion. It should be noted, however, that the discouragement to incorporation applies only insofar as the business is financed by equity. A corporate tax on equity income allows interest payments to the company's creditors to be deducted from the tax base. Hence, when investment is financed at the margin by debt rather than equity, the resulting income bears no tax at the corporate level; the only tax paid on the income is the tax on the lender's interest income. Effectively, then, a classical corporate tax is "integrated" in respect of income from debt-financed projects, and hence may not discourage incorporation when the firm is free to vary its financial structure.

5.10 A second adverse incentive effect of a classical corporate tax is that it encourages companies to finance their projects by using debt rather than equity finance. This distortion increases the risk of bankruptcy. It will, therefore, bias companies toward relatively secure investments and discourage risks. Further, this bias in favor of debt financing gives companies an incentive to disguise the returns they provide to their shareholders, as far as possible, as "interest" payments rather than dividends. Most classical corporation taxes thus require extensive anti-avoidance provisions to limit what may be deducted from the tax base in the form of interest payments.

5.11 Third, given the imperfections of the capital market and lack of perfect foresight on the part of equity holders, a classical corporation tax encourages a company to retain its equity earnings rather than distributing them to its shareholders. When dividends are paid, the shareholder is subject to income tax at the appropriate rate. When earnings are retained, the shareholder should benefit, instead, from an increase in the market value of the company. In many countries, that capital gain is not subject to tax; and when there is a tax on capital gains, it is usually levied at a lower effective rate than the income tax on dividends. As a result of this bias in favor of retentions, equity funds may be "trapped" within particular companies rather than allocated between companies in the most efficient manner by financial markets, according to the investment opportunities that the companies face. Fourth, a classical corporate tax system reduces the incentive to invest, and may therefore inhibit growth. The additional tax that is levied on company income under a classical system, however, represents an additional discouragement.

5.12 Combined, these four points represent a powerful case against the classical form of corporate income tax. This case has in practice been influential one; there has been a general though not entirely universal tendency over the last two decades for existing classical systems to be replaced by some form of integration of corporate and individual income taxes.

The case for retaining a classical system

513. The first, and most powerful, argument for retaining a classical system or against integration is that it will generally entail a loss of revenue, compared with what was generated by the classical system that is replaced. This revenue loss must be made up in some way; the corporate tax rate might be increased, or some other taxes might be imposed. In either case, there are likely to be economic costs that must be set against the benefits of integration.

5.14 Second, doubts have often been expressed about empirical significance of particular benefits from integration, such as the reduction in bankruptcies, and in the costs of recognizing the activities of bankrupt firms. In addition, to the extent that equity is trapped within companies by an existing classical system, the burden of the additional tax that is payable on dividends when those earnings are eventually distributed may already be capitalized into share prices. In this case, much of the benefit of a shift to an integrated system could simply accrue as a windfall gain to existing shareholders.

5.15 Finally, some major benefits that may be claimed for a classical system, compared with most integrated systems that have been adopted in practice, are its simplicity and transparency. These features generally make a classical corporate tax system easier to administer than an integrated system. They also avoid most of the severe difficulties that arise in devising an appropriate tax treatment, in an integrated system, of dividends paid or received from abroad.

The meaning of "integration"

5.16 The term "integration" has been used in different ways. Traditionally, "full integration" has been used to denote an arrangement under which the incomes of all entities, both distributed and retained, would be attributed in an appropriate manner to the individual shareholders who are their ultimate owners. The income tax due would then be collected from those individual shareholders at the marginal tax rates, depending on their total incomes.

5.17 "Full integration" in this sense may be an ideal arrangement in principle but it is administratively impracticable. The first reason is that there would be an enormous amount of information reporting required: in many economies, a single company may have a very high number of ultimate owners, many of whom will have held shares for only a part of any tax year. Second, attributing retained earnings to different owners is problematic when there are different classes of corporate security holders, with heterogeneous claims such as ordinary shares, and convertible notes. Third, many company shares are held by other companies. Hence, tracing the ultimate owners can often be difficult. A fourth general difficulty is that if tax were to be levied on shareholders' earnings whether they are retained or distributed, it could result in shareholders often being liable to pay large amount of tax without having received cash with which those liabilities could be met. No country has tried to apply a full integration scheme of this kind to the taxation of all corporate income. Many countries, however, do effectively integrate company and individual income taxation, along these lines, in the case of small companies with a limited number of owners[57].

5.18 In particular circumstances, full integration could be achieved in principle by several systems besides the partnership method discussed above. One such system would be to abolish the corporate income tax completely and let shareholders pay taxes under the personal income tax on the dividends received plus net accrued capital gains on shares — that is, on a comprehensive income base. However, such a system is extremely burdensome in terms of both administrative and compliance cost. Further, it will also lead to considerable revenue loss, particularly in the transition, since the income in the hands of the shareholders will be very thinly distributed. Second, full integration could be achieved straightforwardly, in the special case where the personal income tax is levied at a single rate, by levying tax on corporate income at the same rate, while exempting dividends and capital gains on company shares from the personal tax. Such a corporate tax should serve as a scheduler final tax on income from equity capital.

5.19 The results of the full integration method can also be substantially achieved in a two rate personal income tax structure where the corporate tax is levied at the higher of the two rates and it is assumed that most (if not all) individual shareholders are subjected to tax at the highest marginal rate of personal income tax. Under this system, a company would not be able to defer tax simply by not paying dividends and therefore there would not be any loss of efficiency. Further, because the number of corporate entities are few than there are individual shareholders, and because they are more easily identifiable, having a corporate as a principal taxpayer makes administration much easier than having only the investors as legal taxpayers. It also makes it much easier for the tax administration to distribute refunds or collect adjustment resulting from scrutiny assessments (audit). In view of the above, the Task Force recommends the adoption of this method of full integration of corporation or personal income tax, that is, levy a tax at the corporate level at the rate of 30 per cent being the maximum rate of personal income tax and exempt all dividends and long-term capital gains from tax in the hands of the shareholders. This method would not undermine any equity since most direct equity investors in the companies in India are likely to be taxed at the top marginal rate of personal income tax.

5.20 The above system recommended by us would serve as a full integration model only if the accounting profits bear the full burden of corporate tax i.e., the effective corporate tax liability is equivalent to the statutory corporate tax rate. This is possible if there is no divergence between the taxable base for companies and accounting profits, which generally arises due to various tax incentives and artificial deductions. Therefore, where there is empirical evidence to establish that corporate profits (accounting profits) have indeed suffered full taxation, the case for taxation of dividend again in the hand of shareholders would be extremely weak. In such a case, dividend distribution should be seen as mere application of income (or transfer of capital).

Economics of Tax Incentives

5.21 The source of the problem of double taxation is, therefore, tax incentives, which are a prominent feature of many tax codes in both developed and developing countries. Tax incentives have been used by countries to achieve a variety of different objectives, not all of which are equally compelling on conceptual grounds. Such incentives have either been for stimulating investment in general, or as a matter of economic or social policy and addressing regional development needs[58]. Quite often, countries pursue multiple objectives with overlapping tax incentives.

5.22 The various factors that could have a bearing on an (domestic or foreign) investor's decision to undertake an investment project in any country could be grouped under four broad categories : (1) tax-related considerations; (2) non-tax-related economic considerations; (3) non-economic considerations ; and (4) social policy considerations. An examination of these factors is necessary before we analyse the conceptual validity of the various objectives of tax incentives.

5.23 Tax-related considerations refer to features in the tax system as a whole that impact on the effective tax burdens on investment projects. If there are limitations in these features that impede investment, the first-best policy is to correct the limitations directly via appropriate tax reform, rather than to compensate for them through enacting tax incentives. If, for example, depreciation allowances are too restrictive or the corporate income tax rate is too high in relation to international norms, then restructuring depreciation allowances or lowering the CIT rate to competitive levels would be far more preferable than introducing tax incentives in restoring a favorable investment climate.

5.24 Non-tax related economic consideration refer to those that affect either the general macroeconomic or the microeconomic/ structural environment, or both. If there are deficiencies in these environments that impede investment, the first-best policy is to implement sound macroeconomic policies and/or undertake relevant structural reforms, rather than to resort to tax incentives that do not address the root-cause of the deficiencies. For example, large budgetary imbalances can raise questions about the sustainability of present tax rates, and high inflation rates can generate considerable uncertainty about prospective macroeconomic developments. Likewise, rigidities in labour markets can raise labor costs above internationally competitive levels, and poor communication and transportation infrastructures can increase the costs of doing business significantly. When such macroeconomic imbalances occur and / or structural deficiencies exist, tax incentives alone are unlikely to provide sufficient underpinning for investors' confidence — they may, in fact, be counterproductive if investors view them as steps in the wrong direction for addressing the underlying problems. Tax incentives attempt to overcome structural rigidities by pushing fundamental reform to the background.

5.25 Non-economic considerations refer to those related to the legal, regulatory and political economy environment. These considerations are often as important as tax and other economic considerations in fostering an environment that is conducive to investment. For example, investors are frequently concerned about the clarity of the law that governs the investment regime, and the transparency with which regulations (rules and procedures) associated with the investment law are enforced. Again, if there are deficiencies in this environment that impede investment, the first-best policy is to undertake corrective actions to remove the deficiencies. Investors' concerns about deficient legislation and onerous regulations, as well as perception of corruption on the part of those officials responsible for approving investment projects, can seldom be overcome by the availability of even generous tax incentives.

5.26 Social policy consideration refers to those that arise from equity concerns. Producers in certain sectors (e.g., agriculture) may be regarded as economically disadvantaged relative to other, more developed sectors (e.g., industry), and the provision of tax incentives to the former sectors may be considered as a way to advance equity objectives. However, such objectives can be more effectively addressed by an appropriately designed expenditure policy that targets individuals on the basis of their levels, rather than by tax incentives that target economic activities on a sectoral level.

5.27 The above discussions suggest that tax incentives are often not the first-best policy instrument to achieve the kind of objectives that they have commonly been used for. Indeed, since tax incentives, if effective, would by definition create an economic distortion between favored and regular investment projects, an economically compelling justification for their use is the rectification of market failures. Specifically, there are some types of investments that generate positive externalities (benefits that the market fails to internalize) for the economy as a whole. Since the amount of such investments would be socially suboptimal if left entirely to market forces, tax incentives could play a legitimate role in encouraging them. Tax incentives justified on this basis would typically include those given to project located in less-developed regions of a country (either to reduce congestion and/or pollution in the developed regions, or to reduce the disparity in income distribution that could be viewed as having some public good characteristics); projects entailing the use of advanced technologies that could raise the general technological absorption capacity of a country; projects that have a high propensity of leading to a build-up of key types of human capital whose benefits usually extend beyond the persons embodying them; and projects that involve R&D activities in targeted areas deemed important for whatever policy reasons. In all such cases, a compelling economic justification, could be made for the use of tax incentives as a corrective policy instrument.

5.28 Another plausible justification for the use of tax incentives could rest on the well known argument that, in small and open economies with mobile capital, the incidence of any tax on capital income would be shifted to less mobile factors such as labour, in which case it would be better to tax the latter factors directly rather than indirectly by taxing capital income. However, even in such economies, having some form of a corporate income tax could be essential as a backstop to labor taxes to prevent the artificial shifting of income from labor to corporations (e.g., owners of firms could incorporate, transform their wage income into corporate retained earnings, and receive returns in the form of capital gains from selling their shares). The optimal form of the corporate income tax under these circumstances would be a cash flow tax. The granting of certain forms of tax incentives could then be viewed as a means of achieving this end.

5.29 Once one departs from the position that no tax incentives should ever be granted, and accepts the proposition that the use of such incentives could be justified under certain circumstances, especially those that are associated with the presence of positive externalities, questions about targeting and measurement will inevitably arise. For example, how would one go about identifying investment projects that would generate the kinds of positive externalities that are deemed to be deserving of tax incentives? Once identified, how would the externalities be measured so as to determine that appropriate amount of tax incentives to be granted? These questions have no easy and clear cut answers, but they like most other policy matters involving difficult choices, nevertheless have to be resolved, by a rational and objective decision-making process informed of all relevant facts and constraints.

5.30 A crucial consideration that bears on the decision to grant tax incentives should be their cost-effectiveness. This implies that the mere identification of the existence of positive externalities associated with certain types of investment projects is not sufficient for justifying the use of such incentives in all instances. Rather, their use should be predicated on the belief that the benefits to the economy that can be expected from an increase (if any) in the incentive-favored activities would actually outweigh the total costs of the tax incentives granted.

5.31 Granting tax incentives entails four types of costs : (1) distortions between investments granted incentives and those without incentives; (2) forgone revenue (on the assumption that the government operates under a revenue constraint, so that the lost revenue would have to be compensated from alternative distortive taxes); (3) administrative resources required to administer them; and (4) the social costs of corruption and/or rentseeking activities connected with abuse of tax incentive provisions. While these costs could be substantial, the benefits to the economy that could be attributed solely to tax incentives are less clear and not easily quantifiable. Hence, the cost-effectiveness of tax incentives is often questionable.

5.32 The distortion cost of the incentives could arise even if such incentives are used to correct for externalities, since the amount of incentives granted may not conform exactly to the extent of the externalities involved, due to the inherent difficulties in measuring the latter. By extension, such costs would also arise whenever tax incentives are erroneously granted to investment projects with no positive externalities, as could happen (for example) through abuse and leakage in the system.

5.33 The revenue costs of tax incentives have two different dimensions. First, investment projects could have been undertaken even if there had been no tax incentives. For these projects, which typically comprise those of the highest profitability and, therefore, having the greatest economic merits, the availability of tax incentives would simply represent a free gift from the government to either the investors or, if they are of foreign origin, the treasury of their home countries. The latter outcome would come about if any income that is spared from taxation by the host country is taxed by the investor's home countries - as it would be the case when these countries have tax systems that are based on the residence principle.

5.34 The second dimension of the revenue costs of tax incentives is that, even when tax incentives are ineffective in attracting additional investments perhaps because of their failure to overcome other impediments to investment, they may still entail a revenue loss because their mere availability opens the door to potential abuse by investors not eligible to receive them.

5.35 Indeed, abuse and leakage are perennial problems with tax incentives, and their effective prevention can often absorb a substantial amount of quality administrative resources – a scarce commodity in most developing countries. The more scare resources are devoted to administering tax incentives, the other more important administrative tasks would be impaired – thus jeopardizing tax collection as a whole.

5.36 Administrative costs would clearly escalate with increased scope and complexity of the tax incentives provided. If the aim is to properly enforce them, a far more serious problem with incentive provisions has often to do with the unofficial condoning - or even encouragement – of abuse of such provisions by officials charged with the responsibility for their administration. Tax incentives also inevitably induce socially unproductive rentseeking behavior. Once the incentive system gets going, those who are fortunate enough to have captured the rents will have an inherent interest to maintain the status quo. This explains, quite apart from economic reasons, why it is so difficult in reality to terminate or even phase out tax incentives once they are granted, even if such incentives are formally time-bound. The most effective way of overcoming these political economy problems of tax incentives is to ensure that the incen.ive-granting process is transparent and has accountability.

5.37 Transparency in granting tax incentives has three dimensions. First, there is the legal and regulatory dimension :all tax incentives should have a statutory basis in the relevant tax laws, and changes to such incentives should require amendments to these laws. This implies that incentive provisions should not be embedded in laws unrelated to taxation to avoid possible conflicts, inconsistencies, and overlaps across different laws; they should certainly not be embedded in instruments that have a lesser degree of legal standing than a law, such as regulations, decrease, or orders that could be issued by various government entities or officials on an ad hoc basis. Similar reasoning would then also indicate that statutory provisions in the relevant tax laws should not confer on any government entity or official discretionary incentive granting powers; tax incentives should be granted, without exception, on the basis of clearly specified qualifying criteria.

5.38 The second dimension is economic, which involves making explicit the rationale for granting any tax incentives on the basis of well thought out economic arguments; estimating the economic impact and revenue cost of granting incentives based on clearly stated assumptions and methodologies; and subjecting the estimated revenue costs to public scrutiny in the budgetary process as tax expenditures. Explicit recognition of tax expenditures is a practice that can be found in many developed and an increasing number of developing countries, and can greatly facilitate the reviewing by policy makers on a continuing basis of the cost effectiveness of granting tax incentives to achieve specified policy objectives.

5.39 Finally, there is the administrative dimension of transparency, which involves formulating qualifying criteria for tax incentives that are simple, specific, and objective to minimize the need for subjective interpretation and application by the administering officials of the incentive system, as well as to ease monitoring and enforcement responsibilities on the part of tax administrators. These considerations clearly suggest that the triggering mechanism for granting tax incentives should be rendered as automatic as possible, i.e., one that allows an investment project to receive the incentives automatically once it satisfies the stipulated qualifying criteria, such as a minimum amount of investment in certain sectors of the economy. In granting the tax incentives, the relevant authorities would only undertake to ensure that the qualifying criteria are met. All other aspects of the investment are irrelevant.

5.40 In contrast, a discretionary triggering mechanism involves the approving or denying an application for tax incentives on the basis of a subjective value judgement of the relevant incentive-granting authorities after taking into account a variety of considerations, irrespective of any formally stated qualifying criteria. If such criteria exist, they are stated either as minimum conditions or in very general terms, thus requiring subjective interpretation. The discretionary application of tax incentives is one of the most important contributing factors to corruption in many countries.

5.41 Tax incentives are, therefore, inefficient, inequitous, impose greater taxpayer compliance burden and administrative burden, result in revenue loss and complexity of the tax laws, and encourage tax avoidance and rent seeking behaviour.

Widening the Corporate Tax Base

5.42 At present, the Income Tax Act is riddled with tax concessions, which take the form of full or partial exemptions, deductions, and tax. Inspite of economic distortions, which are caused by the various tax incentives, these have continued[59]. These concessions may have been justified in the era when the marginal tax rates were exorbitantly high. However, over the year the marginal corporate tax rates have been reduced substantially. Therefore, the exemptions and notional deductions should be discouraged and wherever necessary political environment created to purge the tax statute of such incentives. It is important to review the large number of these exemptions/deductions/holidays so as to expand the tax base and also increase the average tax liability. Given the government's bold initiative in eliminating the incentives relating to exports of goods and services, the die is now cast for eliminating other incentives[60].

5.43 The Task Force does not consider it necessary to reinvent the wheel by examining the efficacy of the various tax incentives. The adverse impact of various incentives have been well documented in the numerous reports of Committees, Task Force, and Study groups. A cursory look at the annual report of the Comptroller and Auditor General of India in respect of the Income Tax Department will bear out the fact that these incentives have become a source of abuse. The mounting appeals at all levels are an eloquent testimony to the complexity and the ambiguity in the tax law on account of the various incentives. The erosion in the tax base is evidenced by the divergence between the statutory corporate tax rate and the effective tax rate. The effective tax rate of a sample of 3777 companies in 1999-00 was 21.7 per cent as against the statutory rate of 38.5 per cent. Similarly, the effective tax rate of a sample of 2585 companies in 2000-01 was 21.9 per cent as against the statutory rate of 39.55 per cent. This is inspite of the provisions of Minimum Alternate Tax (MAT) which, by itself, is a sore point with trade and industry. The Task Force was also of the strong view that the divergence between taxable income and book profit also undermines corporate governance.

5.44 Therefore, the Task Force considers it necessary to redesign the corporate profits tax so as to align taxable income and the book profit. This is possible only by eliminating the various tax incentives/preferences as well as rationalising the various other allowances which are inconsistent with accounting practice. Similarly, some of the artificial disallowances in the Income Tax Act which are neither anti-avoidance in nature nor consistent with accounting practice, also needs to be reviewed. As a result, the divergence between accounting profits and taxable income would be minimised (if not eliminated), and the corporate profits would bear the full burden of corporate tax. It would, therefore, be possible to further simplify the personal income tax by fully exempting the taxation of dividends in the hands of the shareholders. Further, since the retained earnings would have also borne full tax, it would not be necessary to levy separate tax on the capitalized value reflected in the long-term capital gains on equity. Yet another beneficial impact of aligning of book profits to taxable profits would be enhanced corporate governance, a key requirement for healthy capital markets.

Exemption for Exports (Section 10A and 10B)

5.45 Section 10A of the Income tax Act provides for deduction of profits and gains derived by an undertaking from the export of–

i) Articles or things; or

ii) Computer Software.

Further, the undertaking must be located in one of the economic zones/parks and begins to manufacture after the date mentioned in the schedule below:

Location	Date of Commencement of Manufacturing
Free trade zone	01-04-1981
Electronic Hardware Technology park	01-04-1994
Software Technology park	01-04-1994
Special economic zone	01-04-2001

This deduction is available for ten consecutive assessment years beginning with the assessment year relevant to the year in which the undertaking begins to manufacture/ produce. The tax benefit u/s 10A for assessment year 2003-04 is restricted to 90 per cent of the profits and gains from exports. Further, no benefit u/s 10A will be available to any undertaking in assessment year 2010-11 and subsequent years.

5.44 The Finance Act, 2002 has amended the provisions of section 10A to provide that any undertaking established in SEZ in a previous year relevant to any assessment year commencing on or after 1-4-2003, shall be entitled to –

1. 100 per cent deduction for five consecutive assessment years (beginning from the assessment year relevant to the previous year in which it begins to manufacture or produce articles or things or computer software); and

2. a deduction of 50 per cent for further two assessment years.

Similarly, section 10B of the Income Tax Act provides for deduction of profits and gains derived by a hundred per cent export oriented undertaking from the export of any article or thing or computer software. This deduction is available for ten consecutive assessment years beginning with the assessment year relevant to the year in which the undertaking begins to manufacture/produce. The tax benefit u/s 10A for assessment year 2003-04 is restricted to 90 per cent of the profits and gains from exports. Further, no benefit u/s 10A will be available to any undertaking in assessment year 2010-11 and subsequent years.

5.45 The undertakings enjoying tax benefits u/s 10A and 10B of the Income Tax Act derive profits from the following revenue streams:-

1. Goods or services provided within the national boundaries of India (referred to as "domestic sales")
2. Goods and services provided from India to clients in foreign countries (referred to as "off-site exports").
3. Goods and services provided on-site in foreign countries, often involving the stationing of Indian employees in foreign countries(referred to as "onsite exports").

5.46 The profits from "domestic sales" does not enjoy any tax exemption and is therefore subject to tax like profits from goods or services provided within the national boundaries of India from any other location. However, profits from "off-site exports" enjoy hundred percent exemption. Such exemption is neither justified on grounds of efficiency, equity or effectiveness.

5.47 The Finance Act 2000 amended the Income Tax Act to provide for a phased withdrawal of the export related incentives over a period of four years. The full deduction of the profits from exports allowed in assessment year 2000-01 has now been reduced to 50 per cent in assessment year 2003-04, 30 per cent in assessment year 2004-05 and full taxation in assessment year 2005-06. To the extent exports by undertakings covered u/s 10A and 10B continue to enjoy hundred per cent exemption in respect of profits from exports, undertakings located outside the economic zones or not declared as hundred per cent EOUs suffer a competitive disadvantage viz. a viz. the former. Such disadvantage arising solely from tax considerations will result in trade diversion and hence encourage inefficiency.

5.48 The FTZs/HTPs/STPs/SEZs are also endowed with better

infrastructural facilities and input tax regime. Therefore, undertakings in such locations manufacture in an international environment. Inspite of the competitive advantage these undertakings enjoy higher tax benefits in comparison to undertakings located outside such zones/parks. Hence, the exemption u/s 10A and 10B for "off-site exports" also violate both horizontal and vertical equity. Furthermore, the need for continuing monitoring of exemptions degrades the effectiveness of the tax administration as well.

5.49 The tax treatment of profits from "on-site exports" is complex. Such profits are first subjected to income tax in the foreign country; in many countries it could be at two different levels: state and federal level. Further, the Indian taxpayer would also be required to compensate its employees for the non-refundable/non-transferable social security contribution (tax)[61]. As a result the aggregate burden of foreign income tax (excluding social security contributions) on such profits is extremely high in comparison to their liability in India.

5.50 Under the scheme of the income tax act, the global profits (including profits from "on-site exports") of the undertaking would be subject to tax in the absence of tax exemption u/s 10A and 10B of the Income Tax Act. The Indian undertaking is allowed to claim credit for income tax paid in the foreign country. However, such credit is restricted to federal income tax and also to the amount payable on the profits from "on-site exports", at the Indian rates. If the amount of tax payable on such profits at Indian rates is less then the federal income tax paid in the foreign country, no adjustment is given for access federal income tax paid in the foreign country. Similarly, no tax credit is allowed for the state income tax paid in the foreign country. With the proposed corporate tax rate at 30 per cent, large amount of credit for federal income tax and state income tax paid in the foreign country would not be allowable.

5.51 In the course of its consultations with representatives from the Information Technology Sector, it was argued that the exemption u/s 10A and 10B was essentially restricted to exemption from income tax of profits from the exports of goods and services from India. It was pointed out that a significant proportion of the profits of the undertakings in the IT sector enjoying benefits u/s

10A and 10B of the Income Tax Act was from services provided on-site abroad. Since, the aggregate of the foreign county's federal and state income taxes was estimated as high as 45 per cent compared to 36.75 per cent liability in India, the exemption u/s 10A and 10B essentially served as compensation for the increased burden on off-site revenues, that is, the exemption from the point of view of the industry was a "tax cross-subsidy" between on-site and off-site exports. Further, the representatives also argued that in the absence of a totalisation agreement between India and its major trading partners, they (and therefore India) had also to suffer the additional burden of both employer and employee contribution to social security in the foreign country and the same was non-refundable/non-transferable to India on return of the Indian employee[62].

5.52 The Task Force recognises that any company whose activities are spread across international borders could potentially incur a higher income tax burden on its global profits in comparison to a company whose activities are confined to the national boundaries. While companies exporting goods can potentially avoid the liability of the foreign country's federal and state income tax, the companies in the IT sector must necessarily bear the burden because of the very nature of their activities[63]. Potentially though the problem could be faced across sectors, in practice it is acute in the IT sector[64]. Infact, for companies whose revenues from on-site abroad are disproportionately large, the exemption u/s 10A and 10B may not offer any significant compensation. The Task Force therefore recommends the elimination of the tax incentive u/s 10A and 10B of the Income Tax Act for all taxpayers other than those engaged in manufacturing computer software.

5.53 We also recommend that in the case of taxpayers engaged in manufacturing computer software, the Government of India must take immediate steps to negotiate with foreign governments to enter into a comprehensive totalisation agreement leading to a single point incidence of taxes. It may be noted that a number of countries across the globes already have totalisation agreements with each other related to payment of social security and other taxes[65]. However, in the interim, the Task Force recommends the following alternatives:-

1. Eliminate the tax exemption u/s 10A and 10B and amend Section 91 of the Income Tax Act to allow full credit for payment of foreign country's federal and state income tax. However, no refund of such foreign tax credit should be allowed;

OR

2. Since the arrangement is transitory in nature the benefit of tax exemption u/s 10A and 10B for manufacturing of computer software only may be continued till we enter into a totalisation agreement with trading partners. However, the distribution of dividend by computer software manufacturing companies availing of deductions u/s 10A or 10B should be subjected to a dividend distribution tax of 30 per cent. Similarly, the long-term capital gains arising from transfer of equities of such companies should also be subjected to tax like long-term capital gains from any other asset.

The Task Force could not arrive at unanimity on the preferred alternative amongst the above two.

Depreciation

5.54 Under a corporate income tax designed to tax net income including returns from capital, corporations should be provided with deductions for the economic depreciation of capital inputs. In the absence of inflation, the amount of depreciation for tax purposes (i.e., capital cost allowances) over the lifetime of a capital asset used in production should equal to original investment expenditure. This tax treatment allows the taxpayer to recover tax-free the original investment, leaving tax applicable only to the return on the investment. The timing of depreciation claims is equally important for the proper measurement of the return to capital in each period. If the portion of the capital cost that a taxpayer is allowed to write-off in one year is greater (less) than the true cost, income will be understated (overstated).

5.55 In theory, depreciation claims should match economic depreciation, which, for a given asset, will follow a specific pattern over time. This pattern will depend on the length of time the asset is used in production and the pattern of income arising from the use of the asset in each of the years in which it is employed. The pattern of income arising from the use of the asset in each of the years in which it is employed. The pattern will also depend on relative output and capital input price changes arising, for example as a result of technological change or obsolescence, and on the asset's residual value at the end of its useful life.

5.56 In principle, these considerations will be captured by movements in the inflationadjusted value of the asset in each year, and depreciation could be measured by observing the value of second hand capital assets. In practice, the lack of an active market for used assets means that economic depreciation is generally unknown and must be inferred. For some assets, the contribution of an asset to output and thus income may remain roughly constant over time. In such cases, a reasonable (annual) depreciable amount may be a constant percentage of its original cost as under the straight line depreciation method. Other assets may contribute to income mainly in the early years of production, or may become obsolete relatively quickly, suggesting that relatively high depreciation charges should be taken in early year with successively lower charges in subsequent years as under the declining-balance method. In either case, a representative depreciation rate must be chosen. Typically these are based on rough estimates of the useful-life of assets, with additional precision being lost where a single depreciation rate is assigned to a basket of different assets, as is generally the case. In certain cases, taxpayers may be allowed to use for tax purposes depreciation rates that are in excess of what are estimated to be economic depreciation rates in order to encourage investment in the target capital asset.

5.57 The Income Tax Act read with the Income Tax Rules classifies capital assets into a basket of different assets and provides different percentage rates of depreciation for each such basket (known as a block of assets). The depreciable amount is determined on the declining-balance method. The general rate of depreciation for plant and machinery under the tax law is 25 per cent. This was first prescribed in 1991-92. Such high rate of depreciation was justified in 1991-92 because of the high corporate tax rate of 51.75 per cent which adversely affected internal accrual of resources for replacement and modernization. Consequent to our recommendation to reduce the corporate tax rate to 30 per cent from the existing levels of 36.75 per cent, it is now necessary to review the general rate of depreciation for plant and machinery.

5.58 The adequacy of the rate of depreciation depends on the (presumed) period of the useful life of the asset, the mode of granting depreciation, i.e., whether by the diminishing balance method or by the straight line method, and the past and expected rates of growth of prices of capital goods. For the general category of plant and machinery, it would seem reasonable to assume an average period of service life of ten years. Although in practice, machinery has come to be replaced in industry after a period much longer than ten years, nevertheless, in view of the rapidity of technological change, it would be prudent to keep in mind the notional period of ten years of useful life for machinery. Having made this assumption, we should aim at a shorter recovery period through higher or accelerated rate of depreciation. When this is done, the interest (net of tax) earned on the amounts recovered should also be taken into account in computing the accumulated balance at the end of the presumed life of the assets. It would seem reasonable to assume a 9 per cent rate of interest under the prevailing circumstances subject to tax at the rate of 36.75 per cent, for the purpose of an illustrative calculation. We find that depreciation allowances granted at 25 per cent on the basis of the diminishing balance method, if invested at 9 per cent rate of interest, would yield an accumulated balance at the end of ten years of Rs. 126.76 net of tax on interest, for an original cost of Rs. 100 including a Cenvat of Rs. 12.54 and a state VAT of Rs. 9.09[66] (Table-5.1). In the context of our proposal to reduce corporate tax rate to 30 per cent, the depreciation rate corresponding to an equivalent yield at the end of 10 years, is 15 per cent (Table-5.2). Infact, accounting for the residual value of the machinery at the end of the 10 year the accumulated balance would be greater then the replacement value of the machine assuming that the historical rate of inflation of capital goods at 3.5 per cent will continue in the future. In any case, the improved internal generation of resources due to reduction in the corporate tax rates will help faster replacement. In view of the above, the Task Force recommends that the general rate of depreciation for plant and machinery should be reduced to 15 per cent from the existing level of 25 per cent. We also recommend that the rates of depreciation for other blocks of assets must be reviewed along the

Assumptions :	
Capital Cost	Rs. 100
Interest rate applied	9%
Depreciation	25%
Corporate Tax Rate	36.75%
Inflation (capital Goods)	3.5%

Table : 5.1

Computation of accumulated balance under Declining balance Method of Depreciation (with tax on Interest)

Year	Balance at the beginning of the year	Cenvat	State VAT	Depreciation (declining balance)				Interest	Tax on interest	Interest net of tax	Amount accumulated at the end of the year	Replacement value of machinery
				Cost	Cenvat Credit	State VAT Credit	Total					
1	78.37	12.54	9.09	19.59	6.27	3.03	28.89	0.00	0.00	0.00	28.89	100.00
2	58.78	6.27	6.06	8.82	6.27	3.03	18.12	2.60	0.96	1.64	48.65	103.50
3	49.96	0.00	3.03	7.49	0.00	3.03	10.52	4.38	1.61	2.77	61.95	107.12
4	42.47	0.00	0.00	6.37	0.00	0.00	6.37	5.58	2.05	3.53	71.84	110.87
5	36.10	0.00	0.00	5.41	0.00	0.00	5.41	6.47	2.38	4.09	81.35	114.75
6	30.68	0.00	0.00	4.60	0.00	0.00	4.60	7.32	2.69	4.63	90.58	118.77
7	26.08	0.00	0.00	3.91	0.00	0.00	3.91	8.15	3.00	5.16	99.65	122.93
8	22.17	0.00	0.00	3.33	0.00	0.00	3.33	8.97	3.30	5.67	108.65	127.23
9	18.84	0.00	0.00	2.83	0.00	0.00	2.83	9.78	3.59	6.18	117.66	131.68
10	16.02	0.00	0.00	2.40	0.00	0.00	2.40	10.59	3.89	6.70	126.76	136.29
11	13.61	0.00	0.00	2.04	0.00	0.00	2.04	11.41	4.19	7.22	136.02	141.06
12	11.57	0.00	0.00	1.74	0.00	0.00	1.74	12.24	4.50	7.74	145.49	146.00
13	9.84	0.00	0.00	1.48	0.00	0.00	1.48	13.09	4.81	8.28	155.25	151.11
14	8.36	0.00	0.00	1.25	0.00	0.00	1.25	13.97	5.13	8.84	165.34	156.40
15	7.11	0.00	0.00	1.07	0.00	0.00	1.07	14.88	5.47	9.41	175.82	161.87
16	6.04	0.00	0.00	0.91	0.00	0.00	0.91	15.82	5.82	10.01	186.74	167.53
17	5.13	0.00	0.00	0.77	0.00	0.00	0.77	16.81	6.18	10.63	198.14	173.40
18	4.36	0.00	0.00	0.65	0.00	0.00	0.65	17.83	6.55	11.28	210.07	179.47
19	3.71	0.00	0.00	0.56	0.00	0.00	0.56	18.91	6.95	11.96	222.59	185.75
20	3.15	0.00	0.00	0.47	0.00	0.00	0.47	20.03	7.36	12.67	235.73	192.25

Assumptions :	
Capital Cost	Rs. 100
Interest rate applied	9%
Depreciation	15%
Corporate Tax Rate	30%
Inflation (capital Goods)	3.5%

Table : 5.2

Computation of accumulated balance under Declining balance Method of Depreciation (with tax on Interest)

Year	Balance at the beginning of the year	Cenvat	State VAT	Depreciation (declining balance)				Interest	Tax on interest	Interest net of tax	Amount accumulated at the end of the year	Replacement value of machinery
				Cost	Cenvat Credit	State VAT Credit	Total					
1	78.37	12.54	9.09	11.76	6.27	3.03	21.06	0.00	0.00	0.00	21.06	100.00
2	66.61	6.27	6.06	9.99	6.27	3.03	19.29	1.89	0.57	1.33	41.67	103.50
3	56.62	0.00	3.03	8.49	0.00	3.03	11.52	3.75	1.13	2.63	55.82	107.12
4	48.13	0.00	0.00	7.22	0.00	0.00	7.22	5.02	1.51	3.52	66.56	110.87
5	40.91	0.00	0.00	6.14	0.00	0.00	6.14	5.99	1.80	4.19	76.89	114.75
6	34.77	0.00	0.00	5.22	0.00	0.00	5.22	6.92	2.08	4.84	86.95	118.77
7	29.56	0.00	0.00	4.43	0.00	0.00	4.43	7.83	2.35	5.48	96.86	122.93
8	25.12	0.00	0.00	3.77	0.00	0.00	3.77	8.72	2.62	6.10	106.73	127.23
9	21.36	0.00	0.00	3.20	0.00	0.00	3.20	9.61	2.88	6.72	116.66	131.68
10	18.15	0.00	0.00	2.72	0.00	0.00	2.72	10.50	3.15	7.35	126.73	136.29
11	15.43	0.00	0.00	2.31	0.00	0.00	2.31	11.41	3.42	7.98	137.03	141.06
12	13.11	0.00	0.00	1.97	0.00	0.00	1.97	12.33	3.70	8.63	147.63	146.00
13	11.15	0.00	0.00	1.67	0.00	0.00	1.67	13.29	3.99	9.30	158.60	151.11
14	9.48	0.00	0.00	1.42	0.00	0.00	1.42	14.27	4.28	9.99	170.01	156.40
15	8.05	0.00	0.00	1.21	0.00	0.00	1.21	15.30	4.59	10.71	181.93	161.87
16	6.85	0.00	0.00	1.03	0.00	0.00	1.03	16.37	4.91	11.46	194.42	167.53
17	5.82	0.00	0.00	0.87	0.00	0.00	0.87	17.50	5.25	12.25	207.54	173.40
18	4.95	0.00	0.00	0.74	0.00	0.00	0.74	18.68	5.60	13.08	221.36	179.47
19	4.20	0.00	0.00	0.63	0.00	0.00	0.63	19.92	5.98	13.95	235.94	185.75
20	3.57	0.00	0.00	0.54	0.00	0.00	0.54	21.23	6.37	14.86	251.34	192.25

above lines. Consequently, the depreciation amount charged for tax purposes will be similar to those charged under the Companies Act.

Tax incentives for Shipping Industry

5.59 Section 33AC of the Income Tax Act provides for a deduction from the profits of a shipping company, of any amount transferred to a special reserve account. The total amount transferred to such reserve account is subject to a ceiling of twice the aggregate of the paid up share capital, the general reserves and share premium. The reserve must be used for the purpose of acquiring new ships. The use of these reserves for distribution of dividend is prohibited. The underlying objective of allowing this special deduction is to enable shipping companies to build up own capital for new acquisitions. The justification for this special dispensation is far too weak; this argument holds equally good for every other industry. This being so, it should be extended to all industries across the board which would be equivalent to an across the board rate reduction. Our proposal to affect a 18.38 per cent cut in the corporate tax rate[67] is a step towards a sector neutral tax regime. Accordingly, we recommend that there is no further case for retaining the tax benefit u/s 33AC of the Income Tax Act and should, therefore be abolished.

5.60 The shipping industry represented to the Task Force for the introduction of a tonnage tax for shipping companies as an option to the existing tax regime under the Income Tax Act. The Task Force was also informed that the Rakesh Mohan Committee had indeed recommended the introduction of such a tax and the recommendations were under the active consideration of the Ministry of Finance. We have also been informed that the Union Cabinet has, at the instance of the Cabinet Committee on Security, directed the Ministry of Finance/ Ministry of Shipping to separately examine the issue relating to the introduction of a tonnage tax. The Task Force considers it only appropriate to refrain from making any recommendations on the introduction of the tonnage tax.

Tax incentives for Scientific Research and Development

5.61 Companies undertaking research and development

generally ignore the positive spillover benefits (externalities) that accrue to others (e.g. transfer of knowledge) when they decide upon the amount of R&D to undertake, which may result in an inefficiently low level of investment from society's perspective. Tax incentives targeted at research activities, or at the development and the implementation of production processes and products, are introduced to encourage companies to increase their investments in these areas

5.62 The income tax system in India also allows for concessional treatment of expenditure on Scientific Research and Development (Section 35). These take the form of deductions for both revenue and capital expenditure (other than land) on scientific research in the year in which these are incurred. While the treatment for the revenue expenditure is no different from any other expenditure, the treatment for capital expenditure tantamount to 100 per cent depreciation. Further, section 35(2AB)(1) also allows weighted deduction of 150 per cent of the expenditure (other than on land and building) on in-house research by companies engaged in the business of bio-technology, drugs and pharmaceuticals, electronic equipments, computers, tele-communication equipments, chemicals and any other article notified by the CBDT.

5.63 Given the fact that, the use of capital assets is fungible[68], it is rather difficult to identify whether the asset has been used only for scientific research. The full expensing of the capital expenditure on scientific research in the year in which it is incurred, creates a perverse incentive for fungibility. This leads to avoidable disputes between the revenue officials and the taxpayer. Further, the weighted expenditure linked deductions encourage shifting of expenditure from one head to another and making false expenditure claims. The recommendation to reduce the tax rates for corporate profits will now substantially enhance reward for research outcomes. Such outcome-based incentives are more efficient than input based incentives. Accordingly, we recommend the abolition of section 35 of the Income Tax Act. As a result, the revenue expenditure on scientific research will qualify for deduction u/s 37 of the Income Tax Act and capital expenditure on scientific research will be eligible for depreciation under section 32 of the Income Tax Act. Since, expenditure link weighted deduction will also be abolished, there will be no perverse incentive to shift expenditure or make false claims.

5.64 The provision of section 35 also allows weighted deduction in respect of donation to scientific research associations, university, college and other institutions engaged in scientific research, social science research and statistical research. It also allows weighted deduction for donation to approved scientific research programmes. In view of the fact that these confer higher benefit to donors engaged in business in comparison to non-business donors, we recommend the rationalisation of the deduction for donation for scientific research, so as to be more equitable across taxpayers. Therefore, a tax rebate calculated at 20 per cent of the amount of donation for research (scientific, social sciences or statistical) should be allowed to all taxpayers irrespective of their source of income. A comparative analysis of the tax treatment of expenditure on scientific research under the existing law and on the basis of our recommendations is contained in Table 5.3.

Deduction for payment of interest on borrowed capital.

5.65 Section 36(1)(iii) of the Income Tax Act provides for a deduction in respect of interest paid on capital borrowed for the purposes of the business or profession. The Courts have interpreted that, unlike Section 37(1) of the Income Tax Act, there is no prohibition on the allowability of interest paid on capital borrowed for acquisition, construction or production of a capital asset. Therefore, such interest, even though capital in nature is allowable as revenue expenditure. As a result, the interest relating to the period prior to the completion of the project is being claimed as revenue expenditure in the computation of the taxable income. However, for the purposes of reporting to its shareholders, the same interest is capitalised as part of the cost of the capital asset in accordance with the Accounting Standards 16 issued by the Institute of Chartered Accountants of India. The Department continues to disallow the claim for deduction based on the Accounting Standards thereby giving rise to considerable dispute and uncertainty.

5.66 With a view to aligning the provisions relating to the allowability of deduction u/s 36(1)(iii) with those of the Accounting Standard 16 issued by the Institute of Chartered Accountants of India, it is recommended that a suitable clarificatory amendment

Table – 5.3

Comparative analysis of the tax treatment of expenditure on Scientific Research.

Section	Nature of Expenditure / Donations under the existing law (assessment year 2003-04)	Amount of deduction Force recommendations (assessment year 2004-05)	Amount of deduction as per Task	Remarks
35(1)(i)	Revenue expenditure on Scientific Research related to the business	100 per cent of the expenditure	100 per cent of the expenditure to be allowed u/s 37(1)	
35(1)(ii)	Donation to – • a Scientific Research Association set-up for scientific research; • University, College or other institution to be used for scientific research	125 per cent of the donation	20 per cent tax rebate on 100 per cent of the donation (to be merged with the new provision for replacing section 80G)	Aligned to the tax benefit for non-business taxpayers. Hence equitable.
35(1)(iii)	Donation to a university, college or other institution to be used for research in social science or statistics	125 per cent of the donation	20 per cent tax rebate on 100 per cent of the donation (to be merged with the new provision for replacing section 80G)	Aligned to the tax benefit for non-business taxpayers. Hence equitable.
35(1)(iv)	Capital expenditure on scientific research related to the business	100 per cent of the expenditure	Depreciation to be allowed u/s 32	

(Contd...)

...contd...

35(2AA)	Donation to – • A National Laboratory • University or an Indian Institute of Technology or a specified person The donation must be with a specific direction to use for approved scientific research programme.	125 per cent of the donation	20 per cent tax rebate on 100 per cent of the donation (to be merged with the new provision for replacing section 80G)	Aligned to the tax benefit for non-business taxpayers. Hence
35(2AB)(1)	Expenditure (other than on land and building) on in-house research by companies engaged in the business of – • Biotechnology • Drugs and pharmaceuticals • Electronic equipments • Computers • Tele communication equipments • Chemicals • Any other article notified by the CBDT.	150 per cent of the expenditure	• 100 per cent deduction for revenue expenditure to be allowed u/s 37. • Depreciation to be allowed u/s 32.	

to Section 36(1)(iii) should be made to provide for the disallowance of the borrowing costs that are directly attributable to the acquisition, construction or production of a capital asset, as a revenue expenditure. Such borrowing costs will now have to be capitalized as part of the cost of the capital asset in accordance with the Accounting Standards 16 issued by the Institute of Chartered Accountants of India. Other borrowing costs should continue to be recognised as an expense in the period in which they are incurred and continue to be allowed as a deduction u/s 37(1) of the Income Tax Act.

Tax Treatment of Non-performing Assets of the Financial Sector

5.67 Under the general expense rule in the Income Tax Act, an expenditure is an allowable deduction if the liability is crystallized and quantified. Therefore, any provisioning for an expenditure is not an allowable deduction in the determination of the tax base if such provisioning is not a statutory obligation.

5.68 Section 36 (1)(viia) of the Income Tax Act, however, provides for a deviation from this general expense rule by allowing any provision for bad and doubtful debts made by commercial banks and public financial institutions subject to specified limits. The scope of the provision is summarized in Table 5.4.

5.69 The existing position is that in exercise of its statutory authority, the Reserve Bank of India mandates the banks and public financial institutions for provisioning of Non-Performing Assets (NPAs). Compliance to this is a statutory obligation[69]. However, for tax purposes, this statutory obligation is disregarded even though under the general expense rule, a statutory liability is a fully allowable deduction. As a result, the banks and public financial institutions face a double jeopardy: they have to statutorily provide for such nonperforming assets thereby undermining actual profits as well as pay tax on such provisioning which further undermines the profits. Accordingly, we recommend that the provisions of section 36(1)(viia) of the Income Tax Act should be amended to provide that the provision for bad and doubtful debts will be restricted to the amount of provision debited to profit and loss account as audited subject to the maximum amount of provisioning permitted under the prudential guidelines issued by the Reserve Bank of India.

Table – 5.4

Tax Treatment of Provisions for Non-performing Assets of Banks and Financial Institutions

Section	Eligibility	Amount of deduction	Period
36(1)(viia)(a)	Scheduled Bank (other than foreign banks)	(I) Amount not exceeding the sum of 5 per cent of adjusted gross total income and 10 per cent of aggregate average advances made by rural branches; OR (II) 5 percent of the Non-performing Assets identified on the basis of RBI guidelines (10 per cent for assessment years 2003-04 and 2004-05).	Option I is available in every assessment year. Option II is available for assessment years 2000-01 to 2004-05.
36(1)(viia)(b)	Foreign Bank	An amount not exceeding 5 percent of adjusted gross total income	Every assessment year.
36(1)(viia)(c)	Public Financial Institution or State Finance Corporation or State Industrial Investment Corporation	I. Amount not exceeding 5 per cent of adjusted gross total income; OR II. 10 percent of the NPA identified on the basis of RBI guidelines.	Option I-Every assessment year. Option II-For assessment years 2003-04 and 2004-05.

Tax Treatment Of Statutory Liabilities

5.70 In terms of the provisions of Section 43B of the Income Tax Act, deduction for statutory payments relating to labour, taxes and state and public financial institutions are allowed as deductions if they are paid during the financial year. However, under the provisions payment of taxes and interest to state and public financial institutions are deemed to have been paid during the financial year even if they are paid by the due date of filing of return. Further, if the liability is discharged in the subsequent year after the due date of filing of return, the payment is allowed as a deduction in the subsequent year. In the case of statutory payment relating to labour, the deduction for the payment is disallowed if such payment is made any time after the last date for payment of the labour related liability. Trade and industry across the country represented that the delayed payment of statutory liability related to labour should be accorded the same treatment as delayed payment of taxes and interest i.e. they should be allowed in the year of payment.

5.71 Since, the objective of the provision is to ensure that a taxpayer does not avail of any statutory liability without actually making a payment for the same, we are of the view that these objectives would be served if the deduction for the statutory liability relating to labour are allowed in the year of payment. The complete disallowance of such payments is too harsh a punishment for delays in payment. Therefore, we recommend that the deduction for delayed payment of statutory liability relating to labour should be allowed in the year of payment like delayed taxes and interest.

The treatment of corporate tax losses

5.72 Most income tax systems permit businesses that earn a tax loss in one year (where taxable revenues are less than tax deductions in the same year) to carry the tax loss (i.e., the negative amount of taxable income) forward to future years, or (in a more limited number of cases) back to previous years, to be used to offset income in those years. The carry-back and carry-forward provisions are typically limited (e.g., a three year carryback and a seven year carryforward). These provisions are provided in recognition of the arbitrary choice of a fixed period (e.g., 12 months) for which to assess tax. The practice recognises that many companies/firms encounter negative cash flows during their initial phases, despite being profitable over the longer term or on a present value basis. Moreover, in certain high-risk industries, even very efficient and profitable firms may experience wide fluctuations in their earnings over both negative and positive ranges. Disallowing loss transfers over time would be inconsistent with a proper matching of revenues and expenses, would impose a higher tax burden on firms with unstable profit profiles, and would discourage risk-taking.

5.73 Unless a tax loss in one year can be carried back to offset tax paid in a prior year, less than full loss- offsetting occurs, as when losses are carried forward, they typically may not be carried forward with an interest adjustment (to reflect the opportunity cost of funds). Therefore, the present value of losses deducted in the future will be less than the value of those losses if they could be currently used. Countries do not typically offer a cash refund for tax losses, for primarily two reasons. First there is a fear that refundability would encourage unprofitable or inefficient businesses. Second, providing for refundability would impose significant up-front revenue costs, and difficult transitional issues would be met in a move to such a system (i.e., how to treat accumulated pools of losses).

5.74 Finally, it is important to recognise that (conceptually) tax losses can be subdivided into three categories: i) operating business losses, ii) capital losses, and iii) tax incentive losses. Under the Indian income tax system, typically capital losses arising from depreciation are allowed to be carried forward indefinitely however the operating business losses are allowed to be carried forward only for the period of eight years. This discourages projects with long gestation period as well as those which incur losses in the initial years of their operations. With a view to eliminating this bias, we recommend the removal of distinction between unabsorbed depreciation and unabsorbed business loss. In other words unabsorbed depreciation would be merged with business loss and lose its separate identity. Further, business loss would be allowed to be carried forward indefinitely.

Tax Incentives under sections 80IA and 80IB

5.75 The deductions u/s 80IA and 80IB are allowed in respect of profits from the eligible business at the rates and for the number of years as indicated in Tables 5.5 and 5.6. These deductions, in so far as they relate to backward areas and other specific locations, have not served their intended objective[70]. Similarly, like any other incentives, these also cause serious distortions in economic efficiency, equity and administrative effectiveness. If incentive for development of backward areas need to be protected, the objective would be well served by an expenditure grant either in the form of a capital or output subsidy. Such an incentive mechanism would be relatively more efficient and equitable.

5.76 Most often, the case for deduction in respect of profits of the eligible businesses referred in sections 80IA and 80IB is justified on the ground that these businesses have large gestation period and generate huge losses in the first five to seven years. The tax benefit from such losses is often lost out due to the arbitrary cut off period for carry forward and allowability of losses. Since, we have recommended in the earlier section, that business losses, like depreciation, should be allowed to be carried forward indefinitely, the inherent problem associated with such eligible business would stand resolved.

5.77 Further, most of the eligible businesses are regulated and therefore assured of a fixed rate of return. The fixation of tariffs in such cases renders tax payable to be a pass through. Thus the incidence of income tax does not by itself reduce the attractiveness of the project for the investors.

5.78 In a large number of cases covered under these provisions, the exemption is in respect of partial profits. Since, these provisions were introduced when the tax rate was 40.25 per cent (35 per cent plus 15 per cent surcharge), the substantial benefit flowing from our recommendation to reduce the tax rate to 30 per cent and exempt dividends and long-term capital gains on equity, is compensatory for the withdrawal of the benefit u/s 80IA and 80IB.

5.79 Another aspect of the tax benefit u/s 80IA and 80IB that needs to be placed on record is that such benefits only helped to camouflage the under performance of corporate managers. These benefits did not protect the shareholders; the dividends distributed from exempt profit were also taxable along with long-term capital gains. Further, these have also been a source of both abuse and large number of litigation increasing transaction costs all around.

Table – 5.5

Tax incentives Under Section 80IA – At a glance.

Section	Eligible business	Nature of deduction	Number of years for which deduction can be claimed	Remarks
80IA	Development or maintenance or operation of the following infrastructure facility:- 1. Roads including toll road, a bridge or a rail system. 2. A highway project including other or inland port activities which are integral part of the project. 3. Water supply project. 4. Water treatment system. 5. Irrigation project. 6. Sanitation and sewerage system. 7. Solid waste management system. 8. Port, air-port, inland waterway or inland port.	100 per cent of the profits derived from the eligible business.	• 10 consecutive assessment years out of 20 years • 10 out of 15 years for ports, air-ports, inland waterways or inland port	Regulated Industry (other than highway project)
80IA	Provision of Tele-communication	• 100 per cent of the profits derived from the eligible business. For the first 5 years. • 30 per cent of the profits derived from the eligible business. For the next 5 years	10 consecutive assessment years out of 15 years.	Regulated Industry
80IA	Development of industrial park	100 per cent of the profits	10 consecutive assessment years.	
80IA	Development of special economic zone	100 per cent of the profits	10 consecutive assessment years.	
80IA	Development and operation of special economic zone	100 per cent of the profits	10 consecutive assessment years.	
80IA	Maintenance and operation of special economic zone	100 per cent of the profits	10 consecutive assessment years.	
80IA	Generation of power	100 per cent of the profits	10 consecutive assessment years.	Regulated Industry
80IA	Transmission of power	100 per cent of the profits	10 consecutive assessment years.	Regulated Industry
80IA	Distribution of power	100 per cent of the profits	10 consecutive assessment years.	Regulated Industry

Table – 5.5

Tax incentives Under Section 80IA – At a glance.

Section	Eligible business	Nature of deduction	Number of years for which deduction can be claimed	Remarks
80IB(3)(i)	Industrial Undertaking notified by the Central Government	25 per cent (30 per cent for company)	10 consecutive assessment years (12 year for cooperative societies)	Operations must begin before the date specified by notification with reference to any particular undertaking.
80IB(3)(ii)	Small Scale Industrial Undertaking	25 per cent (30 per cent for company)	10 consecutive assessment years (12 year for cooperative societies)	Operations must begin between 1-04-1995 and 31-03-2002
80IB(4)	Industrial undertaking in an industrially backward state specified in the Eighth Schedule	• 100 per cent of the profits derived from the eligible business in the first five years. • 25 per cent (30 per cent for companies) of the profits derived from the eligible in the next 5 years	10 consecutive assessment years	Begins to manufacture before 1-04-2004

(Contd...)

...contd...

80IB(5)(i)	Industrial undertaking located in backward district of category "A"	• 100 per cent of the profits derived from the eligible business in the first five years. • 25 per cent (30 per cent for companies) of the profits derived from the eligible in the next 5 years	10 consecutive assessment years	Begins to manufacture before 1-04-2004
80IB(5)(ii)	Industrial undertaking located in backward district of category "B"	• 100 per cent of the profits derived from the eligible business in the first three years. • 25 per cent (30 per cent for companies) of the profits derived from the eligible business in the next 5 years	8 consecutive assessment years 9 12 assessment years for co-operative societies)	Begins to manufacture before 1-04-2004
80IB(6)	Business of ship	30 per cent of the profits	10 consecutive assessment years	Ship brought into use between 1-04-1991 and 31-03-1995
80IB(7)(a)	Business of Hotel in hilly areas or pilgrimage centres	50 per cent of the profits	10 consecutive assessment years	Operations must begin before 1-04-2001
80IB(7)(b)	Business of Hotel in any other areas	30 per cent of the profits	10 consecutive assessment years	Operations must begin before 1-04-2001
80IB(7A)	Business of building, owning and operating a multiplex theatre	50 per cent of the profits	5 consecutive assessment years	Operations must begin between 1-04-2002 and 31-03-2005

(Contd...)

...contd...

80IB(7B)	Business of building, owning and operating a convention centre	50 per cent of the profits	5 consecutive assessment years	Operations must begin between 1-04-2002 and 31-03-2005
80IB(8)	Scientific Research and Development company	100 per cent of the profits	5 consecutive assessment years	Operations must begin befire 1-04-1999
80IB(8A)	Scientific Research and Development company	100 per cent of the profits	5 consecutive assessment years	Operations must begin between 31-03-2000 and 1-04-2003
80IB(9)	Commercial production or refining of mineral oil	100 per cent of the profits	7 consecutive assessment years	
80IB(10)	Development and building of housing project approved by a local authority	100 per cent of the profits		Operations must begin before 31-03-2001 and completed before 31-03-2003
80IB(11)	Business of setting up and operating a cold chain facility for agriculutral produce	• 100 per cent of the profits in the first 5 years • 25 per cent (30 per cent for companies) of the profits in the next 5 years.	10 consecutive assessment years	Operations must begin after 1-04-1999 but before 31-03-2003
80IB(11A)	Integrated business of handling, storage and transportation of food grains	• 100 per cent of the profits in the first 5 years • 25 per cent (30 per cent for companies) of the profits in the next 5 years.	10 consecutive assessment years	Operations must begin on or after 1-04-2001

5.80 In view of the above, the Task Force recommends the elimination of the provisions of section 80IA and 80IB with immediate effect (and not by a sunset clause).

Promissory Estoppel

5.81 While considering the elimination of a various tax incentives particularly those under section 10A, 10B, 80IA and 80IB, with immediate effect and not by grandfathering them, the Task Force deliberated upon whether such a step would violate the principle of promissory estoppel.

5.82 The doctrine of promissory estoppel, though of ancient vintage, was rescued from obscurity by the decision of Justice Denning in the celebrated High Trees case[71]. This principle has been restarted by him in his book[72] in the following words: "it is a principle of justice and of equity. It comes to this: When a man by his words or conduct has led another to believe that he can safely act on the faith of them and the other does act on them – he will not be allowed to go back on what he has said or done when it would be unjust or unequitable for him to do so". Estoppel is thus a rule of equity.

5.83 In India the doctrine started in a significant way with the Indo-Afghan case in 1968 and after some vicissitude stabilised since mid-eighties with authoritative pronouncements in the cases of Godfrey Phillips, Pournami Oil Mills, Usha Martin, Filterco, Bakul cashew, Bakul oil etc. It is now well-recognised by the Courts and wellestablished in the administrative law of India.

5.84 The rule of interpretation that emerges from the plethora of judgments that if the government promises something about tax or benefit of import etc. To a citizen, the doctrine of promissory estoppel will apply provided the promise made itself is not against the statute (there is no estoppel against statue) and the person promising is compctent to make a promise. The settled law is now that where the Government makes a promise knowing or intending that it would be acted upon by the promisee and in fact the promisee acting in reliance on it, alters its position, the Government would be held bound by the promise and the promise would be enforceable against the Government at the instance of the promisee, notwithstanding that there is no consideration for the promise and the promise is not recorded in the form of a formal contract as required by Article 299 of the Constitution.

5.85 The Supreme Court through its various judgements have decided that promissory estoppel applies against executive powers and not against legislative powers of the Government. The first limitation to the doctrine is that there can be no estoppel against the statute. There is also no estoppel against legislative function exercised by the legislature itself. There is also no estoppel against the taxpayer but only against the Government and public bodies. Promissory estoppel can operate even when the promise is not held out to one person but given in general as a scheme but no promise can be taken as estoppel if it is vague or derived in an indirect manner or given by an unauthorised person. If the concession promised is misused, then the government can withdraw the promised concession. Promise must be acted upon and the taxpayer must have altered his position in order that the promise upon and the assessee must have altered his position in order that the promise constitutes an estoppel. Against classification of goods there cannot be an estoppel. Since promissory estoppel is itself a creature of equity demands for the public good the discontinuance of a promise to an individual or to a class, then promissory estoppel will not apply. Public good will override private injury.

5.86 The Supreme Court in its judgement delivered as late as December, 2001 in the case of Sharma Transport Vs. Government of A.P. and Others[73] has reiterated the principles in the following observations:-

> "Next plea is the oft-repeated one of promissory estoppel. It has to be noted that even though a concession is extended for a fixed period, the same can be withdrawan in public interest. In STO vs. Shree Durga Mills ((1998) 1 SCC 572 : (1997) 7 Scale 726) it has been held by this court that a notification granting exemption of tax can be withdrawn at any point of time. There cannot be estoppel against any statute. Where it is in public interest, the Court will not interfere because public interest must override any consideration of private loss or gain (see Kasinka Trading Vs. Union of India ((1995) 1 SCC 274). In Shrijee Sales Corpn. V. Union of India ((1997) 3 SCC 398) it was observed that where there was supervening public interest, the Government is free to change its stand and withdraw the exemption already granted. One such reason for changing its policy decision can be resource crunch and

the loss of public revenue. There is preponderance of judicial opinion that to invoke the doctrine of promissory estoppel, clear, sound and positive foundation must be laid in the petition itself by the party invoking the doctrine and that bald expressions, without any supporting material, to the effect that the doctrine is attracted because the party invoking the doctrine has altered its position relying on the assurance of the Government would not be sufficient to press into aid the doctrine............................ It has been pleaded as noted above that withdrawal is without any rational or relevant consideration. In this context, it has to be noted that the operators in the State of Andhra Pradesh are required to pay the same tax as those registered in other states. Therefore, there cannot be any question of irrationality. The tests of arbitrary action applicable to executive action do not necessarily apply to delegated legislation. In order to strike down a delegated legislation as arbitrary it has to be established that there is manifest arbitrariness. In order to be described as arbitrary, it must be shown that it was not reasonable and manifestly arbitrary. The expression "arbitrarily" means : in an unreasonable manner, as fixed or done capriciously or at pleasure, without adequate determining principle, not founded in the nature of things, non-rational, not done or acting according to reason or judgement, depending on the will alone. In the present cases all persons who are similarly situated are similarly affected by the change. That being so, there is no question of any discrimination. That plea also fails."

5.87 Since, the promise to confer the tax benefits under sections 10A, 10B, 80IA and 80IB for specified periods is by the legislature and there is no promissory estoppel either against the statute or against the legislature itself, the elimination of these provisions with immediate affect is perfectly legal in view of the various Supreme Court decisions.

5.88 As regards the ethics of such a course of action, the rule of promissory estoppel is essentially a rule of equity and not a fiction of law. If an action is equitable (and all actions of the legislature are deemed as equitable if the rule of promissory estoppel does not apply to legislative functions), then it must necessarily be ethical. Even otherwise, promises are made to human beings and therefore, in effect to shareholders; the company is only a conduit. The proposed package for corporate tax reforms do not in anyway alter the inter-temporal liability of shareholders.

Under the existing law, the tax exemptions to companies are not protected in the hands of the shareholders. Therefore, while the company avoids payments of taxes, the shareholders suffer the full impact of the tax when they receive the profits as dividends. Consequent to our recommendations, the full burden of the tax will fall at the corporate level and the shareholders will be fully exempt. In other words, there will be no change in the cumulative burden on corporate profits. Hence, in reality, there is no violation what so ever of the principle of promissory estoppel.

5.89 The existing system protects managers and undermines corporate governance. In theory a shareholder has a right to decide on the dividend pay out ratio. However, given the thin distribution of the voting powers of shareholders, the decision, in reality, is that of the managers. The emphasis therefore shifts to retention of profits resulting in deferment of taxes in perpetuity. Further, the tax incentives serve to camouflage poor corporate performance of managers. This undermines corporate governance.

5.90 It is also important to place on record the implication of the principle of promissory estoppel on the very process of economic reforms. It must be mentioned that the various "promises" made by the government were in the context of an economic regime characterized by high tax rates (both personal and corporate), high inflation, high tariffs and high interest rates. With considerable change in the economic regime (tax rates, import tariffs, interest rates and inflation have substantially reduced since then), it is imperative to realign the tax regime with these changes. If indeed promissory estoppel to the tax incentives has to be applied, the benefits flowing from reduced tax rates, import tariffs, interest rates and inflation would also have to be withdrawn. In other words, economic reforms must be reversed in its entirety. This will not be in the overall public interest.

5.91 Further, if incentives are retained on grounds of promissory estoppel, the effective tax burden shifts to the salaried and other vulnerable taxpayers who are not shareholders of equity. Therefore, the rule of promissory estoppel flowing from the rule of equity will, in effect, be inequitable.

5.92 In the light of the above, the Task Force is firmly of the view that there is no violation of the principle of promissory estoppel either legally or ethically. If the cause of economic reforms (in particular tax reforms) has to be advanced, it is necessary to simplify the tax system by eliminating the tax incentives across the board with immediate effect. The interest of the multitude of taxpayers should not be allowed to be sacrificed at the altar of some corporate managers.

Corporate Tax Reforms: Implementation Strategy

5.93 The Task Force discussed the possible strategy for the successful implementation of the corporate tax reforms. Towards this, the Task Force recommends two alternate options for reform of corporate income tax:-

Option - I : The following measures to be introduced for the financial year 2003-04:-

(i) Reduction in corporate tax rate from the existing levels of 36.75 per cent to 30 per cent for domestic companies and to 35 per cent for foreign companies.

(ii) Exemption of dividend from taxation in the hands of the shareholders. There will also be no tax on distribution of dividends by a company.

(iii) Exemption of long-terms capital gains on listed equity.

(iv) Elimination of Minimum Alternate Tax under Section 115JB.

(v) Removal of the distinction between unabsorbed depreciation and unabsorbed business loss. In other words unabsorbed depreciation would be merged with business loss and loose its separate identity. Further, business loss would be allowed to be carried forward indefinitely.

(vi) Removal of the following deductions under Section 10 and Chapter VI A of the Income Tax Act with immediate effect and not by a sunset clause :-

(a) Elimination of Section 10A and 10B of the Income Tax Act for all tax payers other than those engaged in manufacturing computer software.

(b) In the case of taxpayers engaged in manufacturing

computer software, the Government of India must take immediate steps to negotiate with foreign governments to enter into a comprehensive totalisation agreement leading to a single point incidence of taxes. However, in the interim, the Task Force recommends the following alternatives:-

1. Eliminate the tax exemption u/s 10A and 10B and amend Section 91 of the Income Tax Act to allow full credit for payment of foreign country's federal and state income tax. However, no refund of such foreign tax credit should be allowed; OR

2. Since the arrangement is transitory in nature the benefit of tax exemption u/s 10A and 10B for manufacturing of computer software only may be continued till we enter into a totalisation agreement with trading partners. However, the distribution of dividend by computer software manufacturing companies availing of deductions u/s 10A or 10B should be subjected to a dividend distribution tax of 30 per cent. Similarly, the long-term capital gains arising from transfer of equities of such companies should also be subjected to tax like long-term capital gains from any other asset.

The Task Force could not arrive at unanimity on the preferred alternative amongst the above two.

(c) Section 80 IA in respect of profit and gains from industrial undertakings or enterprises engaged in infrastructure development or telecommunication service or development of industrial park or special economic zones or generation, transmission or distribution of power.

(d) Section 80 IB in respect of profits and gains from certain industrial undertakings other then infrastructure development undertakings (this includes backward areas also).

(e) Section 80 JJA in respect of profits and gains from business of collecting and processing of biodegradable wastes.

(f) Section 80 JJAA in respect of employment of new workman.

(g) Section 80 M in respect of inter corporate dividends.

(h) The phase out programme in respect of sections 80HHB, 80HHBA, 80HHC, 80HHD, 80HHE, 80HHF, 80-O, 80R, 80RR and 80RRA will continue.

(vii) Depreciation rates for the purposes of depreciation allowance under section 32 should be reduced to 15 per cent for the general category of plant and machinery and to appropriate lower rates for other categories of block of assets. The revised rates of depreciation will minimize the divergence between the depreciation charged to the profit and loss account in accordance with the provisions of the Companies Act and depreciation claimed for tax purposes.

(viii) Elimination of Section 33 AB relating to Tea development account.

(ix) Elimination of Section 33 AC relating to reserve for Shipping business.

(x) Elimination of Section 33 B relating to Rehabilitation allowance.

(xi) Elimination of Section 35 relating to expenditure on Scientific Research. However, donations to trusts, institutions etc. engaged in scientific research will continue to be allowed but in the form of a tax rebate like in the case of Section 80G.

(xii) Elimination of Section 35 AC relating to expenditure on eligible projects. However, expenditure on projects already approved will continue to enjoy tax benefit in the form of rebate at the rate of 20 per cent.

(xiii) Elimination of Section 35 CCA relating to expenditure by way of payment to associations and institutions for carrying out rural development programmes.

(xiv) Elimination of Section 36(1)(iii) in respect of interest on borrowed capital.

(xv) The provision for bad and doubtful debts allowable under Section 36(1)(viia) of the Income Tax Act will henceforth be restricted to the amount of provision debited to profit and loss account as audited subject to the maximum amount of provisioning permitted under the prudential guidelines issued by the Reserve Bank of India.

Option - II : The package of measures along with their phased implementation, to be introduced through the Finance Bill 2003, in the following manner:-

(i) Reduction in corporate tax rate from the existing levels of 36.75 per cent to 30 per cent for domestic companies and to 35 per cent for foreign companies over a period of three years. The rates for domestic companies will be 34 per cent in financial year 2003-04, 32 per cent in 2004-05 and 30 per cent in 2005-06. The rates for foreign companies will be 38.50 per cent in financial year 2003-04, 37 per cent in 2004-05 and 35 per cent in 2005-06.

(ii) No tax on dividend in the hands of the shareholders.

(iii) No tax on long terms capital gains on listed equity.

(iv) Elimination of Minimum Alternate Tax under Section 115JB.

(v) Removal of the distinction between unabsorbed depreciation and unabsorbed business loss. In other words unabsorbed depreciation would be merged with business loss and loose its separate identity. Further, business loss would be allowed to be carried forward indefinitely.

(vi) Levy of a distribution tax on dividends at the rate of 15 per cent for dividends distributed in 2003-04, 7.5 per cent in 2004-05 and Nil in 2005-06.

(vii) Removal / Phasing out of the following deductions under Section 10 and Chapter VI A of the Income Tax Act with immediate effect and not by a sunset clause :-

(a) Phasing out of the provisions of Section 10A and 10B of the Income Tax Act. over a period of 3 years i.e. the deduction will be reduced to 60 per cent of the profits in 2003-04, to 30 per cent of the profits in 2004-05 and NIL in 2005-06.

(b) Phasing out of Section 80 IA in respect of profit and gains from industrial undertakings or enterprises engaged in infrastructure development or telecommunication service or development of industrial park or special economic zones or generation, transmission or distribution of power, over a period of 3 years i.e. the deduction will be reduced to two – third of the profits in 2003-04, to one – third of the profits in 2004-05 and NIL in 2005-06.

(c) Phasing out of Section 80 IB in respect of profits and gains from certain industrial undertakings other then infrastructure development undertakings (this includes backward areas also), over a period of 3 years i.e. the deduction will be reduced to two – third of the profits in 2003-04, to one – third of the profits in 2004-05 and NIL in 2005-06.

(d) Section 80 JJA in respect of profits and gains from business of collecting and processing of biodegradable wastes.

(e) Section 80 JJAA in respect of employment of new workman.

(f) Section 80 M in respect of inter corporate dividends

(g) The phase out programme in respect of sections 80HHB, 80HHBA, 80HHC, 80HHD, 80HHE, 80HHF, 80-O, 80R, 80RR and 80RRA will continue.

(viii) Depreciation allowance under section 32 will be

restricted to the allowance, charged to the profit and loss account in accordance with the provisions of the Companies Act. 161

(ix) Elimination of Section 33 AB relating to Tea development account will be eliminated.

(x) Elimination of Section 33 AC relating to reserve for Shipping business.

(xi) Elimination of Section 33 B relating to Rehabilitation allowance.

(xii) Elimination of Section 35 relating to expenditure on Scientific Research. However, donations to trusts, institutions etc. engaged in scientific research will continue to be allowed but in the form of a tax rebate like in the case of Section 80G.

(xiii) Elimination of Section 35 AC relating to expenditure on eligible projects. However, expenditure on projects already approved will continue to enjoy tax benefit in the form of rebate at the rate of 20 per cent.

(xiv) Elimination of Section 35 CCA relating to expenditure by way of payment to associations and institutions for carrying out rural development programmes.

(xv) Elimination of Section 36(iii) in respect of interest on borrowed capital.

(xvi) The provison for bad and doubtful debts allowable under Section 36(1)(viia) of the Income Tax Act will henceforth be restricted to the amount of provision debited to profit and loss account as audited subject to the maximum amount of provisioning permitted under the prudential guidelines issued by the Reserve Bank of India.

5.93 The Task Force deliberated upon the two packages. It was unanimously agreed that it is rather difficult for any government to give a credible ex-ante time commitment. Such commitments are rarely sustainable. Past experience shows that while tax rates were reduced, successive governments failed to implement the phased withdrawal of incentives. As a result, we have reached a point where the corporate tax rates are close to their resting points and yet the statute continues to be riddled with exemptions and deductions. Any attempt to sequence the reduction in the corporate taxes and the withdrawal of exemptions and deductions could lead to disastrous impact on revenue flows. The two must necessarily be implemented simultaneously. Phasing also gives rise to uncertainty and a "hope" that reforms could be reversed. In addition, in the present state of international economy and the decline in the growth momentum of the domestic economy, implementation in "one go" will be a powerful counter cyclical demand push to the domestic economy particularly given the projected policy initiatives on the indirect taxes front. Therefore, the Task Force unanimously recommends Option - I for implementation.

Notes

56 When the U.S. corporate income tax was introduced in 1909, it was seen, for example, as an "excise tax" on the privilege of limited liability. Defenders of a classical system now usually place little weight on this argument, however. The reason is that it is difficult to establish any direct connection between the benefit of limited liability and the income of a company.

57 For example, in the United States, certain companies with no more than 35 shareholders can qualify (as "Subchapter S" companies) to be taxed in a similar way to partnerships, with their income being allocated directly to their shareholder in the appropriate proportions. A similar effect may be achieved indirectly if the tax system allows small companies to pay out all of their taxable income to their owners in the form of tax-deductible directors" remuneration. This is sometimes referred to as "self-help integration".

58 In many developing countries such incentives are extended to promote FDI, reduce unemployment and promote specific economic sector or types of activities.

59 Introduction of tax incentives creates a clientele for their continuation and spread. The fact that many industrial countries maintain some tax incentives after the tax reforms of the 1980s is less a statement that they are considered to be effective and more a testament to the political difficulty in removing them once they have been introduced. It is because of this tendency that many "temporary" measures, designed to respond to particular perceived disincentives, remain in force long after the conditions that originally led to their introduction have changed.

60 Report of the Advisory Group on Tax Policy and Tax Administration.

61 The non-refundable/non-transferable social security tax serves as a labour input tax from which no unemployment and pension related benefits are derived.

62 It was pointed out that the annual loss to India in the absence of totalisation agreement was US $500 million and such loss was increasing rapidly.

63 Their activities are services in nature which, in most cases, has to be provided on-site abroad.

64 Overtime, this could threaten the international competitive advantage of the IT sector in India.

65 For instance, 17 countries have Totalisation Agreements with the US.

66 We assume a Cenvat rate of 16 per cent and a state VAT of 10 per cent on capital goods. We also assume that the credit against Cenvat on capital goods will be spread over two years and in the case of state VAT over a period of three years.

67 A 6.75 percentage point reduction in the existing corporate tax rate of 36.75 per cent is equivalent to 18.68 per cent reduction.

68 It is rather impossible to identify whether a particular capital asset is used only for scientific research or also in the regular production process.

69 It is neither a contractual obligation nor a case of diversion of profits.

70 Planning Commission (2001) Report of the Advisory Group on Tax Policy and Tax Administration for the Tenth Plan.

71 [1947] KB 130.

72 Discipline in Law 1988 edition P 223

73 2002-(089)-AIR-0322-SC

6

Taxation of Capital Gains

Treatment of Capital Gains

Under the existing law, profits and gains arising from the transfer of capital asset made in a previous year is taxable as capital gains. A capital asset is distinguished on the basis of the period of holding. A capital asset, which is held for more then three years, is categorised as a long-term capital asset. However, if the capital asset is in the nature of equity, it is categorised as a long-term capital asset if it is held for more then one year. All capital assets other then long-term capital asset is termed as a short-term capital asset.

6.2 The profits and gains arising from the transfer of a short-term capital asset are treated as short-term capital gains and included in the total income of the taxpayer for taxation at the rates applicable to him. Where a taxpayer incurs a loss from the transfer of a short-term capital asset (such loss is termed as "short-term capital loss") the same is allowed to be set off only against gain from the transfer of another short-term or long-term capital asset. In a case where the short-term capital loss remains unabsorbed, the same is allowed to be carried forward for set off only against gain from the transfer of another short-term and long-term capital asset in the subsequent year. However, such carry forward is restricted for a period of eight years. In other words, a short-term capital loss cannot be set off against income from salaries, house property, business or profession or income under the head "other sources".

6.3 Similarly, the profits and gains arising from the transfer of a long-term capital asset are treated as long-term capital gains.

Since long-term capital gains represent accumulation of income over a period of time, these could turn out to be illusory in real terms. Accordingly, the cost of the asset is adjusted for inflation during the period of holding. The increased cost is set-off against the sale consideration of the long-term capital asset to determine the long-term capital gain. Such long-term capital gain is subjected to a concessional rate of tax to eliminate the bunching effect[74]. Furthermore, the long-term capital gains are fully exempt if the proceeds are invested in specified savings plan / schemes. In view of the liberalized personal income tax rate schedule comprising of only two rates, the adverse impact in the form of increased tax burden arising from bracket creep due to bunching of capital gains would be considerably reduced and in most cases eliminated. Therefore, we recommend that concessional treatment of long-term capital gains through a reduced scheduler rate of tax must be abolished. In other words, the long-term capital gains would be aggregated with other incomes and subjected to taxation at the normal rates. Further, since we have recommended the abolition of various saving incentives, we do not consider necessary to allow any exemption for roll over of long-term capital gains. However, we do recognise that a large number of small taxpayers feel the necessity to finance their basic requirement of a house by selling other capital assets like equity etc. Similarly, the financing of the construction of the Golden Quadrilateral and the North-South & East-West corridors is dependent on the funds mobilize through investment of the long-term capital gains. Given the public nature of the project, it is necessary to maintain the flow of funds. Therefore, we recommend that long-term capital gains should continue to be exempt if invested in a house or in the bonds of National Highway Authority of India until completion of the Golden Quadrilateral and the North-South & East-West corridors.

6.4 In the section on corporate taxation, we have recommended the elimination of all tax preferences thereby increasing the effective tax burden on corporate profits to the statutory rate of 30 per cent. The divergence between the effective corporate tax rate and the statutory tax rate would be eliminated. Consequent to these recommendations, the retained earnings of a company would bear the full impact of the corporate tax. A substantial portion, if not all, of the long-term capital gains on equity represent the value of retained earnings. Since the profits of the company would bear the full burden of the tax, the retained earnings would have also suffered full taxation. Any tax on such long-term capital gains on equity would tantamount to "double taxation" of the retained earnings.

6.5 The case for taxation of capital gains on equity is often built around the argument that a part of the long-term capital gains on equity will represent the unrealized gains in the value of the assets, which would not have suffered taxation at the corporate level. Consequent to the exemption of long-term capital gains on equity, such unrealized gains would escape taxation. Such unrealized gains are assessed on realization at a future date, as part of the corporate tax base. The exemption of the long-term capital gain would essentially result in deferral of tax revenue. The revenue loss will be restricted to the extent of erosion in the time value of money. Given the simplification, which will follow from exemption of the long-term capital gains, there will be substantial reduction in dead weight loss. Therefore, the net loss from deferral of revenues may not be very significant. Similarly, the exemption will also not impair any equity. The buyer of the equity would have discounted the future value of unrealized gains to the extent of the potential tax liability resulting in lower long-term capital gains to the seller. Hence, the seller would have in any case suffered implicit taxation through lower prices.

6.6 Another argument offered against the proposal to exempt long term capital gains on equity is that part of such gains represent the "goodwill gains" those arising from such factors as improved market position, technological developments and discoveries. Such goodwill gains will be reflected in the monopoly profits of the company, which in any case would suffer full taxation. Hence there is neither any loss of revenue or equity.

6.7 In view of the above, the case for taxation of long-term capital gains on equity is not sustainable. The Task Force recognizes that capital gains on equity could be related to a systemic shift in stock market prices, which may not in any way be related to the economic income of the company. Such gains would not have suffered any taxation at the corporate level. This is likely to be so only in the short term. Accordingly, we recommend that while short-term capital gains on equity should continue to be taxed, the long-term capital gains on equity should be eliminated. However, recognising the possibility of abuse by transferring real assets through the corporate vehicle, we also recommend that the exemption on long-term capital gain on equity should be restricted to listed securities as defined in section 112 of the Income Tax Act.

6.8 A large number of taxpayers pleaded before the Task Force that long-term capital gains on other assets should also be eliminated so as to give a boost to other asset markets. We must clarify that the proposal to exempt long term capital gains on equity is founded on the argument of double taxation and not as an incentive to boost capital market. We do not find double taxation in any other asset market. For example in the case of a house, the investment in a house is essentially out of taxed income. The accumulation of the gain in the value of the house remains untaxed since unrealized gains are exempt. As and when the house is sold, the original investment in the house is allowed as a deduction in the computation of capital gains from the house since the original investment was out of taxed income. Hence, there is no double taxation of the investment in the house. Similarly, the taxation of capital gains on realization does not lead to any double taxation, since such gain was not subjected to any form of tax during the holding period.

Note

74 The rate of tax on long-term capital gains is 20 per cent. However, if the long-term capital asset is in the nature of listed securities (equity) or units, the rate of tax on long-term capital gains is 10 per cent of gains computed without inflation indexation or 20 per cent of gains computed after indexation, whichever is lower.

7

Treatment of Other Entities

Taxation of Investment Funds

Investment funds (mutual funds) are entities owned by many persons and whose primary activity is investing in operating companies. The investment fund acts as an intermediary between the individual investor and the ultimate user of the capital. Several types of investment funds exist. An "open-end" fund issues and redeems fund units from investors. In contrast, "closed-end" funds issue a fixed number of units, and investors trade units with other investors.

7.2 Basic decisions made in designing the overall tax system for individuals and enterprises frame the design of a tax regime for investment funds. Decisions are required on such questions as how to tax dividends and interest received by individuals and enterprises, how to tax capital gains and losses, how to tax foreign source income, and whether and how to adjust for inflation.

7.3 Within the framework defined by these decisions, the choice of tax rules for investment funds requires balancing three objectives: first, not to hamper the development of financial intermediaries, such as investment funds; second, to devise tax rules that are comparable to those that apply to other investments; and, third, to adopt tax rules that can be administered and enforced.

7.4 The tax regimes for investment funds in many countries rest, on the one hand, on the ability of investment fund managers to process substantial amounts of information and to allocate tax items to individual investors and, on the other hand, on the ability of tax administrators to receive information from investment fund managers and match this information with the individual tax returns of millions of taxpayers. The investment funds are likely to have the computer capability to process the information and allocate the tax items. The ability of the tax administration to develop a system to ensure enforcement and compliance with a tax regime that requires monitoring the tax consequences to many investors is much more problematic and, in many countries, may not be worth the expenditure of substantial administrative resources, given the amount of tax revenue involved.

7.5 Another potential compliance problem that may be associated with a special tax regime for investment funds is the ease with which taxpayers can meet the tax and regulatory requirements for investment fund status. If qualification is easy, then adopting a favorable regime for investment funds will create strong incentives for taxpayers to arrange their affairs to obtain favorable tax treatment. If qualification is difficult, then the potential tax motivation for adopting this form of organization is reduced.

7.6 While designing a tax regime for investment funds and their investors, it is necessary to keep in mind: (1) the greater the variation in the treatment of different types of income in the hands of different types of investors, the greater the pressure to tax the income directly at the investor level; and (2) the lesser the variation in the tax regime by type of income in the hands of different types of investors, the stronger is the argument for simply taxing all income at the investment fund level and imposing no further taxes at the investor level.

7.7 There are broadly three different approaches to reducing or eliminating the double – or in some cases triple – taxation of dividends, interest and capital gains attributable to investment funds and their underlying investments. The first method would be to treat the investment fund as a pass through. In its purest form, this approach treats investors as if they earned the income directly and taxes them accordingly, even if the investment fund does not distribute the income to them. This method scores high on market neutrality. However, it scores low on administrative and compliance grounds, especially as a number of investors and the number of fund investments become quite large. Therefore, no country uses this system for investment funds.

7.8 The second method is to tax the fund and exempt the investors. The tax on the income of the Fund is treated as a final withholding tax This method scores high on administrative and compliance grounds but it imposes a uniform tax burden irrespective of the size of the taxpayer.

7.9 The third method imposes tax on the investment fund on any income it receives at a rate that could be either the highest rate applicable to investors or, alternatively, the one that is most common to investors. This approach allocates to investors their share of the income of the fund and provides a credit for taxes paid by the fund allocable to that income. Investors may then file for a refund if the amount of tax paid exceeds their liability, or they could be assessed additional tax if the amount of tax paid exceeds their liability, or they could be assessed additional tax if the amount paid by the investment fund is less than their tax liability. This variation also requires rules for calculating an investor's basis in his or her investment in the fund to determine whether an investor would recognize gain when shares are redeemed.

7.10 Under the existing system in India, the investment fund is exempted from tax. The dividend received by the investor from such fund is subjected to tax at his level at his personal marginal rate of tax applicable to him. The retained earnings by the fund therefore remain untaxed. Therefore, the existing model is not a typically pass-through prototype. The system is biased against dividend distribution and also imposes higher administrative and compliance burden.

7.11 The dividend distributed by the investment funds comprises of the following categories of income:

1. Dividends earned from investments by the Fund in equity.
2. Long-term capital gains from sale of investment.
3. Short-term capital gains from sale of investment.
4. Interest received from investment in debt.

7.12 In our package for corporate tax reform we have recommended the abolition of any form of tax on dividend and long-term capital gains on equity. To the extent, the dividend distributed by the investment fund comprises of these exempt incomes, the full taxation of dividends from the investment fund would result in double (multiple) taxation. Therefore, the proportion of dividend income and long-term capital gain on equity comprised in the dividend distributed by the investment fund must necessarily be exempted. If this be so, the dividend folio must indicate such proportion. This will further add to the complexity of administration and compliance.

7.13 Where there is a conflict between simplicity of equity, the Task Force has a preference for simplicity. Complexity is, inherently, regressive and non-transparent. Therefore, what may appear to be equitable could, in effect, be inequitable. In the light of the problems associated with the existing system of taxation of investment fund and the package for corporate tax reform, we recommend the following:-

1. The income of the mutual fund derived from short-term capital gains and interest should be taxed at a flat rate in the hands of the mutual fund.

2. Since most investors in units are generally smaller taxpayers, we recommend that the rate of tax should be the minimum marginal rate of personal income tax i.e. 20 per cent.

3. With a view to overcoming double taxation, the dividends received by the unit holders should be fully exempted since the distributable surplus would have suffered the full burden of the tax.

4. The short-term capital gain arising to the investor from sale of units of investment funds should be taxed at his level at the personal marginal rate of tax.

5. The long-term capital gain arising to the investor from sale of units of mutual fund should be exempt from income tax.

6. The tax treatment of mutual funds and their investors should also be extended to venture capital funds[75], private equity funds[76] and hedge funds[77]. However, the tax rate for these funds should be 30 per cent since their investors are likely to be those in the highest tax slab.

7. All funds must necessarily obtain the PAN of the investor and the Databases about every payment made by the fund manager back to the investor, tagged with PAN, should be furnished to the tax authorities as a information return.

Tax Treatment Of Partnership Firms

7.14 At present, the profits of a partnership firm are subjected to tax at the same rate of tax applicable to a domestic company. In view of our recommendations, for corporate tax reform, we recommend that the rate of tax for partnership firms should be reduced to the same level as corporate rate of tax.

Tax treatment of Charitable Trusts

7.15 The gross domestic product (GDP) from community services comprising educational services research and scientific services, medical and health services and religious and other community services has sharply increased from 247 crores in 1950-51 at current prices to Rs. 87529 crores in 1998-99 at current prices.

7.16 This unprecedented growth has outpaced with the growth of GDP at market prices at current prices. Accordingly, the share of GDP from community services to GDP at market prices has increased from 2.49 percent in 1950-51 to a high of 4.99 per cent in 1998-99. The share of this sector will continue to increase rapidly as per capita income increase since the demand for those services is generally income-elastic.

7.17 The activities of this sector are mostly through the vehicle of charitable trusts and institutions. These trusts have enjoyed tax support like in most countries across the globe. Under the present system, donations to trust are allowed as a deduction from the gross income to the donor. Empirically tax exemption for donations have been found to be efficient. However, the deductions from gross income are iniquitous in as much as they confer greater benefit to those the higher income levels. Therefore, we recommend that the tax benefit to donations must take the form of tax rebate at the minimum marginal rate of tax at 20 per cent[78]. Further, we also recommend that there should be no quantitative ceiling either in absolute terms or as a fraction of the gross income as is presently provided under Section 80G.

7.18 The income of the Charitable Trust from property held under trust is exempt to the extent it is applied for charitable purposes. The surplus if any is allowed to be accumulated for future application, subject to certain specified conditions. The benefit of the exemptions is either enjoyed under various clauses of Section 10 or under Section 11 to 13. The compliance burden under the two schemes is different. Infact, the Task Force received large number of grievances particularly relating to delay in the issue of exemption notification under Section 10 by the Central Board of Direct Taxes. Such delays are inherent in the very procedure for issuing any statutory notification. Therefore, the Task Force recommends that the exemptions under Section 10(21), 10(23B) and 10(23C)(iiiab) to (via), 10(29A) should be merged with Section 11 to 13A of the Income Tax Act. We also recommend that:-

1. The present practice of exempting a class of Charitable trust and Institutions through notifications should be abolished. However, the requirement to file a return of income by such trust and institutions as proof of fulfilling the various conditions stipulated u/s 10(23C), should continue.
2. Returns to be identified for scrutiny / audit only through a computerised risk assessment system.
3. Where a return is identified for scrutiny and the assessing officer is of the opinion that the activities of the trust are not charitable in nature, such a case will be referred to a rating agency from amongst the panel drawn up by the C&AG[79]. An "A+" rating for the trust will mean that it is indeed a charitable trust. An "A" rating for the trust will mean that it will enjoy exemption during the current year and will be subjected to review again in the following year. A "B" rating for the trust will disqualify it from any tax exemption. The new procedure should be introduced from 01-04-2004 and the interregnum should be utilized to work out the details and also allowing the trust to adapt to the new procedures.
4. Since a large number of provisions in the Income Tax Act

are regulatory in nature, we also recommend the creation of a National Charities Board to assist the government in regulating and promoting charities on the lines of the National Charities Commission, U.K. Since, a number of States in India already have Charity Commissioners, the proposed Board may have to be advisory.

5. The Income Tax Department should reimburse to trusts, the fees payable to the rating agency.

7.19 Consequent to the merger of all the provisions, there will be no requirement for any statutory notification to be issued by the CBDT. The Board will hereafter be able to devote more time on designing tax enforcement strategy rather than deal with individual cases of exemptions.

Tax Treatment of Cooperative Societies

7.20 Under the existing provision of Section 80P of the Income Tax Act, a cooperative society is entitled to 100 per cent exemption in respect of profits / income from a large number of activities like banking, credit facilities, cottage industries, market of agricultural produce, pisciculture, milk, fruits and vegetables. Further, the income from letting of godowns and warehouses is also fully exempt. Similarly, the income of a consumer cooperative society is exempt up-to a specified limit.

7.21 Consistent with our recommendations for personal income tax and corporate income tax, we recommend the elimination of Section 80P of the Income Tax Act. However, the existing exemption limit of Rs. 10,000/- prescribed as part of the rate schedule, should be increased to Rs. 1,00,000/- and the revised income tax rate schedule for cooperatives should be as indicated in Table 7.1 below.

Table 7.1

Proposed Income Tax Structure for Cooperative Societies

Income level	Tax rates
Below 1,00,000	NIL
1,00,000 – 4,00,000	20 per cent of the Income in excess of Rs. 1,00,000-
Above 4,00,000	Rs. 60,000/- plus 30 per cent of the Income in excess of Rs. 4,00,000/-

Tax Treatment Of Non-Residents

7.22 In the course of discussion with various Chamber of Commerce, Trade and Industry, a large number of issues relating to taxation of non-residential individuals and companies were raised. *Inter-alia*, some of the issues related to the following:-

1. The inability of the Foreign Tax Division (FTD) in the Central Board of Direct Taxes to respond swiftly to the various clarifications sought by trade and industry.
2. The delay in the outcome of the Mutual Agreement Procedure (MAP).
3. The absence of an institutional framework to deal with issues arising out of Foreign Tax Credit (FTC).
4. The absence of the mechanism of Advance Pricing Agreements (APA).
5. The existing procedure for issue of remittance certificate. A large number of representatives expressed concern on the new procedure of remittance without obtaining clearance from the income tax department.
6. The absence of any guideline regarding the database to be used for the purposes of transfer pricing.
7. The high level of penalty on transfer pricing contrary to international practice.
8. The restrictive scope of advance ruling. Representatives suggested that the Indian partner in a Joint Venture with a foreign entity should also be eligible for advance ruling.

7.23 The Task Force was informed that the issues at serial number 1 to 3 arose primarily because the composition of the FTD in the CBDT has remained unchanged for over three decades even though there has been a substantial increase in the work particularly in the last one decade. The Task Force was therefore of the view that the manpower strength of FTD should be immediately augmented so as to assign one team each for America, Europe, South East Asia and Australia, and Rest of the World. Each of the four teams should be headed by an officer in the rank of Joint Secretary to Government of India. However, these posts should be created by diverting them from the different field formations and not by creating new posts. Further, the Task Force was also of the view that the issues involved in the taxation of non-residents were far too technical and therefore needed an extended period of deliberation. We understand that, as recommended by us in our Consultation Paper, the CBDT has already set up a working group headed by the Director General of Income Tax (International Taxation) and comprising of representatives also from trade and industry to examine the various issues relating to taxation of non-resident individual and foreign companies. We also understand that the working group is expected to submit its report by the end of December. We suggest that the recommendations should be processed during the forthcoming budget exercise.

Notes

75 Venture capital funds invest in greenfield ventures.

76 Private equity funds invest in firms, which have crossed the greenfield stage, but are not yet listed.

77 Hedge funds are structures where each customer brings in a minimum of (say) Rs. 10 lakh of capital, so that the securities regulator ceases to work for investor protection, and only focuses on contract enforcement and fraud.

78 Suppose a taxpayer makes a donation of Rs. 100/- to a trust for which 50 per cent deduction is allowed u/s 80G. Under the present arrangement, the tax benefit on the donation will vary depending upon the marginal rate of tax applicable to the taxpayer. If the marginal rate is 20 per cent, the 50 per cent deduction from income is effectively a tax relief of Rs. 10/-. If the marginal rate is 30 per cent, the tax relief is Rs. 15/-. The rebate under the proposed scheme will be Rs.100*0.5*0.2= Rs.10/-. This will be the same for all class of taxpayers irrespective of their marginal rate of tax.

79 A number of taxpayers were apprehensive whether such rating agencies indeed exist in India. We have been informed that Crisil is already engaged in rating NGOs for multilateral agencies.

8

Other Taxes

Wealth Tax

The levy of wealth tax is justified on the ground that it is a measure of taxable capacity and enables top marginal income tax rates to be reduced without sacrificing overall tax progressivity. A wealth tax also serves as a source of information to other tax administrations. Further, a separate wealth tax can help ensure that taxes evaded on income might be collected. However, if wealth tax has to serve the purpose of efficiency and equity, it is necessary to minimise the cost of administration and the compliance cost. Given the problems associated with the administration of the wealth tax and cross-country experience, "net wealth tax, although attractive in principle, must be judged impractical in most developing countries"[80].

8.2 Under the existing scheme a tax at the rate of one percent is levied if the aggregate value of the selected assets exceeds Rs. 15 lakhs. The selected assets are mostly unproductive assets in the nature of jewellery, vacant urban land and certain categories of house property. Since, the levy is based on current market value of the asset, these are often subject matter of immense dispute. Both the administrative and compliance cost is disproportionate to the revenues realised. (Table: 8.1). While at current prices, the revenues have almost stagnated at the measly level of approximately Rs 135 crores, in real terms there has been a sharp decline. While no official estimates of the cost of administering the wealth tax were available, it was widely accepted in the official circles that the cost would not be less than Rs 50 crores. Given the large-scale disputes on valuation an equal amount (if not more) could be reasonably estimated towards compliance cost.

Table – 8.1

Trend of Wealth Tax Revenues

Financial Year	Collections (in Rs. crores)	Financial Year	Collections (in Rs. crores)
1988-89	122	1995-96	74
1989-90	179	1996-97	78
1990-91	231	1997-98	113
1991-92	307	1998-99	162
1992-93	468	1999-00	133
1993-94	154	2000-01	132
1994-95	105	2001-02	135

Source: Government of India, Receipts Budget (of different years)

8.3 Further, one of the objectives of this levy was to help verify income earned between the two valuation dates. This objective could have been served if the valuation of the assets was based on historical costs and the scope of the levy was comprehensive. In fact, wealth tax assessments have thrown up large scale disputes at all levels particularly on the issue of valuation.

8.4 In view of the smallness of revenue from wealth tax and the large-scale problems of administration and compliance, the tax can hardly be said to have increased progressivity. The ends of progressivity would be better served if the income tax law is simplified to encourage voluntary compliance and income tax evasion is prevented. Accordingly, we recommend the abolition of wealth tax.

Expenditure Tax

8.5 Expenditure tax was introduced in 1987 on the plea that "those who can afford to patronize high class hotels should also be afforded the further pleasure of contributing to the national exchequer."[81] To begin with, the tax was levied at 10 percent on expenditure in hotels where the room tariff was Rs.400 per individual. At present, it continues to be levied at 10 percent but on expenditure in hotels where the room tariff is Rs. 3000/- or more. In addition, most states also continue to levy a luxury tax on hotels.

8.6 The present tax on expenditure in hotels is in the nature of a consumption tax. It was introduced as a separate tax in the absence of a tax on services. Since tax on services has since been introduced, it is only appropriate that this levy is merged with service tax. We recommend accordingly.

Notes

80 Richard Goode, Government Finance in Developing Countries (1984)

81 Paragragh 73 of the Union Budget Speech for the year 1987-88.

9

Impact of the Recommendations

The impact of our recommendations on equity, revenue collections, savings, financial sector and transaction costs have already been indicated in various sections of this report. Nevertheless we consider it appropriate to summarise the multidimensional impact of our recommendations.

On Equity

9.2 The recommendations relating to personal income tax also enhance progressivity to the highest level in the last two decades (Table 4.3 and Chart 1). Taxpayers with incomes below Rs. 1 lakh will not have to bear the rigors of complying with a progressive tax. The consumption tax burden borne by such taxpayers would be adequate contribution to the treasury. The taxpayers at the relatively higher level of income will now contribute a relatively higher proportion of the income tax revenues.

9.3 The proposals to eliminate exemptions particularly those relating to savings will enhance the equity of the overall tax system. Individual with same gross income will now be treated equally. Since the corporate profits will now bear the full burden of the corporate tax, the effective burden on individual shareholders will be substantially higher inspite of the elimination of the tax on dividend and on long-terms capital gains. To the extent, the individual shareholders are likely to be higher income groups, the effective burden will be higher. As a result the recommendations should further improve the progressivity than what is reflected in the chart. Other recommendations which will enhance equity relate to the elimination of various sectoral/activity based incentives and the extensive use of information technology to identify tax evaders.

On Revenues

9.4 The Task Force conducted an elaborate exercise to analyse the revenue impact of the recommendations and identify the change in the incidence of the recommendations on different categories of taxpayers. During the assessment year 2001-02, 2,04,70,771 tax returns were filed by individual taxpayers. Based on the actual distribution of these returns across income groups and the recent trend in the annual growth of tax returns, we have estimated the number of returns which are expected to be filed in assessment year 2003-04 and there distribution across income groups (Table-9.1).

9.5 In order to obtain a typical taxpayer profile for each income group, income tax return data of 9.25 lakh individual taxpayers was collected from the city of Mumbai which accounts for 35 per cent of the country's direct tax collections. The data related to four assessment years[82] : 1998-99, 1999-00, 2000-01 & 2001-02.

9.6 The sample data for the four years was segregated into two categories, i.e. salaried and non-salaried taxpayers[83]. For each income group and category, a typical taxpayer profile for each of the four assessment years was separately obtained. There after, we further determined the four years average of such profiles for each income group to obtain a typical taxpayer profile for all income groups for the purposes of revenue estimation.

9.7 Table-9.2 indicates the tax liability of a typical non-salaried men tax payer in each income group based on the tax law for assessment year 2003-04 and the total revenue collected from each income group. Similarly, Table-9.3 indicates the tax liability for a typical salaried men taxpayer. The total revenues collected from these two categoriesof tax payers is Rs.24,629 crores, excluding the tax on dividends in the hands of the shareholders. Table-9.4 and Table-9.5 indicate the tax liability for a typical non-salaried and salaried men taxpayer consequent to our recommendations. The revenue collections at the existing level of compliance is estimated to be Rs. 17,345 crores, thereby resulting in a tax relief of Rs. 7,284 crores to such individual tax payers.

9.8 The impact of our recommendations on senior citizens is

also expected to be beneficial. Under the existing law, a senior citizen with income up-to Rs. 1,30,000/- does not have to pay any income tax. Table 9.6 indicates the revenue collection from senior citizens across income groups, under the existing law. Our recommendation to provide a higher exemption limit of Rs. 50,000/- for senior citizens means that senior citizens with income up-to Rs. 1,50,000/- will not have to pay any income tax. Table 9.7 indicates the estimated revenue collection consequent to our recommendations. Those with income above Rs. 1,50,000/- will benefit significantly from a 10 percentage point reduction in the tax rate. Therefore, senior citizens at all income levels stand to gain by an estimated Rs.190 crores from our recommendations.

9.9 The demographic profile of taxpayers is in favour of relatively younger taxpayers. The income of such taxpayers can reasonably be expected to increase (in large number of cases rather rapidly) over the years. Under the existing law, the maximum marginal rate of personal income tax is leviable at a rather low income level i.e. Rs. 1,50,000/-. Most of the younger taxpayers therefore can be expected to pay at the highest rate rather early in life. The recommendation to levy the highest rate of 30 per cent only on incomes above Rs. 4 lakhs would benefit this generation of younger taxpayer substantially. Infact as their incomes approach Rs. 4 lakhs, this threshold for the highest rate would have increased due to inflation indexing overtime. Therefore, the lifetime income tax rate for most younger taxpayers would be the lower rate of 20 per cent.

9.10 Table-9.8 summarizes the tax benefit for senior citizens, salaried and non-salaried (other than senior citizens) taxpayers for each income group, arising from the recommendations made in this report. It shows that taxpayers of all categories and in every income group benefit substantially from the recommendations. Similarly, women as a class of tax payers will also benefit from the package of our recommendations. In the case of a married couple, the recommendations are likely to reduce tax liability on the family as a unit. The recommendation to abolish wealth tax will also benefit the female taxpayer. Women as a class of tax payers will benefit from a relief of Rs.404 crores. With reduced tax burden for each income group, disposable income will be higher for every class of taxpayer. This also means that the entire middle class will benefit from our proposals.

9.11 However, the calculations do not reflect the impact of taxation of dividend in the hands of the individual shareholders introduced by the Finance Act, 2002. Adjusting for an estimated Rs. 1,500 crore in tax collection from dividends[84], the total revenue collection from individual taxpayers is estimated at Rs. 32340 crores representing about 75 per cent of the total income tax collection. The balance amount is collected from partnership firms, HUFs, etc., but does not include collection from companies.

9.12 Our recommendation to reduce the tax rate for partnership firms from the existing levels of 36.75 per cent to 30 per cent will result in a loss in the revenues 18.37 per cent. The current revenues from partnership firms is estimated to be Rs. 10,000 crore, thereby resulting in a revenue loss of Rs. 1,837 crore.

9.13 The package of recommendations relating to corporate tax will result in a estimated revenue gain of Rs. 10,762 crore (Table-9.9). This estimate is based on the financial results of 1,334 profit making companies for the financial year 2001-02. This sample of 1.334 companies comprised of 59 banking companies reporting a corporate tax payment of Rs. 5,844 crores and 1,275 companies reporting a corporate tax payment of Rs. 13,420 crores. The effective corporate tax rate for assessment year 2002-03 for the sample non-banking companies and banking companies was 21.75 per cent and 35.01 respectively as against the statutory rate of 35.7 per cent. In the assessment year 2003-04, these effective rates are estimated to increase by 3 per cent on account of the increase in the surcharge. Adjusting for the measures recommended for the corporate tax reform, the revenue collection from the sample non-banking companies is estimated to increase by 34 per cent while in the case of banking companies it is expected to reduce by 35.5 per cent. In the aggregate the corporate tax revenues are estimated to increase by 22.42 per cent.

9.14 Table-9.10 summarises the revenue impact of the recommendations. Overall, the recommendations are revenue neutral at the existing level of compliance. To the extent the new simplified and liberalized tax regime will induce compliance, the revenue gains are likely to be substantially higher and it will enhance buoyancy by widening the personal and corporate income tax bases.

On Savings

9.15 As indicated in the earlier chapters, the existing tax incentives for investment in savings instruments are inefficient. The recommendations to eliminate them will improve efficiency of the economic system in as much as it will result in reduction in interest rates. Further, the proposed doubling of ceiling on contributions to the pension plan under Section 80CCC to Rs.20,000/- will achieve the social objective of promoting genuine long term savings for increasing old age economic security.

On Financial Sector

9.16 Our recommendations for aligning the corporate tax base with real income means that banks will henceforth enjoy full tax credit for complying with the RBI prudential standards for NPA provisioning. This would encourage banks to "clean" their balance sheets, achieve improved capital adequacy ratio and help the country to move towards a sound and robust banking system. Since banks do not avail of any capital allowances, the benefits will lower tax rates will increase retained profits of the financial sector which will facilitate an increased supply of commercial credit. Banking companies will gain by as much as Rs.2,840 crores in tax reliefs from our recommendations.

On Transaction Costs

9.17 In the earlier chapters we had referred to a NIPFP study commissioned by the Planning Commission which had estimated the compliance cost of personal income tax to be as high as 48 per cent. Such high cost raise serious doubts about income tax as an efficient source of revenue. Therefore, the Task Force was singularly concerned with designing a new simplified system which will foster compliance, impart transparency and discourage rent seeking and crony capitalism. We must reiterate at the cost of being repetitive that our recommendations for eliminating the exemptions, the extensive use of information technology and privatization of non-core activities of the tax administration will result in sharp reduction in transaction cost. A 10 per cent reduction in the transaction cost for personal income tax would help taxpayers to save an estimated Rs. 4,000 crores. Since the burden of compliance cost is essentially regressive, such reduction in transaction cost is, by corollary, progressive.

Conclusion

9.18 The Task Force is convinced that if its recommendations are fully adopted, our tax system will become more transparent and it will align the obligations of taxpayers with the objectives of the tax administration – this is crucial in engendering a trust-based system in place of the present one based on punitive enforcement (often bordering on harassment), This is crucial to both attracting and retaining young taxpayers with their demand for customer-oriented procedures, as well as to bring the "missing middle" – mainly service professionals who are currently outside the tax-net into compliance. The best tax systems in the world deal with taxpayers in a professional customer-relationship environment, which requires the system to be responsive and non-discriminatory. This reduces transaction costs for both taxpayers and the tax administration. We have sought to replace the present "exemption raj" with a tax system that is outcome oriented rather than input aligned, viz., higher productivity of income taxpayers and increased profitability of businesses is encouraged. This is the case with most dynamic countries among the emerging markets.

Notes

82 Assessment year means the year following the financial year.

83 A taxpayer deriving 90 per cent or more of his gross total income from salary has been categorised as a "salaried taxpayer".

84 The collection from the 10 per cent dividend distribution tax was Rs. 1,480 crores in 2001-02. A significant proportion of the dividends is received by the government and a large number of other nontaxable entities such as charitable trusts. Therefore, the average tax on dividends in the hands of the shareholders is not likely to exceed 10 per cent.

Table – 9.1

Distribution of returns for Assessment Year 2003-04

Income Range (in Rs.)	Distribution of returns filed for Assessment Year 2001-02 — Parcentage Distribution			Estimated Distribution of Returns for Assessment Year 2003-2004		
	Salaried	Non-salaried	Total	Salaried	Non-salaried	Total
0-40,000	5.52	26.00	17.73	602942	4194541	4797483
40,000-50,000	2.01	9.44	6.44	219549	1522838	1742387
50,000-60,000	11.26	17.31	14.87	1229913	2793270	4023184
60,000-80,000	17.09	14.74	15.69	1866716	2378324	4245040
80,000-1,00,000	10.18	8.79	9.35	1111947	1417762	2529709
1,00,000-1,50,000	27.77	13.30	19.14	3033277	2145185	5178462
1,50,000-2,00,000	17.32	7.04	11.19	1891839	1135695	3027534
2,00,000-3,00,000	5.05	1.33	2.83	551604	214072	765676
3,00,000-4,00,000	1.62	0.43	0.91	176950	69257	246207
4,00,000-5,00,000	0.73	0.21	0.42	79737	33897	113634
5,00,000-10,00,000	1.2	1.15	1.17	131074	185478	316552
>10,00,000	0.25	0.27	0.26	27307	43038	70345
Total	100	100.00	100	10922855	16132851	27055706

Note: The distribution of returns across income range is based on information given by the Chief Commissioners in April, 2002, on actual returns filed during F.Y. 2001-02. Total number of returns filed during F.Y.2001-02 is 2.05 crores and a 15 per cent annual increase in number of returns has been assumed to arrive at the population size for A.Y. 2003-2004.

Table – 9.2

Revenue Collection from Non-Salaried Men as per the Law for Assessment Year 2003-04

Income Range (in Rs.)	Number of Returns	Average Total Income	Average Tax At Current Rate without surcharge	Average Historical Investment in Securities Specifies u/s 88	Average Rebate Claimed u/s 88	Average Tax After Rebate	Average Surcharge	Average Tax Including Surcharge at Current Rate	Revenue Collection (Without Surcharge (in Rs. crores)	Revenue Collection on Account of Surcharge (in Rs. crores)	Total Revenue Collection at Existing Rates (in Rs. crores)
0-40,000	2096737	21884	0	105	21	0	0	0	0	0	0
40,000-50,000	912891	46098	0	131	26	0	0	0	0	0	0
50,000-60,000	1801169	54667	467	423	85	382	0	382	69	0	69
60,000-80,000	1650294	68482	2696	3024	605	2092	105	2196	345	17	362
80,000-1,00,000	987577	89130	6826	8168	1634	5192	260	5452	513	26	538
1,00,000-1,50,000	1504307	121877	13375	15938	3188	10188	509	10697	1533	77	1609
1,50,000-2,00,000	836005	171719	25516	20762	3114	22401	1120	23522	1873	94	1966
2,00,000-3,00,000	161935	241091	46327	24210	3632	42696	2135	44830	691	35	726
3,00,000-4,00,000	52841	343431	77029	25557	3834	73196	3660	76855	387	19	406
4,00,000-5,00,000	25791	445863	107759	26816	4022	103737	5187	108923	268	13	281
5,00,000-10,00,000	141981	685623	179687	25873	0	179687	8984	188671	2551	128	2679
>10,00,000	33170	3824798	1121439	26230	0	1121439	56072	1177511	3720	186	3906
Total	10973816								11949	594	12543

Table – 9.3

Revenue Collection from Salaried Men as per the Law for Assessment Year 2003-04

Income Range (in Rs.)	Number of Returns	Average Total Income	Average Tax At Current Rate without surcharge	Average Historical Investment in Securities Specified u/s 88	Average Rebate Claimed u/s 88 as per Existing Law	Average Tax After Rebate	Average Surcharge	Average Tax Including Surcharge at Current Rate	Revenue Collection (Without Surcharge (in Rs. crores)	Revenue Collection on Account of Surcharge (in Rs. crores)	Total Revenue Collection at Existing Rates (in Rs. crores)
0-40,000	301394	24746	0	292	88	0	0	0	0	0	0
40,000-50,000	131613	45312	0	1943	583	0	0	0	0	0	0
50,000-60,000	793078	54975	498	5183	1555	0	0	0	0	0	0
60,000-80,000	1295295	68898	2780	11499	3450	0	0	0	0	0	0
80,000-1,00,000	774554	89300	6860	17830	5349	1511	76	1587	117	6	123
1,00,000-1,50,000	2127080	120769	13154	23382	4676	8477	424	8901	1803	90	1893
1,50,000-2,00,000	1392615	171818	25545	24926	3739	21806	1090	22897	3037	152	3189
2,00,000-3,00,000	417261	237410	45223	26228	3934	41289	2064	43353	1723	86	1809
3,00,000-4,00,000	135008	342313	76694	31293	4694	72000	3600	75600	972	49	1021
4,00,000-5,00,000	60669	442347	106704	34263	5139	101565	5078	106643	616	31	647
5,00,000-10,00,000	100336	675284	176585	33028	0	176585	8829	185415	1772	89	1860
>10,00,000	21046	2415767	698730	23601	0	698730	34936	733666	1471	74	1544
Total	7429896								11510	576	12086

Table – 9.4

Revenue Collection from Non-Salaried Men as per Final Recommendations of the Task Force

Income Range (in Rs.)	Number of Returns	Average Salary Income	Average Total Income	Average Standard Deduction	Average Deduction Under Section	Average Other Deductions Under Chapter VI-A	Average Adjusted Total Income	Tax on Average Adjusted Total Income	Savings Under 80-CCC	Average Rebate on Savings Under 80-CCC	Average Other Deductions Under Chapter VI-A (Other Than 80-CCC	Rebate on Other Deductions Under Chapter VI-A	Total Average Tax After Rebate	Total Tax Payable At New Tax Rates (in Rs. crores)
0-40,000	2096737	1899	21884	949	3441	906	27180	0	105	21	696	139	0	0
40,000-50,000	912891	4697	46098	2348	2339	496	51280	0	131	26	450	90	0	0
50,000-60,000	1801169	4083	54667	2042	1593	302	58603	0	423	85	292	58	0	0
60,000-80,000	1650294	6289	68482	3144	2694	625	74945	0	3024	605	595	119	0	0
80,000-1,00,000	987577	9546	89130	4773	4198	1289	99390	0	8168	1634	1073	215	0	0
1,00,000-1,50,000	1504307	16597	121877	8299	5844	2048	138068	7614	15938	3188	1842	368	4057	610
1,50,000-2,00,000	836005	25539	171719	12770	6952	2572	194013	18803	20000	4000	2167	433	14369	1201
2,00,000-3,00,000	161935	49917	241091	24959	7799	3515	277364	35473	20000	4000	3004	601	30872	500
3,00,000-4,00,000	52841	71038	343431	30000	8797	4663	386891	57378	20000	4000	4011	802	52576	278
4,00,000-5,00,000	25791	90469	445863	30000	9733	5951	491547	87464	20000	4000	4372	874	82590	213
5,00,000-10,00,000	141981	119173	685623	30000	9068	6354	731044	159313	20000	4000	5724	1145	154168	2189
>10,00,000	33170	363776	3824798	20000	10079	19308	3874186	1102256	20000	4000	18449	3690	1094566	3631
Total	10973816													8622

Table – 9.5

Revenue Collection from Salaried Men Taxpayers As Per Final Recommendation by the Force

Income Range (in Rs.)	Number of Returns	Average Salary Income	Average Total Income	Average Standard Deduction	Average Deduction Under Section 80-L	Average Other Deduction Under Chapter VI-A	Average Adjusted Total Income	Tax on Average Adjusted Total Income	Savings Under 80-CCC	Average Rebate on Savings Under 80-CCC	Average Other Deductions Under Chapter VI-A (Other Than 80-CCC)	Rebate on Other Deductions Under Chapter VI-A	Average Tax After Rebate At the New Tax Rates	Total Tax Payable At New Tax Rates
0-40,000	301394	27086	24746	13543	235	586	39111	0	292	58	572	114	0	0
40,000-50,000	131613	46375	45312	23187	130	310	68939	0	1943	389	294	59	0	0
50,000-60,000	793078	56047	54975	28024	132	241	83372	0	5183	1037	223	45	0	0
60,000-80,000	1295295	70246	68898	30000	166	267	99331	0	11499	2300	247	49	0	0
80,000-1,00,000	774554	90903	89300	30000	312	378	119990	3998	17830	3566	345	69	363	28
1,00,000-1,50,000	2127080	123287	120769	30000	768	684	152221	10444	20000	4000	549	110	6334	1347
1,50,000-2,00,000	1392615	175833	171818	25000	1530	1347	199695	19939	20000	4000	964	193	15746	2193
2,00,000-3,00,000	417261	241923	237410	25000	2302	1950	266662	33332	20000	4000	1372	274	29058	1212
3,00,000-4,00,000	135008	348288	342313	20000	3519	2801	368633	53727	20000	4000	1958	392	49335	666
4,00,000-5,00,000	60669	448346	442347	20000	4657	3429	470432	81130	20000	4000	2336	467	76662	465
5,00,000-10,00,000	100336	680533	675284	0	5564	4114	684963	145489	20000	4000	3014	603	140886	1414
>10,00,000	21046	2394841	2415767	0	7607	8258	2431631	669489	20000	4000	7099	1420	664070	1398
Total	7429896													8723

Table – 9.6

Revenue Collection from Senior Citizens As Per the Law For Assessment Year 2003-04

Income Range (in Rs.)	Number of Returns	Average Total Income	Average Tax at Current Rate Without Surcharge	Rebate Under Section 88B	Average Tax After Rebate Under Section 88B	Average Historical Investment in Securities Specified u/s 88	Average Rebate Claimed u/s 88	Average Tax After Rebate	Average Surcharge	Average Tax Including Surcharge At Current Rate	Revenue Collection (Without Surcharge) (in Rs. crores)	Revenue Collection on Account of Surcharge (in Rs. crores)	Total Revenue Collection at Existing Range (in Rs. crores)
0-40,000	239,874	21,883.85	0.00	0.00	0.00	105.02	21.00	0.00	0.00	0.00	0.00	0.00	0.00
40,000-50,000	87,119	46,097.57	0.00	0.00	0.00	131.36	26.27	0.00	0.00	0.00	0.00	0.00	0.00
50,000-60,000	201,159	54,667.13	466.71	466.71	0.00	422.73	84.55	0.00	0.00	0.00	0.00	0.00	0.00
60,000-80,000	212,252	68,481.54	2,696.31	2,696.31	0.00	3,024.02	604.80	0.00	0.00	0.00	0.00	0.00	0.00
80,000-1,00,000	126,485	89,129.74	6,825.95	6,825.95	0.00	8,168.47	1,633.69	0.00	0.00	0.00	0.00	0.00	0.00
1,00,000-1,50,000	258,923	121,877.04	13,375.41	13,375.41	0.00	15,938.41	3,187.68	0.00	0.00	0.00	0.00	0.00	0.00
1,50,000-2,00,000	151,377	171,719.09	25,515.72	15,000.00	10,515.72	20,761.62	3,114.24	7,401.48	370.07	7,771.55	112.04	5.60	117.64
2,00,000-3,00,000	38,284	241,090.82	46,327.25	15,000.00	31,327.25	24,210.23	3,631.53	27,695.71	1,384.79	29,080.50	106.03	5.30	111.33
3,00,000-4,00,000	12,310	343,430.57	77,029.17	15,000.00	62,029.17	25,557.20	3,833.58	58,195.59	2,909.78	61,105.37	71.64	3.58	75.22
4,00,000-5,00,000	5,682	445,863.24	107,758.97	15,000.00	92,758.97	26,816.38	4,022.46	88,736.52	4,436.83	93,173.34	50.42	2.52	52.94
5,00,000-10,00,000	15,828	685,623.00	179,686.90	15,000.00	164,686.90	25,872.71	0.00	164,686.90	8,234.34	172,921.24	260.66	13.03	273.69
>10,00,000	3,517	3,824,798.33	1,121,439.50	15,000.00	1,106,439.50	26,230.33	0.00	1,106,439.50	55,321.97	1,161,761.47	389.16	19.46	408.62
Total	1,352,785												1,039.45

Table – 9.7

Revenue Collection from Senior Citizens As Per Final Recommendations of the Task Force

Income Range (in Rs.)	Number of Returns	Average Salary Income	Average Total Income	Average Standard Deduction	Average Deduction Under Section 80-L	Average Other Deduction Under Section VI-A	Average Adjusted Total Income	Tax on Average Adjusted Total Income	Saving Under 88-CCC	Average Rebate on Savings Under 80-CCC	Average Other Deductions Under Chapter VI-A (Other than 80-CCC)	Rebate on Other Deductions Under Chapter VI-A)	Total Average Tax After Rebate	Total Tax Payable at New Tax Rates (in Rs. crores)
0-40,000	239,874	1899	21884	949	3441	906	27180	0	105	21	696	139	0	0.00
40,000-50,000	87,119	4697	46098	2348	2339	496	51280	0	131	26	450	90	0	0.00
50,000-60,000	201,159	4083	54667	2042	1593	302	58603	0	423	85	292	58	0	0.00
60,000-80,000	212,252	6289	68482	3144	2694	625	74945	0	3024	605	595	119	0	0.00
80,000-1,00,000	126,485	9546	89130	4773	4198	1289	99390	0	8168	1634	1073	215	0	0.00
1,00,000-1,50,000	258,923	16597	121877	8299	5844	2048	138068	0	15938	3188	1842	368	0	0.00
1,50,000-2,00,000	151,377	25539	171719	12770	6952	2572	194013	8803	20000	4000	2167	433	4369	66.14
2,00,000-3,00,000	38,284	49917	241091	24959	7799	3515	277364	25473	20000	4000	3004	601	20872	79.91
3,00,000-4,00,000	12,310	71038	343431	30000	8797	4663	386891	47378	20000	4000	4011	802	42576	52.41
4,00,000-5,00,000	5,682	90469	445863	30000	9733	5951	491547	77464	20000	4000	4372	874	72590	41.24
5,00,000-10,00,000	15,828	119173	685623	30000	9068	6354	731044	149313	20000	4000	5724	1145	144168	228.18
>10,00,000	3,517	363776	3824798	20000	10079	19308	3874186	1092256	20000	4000	18449	3690	1084566	381.47
Total	1,352,785													849.35

Table – 9.8

Impact of the Recommendations Made by the Task Force

Income Range	Salaries Taxpayers			Non-Salaried Taxpayers			Senior Citizens		
	Existing Tax Liability	Proposed Tax Liability	Tax Relief (in Rs.)	Existing Tax Liability	Proposed Tax Liability	Tax Relief (in Rs.)	Existing Tax Liability	Proposed Tax Liability	Tax Relief (in Rs.)
0-40,000	0	0	0	0	0	0	0	0	0
40,000-50,000	0	0	0	0	0	0	0	0	0
50,000-60,000	0	0	0	382	0	382	0	0	0
60,000-80,000	0	0	0	2196	0	2196	0	0	0
80,000-1,00,000	1587	363	1224	5452	0	5452	0	0	0
1,00,000-1,50,000	8901	6334	2567	10697	4057	6640	0	0	0
1,50,000-2,00,000	22897	15746	7151	23522	14369	9152	7772	4369	3402
2,00,000-3,00,000	43353	29058	14295	44830	30872	13959	29080	20872	8209
3,00,000-4,00,000	75600	49335	26265	76855	52576	24279	61105	42576	18529
4,00,000-5,00,000	106643	76662	29980	108923	82590	26334	93173	72590	20584
5,00,000-10,00,000	185415	140886	44528	188671	154168	34503	172921	144168	28753
Above 10,00,000	733666	664070	69597	1177511	1094566	82946	1161761	1084566	77196

Table – 9.9

Revenue Impact of Corporate Tax Reforms

Particulars	Non-Banking Companies	Banking Companies	All Companies
Sample Size	1275	59	1334
Statutory Corporate Tax Rate (Assessment Year 2002-03)	35.70	35.70	35.70
Profits before Tax (Assessment Year 2002-03)	61707	16695	78402
Corporate Tax Paid (Assessment Year 2002-03)	13420	5844	19264
Surcharge of 3 per cent (Assessment Year 2003-04)	395	172	567
Corporate Tax Collection (adjusted for Assessment Year 2003-04)	13815	6016	19831
Effective Corporate tax Rate (Assessment Year 2002-03)	21.75	35.01	24.57
Effective Corporate tax Rate (Assessment Year 2003-04)	22.39	36.04	25.29
Pre-Reform Corporate Tax Base	37591	16371	53961
Post-Reform Corporate Tax Base	61707	16695	78402
Post Reform Tax Collection @ 30 per cent)	18512	5009	23521
Increase in Collection	4697	-1008	3690
Percentage increase in collection	34.00	-16.75	18.61
Tax Collection in 2002-03 (Assessment Year 2003-04)	40000	8000	48000
Revenue Impact of Recommendations	13601	-1340	12262
Impact of Full Allowance for NPAs	0	-1500	-1500
Net Revenue Impact of Recommendations	13601	-2840	10762

Table – 9.10

Summary of Revenue Impact

(Rs. in crores)

Particulars	Proposed	Existing	Loss	Gain
Salaried taxpayers	8723	12086	3363	
Non-Salaried Taxpayers	8622	12543	3921	
Senior Citizens	849	1039	190	
Women	4767	5172	404	
Partnership Firms	8150	10000	1850	
Mutual Funds	1500	NIL	-	1500
Taxation of Dividends	-	1500	1500	
Long Term Capital gains	-	1000	1000	
Corporate Tax	58762	48000	-	10762
Total	91373	91340	12228	12262

10

Summary and Recommendations

Reform of Tax Administration

The fundamental role of tax administration is, in order of priority:

1. To render quality taxpayer services to encourage voluntary compliance of tax laws; and
2. To detect and penalise non-compliance.

The extent of success of the tax administration in its role would be reflected in higher revenue growth. (Paragraph 3.6)

10.2 Traditionally, the role of the tax administration has been to enforce the tax laws and provide at least minimal taxpayer service. Most employees unable to reconcile to their new role continue to resist this shift in the role perception from an enforcement officer to a facilitator. (Paragraph 3.8)

10.3 Given the best international practice in the area of taxpayer service and the future programme for widening the tax base through voluntary compliance, the following measures should be undertaken to expand the present scope of the taxpayer service programme:

(i) The income tax department must expand, qualitatively and quantitatively, the present scope of taxpayer service. These should cover the range of taxpayer services indicated in Table–3.1 and, inter alia, include the introduction of a telephonic system (by voice message) to remind taxpayers of important dates and the provision of pre-formatted programmed floppy diskettes through retail outlets.

(ii) The expenditure on taxpayer service must be increased from the present level of about one percent of the total expenditure on tax administration to at least five percent. In this regard, an important start should be made by the establishment of taxpayers' clinic in different parts of the country to enable taxpayers to walk in for assistance. A better treatment of existing taxpayers has an important role in encouraging those outside the tax net to become taxpaying citizens.

(iii) The department should provide easy access to taxpayers through Internet and e-mail and extend facilities such as tele-filing and tele-refunds. It should design special programmes for retired people, low-income taxpayers and other such groups with special needs who cannot afford expensive services of tax consultants.

(Paragraph 3.11)

10.4 Given the ongoing and new initiatives by the Ministry of Home Affairs for issuing a Citizen Identification Number and by the Ministry of Labour for issuing a Social Security Number, PAN can be used to effectively integrate, on the lines of the US Social Security Number system, multiple tasks of tax and commercial enforcement, targeting government subvention, improving governance and enhance national security, both at the Central and State level. The Task Force, therefore, recommends that:

(i) The PAN should be extended to cover all citizens and therefore serve as a Citizen identification number. This will obviate the need for the Home and Labour Ministries to issue new numbers.

(ii) Given the manifold increase in the coverage of PAN, the responsibility for issuing should be transferred to an independent agency outside the income tax department. However, the income tax department should have online access to the database for tax enforcement like any other agency.

(iii) The requirement of quoting PAN may be expanded to cover most financial transactions. (Paragraph 3.15)

10.5 In view of the extant method of collection of information and constraints in digitising the volume of information received by the tax administration, the Task Force recommends :

(i) Income Tax Act should be amended to provide for submission of 'annual information return' by third parties in respect of various transactions as may be prescribed. For this purpose, a proper format of the return also needs to be prescribed. Consequently, the flow of information will be continuous and the discretionary power with the CIB to collect information will be eliminated.

(ii) Such annual return of information (including returns relating to tax deducted at source) should be mandatorily required to be submitted on electronic format.

(iii) Many of the Departments involved in transactions specified in Rule 114B do not have any mechanism for obtaining the PAN of the concerned person. It is, therefore, necessary that the pro forma used by them for their departmental purposes, e.g., the application form for transfer of motor license, should have the necessary column requiring the applicant to disclose his Permanent Account Number (PAN).

(iv) The Department should set up a structure for Electronic Data Interchange (EDI) with some of the major departments and organisations involved in the transactions specified in Rule 114B, such as, Banks, Stock Exchanges, Telephone Companies, Regional Transport Authority etc.

(Paragraph 3.17)

10.6 In view of the diminition in the deterrence effect of search and seizure operations, —

(i) Special procedure for assessment of search cases in chapter XIV B (Block Assessment) which provides for tax at the rate of 60 per cent, be omitted. As and when concealment is detected and established, it should suffer full penal consequences of interest, penalty and prosecution.

(ii) Power of Settlement Commission to grant immunity from interest, penalty and prosecution may be restricted to cases other than those where the assessee admits of tax evasion consequent to search and seizure action taken by the department in his case.

(iii) The scheme of rewarding officers engaged in search and seizure activity be abolished.

(iv) The stocks found during the course of search and seizure operation under the Income Tax Act may only be inventorised but not seized. This can be done by issuing administrative instruction. (Paragraph 3.26)

10.7 The Central Board of Direct Taxes must issue immediate instructions to the effect that no raiding party should obtain any surrender whatsoever. Where, a taxpayer desires to voluntarily make a disclosure, he should be advised to make so after the search. As a result, the taxpayer will not be able to allege coercion and successfully distract investigations. All cases where surrender is obtained during the course of the search in violation of the instructions of the CBDT, the leader of the raiding party should be subjected to vigilance enquiry. All statements recorded during the search should be video recorded. This will, indeed, add to the confidence of the taxpayer in the impartiality of the system. (Paragraph 3.27)

10.8 The Task Force took note of the recent amendments conferring power to seize books of accounts during a survey operation. Accordingly, it recommends —

(i) A survey should be authorised after recording the reasons in writing and the power of authorization should not be vested in any officer below the rank of a Joint Commissioner of Income Tax.

(ii) The books of accounts impounded by the survey team should not be retained beyond a period of seven days since it has the potential of disrupting the business of a taxpayer. Where it is felt that the books need to be retained beyond the period of seven days, the department may obtain photocopies duly attested by the taxpayer for further investigation. (Paragraph 3.28)

10.9 In line with our view that the tax department should concentrate on its core functions, the department should be allowed to outsource data entry work and clear the backlog of returns (which number 2.8 crores as on 30th September, 2002) by end

February 2003. Similarly, all returns must be processed within four months of receipt. For this purpose, it would be necessary for the department to either hire additional personnel on a temporary basis during the peak period for filing returns, or, outsource data entry work, as is done routinely by national tax administrations all over the world. Further, we must emphasis that outsourcing of such data entry work relating to processing of returns should be done only to supplement the efforts of the departmental staff and officers and not as a substitute. The cost of hiring additional personnel or outsourcing data entry work would be far less in comparison to the benefit from reduced interest burden on refunds and taxpayer satisfaction. (Paragraph 3.30)

10.10 The existing discretion based system of selection of returns should be immediately abolished. The department should progressively develop an audit selection system for risk analysis and assessment, which forms a scientific (and, therefore, objective) basis for identifying cases of potential tax evasion for in-depth scrutiny. However, before an audit selection system can be driven by risk analysis, good quality data has to be obtained over a number of years. Risk analysis will help to rank taxpayers and any local knowledge and intelligence must be factored to make a risk assessment. This will provide the most efficient and effective means of targeting tax officials to areas of greatest risk. It is important that cases for audit are selected on the basis of perceived risk and not simply by intelligence or speculation since intelligence would be available for only a few taxpayers. Further, selection of cases based on risk analysis and assessment must be combined with a certain small percentage of random audit, and carrying out issue-specific audits, such as refund audits. In the interim, we recommend the identification of cases through a random non-discretionary centralised method deploying the PAN database. The current practice of issuing guidelines for selection of cases for scrutiny, which eventually finds its way to the public, must be given up.

(Paragraph 3.32 to 3.34)

10.11 Once a case is selected for scrutiny, it should be fully investigated, covering investments, accretion to assets, expenses incurred, savings, transactions entered and profits made, turnover etc. The scrutiny assessment will then serve its purpose of deterrence against tax evasion and contribute to revenue realisation.

The present practice in scrutiny assessments is mostly to make statutory disallowances of exemptions, deductions and other claims made in the return to achieve zero error assessments from the point of audit objections. Since hundred per cent policing is not possible, the number of cases selected for effective scrutiny should be on the basis of available manpower, their number and capability. (Paragraph 3.35)

10.12 Section 275 of the Income Tax Act should be suitably amended to provide that the penalty order should be passed within one year from the end of the financial year in which the first appellate order is received. Consequently, the delay in passing the order-levying penalty for concealment would be considerably reduced to about two years. (Paragraph 3.37)

10.13 The tax department should be allowed to concentrate on its core functions – an increasing emphasis on assessment and enforcement duties, rather than logistics and support services – which will surely lead to increased effectiveness of the tax administration. In this context, rapid and progressive outsourcing of many tasks of the tax department is not only feasible, given the significant pool of talent in the Indian software industry, but it is also desirable. In order to make IT infrastructure commensurate with the requisite processing tasks, the Task Force would like to explicitly put on record that implementation of this enhanced integration-software requires considerable investment in upgrading associated IT hardware and sufficient access to high-capacity bandwidth for implementing the network. (Paragraph 3.40)

10.14 To speed up the process of modernisation, –

(i) The Government should establish a national Tax Information Network (TIN) on a build, operate and transfer basis. This will comprise of a world class (common carrier) network system and have access to state-of-the-art IT infrastructure. A requisite in-built feature of the system is that it should be scalable to offer ease of access across tax administration and taxpayers. The network that is envisaged will facilitate transactions, akin to securities markets, and establish secure and seamless logistics of tax collection through integration of primary information, record keeping, dissemination and retrieval. It should be a repository of information, with a database of all tax payments and refunds. Data mining software associated with such relational databases will allow a quick and systematic identification of non-compliance and abuses, thereby helping to improve compliance. The existing facilities of the National Securities Depository Ltd. (NSDL) can be relatively quickly deployed to make a systemic improvement in processes and reduce transaction cost.

(ii) TIN will receive, on behalf of the tax administration, all TDS returns and other information returns for digitisation. The information would be received either online, or through magnetic media or in printed format. The digitised information will be downloaded by the National Computer Centre / Regional Computer Centres of the income tax department for further processing.

(iii) TIN will also receive online information about collection of taxes from the banks. The information could be downloaded by the income tax department as and when required.

(iv) The taxpayer will have the facility of accessing the TIN system through a secure and confidential Permanent Account Number (PAN)-based identification to ascertain tax payments credited to his/her account and the status of returns and refunds.

The TIN will therefore serve as a gateway to the National Computer Centre of the Income Tax Department. It will help overcome the paucity of technical manpower and inadequate technical infrastructure. (Paragraph 3.42)

10.15 Firms and individuals whose total sales, gross receipts or turnover from the business or profession carried on by it is less than the monetary limits specified under clause (a) or clause (b) of section 44AB should continue to be exempted from the liability of deducting tax at source. However, once the TIN, which has been recommended by this Task Force, is fully operationalised, the requirement to issue TDS certificates to the payee can be dispensed and the scheme can be extended to the smaller taxpayers. (Paragraph 3.45)

10.16 Where a payee receiving salary fails to furnish his PAN, tax should be deducted at a flat rate of 30 percent. In all other cases of such failure, tax should be deducted at twice the normal rate or 30 percent, which ever is lower. Further, —

(i) Tax should be required to be deducted at source irrespective of the amount of payment.

(ii) A payee should be allowed to claim exemption from TDS if she/he furnishes a self declaration to the payer that the tax on her/his estimated total income in which the income is to be included will be NIL and quotes her/his Permanent Account Number (PAN) on such.

(iii) The present system of obtaining a certificate from the assessing officer for deduction at lower rate should be abolished so as to minimize the interface between the taxpayer and tax authorities. (Paragraph 3.46 & 3.48)

10.17 In view of the recommendation for the establishment of TIN, a revised procedure for collection of taxes and their accounting may be designed along the following lines :–

(i) A taxpayer will be required to fill up only one copy of the challan while making payment of taxes in the bank. The present requirement of filling up four copies of challan for payment of any tax will be given up.

(ii) The banks will be networked to the TIN and receive payments online. The banks will be required to issue a computerised receipt to the taxpayer instantaneously. The date of presentation of a cheque will be treated as the date of payment. If a cheque bounces, the bank will reverse the receipt online, and the department would then be expected to prosecute the delinquent taxpayer.

(iii) With instant accounting of tax collection, the requirement of enclosing a copy of the challan as evidence of tax payment, along with the annual return of income could be done away.

(iv) Since the TIN will digitise all TDS returns, the requirement to file TDS certificates along with the return of income will also be dispensed with.

(v) At present, taxes are collected through approximately 10,500 bank branches. Since the proposed procedure requires banks to receive online payment, those banks that do not have adequate infrastructure for establishing online connectivity will be debarred from collecting taxes. Accordingly, the Government, in consultation with the Reserve Bank of India, should also consider paying higher charges for services rendered by banks.

The process outlined above will facilitate real-time accounting of TDS, Advance Tax and Self-Assessment Tax, and help the tax administration to swiftly identify non-compliance. Furthermore, the new procedure of tax accounting will facilitate electronic filing of tax returns. (Paragraph 3.54)

10.18 The existing cumbersome and manually-operated procedures for issue of refunds must be replaced by a more efficient IT-based system. Under the new system the department will prepare a separate file of all refunds daily which will be downloaded by a payment intermediary, i.e., a designated bank. The designated bank will be authorised to issue computerised refunds as is the current practice for issuing dividend and interest warrants by companies. The designated bank will be required to transmit the information relating to the issue of refunds to the TIN, which will also allow a taxpayer to verify the status of his/her refund claim.

(Paragraph 3.55)

10.19 The present requirement of obtaining a tax clearance certificate before leaving the country must be abolished. However in order to protect the interest of revenue, we can continue to allow the income tax authorities to notify the immigration/custom authorities to prevent any particular person from leaving the country if such person is considered to be a proclaimed offender. As a result only a handful of notified persons will be subjected to the process of tax clearance as against the present practice of requiring all and sundry to comply with the requirement of obtaining tax clearance before leaving the country.

(Paragraph 3.60)

10.20 The system of issuing Income Tax Clearance Certificates to contractors and others should be eliminated forthwith. However, to help in enhancing effective tax enforcement, all government agencies should be required to obtain the PAN of entities participating in tenders, being designated as vendors to the government, etc., and periodically submit (pre-specified) relevant information to the tax administration. (Paragraph 3.65)

10.21 On the issue of dispute resolution, the Task Force recommends the following:–

(i) the Income tax Act should be amended to provide that all orders/intimation imposing any additional burden should be made appealable.

(ii) The institution of Ombudsman should be established in the top ten-taxpaying cities and all state capitals along the lines of that in the banking sector. This institution will provide an independent system to assure that tax problems, which have not been resolved through normal channels, are promptly and fairly handled. It will also identify issues that increase burden or create problem for taxpayers, and bring those issues to the attention of the Central Board of Direct Taxes (CBDT). The Ombudsman will also enquire into, should a complaint be filed, the practices and performance of all classes of tax professionals. Where necessary, it will also make appropriate legislative proposals. This institution will be independent of the local tax office. Its goal will be to protect individual taxpayer rights and to reduce taxpayer burden. A consolidated annual report of the Ombudsman system will be tabled in Parliament.

(Paragraph 3.66 & 3.67)

10.22 Central Board of Direct Taxes (CBDT), which is responsible for administering the direct tax laws, should be given the requisite autonomy in the following manner so that it is made more accountable :–

(i) The control of the Central Government over the tax administration be exercised through a Memorandum of Understanding (MOU) between the Central Board of Direct Taxes and the Central Government (we understand that there is already a Cabinet decision to this effect). The Central Board of Revenue Act provides that the two boards (CBDT and CBEC) must function subject to the control of the Central Government, but the mechanism and the extent of control still remains unspecified.

(ii) The MOU should, inter alia, specify the financial commitment of the Central Government for tax administration. It should provide for full financial autonomy and control over deployment of human resources to the CBDT. The Central Government should only specify the general guidelines for financial expenditure and deployment of human resources. The CBDT should have exclusive power for designing the enforcement strategy, subject to the condition that it is non-discriminatory and transparent. The MoU should be for a period of five years specifying observable performance indicators for CBDT and the financial resources that would be made available to CBDT on a year-to-year basis. (Paragraph 3.69 & 3.70)

10.23 The rules for appointment of Members should provide for selection on criteria of merit-cum-seniority from amongst those who have a minimum period of two years of service before retirement as on the date on which the vacancy arises. Further, an officer once appointed as member of the Board should be debarred from any appointment either in the ITAT or Settlement Commission. Similarly, the Chairman, CBDT should be selected on criterion of merit cum seniority and once appointed should have a minimum tenure of two years. (Paragraph 3.71)

10.24 Expressing deep concern at the lack of accountability, the Task Force considers it necessary to reiterate the direction by the Honorable Supreme Court that disciplinary action must be taken in the following cases:

(i) Where the officer had acted in a manner as would reflect on his reputation for integrity or good faith or devotion to duty;

(ii) If there is prima facie material to show recklessness or misconduct in the discharge of his duty;

(iii) If the officer has acted in a manner which is unbecoming of a Government servant;

(iv) If the officer has acted negligently or that he omitted the prescribed conditions which are essential for the exercise of the statutory powers;

(v) If the officer has acted in order to unduly favour a party;

(vi) If the officer has been actuated by corrupt motive, however small the bribe may be because Lord Coke said long ago 'through the bribe may be small, yet the fault is great'. (Paragraph 3.73)

10.25 As a confidence building measure, the Central Board of Direct Taxes should release annual information (giving Chief Commissioner-wise break-up) of number of complaints received from the public or acts of omission or commission identified through internal mechanism or by external agencies and the result of official enquiry into such complaints. The information must be provided separately for officers and staff. Such information may relate to tax payer profiles, returns received, headwise breakup of income, number of appeals filed and disposed of, penalty orders, rectification applications, reopening of assessment, refund orders, refunds issued, returns selected for scrutiny assessment and their results, break up of collection, etc. (Paragraph 3.74)

10.26 With a view to further enhancing accountability of (and transparency in) tax administration, it is important that the CBDT publishes an annual report of its own, along the lines of the UPSC/CVC, that is tabled in Parliament and put on its web site. The annual report must separately provide for performance achievements of each Chief Commissioner/ Commissioner. In addition, the quarterly progress of achievement must be displayed on the web site, so that taxpayers have an opportunity to respond. While defining a stricter accountability structure, however, care must be taken to eschew an excessive and regimented accountability system which over-burdens AOs with onerous and fragmented oversight that ultimately only serves to reduce its overall effectiveness. (Paragraph 3.75)

10.27 Lack of financial autonomy was identified as an important constraint in the functioning of the CBDT. Therefore, The Task Force is of the view that the position should be immediately rectified through adequate delegation of financial powers to bring in synergy and effectiveness in management functions.

(Paragraph 3.81)

10.28 The absence of control over human resources has further undermined accountability. Therefore, it is recommended that the Central Government should delegate to CBDT full authority and responsibility regarding staff of the income tax department and its secretariat. The CBDT should, however, exercise such delegated powers in a transparent manner within the framework of rules and guidelines framed for this purpose. Such rules and guidelines should be framed with the approval of the government.

(Paragraph 3.82)

10.29 To institute changes for modernization of the tax administration —

(i) CBDT should request Chief Commissioners to identify the shortcomings in their offices by 1st April 2003 and send their proposals to CBDT for creating model tax offices.

(ii) By 1st August 2003 a model Commissionerate including the offices at the range, circle and ward levels should be established in each zone.

(iii) CBDT should seek the requisite financial sanction to replicate the model offices by either upgrading existing offices or, where necessary, by purchasing new premises, etc. The entire exercise should be time bound so that by January 2005 modern offices are in place in all Commissionerates. (Paragraph 3.83)

Personal Income Tax Reform

10.30 At the beginning of the 21st century, some truths about taxation have become self evident. Even so, they bear repetition.

(i) First, the design of tax policy is of paramount importance for tax administration.

(ii) Second, if the objective is to have a transparent, efficient and feasible tax administration, then the structure of all taxes should comprise common elements. These are low rates, few nominal rates, a broad base, few exemptions, few incentives, few surcharges, few temporary measures.

And in the rare instances where there are exceptions, there should be clear guidelines. The Task Force is unanimously in favour of these overarching fiscal principles. The numerous recommendations derive from these objectives. (Paragraph 4.12 & 4.13)

10.31 The Task Force endorses the following principles identified in the Report of the Advisory Group on Tax Policy and Tax Administration for the Tenth Plan, for designing the rate schedule:

(i) The basic exemption limit must be at a moderate level — an appropriate balance between the tax liability at the lowest levels, administrative cost of collection and compliance burden of the smallest taxpayers. The ability of the tax administration to render quality services to taxpayers will also significantly affect the choice of the exemption limit.

(ii) The number of tax slabs should be few and their ranges fairly large to minimise distortions arising out of bracket creep.

(iii) The maximum marginal rate of tax should be moderate, so that the distortions in the economic behaviour of taxpayers and incentive to evade tax payment are minimised. (Paragraph 4.14)

10.32 In view of the principles endorsed above, —

(i) the imposition of a single individual income tax rate is rejected in preference for a reformed system of personal income tax with more than one rate. The Task Force believes that the alternative lies in a multiple rate schedule, but with very little spread between such rates;

(ii) and in view of the distortionary impact of multiple slabs, the Task Force opts for a two rate personal income tax schedule;

(iii) and if the full effect of lower tax rates has to be realised, it is not only necessary to have an optimal enforcement strategy but also ensure that the benefits of a tax cut apply to all class of taxpayers — rather than be restricted to a handful of taxpayers at the top end. This is possibly achieved by broad basing the tax slabs.

Accordingly, the Task Force recommends the following personal income tax rate schedule :

Proposed Personal Income Tax Structure.

Income level	Tax rates
Below Rs. 1,00,000	Nil
Rs. 1,00,000-4,00,000	20 percent of the Income in excess of Rs. 1,00,000/-
Above Rs. 4,00,000	Rs. 60,000/- plus 30 percent of the Income in excess of Rs. 4,00,000\-

Further, the revenue gain from levy of surcharge is generally illusory since such a levy has the effect of increasing the marginal rate of tax, which adversely affect compliance. Therefore, the present surcharge of 5 per cent on taxpayers with incomes above Rs. 60,000/- must be eliminated. (Paragraph 4.21, 4.23 to 4.26)

10.33 If compliance is to be fostered and nurtured and economic incentive sustained, it is necessary to move towards a comprehensive tax regime by reviewing the various exemptions, deductions and rebates. (Paragraph 4.38)

10.34 Tax payers who are residents but not ordinarily residents must be subjected to tax on their global/world-wide income at par with residents. To do so, this unusual category of resident but not ordinarily resident taxpayers must be deleted. This will not only enhance the income tax base, but also remove an antiquated anomaly and simplify the law. (Paragraph 4.42 & 4.43)

10.35 The standard deduction under Section 16(1) of the Income Tax Act should be eliminated. However, the exemption of conveyance allowance subject to a ceiling of Rs. 9,600/- should be continued. This should serve as a reasonable deduction for employment related expenses. The additional liability of a taxpayer on this account will be more than met by the reduction in rates of personal income tax proposed by the Task Force. (Paragraph 4.53)

10.36 Individual myopia, particularly amongst the smaller taxpayer and the non-taxpayer may result in sub-optimal investment in the housing sector – a necessity for providing social security.

This problem would not be resolved through the existing scheme of tax treatment of mortgage interest for owner occupied dwelling which is targeted to taxpayers alone. Therefore, the first best policy option would be to incentivise borrowings for housing by providing 2 per cent interest subsidy on all loans below Rs. 5 lakhs. This subsidy should be granted by the Government through the National Housing Bank. This will indeed target such loanees who suffer from individual myopia. The second best policy measure for this purpose would be to continue with the tax treatment of mortgage interest for owner occupied houses. However, given the average size of the home loan (around Rs. 3.5 lakhs), we recommend that the ceiling on the amount of mortgage interest deductible for taxable income purposes should be reduced from the existing level of Rs. 1,50,000/- to Rs. 50,000/- only. (Paragraph 4.66)

10.37 With a view to encourage the States to tap the full potential of their taxing powers and to prevent laundering of non-agricultural income as agricultural income, the Task Force recommends —

(i) A tax rental arrangement should be designed whereby States should pass a resolution under Article 252 of the Constitution authorising the Central Government to impose income tax on agricultural income. The taxes collected by the Centre would however be assigned to the States.

(ii) Tax from agricultural income for the purposes of allocation between States will be the difference between the tax on total income (including agricultural income) and the tax on total income net of agricultural income.

(iii) Where a taxpayer derives agricultural income from different States, the revenues attributable to a State will be in the ratio of the income derived from a particular State to the total agricultural income.

(iv) A separate tax return form should be prescribed for taxpayers deriving income from agriculture.

These recommendations will help mobilise additional resources for the States without the attendant problem of administering the agricultural income tax. Further, given our recommendations on increasing the exemption limit to Rs.1,00,000 per individual, most agricultural farmers would continue to remain out of the tax net. The proposed rental arrangement with the States could be packaged with the rental arrangement for taxation of services.

(Paragraph 4.68)

10.38 The tax incentives for savings under Section 88, Section 80L, Section 10(15)(i), Section 10(15)(iib), Section 10(15)(iic), Section 10(15)(iid), Section 10(15)(iv)(h) and Section 10(15)(iv)(i) of the Income Tax Act must all be eliminated. These benefits must be withdrawn with immediate effect and not through a sunset clause. (Paragraph 4.98)

10.39 Further, with a view to overcoming the problem thrown up by individual myopia, we also recommend the continuation of the deduction under section 80CCC for contribution to the pension fund of LIC or any other insurance company. The ceiling on the deduction should, however, be increased from the existing levels of Rs. 10,000/- to Rs. 20,000/-. This income-based deduction u/s 80CCC be converted to a tax rebate at the minimum marginal rate of 20 per cent. Consequently, the ceiling on tax rebate for contribution to the pension fund should be Rs. 4,000/-. The new ceiling has been proposed keeping in view the needs of the smaller taxpayers with income below Rs. 2 lakhs. The scope of section 80CCC may also be extended to a larger number of pension/annuity schemes within the overall ceiling of Rs. 20,000/-. Since savings in these pension funds will be taxable at the withdrawal stage, the tax benefit for such savings will be consistent with the EET method of tax treatment. (Paragraph 4.99)

10.40 In view of the International practice and the fact that education is one of the basic amenities of life, generating positive externalities, it is necessary to provide continued support to education under the tax law. However, on grounds of equity, we also recommend that the income based deduction under Section 80E should be converted to a tax rebate at the minimum marginal rate of personal income tax. The maximum amount of tax rebate should be restricted to Rs.4,000. (Paragraph 4.102)

10.41 Since health is also one of the basic amenities in life, support under the tax law will continue to be provided under section 80D of the Income Tax Act for contribution to the mediclaim insurance schemes, subject to a ceiling of Rs.15,000/-.

However, the tax support would take the form of a tax rebate at the minimum marginal rate of 20 percent subject to a ceiling of Rs. 3,000/- in tax relief. Similarly, the income based deduction for medical expenses under section 80 DDB is proposed to be restricted to senior citizens subject to a reduced ceiling of Rs. 20,000/-. The deduction would take the form of a tax rebate at 20 per cent subject to a maximum of Rs. 4,000/-. (Paragraph 4.104)

10.42 With a view to providing a human face to the tax reform, we recommend that the basic exemption limit for senior citizens should be Rs. 50,000/- more then the exemption limit for the general class of individual taxpayers. In other words, the exemption limit for senior citizens should be Rs. 1,50,000/- as against Rs. 1,00,000/- for the general category of individual taxpayers recommended by us in Table-4.1. The exemption limit for senior citizens should be revised as and when the exemption limit for the general category of individual taxpayers is revised. We also recommend that this benefit of higher exemption limit should also be extended to widows. (Paragraph 4.106)

10.43 Given the personal circumstances of handicapped, the Task Force recommends the continuation of the personal deductions under Sections 80DD and Section 80U. However, on grounds of equity between handicapped taxpayers, we also recommend that the income based deduction under these provisions should be converted to a tax rebate at the minimum marginal rate of personal income tax. (Paragraph 4.108)

10.44 Further, in view of our recommendations for increase in the exemption limit to Rs. 1,00,000/- and deduction of medical expenses for senior citizens and widows, we recommend that the personal deductions in the form of tax rebate for senior citizens (Section 88B) and women (Section 88C) should be deleted. (Paragraph 4.109)

10.45 The policy measures for the reform of personal income tax therefore comprises of the following elements:-

(i) Increase in the generalised exemption limit from Rs.50,000/- to Rs.1,00,000/-for all individual and HUF taxpayers. The exemption limit for senior citizens and widows would, however, be at an enhanced level of Rs. 1,50,000/-.

(ii) The existing three slabs in the personal income tax rate schedule will be replaced by two slabs. Incomes between Rs.1,00,000/- and Rs.4,00,000 will be subjected to tax at the marginal rate of 20 per cent. All incomes above Rs.4,00,000/-will be subjected to tax at the marginal rate of 30 per cent.

(iii) Dividends received from Indian companies will be fully exempt.

(iv) Long term capital gains on listed equity will be fully exempt.

(v) The standard deduction for salaried taxpayers will be reduced to NIL. However, exemption for conveyance allowance subject to a ceiling of Rs. 9,600/- will continue.

(vi) The income based deduction under Section 80D subject to a ceiling of Rs. 15,000/- in respect of payment of medical insurance premium will be converted to a tax rebate at the rate of 20 per cent subject to a maximum of Rs.3,000.

(vii) The benefit of deduction under Section 80DDB will be withdrawn in so far as it relates to the general category of taxpayers. However, consistent with international practice and in view of the special circumstances of senior citizens, deduction for medical expenses may continue to be allowed in the form of a tax rebate at the rate of 20 per cent of the medical expenses, subject to a maximum rebate of Rs.4,000.

(viii) The income based deduction under Section 80E for repayment of educational expenses will continue to be allowed. However, on grounds of equity, the same should be allowed as a tax rebate at the rate of 20 per cent subject to maximum of Rs.4,000.

(ix) The tax rebate schemes under Sections 88 for savings will be eliminated.

(x) The rebate under Section 88B for senior citizens will be eliminated in view of the enhanced exemption limit for them.

(xi) The rebate under Section 88C for women taxpayers below the age of 65 years, will be eliminated.

(xii) The income based deduction for handicapped under Section 80DD and 80U will however continue.

(xiii) The income based deduction under Section 80L for interest income and dividends will be eliminated.

(xiv) The exemption under Section 10 in respect of interest income from bonds, securities, debentures etc. will be eliminated.

(xv) The deduction for mortgage interest in respect of loans for acquiring a owner occupied dwelling will be reduced to Rs. 50,000/-.

(xvi) The residential status of 'Resident but Not Ordinarily Resident' will be eliminated.

The Task Force would like to place on record that the various recommendations relating to personal income tax in this report are interwoven and therefore indivisible. The recommendations must be seen as a package and piecemeal implementation must be avoided at all cost. (Paragraph 4.110 & 4.111)

Corporate Tax Reforms

10.46 A corporate entity should be viewed as a 'conduit' and therefore the need for integration of corporate tax and personal income tax. Given the pros and cons of the various full/partial integration methods, the Task Force recommends the adoption of this method of full integration of corporation and personal income tax whereby a tax at the corporate level is levied at the same rate as the maximum rate of personal income tax and all dividends and capital gains is exempted from tax in the hands of the shareholders. Accordingly, the Task Force recommends that a corporate tax rate of 30 per cent for domestic companies, being the top marginal rate for personal income tax, and exempt from tax all dividends and long term capital gains from listed equity. This method would not undermine any equity since most direct equity investors in the companies in India are likely to be taxed at the top marginal rate of personal income tax. (Paragraph 5.19)

10.47 This system recommended by us would serve as a full integration model only if the accounting profits bear the full burden of corporate tax i.e., the effective corporate tax liability is equivalent to the statutory corporate tax rate. This is possible if there is no divergence between the taxable base for companies and accounting profits, which generally arises due to various tax incentives and artificial deductions. (Paragraph 5.20)

10.48 The tax incentive u/s 10A and 10B of the Income Tax Act must be eliminated for all taxpayers other than those engaged in manufacturing computer software. (Paragraph 5.52)

10.49 The Task Force recommends that in the case of taxpayers engaged in manufacturing computer software, the Government of India must take immediate steps to negotiate with foreign governments to enter into a comprehensive totalisation agreement leading to a single point incidence of taxes. It may be noted that a number of countries across the globes already have totalisation agreements with each other related to payment of social security and other taxes. However, in the interim, the Task Force recommends the following alternatives:-

1. Eliminate the tax exemption u/s 10A and 10B and amend Section 91 of the Income Tax Act to allow full credit for payment of foreign country's federal and state income tax. However, no refund of such foreign tax credit should be allowed;

   OR

2. Since the arrangement is transitory in nature the benefit of tax exemption u/s 10A and 10B for manufacturing of computer software only may be continued till we enter into a totalisation agreement with trading partners. However, the distribution of dividend by computer software manufacturing companies availing of deductions u/s 10A or 10B should be subjected to a dividend distribution tax of 30 per cent. Similarly, the long-term capital gains arising from transfer of equities of such companies should also be subjected to tax like long-term capital gains from any other asset. The Task Force could not arrive at unanimity on the preferred alternative amongst the above two. (Paragraph 5.53)

10.50 The general rate of depreciation for plant and machinery should be reduced to 15 per cent from the existing level of 25 per cent. The rates of depreciation for other blocks of assets must be reviewed along the same lines as in the case of plant and machinery. Consequently, the depreciation amount charged for tax purposes will be similar to those charged under the Companies Act.

(Paragraph 5.58)

10.51 The tax benefit u/s 33AC of the Income Tax Act should be abolished. (Paragraph 5.59)

10.52 The Task Force recommends the abolition of section 35 of the Income Tax Act. As a result, the revenue expenditure on scientific research will qualify for deduction u/s 37 of the Income Tax Act and capital expenditure on scientific research will be eligible for depreciation under section 32 of the Income Tax Act. Since, expenditure link weighted deduction will also be abolished, there will be no perverse incentive to shift expenditure or make false claims. (Paragraph 5.63)

10.53 In view of the fact that deduction for donations to scientific research institutions confer higher benefit to donors engaged in business in comparison to non-business donors, we recommend the rationalisation of the deduction for donation for scientific research, so as to be more equitable across taxpayers. Therefore, a tax rebate calculated at 20 per cent of the amount of donation for research (scientific, social sciences or statistical) should be allowed to all taxpayers irrespective of their source of income. (Paragraph 5.64)

10.54 With a view to aligning the provisions relating to the allowability of deduction u/s 36(1)(iii) with those of the Accounting Standard 16 issued by the Institute of Chartered Accountants of India, it is recommended that a suitable clarificatory amendment to Section 36(1)(iii) should be made to provide for the disallowance of the borrowing costs that are directly attributable to the acquisition, construction or production of a capital asset, as a revenue expenditure. Such borrowing costs will now have to be capitalized as part of the cost of the capital asset in accordance with the Accounting Standards 16 issued by the Institute of Chartered Accountants of India. Other borrowing costs should continue to be recognised as an expense in the period in which they are incurred and continue to be allowed as a deduction u/s 37(1) of the Income Tax Act. Accordingly, it is recommended that the provisions of section 36(1)(viia) of the Income Tax Act should be amended to provide that the provision for bad and doubtful debts will be restricted to the amount of provision debited to profit and loss account as audited subject to the maximum amount of provisioning permitted under the prudential guidelines issued by the Reserve Bank of India. (Paragraph 5.66 & 5.69)

10.55 Since, the objective of the provisions of section 43B is to ensure that a taxpayer does not avail of any statutory liability without actually making a payment for the same, we are of the view that these objectives would be served if the deduction for the statutory liability relating to labour are allowed in the year of payment. The complete disallowance of such payments is too harsh a punishment for delays in payment. Therefore, it is recommended that the deduction for delayed payment of statutory liability relating to labour should be allowed in the year of payment like delayed taxes and interest. (Paragraph 5.71)

10.56 The distinction between unabsorbed depreciation and unabsorbed business loss should be eliminated. In other words unabsorbed depreciation would be merged with business loss and lose its separate identity. Further, business loss would be allowed to be carried forward indefinitely. (Paragraph 5.74)

10.57 The Task Force recommends the elimination of the provisions of section 80IA and 80IB with immediate effect (and not by a sunset clause). (Paragraph 5.80)

10.58 The Task Force discussed the possible strategy for the successful implementation of the corporate tax reforms. Towards this, the Task Force recommends two alternate options for reform of corporate income tax :-

Option - I : The following measures to be introduced for the financial year 2003-04:-

(i) Reduction in corporate tax rate from the existing levels of 36.75 per cent to 30 per cent for domestic companies and to 35 per cent for foreign companies.

(ii) Exemption of dividend from taxation in the hands of the shareholders. There will also be no tax on distribution of dividends by a company.

(iii) Exemption of long-terms capital gains on listed equity.

(iv) Elimination of Minimum Alternate Tax under Section 115JB.

(v) Removal of the distinction between unabsorbed depreciation and unabsorbed business loss. In other words unabsorbed depreciation would be merged with business loss and loose its separate identity. Further, business loss would be allowed to be carried forward indefinitely.

(vi) Removal of the following deductions under Section 10 and Chapter VI A of the Income Tax Act with immediate effect and not by a sunset clause :–

(a) Elimination of Section 10A and 10B of the Income Tax Act for all tax payers other than those engaged in manufacturing computer software.

(b) In the case of taxpayers engaged in manufacturing computer software, the Government of India must take immediate steps to negotiate with foreign governments to enter into a comprehensive totalisation agreement leading to a single point incidence of taxes. However, in the interim, the Task Force recommends the following alternatives:-

1. Eliminate the tax exemption u/s 10A and 10B and amend Section 91 of the Income Tax Act to allow full credit for payment of foreign country's federal and state income tax. However, no refund of such foreign tax credit should be allowed;

OR

2. Since the arrangement is transitory in nature the benefit of tax exemption u/s 10A and 10B for manufacturing of computer software only may be continued till we enter into a totalisation agreement with trading partners.

However, the distribution of dividend by computer software manufacturing companies availing of deductions u/s 10A or 10B should be subjected to a dividend distribution tax of 30 per cent. Similarly, the long term capital gains arising from transfer of equities of such companies should also be subjected to tax like long-term capital gains from any other asset.

The Task Force could not arrive at unanimity on the preferred alternative amongst the above two.

(c) Section 80 IA in respect of profit and gains from industrial undertakings or enterprises engaged in infrastructure development or telecommunication service or development of industrial park or special economic zones or generation, transmission or distribution of power.

(d) Section 80 IB in respect of profits and gains from certain industrial undertakings other then infrastructure development undertakings (this includes backward areas also).

(e) Section 80 JJA in respect of profits and gains from business of collecting and processing of biodegradable wastes.

(f) Section 80 JJAA in respect of employment of new workman.

(g) Section 80 M in respect of inter corporate dividends.

(h) The phase out programme in respect of sections 80HHB, 80HHBA, 80HHC, 80HHD, 80HHE, 80HHF, 80-O, 80R, 80RR and 80RRA will continue.

(vii) Depreciation rates for the purposes of depreciation allowance under section 32 should be reduced to 15 per cent for the general category of plant and machinery and to appropriate lower rates for other categories of block of assets. The revised rates of depreciation will minimize the divergence between the depreciation charged to the profit and loss account in accordance with the provisions of the Companies Act and depreciation claimed for tax purposes.

(viii) Elimination of Section 33 AB relating to Tea development account.

(ix) Elimination of Section 33 AC relating to reserve for Shipping business.

(x) Elimination of Section 33 B relating to Rehabilitation allowance.

(xi) Elimination of Section 35 relating to expenditure on Scientific Research. However, donations to trusts, institutions etc. engaged in scientific research will continue to be allowed but in the form of a tax rebate like in the case of Section 80G.

(xii) Elimination of Section 35 AC relating to expenditure on eligible projects. However, expenditure on projects already approved will continue to enjoy tax benefit in the form of rebate at the rate of 20 per cent.

(xiii) Elimination of Section 35 CCA relating to expenditure by way of payment to associations and institutions for carrying out rural development programmes.

(xiv) Elimination of Section 36(1)(iii) in respect of interest on borrowed capital.

(xv) The provision for bad and doubtful debts allowable under Section 36(1)(viia) of the Income Tax Act will henceforth be restricted to the amount of provision debited to profit and loss account as audited subject to the maximum amount of provisioning permitted under the prudential guidelines issued by the Reserve Bank of India.

Option - II : The package of measures along with their phased implementation, to be introduced through the Finance Bill 2003, in the following manner:–

(i) Reduction in corporate tax rate from the existing levels of 36.75 per cent to 30 per cent for domestic companies and to 35 per cent for foreign companies over a period of three years. The rates for domestic companies will be 34 per cent in financial year 2003-04, 32 per cent in 2004-05 and 30 per cent in 2005-06. The rates for foreign companies will be 38.50 per cent in financial year 2003-04, 37 per cent in 2004-05 and 35 per cent in 2005-06.

(ii) No tax on dividend in the hands of the shareholders.

(iii) No tax on long terms capital gains on listed equity.

(iv) Elimination of Minimum Alternate Tax under Section 115JB.

(v) Removal of the distinction between unabsorbed depreciation and unabsorbed business loss. In other words unabsorbed depreciation would be merged with business loss and loose its separate identity. Further, business loss would be allowed to be carried forward indefinitely.

(vi) Levy of a distribution tax on dividends at the rate of 15 per cent for dividends distributed in 2003-04, 7.5 per cent in 2004-05 and Nil in 2005-06.

(vii) Removal / Phasing out of the following deductions under Section 10 and Chapter VI A of the Income Tax Act with immediate effect and not by a sunset clause :–

(a) Phasing out of the provisions of Section 10A and 10B of the Income Tax Act. over a period of 3 years i.e. the deduction will be reduced to 60 per cent of the profits in 2003-04, to 30 per cent of the profits in 2004-05 and NIL in 2005-06.

(b) Phasing out of Section 80 IA in respect of profit and gains from industrial undertakings or enterprises engaged in infrastructure development or telecommunication service or development of industrial park or special economic zones or generation, transmission or distribution of power, over a period of 3 years i.e. the deduction will be reduced to two-third of the profits in 2003-04, to one-third of the profits in 2004-05 and NIL in 2005-06.

(c) Phasing out of Section 80 IB in respect of profits and gains from certain industrial undertakings other then infrastructure development undertakings (this includes backward areas also), over a period of 3 years i.e. the deduction will be reduced to two-third of the profits in 2003-04, to one-third of the profits in 2004-05 and NIL in 2005-06.

(d) Section 80 JJA in respect of profits and gains from business of collecting and processing of biodegradable wastes.

(e) Section 80 JJAA in respect of employment of new workman.

(f) Section 80 M in respect of inter corporate dividends

(g) The phase out programme in respect of sections 80HHB, 80HHBA, 80HHC, 80HHD, 80HHE, 80HHF, 80-O, 80R, 80RR and 80RRA will continue.

(viii) Depreciation allowance under section 32 will be restricted to the allowance, charged to the profit and loss account in accordance with the provisions of the Companies Act.

(ix) Elimination of Section 33 AB relating to Tea development account will be eliminated.

(x) Elimination of Section 33 AC relating to reserve for Shipping business.

(xi) Elimination of Section 33 B relating to Rehabilitation allowance.

(xii) Elimination of Section 35 relating to expenditure on Scientific Research. However, donations to trusts, institutions etc. engaged in scientific research will continue to be allowed but in the form of a tax rebate like in the case of Section 80G.

(xiii) Elimination of Section 35 AC relating to expenditure on eligible projects. However, expenditure on projects already approved will continue to enjoy tax benefit in the form of rebate at the rate of 20 per cent.

(xiv) Elimination of Section 35 CCA relating to expenditure by way of payment to associations and institutions for carrying out rural development programmes.

(xv) Elimination of Section 36(iii) in respect of interest on borrowed capital.

(xvi) The provison for bad and doubtful debts allowable under Section 36(1)(viia) of the Income Tax Act will henceforth be restricted to the amount of provision debited to profit and loss account as audited subject to the maximum amount of provisioning permitted under the prudential guidelines issued by the Reserve Bank of India.

The Task Force deliberated upon the two packages. It was unanimously agreed that it is rather difficult for any government to give a credible ex-ante time commitment. Such commitments are rarely sustainable. Past experience shows that while tax rates were reduced, successive governments failed to implement the phased withdrawal of incentives. As a result, we have reached a point where the corporate tax rates are close to their resting points and yet the statute continues to be riddled with exemptions and deductions. Any attempt to sequence the reduction in the corporate taxes and the withdrawal of exemptions and deductions could lead to disastrous impact on revenue flows. The two must necessarily be implemented simultaneously. Phasing also gives rise to uncertainty and a 'hope' that reforms could be reversed. In addition, in the present state of international economy and the decline in the growth momentum of the domestic economy, implementation in 'one go' will be a powerful counter cyclical demand push to the domestic economy particularly given the projected policy initiatives on the indirect taxes front. Therefore, the Task Force unanimously recommends Option - I for implementation. (Paragraph 5.93)

Taxation of Capital Gains

10.59 The concessional treatment of long-term capital gains through a reduced scheduler rate of tax must be abolished. In other words, the long-term capital gains would be aggregated with other incomes and subjected to taxation at the normal rates. Further, since we have recommended the abolition of various saving incentives, we do not consider necessary to allow any exemption for roll over of long-term capital gains. (Paragraph 6.3)

10.60 Given the public nature of the project, it is necessary to maintain the flow of funds. Therefore, we recommend that long-term capital gains should continue to be exempt if invested in a house or in the bonds of National Highway Authority of India until completion of the Golden Quadrilateral and the North-South & East-West corridors. (Paragraph 6.3)

10.61 We have also recommended that while short-term capital gains on equity should continue to be taxed, the long-term capital gains on equity should be eliminated. However, recognising the possibility of abuse by transferring real assets through the corporate vehicle, we also recommend that the exemption on long-term capital gain on equity should be restricted to listed securities as defined in section 112 of the Income Tax Act. (Paragraph 6.7)

Treatment of Other Entities

10.62 Where there is a conflict between simplicity of equity, the Task Force has a preference for simplicity. Complexity is, inherently, regressive and non-transparent. Therefore, what may appear to be equitable could, in effect, be inequitable. In the light of the problems associated with the existing system of taxation of investment fund and the package for corporate tax reform, we recommend the following:–

(i) The income of the mutual fund derived from short-term capital gains and interest should be taxed at a flat rate in the hands of the mutual fund.

(ii) Since most investors in units are generally smaller taxpayers, we recommend that the rate of tax should be the minimum marginal rate of personal income tax i.e. 20 per cent.

(iii) With a view to overcoming double taxation, the dividends received by the unit holders should be fully exempted since the distributable surplus would have suffered the full burden of the tax.

(iv) The short-term capital gain arising to the investor from sale of units of investment funds should be taxed at his level at the personal marginal rate of tax.

(v) The long-term capital gain arising to the investor from sale of units of mutual fund should be exempt from income tax.

(vi) The tax treatment of mutual funds and their investors should also be extended to venture capital funds, private equity funds and hedge funds. However, the tax rate for these funds should be 30 per cent since their investors are likely to be those in the highest tax slab.

(vii) All funds must necessarily obtain the PAN of the investor and the Databases about every payment made by the fund manager back to the investor, tagged with PAN, should be furnished to the tax authorities as a information return.

(Paragraph 7.13)

10.63 At present, the profits of a partnership firm are subjected to tax at the same rate of tax applicable to a domestic company. In view of our recommendations, for corporate tax reform, we recommend that the rate of tax for partnership firms should be reduced to the same level as corporate rate of tax.

(Paragraph 7.14)

10.64 The tax benefit for donations to charitable trusts must take the form of tax rebate at the minimum marginal rate of tax of 20 per cent. Further, we also recommend that there should be no quantitative ceiling either in absolute terms or as a fraction of the gross income as is presently provided under Section 80G.

(Paragraph 7.17)

10.65 Therefore, the Task Force recommends that the exemptions under Section 10(21), 10(23B) and 10(23C)(iiiab) to (via), 10(29A) should be merged with Section 11 to 13A of the Income Tax Act. We also recommend that:-

(i) The present practice of exempting a class of Charitable trust and Institutions through notifications should be abolished. However, the requirement to file a return of income by such trust and institutions as proof of fulfilling the various conditions stipulated u/s 10(23C), should continue.

(ii) Returns to be identified for scrutiny/audit only through a computerised risk assessment system.

(iii) Where a return is identified for scrutiny and the assessing officer is of the opinion that the activities of the trust are not charitable in nature, such a case will be referred to a rating agency from amongst the panel drawn up by the C&AG. An "A+" rating for the trust will mean that it is indeed a charitable trust. An "A" rating for the trust will mean that it will enjoy exemption during the current year and will be subjected to review again in the following year. A "B" rating for the trust will disqualify it from any tax exemption. The new procedure should be introduced from 01-04-2004 and the interregnum should be utilized to work out the details and also allowing the trust to adapt to the new procedures.

(iv) Since a large number of provisions in the Income Tax Act are regulatory in nature, we also recommend the creation of a National Charities Board to assist the government in regulating and promoting charities on the lines of the National Charities Commission, U.K. Since, a number of States in India already have Charity Commissioners, the proposed Board may have to be advisory.

(v) The Income Tax Department should reimburse to trusts, the fees payable to the rating agency. (Paragraph 7.18)

10.66 We recommend the elimination of Section 80P of the Income Tax Act. However, the existing exemption limit of Rs. 10,000/- prescribed as part of the rate schedule, should be increased to Rs. 1,00,000/- and the revised income tax rate schedule for cooperatives should be the same as recommended for personal income tax. (Paragraph 7.21)

10.67 The manpower strength of FTD should be immediately augmented so as to assign one team each for America, Europe, South East Asia and Australia, and Rest of the World. (Paragraph 7.23)

10.68 We understand that, as recommended by us in our

Consultation Paper, the CBDT has already set up a working group headed by the Director General of Income Tax (International Taxation) and comprising of representatives also from trade and industry to examine the various issues relating to taxation of non-resident individual and foreign companies. We also understand that the working group is expected to submit its report by the end of December. We suggest that the recommendations should be processed during the forthcoming budget exercise. (Paragraph 7.23)

Other Taxes

10.69 The Task Force recommends the abolition of wealth tax. (Paragraph 8.4)

10.70 The present tax on expenditure in hotels is in the nature of a consumption tax. It was introduced as a separate tax in the absence of a tax on services. Since tax on services has since been introduced, it is only appropriate that this levy is merged with service tax. We recommend accordingly. (Paragraph 8.6)

Impact of Recommendation

10.71 Individual Taxpayers of all categories and in every income group benefit substantially from the package of recommendation. (Paragraph 9.8)

10.72 Overall, the recommendations are revenue neutral at the existing level of compliance. To the extent the new simplified and liberalised tax regime will induce compliance, the revenue gains are likely to be substantially higher and it will enhance buoyancy by widening the personal and corporate income tax bases. (Paragraph 9.14)

10.73 The recommendations for eliminating the exemptions, the extensive use of technology and privatization of non-core activities of the tax administration will result is sharp reduction in transaction cost. A 10 per cent reduction in transaction cost for personal income tax would help taxpayers to save an estimated Rs. 4,000 crores. Such reduction in transaction cost is progressive. (Paragraph 9.17)

Annexure 'A'

F.No.153/191/2002-TPL

Government of India
Ministry of Finance & Company Affairs
Department of Revenue
Central Board of Direct Taxes

New Delhi, the 6th September, 2002

ORDER

Subject: Task Force on Direct Taxes — Constitution regarding.

Ministry of Finance and Company Affairs has decided to set up a Task Force on Direct Taxes. The objective is to rationalize and simplify the Direct Tax Laws and re-design procedures to bring them at par with best international practices so as to encourage voluntary compliance and reduce compliance cost. Accordingly, the Task Force on Direct Taxes is constituted as under:

1.	Dr. V.L. Kelkar, Advisor to the Minister of Finance and Company Affairs	Chairman
2.	Dr. Ashok Lahiri, Director, NIPFP, New Delhi	Member*
3.	Shri S.N.L. Agarwala, Advocate and former Chief Commissioner of Income-tax, Ahmedabad	Member
4.	Shri Arvind Sonde, Advocate, Mumbai	Member
5.	Dr. Omkar Goswami, Chief Economist, Confederation of Indian Industries, New Delhi	Member
6.	Dr. Urjit Patel, Executive Vice-President, IDFC Ltd., Mumbai	Member
7.	Shri S. Ananthanaryanan, Executive Director, AMCO Batteries Ltd., Bangalore	Member
8.	Shri Dipankar Chatterji, Chartered Accountant, Kolkata	Member
9.	Shri T.V. Mohandas Pai, Chief Financial Officer, Infosys Technologies Ltd., Bangalore	Member
10.	Shri P.C. Parmar, Chartered Accountant, Pune	Member
11.	Shri A.J. Majumdar, Joint Secretary, CBDT, Department of Revenue	Member-Secretary

* Dr. Ashok Lahiri resigned from the Task Force on 11.11.2002 upon his taking over the post of Chief Economic Advisor in the Ministry of Finance and Company Affairs.

Tax Policy and Legislation (Unit-II), Central Board of Direct Taxes, Department of Revenue will serve as the Secretariat of the Task Force.

2. The terms of Reference of the Task Force are as follows:

(i) Rationalisation and simplification of the direct taxes with a view to minimizing exemptions, removing anomalies and improving equity.

(ii) Improvement in tax-payer services so as to reduce compliance cost, impart transparency and facilitate voluntary compliance.

(iii) Re-designing procedures for strengthening enforcement so as to improve compliance of direct tax laws.

(iv) Any other matter related to the above points.

3. The terms and conditions of the Task Force will be as follows:

(a) The Task Force should furnish to the Government a Draft Consultation Paper containing its recommendations by 31.10.2002. The same will be made available to the public for feedback and comments by 07.11.2002, which shall be considered by the Task Force and a Final Report submitted to Government by 15.12.2002.

(b) The Task Force is empowered to interact with departmental officials, trade interests and individuals and visit field formations as it may choose.

(c) The non-official Task Force members would be entitled to TA/DA as per norms.

(Deepika Mittal)

Under Secretary to the Government of India

To

Chairman and Memebrs of Task Force

Copy to:

1. Director (Finance Minister's Office)
2. PS to Advisor to F.M. & CA
3. PS to MOS (Revenue)
4. PS to MOS (Expenditure, Banking & Insurance)
5. Sr. PPS to Finance Secretary
6. PPS to Secretary (Revenue)
7. PPS to Secretary (Expenditure)
8. PPS to Secretary (Banking & Insurance)
9. PPS to Chief Economic Advisor
10. PPS to Chairman, CBDT
11. PPS to Chairman, CBEC
12. PS to Members, CBDT
13. Financial Adviser, Ministry of Finance & Company Affairs
14. All Directors General/Chief Commissioners of Income-tax

(Deepika Mittal)

Under Secretary to the Government of India

Report of the Task Force on Indirect Taxes

2002

Report of the Task Force on Indirect Taxes

CONTENTS

Preface *258*

Executive Summary *261*

Chapter 1 – Reactions to Consultation Paper : Our Response **303**

Chapter 2 – Macro-perspective and Approach to Reforms **311**

Macro-perspective

Approach to reforms

Chapter 3 – Customs Procedures and Trade Facilitation : Basic Reforms **321**

Overview of Procedures

Trust Based Systems (TBS) : Universal Green Channel

Other measures for improved Customs Administration

Custom House Agents (CHAs)

Chapter 4 – Central Excise Procedural Simplification **334**

Introduction

Manufacture

Assessment

Cenvat

Exports

Manner of payment of duty

Budget Day restrictions

Removal of goods for job-work

Collection of information from tax payers

Dispute resolution
Filing of Returns
Voluntary filing of documents by tax payers
Arrest
Tax Clinics for Small Scale Sector manufacturers

Chapter 5 – Export Promotion 361
Introduction
Viable export strategy
SEZ and EOU schemes
Drawback scheme
Duty Entitlement Pass Book (DEPB) scheme
Coordination between DGFT and Customs

Chapter 6 – Automation of Indirect Tax Systems and Procedures 379
Introduction
Automation driven tax administration

Chapter 7 – Improving Indirect Tax Administration 384
Directorate of Anti-dumping and Safeguards duties
Advance Ruling
Prosecution of individuals
Adjudication and Appeal
Strengthening Internal Audit
Trade facilitation
C.B.E.C. Administration
Human Resource Development and training

Chapter 8 – Revenue Augmentation, Tax Levies and Rates 406
Tax to GDP ratio
Customs Tariff and Exemptions
Central Excise Tariff and Exemptions
Central Excise duty structure for Petroleum sector
Central Excise duty structure for Textile sector
Central Excise duty exemptions
Small Scale Sector duty exemption

Location based exemptions
Relevant date of Notification
Zero rating of exports

Chapter 9 – Value Added Tax **456**
Introduction
Preparedness for State VAT
Uniformity of definitions
Compensation to States
VAT to unify all local taxes
VAT and AED
Credit on inter-state transactions
Stability and continuity of the VAT regime

Chapter 10– Service Tax **463**
Introduction
Comprehensive Service Tax
Extension of duty credit scheme to service sector
Rate of Service Tax
Threshold limit of exemption
Separate enactment for Service Tax
Classification of services
Dispute resolution
Non-recovery of Service Tax in certain situations
Service Tax as the first E-tax

Customs Duty Rate Structure – **Annexure 'A'** **471**
Central Excise Duty Rate Structure – **Annexure 'B'** **499**
Order Constituting Task Force – **Annexure 'C'** **521**

Preface

On 25th October, 2002, as mandated, the Task Force presented the Consultation Paper to the Government with a request that the same may be made available to the public at large for a discussion on the proposals contained therein. The response has been overwhelming. An intense public debate was generated and Trade and Industry Associations, professionals and individuals from all walks of life contributed by sending hundreds of e-mails and letters and participating in discussions in the media. On its part, the Task Force interacted with a large number of Trade and Industry Associations and individuals at Pune, Ludhiana, Chennai, Bangalore, Mumbai and Delhi. Needless to state the process reinforced the view that the stakeholders in the fiscal policy are keen to be a part of the decision making process and there has been universal appreciation of the Finance Minister for bringing transparency in the formulation of tax policies.

The Task Force has been mandated to make suggestions to bring our indirect tax system at par with the best international practices. An important element of the terms of reference related to taking advantage of information technology and automation for a user friendly and transparent tax administration. The bottom line was to facilitate the tax payers, improve compliance, promote growth, reduce transaction costs and thus to increase tax to GDP ratio. The recommendations contained in the Report can broadly be divided into three categories. First are those relating to tax administration and its reform, second deal with automation and computerisation of the business processes and the third set of recommendations concern the tax structure and rates. When implemented as a package the Task Force is convinced that these would combine to achieve the desired objectives.

While firming up the recommendations far greater debate was generated in respect of the suggested tariff rates than on the measures for improving quality of tax administration including increased automation. Therefore, it need to be re-emphasised that expected results would be achieved by a holistic approach and not by attention to only one aspect of this Report viz. relating to the tariff. As mentioned in the Consultation Paper, the potential benefits to the economy from the implementation of the package of recommendations can be considerable, with the reduction in the transaction costs itself estimated at 50 per cent and the potential gains to the economy in the range of Rs. 4000-5000 crores annually. The gains would reflect in increased exports, greater compliance leading to higher revenues and increase in tax to GDP ratio thus reinforcing the fiscal consolidation. The Task Force reiterates the importance of these gains.

The consultation process identified a number of areas where a re-look will be helpful for improving the proposals. The Task Force has modified the proposals while maintaining the thrust of the approach to the systemic reforms. It is a matter of satisfaction that as per the response received there was near unanimity in regard to the majority of the proposals contained in the Consultation Paper. However, what came to the forefront was a pronounced sense of urgency to act quickly and effectively to bring our indirect tax system at par with the international best practices. This reinforced the view of the Task Force that half-measures would not do and there is a need to provide a 'big push' to the systemic reforms. The bottom line is that immediate time bound investment in information technology, including automation, with human resource development and training and introduction of the simplified tax structure would improve all-round performance in exports as well as lead to higher revenue mobilization and the overall fiscal well being of the country. Thus, it is hoped that this Report serves as an input for the Budget 2003-04, though some recommendations can be considered for implementation even earlier.

The Task Force is grateful for the help rendered in its deliberations by Shri S. Mukhopadhyay, former Member, C.B.E.C., Dr. M. Govinda Rao, Director, Institute of Social and Economic Change, Bangalore, Shri Anupam Dasgupta, Additional Secretary, Department of Revenue, Shri T.R. Rustagi, Chief Commissioner, C.B.E.C. and Shri Arbind Modi, O.S.D. to the Chairman of the Task Force. The Task Force also wants to give a special thanks to Shri Suresh Kumar, T.O., TRU and Shri S. Ravi, P.P.S to the Chairman of Task Force for their dedicated contribution to its work. A number of organizations, associations and individuals also assisted the Task Force through comments and constructive suggestions. While the response has been of such magnitude that it is simply not possible to individually mention the names of all who contributed, the Task Force would like to sincerely thank all of them.

The Task Force would like to express our gratitude to Chairman and Members of the Central Board of Excise and Customs and officers of the Department of Revenue for their full support and cooperation. The Task Force is grateful to the Ministries and Departments of the Government which commented on the proposals and made valuable suggestions which are now a part of this Report.

In conclusion, the Task Force expresses its sincere thanks to Ministry of Finance and Company Affairs for effectively involving all concerned including the common citizen in tax administration and policy through its medium. Truly, this was a path breaking exercise in the democratization of fiscal policy formulation.

Sd/-
Vijay Kelkar
Chairman of the Task Force on Indirect Taxes

Sd/- Prof. Jayanta Roy Member Task Force	Sd/- K.S. Suresh Member Task Force
Sd/- Gautam Ray Member Task Force	Sd/- Sunil Kant Munjal Member Task Force
Sd/- Nihal Kothari Member Task Force	Sd/- Deepak Puri Member Task Force
Sd/- Sanjay Bhatia Member Task Force	Sd/- Y.P. Suri Member Task Force
Sd/- K.S. Ravi Shankar Member Task Force	Sd/- S.M. Bhatnagar Member-Secretary

New Delhi, 26 December, 2002

Executive Summary of Recommendations

1. Reactions to Consultation Paper : Our Response

By and large the proposals contained in the Consultation Paper were appreciated. However, there was also constructive criticism in respect of some proposals, particularly relating to tax rates of some items. Suggestions for improvement of some other proposals were also received. This Report takes into account all responses received. An endeavour has been made to now make recommendations based on consensus, which reflect the concerns and aspirations of all concerned, while adhering to certain principles considered critical for having an indirect tax system and administration at par with the dynamic economies of the world. What follows in this Report are recommendations which, in the view of the Task Force, combine together to simplify and rationalise the tax system, effectively reduce transaction costs, encourage voluntary compliance and, in short, bring our indirect tax system and administration at par, if not better, than the best international practices.

2. Macro-Perspective and Approach to Reforms

Our economy is at a critical juncture in its efforts to accelerate growth and employment in order to rapidly reduce poverty. Towards this, one of the key components of the strategy will have to be to exploit the opportunities afforded by more rapid globalization. While our economy has succeeded in maintaining one of the highest GDP growth rates in the world in the last decade with very low inflation, there are several areas where immediate improvements are required to sustain the growth momentum. The principal concerns are the deteriorating public finances, with the consolidated public sector deficit estimated to be over 11 percent of GDP, decline in investment dynamism and relatively weak performance of exports and FDI, the two pillars of trade and financial sector integration. The most direct way to raise tax to GDP ratio is to remove most of the plethora of exemptions granted on import and excise taxes for a variety of reasons, mostly for non economic considerations; widen the net by expanding the service tax base; and to improve taxpayers compliance. To boost exports and FDI, the government must sharply reduce the transaction costs associated with trade and doing business with India. Apart from maintaining a realistic marketdriven exchange rate, and liberalization of imports, this will involve changes in policies and procedures involving improvements in trade logistics to allow exporters to compete in today's time-dependent markets. This will require a change in mindset away from controls rigidly administered, towards a more liberal policy environment in line with international standards. Trade facilitation revolves around the reduction of all the transaction costs associated with the enforcement of legislation, regulation, and administration of trade policies.

With the proposed reforms, it is estimated that the reduction in the transaction costs could be as much as 50%, the potential gains to the economy would be Rs. 4000-5000 crores per annum i.e. this large benefit would accrue to the economy every year. In a dynamic sense, in terms of exports foregone on account of high transaction costs, the reduction in costs will be several times higher. Reducing transaction costs and costs of doing business is important not only for boosting exports and FDI but even for creating an appropriate framework for vibrant domestic business.

It is the view of the Task Force that if the indirect tax administration frames its laws and procedures in adherence to the principles enunciated viz. Trust, Best International Practices, Simplicity, Transparency, Stability and Service coupled with the use of the full potential of information technology the net result would be beneficial to the trade, industry and the Government. There would be improved tax to GDP ratio through enhanced voluntary compliance at reduced costs, and less disputes and litigation. Also the confidence of the tax payer in the administration would be restored. It is the expectation that the individual recommendations would, when implemented, combine to change the face of the indirect tax administration in the country.

3. Customs Procedures and Trade Facilitation : Basic Reforms

The role of customs is both of a facilitator and a regulator. Whereas it must facilitate the honest importer and exporter it has also to ensure the laws of the country are applied strictly. Therefore, there has to be a very fine balancing. Taking into account all factors it is the view that the bottom line in regard to customs procedures is that these must be based upon trust, which presupposes absence of selectivity. Modern best practice calls for a systems approach that relies on self-compliance (through the maintenance of business records by tax payers), risk analysis and management (development of profiles of risky transactions), and supported by periodic post audits of records. This approach reduces delays for legitimate transactions while allowing full scrutiny of high-risk transactions. In this background, systemic changes are recommended.

3.1 Trust Based System (TBS) : Universal Green Channel

Customs clearance procedures should be based upon trust and be uniformly applied to all importers and exporters and all goods.

EDI network should be expanded to all ports/airports and should include all processes in the automation programme by 1st January 2004. In this direction, one major port and one airport should be made fully EDI operational by 1st April 2003.

The verification of declaration through pre-clearances examination, where necessary, should be based upon Risk Assessment techniques.

There should be increased use of post clearance audit

A system of self-assessment of Bill of Entry by the importer should be introduced.

Release of imported goods should be allowed on minimum documentation for certain importers of good track record of compliance.

Enhanced Systems Appraisal should be progressively extended

and compliance would be ensured through Risk Management techniques.

Release of goods should be allowed in offence cases provided the goods are not liable to absolute confiscation.

Issue of amendments to Bill of Entry should be allowed settled at the service centre itself.

On-line filing of electronic declarations on internet etc. should be encouraged.

The custodians (IAAI/Port Trust Authorities etc.) should encourage establishment of warehouses by shipping airlines/ airlines/couriers/freight forwarders and consolidators within the port/airport for reducing dwell time.

It should be provided that a complete Import General Manifest (IGM) with house level details is filed with the Customs before the arrival of the vessel/aircraft; the carrier/ steamer agents should file the IGM at Master level and the consol/ forwarding/ break-bulk agents should file the House level details; and the carrier/ steamer agents shall alone be responsible for correct and proper filing of complete IGM (including House level details) with the Customs.

A High level Inter-Ministerial Committee may be set up under the Chairmanship of Chairman, CBEC to resolve inter-agency issues to ensure a steady progress of clearance of import and export goods with reference to international norms.

A Permanent Trade Facilitation Committee should be constituted at each Port/airport/ICD/CFS comprising senior representatives of all agencies including Custom House Agents (CHAs) under the chairmanship of the Commissioner of Customs.

Customs should lay down a time limit within which an import or an export document shall be processed.

Customs should rely increasingly upon Pre-shipment inspections.

[Chapter 3 : Paragraph 2]

3.2 Other measures for improved Customs administration

The Intelligence, Investigation and Audit Sections of the

Custom House may be strengthened.

It is recommended that the instructions on the functioning of the Special Valuation Branch should be reviewed to provide for time bound finalization of cases in practice. Further, pre-deposit of duty should be dispensed with.

There should be sharing of Merchant overtime fees for activities done in Customs area.

Export valuation rules should be framed for export promotion schemes.

Customs should allow abandonment of warehoused goods.

Customs duty payment may be through cheques.

The scope of confiscation provisions in respect of export goods should be expanded to include non-dutiable goods as well as goods not covered under Drawback scheme.

It should be provided that Export Obligation Discharge Certificate issued by DGFT is accepted by customs without delay.

Customs officers may be empowered to enforce IPR by a suitable amendment to the Trade and Merchandise Marks Act and the Copyrights Act.

[Chapter 3 : Paragraph 3]

3.3 Custom House Agents (CHAs)

CHAs should be licensed through an All India entrance examination to be conducted by Directorate General of Inspection, C.B.E.C. once a year at Delhi and at its Zonal Units for licensing of CHAs.

CHAs once licensed should be allowed to operate at any Custom House/Port/Inland Container Depot anywhere in the country subject to simple registration of the business premises with the jurisdictional Commissioner of Customs.

Once a CHA licence is issued it should be valid for all time unless the CHA comes to adverse notice of Customs on account of misconduct, delay, etc. for which penal provisions, including suspension/revocation of Licence may be applicable.

Rates for CHA work should be determined by market forces, which will induce a healthy competition amongst CHAs resulting in competitive rates and better service and accountability towards the clients.

There should be a review of the technical qualifications of the CHAs to include knowledge of computer, Prevention of Corruption Act, etc.

[Chapter 3 : Paragraph 4.1]

4. Central Excise Procedural Simplification

Being the single largest contributor to the tax revenues of the Government, central excise revenues and administration have a critical role in the Indian economy. Naturally, any set back or slow down in central excise revenue mobilization adversely impacts economic planning. Therefore, it is important to devise a suitable tax administration which facilitates voluntary compliance by the tax payer and leads to the collection of revenue at minimum cost. The steps taken so far have not materially altered the general perception that the central excise administration is not tax payer friendly and the systems and procedures are even now far too complex. Therefore, much more need to be done. Importantly, to make a visible impact it is necessary to make fundamental changes without further loss of time. Accordingly, the recommendations are aimed at comprehensively changing the essence of central excise administration with the twin objective of tax payer facilitation and encouraging compliance for increased revenue.

4.1 Manufacture

It is recommended that through suitable legislative changes, the levy of central excise should be progressively based upon value addition to be applied only to the processing stage (of manufactured goods) while ensuring that the other areas of value addition not relating to the processing activity (such as Sales Tax) is not entered into and possibility of double taxation is avoided.

[Chapter 4 : Paragraph 2.1.5]

It is recommended that the said provision should not be used routinely. Moreover, a suitable amendment is necessary so that it is applied prospectively.

[Chapter 4 : Paragraph 2.2.3]

In order to prevent any misuse of the MRP provisions, it is recommended that the wherever MRP based levy is applied on an item, the act of repacking, re-labelling and putting the item into unit container for retail sale may be deemed to be amounting to manufacture.

[Chapter 4 : Paragraph 2.3.2]

4.2 Assessment

It is recommended that the officers should be make responsible for assessments of ER 1 returns, and for this purpose clear cut instructions should be issued. Some monetary limit may be fixed for confirmation of assessment by each level of Central Excise officer upto Additional Commissioner.

[Chapter 4 : Paragraph 3.1.4]

4.3 Valuation

Guidelines on determination of cost of production should be issued at the earliest, and till such time all disputes be kept pending.

[Chapter 4 : Paragraph 3.3.3]

The present stipulation of valuing at 115% of cost of production when the goods are removed to sister units should be brought down to 105%. Moreover, there should be a moratorium on this figure, so that there is certainty in taxation.

[Chapter 4 : Paragraph 3.4.2]

The recommendations as regards the MRP based levy are that the system of MRP based valuation may be expanded; Explanation 1 to Section 4A should be amended to delete reference to the term "sole consideration" and it should only be provided that there is no additional flow back to the manufacturer over and above his selling price; and for transparency in mechanism of fixing abatement C.B.E.C. is advised to consider setting up an advisory Committee (including representatives of Chambers of Trade and Industry Associations) on the subject.

[Chapter 4 : Paragraph 3.5.4]

4.4 Cenvat

The Cenvat Credit Rules, 2002 should be amended to abolish the distinction between capital goods and inputs and allow credit on all inputs brought into the factory except for those figuring in a small negative list, such as office furniture, motor vehicles, MS, HSD, etc.

[Chapter 4 : Paragraph 4.1.4]

It is recommended that the Cenvat Credit Rules, 2002 should be amended to allow with effect from 1.4.2004 full credit of the duty paid on the capital goods immediately on receipt, as in the case of inputs. As an interim measure, 75% of the credit may be so allowed from 1.4.2003.

[Chapter 4 : Paragraph 4.2.3]

Suitable provision should allow Deputy/Assistant Commissioner to condone technical lapses/ infirmities while allowing Cenvat credit.

[Chapter 4 : Paragraph 4.3.2]

An explanation may be inserted in rule 16 to the effect that the amount paid on removal of returned goods can be taken as Cenvat credit in the hands of the recipients.

[Chapter 4 : Paragraph 4.4.2]

A specific provision may be introduced to charge duty on the dismantled capital goods when removed from the factory.

[Chapter 4 : Paragraph 4.5.2]

Cenvat credit should not be allowed on deemed credit basis.

[Chapter 4 : Paragraph 4.6.3]

Rule 12 of the Cenvat Credit Rules, 2002 should be amended to provide for recovery of Cenvat credit erroneously refunded.

[Chapter 4 : Paragraph 4.7.3]

Cenvat inputs maybe allowed to be stored outside the factory in an identified place of storage subject to procedural safeguards for due accountal of the inputs.

[Chapter 4 : Paragraph 4.8.2]

4.5 Exports

It is recommended that sealing of export consignments by Central Excise officers should be replaced by self-sealing by the exporter. This should be granted as a matter of right and not on case to case basis.

[Chapter 4 : Paragraph 5.1.3]

The following recommendations are made to improve the system of grant of rebate :

(i) The work of grant of rebate should be centralized at the Custom House itself. In the alternative, an EDI link can be provided between the Customs House and the Maritime Commissioner. This measure is in addition to the grant of rebate by the Deputy/Assistant Commissioner of Central Excise having jurisdiction over the factory of the manufacturer or warehouse, as at present.

(ii) Notification No. 40/2001 CE (N.T.), dated 26.06.2001 should be amended to provide grant of full rebate in respect of mineral oil products falling under chapter 27 of the schedule to the Central Excise Act, 1985, which are exported as stores for consumption on board an aircraft on foreign run.

[Chapter 4 : Paragraph 5.2.5]

In order to reduce contact points and speed up the disbursal of the rebate/refund the same should be directly credited to the tax payer's own bank account.

[Chapter 4 : Paragraph 5.3.2]

4.6 Manner of payment of duty

Fortnightly payment of duty may be replaced by monthly payment.

[Chapter 4 : Paragraph 6.1.2]

The date of payment of central excise duty may be prescribed as the date of presentation of the cheque to the Bank subject to its realization.

[Chapter 4 : Paragraph 6.2.2]

It is recommended that in case of default in payment of duty :

(i) The provision of withdrawing the facility of payment of duty in installments in case of default should be revoked.

(ii) There should be automatic charge of interest and penalty in the event duty is not paid on time.

(iii) In the event it is decided to retain the provision of withdrawing the facility the assessee should be allowed to pay duty during this period through Cenvat credit.

[Chapter 4 : Paragraph 6.3.5]

4.7 Budget Day restrictions

The Budget Day restrictions are out of tune in present day world and should be removed.

[Chapter 4 : Paragraph 7.3]

4.8 Removal of goods for job-work

There should be a provision for allowing the movement of dutiable goods without payment of duty to job worker even in situations when the principal manufacturer is not working under Cenvat Scheme.

[Chapter 4 : Paragraph 8.2]

4.9 Collection of information from tax payer

Fortnightly statement of revenue paid, which is presently being collected from tax payers, may be discontinued. Further, as a policy, no information should normally be asked for (from departmental officers or industry) unless it is being obtained in the prescribed returns from the tax payer.

[Chapter 4 : Paragraph 9.2]

4.10 Dispute resolution

It is recommended that :

(i) Scope of Section 11A(2)(B), i.e. non-issue of SCN to be expanded to include cases of non-payment detected by Audit/ Department.

(ii) Section 11A should be amended to provide for the issue of a Show Cause Notice which automatically collapses if the tax payer voluntarily pays the duty and interest and 25% penalty within a period of 30 days of the issue of the notice. This would apply to cases involving fraud, suppression etc. In such cases the Notice should also mention in its preamble that there would also be no prosecution proceedings. The provision regarding collapse of the Show Cause Notice should apply to 'other' cases but without the requirement of payment of 25% penalty.

[Chapter 4 : Paragraph 10.3]

4.11 Filing of Returns

It is recommended that :

(i) Date of filing return may be shifted to the 15th of the close of the month/quarter, as the case may be, for all tax payers i.e. including those in the SSI sector. However, the large units would furnish on-line or otherwise, by the 6th of each month, the information of total duty paid.

(ii) As a first step towards on-line filing of returns, the monthly/quarterly submission of TR6 challans may be discontinued and steps should be taken to eventually allow on-line filing of returns. The details of TR 6 Challans will be mentioned in the returns.

[Chapter 4 : Paragraph 11.3]

4.12 Voluntary filing of documents by tax payers

It is recommended that it must be made binding on the field officials to accept documents and give an acknowledgement in writing, if needed, in order to safeguard tax payers interest.

[Chapter 4 : Paragraph 12.2]

4.14 Arrest

The arrest in central excise cases, if warranted, should be made with the sanction of a Magistrate. This would require suitable amendment to the Central Excise Act, 1944.

[Chapter 4 : Paragraph 13.3]

4.15 Tax Clinics for Small Scale Sector Manufacturers

It is recommended that by 1st April 2003 each Central Excise Commissionerate should establish one Tax Clinic for the Small Scale Sector, under the charge of Deputy/Assistant Commissioner to guide small scale manufacturers. This Cell should closely coordinate with the Small Scale Manufacturers Associations.

[Chapter 4 : Paragraph 14.2]

5. Export Promotion

Sustained export growth is crucial for maintaining and accelerating the GDP growth momentum, increasing employment and alleviating poverty. Since full liberalization of imports and sharp reduction in transaction costs were expected to take time to implement, several export promotional schemes were introduced in the last two decades. It is the view that a viable export strategy must rest upon two basic premises. Firstly, to be competitive in the international market, the export product must match, if not better, the competition in terms of pricing and quality. Secondly, the exporter must have an incentive to enter the highly uncertain export market. Both these objectives are achieved through wideranging facilities, infrastructure, financing, income tax relief, trade facilitation, etc. and indirect taxes play a critical role. Taking up indirect taxes, it is evident that the strategy so far has been to grant customs and central excise duty exemptions on the raw materials, inputs etc. used in the export product. Particularly on the customs side this leads to making available the international high quality raw materials, inputs etc. at the international price and our exporters are thus not disadvantaged viz. a viz. their competitors abroad. Moreover it ensures that the price of the export product is not loaded with any tax element.

5.1 Viable export strategy

Multiple schemes cause difficulties in administration and are liable for some misuse. It is recommended that the export strategy should focus upon the following schemes :

(i) SEZ and EOU schemes – This is for the grant of duty exemption on all goods (capital goods, raw materials etc.) required by the units for their export production.

(ii) Advance Licensing (actual user) scheme - This would grant duty exemption to actual users on capital goods, raw materials etc. used for export production subject to post-clearance intelligence and audit-based verification.

(iii) Drawback scheme – Here, the relief from duties on the inputs, raw materials, capital good etc. would be provided through a mechanism of refund of the duties paid.

[Chapter 5 : Paragraph 2.2]

5.2 SEZ and EOU schemes

It is recommended that the C.B.E.C. must immediately work upon consolidating the numerous notifications, circulars and instructions, on both customs and central excise side in respect of the SEZ and EOU/EPZ schemes. This may be done by 1st April 2003. Ideally, all the notifications should be combined into one, and the circulars and instructions issued as a compendium, subject wise.

[Chapter 5 : Paragraph 3.2.2]

The following recommendation is made as regards the facility of DTA access to the EOU/EPZ units subject to the unit meeting the requirement of the EXIM Policy as regards the eligibility of access to DTA :

(i) EOU/EPZ units using wholly indigenous raw materials - status quo to be maintained i.e. DTA access of 50% on payment of duty equal to the central excise duty unless the central excise duty is nil in which case duty paid will be equal to 30% of the customs duty on like goods, as if imported.

(ii) Other EOU/EPZ units - 100% DTA access subject to payment of full customs duty on like goods, as if imported.

[Chapter 5 : Paragraph 3.3.2]

5.3 Drawback Scheme

It is recommended that C.B.E.C. may work out a mechanism to formally associate a representative of the Department of Commerce in the process of fixing the All Industry rates of Drawback.

[Chapter 5 : Paragraph 4.3.2]

It is recommended that through suitable legislative changes the scope of the Drawback scheme should be expanded to provide for rebate of all duties – central, state and local – and on all goods which go into export product including capital goods. Similar action should be taken to include capital goods in the Advance Licencing (actual user) Scheme.

[Chapter 5 : Paragraph 4.4.3]

It is recommended that Customs should accept self- declaration from the Merchant Exporters that their supporting manufacturers are not registered with Central Excise and they do not avail Cenvat benefit. Similar self declaration should be accepted from manufacturer-exporters. Such claims may be subjected to post disbursal verification on basis of intelligence and risk assessment techniques.

[Chapter 5 : Paragraph 4.5.2]

It is recommended that that Drawback should be sanctioned on the basis of Let Export Order without waiting for the EGM.

[Chapter 5 : Paragraph 4.6.3]

The following recommendations are made in respect of improving the mechanism of sanction of Brand rate of Drawback:

(i) In cases where the exporter has applied for fixing the Brand Rate of Drawback, the amount at the All Industry Rate of Drawback may be immediately released once the Let Export order is given. The balance amount may be released upon the determination of the Brand Rate of Drawback.

(ii) Drawback Rules should be modified to provide for an appeal to CEGAT in case an exporter is dissatisfied with the Brand Rate or Special Brand Rate of Drawback fixed for him. Similar redressal mechanism may be explored in respect of orders relating All Industry rate of Drawback and rebate of duty on export goods.

[Chapter 5 : Paragraph 4.7.4]

It is recommended that the Deputy Commissioner (Export) may be made fully responsible for "Let Export" and also sanction of Drawback amount.

[Chapter 5 : Paragraph 4.8.2]

It is recommended that there should be an immediate software modification such that amount of Drawback blocked should not at any one point of time exceed the amount under dispute.

[Chapter 5 : Paragraph 4.9.2]

For expeditious recovery of inadmissible export benefits, it is recommended that the Export Outstanding Statement (XOS) must include a reference to the Code Number of the Custom House/port/airport/ICD/CFS of export. There should also be electronic exchange of information between the RBI and the nodal Custom House.

[Chapter 5 : Paragraph 4.10.4]

It is recommended that to avoid un-necessary issue of demand notices, the Customs may accept from the exporters themselves Bank Realisation Certificates as a proof of realisation of sale proceeds.

[Chapter 5 : Paragraph 4.11.2]

It is recommended that as a general policy the weight declared by the exporters should be accepted. Verification should be done only in case of doubt or there is intelligence to the contrary.

[Chapter 5 : Paragraph 4.12.2]

It is recommended that after issuance of Brand Rate (including Special Brand Rate) letter, a copy should be forwarded to Customs EDI system for data feeding. The amount of Drawback should then be credited automatically in the exporter's bank account as in case of claim of All Industry rate of Drawback.

[Chapter 5 : Paragraph 4.13.2]

It is recommended that at the option of the exporter C.B.E.C. should work out an arrangement with its designated Bank which, when authorized, should send a mail transfer of the Drawback amount direct to the tax payer's bank account, wherever located.

[Chapter 5 : Paragraph 4.14.3]

It is recommended that in case, the sanction of Drawback is delayed beyond a period of one week of the receipt of listed documents, the Department should be liable to pay interest on the amount of Drawback. On its part the C.B.E.C. should list out the documents required for sanction of Drawback, which should be made known to the exporters.

[Chapter 5 : Paragraph 4.15.2]

5.4 Duty Entitlement Pass Book (DEPB) scheme

It is recommended that DEPB should be merged with the Drawback scheme from 1st April 2005.

[Chapter 5 : Paragraph 5.2]

5.5 Coordination between DGFT and Customs

It is recommended that towards improved coordination between the DGFT and customs the following steps may be taken :

(i) Duty exemptions, which are in general a critical

component of the export promotion schemes, should be notified along with the EXIM Policy announcement. For this purpose the EXIM Policy should be made available to the Department of Revenue by 15th of March each year.

(ii) Both Customs and DGFT should make use of EDI technology for exchange of information, which would cut the delays.

(iii) There should be an institutional arrangement to resolve the coordination problems between the DGFT and Customs. The recommended structure is as follows :

(a) 'Export and Import Co-ordination Committee' co-chaired by Member (Customs), C.B.E.C. and DGFT and having as its members J.S. (Customs), C.B.E.C., J.S. (Drawback), C.B.E.C, Additional DGFT, Director (Customs), C.B.E.C. and Joint DGFT and members of Exporters', Importers' and CHA Associations. The Committee would meet once in a quarter to examine and resolve all co-ordination issues. It would also oversee the work of the Regional Export and Import Coordination Committees.

(b) 'Regional Export and Import Co-ordination Committee' at each of the ports/airports/ICDs/CFS. This Committee would be chaired by Chief Commissioner of Customs. Senior most member of the DGFT at the port/airport/ICD/CFS would be a member. The Committee would also include all concerned departments and agencies such as custodians, banks, etc. and members of Exporters, Importers and CHA Associations. The Committee would meet once in a quarter to resolve all co-ordination problems. It is expected that since the customs is the chief implementation agency of the DGFT policies this Committee under the Chief Commissioner would ensure early resolution of the problems.

[Chapter 5 : Paragraph 6.4]

These Export and Import Coordination Committees should be notified in the EXIM Policy and the C.B.E.C. Circular.

[Chapter 5 : Paragraph 7.5]

6. Automation of Indirect Tax Systems and Procedures

It is clear that the success of an efficient tax administration rests upon making full use of the potential of automation and related technologies. The bottom line is that change shall, and indeed must, be automation driven. The major benefit of an automation programme is experienced in the area of trade facilitation. Automation leads to quicker clearances, standardization of procedures, reduced discretion, less interface and faster decision making, all of which greatly benefit the trade and industry. At the same time, compliance issues are not neglected and, in fact, there is far greater control, though unobtrusive, which is desirable. However, a successful automation programme rests upon committed administrative support backed by significant financial investment.

6.1 Automation driven tax administration

The following recommendations are made for an automation driven tax administration.

(i) All Customs and Central Excise Commissionerates should fully automate their processes by 1st January 2004. This requires a Commissionerate-wise work programme to identify the requirement of each station in terms of resources required.

(ii) EDI must be expanded to cover each Customs and Central Excise Commissionerate by January 2004 for on-line processing of returns and applications (for e.g. refund), risk analysis, profiling and management, message exchange with related agencies, etc. In this direction, one major port and one airport should be made fully EDI operational by 1st April 2003.

(iii) C.B.E.C. and its Directorates should be included in the automation programme. All processes should be automated by January 2004.

(iv) Facility of video conferencing between the C.B.E.C. and the Chief Commissioners should be created.

(v) Research capabilities in TRU should be enhanced by intensive automation and development of new software tools, particularly in the context of emerging challenges once VAT is introduced and integration of Service Tax and Central Excise take place.

(vi) On-line filing of returns and documents should be encouraged. For this, Service Centers may be established with a computer link to the Customs and Central Excise Commissionerates for providing the facility. For instance, Excise-Return data is at present entered by the data-entry-operators of the Department. In order to improve the data accuracy and timely capture of data, entry of the particulars by the assessees through a web-based application at their own premise or at Service Center should be allowed.

(vii) Telephone help-line system should be made available in all Custom Houses and Central Excise Commissionerates for providing information support to trade in respect of status of pending documents/claims and other information on procedures etc. In the long run this should become a centrally operated facility.

(viii) Implementation of the automation programme in a time bound manner requires four dedicated teams to oversee the timely implementation of this work, one for Customs, other for Central Excise, the third for Service Tax, and the last for automation of C.B.E.C. and its Directorates. These should be created in the Systems Directorate, from the staff available consequent to cadre restructuring. The teams would work under the Commissioner, Systems and lay down the road map for automation including resource requirement.

(ix) Sufficient resources must be made available at one go to the C.B.E.C. for the automation project. This step will obviate the necessity of taking sanctions and seeking release of funds each time. Importantly, the resources should include an element for an 'Upgradation Fund' for the timely upgradation of the hardware and software on regular basis.

(x) To the extent possible, the automation work should be out sourced as it is not within the core competence of the department. On the other hand India is a leader in software and full use must be made of the local available expertise.

(xi) Senior officers of the Department must take an active interest in computerization by using computers and relying upon the information generated. They should also ensure its use by others. In short, there has to be better ownership at senior levels.

(xii) Systems wing of C.B.E.C. should be strengthened (in terms of both manpower and resources) to ensure immediate dissemination of information through an updated website.

(xiii) Simplification, standardization and stability of law and procedures are essential prerequisites of a successful automation programme.

(xiv) Providing lead-time for software changes when laws are changed is essential for successful automation. For example, a notification must not come into force immediately from the date of its issue but from the next day. Similarly, new procedures should be implemented after a time gap of at least 30 days.

(xv) All procedures must be devised in consultations with the systems personnel who can advise on their adaptability to computerization.

(xvi) Multiple levies create complexities in development of software and retrieval of data. Accordingly, there must be an attempt to reduce the number of levies. Similar is the case in respect of multiple rates of duties. By and large an item should be subject to one duty rate.

(xvii) Levies and exemptions must be aligned to tariff headings. At present levies and exemptions are, at times, announced with reference to the description of the goods. Since the descriptions are not standardized, it creates difficulty in automation.

(xviii) Automated processes should provide for bifurcation of total duty paid into individual heads. In other words, for each Tariff Heading read with the exemption notification, there should be one duty amount to be deposited by the importer. Once deposited, the system should do the further allocation of this amount under the respective duty heads. Presently this work is done by the tax payer. For this purpose to facilitate the tax payer, C.B.E.C. should come out with a Working Schedule indicating the break up of the duties.

[Chapter 6 : Paragraph 2.2]

7. Improving Indirect Tax Administration

7.1 Directorate of Anti-dumping and Safeguards duties

It is recommended that an independent body such as the Tariff Commission should be suitably strengthened to conduct the work of investigations such as injury determination, dumping margin, etc. relating to Safeguard duties and Anti-dumping.

[Chapter 7 : Paragraph 1.4]

7.2 Advance Ruling

It is recommended that suitable legislative changes may be made to include within the ambit of the Authority on Advance Ruling:

(i) A wholly owned subsidiary Indian company, of which the holding company is a foreign company, proposing to undertake an activity in India, and

(ii) Notifications issued under the Finance Acts in respect of duties collected as excise or customs duties, and notifications issued under the Customs Tariff Act.

(iii) Admissibility of Cenvat credit.

[Chapter 7 : Paragraph 2.4]

7.3 Prosecution of individuals

It is recommended that the prosecution provisions under the Central Excise and Customs laws be suitably amended to restrict their applicability to the persons actually responsible for the offence.

[Chapter 7 : Paragraph 3.3]

7.4 Adjudication and Appeal

It is recommended that in order to restore the confidence of the tax payers, Section 11A of the Central Excise Act, 1944 and Section 28 of the Customs Act, 1962 should be amended to restore the earlier position of issue of Show Cause Notice for demand of duty by an officer of the level competent to adjudicate the case.

[Chapter 7 : Paragraph 4.1.3]

It is recommended that pre-deposit of duty should not be taken at the first stage of appeal, i.e. at the level of Commissioner (Appeals).

[Chapter 7 : Paragraph 4.2.3]

It is recommended that the relevant provisions should be modified to provide for the finalisation of the case (wherein stay is granted) within a period of six months so far as it is possible to do so. This would act as a signal to the CEGAT to decide the cases in a time bound manner. The provision that the stay is automatically vacated when the case is not finalized in six months should be revoked.

[Chapter 7 : Paragraph 4.3.2]

It is recommended that suitable measures may be taken to authorize Commissioners of Customs and Central Excise to appoint Special Fee Counsels upto a certain monetary limit. The Chief Commissioners may also be suitably authorized for appointment of Counsels beyond the monetary limit prescribed for Commissioners.

[Chapter 7 : Paragraph 4.4.2]

It is recommended that in like manner of CEGAT, Departmental representatives should be appointed at the benches of the Settlement Commission. Subsequently, this practice can be replicated in case of Authority for Advance Rulings.

[Chapter 7 : Paragraph 4.5.2]

7.5 Strengthening Internal Audit

It is recommended that the following steps may be explored to strengthen the system of audit for the benefit of both revenue and the tax payer:

(i) Instruction may be issued that Audit should be participative and a fact finding mission with the objective of guiding the tax payer; the attempt should be to evolve a consensus on the issues and Audit teams should not be empowered to issue show cause notices for duty demand.

(ii) C.B.E.C. and CAG should identify posts within their organizations for exchange of officers on deputation basis.

(iii) Rule 22(3) of the Central Excise Rules, 2002 may be amended to exclude reference to audit party deputed by the CAG so that they need not visit the tax payers premises.

[Chapter 7 : Paragraph 5.1.5]

7.6 Trade facilitation

Keeping in mind that the objective of tax administration should be to provide certainty and transparency, the following recommendations are made in so far as introduction of new procedures are concerned:

(i) An institutional mechanism, namely Standing Committee on Procedures chaired by Chairman CBEC and including trade and industry representatives, should be established to identify and resolve the problem areas in present procedures and evolve new procedures on a need basis. This Committee should meet once a quarter.

(ii) A new procedure should come into force after minimum 30 days of its announcement.

[Chapter 7 : Paragraph 6.1.3]

The following is recommended in respect of fixing revenue targets :

(i) Revenue targets must be fixed realistically. The target must be broken into POL and Non-POL which would enable the Commissionerates to make realistic attempts to reach the target through legal measures and trade facilitation.

(ii) On the customs side, as an export facilitation measure, the revenue target should be fixed by including Drawback disbursed and refund sanctioned. This will ensure against blockage of Drawback and refunds. It would also encourage the Commissionerates to release Drawback in order to meet the target.

(iii) On the central excise side the revenue target should take into account duty paid through both Personal Ledger Account (PLA) and Cenvat credit. Refunds sanctioned should also be taken into account. This will ensure against stoppage of payment through Cenvat during revenue drive and withholding of refunds.

[Chapter 7 : Paragraph 6.2.4]

It is recommended that the 8-digit Common Commodity Classification Code should be implemented at the earliest and latest by 1st April 2003. This should be used by all other agencies (DGFT, DG, CIS, custodian, etc.) also.

[Chapter 7 : Paragraph 6.3.4]

It is recommended that a time bound programme should be initiated for the ISO Certification of all Custom Houses and Central Excise Commissionerates – to be started in 2003 and completed by 1st January 2005. This presupposes standardization of procedures.

[Chapter 7 : Paragraph 6.4.2]

The following recommendations are made as regards role of the Banks in indirect tax collection :

(i) Multi-banking should be encouraged by recognizing new banks including private sector banks to handle receipt of Government revenue.

(ii) A pre-condition to the appointment of the banks should be establishment of an EDI link with the Custom House/ Central Excise Commissionerate to facilitate recon-ciliation of revenue.

(iii) Banks should have the responsibility of issue/transfer of refund checks/amount direct to the tax payers bank account on the basis of a release advise from the Commissionerate.

(iv) Option of payment of duty through debit card and the like should be explored for implementation.

(v) Appointed banks should give the tax payer the option of internet banking for deposit of duty and transfer of funds.

[Chapter 7 : Paragraph 6.5.1]

On matter of interest rates it is recommended that :

(i) The interest payable by the tax payer and the department may be made uniform.

(ii) The interest so determined must be uniformly applied in each and every situation where it is decided to charge interest.

(iii) The law should itself clarify that the interest is simple and not compounded.

(iv) The rate of interest should be reviewed each year at the time of the Budget and brought in line with the prevailing market rate. Rate determined should not be changed during the year.

[Chapter 7 : Paragraph 6.6.2]

It is recommended that the provision in respect of Unjust Enrichment may be amended to the effect that it would not apply when the refund arises in respect of provisional assessment, goods captively consumed and predeposit of duty.

[Chapter 7 : Paragraph 6.7.2]

It is recommended that the system of receipt and acknowledgement of dak and correspondence should be reviewed and it should be ensured that a receipt counter manned at all hours during office hours is positioned at an easily accessible place. In the case of small offices where there is a paucity of staff, a Mail box should be provided and acknowledgements issued next day. Every correspondence should be acknowledged and timely replies sent.

[Chapter 7 : Paragraph 6.8.2]

It is recommended that C.B.E.C should codify all circulars/ instructions in one cover, subject-wise by 1st April 2003.

[Chapter 7 : Paragraph 6.9.2]

It is recommended that C.B.E.C should ensure by 1st April 2003 that all its tax payers are entered into its computer record on the basis of PAN.

[Chapter 7 : Paragraph 6.10.2]

The recommendations in respect of search and seizures are as follows:

(i) Central Excise officers should not be required to wear uniform. This would change the mind set on both side (Department and taxpayer) and contribute to freer communication.

(ii) Videography should be done whenever statements are recorded and searches made.

(iii) Seizure of documents and records adversely affect the conduct of business. Accordingly, these should be mandatorily released upon the completion of adjudication. [Chapter 7 : Paragraph 6.11.1]

7.7 C.B.E.C. Administration

As long term measures to give stability and direction to the indirect tax administration, which is so critical for the economic well being of the country it is recommended that Chairman, C.B.E.C. should be selected on criterion of merit cum seniority and once appointed (at whaιever age before 60 years) should have a minimum tenure of 2 years.

[Chapter 7 : Paragraph 7.1.3]

It is recommended that a mechanism may be found to give C.B.E.C. financial autonomy. The Chief Commissioner and the Commissioners may also be given enhanced financial powers.

[Chapter 7 : Paragraph 7.2.2]

It is recommended that the C.B.E.C. should evolve a time bound strategy to improve the office accommodation as follows:

(i) A Task Force should be set up to standardize the requirement of a modern customer friendly office (model office) which should furnish its report by 31st January 2002. The report should include financial estimates.

(ii) Based on the report of the Task Force, the C.B.E.C should ask the Chief Commissioners to identify the shortcomings in each of their offices in their jurisdiction by 1st April 2003 and send a consolidated proposal to C.B.E.C.

(iii) By 1st August 2003, a model Commissionerate (Customs

and Central Excise), Central Excise Division and Central Excise Range office should be set up in each of the Chief Commissioner zones.

(iv) C.B.E.C. should seek financial sanctions and replicate the model offices by upgrading the existing offices and purchasing land, building, etc., where necessary. The entire exercise should be time bound, so that by 2005, modern offices are in place in each Commissionerate.

(v) Modernisation of C.B.E.C and its Directorates should be done by setting up a Task Force to identify the areas of improvement and thereafter taking time bound action.

(vi) Facility of video conferencing between the C.B.E.C. and the Chief Commissioners should be created.

(vii) Research capabilities in TRU should be enhanced, particularly in the context of emerging challenges once VAT is introduced and there is integration of Service Tax and Central Excise.

[Chapter 7 : Paragraph 7.3.2]

7.8 Human Resource Development and training

In the area of training and human resource development it is recommended that :

(i) The infrastructure available for training at regional level should be upgraded. Training should be accorded priority and sufficient infrastructure needs to be created to impart training especially in areas of use of information technology, managerial skills and attitude changes at the cutting edge level. Each Chief Commissioner of a Zone should have an in-house training center equipped with latest training aids and adequate infrastructure to take care of the training requirements in addition to the proposed regional training centers in the Cadre Restructuring proposal.

(ii) The C.B.E.C. should make full use of the technical assistance of multilateral agencies such as World Bank, Asian Development Bank and World Customs Organization, especially their reform and modernization projects and programmes, that support customs reform through training in diagnostic study and in customs needs analysis. These help domestic customs authorities implement the required changes that have been identified and evaluate their impact on trade facilitation and customs compliance.

(iii) A relevant UN body to be contacted for assistance is the Center for Facilitation of Procedures and Practices for Administration, Commerce, and Transportation (CEFACT-UN/ECE).

(iv) Group 'B' and 'C' officers who are at the cutting edge should be given training to change the mind-set for bringing about proclient/customer orientation.

(v) Entry level training to officers who are promoted from Group 'B' to Group 'A' should be mandatorily provided at NACEN, for a minimum period of 3 months covering both Customs & Central Excise. This is essential as officers promoted from Customs are often posted to Excise Commissionerates and vice versa.

(vi) Cadre training should be compulsory in respect of all Group 'A' officers and periodical refresher courses should be organized to impart training of managerial skills.

(vii) Senior Group 'A' officers of the rank of Commissioners and above should be deputed to attend Executive Development Programmes in premier management institutes in the country such as, IIM, IIFT, ASCI etc.

(viii) Group 'A' officers should be exposed to the tax administrations abroad and international best practices in training followed to enhance their skills.

[Chapter 7 : Paragraph 8.2]

8. Revenue Augmentation, Tax Levies and Rates

It is but evident that there is an urgent need to arrest the trend of falling indirect tax to GDP ratio if an impact is to be made on the fiscal deficit. Broadly, this calls for action in two areas of tax policy. First is the tax structure and second is tax implementation. Widening the tax base by reviewing and removing to the extent possible the duty exemptions; reducing the types of tax levies and the number of duty rates; expanding coverage of Service Tax and integration of Central Excise (goods) and Service Tax legislation; and implementing VAT are some of the measures.

8.1 Customs Tariff and Exemptions

As a policy, multiplicity of levies must be reduced. Accordingly, it is recommended that there should be only three types of duties, viz. Basic Customs Duty, Additional Duty of Customs (or Countervailing duty) and Anti-dumping/Safeguard duties. All other duties should be removed. However, removal of SAD should be linked to implementation of State level VAT, where SAD would get replaced by the State VAT to be levied on imports.

[Chapter 8 : Paragraph 2.1.2]

The following road map for the future is recommended in respect of customs duties so that there is no uncertainty in the minds of the investors and industry.

(i) O% - for items like life-saving drugs and equipments, sovereign imports (defence and security related goods etc.) and imports by RBI.

(ii) For other goods -

By 2004-05
- 10% for raw materials, inputs and intermediate goods.
- 20% for consumer durables.

By 2006-07
- 5% for basic raw materials like coal, ores and concentrates, xylenes, etc.
- 8% for intermediate goods which will be used for future manufacture (capital goods, basic chemicals, metals etc.).
- 10% for finished goods other than consumer durables
- 20% for consumer durables.

[The duty reduction to the level of 5%-8%-10% should start only after introduction of State VAT so that imported goods are also made subject to the same State VAT (in lieu of SAD) by way of Additional Duty of Customs.]

(iii) Motor vehicles - nominal reduction in the duty from 60% to 50%. The import duty on second hand cars may continue at the existing rates. Higher import duty on defective steel items may continue.

(iv) Cellular phones - the exemption from CVD may be withdrawn but the basic import duty may be reduced to zero in 2003-04. The SAD on this item should also be abolished, so that the total incidence of duty goes up only marginally.

(v) 2003-04 : - 8% on crude oil.

- 15% on the petroleum products.

2004-05 : - 5% on crude oil.

- 10% on the petroleum products.

(vi) Higher duty rate upto 150% for specified agriculture produce and demerit goods.

[Chapter 8 : Paragraph 2.2.11]

Hence, it is recommended that as a general policy, the downward revision of duty rates should be in stages of (–) 5% each year. However, having regard to our commitment to reform, it is recommended that to the extent possible, for no item should the present duty rate be increased, unless the item is charged to nil duty, in which case a minimum duty of 5% can be imposed. Some increases may be resorted to only on administrative consideration to avoid multiple rates depending upon end use.

[Chapter 8 : Paragraph 2.2.12]

It is recommended that the grant or continuance of exemptions must be judged against the following criterion and if this done it would widen the tax base, improve the tax to GDP ratio and improve the tax administration :

(i) As a policy, all exemptions must be removed except in case of :

(a) Life-saving goods.

(b) Goods of security and strategic interest.

(c) Goods for relief and charitable purposes.

(d) International obligations including contracts.

(ii) As a general policy, when exemptions are removed but the relief is justified, the targeted beneficiary may be assisted by upfront transparent budgetary support based on a prior stated objective criteria. By such method, the expenditure would be subject to Parliamentary scrutiny and there would be public debate besides CAG audit.

(iii) In case an exemption is justified, it should not be end-use based conditional exemption. However, in the event the end-use condition cannot be avoided, the confirmation of end-use should be done on the basis of selective post clearance checks by using Risk Assessment techniques. It should not be based upon the Customs (Import of Goods at Concessional Rate of Duty for Manufacture of Excisable Goods) Rules, 1996, as the implication in terms of registration with central excise, execution of bond etc. increases contact points and the cost of compliance.

(iv) As a general policy, there should be no exemption from Countervailing duty (CVD), which is at par with the duty paid by the domestic manufacturers of similar goods, including in cases where the exemption from basic customs duty is merited. An exemption from CVD places domestic industry (including potential industry) at disadvantage and discourages domestic investment in these areas, which is not desirable.

(v) Best international practices should be one criteria for determining the requirement of otherwise of an exemption.

[Chapter 8 : Paragraph 2.4.7]

As a policy there should be a move away from specific rates towards advalorem rates.

[Chapter 8 : Paragraph 2.5.1]

The suggested customs duty structure on imports is given in Annexure 'A'. Since agricultural products stand on a different footing, the Task Force has refrained from suggesting the proposed rates and recommends an Expert Group should be set up for the same.

[Chapter 8 : Paragraph 2.6]

8.2 Central Excise Tariff and Exemptions

It is recommended that as a policy, we should review all levies and have only one levy, i.e. the Cenvat.

[Chapter 8 : Paragraph 3.1.3]

It is recommended that till such time as there are multiple levies, there should be a working schedule indicating the total tax payable on a particular product and the system should internally segregate the same into the respective levies.

[Chapter 8 : Paragraph 3.1.5]

The following recommendations are made for the central excise duty structure:

(i) 0% - for life-saving drugs and equipments, security items, food items, necessities and the like, agricultural products.

(ii) 6% - for processed food products and matches.

(iii) 14% - standard rate for all items not mentioned against other rates.

(iv) 20% - for motor vehicles, airconditioners and aerated water.

(v) Separate rates for tobacco products and their substitutes (like Pan Masala).

(vi) The specific rate of excise duty of Re.1 per kilo on bulk tea today translates to about 1% in ad-valorem terms. Raising it to 6% may not be desirable, more so when coffee is already exempt from excise duty. Thus, bulk tea may also be exempted from duty. This is anyway a plantation product.

(vii) Specific duty on cement may continue as most of the clearances are to the depots where the prices vary from day to day and ad valorem levy would necessitate provisional assessments, and may result in uncertainty.

[Chapter 8 : Paragraph 3.2.6]

It is recommended that the road map of duty rates should lead towards the identified duty rate (for the product) through a mechanism of (+) 2% or (+) 6% or (+) 8%, as the case may be or (-) 4% each year, depending upon its current rate of duty.

[Chapter 8 : Paragraph 3.2.7]

It is recommended that Government may move down to the long term rates even quicker, in case there is adequate revenue buoyancy from other tax proposals such as taxes on services sector.

[Chapter 8 : Paragraph 3.2.8]

8.3 Central Excise duty structure for Petroleum sector

The following recommendation is made in respect of the duty structure of the Petroleum sector :

(i) Central excise duty on petroleum products, particularly HSD and motor spirit, may be fixed at specific rates. But keeping in view the importance of the petroleum sector to the revenue, there should be a quarterly review of the specific duties by joint discussions between the Department of Revenue and Ministry of Petroleum so that the duty rates can be adjusted to take account of fluctuation of prices in the prevailing quarter.

(ii) Central excise duty on kerosene may be raised by Rs.1/litre. An additional duty of Rs.1/litre may be imposed on LDO to make the duty at par with diesel.

(iii) Warehousing facility for petroleum products should be withdrawn.

[Chapter 8 : Paragraph 4.4]

8.4 Central Excise duty structure for Textile sector

The following recommendations are made as regards the central excise levy on Textile sector :

(i) A uniform duty of 16% (to be reduced to 14% in 2004-2005) on all fibres and yarns by raising duty on cotton yarn from 8% to 14% and bringing down the duty rates on polyester filament yarn. The duty on polyester filament yarn to be brought down to 14% in four installments.

(ii) A uniform duty of 12% on all fabrics,(knitted or woven) which are not processed, till 2004-2005.

(iii) All exemptions should be removed except for the following :

(a) Fabrics woven on handlooms (unprocessed);

(b) Fabrics processed without the aid of power or steam. Articles of yearn, strip, twine, cordage, rope, cables (56.07/09) manufactured without the aid of power;

(c) Handloom fabrics (whether cotton, woollen, etc.) certified, as khadi as well as Polyvastra;

(d) Silk yarn spun from silk waste and manufactured without the aid of power;

(e) Woolen yarn spun without the aid of power;

(f) Fabrics processed without the aid of power or steam (but using power for certain specified processes) may be brought under the SSI exemption, when the present exemption is removed;

(g) Dyeing/printing/bleaching/mercerizing of filament & spun yarns without aid of power or steam in a factory which does not have the facilities for producing single yarn;

(h) Yarns manufactured without aid of power;

(i) Jute and jute products (being natural fibres and used mainly for industrial purposes. These are extremely eco-friendly), and also impregnated, coated, covered or laminated with plastics;

(j) Strips of jute (5806.39);

(k) Rot proofed jute products, laminated jute products and fire resistant jute products; and

(l) Blankets of wool/shoddy yarn of value not exceeding Rs. 150 per square metre.

(m) Processing of woolen fabrics (woven on powerlooms), not containing worsted yarn or made of shoddy yarn or melton cloth (made of shoddy yarn), where the fabric value does not exceed Rs. 150 per square metre.

(n) Synthetic fabrics, manufactured from shoddy yarn and consumed in the factory of production for manufacture of shoddy blankets of value not exceeding Rs. 150 per square metre.

(o) Captive consumption of Printing frames for use in printing of fabrics

(iv) Following full exemptions may be withdrawn, and the items brought under the general SSI duty exemption scheme, if not already covered:

(a) Sisal and manila twist yarn, thread, ropes and twine (Ch. 53/56), if consumed within the factory where it is produced for manufacture of sisal and manila products falling under Ch. 53, 56, 57 or 63;

(b) Hair belting of wool (5806.39); and

(c) Raincoats, undergarments & clothing accessories.

(v) Exemption to all other handloom fabrics processed by any agency may be withdrawn and replaced by an outright transparent subsidy similar to the Hank Yarn Subsidy Scheme.

(vi) Excise duty on coated and bonded fabrics (Chapter 59) should be rationalized to 16% (and subsequently to 14%) instead of 21% (16% + 5%) as at present.

(vii) The deemed credit schemes should be immediately withdrawn, and credit given only on production of duty paying documents. The Task Force recognizes that Textile industry is to a large extent controlled by traders. With the withdrawal of the deemed credit scheme, if the users are to avail of the credit of duty paid on inputs, all down stream manufacturers would have to come under the excise net. This might create some problems for the power looms which can, however, be obviated if the supplier of yarn to the power looms is deemed to be the manufacturer, so that all excise formalities including taking of credit undertaken by the traders. Similar dispensation can be made in the case of processed fabric in cases where the traders send grey fabrics to the processors for further processing. Such scheme already exists in the garment sector. Needless to say, the procedure for payment of duty by the traders will have to be simplified so as to encourage the acceptance of the scheme. However, optional levy on unprocessed fabrics may continue.

(viii) There may be a problem when the general SSI duty exemption for ready-made garments is removed, as in that case, even tailors may have to be brought under the excise net. To overcome this, it can be provided that when ready-made garments are made on job-work basis for use and not intended for sale, no excise duty should be charged.

(ix) As regards rate structure, the existing 12% rate may continue till 2005, as a commitment has already been made in this year's Budget to that effect.

(x) The Additional Duty of Excise (Goods of Special Importance) Act, 1957, should be amended from 2005 in respect of textile fabrics so that like any other goods, the States can levy sales tax on such goods also.

[Chapter 8 : Paragraph 5.7]

8.5 Central Excise duty exemptions

It is recommended that the following factors must be taken into account while considering the grant of a duty exemption :

(i) Income elasticity of the product; cost of compliance; international best practices; and canon of transparency;

(ii) Instead of duty exemption whether it is possible to extend the same benefit through a budgetary mechanism; and

(iii) If an exemption is issued it should indicate the period of its validity with a proviso that changed circumstance may warrant a mid-term review.

[Chapter 8 : Paragraph 6.6.6]

8.6 Small Scale Sector duty exemption

The following recommendations are made as regards the central excise duty exemption for the small scale sector:

(i) The duty exemption should be extended to only small units with a turnover of Rs. 50 lakhs

(ii) The duty exemption limit for the larger SSI units should be gradually brought down to Rs. 50 lakhs. The time frame is suggested, as follows :

(a) Year 0 (2004-05) – From Rs.100 lakhs to Rs. 75 lakhs.

(b) Year 1 (2005-06) – From Rs.75 lakhs to Rs. 50 lakhs.

However, on reduction of the exemption limit, the unit would have the option of payment of duty at 4% (without Cenvat) on the value of clearance upto Rs. 100 Lakhs. The other option available at present of paying duty at a certain percentage of the normal rate would continue to be available.

It is important to note that the downward revision in exemption is proposed to be complemented by a transparent and hassle free tax collection mechanism, which must be in place from April 2004.

(iii) The duty exemption should provide for determining the turnover based on value of total clearances including exempted goods. However, in view of the special contribution of the sector towards the overall exports and to encourage exports, it is proposed that the clearances for exports may continue to be excluded for this purpose, as at present.

(iv) On principle duty exemption for SSI sector should not subsidise consumption of luxury items by the affluent

(v) It is proposed that with effect from 1st April 2003 a Declaration should be filed by the unit when value of its clearances touches Rs.50 lakhs.

[Chapter 8 : Paragraph 7.5]

It is recommended that the present list of items to which the small scale sector duty exemption has not been extended should be subjected to a comprehensive review and to the extent possible the exemption should be extended. A relevant factor would also be the nature of the item and it should not be the case that grant of exemption subsidizes consumers of luxury items.

[Chapter 8 : Paragraph 7.6]

8.7 Small Scale Sector duty exemption to Matches

It is recommended that :

(i) The small scale sector duty exemption should be extended to Matches - the vast majority of the manufacturers would then be outside the scheme of excise procedure i.e. – no registration, no records, no returns and no payment of duty. This would be source of great relief to the small and cottage sector units.

(ii) The duty structure may be made ad-valorem. Since, the duty would be paid only by the large units (semi-mechanized and mechanized) only, the Cenvat credit scheme can be extended. Such step would also clean up the Central Excise Rules as the rules 13 and 14 may be deleted. The present duties incidence various from less than 1% to about 8%. Since it is an item of necessity, a duty of 6% is recommended.

[Chapter 8 : Paragraph 7.7.4]

In the light of all the above recommendations, the suggested central excise duty structure is given in Annexure 'B'.

[Chapter 8 : Paragraph 8]

8.8 Location based exemptions

It is recommended that there is a need to review the policy of granting exemption based upon location and no further exemption should be granted.

[Chapter 8 : Paragraph 9.2]

8.9. Relevant date of Notification

It is recommended that a notification should come into force from the day after the day of its issue.

[Chapter 8 : Paragraph 10.3]

8.10 Zero rating of exports

It is recommended that from 1st April 2003 exports should be zero rated.

[Chapter 8 : Paragraph 11.4]

9. Value Added Tax

Value Added Tax (VAT) is unanimously acknowledged to be a major reform in the indirect taxation system. By adopting VAT the country would soon be joining the majority of the countries and hopes to derive the advantages thereof in like measure. The Task Force has had the benefit of meeting with the Empowered Committee of the Finance Ministers of the States, constituted for the purpose of implementing a nationwide State-level VAT. Most all vital areas have been covered by the Empowered Committee and it would not be appropriate, nor is it considered necessary for this Task Force to reexamine these issues. The Task Force would like only to highlight few issues to ensure successful implementation of VAT, and its continuity and stability in a dynamic sense. These matters assume importance in view of the limited time now left for the proposed implementation of State VAT, from 1st April 2003.

9.1 Preparedness for State VAT

It is recommended that a publicity awareness programme should be started jointly by the Central Government and the State Governments and the former should extend financial support for this, if required. Since the State VAT is expected to be implemented from 1.4.2003 it is also necessary that the publicity awareness programme should be implemented at the earliest.

[Chapter 9 : Paragraph 2.2]

9.2 Uniformity of definitions

It is recommended that an attempt should be made towards uniformity of all State legislations, procedures and documentation relating to VAT.

[Chapter 9 : Paragraph 3.2]

9.3 Compensation to States

It is recommended that issue of compensation, if it arises, must be tackled through mutually acceptable mechanism of additional resource mobilization through Service Tax and not through Budgetary support.

[Chapter 9 : Paragraph 4.2]

9.4 VAT to unify all local taxes

It is recommended that with the introduction of VAT, all other local taxes be discontinued, and the same should be taken into account in determining the RNR.

[Chapter 9 : Paragraph 5.3]

9.5 VAT and AED

It is recommended that whereas AED may continue for textiles upto 2005, it may continue even thereafter for cigarettes which should not be subjected to VAT.

[Chapter 9 : Paragraph 6.4]

9.6 Credit on Inter-state transactions

It is recommended that the VAT scheme should provide for grant of credit of duty by the importing State for the duty paid in the exporting State, in the course of inter-State movement of goods.

[Chapter 9 : Paragraph 7.3]

9.7 Stability and continuity of the VAT regime

It is recommended that for the stability and continuity of VAT, a VAT Council or a permanent suitable alternative vested with adequate powers to take steps against discriminatory taxes and practices and eliminate barriers to free flow of trade and commerce across the country should be explored.

[Chapter 9 : Paragraph 8.3]

10 Service Tax

The service sector contributes roughly 48.45% of the GDP (2000-01) and, as has been the experience worldwide, its contribution to GDP is expected to grow over the time. The scope has been considerably enhanced it is expected the importance of Service Tax, as a source of revenue to the exchequer shall further increase. Whereas the expansion of Service Tax in the coming days is not debatable certain critical issues need to be addressed at this juncture to ensure smooth administration of this tax. The matter assumes importance considering that the country is progressing towards implementation of VAT and the compensation of revenue to the States (in the case there is revenue loss in the transition period) through revenue from Service Tax is under consideration. At the same time, it is learnt that the Government has already taken a view in the matter of levy of Service Tax in the future. Accordingly, it would not be appropriate at this stage to re-open the issues on which a consensus appears to have been arrived at after much deliberation. In this background, the Task Force has examined the critical issues which, in its opinion, would facilitate the early implementation of a modern Service Tax administration and its integration with central excise and VAT.

10.1 Comprehensive Service Tax

It is recommended that to the extent possible Service Tax should be levied in a comprehensive manner leaving out only few services by including them in a negative list.

[Chapter 10 : Paragraph 2.2]

10.2 Extension of duty-credit scheme to service sector

It is recommended that the following measures should be taken to allow the credit of duty paid by a service provider on the goods and services procured:

(i) There should be complete integration of the Cenvat credit and Service Tax credit schemes with effect from 1.4.2003.

(ii) Credit of Central duties (on goods and services) should be utilized for payment of Service Tax collected and appropriated by the Central Government.

[Chapter 10 : Paragraph 3.3]

10.3 Rate of Service Tax

It is recommended that along with integration of the goods and services credit schemes from 1.4.2003, the rate of Service Tax should be suitably enhanced so as to achieve parity with the Cenvat rate by 2006-2007. However, there should be two rates, one for service providers who avail credit and a lower rate for those who do not.

[Chapter 10 : Paragraph 4.3]

10.4 Threshold limit of exemption

It is recommended that the service providers who provide services upto a value of Rs. 10 lakhs in a financial year should be subjected to a total tax of 1% on the value of the services on an annual basis on the basis of simple declaration. Such service providers would be exempt from the normal procedures of returns and documentation. This scheme does not envisage availment of the credit of the duty paid on the input goods and services.

[Chapter 10 : Paragraph 5.3]

10.5 Separate enactment for Service Tax

It is recommended that there should be a separate legislation for levy of Service Tax, which should eventually be integrated with the central excise law.

[Chapter 10 : Paragraph 6.2]

10.6 Classification of services

It is recommended that the services should be classified on the basis WTO classification, which should be made a part of the Service Tax legislation.

[Chapter 10 : Paragraph 7.2]

10.7 Dispute resolution

It is recommended that as a measure of early settlement of disputes :

(i) Suitable legal provision should be provided to allow voluntary payment of Service Tax not paid when detected either suo-motto by the service provider or by Department.

(ii) Suitable legal provision should provide for the automatically collapse of a Show Cause Notice if the duty is voluntarily paid along with interest and 25% penalty within a period of 30 days of the issue of the notice in cases involving fraud, suppression of fact etc. In such cases the Notice should also mention in its preamble that there would also be no prosecution proceedings. The provision regarding collapse of the Show Cause Notice should apply to 'other' cases but without the requirement of payment of 25% penalty.

[Chapter 10 : Paragraph 8.2]

10.8 Non-recovery of Service Tax in certain situations

It is recommended that a provision similar to that contained in Section 11C of the Central Excise Act, 1944 should be provide in respect of levy of Service Tax.

[Chapter 10 : Paragraph 9.2]

10.9 Service Tax as the first E-tax

It is recommended that there should be a time bound review of the automation needs of the service tax administration and in like manner as proposed for other indirect taxes steps should be taken to automate the processes and allow online filing of returns and payment of Service Tax.

[Chapter 10 : Paragraph 10.2]

1

Reactions to Consultation Paper : Our Response

The consultation process for formulating the recommendations of the Task Force is now over. What has been witnessed in the past almost 2 months, after the Consultation Paper was made available on 29th October 2002 on the website of the Ministry of Finance & Company Affairs (http://finmin.nic.in), in terms of intense public debate, is in many respects unprecedented in the history of fiscal policy making in the country. The debates and discussions that took place and the response received through memoranda, e-mails, op-eds and other articles in national dailies and regional newspapers were naturally thought provoking and very useful for firming the recommendations. However, the success of the process is reflected not so much in terms of the number of new ideas now included in this Report but that it enthused so many across the country to convey their thoughts with the common objective of improving our fiscal condition.

2. By and large the proposals contained in the Consultation Paper were appreciated. However, there was also constructive criticism in respect of some proposals, particularly relating to tax rates of individual items. Suggestions for improvement of some other proposals were also received. This Report takes into account all responses received. An endeavour has been made to now make recommendations based on consensus, which reflect the concerns and aspirations of all concerned, while adhering to the principles considered critical for our indirect tax system and administration at par with the dynamic economies of the world.

3. Interestingly, though not entirely unexpected, the maximum

reaction and debate was generated with regard to the proposed customs and central excise duty structure and its road map, and not the measures to improve tax administration. It transpires that the tax administration is largely viewed as being internal to the Government and the public is not so far attuned to being asked to comment upon it. Notwithstanding this general observation, suggestions were received and the proposed measures to expedite decision making, increase transparency and intensify automation were taken on board.

4. In the context of the recommendations for improving customs administration by making available the officers round the clock for clearance of jewellery for export and doing away with merchant overtime fees for work in customs area, attention of the Task Force was drawn to the provisions of Kyoto Convention and the practical constraint of not having the adequate number of officers to provide the facilities. At the same time, it was informed that whenever an individual exporter or importer requires the services of customs officers the same is being provided and clearances are not held up. The Task Force found substance in this assertion.

5. In the area of tax administration, the proposal to improve the credibility of adjudication by appointing a two member bench to adjudicate matters was by and large not welcomed. The majority view felt that this would delay the proceedings. Apprehension was also voiced that this would not guarantee a judicious approach as the view of the senior member of the bench is likely to prevail. Hence, while recognizing the issue of bringing credibility to adjudication proceedings and restoring the confidence of the tax payer needs resolution, the Task Force has refrained from reiterating its earlier proposal. However, it is urged that C.B.E.C. should initiate administrative measures to ensure a judicious approach is adopted by the adjudicating officers and a pronounced pro-revenue bias, as at present is avoided. No doubt the recommendation to do away with the pre-deposit of duty at the first appeal stage, which is being reiterated, would benefit the tax payers who are aggrieved of the adjudication order.

6. Another matter which attracted enormous attention was export promotion. While almost all concerned concurred with the proposal to reduce the multiplicity of export promotion schemes, a case was made out that DEPB should be allowed to continue

for some more time. It was also opined that Drawback would be the preferred scheme in the long run subject to steps being taken to reduce the delays in its sanction. An important suggestion was that Drawback scheme should be made comprehensive to include in its ambit not only capital goods but also state level taxes imposed on the export products. Accordingly, the Task Force has suitably modified its earlier proposals while reiterating the principle that the multiplicity of schemes should be reduced. The objective is that the exporting community should continue to be facilitated by neutralizing the domestic taxes through transparent schemes and the future scenario should rest upon the schemes for EOU/SEZs, Advance Licensing (actual user) and Drawback.

7. In respect of Export Oriented Units, the proposal that the DTA access should be reduced in respect of the units to bring back their focus on exports was endorsed by many. However, many others contended that so long as the export obligation is met there should be no restriction on DTA access subject to payment of full Customs duty. This view took support from the provisions of the SEZ scheme, which is being projected as a scheme in line with the best international practices. It was also mentioned that that the underlying philosophy that the units are 'as if abroad' needs to be reinforced. Hence, taking into account the pros and con of the proposal, the Task Force decided to adopt the SEZ scheme as the role model and recommend suitably the dispensation for the access of the Export Oriented Units to the DTA.

8. In so far as the tax structure is concerned, there was near unanimous view that indeed the time has come to remove the multiplicity of levies and rates. In fact, on the customs side there was a suggestion that there should be only one rate of duty instead of the two tier structure (10% and 20%) proposed by the Task Force. However, this was not found feasible due to presence of the local taxes and indeed the international practice amongst of the open economies is to have more than one rate of duty, though few in number and at low rates. The Task Force had also taken into account the fact that categorization of goods as intermediate or final for the purpose of fixing the rate of duty may be considered a subjective exercise. Hence, the idea had been to evolve a consensus on the categorization and then apply the

yardstick to specific items. Expectedly, many views and counter views were received on this, which are now attempted to be reconciled and the broad categorization of the items has been achieved.

9. In relation to the rates of customs duties, references were also received from many quarters on the need to remove distortions such as inverted duty structure, where existing. While many viewed high customs duty as a protection that should continue, others commented adversely upon the conservative approach of the Task Force in reducing the duty rates! By and large the majority view was that the downward movement should be faster. It was also mentioned that if the avowed objective is to be at par with the international practices, particularly the dynamic ASEAN States, then we can ill afford high duty rate of 20%, as proposed. Accordingly, the customs duty rates have been comprehensively reviewed and the road map extended taking into account the suggestions received. The proposal now is that we shall aim at the lower rates with a peak of 10%, though specified final consumer goods would continue at higher rate, and this may be achieved during the Tenth Plan period.

10. As regards the central excise rates of duties, the sanctity of adhering to the 16% rate was questioned by many. Considering that central excise duty rates tend to impact demand and there is a pressing need to revive both demand and investment, the Task Force found force in the argument for a lower rate of duty. Concern was also expressed in some quarters regarding the removal of few duty exemptions and the criterion for categorization of the goods for the lower rate of duty (8%). An attempt was made to justify that other items (and not only food products) also warrant a low rate of duty. Likewise a case has been made out for placing certain other items which have a high income elasticity in a distinct category and at a higher rate. The Task Force saw considerable merit in the arguments. Accordingly, the Task Force has re-examined the entire duty structure and exemptions and this Report recognizes the need for a three-tier structure (other than nil) viz. a low rate of 6% only for the processed food items, a rate of 16% (moving towards 14%) for all the other items, and a higher (though lower than at present) rate of 28% (moving towards 20%) for few items, namely motor

vehicles, airconditioners and aerated waters. The Task Force have proposed that the target of 6% - 14% - 20% rate structure be achieved by 2004-2005.

11. Petroleum and textiles sectors occupy a special place in the economy and the proposals thereon attracted considerable reaction. In respect of the petroleum sector there was a demand for continued high protection by keeping a suitable differential between the custom duties on crude and petroleum products. Problems of valuation of the indigenous petroleum products was also pointed out on account of matters such as transit losses during pipe line movement. In so far as textiles are concerned, a case was made out for continuing with certain duty exemptions and having lower rate of duty, at least upto 2005 in line with MFA. Accordingly, the Task Force comprehensively reviewed the duty structure, both customs and central excise, in respect of these sectors and has come up with revised recommendations which, in its view take care of the reported problems and is also in line with the best international practices.

12. On the small scale sector duty exemption, there was a view that the exemption limit had been extended upto Rs. 100 Lakhs only two years back and should continue for some more time. The other view was that the duty exemption should benefit the genuinely small scale units and the high exemption limit has encouraged horizontal proliferation and is anti-growth, adversely impacting economies of scale and efficiency. Further the road map for reduction in duty exemption was supported as a transparent move that would give this sector time to adapt. It was also contended that in so far as the duty exemption allows the small scale sector units to pay concessional duty (upto Rs.100 Lakhs value of clearances), in actual fact the concession gets extended beyond this limit on account of the accumulation of the Cenvat credit. By and large the view was that it is necessary to quickly integrate the small scale sector units into the mainstream of central excise administration by reviewing the duty exemption limit such that it benefits the genuinely small units. The Task Force endorsed this view with the caveat that confidence building measures are also undertaken by the central excise administration.

13. In so far as VAT is concerned, the Task Force interacted with the Empowered Committee of State Finance Ministers. This

was educative and the Task Force learnt of the many initiatives taken over the time and achievements of this unique experiment in federal fiscal administration, namely the Empowered Committee. There was a lot of common ground and the Task Force was sensitized to the enormity of the task relating to the implementation of the State VAT. It recognized that the hands of the Empowered Committee need to be strengthened through support of the Government of India in all matters of concern including publicity, computerization and compensation. Accordingly, an endeavour is now being made to place in perspective the critical contribution of the Empowered Committee and the important areas requiring immediate attention for the smooth transition to and implementation of VAT.

14. On the subject of VAT, a case was made out for keeping tobacco products particularly cigarettes outside its scope. The rationale is that this item i.e. cigarettes is a high tax item and subjecting it to State level taxes would adversely impact the industry through encouraging illicit cross border movements. The impact on revenue would be significant. Similar rationale was applied to textiles, particularly in the background of expected move towards post MFA period. The Task Force found considerable force in the arguments and has accordingly modified its earlier proposals suitably.

15. In the Consultation Paper, the Task Force had mentioned that it would discuss issues relating to the Service Tax in its Report. In this regard, it was found that the Government has since taken a view on Service Tax. Therefore, it was felt that not much point will be served in examining the entire gamut of issues relating to Service Tax afresh. At the same time it has been considered necessary to re-emphasize that Service Tax shall be a major revenue source in the coming years, as is also the experience worldwide. Accordingly, certain fundamental propositions such as extension of the credit scheme to services sector are being presented for efficient administration of Service Tax and its eventual merger with central excise and State level VAT.

16. The Task Force is mindful that one of the tests of a good tax system, other than encouraging compliance, reducing transaction costs, facilitating investment decisions etc. is its capacity to facilitate revenue generation for the exchequer. This

criterion assumes far greater importance in a developing country such as ours. Hence, an exercise has been done to assess the impact of the recommendations contained in this Report on the revenue. The finding is that revenue buoyancy is a function of the administration on the one hand and the tax rates on the other. Thus, recommendations such as relating to reduced complexities in levies, better administration, training, increased use of automation, bolstering tax payer confidence in the administration, better enforcement, etc. would certainly improve revenue collections through improved compliance and lower leakages. The other positive fall out is in terms of increased economic activities such as enhanced exports, which does not directly translate into revenue for the Government but boosts the economy through employment generation and other benefits. It is, however, difficult to quantify and put a figure on the net gains on these accounts.

17. The rationalized and lower tax rates and removal of exemptions also positively impact the compliance and, in turn, the revenue. Expectedly, both the accountal of transactions as well as the transaction volumes themselves improve when the tax rates are low. However, it is also a fact that the revenue impact on this count may not be felt in the immediate short run as there is invariably a lead time for investment decision to fructify. It also merits appreciation that the manufacturing sector contributes roughly 16.8% of the GDP and India's share in world trade is also nominal at present. Thus, on expected lines the net impact on revenue, both central excise and customs, on account of the general reduction in the duty rates may initially be marginally negative despite the removal of exemptions. However, even in the short run the total package (on indirect taxes) would be revenue neutral once we take into account the greater buoyancy which will be possible from service tax revenue, this sector presently contributes roughly 48.45% of the GDP. Undoubtedly in the near future the proposed lower rates of duties would encourage greater transaction volumes and revenue even from central excise and customs. Thus, the outcome of the implementation of the recommendations of the Task Force would be revenue neutral in the immediate short run and lead to positive revenue growth in the near future.

18. As aforestated, the proposals contained in the Consultation

Paper have been broadly endorsed by all concerned. Accordingly, these are now being reiterated with modifications, where warranted. A few proposals have had to be dropped in the light of the response received. Some others have been dispensed with as these have already been implemented, such as the decision not to issue protective duty demands on the basis of an audit objection which is in contrast to the instruction or circular of the C.B.E.C. At the same time, few new proposals have also been included as these were found to be in conformity to the principles enunciated by the Task Force and serve to give further boost to the economy. What follows in this Report are recommendations which, in the view of the Task Force, combine together to simplify and rationalise the tax system, effectively reduce transaction costs, encourage voluntary compliance and, in short, bring our indirect tax system and administration at par, if not better, than the best international practices.

2

Macro-Perspective and Approach to Reforms

1. Macro-perspective

Our economy is at a critical juncture in its efforts to accelerate growth and employment in order to rapidly reduce poverty. Towards this, one of the key components of the strategy will have to be to exploit the opportunities afforded by more rapid globalisation. While our economy has succeeded in maintaining one of the highest GDP growth rates in the world in the last decade with very low inflation, there are several areas where immediate improvements are required to sustain the growth momentum. The principal concerns are the deteriorating public finances, with the consolidated public sector deficit estimated to be over 11 percent of GDP, decline in investment dynamism and relatively weak performance of exports and FDI, the two pillars of trade and financial sector integration. On the fiscal side, while the Government needs to focus on expenditure rationalization, a more critical area which needs immediate attention is to raise the declining tax to GDP ratio. This will also facilitate greater emphasis on public investment in infrastructure: a key for overall investment dynamism. On the external front, India's success in integrating into the world economy critically hinges upon raising the share of its exports in world trade closer to it's pre-independence level of over 2 percent from the current level of 0.6 percent, and increasing the inflow of FDI to at least $ 10 billion annually in the current plan period (China receives close to $ 46 billion) from the current dismal level of $ 2 billion.

1.2 The stated objective of the Ministry of Finance and

Company Affairs in setting up the Task Force on Indirect Taxes is "to take advantage of information technology and bring the indirect tax systems and procedures at par with the best international practices and thus, encourage compliance and reduce transaction costs". This mandated the review of the extant indirect tax laws and procedures - Customs, Central Excise and Service Tax - with an eye toward removing complexities and facilitating voluntary compliance. The bottom line is to set in place a user friendly and transparent tax administration in tune with the best international practices. The understanding is that such measures would improve voluntary tax compliance and reduce the transaction costs and, thus arrest the trend of falling tax to GDP ratio.

1.3 The most direct way to raise tax to GDP ratio is to remove most of the plethora of exemptions granted on import and excise taxes for a variety of reasons, mostly for non economic considerations; widen the net by expanding the service tax base; and to improve taxpayers compliance. Recent research in tax policy suggests that, in general, indirect tax incentives are very prone to abuse, as qualified purchases can easily be diverted to buyers not intended to receive incentives. Thus they are difficult to justify on policy grounds. Their use should, therefore, be limited to removing import duties on inputs used in the direct production of exports. Granting indirect tax incentives to exportoriented industries is a prevalent practice worldwide. Conceptually, relieving inputs used in the direct production of exports from the burden of indirect taxes is clearly justifiable on the principle of destination-based taxation, and should, in general, be supported. Such measures will also revive growth and stimulate investment, the tax system in general is in conformity with international norm, supported by suitable macroeconomic, structural, legal, and regulatory environments.

1.4 To boost exports and FDI, the government must sharply reduce the transaction costs associated with trade and doing business with India. Apart from maintaining a realistic market-driven exchange rate, and liberalization of imports, this will involve changes in policies and procedures involving improvements in trade logistics to allow exporters to compete in today's time-dependent markets. This will require a change in mindset away from controls rigidly administered, towards a more liberal policy environment in line with international standards. Trade facilitation revolves around the reduction of all the transaction costs associated with the enforcement of legislation, regulation, and administration of trade policies. It involves several agencies such as customs, airport authority, port authority, central bank, trade ministry etc. The main objective is to reduce the cost of doing business for all parties by eliminating unnecessary administrative burdens associated with bringing goods and services across borders. The means to achieve this objective are the modernization and automation of clearance procedures to established international standards. There is a dire need to streamline trade administration so that exports and imports are cleared in line with international norms. It takes days in major ports/airports to clear goods as against hours in most successful globalized countries. This is a key step to stimulate a rapid export drive and to attract a sizeable FDI. In this context, the Task Force would like to recommend the Government to take a more proactive stance towards trade facilitation in the coming WTO round. The Government is in dire need to streamline trade administration so that exports and imports are cleared in line with international norms. This is a key step to stimulate increased investments, attract a sizeable FDI and promote exports and employment. A positive stance by India in WTO on trade facilitation would serve two purposes. We could use it to get some concessions from the developed countries who are championing this idea. Secondly, this would improve our international image as a committed reformer.

1.5 It is important to note that once Universal Green Channel and EDI in all major ports/airports are in place, transaction costs will be substantially reduced. This will sharply bring down the anti-export bias in the economy. According to a recent EXIM Bank study (October 2002) - "Transaction cost of Indian exports : an update", transaction cost which has come down in the last four years, continues to be high. For example, for dynamic sectors of textile and garments and pharmaceuticals such costs are 10% and 8%, respectively. With the proposed reforms, it is estimated that the reduction in the transaction costs could be as much as 50%, the potential gains to the economy would be Rs.4000-5000 crores per annum i.e. this large benefit would accrue to the economy every year. In a dynamic sense, in terms of exports foregone on account of high transaction costs, the reduction in costs will be several times higher. Reducing transaction costs and costs of doing business is important not only for boosting exports and FDI but even for creating an appropriate framework for vibrant domestic business.

1.6 What ails the indirect tax administration beleaguered by low collections, revenue leakages and high cost of compliance has been the subject matter of intense debate over the years. Whereas recent initiatives are directed at a more transparent and rule bound system, there is an increasing realisation that whatever has been done has neither been sufficient nor effective. As a result, it becomes evident that the present system does not lead to confidence building in the tax payer, which has grave implications such as the falling tax to GDP ratio. Accordingly, it is imperative to go to the root of the problems and arrive at long terms solutions.

2. Approach to reforms

2.1 In this background, as a part of its work programme, the Task Force undertook studies and analysed the different aspects of indirect tax laws and administration. It initiated dialogue with a large number of stakeholders from the trade, industry and department and also examined the best international practices in the critical areas of indirect tax administration. A close look was also had at important reports of Expert Committees and Groups which had examined the indirect tax system in the recent past - The Advisory Group on Tax Policy and Tax Administration for the Tenth plan (Chaired by Shri Parthasarathi Shome), Committee on Review of Central Excise Collection System (Chaired by Shri S. V. Iyer), Expert Group on Taxation of Services (Chaired by Dr. M. Govinda Rao) and Inter-Ministerial Working Group on Customs Tariff (Chaired by Shri Arvind Virmani). All these reports have contributed significantly in shaping the final views of the Task Force.

2.2 The finding was that in the recent past Government has initiated a number of steps to improve the indirect tax administration. To list a few such measures, transaction value concept has been introduced for excise duty assessment; MRP based levy introduced on 92 categories of consumer goods; central excise procedures have been substantially simplified such as dispensation of most pre-clearance requirements, fortnightly payment of duty introduced, alongwith dispensation of statutory records etc. Similar positive steps have been taken on the customs side, particularly relating to EDI based assessment and clearance of import and export cargo. However, it is the perception that much more needs to be done. All in all the common refrain which emerged out of the aforestated exercise was that despite all what has been done, the indirect tax system in the country suffers from the following drawbacks :

(i) Lack of confidence in the tax administration on account of too much discretion, absence of accountability and a pro-revenue bias in all matters, especially quasi-judicial.

(ii) Alienation from tax administration, which manifests into corrupt practices and low compliance.

(iii) Uncertainty about tax policy, administration and absence of time bound decision making all of which affects business decisions.

(iv) Complexities of laws and procedures on account of lack of codification which is exploited for private gain by the unscrupulous tax payer and the tax collector.

(v) Too many laws and procedures which create an environment of confusion and mistrust.

(vi) Too many conditions attached to each exemption and procedure delay decision making and increase transaction costs.

(vii) Absence of transparency in tax planning.

(viii) Customer orientation is missing in the tax collectors who view all tax payers with suspicion.

2.3 Inspite of these problems, the experience of recent measures undertaken by the C.B.E.C. clearly shows that a modern, transparent and efficient tax system encompassing the best international practices is certainly possible to implement in an acceptable time frame. Beginning has already been made towards the simplification of indirect tax laws and procedures. There has been also a discernible move towards reducing departmental interface with the tax payer, increased reliance upon automation, particularly in customs, reducing complexities in tariffs and procedures etc. These changes have largely been beneficial to the trade and industry. However, it is evident that whatever has been done so far has not been sufficient to impact positively the face of the indirect tax administration in a manner which results in a 'big push' towards best international practices. Therefore, the finding is that for the desired tax system to be achieved without further loss of time mere tinkering with the present law and procedures would not suffice. It is the need of the hour to move away from incremental changes, from the policy of taking ad-hoc and half-hearted measures. What is required is a formulation for a macro-jump of the Indian economy so that India is no longer perceived as a nation hesitantly approaching globalization .... a strategy that revolutionizes the way things are looked at and causes fundamental changes in the way things are done in indirect tax administration. Only such a strategy would result in a quantum improvement in the administration of indirect tax system in the country. India must be seen as an economy offering the best internationally accepted standards of tax administration and tax payer facilitation .... now and for all time to come. This would no doubt positively impact the tax to GDP ratio also. Basically the strategy must provide the following elements in the tax administration :

(i) Administration should be based on trust. This translates into clearances based on self-certification.

(ii) To the extent necessary all checks should be based either upon risk assessment and intelligence or post-facto audit within a specified time frame.

(iii) To reduce transaction costs there should be no insistence upon securities.

(iv) Disputes and litigation should be minimized and if a dispute does arise early resolution should be ensured.

(v) All procedures should be IT-centered in view of the comparative advantage we have in this field. Increased use of automation ensures greater transparency, accountability and efficiency.

(vi) Reduce contact points by moving to on-line acceptance of documents.

(vii) Decisions to be rule bound not discretionary.

(viii) A modern tax administration depends heavily on change in mind set, which is to be achieved through time bound training and human resource development.

(ix) Confidence to be bestowed upon the tax administrators.

2.4 The outcome of this comprehensive exercise has led the Task Force to postulate certain principles, which in its considered opinion must necessarily govern an efficient and tax payer friendly tax administration. Thereafter, the Task Force has examined each of the critical areas of the present indirect tax laws and administration against the touchstone of these principles. The corollary is that such a tax system based upon these principles would encourage voluntary tax compliance, discourage tax evasion, reduce compliance and transaction costs and improve the tax to GDP ratio.

2.5 The Task Force has also duly recognized that an efficient rule bound system cannot exist in isolation and the human element in terms of tax administrators and other facilitators perform a critical role. In fact, an efficient system would demand matching performance from the implementers and facilitators or else the system would simply not be efficient. Hence, due attention has been paid to the aspects of training, automation, HRD and change in mind-set.

2.6 After giving considerable thought it is the view that the first principle which must govern the tax administration of the country is a system based upon TRUST. So long as the laws and procedures are made with an eye to prevent misuse, and not with the objective of facilitating the honest tax payers, there would be complexities, excessive documentation, avoidable transaction costs, inefficiencies and corruption. Interestingly, no concrete evidence was brought out that even the present such laws, which are based upon checks and counter-checks have really impacted tax evasion. In fact, the contrary appears to be true. Thus, it is the view that our law and procedures should be based upon trust. This is not to state that there should be no checks provided against misuse. However, what is required is that instead of suspecting all tax payers the system should provide for trusting all tax payers by using modern and scientific methods of risk assessment and intelligence gathering to detect misuse by the few unscrupulous persons. Further, trust by its very nature cannot be selective as this would lead to discretion and formation of pressure groups. Hence, it is proposed that as a policy the law and procedures should be based upon the trust that the tax payer is willing to voluntary discharge his legal obligations and is required to be facilitated by providing an efficient and transparent tax administration.

2.7 The second principle which has governed the proposals of the Task Force is that in the age of mobile financial, physical and human capital we must adopt the BEST INTERNATIONAL PRACTICES. It is the view that having committed ourselves to fully integrate into the world economy we can no longer remain unconcerned about having procedures which are not at par with the best in the world. For instance, if the standard in the developed countries is to clear imported goods in 6 hours we should be able to evolve procedures which not only match this but do better. It is only by adopting the best international practices that we can hope to compete internationally. Thus, an endeavour has been made in this direction. It is worth mentioning at this stage that on the customs side we have the advantage of international Conventions (Kyoto and others) which have also been adopted by India. To this extent much has already been done and the C.B.E.C. has taken some steps in aligning the procedures to the extent possible, which is a matter of satisfaction. However, we must act in a hurry and quickly do much more.

2.8 The third principle is that of SIMPLICITY. Too many levies, too many rates of duties, too many procedures, and too much documentation, all contribute to complexities, which go against the grain of efficiency. The underlying assumption is that a simple tax law is not only easy to administer at less cost but would also encourage compliance and positively impact the tax revenues. There is a crying need for simplicity in the indirect tax laws. To illustrate, there are over 300 circulars on the subject of EOUs with some overriding the others and some modifying the others. It can scarcely be expected that these many circulars are available to all in the trade and the departmental officers are no better placed. The net result is an absence of uniformity in application, which is often taken advantage of for private gain. It appears reasonable that the minimum effort to codify the instructions in one place after weeding out those which are no longer relevant would ensure better administration. Thus, there is a need to have a simple law, which should be applied uniformly.

2.9 An equally important principle is that of TRANSPARENCY. Tax administration should be rule bound and transparent. There should be as less discretion as is possible. This would increase the tax payers confidence in the administration. It has also been reported that the industry feels alienated as there is almost no institutionalized mechanism to obtain its response while framing a new policy. The concern of the industry is genuine. A remedy lies in involving the tax payers in the formulation of new policies to the extent possible. This has the inherent advantage that the users would point out the advantages and dis-advantages of the proposals as they know best. Secondly, for obvious reasons, compliance would be much better in such sort of participative and transparent policy formulation.

2.10 The next principle is that of STABILITY. During its many interactions it was oft repeated to the Task Force that sudden and frequent changes in policies adversely impact the business community. The difficulties get compounded when there is sudden change in the practice of assessment which has revenue implications as reportedly, tax payers are burdened by tax demands for the past 5 years. It is also the view that stability of Government policies is an essential input for healthy and prosperous business. Further, any action of the Government which takes the tax payers by surprise is bound to cause compliance problems. It is, therefore, necessary that not only a policy should be framed in consultation with all the stake holders but it should come into force only from a date in the future and not immediately. Giving sufficient notice is necessary for a healthy business environment.

2.11 The last and very important principle is that of customer orientation of the tax collectors towards the tax payers. There is no doubt that the payment of taxes is the statutory and legal obligation of the tax payers. Similarly, it is the legal responsibility of the tax collectors to collect the taxes for the exchequer. However, it is essential to realize that unless the tax payer is also viewed as customer and treated as such there would be an alienation which tax administration can ill afford. Thus, a tax payer friendly administration requires the administrators to adhere to the principle of SERVICE while interacting with the tax payer cum customer. This approach rests upon the assumption that tax payer cum customer facilitation is a critical input for greater tax compliance and reducing disputes and compliance costs.

2.12 It is the view of the Task Force that if the indirect tax administration frames its laws and procedures in adherence to the principles enunciated above viz. Trust, Best International Practices, Simplicity, Transparency, Stability and Service coupled with the use of the full potential of information technology the net result would be beneficial to the trade, industry and the Government. There would be improved tax to GDP ratio through enhanced voluntary compliance at reduced costs, and less disputes and litigation. Also the confidence of the tax payer in the administration would be restored. All in all a healthy economic environment. However, it is also important to appreciate that what is essential is not mere lip service to these principles. These have to be implemented immediately and forcefully. The attempt must bring about systemic and fundamental changes in the indirect tax administration so that we have in place an efficient and transparent tax administration, second to none in the world, facilitating the honest tax payers in the conduct of his business in the overall interest of the country. Accordingly, each of the recommendations of the Task Force must be viewed against the backdrop of the aforestated principles. It is the expectation that the individual recommendations would, when implemented, combine to change the face of the indirect tax administration in the country.

3

Customs Procedures and Trade Facilitation

Basic Reforms

1. Overview of procedures

Custom clearance in India has so far been based on physical control where each consignment is examined and assessed to duty, a legacy, no doubt, of the strict import control regime implemented with the purpose of protecting domestic industry. High import tariffs and multiplicity of exemptions and export promotion schemes also contribute in complicating the documentation and procedures resulting in a major gap between the customs import and export procedures at home and the best international practices. The major problems associated with the customs clearance procedures with reference to international best practices are:

(i) Excessive documentation requirements;

(ii) Less use of automation and information technology;

(iii) Lack of transparency; unclear and unspecified import and export requirements;

(iv) Inadequate procedures; especially a lack of audit-based controls and risk assessment techniques;

(v) Lack of modernization of, and cooperation among other governmental agencies, which thwarts efforts to deal effectively with increased trade flows;

(vi) Procedures are transaction based. Every document has to be checked, double-checked, signed and countersigned and most import and export goods are physically examined, which also breeds corruption;

(vii) Documentary inspection for all export cargo is intensive though less than in the case of imports; and

(viii) In spite of computerization, the administrative philosophy remains that of a paper-based system with many opportunities for face-to-face contacts on routine matters.

1.2 In this context the Vision Document published by the C.B.E.C., in 1998, shows that trade facilitation and creating a climate for voluntary compliance have been given the same thrust as realizing revenue and combating duty evasion. Therefore it is clear that there is a need for change and attempts are also being made in this direction. C.B.E.C. has taken a number of steps to put in place procedures at par with the best international practices, as expounded in the Kyoto Convention and other international Conventions. It is particularly heartening to note that a major push is being given to EDI and 'System based appraisal'. The fact that C.B.E.C. has suo moto taken up the exercise of evolving modern and efficient procedures reflects the changed mind-set, which must necessarily lead to trade facilitation in all its facets. At the same time care should be taken to ensure that simplification is not at the cost of compliance and accountability is ensured.

1.3 On the subject of trade facilitation it is worthwhile to take a look at the Green Channel system currently in place. As seen, this is a selective approach to trade facilitation restricted to specific importers (Government, PSUs, EOU/EPZ units, approved research institutes, top 20 importers, and importers of specified goods like pulses, sulphur etc.) at specific ports, Air cargo complexes (at Kandla, Vishakhapatnam, Cochin, Mumbai, Nhava-Sheva, Kolkata, Chennai, Bangalore, Delhi, Sahar) and ICD at Tughlakabad. Further, the system is product specific and does not apply to about 20 items including variety of engineering products, electronic items, plastics, textiles fibres, yarns, fabrics, miscellaneous item like dry fruits, marble, ash/dross of zinc etc. Goods requiring an import licence or execution of a Bond/Bank guarantee are also kept out. To obtain the facility the eligible importer gets registered with the concerned Customs House. Basically, the normal appraisement procedure is followed except that there is no physical examination of goods unless there are specific doubts about correctness of declaration. The scheme envisages post clearance audit within 48 hours of receipt of Bill of Entry, for which traders are not to dispose of the goods within 3 days including transit time.

1.4 Simply put the Green Channel scheme did not take off in view of its restrictive approach to trade facilitation and complexities which rule out majority of importers. Evidently, the focus on selectivity was mis-directed. Therefore, the present Green Channel has failed to effectively address the twin issues of trade facilitation and ensuring compliance. As a result our clearance time at ports/airports is still far from the best international practices. Delays increase not only the cost of compliance, the other adverse effects are corruption, congestion in the ports etc. Complex assessment procedures, insistence upon bonds and securities are some of the other problems associated with the customs. Thus, there is an urgent need to re-examine the present procedures and identify the critical areas, which may be improved so that we have in place a world class customs administration.

1.5 The role of customs is both of a facilitator and a regulator. Whereas it must facilitate the honest importer and exporter it has also to ensure the laws of the country are applied strictly. Therefore, there has to be a very fine balancing. While the procedures must provide for expeditious clearance of the goods so that international trade is not delayed, it must also provide for the necessary in-built alert signals to detect cases of infringements of the laws. At the same time it is no longer practical or desirable to develop systems based upon physical checks on consignment to consignment basis. The sheer volume of import and export would not permit this. Naturally there has to be selectivity in checks. There are basically two ways to be selective. Firstly, identify the risk free transactions either in terms of class of importer or exporter or in terms of the nature of goods concerned or both and such identified transactions would either not be subjected to checks or to low level checks on random basis. This class would have the benefit of special procedures whereas all other transactions would be subjected to consignment check and normal procedures would apply. The second method is not to create a special class of trusted or risk free transactions but to treat all at par. This system provides uniformity of procedures for all transactions based upon trust and works on the assumption that risk is uniformly spread. Therefore, in this system modern and efficient procedures are made available to all. At the same time the system provides for confirmation of declarations through a system of risk assessment and post clearance audit. The risk criteria are internalized in the automated system which would pick up transactions for examination on random or advise on selection for purposes of post clearance audit. The net result is that all importers and exporters are treated alike and it the luck of the draw (system based) which will determine which particular transaction would get picked up for examination or post clearance checks. Of course, customs has the undeniable right to intervention on the basis of specific intelligence and information.

1.6 After careful examination of the international procedures, as enunciated in the Kyoto and other Conventions and also the Green Channel system in place in the country it is the view that selectivity does not work and is also not desirable. Selectivity leads to creation of classes and formation of pressure groups. Furthermore, so long as general procedures are not improved (in terms of filing of manifest, availability of goods etc.) no special benefit is available to the selected class. Accordingly, taking into account all factors it is the view that the bottom line in regard to customs procedures is that these must be based upon trust, which presupposes absence of selectivity. If this is done there would be no routine examination of goods and examination, when warranted, would be either on basis of intelligence or on basis of Risk Assessment criteria. At the same time compliance issues are addressed by adopting modern tools of risk profiling and risk management based upon EDI for pre-clearance and post clearance checks. Such tools help in evolving transparent customs clearance procedures applied uniformly thereby increasing the level of facilitation and satisfaction while also obtaining an increased level of control. However, such a system would deliver results provided there are efficient backward and forward linkage with the other agencies concerned with the clearance of the goods. Customs can not work in isolation and the entire (multi-agency) machinery has to work in a finely tuned and cohesive manner for the ultimate benefit of the importer and exporter.

1.7 Modern best practice calls for a systems approach that relies on self-compliance (through the maintenance of business records by tax payers), risk analysis and management (development of profiles of risky transactions), and supported by periodic post audits of records. This approach reduces delays for legitimate transactions while allowing full scrutiny of high-risk transactions. In this background, systemic changes are recommended. As earlier stated, it is appreciated that the C.B.E.C. is also working in the same general direction.

2. *Trust Based System (TBS) : Universal Green Channel*

(i) Customs clearance procedures should be based upon trust and be uniformly applied to all importers and exporters and all goods.

(ii) Expand EDI network to all ports/airports and to include all processes in the automation programme by 1st January 2004 – For this C.B.E.C. may make a station–wise chart and identify the requirement of each station in terms of resources required. A dedicated team should be set up to oversee the timely implementation of this work and where warranted customs should not hesitate to outsource the work. In this direction, one major port and one airport should be made fully EDI operational by 1st April 2003.

(iii) The verification of declaration through pre-clearances examination, where necessary, should be based upon Risk Assessment techniques - As a policy there should be no routine examination of the goods. Examination, where necessary, would be done on the basis of an alert by the system based on risk profiling and risk assessment techniques. Some illustrative risk areas for imported goods could be very high import duty (demerit goods), imports from a country other than the country of manufacture, related party transactions and the like. Detailed profiles of all importers/ exporters are also an input. Importantly, it is the system which would decide the selection of goods (for examination).

(iv) Increased use of post clearance audit – This would be increasingly used to confirm the declarations made at the time of clearance of the goods through customs. This mechanism would allow the clearance of a number of transactions under systems appraisal. This audit could be combined with multi-disciplinary audit (say, including central excise audit) at the importers premises.

(v) Introducing a system of self-assessment of Bill of Entry – Just as in central excise the importer may be allowed to assess the Bill of Entry and pay the duty thereon. The system would confirm the assessment and after examination of the goods, if warranted, give a clearance. In the event an additional duty liability is detected the same would be discharged before clearance.

(vi) Release on minimum documentation: For certain importers of good track record of compliance, a release order could be given on the basis of certain specified minimum information (not documents) to be provided before the import. This minimum information would be name of consignee, name of consignor, country of origin, total assessable value, total quantity, description and H.S.Code. The goods would be released with or without examination as the case may be and on payment of duty. The assessment could be done subsequently after receipt of all other documents within a specified time period.

(vii) Enhanced Systems Appraisal: System Appraisal i.e. the process of automated verification of import declaration based on systems/ directory information to determine duty liability without human intervention would be progressively extended. Compliance would be ensured through Risk Management techniques.

(viii) Release of goods in offence cases - Even where an offence has been detected, the Customs should release the goods before adjudication provided the goods are not liable to absolute confiscation. In this case the importer/ exporter would pay the duties and furnishes security to ensure collection of any additional duty or payment of penalty.

(ix) Amendments to Bill of Entry – Amendment of documents, if required, (other than having revenue impact) should be settled at the service centre itself rather than first being sent to the concerned senior officer for 'No Objection'. This would speed up processing and expedite the clearances.

(x) On-line filing of documents – Filing of electronic declarations on internet etc. for release of import/export goods from any Customs location should be encouraged.

(xi) Storage of import goods - Section 45 of the Customs Act, 1962 lays down that all imported goods unloaded in a Customs area shall remain under the charge of a Custodian approved by the Commissioner of Customs till such time they are cleared for home consumption/ warehoused or transshipped. It is the finding that one of the major reasons for delay clearance of the goods is the multiplicity of handling between the carrier and the custodian. This also results in demurrage and increase in transaction costs. In the event the import cargo is directly transferred from the vessels/ aircrafts to warehouses (owned by carriers) set up in the Port/ Airport the delays would come down. Accordingly, it is recommended that the custodians (IAAI/ Port Trust Authorities etc.) should encourage establishment of warehouses by shipping airlines/airlines/couriers/ freight forwarders and consolidators within the port/airport for reducing dwell time.

(xii) Filing of Import Manifest - Internationally, the practice appears to be to allow the filing of advance Import General Manifest before the arrival of the vessel/aircraft. Also other forwarders file cargo declarations pertaining to their own containers directly with the Customs. It is considered essential for effecting quicker clearances that the Manifest is made available to customs without delay, and in fact before the vessel arrives/flight lands. Accordingly, the following recommendations are made :

(a) A complete Import General Manifest (IGM) with house level details must be filed with the Customs before the arrival of the vessel/ aircraft.

(b) The carrier/ steamer agents should file the IGM at Master level and the consol/ forwarding/ break-bulk agents should file the House level details.

(c) The carrier/ steamer agents shall alone be responsible for correct and proper filing of complete IGM (including House level details) with the Customs.

(xiii) Permanent Trade Facilitation Committee - Constitution of multiagency framework at ports/airports (port trust, shipping companies, custodian, etc.) is a necessary requirement for a long term solution to the day to day problems associated with the clearance of import and export goods. This is since customs clearance procedures are not the sole cause of delay in the import and export of goods - inefficient port and airport logistics play an equally important role. Since delay by any one agency is invariably viewed as a delay in clearance through customs, the multi agency framework should be placed under Commissioner of Customs. Accordingly, it is recommended that :

(a) A High level Inter-Ministerial Committee may be set up under the Chairmanship of Chairman, CBEC to resolve inter-agency issues to ensure a steady progress of clearance of import and export goods with reference to international norms. The Committee should meet quarterly.

(b) A Permanent Trade Facilitation Committee should be constituted at each Port/airport/ICD/CFS comprising senior representatives of all agencies including Custom House Agents (CHAs) under the chairmanship of the Commissioner of Customs. The Committee should meet once a month to resolve all clearance related issues.

(xiv) Customs should lay down a time limit within which an import or an export document shall be processed. This could be implemented through executive instructions which should be made known to public. Such action would bind the department to certain performance standards and enhance confidence of the importers/exporters.

(xv) Increased reliance on Pre-shipment Inspections – At times the clearance of goods is held up on account of inspections from point of view of health and safety considerations, such as in case of food stuff. In such cases increased reliance on certification prior to shipment by internationally recognized inspection firms, a common practice internationally would considerably speed up the pace of clearance. Accordingly, an endeavour should be made to identify the situations requiring certification before customs clearance and explore the possibility of granting the clearance on the basis of pre-shipment certification. However, this exercise should be consistent with the requirements of the other laws of the land being enforced by customs.

3. Other measures for improved Customs administration

(i) The Intelligence, Investigation and Audit Sections of the Custom House may be suitably strengthened – This is necessitated on account of the recommendation to increase the use of risk assessment techniques in customs clearance procedures.

(ii) Functioning of Special Valuation Branch - One issue which was raised at many forums was the working of the Special Valuation Branches of the Custom houses. The common refrain was that cases are registered on flimsy grounds and the importers are asked to make numerous visits for submission of documents and information. Besides it was contended that even in cases where the matter has been finally settled in favour of the importer the refund of the amount pre-deposit is a time consuming and often unproductive exercise as the Department tries to hold on to the amount. It was also informed that the pre-deposit amount is so nominal (1% of the value) that it does not really safeguard the duty. Yet, it leads to harassment as the Department tries to incorrectly adjust this amount in the final duty determined or delays in grant of refund. Accordingly, the functioning of the SVB was examined in the context of the instructions of C.B.E.C. As seen, an attempt has been made to ensure against routine registration of cases for investigation by SVB by providing for approval of Commissioner and periodic reviews. However, it is also a fact that cases once registered are not finalized early. Furthermore, the instructions provide that if no decision has given within 4 months of the registration of the case, the obtaining of extra duty deposit should be discontinued. Considering that discontinuance of the duty deposit is provided for a view may be taken that extra duty deposit is not a safeguard for the revenue and is not warranted. It is also a fact that so long as this nominal duty deposit is taken the importers would be anxious to get the case finalized at the earliest. Thus, it appears that the duty deposit is basically being used as an instrument to obtain the cooperation of the importers. It is the view that this is not desirable and there is a case for doing away with the duty deposit. In any case, the department has sufficient legal methods to obtain the required documents and information from the importers. Accordingly, it is recommended that the instructions on the functioning of the Special Valuation Branch should be reviewed to provide for time bound finalization of cases in practice. Further, predeposit of duty should be dispensed with.

(iii) Sharing of Merchant Overtime Fee for activities done in Customs area – On principle once the goods enter the customs area any activity therein should be done during the office hours. However, at times certain activities such as examination of the goods are required to done after office hours. This facility is extended by customs subject to the payment of overtime fees by the importer or exporter, as the case may be. It also happens that at times there are more than one importer or exporter who ask for the said facility at the same time. The present practice is to charge each importer/exporter individually to make the payment of the overtime fee even though the work of all may be done during the time limit fixed for one. Since overtime fee adds to the cost of the importer or exporter it appears desirable that wherever a custom officer undertakes work for more than importer or exporter during the same time period, the overtime charges should be equally apportioned between the parties concerned, thereby reducing the burden to the individual.

(iv) Export valuation rules for export promotion schemes – Customs Valuation Rules, 1988 apply only to valuation of imported goods. For valuation of export goods, there are no valuation rules. Whereas there appears to be no need for valuation rules for export goods in general, cases of over-valuation can not be ruled out in respect of goods entered for export under an export incentive scheme. At present, in the absence of standardized rules, each Custom House resorts to valuation of such export goods in its own way resulting in non-uniformity and subjectivity, which in turn gives rise to disputes and litigation on many occasions. A clear cut set of rules on export valuation will bring down the number of disputes on the area of export valuation of the goods. This would also ensure transparency and certainty in export valuation matters. Thus, there is a need to have in place valuation rules for determination of value of goods entered for export under an export incentive/promotion scheme.

(v) Customs to allow abandonment of warehoused goods - Presently, under the Customs laws, imported goods which have been warehoused are not allowed to be abandoned. This right should be available to the importers, as is the case in respect of other imported goods.

(vi) Customs duty payment may be through cheques – Facility of payment of customs duty through cheques would facilitate the genuine importers. It is seen that similar practice is followed in respect of payment of Income Tax. However, the stakes are considerably higher on the customs side as the acceptance of the cheque would entitle the importer to take away the imported goods. Accordingly, while recognizing that the facility needs to be extended, as a safeguard this may be first made available to importers who are registered with the Central Excise department.

(vii) Confiscation provisions in respect of export goods - Section 113 of the Customs Act, 1962 deals with the confiscation of export goods on account of mis-declaration, only if the goods are dutiable or prohibited or entered for export under claim of Drawback. Thus, when the goods under export are neither dutiable nor covered by Drawback and there is misdeclaration no action can be taken under the said section. Examples are exports under DEPB, DEEC, or other export promotion schemes or when the goods are covered by a White Shipping Bills i.e. where no benefit is claimed. Accordingly, it appears necessary that there should be no legal lacunae and customs should be empowered to take action even in case of such exports. For this suitable amendment would be necessary to the said section.

(viii) Acceptance of Export Obligation Discharge Certificate (EODC) - EODC Certificates invariably are issued by DGFT without affixing "seal" which is, however, insisted upon by Customs while accepting EODC, which causes delays. It is recommended that ideally DGFT and customs should develop an EDI link so that messages can be exchanged without loss of time. Even otherwise customs should accept the EODC produced by the exporter. In case of doubt the post-facto verification may be done from DGFT.

(ix) Customs officers may be empowered to enforce IPR – custom officers are not empowered to enforce the law on Intellectual Property Rights which is not in keeping with the international practice. No specific reasons could be ascertained for this deviation. At present, the IPR violations are to be first determined by the Registrar of Copyrights or Registrar of Trade and Merchandise Marks, and thereafter a notification is required to be issued under Section 11 of the Customs Act, 1962 whereupon the goods become liable to action (under the Customs Act). However, under TRIPS the border enforcement requires a mechanism such that a holder of IPR informs customs of a violation and requests it to suspend clearance in respect of counterfeit or pirated goods. Present law does not provide such an authority to customs. Incidentally, the same goods may also be liable to action under TRIPS as well as Customs provisions and it is desirable that a common authority viz. customs adjudicate the matter. Accordingly, it is recommended that the customs should be authorized to enforce IPR, by a suitable amendment to the Trade and Merchandise Marks Act and the Copyrights Act.

4. Custom House Agents (CHAs)

4.1 Customs House Agent's Licensing Regulations, 1984 govern the functioning of the Customs House Agents. Whereas the CHAs provide an important role in faciiitating both department and the importing and exporting community, at times complaints are also received against them. Further, it is seen that though the Commissioner of Customs is required to call for fresh applications each year this is not done regularly. Moreover there is a complex procedure for obtaining a CHA license and new entry becomes difficult. It is also found that a CHA registered for operation at one port can not easily do his work at other places. Finally, the charges for customs clearance work by CHAs were fixed long back in 1989 and since then, cost of all services, such as, documentation, warehousing and transport, etc. have gone up manifold. In fact, cases of double billing by CHAs have been noticed where they maintain one set of books in accordance with the prescribed rates while in reality, they had charged their clients at higher rates. Thus, there is a need to identify the areas of improvement so that the CHA community can perform in a professional manner for the benefit of the trade and industry. In this direction the following recommendations are made :

(i) CHAs should be licensed through an All India entrance examination to be conducted by Directorate General of Inspection, C.B.E.C. once a year at Delhi and at its Zonal Units for licensing of CHAs.

(ii) CHAs once licensed should be allowed to operate at any Custom House/Port/Inland Container Depot anywhere in the country subject to simple registration of the business premises with the jurisdictional Commissioner of Customs.

(iii) Once a CHA licence is issued it should be valid for all time unless the CHA comes to adverse notice of Customs on account of misconduct, delay, etc. for which penal provisions, including suspension/revocation of Licence may be applicable.

(iv) Rates for CHA work should be determined by market forces, which will induce a healthy competition amongst CHAs resulting in competitive rates and better service and accountability towards the clients.

(v) There should be a review of the technical qualifications of the CHAs to include knowledge of computer, Prevention of Corruption Act, etc.

4

Central Excise Procedural Simplification

1. Introduction

Being the single largest contributor to the tax revenues of the Government, central excise revenues and administration have a critical role in the Indian economy. Naturally, any set back or slow down in central excise revenue mobilization adversely impacts economic planning. Therefore, it is important to devise a suitable tax administration which facilitates voluntary compliance by the tax payer and leads to the collection of revenue at minimum cost.

1.2 In this regard a number of steps have been taken in the recent past to improve central excise administration. Some of these are :

(i) With exception of cigarettes, self assessment of central excise duty by the manufacturer without reference to or interaction with the department has become the norm of central excise administration.

(ii) Central Excise rules earlier numbering over 234 have been considerably simplified and replaced by new set of Central Excise Rules, wherein the number of rules has been reduced to only 72.

(iii) Payment of duty has been simplified with the introduction of a fortnightly payment system. As a measure of further relaxation the units in the small scale sector are required to pay duty on monthly basis.

(iv) Documentation is reduced to the minimum and largely reliance is placed upon the tax payers own records.

Further, the filing of statutory return with the department has been made less rigorous by increasing the periodicity. Tax payers are required to file a simple monthly return and those in the small scale sector have to furnish the return only on a quarterly basis.

(v) A statutory body has been set up for giving Advance Rulings on matters of classification and valuation of goods and applicability of notifications with the objective of introducing uniformity and certainty in central excise administration.

(vi) Computerisation has been initiated on a large scale in the and the emphasis is on effective monitoring, analysis of data base, and use of Information Technology to carry out day to day functions.

(vii) New PAN based excise registration has been adopted with the objective of moving towards on-line registration to facilitate the tax payer.

(viii) Manufacturer exporters have been facilitated by dispensing with the requirement of bonds and security. Further a simplified procedure has been introduced for self-credit of the duty on the goods exported. In respect of merchant exporters also the requirement of security for exports is not insisted upon.

(ix) Disputes with the tax payer have been sought to be reduced with the introduction of new valuation; rules and extension of the scheme of assessment based on Maximum Retail Price.

(x) To ensure speedy disposal of cases pending adjudication and in appeal a time period for deciding the cases has been prescribed in the law.

(xi) Selective Audit based upon risk assessment has been introduced.

(xii) For greater facilitation the administration has been brought closer to the tax payer by an increase in the number of Central Excise Chief Commissioners from 10 to 23, Commissioners from 61 to 92 and Commissioners of Central Excise (Appeals) from 18 to 71.

1.3 However, it is clear that while the direction is correct, the steps taken so far have not materially altered the general perception that the central excise administration is not tax payer friendly and the systems and procedures are even now far too complex. Therefore, much more need to be done. Importantly, to make a visible impact it is necessary to make fundamental changes without further loss of time. Accordingly, based upon the principles formulated by the Task Force the following recommendations are aimed at comprehensively changing the essence of central excise administration with the twin objective of tax payer facilitation and encouraging compliance for increased revenue.

2. Manufacture

2.1 Increasing scope of central excise levy

2.1.1 In terms of the Constitution provisions [Seventh Schedule, List 1, Entry 84] central excise duty is levied on all articles produced or manufactured (except alcohol for human consumption etc.). "Excise" in our context has, thus, been understood as a duty on "manufacture" of goods, and the expression "manufacture" has been the subject matter of many judicial decisions, and has attained a specific meaning under the law. Now, there are many processes which may not answer the strict definition of "manufacture", but yet result in significant value addition. As a result, such processes do not attract the central excise levy. However, it must be noted that by virtue of residual power under Entry 97 of List 1, the Parliament may levy a tax on such processes also. Interestingly, such a levy on act of 'manufacture' is unique in the sphere of indirect tax administration world over. What we have instead is Value Added Tax (VAT), with over 120 countries adopting one or the other variant of this tax.

2.1.2 In our context, as seen, central excise duty is levied on the manufacture of goods and 'manufacture' has been defined under Section 2(f) of the Central Excise Act, 1944. However, apart from this definition there are a number of deeming provisions under various Chapter Notes of the Central Excise Tariff Act, 1985, which also define 'manufacture'. Over the time Government has been tinkering with the said Chapter Notes in order to expand the scope of the term 'manufacture', particularly to include activities such as packing, labeling and re-labeling in its ambit. As a result more and more activities, which basically are not 'manufacture' in the strict sense of the word but do add value to the product are being covered under the ambit of the central excise levy.

2.1.3 It appears that the traditional approach in defining the taxable event i.e. 'manufacture' has largely lost relevance given the fast changing technology and new emerging markets. In the final analysis what is material in the world of business is whether an activity has added value or not. Accordingly, it is the value addition which must be tapped for purposes of taxation. In this background, the present definition of manufacture resting basically upon the act of 'bringing into existence an article which has a different name, character and use' appears woefully inadequate. A modern tax system requires focus upon value addition, and the central excise must also eventually move towards this concept, which will also gradually pave way towards VAT. Thus, scope of central excise levy which is based upon the concept of tax based upon factum of production or manufacture, as at present, must expand. Besides, there are a number of disputes today whether a particular activity amounts to manufacture or not.

2.1.4 The implication is that the future of central excise lies in taxing any activity which adds value to the product. Of course, the idea is not to encroach upon the territory of sales tax. In this regard it is to be appreciated that even today the central excise levy is basically on the value addition but the critical difference is that the tax is levied only if manufacture takes place. What is now being proposed is that the tax would be levied whenever value addition takes place on account of some processing of the manufactured goods. However, the process must be capable of being distinctly identified. In other words, the concept of production or manufacture would require a relook and this may have constitutional and legal implications. This has the following advantages :

(i) Concept of value addition is easy to understand and implement. It does not suffer from interpretation problems associated with the definition of 'manufacture';

(ii) It widens the tax base and would positively impact the tax to GDP ratio;

(iii) Value addition in contrast to 'manufacture' ensures against tax evasion and avoidance through sub-contracting or segregation of the value addition activities outside the manufacturing premises;

(iv) Basing central excise levy on value addition is a step closer to VAT; and

(v) Uncertainty in the minds of tax payers will be removed.

2.1.5 Accordingly, it is recommended that through suitable legislative changes, the levy of central excise should be progressively based upon value addition to be applied only to the processing stage (of manufactured goods) while ensuring that the other areas of value addition not relating to the processing activity (such as Sales Tax) is not entered into and possibility of double taxation is avoided.

2.2 Powers to notify act of 'Manufacture'

2.2.1 Charge of central excise levy is attracted when goods are produced or manufactured. Thus, the issue when manufacture is said to have taken place has oft been the subject matter of legal debates and judicial decisions. Simply put excisability of particular goods would depend upon the fact of their manufacture and marketability. The matter stands largely settled now and except for stray cases there is certainty in the minds of both tax administrators and the tax payer. In this background concern has been voiced in many quarters about the recent legislative amendments [section 2 (f) of the Central Excise Act, 1944] empowering the executive to rule upon what is manufacture and that the ruling would have retrospective effect over the past one year. In other words once the executive clarifies in a particular case that manufacture has taken place, by virtue of this provision it would be in a position to demand the duty from the tax payer on all production and clearances made over the past one year, which would be a heavy burden. The trade and industry is concerned that such power may be misused.

2.2.2 On a careful perusal of the said provision it is noted that this provision has been introduced only recently and has not been invoked so far. It appears that with the issue of what is manufacture having been judicially settled over the time there may in fact be no occasion to invoke this power. Moreover, there is a positive aspect, which is that should the power be exercised it would ensure uniformity of practice all over the country. Otherwise it is often the case that an issue is raised and decided against one tax payer whereas his competitors in other Commissionerates escape the proceedings. It is expected that these considerations would have weighed with the legislature while empowering the executive. At the same time due importance must be given to certainty in tax matters which boosts the confidence of the tax payer and is necessary for a higher degree of compliance.

2.2.3 It is recommended that the said provision should not be used routinely. Moreover, a suitable amendment is necessary so that it is applied prospectively.

2.3 Expanding definition of 'Manufacture'

2.3.1 Assessment based on the Retail Sale Price [Maximum Retail Price (MRP)] of goods covered under the Standards of Weights and Measures Act, 1976 and provided for under Section 4A of the Central Excise Act, 1944, has been found to be very effective. It has reduced disputes and brought about certainty in assessment. However, the Standards of Weights and Measures Act provides for certain relaxation of the condition of affixation of MRP on goods such as when the goods are sold in bulk quantities for actual industrial use. It is the apprehension that such relation may be used to avoid central excise duty. For instance, a manufacturer may clear the goods from the factory in bulk and get it re-packed outside into retail packages.

2.3.2 In order to prevent any misuse of the MRP provisions, it is recommended that the wherever MRP based levy is applied on an item, the act of repacking, relabelling and putting the item into unit container for retail sale may be deemed to be amounting to manufacture.

3. Assessment

3.1 Confirmation of assessment

3.1.1 Correct assessment of duty is critical to the central excise administration. This entails correct determination of classification, rate of duty and valuation of the excisable goods. Presently we have a system of self-assessment whereby the tax payer determines his duty liability and pays the same suo moto. He later files a return with the Department indicating the production and clearances and duty paid.

3.1.2 It is the perception that the introduction of self-assessment in Central Excise has reduced responsibility of the Central Excise officers in ensuring the correctness of assessment including correct availment of Cenvat credit. By and large the officers feel that since the tax payer is responsible for self-assessment of the return their own responsibility is reduced to mere confirmation of mathematical accuracy. This is not correct. The C.B.E.C. had clearly laid down the responsibilities of the assessing officers right up to the level of Addl. Commissioner in ensuring correctness of assessment and availment of Cenvat credit by the tax payer. The instructions also empower the officers to call for any document to confirm the assessment of the tax payer. However, it is a finding that this is not being done properly, furthermore there is an absence of a monitoring mechanism and as a result proper checks are not carried out. In fact, the assessing officers take the stand that with the introduction of self assessment and the non-submission of invoices with monthly returns the responsibility of finding out short levy is on the Audit or Anti-Evasion.

3.1.3 It is the view that assessment should be the primary function of the Central Excise officers. Self assessment on the part of the tax payer is only a facility and cannot and must not be treated as a dilution of the statutory responsibility of the central excise officers in ensuring correctness of duty payment. No doubt Audit and Anti-Evasion have their roles to play but assessment or confirmation of assessment should remain the primary responsibility of the Central Excise officers.

3.1.4 It is recommended that the officers should be make responsible for assessments of ER 1 returns, and for this purpose clear cut instructions should be issued. Some monetary limit may be fixed for confirmation of assessment by each level of Central Excise officer upto Additional Commissioner.

3.2 Valuation

3.2.1 Valuation of the excisable goods is an important exercise as the duty charged is mostly on ad-valorem basis. Over time, there have been commendable efforts to simplify the valuation norms for levy of central excise duty. The amendments to Section 4 have indeed brought about much needed clarity and certainty to the principles of valuation. Moreover the increasing use of MRP based assessment under Section 4A has increased certainty and is a welcome step. But, the change-over to new rules and the introduction of new norms and the increasing usage of MRP-based levy, may well lead to a new era of disputes, and, therefore, it will be in the interest of both, the Department and the industry, to address these issues proactively. It is appreciated that this is indeed what is being done, such as the recent clarification on matter of treatment of Sales Tax.

3.2.2 At present there are more than one method of valuation applied to the excisable goods, Transaction value, Tariff value and Value based upon Maximum Retail Sale Price (MRP). Transaction value is the most commonly adopted method. By and large no fresh issues have been thrown up in this area as a result of switching over to this method of valuation in July, 2001, from the earlier practiced method of 'normal price'. The transaction value method is tried and adopted the world over and there can be no two views on its acceptance in principle. However, it is noted that there are certain areas which require a clarification lest we enter into fresh disputes on valuation. Primarily these relate to cost of transport, margin of profit and determination of abatement under MRP based assessment etc.

3.3 Cost of Production

3.3.1 The answer to the question "what would constitute cost of production?", which is necessary to determine in order to value goods under rule 8 of the Central Excise Valuation Rules, 2000 is not very clear. In many cases, excise audit parties are directing the assessee to add advertising, marketing, Head Office costs, etc. It is the view of the trade that only the raw material costs, packaging material cost, energy and services cost and factory overheads should form part of the cost of production. Head Office costs are in the nature of Corporate costs which have no direct bearing on the intermediate goods cleared for captive consumption. Further, advertising, sales and distribution costs are also not relevant in this case as such intermediate products are neither advertised nor sold in the trade. The sales and distribution expenses relate to finished goods marketed and sold and, therefore, hold no relevance to the intermediate goods.

3.3.2 Since different views are being taken by the field formation as to what constitutes cost of production, it would only be appropriate that the C.B.E.C. issues clear guidelines on the aspect of valuation of intermediate goods used captively to avoid disputes in the matter. It is understood that such guidelines (CAS4) on the cost of production for goods captively consumed are being issued by the Institute of Cost and Works Accountants of India.

3.3.3 It is recommended that the guidelines on determination of cost of production should be issued at the earliest and till such time all disputes be kept pending.

3.4 Margin of Profit

3.4.1 Under the Central Excise Valuation Rules, 2000, when the goods have been consumed captively by the assessee in the production or manufacturing of other articles or these are sold to the related person for his captive consumption, the duty is to be charged on 115% of cost of production as assessable value. It is the view of the trade that 115% is an abnormal margin as such profits are an exception. However, in the overall interest of ensuring certainty in taxation it was conceded that rather than individual determination of the profit margin, its standardization in the law is a better step. At the same time it was felt that since this is largely going to be a revenue neutral exercise as the recipient unit can claim Cenvat credit, it would be better to review the margin and reduce it. This step would positively impact the cash flow and benefit the industry. There is force in this argument.

3.4.2 It is recommended that the figure of 115% should be brought down to 105%. Moreover, there should be a moratorium on this figure, so that there is certainty in taxation.

3.5 Valuation based upon Retail Sale Price [Maximum Retail price (MRP)]

3.5.1 Section 4A of the Central Excise Act, 1944, provides for levy of central excise duty on the basis of retail sale price in respect of certain specified goods. Essentially, this provision is being enforced by issue of a Notification whereby goods are specified and the duty is chargeable with reference to the retail sale price thereof after giving certain abetment, as mentioned in the Notification. It is observed that notwithstanding certain questions on the rationale for levy of excise duty on the basis of a price over which the manufacturer has no control, the switch over to MRP based value and the increasing use of this method has been welcomed by the trade and industry. Interestingly, it marks a change in the mindset of the tax administrators who were traditionally not looking beyond the factory gate for determining the value of the excisable goods. MRP based levy also has an intrinsic advantage in ensuring certainty of determination and reduces disputes and has been welcomed by the trade and industry. Therefore, this is a step in the right direction. At the same time, it is necessary to see that the provisions do not provide any scope for disputes in future.

3.5.2 In this regard, the discussions with trade and industry have revealed that there is some apprehension in respect of the contents of "Explanation 1" given in the said Section 4A. Herein the definition of retail sale price has been given as "retail sale price means the maximum price at which the excisable goods in packaged form may be sold to the ultimate consumer ... and the price is the sole consideration for such sale". The apprehension is that while the Explanation makes it clear that the price should be the sole consideration, it does not clarify that the sole consideration referred to therein is in respect of the manufacturer. In the normal course the manufacturer will have no control on the ultimate sale price and the term "sole consideration" will difficult to implement. It would also give rise to avoidable disputes. Hence, it appears appropriate to delete a reference to the term "sole consideration" and instead provide that there should be no consideration flowing from the buyer to the manufacturer.

3.5.3 The second issue relates to fixing of abatement from the MRP. Government, by issue of a notification, announces the percentage of abatement to be allowed from MRP in order to arrive at the assessable value for charging excise duty. The finding is that the determination of abatement is not a transparent exercise. For instance, the extent of abatement does not appear to take into account certain standard deductions (delivery charges, secondary packing, etc.) and the changes in rates of various levies. Reportedly, the present quantum of abatement just takes care of the levies of excise duty, sales tax, octroi, etc. Further, the quantum of abatement which had been fixed at the time of bringing the commodities under Section 4A does not appear to have taken into account the subsequent developments such as the adoption of uniform sales tax rates by the State Governments, which has resulted in extra burden ranging from 15 to 20 per cent. No doubt the abatement is done on basis of industry averaging but the manner of its determination leaves doubts in the minds of the affected industry. It is the view that Government policies particularly in matters of taxation must not only be fair but should be transparently fair to all. Hence, wider consultation is required and the industry should be associated in the exercise.

3.5.4 In the aforestated background, the following recommendations are made as regards the MRP based levy :

(i) System of MRP based valuation may be expanded.

(ii) Explanation 1 to Section 4A should be amended to delete reference to the term "sole consideration" and it should only be provided that there is no additional flow back to the manufacturer over and above his selling price.

(iii) For further transparency in mechanism of fixing abatement C.B.E.C. is advised to consider setting up an advisory Committee (including representatives of Chambers of Trade and Industry Associations) on the subject.

4. Cenvat

4.1 Removing distinction between inputs and capital goods

4.1.1 At present, the Cenvat credit is admissible in respect of inputs which are brought into a factory "for use in or in relation to the manufacture of the final products". In contrast the Cenvat credit is admissible in respect of capital goods when these are "used in the factory of the manufacturer". This distinction is a cause of many disputes and litigation.

4.1.2 No doubt the levy of central excise duty is on manufacture. However, there is no reason why the Cenvat credit must also be linked to the act of manufacture. The term manufacture is strictly interpreted and many legitimate business activities such as the use of a computer for calculation of duty may not get covered even though the said goods are indeed required to support the manufacturing activity. Actually, Cenvat credit can be viewed as an exemption and to remove all controversies, we need to allow the input credit on the basis of "use in the factory" rather than on the basis of "use in manufacture of final products". Incidentally, the grant of Cenvat credit on capital goods by using the yardstick of factory of the manufacturer has not led to any disputes and is time tested.

4.1.3 At the same time there may be a possibility of tax payers taking credit on items such as building materials, airconditioners used in guest houses etc, within the factory premises etc. Accordingly, this needs to be taken care of.

4.1.4 It is recommended that the Cenvat Credit Rules, 2002 should be amended to abolish the distinction between capital goods and inputs and allow credit on all inputs brought into the factory except for those figuring in a small negative list, such as office furniture, motor vehicles, MS, HSD, etc.

4.2 Cenvat credit on capital goods

4.2.1 At present, when capital goods are procured the recipient manufacturer is entitled to take 50% of the duty paid thereon as Cenvat credit in the year of their procurement. The balance 50% is availed the next year provided the goods remain in the premises. There is, however, a relaxation in respect of identified components of capital goods on which the entire credit can be taken in the first year itself.

4.2.2 A careful examination of the said provision reveals that this could only have been a measure to stagger the Cenvat credit so that the heavy inflow does not disturb the duty payable by the unit. For instance, in case of a new investment or a new factory the Cenvat credit on the capital goods may be so large that the duty payable by the unit in cash i.e. PLA would be negligible or even nil as the entire duty can be paid through the debit of the accumulated Cenvat credit. Thus, the measure is basically an artificial method to have positive revenue. It is a moot point that even payment of duty through Cenvat credit is nothing but a payment of revenue, though for reasons unknown it is not considered so by the authorities. It is the view that such artificial measures go against the basic philosophy of Cenvat credit scheme. Any person should be entitled to full Cenvat credit of the duty paid so long as the items in question qualify for the credit. At the same time it is recognized that a sudden reversal of the present scheme would adversely impact the revenue in view of the significant amount involved – in 2001-2002 the 50% of the Cenvat credit on capital goods availed was to the tune of approximately Rs. 2500 Crores.

4.2.3 It is recommended that the Cenvat Credit Rules, 2002 should be amended to allow with effect from 1.4.2004 full credit of the duty paid on the capital goods immediately on receipt, as in the case of inputs. As an interim measure, 75% of the credit may be so allowed from 1.4.2003.

4.3 Cenvat credit to be allowed despite technical or procedural violations

4.3.1 Reportedly a large number of Cenvat disputes arise on account of technical or procedural violations or infringements. In such cases it is not in dispute that the said inputs are duty paid, have been received by the claimant for use in the manufacture of the final products, and the final products are dutiable. In the event it appears that while fulfillment of procedural conditions is important the substantive claim of the tax payer should not be denied. Where merited, penalty proceeding may be in order to ensure compliance of the procedures. Accordingly, it is necessary that a clear statement should be made that the procedural violations are not punished in terms of denial of substantive benefits so long there is no revenue loss.

4.3.2 It is recommended that a suitable provision should allow Deputy/Assistant Commissioner to condone technical lapses/ infirmities while allowing Cenvat credit.

4.4 Credit of duty on goods returned to the factory

4.4.1 Rule 16 (1) of Central Excise Rules provides for taking Cenvat credit on returned goods. Sub-Rule (2) provides for payment of an amount equal to the Cenvat credit taken under Sub-Rule (1), if the process carried out on the returned goods does not amount to manufacture. In this context, it is reported that there is no provision or clarification for the recipient of the said goods to take credit of the said amount on receipt of the goods.

4.4.2 It is recommended that an Explanation may be inserted in rule 16 to the effect that the amount paid on removal of returned goods can be taken as Cenvat credit in the hands of the recipients.

4.5 Levy of duty on scrap arising out of dismantled/ broken capital goods.

4.5.1 The Cenvat Credit Rules, 2002 provide that when inputs or capital goods are cleared as such then the manufacturer shall pay an amount equal to the duty of excise which is leviable on the said goods. However, in case capital goods are broken up or dismantled and then removed no duty is being charged. This is in view of the CEGAT orders that no manufacturing activity has taken place on account of dismantling of capital goods. Further, it can also not be said that the capital goods are being removed as such. It is the view that the absence of a provision to charge duty is liable to be misused.

4.5.2 It is recommended that a specific provision may be introduced to charge duty on the dismantled capital goods when removed from the factory.

4.6 Review of grant of Cenvat credit on deemed basis

4.6.1 Rule 11 of the Cenvat Credit Rules, 2002, provide that the Central Government may issue a notification declaring the inputs on which Excise duty or Additional Customs duty shall be deemed to have been paid at the specified rate or equivalent to such amount as may be specified and Cenvat credit of the same would be allowed. Accordingly, a number of notifications have been issued under the authority of this rule indicating the deemed amount of duty which can be availed as Cenvat credit. These notifications are basically for inputs such as yarn used in the manufacture of fabrics and for fabrics used in the manufacture of specified articles of apparel and clothing accessories.

4.6.2 It is the view that as a policy Cenvat credit should be available on actual basis. No doubt, deemed credit appears attractive as it reduces the documentation since evidence of payment of duty need not be insisted upon. However, this is against transparency.

4.6.3 It is recommended that as a policy, Cenvat credit should not be allowed on deemed credit basis.

4.7 Recovery of Cenvat credit erroneously refunded

4.7.1 Rule 12 of the Cenvat Credit Rules, 2002, deals with recovery of Cenvat credit wrongly taken. As mentioned therein, the credit wrongly taken or utilized along with interest shall be recovered from the manufacturer by applying the provisions of Section 11A & 11AB of the Central Excise Act, 1944. These Sections provide for issue of demand notice for Central Excise duty not levied or paid or short levied or short paid or erroneously refunded.

4.7.2 In this regard, it is seen that in terms of rule 5 of the said Cenvat Credit Rules the refund of Cenvat credit can be given to the manufacturer in certain situations. However, in the event a refund is erroneously given there appears to be no provision to recover the same. No doubt, Section 11A would apply to a case of erroneous refund of Central Excise duty but by virtue of rule 12 of the Cenvat Credit Rules it would not apply in case of Cenvat credit erroneously refunded.

4.7.3 It is recommended that rule 12 of the Cenvat Credit Rules, 2002 should be amended to provide for recovery of Cenvat credit erroneously refunded.

4.8 Storage of inputs outside factory after taking Cenvat credit

4.8.1 There is no provision in the Cenvat Credit Rules allowing the recipient of the Cenvat inputs who has availed the credit to store the said goods outside the factory in case there is a shortage of space or for any other reason. Presently, the goods cannot be removed from the factory of manufacture unless the removal is for purpose of job work or these are being cleared permanently. It is the view that the absence of a suitable provision is causing genuine difficulties for the manufacturers who like to get the inputs at the best price by buying in bulk but use the inputs in smalier quantities. There are occasions when a particular input is procured for a specific purpose say, an export order which gets cancelled or postponed necessitating the need to hold the input stocks for a later date. Thus, the facility of storage of the inputs outside the factory would facilitate the trade and industry. It is also not a risk to revenue since a suitable procedure can be drawn up to identify the place of storage and account for the inputs.

4.8.2 It is recommended that Cenvat inputs maybe allowed to be stored outside the factory in an identified place of storage subject to procedural safeguards for due accountal of the inputs.

5. *Exports*

5.1 Self Sealing

5.1.1 Self sealing of container and export goods is allowed under Central Excise provisions subject to prescribed conditions and responsibilities imposed on the exporter which safeguards revenue. Normally these permissions require periodic renewal. At times the field formations are known to refuse this permission. In such situation the exporter has the option of getting the goods sealed by the central excise officers.

5.1.2 In so far as the sealing of export goods by the central excise officers is concerned, it is the view that this invariably causes delays as the officers may not always be present. Further, there is a rise in transaction cost on account of the fact that overtime has to be paid to the department for this work. In any case self-sealing or sealing by central excise officers does not provide a significant relief since the customs at the port of export has the right to re-examine the goods. No doubt the risk attached to goods may be lower when the goods are sealed by the central excise officers. Taking into account all factors related to the sealing of export goods, the pros and cons it is the view that the exports should not be subjected to avoidable transaction costs incurred on account of sealing by the central excise officers. In any case there is a revenue safeguard since the Risk Assessment module at the port of export would take into account the fact that the goods are self-sealed.

5.1.3 It is recommended that sealing of export consignments by Central Excise officers should be replaced by self-sealing by the exporter. This should be granted as a matter of right and not on case to case basis.

5.2 Rebate of Duty.

5.2.1 As per rule 18 of the Central Excise Rules, 2002, rebate is granted on the amount of duty paid on such excisable goods or materials which are used in the manufacture of goods exported out of India. In accordance with the relevant notifications Nos. 40 and 41/2001-CE (N.T.), both dated 26th June, 2001 the rebate is granted by the Deputy Commissioner having jurisdiction over the factory of the manufacture or the Warehouse or the Maritime Commissioner of Central Excise.

5.2.2 In so far as the grant of rebate by the Maritime Commissioner is concerned, at present the exporters after obtaining the proof of export from the Customs officer at the port of shipment have to tender this document to the office of the Maritime Commissioner. Invariably this causes delays. On the other hand if the functions of the Maritime Commissioner are transferred to the Customs Houses located at the said ports the delays would get reduced. Further, such a system would have the following advantages:

(i) Reduction in the transaction costs of the manufacturer-exporters;

(ii) The proof of Export being signed by the Customs officer at the port of shipment would also ensure the genuineness of export within the same office; and

(iii) Reduction in the number of agencies and the paper work both for the department and the exporting community.

5.2.3 Another important issue relates to rebate of duty on specified mineral oils and products. Notification No. 40/2001 CE (N.T.), dated 26.06.2001, deals with the grant of rebate of central excise duty on goods exported. The basic idea is that the export product should not be burdened with domestic taxes. Normally, in the case of goods exported the whole of the duty is rebated. However, the said Notification provides that in respect of specified mineral oil products falling under chapter 27 of the schedule to the Central Excise Act, 1985, which are exported as stores for consumption on board an aircraft on foreign run, the rebate has to be reduced by a specified amount as follows:

S.No.	Description of excisable goods	Amount
1.	Motor Spirit	Rs. 48.88 per kilolitre at fifteen degrees of Centigrade thermometer.
2.	Kerosene and Aviation Turbine Fuel	Rs. 24.94 per kilolitre at fifteen degrees of Centigrade thermometer.
3.	Refined Diesel Oil, other than High Speed Diesel Oil	Rs. 60.00 per kilolitre at fifteen degrees of Centigrade thermometer.
4.	High Speed Diesel Oil	Rs. 24.94 per kilolitre at fifteen degrees of Centigrade thermometer.
5.	Vaporizing Oil	Rs. 50.00 per kilolitre at fifteen degrees of Centigrade thermometer.
6.	Diesel Oil not otherwise specified	Rs. 53.39 per kilolitre at fifteen degrees of Centigrade thermometer.
7.	Furnace Oil	Rs. 21.05 per kilolitre at fifteen degrees of Centigrade thermometer.

5.2.4 The rationale for reducing the amount of rebate in respect of the specified items, as above, is not clear. There is one view that this may have been done in order to take care of the fuel consumed during the domestic run of an aircraft on foreign drum. However, similar approach has not been adopted in the case of aircraft on foreign run using duty free imported fuel. Logically the custom duty should have been demanded on the fuel so used but this is not done. Thus, it is the view that the denial of rebate to the extent specified in the Notification does not appear justified. More so, when we note that the percentage of duty which is denied as rebate is nominal. Incidentally, full rebate of duty is being provided in respect of these items in the case of aircraft on foreign run to Nepal.

5.2.5 The following recommendations are made to improve the system of grant of rebate :

(i) The work of grant of rebate should be centralized at the Custom House itself. In the alternative, an EDI link can be provided between the Customs House and the Maritime Commissioner. This measure is in addition to the grant of rebate by the Deputy/Assistant Commissioner of Central

Excise having jurisdiction over the factory of the manufacturer or warehouse, as at present.

(ii) Notification No. 40/2001 CE (N.T.), dated 26.06.2001 should be amended to provide grant of full rebate in respect of mineral oil products falling under chapter 27 of the schedule to the Central Excise Act, 1985, which are exported as stores for consumption on board an aircraft on foreign run.

5.3 All refunds/rebates to be directly credited to Bank account.

5.3.1 At present, refund/rebate is sanctioned by the competent authority and the payment is made by issue of cheque. The practice is that the cheque is physically delivered to the tax payer, and reportedly this is an avoidable contact point. On the other hand the exporting community is happy with the system of disbursal of the drawback by credit directly to their bank account.

5.3.2 It is recommended that in order to reduce contact points and speed up the disbursal of the rebate/refund, the same should be directly credited to the tax payers' own bank account.

6. Manner of payment of duty

6.1 Periodicity of payment of duty

6.1.1 At present, in terms of rule 8 of the Central Excise Rules, 2002 SSI units pay duty on a monthly basis while non-SSI units pay the same on a fortnightly basis. A condition has also been imposed that Cenvat credit of inputs, raw materials etc. available as on the fifteenth day of the month alone should be utilized while discharging the duty liability for the fortnight. This increases the documentation on the part of the tax payer. It also increases the checks to be performed by the Department while doing the scrutiny of the prescribed return. Accordingly, it is the view that a uniform periodicity of payment of duty would be convenient to administer and would increase transparency. It would also reduce the number of duty payment challans and facilitate revenue reconciliation. Finally, it would be in line with the practice of monthly filing of returns by assesses. However, no change is suggested for the SSI sector.

6.1.2 It is recommended that fortnightly payment of duty may be replaced by monthly payment of duty.

6.2 Date of payment of duty

6.2.1 Explanation to Rule 8 of the Central Excise Rules 2002 dealing with manner of payment of duty clarifies that duty liability shall be deemed to be discharged only if the amount payable is credited to the account of the Central Government by the specified date. Also C.B.E.C. has clarified that the date of affixation of 'receipt stamp' on duty payment document (TR-6), against duly cleared cheque shall be treated as the date on which the amount is credited to the Central Government account. However, it is a fact that it is difficult to ascertain exactly when the amount paid is credited to the Government account. Moreover there is invariably few days delay in realisation of the amount when payment is by cheque. Such instances are treated as default in payment of duty and penal action is initiated against the assessee even though he has deposited the cheque by the due date. However it would be unfair if despite having deposited the duty amount by the due date and the cheque having been honoured, the tax payer is penalized on account of the delays in banking channel. In fact, on the Service Tax side and also in Income Tax Department the date of payment of duty is the date of deposit of cheque. This is considered a better method.

6.2.2 It is recommended that the date of payment of central excise duty may be prescribed as the date of presentation of the cheque to the Bank subject to its realization.

6.3 Default in payment of duty

6.3.1 Rule 8 (4) of the Central Excise Rules, 2002, provides that in case an assessee defaults in payment of installment of duty, as specified, then he shall forfeit the facility to pay the dues in installments for a period of two months starting from the date of communication of an order passed by the Deputy/ Assistant Commissioner or till such date on which all dues are paid, whichever is later. Further, during the period the facility is withdrawn, the assessee has to pay duty on consignment basis by debit to account current (PLA).

6.3.2 Three issues arise out of the above provision. Firstly, basis by debit in account current. In other words, during the period the facility of payment of duty in installments has been withdrawn the assessee cannot pay duty by using the accumulated Cenvat credit. It is the view that this is too harsh a measure. Government should be concerned with payment of duty and not whether it is being paid through debit and account current or through Cenvat credit. Accordingly, it is the view that this condition should be withdrawn.

6.3.5 It is recommended that :

(i) The provision of withdrawing the facility of payment of duty in installments in case of default should be revoked.

(ii) There should be automatic charge of interest and penalty in the event duty is not paid on time.

(iii) In the event it is decided to retain the provision of withdrawing the facility the assessee should be allowed to pay duty during this period through Cenvat credit.

6.3.6 At the same time it should not happen that an assessee continues to default stating that he would pay the interest and penalty in due course. Accordingly, in such case the recovery proceedings under the law should be initiated.

7. Budget Day restrictions

7.1 Rule 32 of the Central Excise Rules, 2002, indicates the restrictions on removal of goods on Budget Day. Essentially it provides that between the time the Budget/ Finance Bill is presented and 2400 hrs midnight on the said day no excisable goods can be removed from a factory or warehouse unless specific permission is obtained from the Commissioner of Central Excise. Moreover, an application for removal of goods has to be presented before 1700 hrs on the working day immediately before the Budget Day.

7.2 Budget Day restrictions had been present in Central Excise law from the very beginning. Earlier, the restrictions were more rigid. Even at present, the net result is that on the Budget Day, clearances of excisable goods all over the country come to a stand still. Reportedly, factories shutdown and there are no economic activities. The Central Excise officers also resort to physical verification of stocks and clearances from the factory, if permitted, take place under physical supervision. Expectedly, transactions costs go up and it is a fertile ground for corrupt practices. Evidently, the restrictions were earlier imposed to ensure against speculation and evasion of duty as during these times the central excise duty was usually revised upwards. Moreover during these times the central excise duty was discharged consignment wise. This is not the case now. In any case, it appears incongruous that the Budget, an instrument to boost economic activity starts with the complete stoppage of all such activity. As regard the likely misuse, no doubt, there may be small clearances of goods at lower duty (if the duty rates go up) but this should be ignored in the interest of encouraging free trade and commerce. Also, under the self-assessment system a procedure is in place to ensure proper accountal and discharge of duty.

7.3 It is recommended that the Budget Day restrictions are out of tune in present day world and should be removed

8. Removal of goods for job-work

8.1 Central Excise Rules, 2002 do not contain any provisions for removal of goods without payment of duty from one factory to another for the purpose of processing when the manufacturer is not working under Cenvat scheme. For instance, earlier rule 96E of the Central Excise Rules, 1944 provided a special procedure for removal of cotton yarn for processing like winding, doubling, reeling etc. or for conversion into hank yarn in plain Reel hank. Thus, the manufacturers not working under Cenvat scheme would have to pay duty on the goods at the time of removal to other factories for the purpose of further processing. This requires redressal.

8.2 It is recommended that there should be a provision for allowing the movement of dutiable goods without payment of duty to job worker even in situations when the principal manufacturer is not working under Cenvat Scheme.

9. Collection of information from tax payer

9.1 While studying the various contact points between department and tax payer, it was revealed that in order to collect information on central excise duty collections all large assesses are being contacted over telephone and through visits to ascertain the duty paid by them during the fortnight. Reportedly, this information is being collected on behalf of C.B.E.C. It is not clear how this information is made use of. In any case, a separate recommendation has already been made for shifting to monthly payment of duty. In the circumstance, it appears that the information on fortnightly payment of duty need not be collected as it increases contact points and causes harassment.

9.2 It is recommended that fortnightly statement of revenue paid, which is presently being collected from tax payers, may be discontinued. Further, as a policy, no information should normally be asked for (from departmental officers or industry) unless it is being obtained in the prescribed returns.

10. Dispute resolution

10.1 Section 11A of the Central Excise Act, 1944 provides for voluntary payment of duty, with interest, by assessees before issue of a Show Cause Notice. However, cases involving suppression, mis-declaration etc., with intent to evade duty are excluded. It appears that since the intention of the Government is to realize the duty at the earliest the assessee should be given the option of voluntarily depositing duty even in the case of fraud etc. However, to ensure that no undue advantage is taken of this facility, such cases should be subject to payment of interest and 25% penalty. In any case even at present after a long drawn out adjudication proceeding the assessee has the option of paying 25% penalty if he pays the confirmed duty within one month of the order determining the duty.

10.2 A related issue is that as a policy when department detects short levy or payment of duty it should have an open discussion with the assessee before proceeding with the issue of Show Cause Notice, if warranted. This will allow the assessee to exercise the option of voluntary payment of duty thereby saving on time and resource in adjudication proceedings.

10.3 It is recommended that :

(i) Scope of Section 11A(2)(B), i.e. non-issue of SCN to be expanded to include cases of non-payment detected by

Audit/ Department.

(ii) Section 11A should be amended to provide for the issue of a Show Cause Notice which automatically collapses if the tax payer voluntarily pays the duty and interest and 25% penalty within a period of 30 days of the issue of the notice. This would apply to cases involving fraud, suppression etc. In such cases the Notice should also mention in its preamble that there would also be no prosecution proceedings. The provision regarding collapse of the Show Cause Notice should apply to 'other' cases but without the requirement of payment of 25% penalty.

11. Filing of Returns

11.1 Every tax payer is required to submit a return in the prescribed form indicating the production and removal of the goods and other relevant information including duty paid. This is supported by a copy of TR6 challan which evidences the deposit of duty in the Bank. Whereas, an assessee is required to furnish this return by the 10th of each month (for the preceeding month) an assessee in the small scale sector is required to furnish this return by the 20th day following each quarter (for the preceeding quarter). Two issues are raised in respect of the filing of return. Firstly, the duty has to be paid by the 5th of the following month and it becomes difficult to finalise the return in only 5 days thereafter. Secondly, the furnishing of the return is a contact point which is avoidable. Hence, steps must be taken in the interest of transparency and tax payer facilitation.

11.2 In this regard a perusal of the return and a study of the present system shows that on-line filing of return would greatly facilitate both department and assessee. However, there are two constraints in moving towards this mechanism. Firstly, digital signatures are not recognized. Secondly, the submission of the hard copy of the TR6 challan requires manual filing of return. In so far as, the submission of the TR6 challan is concerned it is felt that this can be dispensed with. Presently, this document is used to reconcile the payments by matching with the copy of TR6 challan received separately by the PAO from the Bank. Instead the matching could be done on the basis on declaration of duty paid to TR6 on the return with the TR6 copy with the PAO. In so far as digital signature is concerned, steps have to be taken for its recognition.

11.3 It is recommended that :

(i) Date of filing return may be shifted to the 15th. of the close of the month/quarter, as the case may be for all tax payers i.e. including those in the SSI sector. However, the large units would furnish online or otherwise, by the 6th of each month, the information of total duty paid.

(ii) As a first step towards on-line filing of returns the monthly/quarterly submission of TR 6 challans may be discontinued and steps should be taken to eventually allow on-line filing of returns. The details of TR 6 Challans will be mentioned in the returns.

12. Voluntary filing of documents by tax payers

12.1 Sometimes the tax payer would like to voluntarily file some documents in connection with his manufacturing activity with his jurisdictional excise department even though the same are not statutorily prescribed. This is done as a matter of abundant caution so as to preempt allegation of suppression of facts and creating hardship and loss through imposition of fine and penalty. Such a refusal appears unfair and unwarranted. Voluntary filing of documents and papers to safeguard the tax payers interest cannot be denied. Moreover, this has no risk to revenue and instead helps in dispensing justice.

12.2 It is recommended that it must be made binding on the field officials to accept documents from the tax payers and give an acknowledgement in writing, if needed, in order to safeguard tax payers interest.

13. Arrest

13.1 Arrest provision in central excise as contained in Section 13 of the Central Excise Act, 1944 has been reported to be misused to the detriment of tax payer confidence. Reportedly there are many cases when the officers at the cutting edge have threatened the tax payer with the use of this provision for their personal gain. There is no doubt that a tax evader deserves no leniency but the finding is that the vast body of the honest tax payers remain in constant fear of the misuse of this provision. There is, accordingly, a need to review the provision.

13.2 In this regard an attempt was made to ascertain the best international practices. By and large it was seen that the law is severe on the tax evader. Accordingly, it was also examined whether in our context certain safeguards could be built into the provisions so that the honest tax payer is not harassed and the provision is not misused. One safeguard could be that the arrest is made with the written sanction of the Commissioner and another that the Citizen Charter clearly indicates the rights of the arrested person. However, due cognizance was given to the fact that the large number of the taxpayers and the potential tax payers particularly in the small scale sector do not have access to the information and the provision could still be misused. In this background, keeping in mind all factors of which the most important is to restore tax payer confidence in the tax administration it is the view that the power to sanction arrest should not be exercised by the departmental officer. This is also in line with the best international practices.

13.3 It is recommended that the arrest in central excise cases, if warranted, should be made with the sanction of a Magistrate. This would require suitable amendment to the Central Excise Act, 1944.

14. Tax Clinics for Small Scale Sector Manufacturers

14.1 A critical element of tax payer facilitation is the proper dissemination of information and guidance in the compliance of the legal provisions. This is all the more necessary in respect of our small scale manufacturers who are typically one–man shows and cannot keep abreast of the changes in the law and procedures. In fact, it is the absence of healthy interaction between the taxpayer and the tax administrators that often leads to compliance issues. It is desirable that the confidence of the small scale manufacturer should be restored for which an institutionalized mechanism is necessary. Importantly, it is the tax administrators who must reach out to the small scale manufacturers. Expecting a small scale manufacturer to leave his business and enter the portal of the Commissionerates may not yield results as the mentality is that he would rather avoid the interaction. The interaction which is now proposed would be a step towards educating the small scale manufacturers about their legal responsibilities, guiding them in the conduct of their tax matters and breaking the communication wall which has distanced the small manufacturers for the tax administrators.

14.2 It is recommended that by 1st April 2003 each Central Excise Commissionerate should establish one Tax Clinic for the Small Scale Sector, under the charge of Deputy/Assistant Commissioner to guide small scale manufacturers. This Cell should closely coordinate with the Small Scale Manufacturers Associations. The number of such Clinics can be increased later based upon the experience.

5

Export Promotion

1. Introduction

Sustained export growth is crucial for maintaining and accelerating the GDP growth momentum, increasing employment and alleviating poverty. Since full liberalization of imports and sharp reduction in transaction costs were expected to take time to implement, several export promotional schemes were introduced in the last two decades. In light of the recent changes introduced in removal of all quantitative restrictions in imports and substantial reduction in import duties and the present proposals to introduce Universal Green Channel and full implementation of EDI (in customs clearances), it is an opportune time to take stock of all the schemes and to take a view to remove some of them which may have outlived their roles. However, in the transition period, as also suggested by the Prabhu Committee, export incentives need to be maintained so as not to lose the export momentum.

2. Viable export strategy

2.1 It is the view that a viable export strategy must rest upon two basic premises. Firstly, to be competitive in the international market, the export product must match, if not better, the competition in terms of pricing and quality. Secondly, the exporter must have an incentive to enter the highly uncertain export market. Both these objectives are achieved through wide-ranging facilities, infrastructure, financing, income tax relief, trade facilitation, etc. and indirect taxes play a critical role. Taking up indirect taxes, it is evident that the strategy so far has been to grant customs and central excise duty exemptions on the raw materials, inputs etc.

used in the export product. Particularly on the customs side this leads to making available the international high quality raw materials, inputs etc. at the international price and our exporters are thus not disadvantaged viz. a viz. their competitors abroad. Moreover it ensures that the price of the export product is not loaded with any tax element.

2.2 Neutralizing the tax element in export products is an internationally accepted methodology to encourage exports. However, multiple schemes such as Drawback, DEPB, Advance Licence/DEEC, DFRS, EPCG and EOU/EPZ/SEZ schemes cause difficulties in administration and are liable for some misuse. Accordingly, on a comprehensive review of the present schemes and taking into regard all relevant factors and the best international practices it is recommended that the export strategy should focus upon the following schemes :

(iv) SEZ and EOU schemes – This is for the grant of duty exemption on all goods (capital goods, raw materials etc.) required by the units for their export production.

(v) Advance Licensing (actual user) scheme - This would grant duty exemption to actual users on capital goods, raw materials etc. used for export production subject to post-clearance intelligence and audit-based verification.

(vi) Drawback scheme – Here, the relief from duties on the inputs, raw materials, capital good etc. would be provided through a mechanism of refund of the duties paid.

3. SEZ and EOU schemes

3.1 In so far the SEZ and EOU schemes are concerned, the trade and industry do not have any significant conceptual disagreement with their design. A policy decision has also been taken to convert the existing EPZs into SEZs. The focus is correctly placed on the SEZ scheme which has been conceptualized with care taking into account the experience of implementing similar scheme world-wide. However, upon taking the SEZ scheme as the role model (for the EOU scheme) it is the view that certain measures are required to be taken in order to derive the full potential of the SEZ and EOU schemes.

3.2 Codification of laws and procedures relating to SEZ and EOU/EPZ schemes!

3.2.1 The SEZ and EOU/EPZ schemes has a common philosophy and common objectives. Therefore, by and large the procedures are the same. The one critical difference is that whereas the EOUs are 'stand alone' units, the units in the SEZ/EPZ are in a well defined enclave. However, a perusal of the supporting customs and central excise duty exemption notifications and procedures reveals a confusing scenario. This is since there are an unduly large number of notifications (over 50) and circulars and instructions (over 300) in existence. It can well be contemplated that both the tax administrators and the units themselves would have a lot of doubts in view of the sheer volume of relevant material. It is also quite possible that cases of misuse of the scheme, which are on the rise in recent years are on account of the absence of codification of the law and procedures in respect of the said schemes.

3.2.2 It is recommended that the C.B.E.C. must immediately work upon consolidating the numerous notifications, circulars and instructions, on both customs and central excise side in respect of the SEZ and EOU/EPZ schemes. This may be done by 1st April 2003. Ideally, all the notifications should be combined into one, and the circulars and instructions issued as a compendium, subject wise. Future changes, if any, must be included in the said compendium from time to time so that at any one point of time the units as well as the administrators have up-to-dated information available with them. Not only will this ensure transparency it would reduce the scope of misuse.

3.3 Access to DTA

3.3.1 Initially no DTA sale was allowed to the EOUs, one reason why these were called '100%' EOUs. However, in view of the fact that access to international market may not always be available DTA sale was allowed in a limited way as a buffer, in 1988. However, over time the extent of DTA access has increased, touching a figure of 50% at present. The DTA access is allowed on payment of duty on the goods sold in the DTA. With few exceptions, the EOU/EPZ units which use wholly indigenous raw materials pay duty equal to the central excise duty on the said goods (provided the same is not nil) whereas the other units (i.e. which use imported raw materials) pay duty equal to 50% of the customs duty in the like goods, as if imported. There is one view that there appears to be little or no justification to grant the benefit of concessional duty on DTA sale (i.e 50% of the customs duty) to the units which in any case avail the benefit of procurement of required capital goods, raw materials etc. free of customs and central excise duties. This also places the competing DTA units at a disadvantage.

3.3.2 In this regard a perusal of the SEZ scheme reveals that in so far as DTA access is concerned the units therein are treated as if these are outside India and there is no restriction on their access to DTA. At the same time the goods sold in DTA are subjected to payment of full customs duty, in like manner of imports into the country. As earlier seen, the SEZ scheme has been conceptualized in line with the best international practice and there is appreciable common ground between this scheme and the EOU scheme. Therefore, taking a cue from the SEZ scheme but at the same time noting the concern of the EOU/EPZ units which use wholly indigenous raw materials, the following recommendation is made as regards the facility of DTA access to the EOU/EPZ units subject to the unit meeting the requirement of the EXIM Policy as regards the eligibility of access to DTA :

(iii) EOU/EPZ units using wholly indigenous raw materials - status quo to be maintained i.e. DTA access of 50% on payment of duty equal to the central excise duty unless the central excise duty is nil in which case duty paid will be equal to 30% of the customs duty on like goods, as if imported (with few exceptions, as at present).

(iv) Other EOU/EPZ units - 100% DTA access subject to payment of full customs duty on like goods, as if imported.

4. Drawback scheme

4.1 Drawback scheme provides for rebate of the duty chargeable on the imported or excisable materials, components, packing materials etc. used in the manufacture of the export product. It basically neutralizes the incidence of indirect taxes (customs and central excise) on the export products through the refund of the said duty. The mechanism is to announce the 'All Industry' rate of Drawback for the export products in the form of a schedule, which is determined on annual basis for a large number of export goods. For this purpose, the Drawback Directorate seeks information on consumption norms, the international and local values of the inputs, and the duty levied thereon from the Export Promotion Counsels, Associations and Organizations. Thereafter, the workings are pre-audited by the officers of CAG. Thus, the rate of Drawback is worked out on the basis of statistical study taking into account the average indirect tax borne on each of the export goods. However, when the export product is either not figuring in the schedule or the individual exporter is not satisfied with the Drawback rate and feels that his product has suffered higher input taxation, there is provision for fixing a 'Brand' or Special Brand' rate of Drawback.

4.2 It is the view that the Drawback scheme should be in the forefront of the export promotion schemes as it is transparent, upfront and has lower risks of leakage. However, it imposes a cash-flow burden on exporters, and must, therefore, necessarily efficiently provide disbursal of the Drawback amount without delay if it is to be popular. At the same time the scheme is also not comprehensive such that it does not include in its ambit the capital goods and also various other State level taxes, which are borne by the export goods. On the other hand, though exemptions eliminate the cash-flow burden on qualified exporters completely, but at the price of higher risks of leakage. Thus, as a policy they should only be applied to exporters who meet very restrictive qualifying criteria, such as a high threshold of exports to total sales and a good track record of tax compliance. In the present situation in India there is a strong case to reduce the multiplicity of schemes and rely chiefly on an efficient Drawback system duly revamped to eliminate the reported disadvantages. Recent initiatives such as the credit of Drawback sanctioned directly to the bank account of the exporter, through EDI, and the sanction of Brand rate of Drawback within 15 days subject to ex-post facto verification of the declaration made by the exporter have removed some of the difficulties associated with the scheme. However, there is scope for further improvement.

4.3 Increasing transparency of Drawback scheme

4.3.1 As seen, the methodology of fixing the 'All Industry' rate of Drawback is to obtain data from on consumption norms, values of the inputs, and the duty levied thereon from the Export Promotion Counsels, Associations and Organizations. Thereafter, the workings are pre-audited by the officers of CAG. However, besides routine correspondence, there is no formal mechanism for consulting the Department of Commerce in the matter, which appears surprising since the work of export promotion is allocated to this Department. Moreover, all Export Promotion Counsels, Associations and Organizations work in close interaction with the Department of Commerce. Thus, it would enhance the credibility of the Drawback scheme and improve transparency if the Department of Commerce is formally made a part of the process of fixing All Industry Rate of Drawback.

4.3.2 It is recommended that C.B.E.C. may work out a mechanism to formally associate a representative of the Department of Commerce in the process of fixing the All Industry rates of Drawback.

4.4 Expanding scope of Drawback scheme

4.4.1 Drawback has been considered as amongst the most effective schemes to neutralize the domestic taxes on export goods. Therefore, the Task Force has made certain recommendations to further improve this scheme and remove the deficiencies noticed. However, as seen the domestic taxes on export goods are basically taxes on inputs and raw materials and taxes on capital goods. So far capital goods are outside the scope of Drawback scheme. Furthermore, the present scheme seeks to neutralize the central indirect taxes (customs and central excise) whereas it is a fact that there are a large number of State and Local level taxes incurred on the export goods. Thus, an effective long term export promotion scheme would be one which neutralises all domestic taxes whether imposed at central, state or local level and on all factors of production (inputs, raw materials, capital goods, etc.). Therefore, there is a case for expanding the scope of Drawback scheme in this direction. In so far as the inclusion of State level taxes in the Drawback scheme is concerned the matter would get simplified once State VAT is place. However, as regards, the extension of the scheme to capital goods, the modalities would have to be worked out carefully. Certain issues such as the use of the said capital goods for domestic production, etc., would require to be resolved.

4.4.2 It is also noted that Drawback scheme envisages the rebate of the duty paid on the inputs, raw materials, etc. In other words, the duties have to be first paid and then rebated/refunded. This would, no doubt cause cash flow problems particularly in respect of capital goods wherein the duty amount may be significant. Therefore, it appears that a parallel scheme of allowing duty free procurement of capital goods should continue, as a part of the Advance Licencing (actual user) Scheme.

4.4.3 It is recommended that through suitable legislative changes the scope of the Drawback scheme should be expanded to provide for rebate of all duties – central, state and local – and on all goods which go into export product including capital goods. Similar action should be taken to include capital goods in the Advance Licencing (actual user) Scheme.

4.5 Furnishing of non-availment of Cenvat certificate

4.5.1 Availment of Cenvat credit and Drawback are mutually exclusive benefits. Accordingly, it is provided that while claiming Drawback the exporter should produce a certificate of non-availment of Cenvat credit. In fact to make the matter abundantly clear certain entries of the Duty Drawback schedule specifically provide for the nonrequirement of this certificate when the goods are exempt for central excise duty (e.g. proviso of general note No. 8 of Duty Drawback Schedule – Handicrafts (including handicrafts of brass artwares), handloom products or leather and other products). The requirement of the non-availment of Cenvat credit is insisted upon with each and every shipment. The consignment–wise insistence upon production of the required certificate increases the contact points and transaction cost. However, it is the view that customs should trust the exporter to make a correct declaration. Further, if the requirement of the certificate is dispensed with, the disposal of Drawback claims will also speed up.

4.5.2 It is recommended that Customs should accept self-declaration from the Merchant Exporters that their supporting manufacturers are not registered with Central Excise and they do not avail Cenvat benefit. Similar self-declaration should be accepted from manufacturer-exporters. Such claims may be subjected to post disbursal verification on basis of intelligence and risk assessment techniques.

4.6 Sanction of Drawback on grant of Let Export order

4.6.1 Section 75(1) of Customs Act, 1962 provides that exporter shall be granted Drawback in respect of goods which have entered for export and in respect of which an order permitting clearance and loading thereof for exportation has been made under Section 51 by the proper officers. In fact, Section 75 had been amended in 1983 to enable the payment of Drawback as soon as the order permitting clearance for exportation has been made by the proper officer. In the EDI system, however, Drawback is sanctioned only after Export General Manifest (EGM) is filed and Shipping Bill is reconciled with the EGM. As seen, delays in sanction of Drawback occur due to the late filing of the EGM and also due to errors during reconciliation (of Shipping Bill details and EGM) because of mistakes. Thus, sanctioning the payment of Drawback only after the EGM is filed and reconciled has led to innumerable disputes and pendencies.

4.6.2 In this regard it is noted that EGM is essentially required to confirm the actual export of the goods after Let Export order has been given. In other words the EGM helps to account for the goods and confirms their export. However, once the goods have been entered for export these are out of the control of the exporter and whereas it is possible that in few cases the export may be delayed or may not take place, this is a remote possibility. In any case, the law provides for raising of demands in case Drawback has been wrongly sanctioned and the revenue is safeguarded. Thus, keeping in mind exporters interest in quick sanction of Drawback and that the risk to revenue on account of non-export after the goods are entered for export is minimal, it appears appropriate that the sanction of Drawback is not held up on account of either delay in submission of EGM or errors on account thereof. The matching of the Shipping Bill with EGM may be a post-facto activity and steps may be taken to recover the Drawback sanctioned if in few remote cases the export has not taken place for some reason.

4.6.3 It is recommended that that Drawback should be sanctioned on the basis of Let Export Order without waiting for the EGM.

4.7 Brand Rate of Drawback

4.7.1 As per the procedure prescribed in regard to fixation of Brand Rate of Drawback, where no amount or rate of Drawback has been determined in respect of any goods or the exporter is not satisfied with the amount determined he may, within 60 days (or extended period of 30 days) from the relevant date apply to the Central Government for the determination of the amount or rate of Drawback. For this purpose the exporter is required to required to state all relevant facts including the proportion in which the materials or components are used in the production or manufacture of goods and the duties paid on such materials or components. Based upon the information given and subject to verification thereof the Drawback Directorate determines the amount or rate of Drawback in respect of such goods.

4.7.2 In this regard the finding is that steps have been recently been taken to expedite the fixing of Brand Rate of Drawback on the basis of the exporters application subject to post-facto verification. Notwithstanding it is observed that delays continue to occur and it is worthwhile to explore alternatives to give relief to the exporter. One way is to make available some of the Drawback amount once the Let Export Order has been given. This amount could be on the basis of the All Industry Rate of Drawback since Brand Rate of Drawback would be invariably higher. The differential amount may be released after the Brand Rate of Drawback is determined. It is expected that this system would greatly increase the liquidity of the exporters and the additional work load would not be so much.

4.7.3 Another issue is that Brand Rate or Special Brand Rate of Drawback is fixed by the Directorate of Drawback, C.B.E.C. on an application made by the exporter. This is done on the basis of the declared input-output ratio and duty burden on the goods followed by post-facto verification on random basis. However, it is reported that in case an exporter is dissatisfied with the determined Brand Rate or Special Brand Rate of Drawback no mechanism is provided for redressal. Brand Rate or Special Brand Rate has an impact on exports. Accordingly, it is necessary that an exporter must be fully satisfied that he is getting the export incentive correctly. Absence of a redressal mechanism is against the exporters interest. A related issue is that, at present, exporters aggreived of orders in matters of "All Industry" rate of Drawback and rebate of duty on goods exported, have to approach Joint secretary, Revision Application for redressal. This causes hardip to the exporters in far off places.

4.7.4 The following recommendations are made in respect of improving the mechanism of sanction of Brand rate of Drawback:

(i) In cases where the exporter has applied for fixing the Brand Rate of Drawback, the amount at the All Industry Rate of Drawback may be immediately released once the Let Export order is given. The balance amount may be released upon the determination of the Brand Rate of Drawback.

(ii) Drawback Rules should be modified to provide for an appeal to CEGAT in case an exporter is dissatisfied with the Brand Rate or Special Brand Rate of Drawback fixed for him. Similar redresal mechanism may be explored in respect of orders relating to All Industry rate of Drawback and rebate of duty on export goods.

4.8 Deputy/Assistant Commissioner (Exports) to sanction Drawback

4.8.1 In the existing system Deputy Commissioner (Export) and Deputy Commissioner (Drawback) are separate. Whereas the former deals with the passing of export consignments these are subsequently sent to Deputy Commissioner (Drawback) for sanction of Drawback, in case the export is under claim of Drawback. Invariably the new officer raises unnecessary queries and documents have to go to and fro the two officers. It is the view that all procedural requirement for Drawback such as production of Cenvat certificates etc. should be scrutinized at the time of Let Export. Once the Shipping Bill is passed and Let Export order given, the Drawback claim should be sanctioned subject to post facto ensuring that the goods have been actually exported. It is expected that this would further speed up the disposal of Drawback.

4.8.2 It is recommended that the Deputy Commissioner (Export) may be made fully responsible for "Let Export" and also sanction of Drawback amount.

4.9 Blocking of Drawback

4.9.1 At present the Drawback Rules provide that in the event the exporter does not furnish proof of remittance of sales proceeds within 6 months of exports the amount availed as Drawback has to be returned. This is being enforced on the strength of XOS statements received from RBI. It is seen that once the XOS statement is entered into the system the software is so developed that it automatically blocks further disbursal of Drawback to the exporter concerned. In fact the blockage is so complete that even if the outstanding is a nominal amount all future Drawback claims amounting to Crores of rupees would get blocked. This is a cause of hardship to the genuine exporter who may be in a position to finally satisfy the customs that the foreign exchange has been received. The present procedure is also not sound on equity as the amount blocked has no relation to the amount of Drawback under dispute.

4.9.2 It is recommended that there should be an immediate software modification such that amount of Drawback blocked should not at any one point of time exceed the amount under dispute.

4.10 Management of XOS data

4.10.1 At present, RBI compiles the report of outstanding remittances for exports made under various schemes every six months and sends the same to the nodal Custom House in the form of XOS (Export Outstanding Statement). This statement is sent to the nodal Customs House under each Zonal Office of RBI, which in turn segregates the data manually for each of the concerned Custom House/port/airport/ICD/CFS of export. Thereafter, the concerned Customs officers are required to issue a notice to the exporter to recover Drawback on the unrealized remittance.

4.10.2 The volume of data in the XOS is phenomenal. To illustrate, XOS of only RBI, Delhi contains around 55,000 shipping bills. Such a volume is not amenable to manual sorting. Further, whereas the existing format of XOS provides details of name, address of exporter, number of shipping bill, G.R. number and amount outstanding, it does not provide the following critical information :

(i) Port of export; and

(ii) Scheme under which exported.

4.10.3 It is, therefore, not surprising that invariably there is delay in linking the XOS statement with the port/airport concerned and export benefits wrongly availed can not be easily recovered. At the same it is learnt that each Custom House/port/airport/ICD/CFS is having a unique Code number. Were the XOS to mention the Code number the matter of identifying the outstanding remittance with the Custom House/port/airport/ICD/CFS and exporter concerned would be much simplified. Further, there appears to be no sound reason why the information continues to be dealt on manual basis. Electronic mode of receipt of information would facilitate sorting besides ensuring faster action to recover the outstanding export benefits.

4.10.4 For expeditious recovery of inadmissible export benefits, it is recommended that the Export Outstanding Statement (XOS) must include a reference to the Code Number of the Custom House/port/airport/ICD/CFS of export. There should also be electronic exchange of information between the RBI and the nodal Custom House.

4.11 Confirmation of receipt of remittance

4.11.1 The Drawback Rules provide for recovery of Drawback in cases where the sale proceeds of the exported goods are not realized. It is specified that this verification has to be done on the basis of intimation from the RBI in the form of a Export Outstanding Statement (XOS). The XOS is received on a periodic basis, normally once in six months, after which verification is carried out and demands raised where the foreign exchange remittance has not been realized. Very often these demands are kept pending as exporters claim that foreign exchange has since been realized and would be reflected in the ensuing XOS.

4.11.2 It is recommended that to avoid un-necessary issue of demand notices, the Customs may accept from the exporters themselves Bank Realisation Certificates as a proof of realisation of sale proceeds.

4.12 Duty Drawback on composite items

4.12.1 As per General Note No. 11 of Duty Drawback Schedule, in the case of export of composite items constituent material should be visibly distinguishable and their weights should be unambiguously verifiable. That means unless one piece of each item or entire consignment is broken, the weight cannot be verified for some of the handicrafts items. For such items, at the field level, problems are being faced and the Drawback for the composite items is being denied.

4.12.2 It is recommended that as a general policy the weight declared by the exporters should be accepted. Verification should be done only in case of doubt or there is intelligence to the contrary.

4.13 Credit of Brand Rate of Drawback into Bank

4.13.1 On issue of the Brand Rate (or Special Brand Rate) letter by the Directorate of Drawback, the exporter has to get it registered at the Custom House of export. After registration, a Quantity release order is issued to the Drawback section from where the Drawback amount is released after feeding the data into the computer system, which is linked with the shipping bill details of exports made. This procedure is time consuming, taking approximately 3-4 months before the Drawback amount is credited in the account of exporter. Sometimes shipping bill details are also not readily available, which causes further delay. It appears that a short-cut is necessary to expedite the grant of Drawback. This could be achieved by merging the steps of registration and the issue of Quantity release order.

4.13.2 It is recommended that after issuance of Brand Rate (including Special Brand Rate) letter, a copy should be forwarded to Customs EDI system for data feeding. The amount of Drawback should then be credited automatically in the exporter's bank account as in case of claim of All Industry rate of Drawback.

4.14 Opening of Bank accounts for Drawback

4.14.1 Under the EDI system and even otherwise, the exporter is required to open a Bank account at an identified Bank and the Drawback amount is directly credited to the said account by the Customs. It has been reported that this arrangement is causing difficulties and increasing the transaction cost for the following reasons:

(i) An exporter who has exports through more than one port/ airport has to open that many number of Bank accounts. This entails various formalities, keeping minimum deposit etc.

(ii) When the exporter is located at the interior away for the place of export, the Drawback amount is first received at the designated Bank and subsequently transferred to his own account at the place of his business. This invariably take time and costs the exporter in terms of bank commissions etc.

(iii) When the Bank is located far away the exporter has often to incur wasteful expenditure to ascertain whether the Drawback amount is credited or not.

4.14.2 Accordingly, while the present system of direct credit of Drawback to the designated Bank has its advantages for the exporters who are in the same city it has resulted in increase in transaction cost for other exporters. In this regard, a system whereby the designated Bank transfers the Drawback amount direct to the tax payers Bank account wherever located has obvious advantages and resolves the reported difficulties in the present system being followed by customs. There is no reason why the Banks should not be willing to carry out this additional work as they collection of sizeable revenues is a source of income for them. In the alternative, the exporter would not mind paying the additional bank fees, if any, for the facility of receiving the Drawback amount at this own Bank.

4.14.3 It is recommended that at the option of the exporter C.B.E.C. should work out an arrangement with its designated Bank which, when authorized, should send a mail transfer of the

Drawback amount direct to the tax payer's bank account, wherever located.

4.15 Interest on delayed sanction of Drawback

4.15.1 Reportedly the sanction of Drawback gets delayed at the hands of the customs and this handicaps the export effort. Further, in the event the grand to refund is delayed the department is liable to pay interest thereon. However, there is no such provision in respect of delay in sanction of Drawback. It is the view that the exporter should not be penalized on account of delays by the department.

4.15.2 It is recommended that in case, the sanction of Drawback is delayed beyond a period of one week of the receipt of listed documents, the Department should be liable to pay interest on the amount of Drawback. On its part the C.B.E.C. should list out the documents required for sanction of Drawback, which should be made known to the exporters.

5. Duty Entitlement Pass Book (DEPB) scheme

5.1 As a policy, export promotion should largely rest upon an efficient scheme of Drawback. However, there are presently some difficulties in the Drawback scheme which contribute to delay in the sanction of Drawback. The delay causes a cash flow problem for the exporter which has to be avoided. Accordingly, certain measures have been suggested to improve the Drawback scheme. On its part it is recognized that DEPB is presently largely meeting the requirement of the exporters. It is also seen that the matter of having a long term scheme which efficiently meets the requirement of the exporters and boost exports has been recently examined by the Prabhu Committee set up by the Ministry of Commerce. After detailed examination of the pros and cons of the various schemes it recommended that DEPB should be merged with Drawback. The Task Force endorses this view. The merged scheme should basically rest upon the Drawback model. It is expected that by this time the Drawback scheme would have been further improved to reduce delays and provide immediate relief to the exporters.

5.2 It is recommended that DEPB should be merged with the Drawback scheme from 1st April 2005.

6. Coordination between DGFT and Customs

6.1 It is often reported that there is a need to promote the coordination between DGFT and C.B.E.C. and its customs field formations as otherwise hardship is caused to the importing and exporting community and there is also increase in transaction costs. Instances were reported of delay in registration of DEPB books by customs as they had not received the copy from DGFT, non-acceptance of the DGFT instruction unless the supporting customs notification were issued etc. It is the finding that the grievances are genuine. Effective implementation of the policy provisions is very important to cut delays and achieve export performance.

6.2 From the point of the view of the exporters and importers the Government is one, and so it should be. Both DGFT and Customs are two arms of the Government and it is necessary that they operate together and in harmony while giving effect to Government policies. At the same time it is appreciated that at the field level the individual officer of customs (or DGFT) are bound by their individual laws and would hesitate to act on the basis of a DGFT order unless specifically so authorized to do so under their own law. Thus, the remedy lies in improved coordination between the two departments. Broadly, the difficulties which are faced at the field level and by the industry can be categorized as follows :

(i) Non-issue of supporting customs notifications despite policy announcement - Invariably it is noticed that there is significant time gap between the EXIM Policy announcement on 1st April each year and the issue of the relevant customs and central excise duty exemption notifications. The notifications are issued after a few months and then too with contents inconsistent with the EXIM Policy provisions. At times the notifications are simply not issued which nullifies the DGFTs policy announcements.

(ii) Non-receipt of documents relating to licensing by the customs - For instance, it is reported that the manufacturer exporter experience difficulties in getting registration of DEPB at the customs port on account of the fact that the

Customs authorities may not have got their copy from DGFT.

6.3 The first issue is really one of coordination between two arms of the Government, which has a bearing upon both the delay in release of duty exemption notifications and their contradictions with the EXIM Policy provisions. The matter requires urgent attention. Ideally consensus should be evolved on the Policy prescription before it is announced and the attempt should be to make no changes, which in any way dilute or modify the concessions given earlier, which affect the trade and industry adversely.

6.4 It is recommended that towards improved coordination between the DGFT and customs the following steps may be taken:

(i) Duty exemptions, which are in general a critical component of the export promotion schemes, should be notified along with the EXIM Policy announcement. For this purpose the EXIM Policy should be made available to the Department of Revenue by 15th of March each year.

(ii) Both Customs and DGFT should make use of EDI technology for exchange of information, which would cut the delays.

(iii) There should be an institutional arrangement to resolve the coordination problems between the DGFT and Customs. The recommended structure is as follows :

(a) 'Export and Import Co-ordination Committee' co-chaired by Member (Customs), C.B.E.C. and DGFT and having as its members J.S. (Customs), C.B.E.C., J.S. (Drawback), C.B.E.C, Additional DGFT, Director (Customs), C.B.E.C. and Joint DGFT and members of Exporters', Importers' and CHA Associations. The Committee would meet once in a quarter to examine and resolve all co-ordination issues. It would also oversee the work of the Regional Export and Import Coordination Committees.

(b) 'Regional Export and Import Co-ordination Committee' at each of the ports/airports/ICDs/CFS.

This Committee would be chaired by Chief Commissioner of Customs. Senior most member of the DGFT at the port/airport/ICD/CFS would be a member. The Committee would also include all concerned departments and agencies such as custodians, banks, etc. and members of Exporters, Importers and CHA Associations. The Committee would meet once in a quarter to resolve all co-ordination problems. It is expected that since the customs is the chief implementation agency of the DGFT policies this Committee under the Chief Commissioner would ensure early resolution of the problems.

6.5 It is understood that in some places similar bodies do meet but the result is not satisfactory. Hence, there is a need to place the Committees on a firm footing, as proposed above. These Committees should be notified in the EXIM Policy and the C.B.E.C. Circular.

6

Automation of Indirect Tax Systems and Procedures

1. Introduction

It is clear that the success of an efficient tax administration rests upon making full use of the potential of automation and related technologies. The bottom line is that change shall, and indeed must, be automation driven. This is also the philosophy underlying the many recommendations of the Task Force in the various matters relating to the Indirect taxes. Internationally too, risk profiling and assessment is heavily dependent upon the use of computers, and Information Technology is revolutionizing the work on trade facilitation.

1.2 The major benefit of an automation programme is experienced in the area of trade facilitation. Automation leads to quicker clearances, standardization of procedures, reduced discretion, less interface and faster decision making, all of which greatly benefit the trade and industry. At the same time, compliance issues are not neglected and, in fact, there is far greater control, though unobtrusive, which is desirable. Thus, internationally, on the customs side cargoes, containers, and goods are being tracked around the globe by a variety of automatic identification devices. EDI and electronic commerce are replacing the tedious paper trail and signatures. Most countries are considering the use of smart cards, and satellite tracking system whereby containers are locked electronically and tracked via satellites. It is the view that India with its army of first-rate IT specialists can certainly take the lead in this transformation rather than take the back seat with outmoded practices. The same goes for reform of the central excise administration, which should follow the best international practices and remove most discretionary powers and rely on a transparent, simple, and objective system based on trust, aided by full use of information technology to collect revenues and punish entities who dodge compliance. The use of automation for higher level policy planning is also evident as the computers capture the required data error free.

1.3 In this regard, it is appreciated that C.B.E.C. has taken some steps towards increased use of technology in the conduct of the day to day operation in the Custom Houses. This is particularly evident in the case of customs with the spread of EDI from port to port. Interestingly, not only does EDI speed up decision making, it also ensures accountability as each transaction is time stamped. Recent initiatives on the Central Excise side, such as on-the spot issue of Registration Certificate by use of web based applications are also promising. However, much more needs to be done and at a far quicker pace. In fact, C.B.E.C. itself appears to be lagging behind in terms of infrastructure and use of computer information. Ideally the C.B.E.C. should have available on line access to all Custom Houses and Central Excise Commissionerates. This would obviate the need of calling for information from time to time. This would also speed up decision making. Further, an arrangement for video conferencing between the C.B.E.C. and the field formations would allow the senior field officers to remain in their station and not come to Delhi often. This would be a facility to the trade and industry as the absence of the officers adversely affects the disposal of work.

2. Automation driven tax administration

2.1. The essential requirement of any successful automation process is the standardization of information and absence of frequent changes. Accordingly, it is imperative that a conscious decision must be taken for imposing self-discipline and not making frequent changes in laws, procedures and rates of duties (through exemptions). Once the procedures are standardized and stable the automation can be done and it would deliver results. However, a successful automation programme rests upon committed administrative support backed by significant financial investment.

2.2 The following recommendations, which encompass legislative, administrative and financial areas, are made for an automation driven tax administration.

(i) All Customs and Central Excise Commissionerates should fully automate their processes by 1st January 2004. This requires a Commissionerate-wise work programme to identify the requirement of each station in terms of resources required.

(ii) EDI must be expanded to cover each Customs and Central Excise Commissionerate by January 2004 for on-line processing of returns and applications (for e.g. refund), risk analysis, profiling and management, message exchange with related agencies, etc. In this direction, one major port and one airport should be made fully EDI operational by 1st April 2003.

(iii) C.B.E.C. and its Directorates should be included in the automation programme. All processes should be automated by January 2004.

(iv) Facility of video conferencing between the C.B.E.C. and the Chief Commissioners should be created.

(v) Research capabilities in TRU should be enhanced by intensive automation and development of new software tools, particularly in the context of emerging challenges once VAT is introduced and integration of Service Tax and Central Excise take place.

(vi) On-line filing of returns and documents should be encouraged. For this, Service Centers may be established with a computer link to the Customs and Central Excise Commissionerates for providing the facility. For instance, Excise-Return data is at present entered by the data-entry-operators of the Department. In order to improve the data accuracy and timely capture of data, entry of the particulars by the assessees through a web-based application at their own premise or at Service Center should be allowed.

(vii) Telephone help-line system should be made available in all Custom Houses and Central Excise Commissionerates for providing information support to trade in respect of status of pending documents/claims and other information on procedures etc. In the long run this should become a centrally operated facility.

(viii) Implementation of the automation programme in a time bound manner requires four dedicated teams to oversee the timely implementation of this work, one for Customs, other for Central Excise, the third for Service Tax, and the last for automation of C.B.E.C. and its Directorates. These should be created in the Systems Directorate, from the staff available consequent to cadre restructuring. The teams would work under the Commissioner, Systems and lay down the road map for automation including resource requirement.

(ix) Sufficient resources must be made available at one go to the C.B.E.C. for the automation project. This step will obviate the necessity of taking sanctions and seeking release of funds each time. Importantly, the resources should include an element for an 'Upgradation Fund' for the timely upgradation of the hardware and software on regular basis.

(x) To the extent possible, the automation work should be out sourced as it is not within the core competence of the department. On the other hand India is a leader in software and full use must be made of the local available expertise.

(xi) Senior officers of the Department must take an active interest in computerization by using computers and relying upon the information generated. They should also ensure its use by others. In short, there has to be better ownership at senior levels.

(xii) Systems wing of C.B.E.C. should be strengthened (in terms of both manpower and resources) to ensure immediate dissemination of information through an updated website.

(xiii) Simplification, standardization and stability of law and procedures are essential prerequisites of a successful automation programme.

(xiv) Providing lead-time for software changes when laws are changed is essential for successful automation. For example, a notification must not come into force immediately from the date of its issue but from the next day. Similarly, new procedures should be implemented after a time gap of at least 30 days.

(xv) All procedures must be devised in consultations with the systems personnel who can advise on their adaptability to computerization.

(xvi) Multiple levies create complexities in development of software and retrieval of data. Accordingly, there must be an attempt to reduce the number of levies. Similar is the case in respect of multiple rates of duties. By and large an item should be subject to one duty rate.

(xvii) Levies and exemptions must be aligned to tariff headings. At present levies and exemptions are, at times, announced with reference to the description of the goods. Since the descriptions are not standardized, it creates difficulty in automation.

(xviii) Automated processes should provide for bifurcation of total duty paid into individual heads. In other words, for each Tariff Heading read with the exemption notification, there should be one duty amount to be deposited by the importer. Once deposited, the system should do the further allocation of this amount under the respective duty heads. Presently this work is done by the tax payer. For this purpose to facilitate the tax payer, C.B.E.C. should come out with a Working Schedule indicating the break up of the duties.

7

Improving Indirect Tax Administration

1. Directorate of Anti-dumping and Safeguards duties

Section 9A of Customs Tariff Act, 1975 empowers the Government to impose Anti-dumping duty when any article is exported from any other country in India at less than normal value. Section 8B of the same Act empowers the Government to impose Safeguard duty when any goods are imported into India in such increased quantities and under such conditions so as to cause or threaten to cause serious injury to domestic industry.

1.2 At present the power to register and investigate cases and recommend Anti-dumping duty is vested with the Director General of Anti-Dumping under Ministry of Commerce and Industry. However, on receiving the findings and recommendations from the said authority, the Ministry of Finance, Department of Revenue issues necessary notifications imposing the Anti-dumping duty, which is also levied and collected by Customs officers. On the other hand, the power to register, conduct enquiry and recommend appropriate Safeguard duty lies with the Director General, Safeguard functioning under Ministry of Finance. On the basis of his recommendation, the Ministry of Finance, Department of Revenue issues notification imposing safeguard duty, which is enforced by Customs officers.

1.3 India has an impeccable record in meeting WTO commitments. Alongwith its impressive record in removal of all quantitative restrictions in one stroke, the stage is set for making the anti-dumping body most modern. Towards this objective, reliance on an independent body and a transparent mechanism is critical to conduct an efficient review of cases pertaining to matters such as injury determination, dumping margin, etc. related to safeguards and dumping.

1.4 It is recommended that an independent body such as the Tariff Commission should be suitably strengthened to conduct the work of investigations such as injury determination, dumping margin, etc. relating to Safeguard duties and Anti-dumping.

2. Advance Ruling

2.1 The stated objective of setting up the Authority on Advance Ruling is to meet the "need for foreign investors to be assured in advance of their likely indirect tax liability." The mode of foreign investment envisaged in the legislation is through the joint venture route i.e. investment by a non-resident in collaboration with another non-resident or a resident, or a resident in collaboration with a non-resident. Secondly, as per the existing provisions, the Authority can deliver advance rulings on select issues viz. classification of goods under the Customs and Excise Tariffs, principles of valuation and applicability of exemption notifications.

2.2 In so far as the eligibility of persons to ask for advance ruling is concerned, it is the view that investment through joint ventures is only one method adopted by foreign investors. In fact, foreign direct investment (FDI) through joint ventures is a small component of foreign investment, and the most common method of FDI is through wholly owned subsidiaries of foreign companies. Such companies are presently precluded from seeking an advance ruling on their proposed activity which may attract indirect tax liability. Thus, to avail full advantage of the advance ruling mechanism it is necessary to broaden its scope to allow the ruling to be given in respect of wholly owned subsidiaries of foreign companies.

2.3 As regards the determination of net duty liability, a few aspects under the Customs and Central Excise Acts which have a direct bearing on this issue have been left out of the purview of the Authority. These relate to notifications issued under the Finance Acts in respect of duties collected as excise or customs duties, and notifications issued under the Customs Tariff Act. These elements have a bearing on the overall duty liabilities of a foreign investor. Ideally, the scheme of advance ruling should be comprehensive to include the foreign investor's indirect tax liabilities are concerned. This would include liability net of Cenvat credit. Thus, it appears necessary to expand the scope of the Authority on Advance Ruling to allow comprehensive coverage to foreign investors in respect of their indirect tax liability.

2.4 It is recommended that suitable legislative changes may be made to include within the ambit of the Authority on Advance Ruling:

(i) A wholly owned subsidiary Indian company, of which the holding company is a foreign company, proposing to undertake an activity in India, and

(ii) Notifications issued under the Finance Acts in respect of duties collected as excise or customs duties, and notifications issued under the Customs Tariff Act.

(iii) Admissibility of Cenvat credit.

3. Prosecution of individuals

3.1 Section 9AA and Section 140 of the Central Excise Act, 1944 and the Customs Act, 1962 respectively contain provisions for criminal prosecution of individuals for offences committed by Companies. These two sections are in identical phraseology. Therefore, referring to Section 9AA(1) it is provided herein that if an offence is committed by a company, then "every person who, at the time the offence was committed, was in charge of, and was responsible to, the company for the conduct of the business of the company", as also the company, shall be deemed to be guilty and accordingly liable to be proceeded against and punished. However, if he proves his ignorance of the offence or that it was committed in spite of his due diligence, he shall not be liable to be punished. Thus, every person who is brought in the ambit of this provision is presumed guilty until proved innocent. Notwithstanding it is provided vide Section 9AA(2) that if it is proved that such offence was committed with the consent, connivance or negligence of any director, manager, secretary or other officer, then they are also liable to be proceeded against and punished.

3.2 The implication of the above mentioned provisions is that whereas a director, secretary or manager can be punished if there is proof of their consent, connivance or negligence, they are presumed innocent until proved guilty. In fact, the C.B.E.C circulars are also to the effect that prosecution should be launched against directors and others only if there is sufficient proof of their involvement in the offence. It is only those people who are directly entrusted with the responsibility of payment of duty and such other compliance with the provisions of the Act, who must fall under section 9AA(1), and accordingly subject to the presumption, which they can discharge by proving otherwise. However, the said provision is wide in its scope and can include even persons who have no connection with the acts complained, but by virtue of their designation, are "in charge of and responsible for the conduct of the business of the company". Thus, for every single contravention, however minor it may be, every member of the senior management regardless of his non-involvement, is exposed to criminal proceedings, resulting in harassment and, sometimes, arrest and detention. It appears that there is a need to ensure against excessive prosecution while seeing that the guilty persons do not escape, which is taken care of by Section 9AA(2).

3.3 It is recommended that the prosecution provisions under the Central Excise and Customs laws be suitably amended to restrict their applicability to the persons actually responsible for the offence.

4. Adjudication and Appeal

4.1 Issue of Show Cause Notice

4.1.1 Show cause notices for demand of duty from the tax payers are issued under Section 11A of the Central Excise Act, 1944 and Section 28 of the Custom Act, 1962. It is provided thereunder that, in the case the duty to be demanded is over Rs. One crore the Show cause Notice will be issued with the prior approval of the Chief Commissioner and in all other cases i.e. when the duty to be demanded is less than Rs. One crore the Commissioner's approval is required. The Show Cause Notice is thereafter adjudicated by the competent officer, may be Assistant/Deputy/Additional/Commissioner, as the case may be. This is a fairly recent development and earlier the Show Cause Notices for demand of duty were issued by the same level officer, as the one entrusted with the adjudication thereof. For instance, if the case fell within the competence of the Additional Commissioner for adjudication an officer of the same level would issue the Show Cause Notice.

4.1.2 In this regard, it is observed that the present system has eroded the confidence of the tax payers in the system of quasi-judicial adjudication. After a Chief Commissioner or Commissioner level officer has approved the Show Cause Notice the adjudicating officer, who is a junior functionary, does not usually have the confidence to disagree with the findings of the senior officer. As a result, the duty demand gets confirmed. Even otherwise, the tax payers do not have much confidence in the neutrality of the adjudicating officer and the present position makes it worse. Thus, the present system has given rise to increased litigation as the pro-revenue orders of the junior functionaries are contested in appeal. This matter requires redressal.

4.1.3 It is recommended that in order to restore the confidence of the tax payers, Section 11A of the Central Excise Act, 1944 and Section 28 of the Customs Act, 1962 should be amended to restore the earlier position of issue of Show Cause Notice for demand of duty by an officer of the level competent to adjudicate the case.

4.2 Pre-deposit of duty at first appeal stage

4.2.1 At present appeals against adjudication orders passed by officers up to the level of Addl. Commissioners lie before the Commissioner of Customs or Central Excise (Appeals). Section 35F of the Central Excise Act, 1944, provides that one of the conditions of hearing an appeal is that the appellant shall make a pre-deposit of the amount of duty in question. In fact, the appeal may not be admitted unless this is done. Reportedly, the insistence on pre-deposit is causing hardship on trade and industry more so in view of the fact that the orders of the adjudicating authority are generally prorevenue which in most cases are subsequently set aside. It is also reported that most cases do not get finally settled at the level of Commissioner (Appeals) and insistence on pre-deposit causes cash flow problems.

4.2.2 It is the finding that indeed the majority of cases are being decided at the level of CEGAT. The success rate of the Department is also not very high. In this background the pre-deposit of the duty blocks the tax payers funds and in a large number of cases has to be returned. There is also no provision for payment of interest on this amount.

4.2.3 It is recommended that pre-deposit of duty should not be taken at the first stage of appeal, i.e. at the level of Commissioner (Appeals).

4.3 Stay Orders passed by CEGAT

4.3.1 A recent amendment in Section 35C of the Central Excise Act, 1944 provides that in case a Stay Order is passed by the CEGAT and the case is not finally disposed within a period of 180 days, the stay stands vacated automatically. Similar position is there in respect of the customs cases. It appears that this change was introduced to expedite the disposal of cases since stay orders impact the recovery of revenue. However, looking at it from the point of view of the tax payer and the circumstances governing the grant of stay, it is evident that this provision would work against the interest of the justice and equity. A stay is normally granted when there is merit in the appeal and the operation of the adjudication order would be prejudicial to the tax payers interest. It is logical to assume that the circumstances granting this stay would not materially change in the sixth month period. Hence, if the stay is automatically vacated the tax payer would no doubt file another application for continuance of stay. This would unnecessarily raise the work load of CEGAT.

4.3.2 It is recommended that the relevant provisions should be modified to provide for the finalisation of the case (wherein stay is granted) within a period of six months so far as it is possible to do so. This would act as a signal to the CEGAT to decide the cases in a time bound manner. The provision that the stay is automatically vacated when the case is not finalized in six months should be revoked.

4.4 Appointment of Departmental Counsels

4.4.1 At present the Government appoints Standing Counsels which take up the brief for the revenue when cases are heard by the Tribunal, High Court and Supreme Court. It has been reported that in certain cases involving high revenue stakes or complex law points it is desirable to appoint a counsel from outside the approved panel. This is particularly so, when the opposite side is a big corporate and has at its disposal the best legal brains. It is the view that considering the revenue stakes and the fact that some cases may have long term bearing on revenue, the Commissioners concerned should have the discretion to appoint the special free counsels. Today this is possible though a time consuming procedure requiring the approval of the Ministry. Often, the opposite party manages to get relief through stay, etc., while the process of appointing special fee counsel is not complete. It is the view that the present procedure must change. In this regard, it is learnt that on the Income Tax side the Commissioners are authorized to appoint special fee council upto certain monetary limits (of fees). This system could be followed in the Indirect tax side

4 4.2 It is recommended that suitable measures may be taken to authorize Commissioners of Customs and Central Excise to appoint Special Fee Counsels upto a certain monetary limit. The Chief Commissioners may also be suitably authorized for appointment of Counsels beyond the monetary limit prescribed for Commissioners.

4.5 Institution of SDR/JDR in Settlement Commission

4.5.1 Settlement Commission has been in place for some time. Now increasing number of cases involving high revenue stakes are coming up for settlement. In contrast to the arrangement at CEGAT where the Department has a presence in terms of its representatives, there is no departmental representation at the Settlement Commission. As per the present arrangement, it is the Settlement Commission which is entering into a correspondence with the concerned Customs or Central Excise Commissionerate to get a report whenever a case comes up before it. On their part the Commissionerates follow an ad-hoc approach and at times the departmental view point is not adequately presented. Considering the revenue stakes and the increasing popularity of the Settlement Commission, it appears justified to have an institutional mechanism to represent the department in the cases before the Settlement Commission.

4.5.2 It is recommended that in like manner of CEGAT, Departmental representatives should be appointed at the benches of the Settlement Commission. Subsequently, this practice can be replicated in case of Authority for Advance Rulings.

5. Strengthening Internal Audit

5.1.1 Central Excise officers are empowered to conduct audit of the tax payers business activities to ensure adherance to the rules and correct discharge of duty liability. Further, rule 22 (3) of the Central Excise Rules, 2002 provides that every assessee shall, on demand make available to the audit party deputed by the Comptroller and Auditor General of India (CAG) the specified records maintained by him. Thus, CAG staff also audits the central excise tax payers. In this regard, Article 149 of the Constitution provides that "the Comptroller and Auditor-General shall perform such duties and exercise such powers in relation to the accounts of the Union and of the States and of any other authority or body as may be prescribed by or under any law made by Parliament.. ". Furthermore, vide Sections 10 to 20 of the Comptroller and Auditor-General's (Duties, Powers etc.) Act, 1971 the duties of CAG appear to relate to compilation of accounts of Union and States, and general provisions relating to audit such as audit all accounts and transactions of the Union and the States, audit all trading, manufacturing, profit and loss accounts and balance sheet etc. kept in any department of the Union or the State etc. It also provides for audit of Government companies and corporations and certain authorities or bodies only.

5.1.2 An audit objection invariably results in issue of a duty demand notice against the tax payers, an indicator of dispute and which gives rise to uncertainty. Therefore, it is in the interest of all concerned that disputes should not arise but having arisen should be settled without delay. As seen, one reason for issue of the notice is the objection and observation of the CAG. This is in order when the duty demands are issued in the situation the department agrees with the findings of the CAG. However, notices referred to as 'protective' demands are also issued to protect the revenue even when the Department does not agree with the CAG. These notices are kept pending in the Call Book for years until the issue is decided between C.B.E.C. and CAG, which no doubt adversely affect the tax payer. Incidentally, C.B.E.C. has issued instructions that when the Audit objection runs contrary to its orders issued under Section 37B of the Central Excise Act, 1944 and Section 151A of the Customs Act, 1962 (laying down the correct classification and valuation of goods) or its circulars or instructions, no protective duty demand need be issued. This is a step in the right direction and should reduce the number of duty demands being issued.

5.1.3 In this regard the finding is that internal audit by the Department is now being done in accordance with a recently developed programme of audit titled "EA 2000", which relies chiefly upon the tax payers own records and documents to confirm the compliance of the rules and procedures and payment of central excise duty. Reportedly the results of EA 2000 have been good, in terms of safeguarding revenue and also in ensuring the audit does not disrupt tax payer's business activities. However, there is still some apprehension in the minds of the taxpayers that the Audit teams are driven by revenue targets and conduct their business with the objective of raising a demand for duty. Another area of concern is that visits by different audit teams (Department and CAG) to the tax payers' premises disrupts their work. Finally, the tax payers would like early resolution of issues between the Department and CAG so that duty demands are not kept pending for long.

5.1.4 It is the view that as the Central Excise officers are in any case responsible for ensuring the correctness of the duty payment and visit the tax payers premises to conduct audit for this purpose, the repeat visit for the same job by the CAG officers may not be necessary. EA 2000 has also shown good results and has been accepted by the tax payers. Incidentally, CAG does not visit the Income Tax and Customs tax payers and earlier the provision now found in rule 22(3) was not there in the central excise law. It also appears necessary to create an environment of greater certainty in taxation matters and resolve areas of differences of opinion between C.B.E.C. and CAG. Thus, there must be greater interaction between the two. This would also strengthen internal audit of the department. Once this is done the disputes would firstly not arise and if at all they arise would be quickly resolved. Interaction between the officers of both the sides would lead to appreciation of each others view points and the resolution of differences in a harmonious way. It would result in less paper work, reduction in issue of duty demand notices and a tax payer friendly administration. This would benefit the tax payers.

5.1.5 It is recommended that the following steps may be explored to strengthen the system of audit for the benefit of both revenue and the tax payer:

(i) Instruction may be issued that Audit should be participative and a fact finding mission with the objective of guiding the tax payer; the attempt should be to evolve a consensus on the issues and Audit teams should not be empowered to issue show cause notices for duty demand.

(ii) C.B.E.C. and CAG should identify posts within their organizations to be occupied by the officers of the other department on deputation.

(iii) Rule 22(3) of the Central Excise Rules, 2002 may be amended to exclude reference to audit party deputed by the CAG so that they need not visit the tax payers premises.

6. *Trade facilitation*

6.1 Standing Committee on Procedures

6.1.1 Customs and Central Excise procedures are being changed rather frequently. Invariably, the procedures are framed in consultation with the field officers and there is no apparent involvement of the trade and industry. As a result, each new procedure is invariably accompanied by representations from the tax payers. These are then examined and at times the procedures are suitably modified and at other times no action is taken on the ground that the new procedure must be allowed to settle down. As a result the present system of evolving new procedures, even if these are presumed to be trade friendly, create uncertainty and generates additional work. It is the view that there should be an institutional mechanism to frame new procedures.

6.1.2 Furthermore, new procedures come into effect from the date they are brought to the notice of field formations. Each instruction contains a direction to the field formations to issue suitable public notices/ trade notices to inform the trade. Not only does this catch the trade by surprise but it may also happen that a procedure has been in force but is not complied with for the reason that the trade may not have come to know about it. Invariably, such situation also leads to compliance issuance and disputes. Also, the Departmental Systems personnel are unable to modify their software, if required. It is the view that this matter requires remedy.

6.1.3 In the circumstance, keeping in mind that the objective of tax administration should be to provide certainty and transparency, the following recommendations are made in so far as introduction of new procedures are concerned:

(i) An institutional mechanism, namely Standing Committee on Procedures chaired by Chairman CBEC and including trade and industry representatives, should be established to identify and resolve the problem areas in present procedures and evolve new procedures on a need basis. This Committee should meet once a quarter.

(ii) A new procedure should come into force after minimum 30 days of its announcement.

6.2 Fixing of revenue targets

6.2.1 A major area of concern, both for trade and departmental officers is related to the annual ritual of fixing of Commissionerate-wise revenue targets by the C.B.E.C. There are two issues here. First is the fixing of the target itself. No doubt the targets are necessary for the revenue administration to closely monitor the revenue inflows and it also sensitizes the Commissionerates to their primary responsibility of revenue collection. However, the problem area is that invariably the targets are unrealistically fixed on the higher side. This is revealed on a perusal of the performance vis-a-vis the targets and it is seen that it is an exceptional year when the targets are achieved. It is also reported that the targets are fixed for the total revenue, ignoring that the major share is on account of revenue from POL, which is largely, even today, the subject matter of Government policies on pricing. As a result, there is tremendous pressure on the Commissionerates to achieve the unrealistic targets.

6.2.2 An outcome of the revenue target fixing exercise is that on the customs side the Commissionerates invariably clamp down on disbursal of Drawback and refunds during the last quarter of the financial year. This happens since the disbursal is treated as an outflow of revenue and the net revenue realised comes down. Importers are also made to deposit customs duty in cash instead of using DEPB. Similarly on the central excise side the tax payers are 'persuaded' to pay duty through cash (PLA) and not use the accumulated Cenvat credit for the same. Refunds are also stopped. These are extra legal measures. As seen, the Commissionerates tend to raise all sorts of technical objections on the drawback and refund claims so that the disbursal does not take place during the financial year in question. This entire exercise is avoidable as it is basically revenue neutral. The withheld amount (of drawback and refunds) is promptly released the beginning of the new financial year. Also at times the tax payer is encouraged to make excess payment of duty with the promise that the same would be refunded at the beginning of the new financial year. In fact for these reasons, on the central excise side there is hardly any revenue realisation (in PLA) in the first quarter of the new financial year since the tax payers use the blocked Cenvat credit to pay the duty.

6.2.3 The present system of withholding drawback, refunds and not allowing the central excise tax payers to use Cenvat credit is disturbing. Drawback is an export facilitation measure and denial or withholding drawback causes a set back to the export efforts. Actually the Commissionerates must be encouraged to disburse drawback and facilitate increased exports. Similarly withholding of refunds and not allowing utilization of Cenvat credit to pay duty create cash flow problems for the trade and adversely affects business by either holding up clearances or puts tax payers to severe financial pressure. It is high time that it is realised that payment of duty through Cenvat credit is also duty realization.

6.2.4 On a careful examination of the matters the following remedial action is recommended:

(i) Revenue targets must be fixed realistically. The target must be broken into POL and Non-POL which would enable the Commissionerates to make realistic attempts to reach the target through legal measures and trade facilitation.

(ii) On the customs side, as an export facilitation measure, the revenue target should be fixed by including Drawback disbursed and refund sanctioned. This will ensure against blockage of Drawback and refunds. It would also encourage the Commissionerates to release Drawback in order to meet the target.

(iii) On the central excise side the revenue target should take into account duty paid through both Personal Ledger Account (PLA) and Cenvat credit. Refunds sanctioned should also be taken into account. This will ensure against stoppage of payment through Cenvat during revenue drive and withholding of refunds.

6.2.5 The above measures would boost tax payers confidence in the administration and also reduce the pressures on the departmental officials. All in all a healthy tax compliant environment would be created.

6.3 Harmonization of commodity classification

6.3.1 At present, various Government departments and agencies use their own methods of classification of the goods for taxation or statistical purposes or for deciding the importability or exportability or for any other purpose. For instance, DGFT, Customs, Central Excise, Directorate General of Commercial Statistics and Intelligence, State Sales Tax departments, Central Statistical organization etc. all use different commodity classification codes. Except Customs the codes of the other agencies are not aligned with the internationally adopted HSN.

6.3.2 Multiplicity of classification codes causes hardship to the trade and industry besides coming in the way of establishing a common market. Internationally a common classification is adopted for all trade related transactions. Common classification helps in simplifying procedures and documentation and facilitates trade. It also encourages increased use of electronic data processing which is otherwise not possible. Common classification codes also help in obtaining specific data on need basis more easily and sharing it between various agencies.

6.3.3 It is understood that C.B.E.C. has taken the initiative to prepare an 8-digit Common Commodity Classification Code for both central excise and customs as a standard unit of measurement for all trade related activities, in consultation with other concerned Ministries and Departments. This is appreciated as a step in the right direction.

6.3.4 It is recommended that the 8-digit Common Commodity Classification Code should be implemented at the earliest and latest by 1st April 2003. This should be used by all other agencies (DGFT, DG, CIS, custodian, etc.) also.

6.4 Standardization of service standards

6.4.1 Besides the need for tax payer friendly procedures there is also the need for uniform application of such procedures. It is often reported that different Custom Houses and Central Excise Commissionerates have different practices which is not know o the trade and industry and, at times, gives rise to compliance issues. Hence, it is necessary that there should be standardization of procedures. Also it is very important that there is in place an institutionalized mechanism to periodically review the procedures and the way work is done. It is noticed that very often the systems are personality based and upon the transfer of an officer the new incumbent starts his own procedures and the system changes over night. No doubt the tax payer is legally bound to collect the duty and the tax administrators to collect the same. However, the tax collectors must appreciate that the tax payer is a customer for them. In other words, it is important to set in place high standards of service for customer satisfaction and maintain them over the time. Standardization of the procedures across the Commissionerates in different parts of the country is equally important. This would improve compliance, certainty and tax payer confidence.

6.4.2 It is recommended that a time bound programme should be initiated for the ISO Certification of all Custom Houses and Central Excise Commissionerates – to be started in 2003 and completed by 1st January 2005. This presupposes standardization of procedures.

6.5 Banking

6.5.1 Banks play a critical role in the tax administration through facilitating payment of duty and its reconciliation. So far the payment of duty is being made in the nominated public sector banks. At present, the policy of one Commissionerate - one bank is followed. This has obviously given rise to complaints of monopolistic behaviour and poor service. The move to EDI based reconciliation of duty payment has also not picked up so far, though certain positive moves have been made in this direction. Accordingly, in order to exploit the facilities of modern automated banking for enhanced convenience of the tax payer and the revenue the following recommendations are made :

(i) Multi-banking should be encouraged by recognizing new banks including private sector banks to handle receipt of Government revenue.

(ii) A pre-condition to the appointment of the banks should be establishment of an EDI link with the Custom House/ Central Excise Commissionerate to facilitate reconciliation of revenue.

(iii) Banks should have the responsibility of issue/transfer of refund checks/amount direct to the tax payers bank account on the basis of a release advise form the Commissionerate.

(iv) Option of payment of duty through debit card and the like should be explored for implementation.

(v) Appointed banks should give the tax payer the option of internet banking for deposit of duty and transfer of funds.

6.6 Uniformity of interest rates

6.6.1 At present, there is great disparity between the interest payable by the tax payer (to the department) on the duty short levied or short paid or not levied or not paid and the interest payable by the Department (to the tax payer) on the delayed refunds. Whereas the tax payer is required to pay interest at the rate of 15% per annum the Department pays interest at the rate of 8%. Not only is there no equity, the disparity causes concern that the Government is not treating the tax payer as an equal partner in the economy. In fact, there is also an absence of uniformity in the rate payable by the tax payer. For instance, in the case of warehoused goods the interest payable is 24%. Whereas the vires of charging higher interest and giving lower interest is not questioned it appears that in the interest of boosting tax payer confidence in the fairness of tax administration the disparity need to be removed. Also there is some confusion whether the interest payable is simple interest or compounded. Finally, it is contended that the rate of interest is too high and must move with the PLR.

6.6.2 It is recommended that :

(i) The interest payable by the tax payer and the department may be made uniform.

(ii) The interest so determined must be uniformly applied in each and every situation where it is decided to charge interest.

(iii) The law should itself clarify that the interest is simple and not compounded.

(iv) The rate of interest should be reviewed each year at the time of the Budget and brought in line with the prevailing market rate. Rate determined should not be changed during the year.

6.7 Unjust Enrichment

6.7.1 The Constitutional validity of Section 11B, as amended in 1991, has been upheld by the Supreme Court in the case of Mafatlal Industries. However, it is seen that in certain cases which have been judicially held to be outside the scope of the said provisions the tax payers are asked to produce all sorts of documents and establish the duty burden has not been passed on to their buyers. This causes harassment. Without going into the merit of the legislation it appears that the net result has been to reduce tax payer satisfaction, increase contact points and discretion on the part of the departmental officers. Thus, it merits defining certain situations wherein the tax payer should be given the benefit of refund of duty without going into the question of legality thereof. This would also reduce the transaction cost and avoidable interface between the industry and the Department. This is possible through suitable legislative changes.

6.7.2 It is recommended that the provision in respect of Unjust Enrichment may be amended to the effect that it would not apply when the refund arises in respect of provisional assessment, goods captively consumed and pre-deposit of duty.

6.8 Non-Receipt of Applications/documents

6.8.1 Presently there are no Dak receipt counters at most of the Excise Offices. As a result a tax payer is not able to deposit any application/document and get an acknowledgement. The problem is more acute in Central Excise Range offices as the Excise Inspector/Range Superintendent may not always be available in their office.

6.8.2 It is recommended that the system of receipt and acknowledgement of dak and correspondence should be reviewed and it should be ensured that a receipt counter manned at all hours during office hours is positioned at an easily accessible place. In the case of small offices where there is a paucity of staff, a Mail box should be provided and acknowledgements issued next day. Every correspondence should be acknowledged and timely replies sent.

6.9 Codification of circulars/ instructions

6.9.1 At present there is no practice of codifying the many instructions and circulars issued by the C.B.E.C. from time to time. As a result there is confusion in the trade and industry and also the departmental officers regarding the latest position on any aspect of law and procedure. This leads to absence of uniformity besides giving rise to disputes. It appears that the solution lies in organizing the issue subject-wise booklets including all relevant circulars and instructions. This would also help in weeding out those which are redundant. Importantly, this should not be a mere reproduction or compilation of Circulars and instructions. Effort should be made to state the legal position in simple and clearly understood language. Once this is issued future changes should simply be inserted at the relevant page. For instance, future instructions should mention 'replace paragraph AB on page XYZ'. This mechanism would ensure updated instructions/procedure are available at all times with the trade and industry and the departmental officers.

6.9.2 It is recommended that C.B.E.C should codify all circulars/ instructions in one cover, subject-wise by 1st April 2003.

6.10 PAN as the common identifier in taxation matters

6.10.1 It is essential that for identification of the tax payers and also for exchange of information on the tax payer between different government departments/agencies, there should be a common identifier. It is observed that C.B.E.C has already started using the PAN issued by the Income Tax department as the common identifier for central excise purposes. This should be extended to customs also.

6.10.2 It is recommended that C.B.E.C should ensure by 1st April 2003 that all its tax payers are entered into its computer record on the basis of PAN.

6.11 Enhancing tax players confidence

6.11.1 In order to enhance tax payers confidence in the Central Excise administration with focus on transparency and accountability, it appears necessary to introduce certain changes in the mind-set. This is possible by change in the presentation of the officials as well as in the present system of work of relating to search, seizure and summons. Accordingly, the recommendations are as follows:

(i) Central Excise officers should not be required to wear uniform. This would change the mind set on both side (Department and taxpayer) and contribute to freer communication.

(ii) Videography should be done whenever statements are recorded and searches made.

(iii) Seizure of documents and records adversely affect the conduct of business. Accordingly, these should be mandatorily released upon the completion of adjudication.

7. C.B.E.C. Administration

7.1 Tenure of Chairman, C.B.E.C.

7.1.1 The Chairman, C.B.E.C is in charge of collection of major share of the total tax revenues of the Government. He is in overall charge of administering the tax administration in respect of Customs, Central Excise and Service Tax and some element of Narcotics. Being the head of the Indian Customs Administration Chairman. C.B.E.C. represents the country in all International forums such as WCO. Thus the continuity in the post of Chairman.

C.B.E.C. is of critical importance.

7.1.2 In this regard it is observed that invariably an officer is appointed as Chairman., C.B.E.C when he has scarcely a few months to go before superannuating. As a result he is hardly in a position to give long term direction to the department. The officer is not able to give shape to policies of long term importance to the revenue and an element of ad-hocism creeps in, which is detrimental to the tax administration. Consistency and long term vision are essential for a administration, and much more important in tax administration.

7.1.3 As long term measures to give stability and direction to the indirect tax administration, which is so critical for the economic well being of the country it is recommended that Chairman, C.B.E.C. should be selected on criterion of merit cum seniority and once appointed (at whatever age before 60 years) should have a minimum tenure of 2 years.

7.2 Financial autonomy

7.2.1 C.B.E.C. has no financial autonomy and has to obtain financial sanctions for expenditure from the Financial Adviser (Finance) who is entrusted with the Budget of the Department and reports administratively to the Secretary Revenue. All the field formations of the C.B.E.C. are necessarily required to first take the clearance of the C.B.E.C. in respect of their expenditure proposals, and then obtain the sanction of the Finance wing. This often impacts the projects which works against efficient tax administration and tax payers facilitation suffers. It is the view that as a major revenue earning Department whose top priority is tax payer facilitation, C.B.E.C. should be given financial autonomy. This would allow C.B.E.C. to take immediate steps to create infrastructure, automate etc. for benefit of the tax payers. Similarly the senior officers in the field i.e. Commissioners should be in a position to incur expenditure upto a reasonable limit (higher than at present) without seeking approval of the C.B.E.C. and the Finance wing each time. Chief Commissioners should also be given financial powers.

7.2.2. It is recommended that a mechanism may be found to give C.B.E.C. financial autonomy. The Chief Commissioner and the Commissioners may also be given enhanced financial powers.

7.3 Improving office infrastructure

7.3.1 Customs and central excise officers and the taxpayers are partners in the economic development of the country through the payment and collection of taxes. It is often the case that the taxpayers – importers, exporters, corporate heads, foreign nationals have to visit the customs and central excise offices for the conduct of the tax related businesses. Reportedly, the majority of offices are in bad shape in terms of basic infrastructures and amenities. Most are also in rented accommodation and there is little scope for carrying out improvements. Not only does this distance the tax payers from the tax administrators it also create an unhealthy mind set in the officers who work in unsatisfactory environment. Therefore, it is necessary to develop a corporate culture which is customer friendly by improving the office accommodation of the customs and central excise officers.

7.3.2 It is recommended that the C.B.E.C. should evolve a time bound strategy to improve the office accommodation as follows:

(i) A Task Force should be set up to standardize the requirement of a modern customer friendly office (model office) which should furnish its report by 31st January 2002. The report should include financial estimates.

(ii) Based on the report of the Task Force, the C.B.E.C should ask the Chief Commissioners to identify the shortcomings in each of their offices in their jurisdiction by 1st April 2003 and send a consolidated proposal to C.B.E.C.

(iii) By 1st August 2003, a model Commissionerate (Customs and Central Excise), Central Excise Division and Central Excise Range office should be set up in each of the Chief Commissioner zones.

(iv) C.B.E.C. should seek financial sanctions and replicate the model offices by upgrading the existing offices and purchasing land, building, etc., where necessary. The entire exercise should be time bound, so that by 2005, modern offices are in place in each Commissionerate.

(v) Modernisation of C.B.E.C and its Directorates should be done by setting up a Task Force to identify the areas of improvement and thereafter taking time bound action.

(vi) Facility of video conferencing between the C.B.E.C. and the Chief Commissioners should be created.

(vii) Research capabilities in TRU should be enhanced, particularly in the context of emerging challenges once VAT is introduced and there is integration of Service Tax and Central Excise.

8. Human Resource Development and training

8.1 Human resource development is an important ingredient in administration. Training is essential for upgrading skills and change in mind-set for tax payer facilitation. This is all the more important when the environment in terms of policies and procedures and tax payer expectation is changing rapidly. C.B.E.C. is already having an institutionalized training programme run by NACEN and the Commissionerates also conduct in-house training programmes from time to time. However, the common perception is that much more need to be done in the training the officers, particularly at the cutting edge, in two key areas. The first is the use of computers and the second is the change in mind set. Particular attention needs to be paid to change in mind set at the cutting edge.

8.2 It is also important to appreciate that a long term institutional arrangement is necessary for sustained progress in human resource development. Once the resource centers are identified, C.B.E.C. should enter into a Memorandum of Understanding with them so that the continuity of the arrangement is maintained. Accordingly, it is recommended that :

(i) The infrastructure available for training at regional level should be upgraded. Training should be accorded priority and sufficient infrastructure needs to be created to impart training especially in areas of use of information technology, managerial skills and attitude changes at the cutting edge level. Each Chief Commissioner of a Zone should have an in-house training center equipped with latest training aids and adequate infrastructure to take care of the training requirements in addition to the proposed regional training centers in the Cadre Restructuring proposal.

(ii) The C.B.E.C. should make full use of the technical assistance of multilateral agencies such as World Bank, Asian Development Bank and World Customs Organization, especially their reform and modernization projects and programmes, that support customs reform through training in diagnostic study and in customs needs analysis. These help domestic customs authorities implement the required changes that have been identified and evaluate their impact on trade facilitation and customs compliance.

(iii) A relevant UN body to be contacted for assistance is the Center for Facilitation of Procedures and Practices for Administration, Commerce, and Transportation (CEFACT-UN/ECE).

(iv) Group 'B' and 'C' officers who are at the cutting edge should be given training to change the mind-set for bringing about pro-client/customer orientation.

(v) Entry level training to officers who are promoted from Group 'B' to Group 'A' should be mandatorily provided at NACEN, for a minimum period of 3 months covering both Customs & Central Excise. This is essential as officers promoted from Customs are often posted to Excise Commissionerates and vice versa.

(vi) Cadre training should be compulsory in respect of all Group 'A' officers and periodical refresher courses should be organized to impart training of managerial skills.

(vii) Senior Group 'A' officers of the rank of Commissioners and above should be deputed to attend Executive Development Programmes in premier management institutes in the country such as, IIM, IIFT, ASCI etc.

(viii) Group 'A' officers should be exposed to the tax administrations abroad and international best practices in training followed to enhance their skills.

8

Revenue Augmentation, Tax Levies and Rates

1. Tax to GDP Ratio

Falling tax to GDP ratio in general, and similar trend in respect of indirect tax to GDP ratio, in particular is a matter of serious concern, more so when the ratios are falling in the post liberalization era, since early 1990s, when the expectation was to the contrary. There can be no two views that structural and fiscal policy changes over the last decade have been necessary as otherwise the country would have been isolated in the world economy. However, the falling ratios alert us to the fact that much more need to be done than has been done so far and also that a re-thinking is clearly warranted on certain critical issues if the trend is to be quickly reversed.

1.2 On the subject, it is interesting to study the initiatives taken by countries which were similarly placed as ours in the pre 1990s but which have made significant strides in achieving a higher tax to GDP ratio in the last few years (1996 to 2000), such as Brazil, China and Turkey. The common aspect of the reform process in all these countries was to expand the tax base (focusing on consumption expenditure), rationalize tax structure and improve efficiency of tax administration. An important element in relation to tax structure was to focus on incentives, exemptions and distortions. No doubt India too has followed this general direction but not with the same results.

Trends in tax to GDP ratio in select countries (1996-2000)

	1996	1997	1998	1999	2000
Brazil	11.00	12.00	12.50	14.40	14.80
China[1]	10.20	11.10	11.80	13.00	14.10
Turkey[2]	15.00	19.05	20.21	21.28	22.03

1 Revenue performance of Centre, Provinces, and Municipalities.
2 Tax to GNP ratio

Customs Revenues, tax to GDP ratio and average collection rate

Year	Revenue (Rs. Cr.)	Growth in Customs revenue (%)	GDP (Rs. Cr.)	Tax-GDP ratio	Average Collection rate(%)*	Imports as a% of GDP (at market price)	Revenue foregone on export promotion schemes (Rs. Cr.)
1990-91	20644	N.A.	573444	3.6	74	5.01	N.A.
1997-98	40193	(-)6.2	1522574	2.6	27	12.5	13157
1998-99	40668	1.2	1740935	2.3	23	11.5	15492
1999-2000	48420	19	1929641	2.5	22	12.4	18166
2000-01	47542	(-)1.8	2087988	2.3	21	13.0	21658

* Percentage of total customs revenue to the total value of imports.

Central Excise Revenues and tax to GDP ratio

Year	Revenue (Rs. Cr.)	Growth in Excise revenue (%)	GDP (Rs. Crs.)	Tax - GDP ratio
1990-91	24514	5.73	573444	4.3
1997-98	47962	6.56	1522574	3.2
1998-99	59246	11.02	1740935	3.1
1999-2000	61902	16.26	1929641	3.2
2000-01	68526	10.70	2087988	3.3

1.3 As seen, between 1990-91 and 2000-01 the customs revenue to GDP ratio has fallen from 3.6 to 2.3 and the central excise revenue to GDP ratio from 4.3 to 3.3. One does not have to look far to find the reasons for the reduction and some of the reasons are :

(i) The rate of reduction in duty rates (both customs and central excise) has been much higher than the rate of growth of GDP.

(ii) On the customs side, the reduction in rate has not led to higher revenue in view of lower than expected increase in volumes of import.

(iii) On the central excise side the contribution of manufacturing sector in total GDP has declined and whereas contribution of services has gone up and this sector is not being taxed comprehensively.

1.4 It is but evident that there is an urgent need to arrest the trend of falling indirect tax to GDP ratio if an impact is to be made on the fiscal deficit. Broadly, this calls for action in two areas of tax policy. First is the tax structure including its coverage and second is tax implementation. In so far as the former is concerned, the following measures are necessary, which are subsequently detailed in respect of each of the indirect taxes :

(i) Widen the tax base by reviewing and removing to the extent possible the duty exemptions – as a general principle, duty exemptions tend to create pressure groups, increase discretion and do not always ensure benefits reach the target. The exemption, when merited (such as in case of life saving goods and sovereign imports of security/strategic interest) should be replaced by a more transparent method of ensuring the relief to the target group, through budgetary support.

(ii) The types of tax levies should be brought down to the minimum - too many levies create distortion and inefficiencies in administration, raising compliance issues.

(iii) Move towards a maximum number of three rates of duty in central excise to be achieved in two years and fewer rates from present 20 rates in Customs, in stages. Fewer number of rates and moderate rates would encourage compliance, reduce discretion and create an efficient tax administration.

(iv) Expand coverage of Service Tax and integration of central èxcise (goods) and Service Tax legislation - It is the expectation that in the long run the service sector would contribute significantly more to the GDP, and even at present it is the single largest contributor. Therefore, for improvement in tax to GDP ratio the scope of Service Tax must necessarily expand.

(v) VAT should be implemented to reduce cascading effects of taxes.

2. *Customs Tariff and Exemptions*

2.1 Multiplicity of levies

2.1.1 At present, besides the Basic Customs Duty, we have the following levies :

(i) Additional Duty of Customs (loosely referred to as Countervailing duty or 'CVD')

(ii) Special Additional Duty of Customs (SAD)

(iii) Additional Duty of Customs on Motor Spirit

(iv) Additional Duty of Customs on High Speed Diesel Oil

(v) Export Duty

(vi) Cesses on Exports

(vii) Anti-dumping/Safeguard duties

2.1.2 As a policy, multiplicity of levies must be reduced. Accordingly, it is recommended that there should be only three types of duties, viz. Basic Customs Duty, Additional Duty of Customs (or Countervailing duty) and Anti-dumping/ Safeguard duties. All other duties should be removed. However, removal of SAD should be linked to implementation of State level VAT, where SAD would get replaced by the State VAT to be levied on imports.

2.2 Multiplicity of duty rates

2.2.1 It has been the avowed objective of the Government to reduce the peak rates of customs duty to the ASEAN levels. This is not merely an attempt to follow the other faster growing developing economies but a pragmatic approach to move towards a modern economy producing efficiently according to its dynamic comparative advantage. To achieve this, India needs a large volume of imports which are necessary for technology upgradation. These imports have largely to be paid for by a high level of exports which require import at world prices. That imports are necessary for exports and the development of an economy is a settled proposition and the answer lies in encouraging imports without quantitative barriers, without licensing, and having moderate tariffs. However, revenue considerations are known to affect the pace of reduction of tariffs in most countries, especially developing countries which are heavily dependent upon indirect tax revenues. But experience of successful trading economies have shown that sheer increase in volume of imports has more than offset the fall in revenues on account of cuts in tariff rates, though there may be a transition period. This has to be balanced by a comprehensive reform of the tax system.

2.2.2 The customs tariff, completely aligned to HSN contains 99 chapters wherein all the goods are classified. Each Chapter contains a number of goods and against each Tariff Heading or Sub-Heading the rate of duty is indicated. As seen, the customs duties has continued to remain most complicated even after several years of reforms since 1991. This can be seen from the rates of duty, which are 20 in number (182, 160, 150, 105, 100, 85, 75, 70, 65, 50, 45, 40, 35, 30, 25, 15, 10, 5, 3, and nil). 30% rate is the median rate i.e. the most common rate. Besides some items are subjected to specific duties. It, however, must be conceded that in general rates of import duties higher than the median rate apply to agricultural products. As most countries adopt higher input duties on agricultural products, the multiplicity of rates because of such compensation need not necessarily be called an aberration.

2.2.3 The difficulties in administering such a large number of rates are evident. Importantly the large number of rates lead to discretion which should be best avoided in taxation. Further, such a large number of duty rates can only contribute to complexities of clearance procedures. Accordingly, it is the view that a modern tax system should be based upon the minimum number of duty rates. In fact, even at present, the major share of revenue comes from few rates only. Hence, it is necessary to quickly move to the least number of duty rates.

CUSTOMS-RATE WISE DISTRIBUTION OF REVENUE

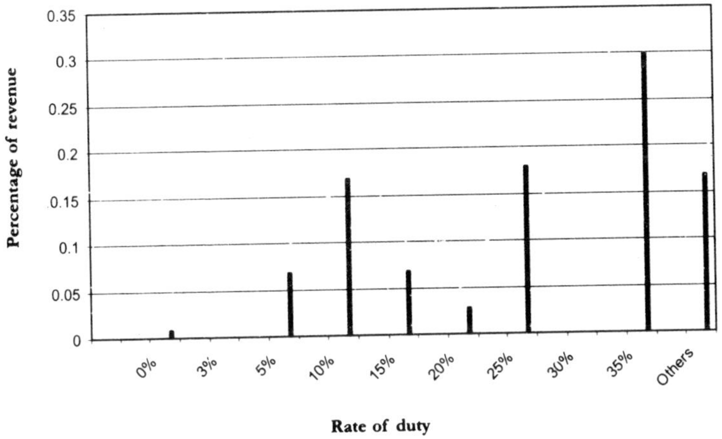

2.2.4 The Task Force had contemplated a 2-tier duty structure to be achieved by 2004- 05, 10% for raw materials, inputs and intermediates and 20% for final goods. During discussions with the trade, it was brought out that there are definitional problems as to what constitutes raw materials and what constitutes final goods because the intermediate for one industry may be raw material for another industry. While one section of the trade was of the view that there should be uniform rate of tariff on all imports, the other view, which was equally powerful, was that there should be a differential duty structure so as to give more protection to the domestic industry which is burdened with additional cost on account of various factors not related to tariff, like high sales tax, octroi, higher interest rates and power costs and to compensate for such increases, a duty differential is essential. Some trade associations also pointed out the anomalies in the duty structure such that the final product attracts the same duty as raw materials.

2.2.5 The Task Force feels that while a uniform tariff would be ideal as it removes all distortions and makes the administration simple, there is no denying that certain disadvantages are faced by the industry and, therefore, a 3-tier duty structure may be considered for adoption. Through suitable grouping of the goods, it can be ensured that this does not give rise to any classification disputes. The problem of raw materials, intermediates, etc., can be sorted out by having a lower duty on goods which are used for further manufacture, as distinct from finished goods which are basically meant for consumer consumption without the need for any further processing. Such finished goods can attract the peak rate of duty. Even today, countries like Malaysia and Indonesia charge import duty of 15% to 30% on consumer durables. The Task Force thus recommends a duty of 20% on finished consumer goods. As regards anomalies, the Task Force subscribes to the view that an anomaly arises only when the input tax is more than the tax on the finished product. What is relevant is effective rates of protection and not the nominal rates. Because of the demand of the industry for a large duty differential in the nominal duty rates on these inputs and final products, the Task Force would like to address some of the misconceptions. There is an excellent exposition of the concept of Effective Protection in the paper "Towards a Competitive Economy : VAT and Customs Duty Reform" by Dr. Arvind Virmani. The Task Force with sincere acknowledgement to Dr. Arvind Virmani would like to reproduce the relevant portions of the report:-

"The protection that directly affects any individual producer is the effective protection rate application to his production operation. Any given producer uses a variety of inputs to produce output. In the process he adds value to the inputs he has bought from others. The process of production is in effect the process of adding value to the inputs, using capital and labour (factors of production). The effective protection that the producer gets on his process of value addition depends on the value added proportion, the average import tariffs/duties on the inputs used and the tariff on the output. A simple formula based on these parameters can be used to calculate the effective protection rate (EPR) based on these three parameters. This can be illustrated through a simple example.

Consider an internationally competitive producer who produces output using only one input. Assume that the input-output ratio for this item is 0.7%. Then the value added ratio is 1-0.7=0.3. In other words for every $1 of output produced he has a value added *of \$0.3. Let the exchange rate of the rupee against the dollar (Rs. per \$) be any number, which we can denote as e. Then the value added by this globally competitive producer measured in rupees is equal to Rs.0.3 e.*

Now consider an Indian producer of the same item, who has a tariff rate of 20% on his output and 15% on his input. The "landed cost" of his imported input will be equal to Rs.1.2 e while the "landed price" of the imported output which competes with his domestically produced output will be Rs.1.15 e. The amount of margin available to the producer (inclusive of wages to be paid to labour) is the difference between the "landed cost" of the output minus the "landed cost" of the inputs used in producing this output. This value is equal to,

$$1.2e-0.7*1.15e=0.395e$$

per unit of output produced by the domestic producers. This is also equal to the value added at domestic prices. The effective protection rate is therefore defined as the difference between this margin and the global value added as a percent of the global value added, that is,

$$EPR=0.395\ e/0.3\ e-1=0.316$$

Thus the effective protection rate for this particular producer is neither 20% (the nominal protection rate) nor 5% (20%-15%) but 31.6%.

The higher the effective protection rate the greater the room for inefficiency. The EPR therefore measures the degree of inefficiency that the domestic producer can have in value addition as a percent of the global efficiency norm of value addition in the production of this item. In the above example the producer can be 40% more inefficient than the globally efficient producer.

The variation of the effective protection rate with different input ratios and input tariffs is illustrated in greater detail in Table 2a and Table 2b. These show the set of cases in which the peak rate of duty is 20% with not even one item having a higher duty. Part I of table 2a illustrates the case of a producer subject to a tariff rate of 20% on his output, but with tariffs on inputs ranging between 0% and 20%. The average input tariff can therefore lie anywhere between nil and 20%. The first row shows that if all inputs used by the producer have an import duty of 20% then the effective protection rate is also 20% no matter what the proportion of value added. This result also implies that a uniform rate of import duty/tariff of 20% ensures an effective protection of 20% for all. Similarly a single uniform rate of basic customs duty of 10% as proposed by us will ensure that all producers of all goods have an effective protection of 10% (last row of part II of this table).

The other rows of part I illustrate the variation in effective protection rate (EPR) arising from differences in proportion of value added and differences in the average tariff rate on inputs. The effective protection rate is inversely related to the proportion of value added by the producer and the average tariff rate on inputs used by the producer. Thus EPR rises as we move from the northwest corner to Southeast corner of the table. For all goods at the peak rate of duty (20%) the effective protection rate ranges (in the table) from 20% to 400%[1]*. Even if the average input duty is only 5% points less than the output duty (i.e. 15%) the effective protection can be higher than 100% (2nd row). A two-tier duty structure with consumer goods at 20% can result in some having an EPR of 200%. Thus with a varying rate of import duty on inputs, the effective protection rate can be quite arbitrary and random*

The second important lesson from this table is that the producers who add the least value tend to get the highest protection. This can be illustrated by considering a case in which all raw material and intermediate goods have customs duty rate of 10% while most consumer goods have a customs duty rate of 20%. For this latter set of goods the effective protection increases from 21% if the value added ratio is 0.9% to an EPR of 30% if the value added ratio is 0.5% to 110% if the value added ratio is 0.1(3rd line, part I, table 2a). In other words the higher the use of imported/importable inputs the higher the level of effective protection.

In contrast to part I, where the produced item was subject to the peak duty of 20%, in part II the item has an output duty of 10%. Thus the average input duty can be higher than the output

1 In general it can even be higher

duty. This can give rise to the problem of negative protection, i.e. instead of protecting the product, the structure ends up penalizing and discouraging the domestic production of some group of commodities. Part II of table 2a shows that negative protection arises when the value added proportion is low and the average input duty is higher relative to the output duty (north east corner of the table). For instance negative protection is seen to arise when the value added proportion is less than 0.5(50%) and the average input duty is 20%(1st row, part II).

The table also shows that negative protection can arise even if the average input duty is even 1% point higher (11%) than the output duty (3rd row of part II). Thus any effort to offer higher effective protection to favoured commodities can result in negative protection to those not so favoured.

Part III of Table 2a shows the effective protection that results from tariff exemptions (i.e. zero tariff). In this case there is negative effective protection if there is even one input that has a positive import tariff. This is irrespective of the degree of value addition in this situation.

There is only one normal situation in which exemption does not create negative protection. That is an exemption, which is available for inputs used for export production. In this case as the product is competing in the international market its output tariff is implicitly zero, while all exempted items are going into its production only. Thus effective protection is also zero in this case.

Table 2b shows the range of effective protection rates that can arise if the peak rate is 20% and there are only three import tariff rates (10%, 15% and 20%) and no exemptions. The weighted average tariff on inputs can lie anywhere between 10% and 20% (e.g. 11% or 18%). Items with a tariff rate of 10% are likely to have negative protection if the value added ratio is less than 0.5. Similarly items with a tariff rate of 15% are likely to be vulnerable to negative protection if the value added proportion is less than 0.25. At the same time effective protection can range as high as 100% (or higher). Items with a tariff rate of 20% and input rates of 10% may have even higher effective protection rates of the order of 200%.

Table 2(a)

Effective Protection Rate [EPR] :
Variation with value added & Input tariff

Average Input Tariff duty								
	Value Added							
	0.9	0.7	0.5	0.4	0.3	0.2	0.1	0.05
	Input ratio							
	0.1	0.3	0.5	0.6	0.7	0.8	0.9	0.95
	I Output Tariff = 20%							
20%	20%	20%	20%	20%	20%	20%	20%	20%
15%	21%	22%	25%	28%	32%	40%	65%	115%
10%	21%	24%	30%	35%	43%	60%	110%	210%
5%	22%	26%	35%	43%	55%	80%	155%	305%
0%	22%	29%	40%	50%	67%	100%	200%	400%
	II Output Tariff = 10%				Negative Protection			
20%	9%	6%	0%	-5%	-13%	-30%	-80%	-180%
15%	9%	8%	5%	3%	-2%	-10%	-35%	-85%
11%	10%	10%	9%	9%	8%	6%	1%	-9%
10%	10%	10%	10%	10%	10%	10%	10%	10%
	III Exemption: Output Tariff = 0%					Negative Protection		
10%	-1%	-4%	-10%	-15%	-23%	-40%	-90%	-190%
5%	-1%	-2%	-5%	-8%	-12%	-20%	-45%	-95%
1%	-0.10%	-0.4%	-1%	-2%	-2%	-4%	-9%	-19%

Table 2(b):

Three Rate Structure (10%, 15% & 20%) :
Effective Protection Rates

	Items with Tariff = 10%				Negative Protection			
20%	9%	6%	0%	-5%	-13%	-30%	-80%	-180%
18%	9%	7%	3%	-1%	-7%	-20%	-58%	-133%
15%	9%	8%	5%	3%	-2%	-10%	-35%	-85%
11%	10%	10%	10%	9%	9%	8%	6%	1%
10%	10%	10%	10%	10%	10%	10%	10%	10%
	Items with Tariff = 15%							
20%	14%	13%	10%	8%	3%	-5%	-30%	-80%
18%	15%	14%	13%	11%	9%	5%	-8%	-32%
15%	15%	15%	15%	15%	15%	15%	15%	15%
11%	16%	17%	20%	22%	26%	33%	56%	101%
10%	16%	17%	20%	23%	27%	35%	60%	110%
	Items with Tariff = 20%							
20%	20%	20%	20%	20%	20%	20%	20%	20%
18%	20%	21%	23%	24%	26%	30%	43%	68%
15%	21%	22%	25%	28%	32%	40%	65%	115%
11%	21%	24%	30%	34%	42%	58%	106%	201%
10%	21%	24%	30%	35%	43%	60%	110%	210%

Note : It is assumed that there are no exemptions."

2.2.6 With this background we can start addressing the issue of the desirable structure of tariff rates. While the Task Force is in agreement with the need for simplifying the tariff by reducing multiplicity of rates, the need for giving some protection beyond the nominal rates also cannot be completely ignored. The Task Force is aware that imported goods are not subjected to all the domestic taxes which domestic goods are subject to. But this can be taken care of with the introduction of VAT, which is supposed to more or less reflect the various taxes currently being imposed. Further, it is the view that basic raw materials should attract the lowest rate and the highest rate should be made applicable to the finished consumable goods. Finally, it is also of the view that we need to eventually come down to rates of 10% and below, which is the trend in the ASEAN States, to make our economy competitive. We must have rates comparable to ASEAN States by 2006-07. However, as mentioned earlier, even in countries like Malaysia and Indonesia, consumer durables attract duty at more than 10%.

2.2.7 As regards automobiles, the Task Force notes that since the quantitative restrictions were removed only last year, the manufacturers will need more time to adjust to reduction of the import duty rates. Even in countries like China, customs duty on new vehicles vary from 70% to 80%. In Indonesia, it varies between 75% to 200% and in Malaysia, the rates vary from 70% to 105%. Present rates of duty on automobiles thus do not require any substantial change for the present. Today, a duty higher than the median rate applies to defective steel plates mainly to check imports of prime material in the guise of seconds. A higher rate on such materials is thus justified.

2.2.8 The Task Force also notes that in respect of goods covered under the IT Agreement, the rates of import duty on a number of items including computers and cellular phones will have to come down to zero. It is, therefore, essential that domestic industry in this sector is able to get raw materials also at zero rate in such eventualities. The capital goods for this sector also need to be given special consideration in order to help this industry to successfully compete with imports. In particular the cellular phones industry has been prone to smuggling and Government had reduced the customs duty to 10% with zero CVD duty in this year's budget.

Under the IT Agreement, the import duty will have to come down to zero. Therefore steps are necessary to give encouragement to the domestic industry to manufacture cellular phones in the country

2.2.9 In the discussions with the trade, there was a very strong plea for reducing the import duty on crude petroleum and naphtha to zero, which is the rate presently prevailing in the ASEAN countries. These are basic raw materials for petrochemical industry, and the trade has prayed for immediate reduction. The Task Force finds considerable merit in this suggestion. With the dismantling of the Administered Price Mechanism, it is essential to allow the prices of the petroleum products in the domestic market to be determined on the basis of import parity price. To protect consumers, the import duty has to be brought down from the present levels. At the same time, as crude is the basic raw material for other petroleum and chemical products there has to be a duty differential. In this regard, it is observed that the international practice is that the differential is around 2 percentage points with the value addition normally around 10- 15%. Accordingly, taking into account all factors including profit margin of refineries, the value addition and need to keep the product prices reasonable for the consumers, the road map for duty structure on petroleum has to be kept distinct from that of other products. The Task Force also recognizes that the effective rate of protection in refining sector is much higher than the nominal protection, as the value addition is only about 10%. As seen from the chart for effective protection, with an output tariff of 20% and input tariff of 10%, with a value addition of 10%, the effective rate of protection is as high at 110%. If along with the reduction of duty on crude to 5%, the duty on the petroleum product is brought down from 20% to 10% this will still give a 55% effective rate of protection. Revenue loss on account of reduction of import duty in the petroleum sector may be made up through suitable increase in excise duty on petroleum products, namely, diesel and petrol. The Task Force, however, feels that duty reduction on crude petroleum should be in phases.

2.2.10. The above analysis is mainly for industrial goods. The Task Force is of the view that agricultural goods stand on a different footing where various other factors like subsidy, market intervention measures, minimum support prices make it necessary to look into each item individually. The Task Force is not equipped to take on this function and recommends that a separate group with the requisite expertise may be set up to look into the duty structure for such products. The Task Force thus has not given any recommendation with regard to the road map for import duty structure on agricultural products, etc. At the same time, the Task Force also recommends that such duty should not exceed 150%.

2.2.11 In the aforestated background the following recommendations are made :

(i) 0% - for items like life-saving drugs and equipments, sovereign imports (defence and security related goods etc.) and imports by RBI.

(ii) For other goods -

By 2004-05 :- 10% for raw materials, inputs and intermediate goods.

- 20% for consumer durables.

By 2006-07 :- 5% for basic raw materials like coal, ores and concentrates, xylenes, etc.

- 8% for intermediate goods which will be used for future manufacture (capital goods, basic chemicals, metals etc.).
- 10% for finished goods other than consumer durables
- 20% for consumer durables.

[The duty reduction to the level of 5%-8%-10% should start only after introduction of State VAT so that imported goods are also made subject to the same State VAT (in lieu of SAD) by way of Additional Duty of Customs.]

(iii) Motor vehicles - nominal reduction in the duty from 60% to 50%. The import duty on second hand cars may continue at the existing rates. Higher import duty on defective steel items may continue.

(iv) Cellular phones - the exemption from CVD may be withdrawn but the basic import duty may be reduced to zero in 2003-04. The SAD on this item should also be abolished, so that the total incidence of duty goes up only marginally.

(v) 2003-04 : - 8% on crude oil.

- 15% on the petroleum products.

2004-05 : - 5% on crude oil.

- 10% on the petroleum products.

(vi) Higher duty rate upto 150% for specified agriculture products and demerit goods.

2.2.12 A word of caution is warranted in the move to the suggested rates of duty. In the event, if the import duty on a particular item is currently high, say, 30% and it has to move to 10% then certainly a sudden reduction to 10% in just 1 year would upset the domestic industry and it would also not be desirable from the point of view of revenue. Thus, certain high rate-high revenue items may require a more gradual move towards 10%. Hence, it is recommended that as a general policy, the downward revision of duty rates should be in stages of (–) 5% each year. However, it is quite possible that Government chooses to move to the identified lower rate at a faster pace particularly in areas where domestic manufacture is not adequate and imports are necessary. All endeavour should be made to move to the identified rates of duty, as above by 2004-05. Further, having regard to our commitment to reform, it is recommended that to the extent possible, for no item should the present duty rate be increased, unless the item is charged to nil duty, in which case a minimum duty of 5% can be imposed. Some increases may be resorted to only on administrative consideration to avoid multiple rates depending upon end use.

2.3 Customs duty exemptions

2.3.1 Whereas the customs tariff indicates the peak rate of duty, also called the tariff rate of duty applicable on a particular item, it is not the case that this is the duty actually leviable when the said item is imported. The leviable duty also called the effective duty is determined in the context of the duty exemption notifications, if any, issued in respect of the said item in terms of Section 25 of the Customs Act, 1962. Thus, on account of an exemption an imported item may be subjected to a duty lower than that prescribed in the tariff. At times, the duty payable may even be nil. The exemptions are mainly of three types as follows:

(i) General exemptions which are non-conditional and can be availed by all importers.

(ii) General exemptions which are subjected to conditions such as end-use.

(iii) Ad-hoc exemptions, which are issued in respect of specific imports for security, strategic or charitable purposes - the number of ad-hoc duty exemptions are coming down, no doubt, due to the effect of the legislative change, in 1999, restricting the scope of the exemptions to imports of strategic, secret interest or for charitable purposes.

2.3.2 At present, the said exemptions can broadly be placed into the following categories:

(i) Importer specific – e.g., Government (defence and police) etc.

(ii) Project and purpose specific – e.g. training, educational, research, Oil exploration etc.

(iii) Social and health sector/objective specific – e.g. handicapped persons, charitable and social welfare organizations, donations and gifts, medicines, drugs and hospital equipments etc.

(iv) Export related – e.g. samples, packaging materials, durable containers, advance licence, passbook etc.

(v) Sports related – e.g. sports goods, prizes, medals and trophies.

(vi) International commitments – There are a number of international agreements that bind customs duties. These include the GATT/WTO bound rates, contractual commitments such as oil exploration contracts, Information Technology Agreements, exemption to privileged persons, organizations, authorities and foreigners, preferential areas etc.

(vii) Others – e.g. exhibitions, seminars, or expeditions, re-imports.

2.3.3 A duty exemption naturally has revenue implication. On their part conditional exemptions also invariably necessitate imposition of regime of certification, verification, discretion, etc., which adversely impact the clearance of goods, result in higher administrative costs, use of discretionary powers, and raise compliance issues on account of misuse. Exemptions are also nothing but a subsidy, and in fact, a discretionary subsidy. Thus, aside from the obvious impact on the tax to GDP ratio, the duty exemptions have undesirable side effects. The fact that exemptions also cause loss of transparency is another aspect of serious concern for the policy makers.

2.4 End-use based exemption

2.4.1 At present, there are a large number of exemptions subject to the condition of end-use, which is sought to be confirmed by the requirement of production of a certificate from a competent authority, usually a Government Officer, that the imported goods are meant for the declared use. To illustrate, in case of sports goods the certification would be done by Sport Authority of India and in the case of IT products by the Information Technology Ministry. There are around 33 such certification agencies. There can be no two views that involvement of multiple agencies would only increase the transaction cost besides contributing to delays in customs clearance.

2.4.2 Besides the problems associated with certification, the end use based notifications require the customs to ensure the goods are indeed meant for the stated use. This is invariably accomplished by calling for literature of the imported item. As a result queries are raised and till the literature is produced and perused the goods cannot be released. Thus, the end use based exemption notifications do not facilitate quick customs clearance and also militate against on-line appraisal and clearance of imported goods. Therefore, as the intention is to expedite the clearance of the goods and that too without examination, to the extent possible, the solution lies in removing all the end usebased exemptions, which necessitates the calling of literature and certificates from different departments.

2.4.3 On the subject, it is increasingly been noticed that there is a move towards removing the requirement of execution of bonds with the customs authorities for the fulfillment of post import conditions. This is a welcome step as it reduces delays in clearances and also transaction costs. However, it is not the case that the bonds are being removed altogether. What is being provided is that such importers must follow the provisions of Customs (Import of Goods at Concessional Rate of Duty for Manufacture of Excisable Goods) Rules, 1996. Invariably this entails the importer to obtain registration with the central excise authorities, followed by execution of bond, filing application for import of goods, maintaining records for verification, obtaining case by case permissions for import etc. Hence, the new procedure is merely a substitute for the system of enduse bonds as instead of the execution of the bonds with the customs authorities the importer registers with the central excise authorities and must satisfy this authority that the goods have been used for the intended purpose.

2.4.4 It is the view that the present procedure is not desirable. Such procedure only increases the contact points and the cost of compliance. On principle it should suffice that customs clear the goods on the basis of the importer's declaration and if misuse is detected on the basis of intelligence or post clearance audit checks, the duty should be recovered along with interest.

2.4.5 As a policy end-use based exemptions must be avoided. However, when this is not possible the customs clearance procedure must provide for the grant of the exemption without insistence upon literature and certification and the customs would reserve the right to carry out a post clearance audit check based upon risk management tools i.e. not as a matter of routine. This is also in line with the best international practices.

2.4.6 To sum up, criticizing all duty exemptions would be a simplistic approach. Exemptions do serve a number of objectives by ensuring that the imported goods are not only available but also at less cost. Exemptions also serve to stimulate domestic economic activity by making available a level playing field. However, it is also true that exemptions once granted tend to continue even if the objective has since been met and even if alternative and more transparent mechanism is available for achieving the desired objective. Exemptions tend to distort the opportunity cost and in the long run adversely impact competitiveness. Invariably the exemptions are conditional and also impact the pace of clearance on account of necessity of verification process. Overall falling tariffs and India's commitment to bringing down the customs rates of duties to international standards by 2004-05 must also influence the decision whether a particular exemption merits continuance or not.

2.4.7 It is recommended that the grant or continuance of exemptions must be judged against the following criterion and if this done it would widen the tax base, improve the tax to GDP ratio and improve the tax administration:

(i) As a policy, all exemptions must be removed except in case of :

(a) Life-saving goods.

(b) Goods of security and strategic interest.

(c) Goods for relief and charitable purposes.

(d) International obligations including contracts.

(ii) As a general policy, when exemptions are removed but the relief is justified, the targeted beneficiary may be assisted by upfront transparent budgetary support based on a prior stated objective criteria. By such method, the expenditure would be subject to Parliamentary scrutiny and there would be public debate besides CAG audit.

(iii) In case an exemption is justified, it should not be end-use based conditional exemption. However, in the event the end-use condition cannot be avoided, the confirmation of end-use should be done on the basis of selective post clearance checks by using Risk Assessment techniques. It should not be based upon the Customs (Import of Goods at Concessional Rate of Duty for Manufacture of Excisable Goods) Rules, 1996, as the implication in terms of registration with central excise, execution of bond etc. increases contact points and the cost of compliance.

(iv) As a general policy, there should be no exemption from Countervailing duty (CVD), which is at par with the duty paid by the domestic manufacturers of similar goods, including in cases where the exemption from basic customs duty is merited. An exemption from CVD places domestic industry (including potential industry) at disadvantage and discourages domestic investment in these areas, which is not desirable.

(v) Best international practices should be one criteria for determining the requirement of otherwise of an exemption.

2.5 Nature of tax rates - specific versus ad-valorem

2.5.1 A perusal of the Customs tariff shows that for a few items there are specific rates of duty. While the administrative convenience of specific rate is not debatable, these are out of place in an economy seeking to maximize its revenue through buoyancy. A modern tax system should not have specific rates at all. Specific rates also do not allow for buoyancy in revenue on account of price changes. Accordingly, as a policy there should be a move away from specific rates towards ad-valorem rates. These findings would also apply to the central excise notifications, to the extent relevant. Textile fabrics are, however, particularly, sensitive to valuation, and after protracted negotiations, a regime of ad-valorem and specific duty, whichever is higher has been introduced. This should continue keeping in view the importance of this sector.

2.6 In the light of the above recommendations, the suggested customs duty structure on imports is given in Annexure 'A'. Since agricultural products stand on a different footing, the Task Force has refrained from suggesting the proposed rates for these items and recommends an Expert Group may be set up for the same. The Annexure has attempted to cover all goods but in the event certain items may have been left out inadvertently, the duty rates on such items may be fixed in the light of the principles laid down earlier.

3. Central Excise Tariff and Exemptions

3.1 Multiplicity of levies

3.1.1 At present there are more than one type of levy administered by the central excise department other than the Cenvat (Central Value Added tax) duty. These other duties include :

(i) Special Duty of Excise (SED) - levied under authority of Finance Act(s).

(ii) Additional Duty of Excise (AED) – levied under authority of Additional Duty of Excise (Goods of Special Importance Act, 1957) on specified goods, sugar, fabrics and tobacco products. This duty is in lieu of sales tax.

(iii) Additional Duty of Excise (AED) – levied under authority of Additional Duty of Excise (Textile & Textile Articles) Act, 1978 on specified fibres, yarn and fabrics.

(iv) Additional duty on Motor Spirit and High Speed Diesel – levied under authority of Finance Acts.

(v) National Calamity Contingent Duty - levied under authority of Finance Act.

(vi) Cess – levied under various enactments such as Jute Cess Act, Tea Cess Act, etc.

3.1.2 It is well known that multiplicity of levies does not contribute to ease of administration. Invariably separate accounts are to be maintained by the tax payer and the tax collector, which pushes up the cost of compliance. Further, the complexities caused by multiple levies also give rise to errors and disputes. In fact, in cases when an item is subject to more than one levy we often have audit pointing out that one or the other levy was not paid. Even conceptually it is not at all clear why we should continue to have the AEDs, which are basically imposed in lieu of sales tax, for those items which would be subjected to VAT, though there may be a case for continuing with it in respect of some items. In general terms so long as this levy continues it would be difficult to move to VAT. Accordingly, in order to have a simple administration which has as its advantage reduced complexities and compliance costs, it is desirable that as a policy there should not be multiple levies.

3.1.3 It is recommended that as a policy, we should review all levies and have only one levy, i.e. the Cenvat. Some exception, however, has been suggested for the textile and petroleum sector.

3.1.4 An alternative scenario is proposed if for some reason it is not found possible to remove multiple levies at one go. At present, both the tax payer and his counterpart, the tax collector indicate the tax paid under each of the levies separately and subject the same to calculations to confirm the correctness of the payment.

This system is not conducive to efficient implementation and given the large number of transactions, mistakes can not be ruled out. It appears that so long as the total tax is correctly paid, the tax payer should not be bothered with the task of giving the break up. This is a job strictly for the administrators who have to later divide the tax proceed under various accounting heads. Accordingly, it should be provided that when a product attracts multiple levies only the total levy (i.e. one figure only) should be indicated against the particular item. This amount would be paid and the system should further break it up into the individual heads. This would save the tax payer and the tax administrator the exercise of carrying out all sorts of complex calculations. Of course, one problem in this system would be that at present, under the Cenvat Credit Rules, the credit of a particular duty can be used to pay the same duty on the final goods. Thus, the tax payer must know the element of each duty for this purpose. This can be done by indicating the break up of the total duty (in percentage terms) into its respective heads – in like manner of the Drawback Schedule. In fact, it is learnt that earlier a 'working schedule' was being prepared for similar purpose. As stated, however, the ideal solution is to have a single levy.

3.1.5 It is recommended that till such time as there are multiple levies, there should be a working schedule indicating the total tax payable on a particular product and the system should internally segregate the same into the respective levies.

Distribution of revenue in 2001-2002

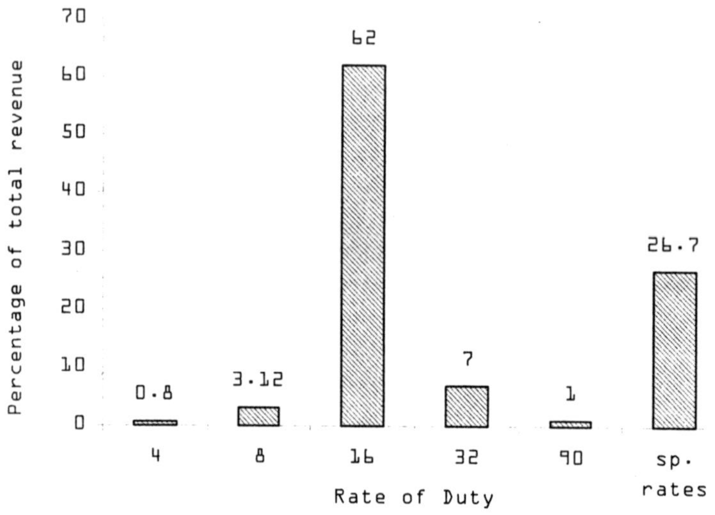

3.2 Multiplicity of duty rates

3.2.1 In so far as the multiplicity of rates on the central excise side are concerned, it is appreciated that recently steps have been taken in the general direction to reduce the multiplicity. For instance, the number of duty rates has been reduced substantially, from 11 rates in 1997-98 to a single rate of 16% at present, except in few cases. Whereas a single rate has many advantages domestic economic considerations do not always permit so. However, it is certainly true that the endeavour should be to have as few number of rates of duty as is possible.

3.2.2 The question of having a single rate of duty for all goods except tobacco products was debated at length. In this regard the VAT structure of a number of developed countries has been examined. The finding is that multiplicity of rates persists in VAT also – with one medium rate for most items, a higher rate for luxuries and a reduced rate for food products. All these countries also levy excise duty on mineral oils, tobacco products and alcohol, which is in addition to the VAT. Besides, they also have exemption for small traders. The VAT structure for some of these countries are as under:-

Belgium

Super reduced rate - 1% (for gold)

Reduced rate - 6% (certain food stuff, agricultural services and pharmaceutical products)

Parking rate - 12% (on certain services)

Standard rate – 21%.

Germany

Reduced rate – 7% (for food, printed matter, health services and public transport)

Standard rate – 16%

France

Minimum rate – 2.1% (medicinal products and newspapers)

Reduced rate – 5.5.% (particularly for agricultural products and most food stuffs)

Standard rate – 20.6%

Ireland

Lowest rate - 0% (books, food stuff, clothing for children).

Minimum rate - 3.6% (supply of live stock)

Reduced rate - 12.5% (energy and certain services)

Standard rate - 21%

Netherlands

Reduced rate - 6% (goods and services which can in general be regarded as necessities).

Standard rate – 17.5%

U.K.

Lowest rate - 0% (food items, passenger transport, children clothing, newspapers).

Reduced rate - 5% (domestic and charity, fuel and power).

Standard rate -17.5%

Basically in all the countries, a large number of products which are considered as necessities are exempt from VAT.

3.2.3 Having regard to the international practices and considering the spread of duty rates in our country presently vary from 0 to 32%, it is the view that there is no great merit in having a single rate of Cenvat on all goods and a 3-tier duty structure with the lowest for food and necessities and highest for luxuries and a standard rate for all other goods may be adopted. If the items are carefully grouped it should not create any problems of classification. Additional taxes by way of surcharge or a SED may be levied on petroleum and tobacco products. In the meetings with various Chambers of trade and industry the common refrain was that any reduction, simplification or alignment of the rates should be resorted to at the earliest and not phased over 3 to 4 years. The Task Force finds considerable merit in these suggestions.

3.2.4 It is also noted that exemption of excise duty in fact acts adversely against the domestic manufacturers because of the taxes paid on the inputs. Therefore, even if the final product is exempt, it bears an effective duty incidence which may work out to 5 to 6% or even more because of the input taxes. This makes imports relatively cheaper. To remedy the situation, the exemptions need to be removed. This will ensure that the protection of the domestic manufacturers vis-a-vis imports is increased, while broadening the tax base. This will ensure that exports can be easily stripped of all taxes and protection of domestic manufacturers will increase without any significant increase in their present liability since credit can be taken of all input duties Some exemptions will, however, continue on other rational considerations.

3.2.5 During interactions with the trade, there was a common refrain that the cumulative domestic taxes (central and state) are very high, and there is a need to bring down the duty rates. The example, of China was cited where the total incidence is reportedly 17%. The Task Force is of the view that there is a need to bring down the Cenvat rate. While it may not be possible to bring down the total incidence to 17% (as State levies are also involved, and tax to GDP ratio also needs to be raised), a Cenvat of 14% would ensure that total incidence is around 20%. A Cenvat of 14% at wholesale level would translate to about 8-10% of the retail price to consumers (we are not concerned with industrial raw material as the manufacturers will get the tax credit) depending upon the commodity, and this coupled with the State VAT (which is expected to be around 10-12%) would bring down the total duty incidences in the range of 20%. This will compare favourably with the VAT rate of 21% in Belgium, 20.6% in France, and 21% in Ireland as well as with the Asian economies. The Task Force thus recommends that the median Cenvat rate showed be brought down from 16% to 14%.

3.2.6 In the aforestated background, the following recommendations are made for the central excise duty structure:

(i) 0% - for life-saving drugs and equipments, security items, food items, necessities and the like, agricultural products.

(ii) 6% - for processed food products and matches.

(iii) 14% - standard rate for all items not mentioned against other rates.

(iv) 20% - for motor vehicles, airconditioners and aerated water.

(v) Separate rates for tobacco products and their substitutes (like Pan Masala).

(vi) The specific rate of excise duty of Re.1 per kilo on bulk tea today translates to about 1% in ad-valorem terms. Raising it to 6% may not be desirable, more so when coffee is already exempt from excise duty. Thus, bulk tea may also be exempted from duty. This is anyway a plantation product.

(vii) Specific duty on cement may continue as most of the clearances are to the depots where the prices vary from day to day and ad valorem levy would necessitate provisional assessments, and may result in uncertainty.

3.2.7 Accordingly, it is recommended that the road map of duty rates should lead towards the identified duty rate (for the product) through a mechanism of (+) 2% or (+) 6% or (+) 8%, as the case may be or (-) 4% each year, depending upon its current rate of duty. To illustrate :

Duty rate at 0% or Nil

Year 0 (2003-04) - from 0 % to 6% (with Cenvat)

Year 1(2004-05) - from 6% (with Cenvat) to 14% (with Cenvat)

Duty rate at 4%

Year 0 (2003-04) - from 4% (without Cenvat) to 6% (with Cenvat)

Year 1(2004-05) - from 6% (with Cenvat) to 14% (with Cenvat)

Duty rate at 32% (except Pan Masala)

Year 0 (2003-04) - from 32 % to 28%

Year 1 (2004-05) - from 28% to 24%

Year 2 (2005-06) - from 24% to 20% (20% will be the parking rate for motor vehicles, air conditioners and aerated waters).

Year 3 (2006-07) - from 20% to 14% (except for motor vehicles, air conditioners, and aerated waters).

3.2.8 The above mentioned approach to the identified duty rates may be taken as the general rule. However, it is recommended that Government may move down to the long term rates even quicker, in case there is adequate revenue buoyancy from other tax proposals such as taxes on services sector.

4. Central Excise duty structure for Petroleum sector

4.1 Petroleum occupies a very important place in the economy in view of its direct and indirect use in practically every sphere of economic activity but also in terms of its direct impact on the revenues of the Government as it is the single largest source of revenue. At present central excise duty rates on petroleum products vary from 14% to 30% - 14% for HSD and 30% for petrol – with

16% being the rate for other petroleum products. Petrol and HSD also attract cess/ surcharge. After the dismantling of the APM, the oil companies now decide on the prices periodically taking into account the behavior of the international oil market. Obviously, therefore, as and when the prices fluctuate, it is expected that the domestic prices would also be fixed accordingly and in fact this is happening. Such periodical revisions in the prices make administration of advalorem levy difficult. Replacing ad-valorem levy by specific duties would ensure certainty in the duty, which the refineries would have to pay. This would facilitate assessment and would also be administratively convenient. The need for ascertaining the market cost, inland freight, margin, etc. would also be obviated. In fact, apart from the Cenvat, these products are already subjected to cesses/surcharge, which are specific, and, therefore, it will be convenient if the Cenvat component which is advalorem is also converted into specific rates.

4.2 Another important issue relating to levy of central excise duty on petroleum products is that of warehousing. Normally, whenever excisable goods are cleared from the factory, excise duty is to be paid. But an exception has been made in the case of petroleum products. Petroleum products can be removed from the factory of production to a warehouse or from one warehouse to another warehouse without payment of duty. This facility has given rise to certain administrative problems particularly with respect to treatment of transit losses. The verification of re-warehousing of non-duty paid petroleum products is time consuming and involves physical verification and substantial scriptory work. With the proposal for introduction of monthly payment of duty, the proposed privatization of this sector and the introduction of specific duty rates, the present facilities for movement of petroleum products without payment of duty would seem to be anachronistic and there is no reason why petroleum products should not be treated at par with other goods. This would also obviate the problems of transit losses, which today result in disputes.

4.3 It has also been brought to the notice of the Task Force that the present duty exemption on kerosene encourages adulteration of petrol and diesel, which attract higher excise taxes. Similarly LDO (Light Diesel Oil) has also a potential to substitute diesel in certain operations. Therefore, a remedy lies in reducing the duty price differentials between the various products, which would disincentives adulteration.

4.4 In the light of the above discussion, the following recommendation is made in respect of the duty structure of the Petroleum sector :

(i) Central excise duty on petroleum products, particularly HSD and motor spirit, may be fixed at specific rates. But keeping in view the importance of the petroleum sector to the revenue, there should be a quarterly review of the specific duties by joint discussions between the Department of Revenue and Ministry of Petroleum so that the duty rates can be adjusted to take account of fluctuation of prices in the prevailing quarter.

(ii) Central excise duty on kerosene may be raised by Rs.1/litre. An additional duty of Rs.1/litre may be imposed on LDO to make the duty at par with diesel.

(iii) Warehousing facility for petroleum products should be withdrawn.

5. Central Excise duty structure for Textile sector

5.1 The Task Force has paid special attention to the duty structure on textiles in view of its importance in the economy and also the complexity in the form of series of exemptions because of attempts to reconcile the various sectoral conflicts. There are broadly the following stages of production in the Textile sector :

- Fibres – natural (like cotton), artificial (like viscose), synthetic (like polyester)
- Yarn spun from the fibres and also filament yarn (artificial and synthetic)
- Knitted and woven fabrics (unprocessed)
- Processed fabrics
- Readymade garments

5.2 Textile and textile products attract duty in terms of the Additional Duties of Excise (Goods of Special Importance) Act, 1957 [AED (ST)] and Additional Duties of Excise (Textiles &

Textile Articles) Act, 1978 [AED (TTA)]. While AED (ST) is leviable @ 4% ad valorem on fabrics, AED (TTA) is leviable on fibres and yarns @ 15% of Cenvat.

5.3 In so far as the fibres and yarns are concerned the duty structure and exemptions are as follows :

(i) All fibres and yarns attract Cenvat of 16% ad valorem, except for cotton yarn (not containing synthetic staple fibres or filament yarns) which attracts Cenvat of 8% (with Cenvat credit) and polyester filament yarn which attracts 32% ad valorem [16% Cenvat + 16% SED] respectively.

(ii) There is a plethora of exemptions on fibres and yarns and broadly, the exemptions apply to the following items:

(a) Carded wool (lefa) for making hand spun yarn of upto 10 counts;

(b) Woolen yarn of upto 10 counts in plain (straight) reel hank form for manufacturing carpets;

(c) Yarns purchased by registered handloom co-operative societies (NHDC & State Government HDC) for use only on handlooms;

(d) Yarn of polyester staple fibres containing cotton and consumed by KVIC for manufacturing Poly Vastra;

(e) Yarn subjected to multiple (folding), cabling or air-mingling manufactured in a factory which does not have facility for producing single yarn;

(f) Dyeing/printing/bleaching/mercerising of cotton / woolen (not containing man-made staple fibres) yarns;

(g) Yarns subjected to beaming, warping, wrapping, winding, reeling; and

(h) Twisting of filament yarns.

(iii) Silk and silk products are exempt from excise duty. Blended silk yarn (containing less than 85% silk), however, attracts 16% adv. [it is exempt from AED (TTA)].

(iv) Following yarns attract specific duty :

(a) Dyeing/printing/bleaching/mercerizing of spun yarns

(Chapters 51, 52, 55)-Rs. 2.50 per kg Cenvat + AED (TTA).

(b) Dyeing/printing/bleaching/mercerizing of filament yarns (Chapter 54)-Rs. 9 per kg Cenvat + AED (TTA).

(c) Textured yarn (including draw twisted & draw wound yarn) of polyesters manufactured by an independent texturiser-Rs. 2.50 per kg Cenvat + AED (TTA).

(v) Specific rates have been worked out so that duty is leviable on the value addition; as such yarn processors may find it difficult to take credit of input taxes as they work mostly on job work basis on behalf of traders.

(vi) Fibres and yarns are generally not covered under the SSI duty exemption scheme except for woolen and shoddy yarn.

5.4 The duty structure and exemptions in respect of Fabrics are as follows :

(i) Fabrics (Chapters 51, 52, 54, 55, 58, 60 & certain fabrics of Chapter 59) attract an 'aggregate' duty of 12% ad valorem [8% CENVAT + 4% AED (ST)]. Fabrics of flax, ramie and other vegetable textile fibres (Chapter 53) attract effective excise of 12% adv. [no AED (ST)].

(ii) Unprocessed (grey) fabrics attract optional 'aggregate' duty of 12% ad valorem. However, once a manufacturer of grey fabrics opts to pay duty, he has to do in respect of all clearances till he opts not to pay duty.

(iii) Textile fabrics generally are not covered under the SSI exemption scheme.

(iv) Following grey fabrics attract compulsory excise duty of 12% ad valorem :

(a) Woven pile & chenille fabrics of cotton & man-made fibres;

(b) Terry toweling & similar woven terry fabrics of cotton & man-made fibres;

(c) Gauze; and

(d) Knitted/crocheted fabrics of a width not exceeding 30 cm and containing elastomeric yarn.

[The general SSI exemption has been extended to these fabrics.]

(v) Grey and processed knitted/crocheted fabrics of cotton attract optional 'aggregate' duty of 12% ad valorem.

(vi) Processed knitted/crocheted fabrics of man-made fibres attract 'aggregate' duty of 12% ad valorem.

(vii) Grey knitted/crocheted fabrics of man-made fibres attract optional levy.

(viii) Broadly, following fabrics are exempt from duty :

(a) Khadi (hand spun yarn woven on handlooms) & Poly Vastra (hand spun yarn, containing cotton & polyester, woven on handlooms):

(b) Fabrics woven on handlooms and processed by a factory owned by Apex/registered Handloom Co-operative Society, State Govt. HDC, KVIC, etc.,:

(c) Fabrics processed without the aid of power. However, woven fabrics of wool/cotton/man-made fibres, even if subjected to specified processes with the aid of power in a factory, are exempt from Cenvat, provided that the factory does not have the facilities of carrying out bleaching/dyeing/printing with the aid of power ("hand processing" sector);

(d) Fabrics woven on handlooms and processed without the aid of power/steam;

(e) Cotton fabrics processed without the aid of power/ steam;

(f) Narrow woven fabrics of cotton and man-made fibres;

(g) Fabrics of cotton/man-made fibres woven in prisons and processed outside;

(h) Pleated/embossed fabrics and fabrics subjected to dew drop process; and

(i) Indian National Flag.

(ix) While in the case of excisable goods, input tax credit is allowed only on the basis of documents evidencing duty payment, in the case of textiles, a special dispensation has been given by way of "Deemed Credit" whereby the users can take credit on a deemed basis without production of duty paying documents. The salient features of the scheme are, as follows :

(a) Independent textile processors manufacturing cotton and manmade fabrics are eligible for deemed credit @ $33\frac{1}{3}$ % and $66\frac{2}{3}$% respectively of aggregate duty leviable on such fabrics;

(b) Deemed credit and actual Cenvat credit can not be availed simultaneously on the same consignment of grey fabrics;

(c) Composite mills can avail of deemed credit when they manufacture processed fabrics from grey fabrics not woven in the said composite mill (job work). The rates are 26% and 60% of the aggregate duty leviable on cotton and man-made fabrics respectively. This is because composite mills avail of actual Cenvat credit in respect of other inputs (dyes, chemicals, consumables, packaging materials), while independent textile processors are not permitted to avail of actual Cenvat credit on the same; and

(d) Deemed credit is allowed in respect of texturised yarn (including draw twisted and draw wound yarn) of polyesters @ Rs. 18 per kg to a composite mill manufacturing processed textile fabrics (Chapters 52/54/55) and fabrics of cotton/man-made fibres (Chapters 58/60).

(x) Embroidery attracts duty under the compounded levy @ Rs. 45 per metre length of the machine per shift.

(xi) Industrial fabrics (Chapter 59) continue to attract Cenvat of 16% ad valorem. Tyre cord fabrics also attract specific AED (ST) of Rs. 10 per kg.

(xii) Jute and goods of jute are exempt from excise duty.

5.5 The duty structure and exemptions in respect of Garments and Made-ups are as follows :

(i) Woven articles of apparel (Chapter 62) and other Made-up textile articles (Chapter 63) attract Cenvat of 12% ad valorem.

(ii) Knitted articles of apparel (Chapter 61) attract optional Cenvat of 12% ad valorem.

(iii) Following goods are exempt:

(a) Undergarments, clothing accessories, raincoats;

(b) Woven garments made of handloom fabrics;

(c) Made up textile articles of handloom fabrics; and

(d) Blankets of wool/shoddy yarn of value upto Rs. 150/ sqrmtr.

(iv) Salient features of scheme of central excise levy on Ready-made garments is as follows :-

(a) Tariff value of 60% of the retail sale price that is declared or required to be declared on the retail packages under Standards of Weights and Measures Act, 1976 has been fixed in respect of garments;

(b) General SSI exemption is applicable to garments;

(c) Liability to pay excise duty and fulfill excise formalities has been fixed on the person (merchant manufacturer/brand name owner) who gets garments manufactured on his account on job work basis, unless he authorizes the job worker to do so and the job worker so authorized undertakes to do so;

(d) In order to enable such person to avail of Cenvat credit, the manufacturer/producer of garments includes the person who is liable to pay excise duty on the same; and

(e) Manufacturer of woven garments are eligible to avail of deemed credit @ 20% of the duty leviable on the finished product, without production of duty paying documents, subject to non-availment of actual Cenvat credit on inputs; and

(v) Metallic yarn (imitation zari), adhesive tape of width not exceeding 20 cm and tubular knitted gas mantle fabric for use in incandescent gas mantles attract excise duty of 4% ad valorem without Cenvat credit facility.

(vi) Imported fabrics, garments and other textile made ups attract CVD of 16% ad valorem.

5.6 The multiplicity of rates and the plethora of exemptions make the textile sector extremely vulnerable to evasion of duty. Apart from this, the deemed credit facility is not strictly in accordance with the rationale of the Cenvat credit scheme. Particularly, the exemption given to handloom sector has been misused in the past and in the recent Budget, exemption to hank yarn, which is used by the handloom sector but reportedly diverted to the power loom sector was withdrawn and replaced by a system of subsidy targeted at the intended beneficiaries. The Task Force would like to stress that in the case of other handloom sector also (except when it is processed without the aid of power or steam), the exemption should be withdrawn and replaced by a transparent system of subsidy which will ensure that benefit goes to the right persons for whom it is intended.

5.7 In the aforestated background, the following recommendations are made as regards the central excise levy on Textile sector :

(i) A uniform duty of 16% (to be reduced to 14% in 2004-2005) on all fibres and yarns by raising duty on cotton yarn from 8% to 14% and bringing down the duty rates on polyester filament yarn. The duty on polyester filament yarn to be brought down to 14% in four installments.

(ii) A uniform duty of 12% on all fabrics,(knitted or woven) which are not processed, till 2004-2005.

(iii) All exemptions should be removed except for the following:

(a) Fabrics woven on handlooms (unprocessed);

(b) Fabrics processed without the aid of power or steam. Articles of yearn, strip, twine, cordage, rope, cables (56.07/09) manufactured without the aid of power;

(c) Handloom fabrics (whether cotton, woollen, etc.) certified, as khadi as well as Polyvastra;

(d) Silk yarn spun from silk waste and manufactured without the aid of power;

(e) Woolen yarn spun without the aid of power;

(f) Fabrics processed without the aid of power or steam (but using power for certain specified processes) may be brought under the SSI exemption, when the present exemption is removed;

(g) Dyeing/printing/bleaching/mercerizing of filament & spun yarns without aid of power or steam in a factory which does not have the facilities for producing single yarn;

(h) Yarns manufactured without aid of power;

(i) Jute and jute products (being natural fibres and used mainly for industrial purposes. These are extremely eco-friendly), and also impregnated, coated, covered or laminated with plastics;

(j) Strips of jute (5806.39);

(k) Rot proofed jute products, laminated jute products and fire resistant jute products; and

(l) Blankets of wool/shoddy yarn of value not exceeding Rs. 150 per square metre.

(m) Processing of woolen fabrics (woven on powerlooms), not containing worsted yarn or made of shoddy yarn or melton cloth (made of shoddy yarn), where the fabric value does not exceed Rs. 150 per square metre.

(n) Synthetic fabrics, manufactured from shoddy yarn and consumed in the factory of production for manufacture of shoddy blankets of value not exceeding Rs. 150 per square metre.

(o) Captive consumption of Printing frames for use in printing of fabrics (Administrative convenience)

(iv) Following full exemptions may be withdrawn, and the items brought under the general SSI duty exemption scheme, if not already covered:

(a) Sisal and manila twist yarn, thread, ropes and twine (Ch. 53/56), if consumed within the factory where it is produced for manufacture of sisal and manila products falling under Ch. 53, 56, 57 or 63;

(b) Hair belting of wool (5806.39); and

(c) Raincoats, undergarments & clothing accessories.

(v) Exemption to all other handloom fabrics processed by any agency may be withdrawn and replaced by an outright transparent subsidy similar to the hank yarn subsidy scheme.

(vi) Excise duty on coated and bonded fabrics (Chapter 59) should be rationalized to 16% (and subsequently to 14%) instead of 21% (16% + 5%) as at present.

(vii) The deemed credit schemes should be immediately withdrawn, and credit given only on production of duty paying documents. The Task Force recognizes that Textile industry is to a large extent controlled by traders. With the withdrawal of the deemed credit scheme, if the users are to avail of the credit of duty paid on inputs, all down stream manufacturers would have to come under the excise net. This might create some problems for the power looms which can, however, be obviated if the supplier of yarn to the power looms is deemed to be the manufacturer, so that all excise formalities including taking of credit undertaken by the traders. Similar dispensation can be made in the case of processed fabric in cases where the traders send grey fabrics to the processors for further processing. Such scheme already exists in the garment sector. Needless to say, the procedure for payment of duty by the traders will have to be simplified so as to encourage the acceptance of the scheme. However, optional levy on unprocessed fabrics may continue.

(viii) There may be a problem when the general SSI duty exemption for ready-made garments is removed, as in that case, even tailors may have to be brought under the excise net. To overcome this, it can be provided that when ready-made garments are made on job-work basis for use and not intended for sale, no excise duty should be charged.

(ix) As regards rate structure, the existing 12% rate may continue till 2005, as a commitment has already been made in this year's Budget to that effect.

(x) The Additional Duty of Excise (Goods of Special Importance) Act, 1957, should be amended from 2005 in respect of textile fabrics so that like any other goods, the States can levy sales tax on such goods also.

6. Central Excise duty exemptions

6.1 Central Excise duty exemption notifications are issued under the provision of Section 5A of the Central Excise Act, 1944. In like manner to the Customs duty exemption notifications, these also provide relief to the tax payer such that the tariff rate of duty need not be paid and only the concessional (or nil) duty has to be paid. A review of the exemptions reveal that over the past 5 years there has been nominal decline in the number of exemptions. However, it is worth noting that the total number of exemptions is not a correct reflection of the number of products being exempted from levy of excise duty. This is due to the fact that one exemption may contain a large number of products spread over a large number of product classifications. For instance, duty exemption notification No. 6/2002-C.E., dated 1.3.2002 is applicable to over hundreds of items, some of which are indicated by their generic descriptions and the actual number of items would be so much more.

6.2 It appears evident that monitoring duty exemptions to ensure that these are issued on sound principles and withdrawn when the objective is met is a critical task for the Government, which impacts the tax to GDP ratio. However, review of duty exemptions does not appear to be done though the ground realities warranting exemption may have undergone change. Also some exemptions may lead to distorted investment decisions as the industry believes that the exemption will continue ad infinitum. It appears that an exemption when issued to meet a specific objective should be reviewed periodically with change in ground conditions. The continuing grant of exemption may not be conducive to efficient utilization of resources. Hence, it is necessary in the interest of transparency that when an exemption is issued it indicates the period of its validity with a proviso that changed circumstance may warrant a midterm review. This would ensure a comprehensive periodic review by the Government which must record the justification for its continuance. It would also put the burden on the beneficiaries to establish the continued justification for the exemptions. This also resolves the problem of promissory estoppel and also ensure transparency and stability.

6.3 Taking into account all factors the the grant of exemptions on the central excise side needs careful consideration and justification based upon the following touchstones :

(i) Income elasticity of the product - an exemption is not justified on items which have high income elasticity. In other words, social equity demands that exemption should not be granted in respect of goods which are purchased or used by the high income groups and can be termed as luxury goods. This is not to justify the grant of exemption in each and every case the goods are consumed by the masses. A careful approach is required before grant of exemptions.

(ii) Cost of compliance is an important element which would justify the grant or otherwise of the duty exemption - in view of the vastness of the economy and that the tax administrators are spread thin it is desirable that the cost of collection should not be high. Hence, an exemption should be weighed both against the revenue mobilization as well as the cost of collection thereof. In the event, the cost of collection is significant it may be an economically viable decision to grant exemption.

(iii) International practices serve as an important input for grant or denial of exemption. No doubt the ground realities and compulsions of other countries may not adequately compare with the situation at home nevertheless tax treatments of goods internationally do reflect the international thinking. For instance, it is a common trait internationally that demerit goods are subject to high tax rates, and the same is done here also. Likewise exemptions to environmental friendly equipment is an international phenomenon and is equally justified at home.

(iv) Whether an exemption meets the canon of transparency or not is an important factor to be taken into account while examining the issue. By and large conditional exemptions run the risk of increase in cost of compliance and inefficient monitoring systems provide scope for misuse. On principle a more transparent methodology is the grant of budgetary support to the activity warranting an exemption. This would ensure accountability, reduce transaction cost, and most importantly lead to periodic monitoring on regular basis. In such scenario the unintended continuance of an exemption would also be ensured against. In other words, while granting exemptions on sound principles the scope of extending the intended benefit through budgetary support should first be examined.

6.4 Applying the aforementioned tests to the present exemptions the consensus is that a number of duty exemptions can be removed. An illustration is the duty Exemption No. 13/2000 C.E., dated 1.3.2000 issued in respect of freight element incurred by Integrated Steel Plants.

6.5 As stated, the general prescription in respect of grant of duty exemption, as indicated in the context of customs duty exemption notifications would equally apply. In other words, it is the view that sound taxation policy demands limited use of exemptions. Further, when exemptions are justified these should not be end use based conditional exemptions, which cause compliance problems and increase contact points which are best avoided. Thus, instead of exemptions we should preferably move to a budgetary mechanism for giving the same relief.

6.6 To sum up, it is recommended that the following factors must be taken into account while considering the grant of a duty exemption :

(i) Income elasticity of the product; cost of compliance; international best practices; and canon of transparency;

(ii) Instead of duty exemption whether it is possible to extend the same benefit through a budgetary mechanism; and

(iii) If an exemption is issued it should indicate the period of its validity with a proviso that changed circumstance may warrant a mid-term review.

7. Small Scale Sector duty exemption

7.1 The Small-Scale Sector Industries (SSIs) have been playing an important role in India's economic development in the form of value addition, employment generation, mobilisation of capital, entrepreneurial skills and contribution to export earnings. At present, the SSI sector with over 40 lakh units spread all over the country accounts for nearly 95 per cent of industrial units in the country and 40 per cent of value-added in the manufacturing sector. Its share is as high as 34 per cent in national export and it contributes roughly 7 per cent to the country's total GDP. Yet its contribution to excise revenue is negligible, only of the order of 3.4% of the total excise revenue.

7.2 Traditionally, the central excise duty exemption has been used to support the SSI sector. But it has been noticed that over the time the exemption is increasing and today no central excise duty need be paid by a unit whose clearances are upto Rs. 100 lakhs in a financial year. Whereas there is no doubt that the smaller units do need the central excise exemption, the flip side is that so long as such a vast sector continues to remain exempted, avoidable distortions are caused, as follows :

(i) The adverse impact on the tax to GDP ratio is an undeniable outcome of the increasing exemption limit for this sector;

(ii) Central excise being a tax at first stage of production, the exemption therefore leads to non-accountal of production which leads to nonpayment of all other taxes (Income Tax, Sales tax etc.) and generation of black money;

(iii) Exemption leads to misuse of Cenvat credit by the duty paying (large) sector which procures the exempted goods from SSI sector but wrongly takes credit on basis of duty payment documents generated elsewhere;

(iv) Non-accountal of transactions encourage a cash economy with its own adverse implications;

(v) The exemption gives benefit to units upto a specified turnover after which, duty has to be discharged at the full rate. Therefore, for obvious reasons the units prefer to keep their turnover within the full exemption limit, either by unaccounted removals or by horizontal proliferation. This is not desirable from the point of view of evasion of tax. It also discourages economies of scale;

(vi) Duty exemptions for the SSI sector cause a break in the Cenvat credit chain and would adversely impact the adoption of a full fledged VAT; and

(vii) An exemption leads to loss of valuable data which proves counterproductive in respect of dissemination of information, tax planning etc.

7.3 In so far as the payment of tax in general is concerned it is important to appreciate that the SSI sector does pay its dues, the sector contributes significantly in the payment of central excise duty on the goods procured from the duty paying sector, payment of income tax, sales tax etc. However, the units do not pay central excise duty. The starkness of this simple statement is brought out when we find that a person owning a phone or residential property is on the records of the Income Tax; a person with a turnover of Rs.40 lakhs is subject to compulsory audit by Income Tax; all such persons pay sales tax and income tax etc. Yet, upto a turnover of Rs. 100 lakhs no central excise duty need be paid and upto clearances of Rs.90 lakhs in a financial year these are not even on the records of the central excise department. The threshold limit for exemption in the developed countries does not exceed Rs.30-40 lakh. It is also the view that the ever increasing exemption limit (from Rs.25 lakhs to Rs.50 lakhs and now to Rs.100 lakhs) has been cornered by the larger of the SSI units and the smaller (tiny and family) units continue to produce at lower levels of output. In fact, being a first point tax non-payment of central excise duty leads to non-accountal of production and income which leads to non-payment of sales tax, income tax, generation of black money etc. Obviously there is something wrong somewhere.

7.4 It is the view that as a policy, SSI sector must also pay central excise duty. In fact since they already pay all other taxes there should be no hesitation in paying the central excise duty also. In any case, being an indirect tax, it gets passed on the consumer. Moreover it is the finding that the SSI sector is not averse to payment of central excise duty so long as they do not have to interact with the department. There is a logical reason for this. Since the units are mostly one-man shows dealing with the tax department would lead to loss of man-hours which they can ill afford. This is especially true of the smaller of the SSI units. The bottom line is that it is not the payment of excise duty rather method of collection of the same i.e. harassment by the department which is bothering the SSI sector. Accordingly, what is required is a moderate tax rate and a transparent mechanism to collect the due tax without interaction with the department to the extent possible. At the same time it needs to be appreciated that the present system of collection of central excise may not be administratively able to cope with over 40 lakh units. Hence, while accepting that the smaller of the SSI units need to be kept out of the tax net it is also necessary to evolve a modern system of tax collection which does not encourage interface, contact points and excessive documentation.

7.5 The matter of SSI sector duty exemption was debated at length and the view was that the exemption must be available to only the really small units with turnover of upto Rs. 50 lakhs. Other units must gradually start paying the duty. This is, however, subject to the condition that the central excise procedures improve appreciably and the procedures are 'small scale sector friendly'. In short, the view regarding the SSI sector duty exemption is that the problem in payment of duty (by the sector) is basically that the present procedures do not encourage participation and confidence building. Accordingly, there is a need for confidence building measures, which may take some time. In this background, the following recommendations are made :

(i) The duty exemption should be extended to only small units with a turnover of Rs. 50 lakhs - This would ensure the really small scale units being run mostly with family labour and having low capital investment get the desired support. It will exempt those units whose compliance cost will be significantly high relative to their tax obligations.

(ii) The duty exemption limit for the larger SSI units should be gradually brought down to Rs. 50 lakhs. The gradual downward revision of the limit would give the industry time to adjust. The time frame is suggested, as follows :

(a) Year 0 (2004-05) – From Rs.100 lakhs to Rs. 75 lakhs.

(b) Year 0 (2005-06) – From Rs.75 lakhs to Rs. 50 lakhs.

However, on reduction of the exemption limit, the unit would have the option of payment of duty at 4% (without Cenvat) on the value of clearance upto Rs. 100 Lakhs. The other option available at present of paying duty at a certain percentage of the normal rate would continue to be available.

It is important to note that the downward revision in exemption is proposed to be complemented by a transparent and hassle free tax collection mechanism, which must be in place from April 2004.

(iii) The duty exemption should be based upon total turnover - Since the exemption is for a small scale unit, the logical criteria to determine the smallness of a unit is its turnover. It can reasonably be expected that if the turnover is few hundreds of lakhs (Rupees) there is really no difference between a small scale and a large scale unit. Accordingly, at present, a unit is entitled to a small scale exemption if the value of its clearances does not exceed Rs.300 lakhs in the previous financial year. This figure is determined after ignoring the value of clearance of exempted goods and goods exported. Thus, if a unit has clearances of Rs.10 crores or even Rs.20 crores it would still qualify for the SSI sector exemption if these are exempted goods! Surely this cannot be the intention of the duty exemption scheme. It is the view that this is a wrong methodology. The central issue is whether a unit is small or not, a factor of its turnover. Thus, the duty exemption should provide for determining the turnover based on value of total clearances including exempted goods. However, in view of the special contribution of the sector towards the overall exports and to encourage exports, it is proposed that the clearances for exports may continue to be excluded for this purpose, as at present.

(iv) On principle duty exemption for SSI sector should not subsidise consumption of luxury items by the affluent - Central Excise duty is an indirect tax and is paid by the consumer of the goods. In case of an exemption on the goods, the benefit actually accrues to its consumer. It is the view that consumers of luxury goods (e.g. Airconditioners) do not merit the subsidy extended indirectly to them through the SSI sector duty exemption. Hence, it is recommended that a negative list of such items should be drawn up and the SSI sector duty exemption should be denied to a unit making these items. One yardstick to define a luxury item may be that item which attracts over 24% duty. However, this is only a guideline.

(v) Declaration of production activity - At present a SSI unit is required to file a declaration with the Department when its clearances touch Rs.90 lakhs. It is proposed that with effect from 1st April 2003 a Declaration should be filed by the unit when value of its clearances touches Rs.50 lakhs. We can simply not have a modern tax system unless there is a data base and proper accountal of all transactions.

7.6 As regards the SSI sector duty exemption it is also observed that at present the exemption is not extended to all items. In fact, there are a large number of such items – watches, blankets of wool, copper circles, ball or roller bearings are few examples. No doubt one rationale for the denial of the duty exemption may have been that the economies of scale do not permit the manufacture of the item in the small scale sector. Another could be the possibility of misuse. Nevertheless this is an important matter and as a policy the small scale sector duty exemption should be extended to all items. Accordingly, it is recommended that the present list of items to which the small scale sector duty exemption has not been extended should be subjected to a comprehensive review and to the extent possible the exemption should be extended. A relevant factor would also be the nature of the item and it should not be the case that grant of exemption subsidizes consumers of luxury items.

7.7 Extension of SSI sector duty exemption to Matches

7.7.1 At present, the small scale sector duty exemption does not apply to Matches. This sector has over 18,000 tax payers, with an overwhelming majority in the cottage sector located in and around Madurai and Chennai, and only few large mechanized units. The revenue from Matches is nominal - only Rs.32 Cr. in 2001-2002. Thus, large number of small scale assessees are subject to nominal tax, which is not desirable particularly as it is in contrast to general policy to exempt from excise duty the small scale sector.

7.7.2 Rules 13 and 14 of Central Excise Rules, 2002 prescribe a special procedure for the assessment and collection of duty on Matches (CETH 36.05). This procedure continues on the statute as a unique dispensation for the Match sector. It envisages payment of central excise duty by the method of affixing to each box or booklet a central excise stamp of the value appropriate to the duty. The stamps are printed at Government Security Printing Press, Hyderabad and kept in safe custody at the District Revenue Treasuries or Sub–treasuries wherefrom these are supplied to the individual Match manufacturers. It is the finding that the special duty structure for the Match sector and the special procedure, which is an aberration in so far as the general procedures of central excise administration is not desirable. Some of the common problems which have been noticed are :

(i) The system is inefficient – reportedly, the cost of collection of revenue ranged from 124% in 1998-99 to 68% in 2001-02 - major share being the cost of purchase and distributions of stamps.

(ii) Cost of compliance is high as a tax payer has to shuttle between the Range Office and the Treasury more than once a week to pay the duty and obtain central excise stamps before effecting clearance.

(iii) The central excise stamps are frequently not available, which dislocates the production activity besides increasing the administrative work on account of Department having to declare 'Stamp Holidays'.

(iv) The specimen of the labels (of stamps) are approved by the Department, and often it is dragged into disputes of

Trade Mark. This is avoidable litigation.

(v) The Treasuries are under the control of State Government and the Security Printing Press under Department of Economic Affairs, Ministry of Finance. Thus, procedural or other delays at either end affect the collection of central excise revenue.

7.7.3 As a result of the unique tax structure and absence of duty exemption there is, reportedly, wide spread corruption and inefficiency. There can be no sound rationale why the poor unorganized sector is being deprived the advantage of the SSI sector duty exemption. In fact, if there is a case for the SSI sector duty exemption for any item it is the Match sector. Accordingly, it is necessary to clean up the central excise law and bring this sector into the main stream.

7.7.4 It is recommended that :

(i) The small scale sector duty exemption should be extended to Matches - the vast majority of the manufacturers would then be outside the scheme of excise procedure i.e. – no registration, no records, no returns and no payment of duty. This would be source of great relief to the small and cottage sector units.

(ii) The duty structure may be made ad-valorem. Since, the duty would be paid only by the large units (semi-mechanized and mechanized) only, the Cenvat credit scheme can be extended. Such step would also clean up the Central Excise Rules as the rules 13 and 14 may be deleted. The present duties incidence various from less than 1% to about 8%. Since it is an item of necessity, a duty of 6% is recommended.

8. In the light of all the above recommendations, the suggested central excise duty structure is given in Annexure 'B'. The Annexure has attempted to cover all goods but in the event certain items may have been left out inadvertently, the duty rates on such items may be fixed in the light of the principles laid down earlier.

9. Location based exemptions

9.1 In 1999, for the first item in the history of central excise the Government issued two exemption notifications aimed at development of the North-Eastern States. While the intention was laudable it has actually translated into shifting of investment to the North-East from other parts of the country. The long terms effect of the exemption, which is valid for 10 years would be to depress the excise revenues for this long period. Another fall out, on expected lines has been the demand from other states for similar exemption. Kutch district and Jammu and Kashmir have been included under this scheme and the day is not far when other States would press for such exemption. The net result would be the creation of areas of exemption, which is most undesirable from the point of view of any tax administration. Such a move would seriously impact the tax to GDP ratio in the coming years.

9.2 It is recommended that there is a need to review the policy of granting exemption based upon location and no further exemption should be granted.

10. Relevant date of Notification

10.1 An important issue relating to exemption notifications, both customs and central excise is the relevant date from which the exemption would come into force. Over time, this has been an area of dispute with some treating the date of issue as the relevant date and others the date from which it is made known to the public. Without going into the legality of the issue, it is the finding that any good tax administration must provide some advance notice to the tax payer before a change is introduced. This has its obvious advantages. In fact, at present the system is that a notification is issued on a particular day and that same day it is placed on the C.B.E.C. web site and comes into force. This is true even if the notification is issued after office hours or late at night, which is usually the case. Reportedly, this situation results in neither the departmental officials or the trade and industry knowing about the notification. As a result, there is invariably an exercise of issue of demand notices (when duty has been increased) and filing of refund claims (when duty is reduced). Another fall out of the sudden introduction of the notification is that the automated clearances on the customs side give the wrong results, since the software modification does take time.

10.2 As stated, it is not reasonable to bring into force a notification from the date of its issue as this increases the work load and adversely affects the efficiency of the system. At the same time, it may not be appropriate to give too much time for the implementation of the notification as this may lead to speculation.

10.3 It is recommended that a notification should come into force from the day after the day of its issue. To illustrate, a notification dated (i.e. issued) 1st December would come into force from 2nd December. This would require each notification to contain a suitable clause, till such time as the law is amended.

11. Zero rating of exports

11.1 There is a misconception that exports are exempt form central excise duty. This is not so. Excisable goods meant for exports are chargeable to duty as any other excisable goods. Today, there are two schemes of giving tax credit in respect of exports, in terms of rules 18 and 19 of the Central Excise Rules, 2002. In one scheme the goods can be cleared without payment of duty and the manufacturers can take credit of the input taxes paid which can be used for payment of duty on their domestic clearances, if any. The other scheme is that the exporters can pay excise duty on their products and subsequently claim rebate of the duty paid.

11.2 In this regard it is the view that since the central excise duty is meant to apply only to consumption of goods in India, obviously export should not be subject to any tax. This is based on the destination based principle of Trade Taxes, whereby domestic taxes are not transmitted across the borders. The international practice is also that exports are treated as zero-rated, that is, to say no VAT is charged on export of any goods and the manufacturers are given the credit of all input taxes which have gone into the manufacture of exported goods and periodically this amount is refunded to the exporters. There appears to be no reason why in our country there is a dual system of giving the export rebates, more so when there is substantial delay in many cases in granting rebates. This only adds to the cost of the exporters.

11.3 In the event exports are zero rated, that is, to say no excise duty is payable on exports, as distinct from exempt goods in respect of which no tax rebate is admissible, manufacturers will no longer have the option to pay duty on exports. Whatever duty has been paid on the tax credits would be regulated and periodically refunded to the manufacturers in case they are not in a position to utilize such credit on their domestic clearances. For this purpose, suitable mechanism will have to be evolved for quick refund of the credit in all such cases, say, at monthly intervals. There would be cases where the goods may not be exported directly from the factory, in which case Cenvat will be payable, and in such cases the Drawback scheme would apply. It is the view that this system would be far more efficient in facilitating the exporting community.

11.4 It is recommended that from 1st April 2003 exports should be zero rated.

9

Value Added Tax

1. Introduction

Value Added Tax (VAT) is unanimously acknowledged to be a major reform in the indirect taxation system for the following reasons:

(i) It eliminates the cascading effect of taxes;

(ii) It promotes competitiveness of exports;

(iii) It has a simple and transparent structure; and

(iv) It Improves compliance.

1.2 In recent time, more and more countries have been adopting VAT for taxation of commodities and services, and presently there are more than 120 countries in which VAT is in force. Only the USA and India are amongst the more populous countries that do not have a VAT. Economists have generally shared the view that VAT is best suited as a Federal or Central tax, and not at the State-level. However, states and provinces in a few large federal countries like Brazil, and, to a lesser extent, Canada, have adopted VAT, with varying degrees of success. By adopting VAT the country would soon be joining the majority of the countries and hopes to derive the advantages thereof in like measure.

1.3 Considering that the implementation of VAT is closely linked to the administration of other indirect taxes and impacts the tax to GDP ratio, it has become necessary to examine the relevant issues. In this direction the Task Force has had the benefit of meeting with the Empowered Committee of the Finance Ministers of the States, constituted for the purpose of implementing a nationwide State-level VAT. The Empowered Committee is indeed a unique experiment in federal fiscal planning and has achieved much in terms of building a consensus on many of the critical issues relating to implementation of VAT in a relatively short spell of time. Most countries have taken several years to implement VAT. As was learnt, decisions have been taken on the important features of VAT relating to replacement of the Sales Tax levied by the States (though some other local taxes like octroi, mandi cess etc. may continue); the Revenue Neutral Rate and other rates; the tax to be a multi-point levy, with the tax paid on inputs within the State being set off against the tax payable on the dealer's sales (subject to a threshold limit); phasing out of CST in 4 years; adoption of uniform classification, etc. Most all vital areas have been covered by the Empowered Committee and it would not be appropriate, nor is it considered necessary for this Task Force to reexamine these issues. The Task Force would like only to highlight few issues to ensure successful implementation of VAT, and its continuity and stability in a dynamic sense. These matters assume importance in view of the limited time now left for the proposed implementation of State VAT, from 1st April 2003.

2. Preparedness for State VAT

2.1 For State VAT to become a reality, a high level of commitment is required for all concerned tax administrators and businesses which include the small traders. Thus, clear and transparent dissemination of information is going to be critical to the success of the implementation of State VAT. In this regard, it is evident that what is required is a comprehensive publicity programme across the country to apprise and educate all concerned regarding the implications of VAT. This programme should take place at National and State level and percolate down to the Districts. Naturally this requires resources. It is the view that the publicity programme must involve both Central and State Governments and the former should be prepared to extend financial support for this.

2.2 It is recommended that a publicity awareness programme should be started jointly by the Central Government and the State Governments and the former should extend financial support for this, if required. Since the State VAT is expected to be implemented from 1.4.2003 it is also necessary that the publicity awareness programme should be implemented at the earliest.

3. Uniformity of definitions

3.1 Reportedly, some of the State VAT legislations are not fully based upon the model legislation and, as a result, there is a variance in the definitions of dealers, distributors, etc. In some cases even the charging section is not uniform. Further there must also be uniformity in the procedures and documentation. In fact, common classification of goods is critical, though there is one view that it would be difficult for the small dealers to adapt to the same. However, uniformity in all these matters is important for the creation of a truly common market. It will also take care of the apprehension that absence of uniformity may give rise to avoidable disputes.

3.2 It is recommended that an attempt should be made towards uniformity of all State legislations, procedures and documentation relating to VAT.

4. Compensation to States

4.1 One of the issues which impact the transition to VAT is the compensation to be given to the States upon the removal of Sales Tax and the introduction of State VAT, in the event the tax revenue drops due to the change over. In this regard it is observed that the experience world-wide has been that a move to VAT results in higher revenue realisation. Therefore, there is no cause for concern. Nevertheless if such eventuality arises any compensation should be through revenue mobilization (by the States) from specified services and not through Budgetary support. One avenue is to allow the States to collect and appropriate the Service Tax on identified services.

4.2 It is recommended that issue of compensation, if it arises, must be primarily tackled through mutually acceptable mechanism of additional resource mobilization through Service Tax and not through Budgetary support.

5. VAT to unify all local taxes

5.1 During the meetings that the Task Force had with several industry and trade bodies, it was represented that the switch-over to VAT must ensure that the desired benefits are achieved, especially in view of the fact that this switch-over will entail a major overhaul of systems and procedures for businesses and governments, and at substantial expenditure of money, time and effort. One of the views that was consistently expressed is that the simultaneous imposition of several taxes on goods, with VAT alone being eligible for credit and set-off, would not serve the purpose. Currently, about 16 States impose Entry Tax on goods, 12 States impose Luxury Tax on goods, in addition to which a number of States impose Mandi Cess and a number of local bodies impose Octroi. The rates of each of these taxes vary widely between the States. It was pointed out that if VAT were to achieve its purpose including removal of the cascading effect then it must replace all these local taxes.

5.2 The Task Force is an agreement with the submission of the industry and trade. At the same time, it is a fact that local taxes such as Entry Tax, Octroi, Luxury Tax etc., in addition to Sales, Purchase and Turnover Taxes, are productive sources of revenue for many States, and that therefore, it would be difficult for the States to forego the revenue from these taxes. The proposed VAT should, therefore, meet both these concerns.

5.3 It is recommended that with the introduction of VAT, all other local taxes be discontinued, and the same should be taken into account in determining the RNR.

6. VAT and AED

6.1 The Additional Duties of Excise (Goods of Special Importance) Act, 1957 imposes Additional Duties of Excise (AED) on sugar, textiles and tobacco products. AED was introduced in lieu of sales taxes being levied at that time by the States. There is once view that the rationale for the Act is no longer valid and States should be allowed to levy sales tax on the goods. Another view is that as a policy multiplicity of levies must be reduced and in this direction AED is not required. A third view is that the goods, particularly tobacco products contribute significantly to the revenue that the matter of changing the methodology of levy and rate of tax must be handled with caution as the country can ill afford uncertainty in revenue generation. Accordingly, the matter has been examined in its entirety.

6.2 It is a fact that if AED is removed and the goods are subject to State level taxes the incidence thereon is likely to increase. Thus, the issue of removal of AED has to be examined in the context of impact of higher and also differential incidence of taxes from State to State. As regards tobacco products, it has been the experience of many countries that differential taxes on such high-excise goods particularly cigarettes, incentives large scale illegal cross-border movement resulting in huge evasion of revenue. Studies also reveal that such revenue losses, as a proportion to revenue collected, range from 10-14% in the case of Canada to 25% in the case of Sweden. Unregulated tax rates on such high value good have also been seen to lead to displacement of domestic tax-paid cigarettes by contraband products, translating to significant losses in revenue. Further, being a final consumer product, there is very little value-addition beyond the manufacturing stage in respect of cigarettes. In our country the entire trade margin is found to average about 10%, with around 7% going to the retailers, who number about 2 million and most of whom would be below the threshold limit for VAT. Considering that the excise duty on cigarettes is as high as 100 to 130% in assessable value terms, the VAT on cigarettes would chiefly be a tax on excise. Further, cigarettes constitute one of the most important sources of excise revenue (over Rs.5000 Cr. in 2001-2002) and in addition, the AED on cigarettes, through a specific rate structure, has achieved a stable and substantial revenue stream. It has also completely eliminated the scope for cross-border arbitrage in an otherwise high evasion-prone category of goods. Thus, there is a justifiable case for keeping cigarettes outside VAT.

6.3 In so far as textiles are concerned, India is bound by the MFA and from 2005 competition would increase. Therefore, while proposing to keep the central excise duty at 12% no doubt the idea had been to allow the industry to upgrade and modernize. To further this objective it appears necessary that the tax rates on the item must not increase, a likelihood with the removal of AED and subsequent multiplicity of State level taxes. Hence, it appears that while conceptually AED must go there is sufficient merit in maintaining status quo for this item upto 2005.

6.4 It is recommended that that whereas AED may continue for textiles upto 2005, it may continue even thereafter for cigarettes which should not be subjected to VAT.

7. Credit on Inter-state transactions

7.1 An important issue is the grant of credit of the tax paid in one State by another State in the course of inter-State movement of goods. There is one view that the States into which goods are imported from other States, may find it difficult to allow credit of tax already paid on such goods. However, if the credit is not given there is apprehension of cascading effect besides placing the 'imported' goods at a competitive disadvantage vis-a-vis the local goods with resultant effect of dividing the common market, since investment decisions will tend towards States where the market within that State is larger than that outside.

7.2 In this regard experience of other federal countries like Brazil and Canada reveals that either the inter-State transactions are zero-rated or the tax paid in the exporting State is allowed to be set off by the importing State. The same is the case between the European Union members also. It appears that in our context once the Central Sales Tax is phased out, as presently contemplated, this would cease to be an issue. However, the denial of credit in inter-State transactions appears to have legal implications, inasmuch as it could well attract the provisions of article 304(a) of the Constitution which prohibits any discrimination between local goods and imported goods in the matter of taxation.

7.3 It is recommended that the VAT scheme should provide for grant of credit of duty by the importing State for the duty paid in the exporting State, in the course of inter-State movement of goods.

8. Stability and continuity of the VAT regime

8.1 VAT is going to be a reality soon chiefly on account of the commitment of the States which have after years of painstaking deliberations built a consensus. As earlier observed, this was possible only due to the tremendous efforts of the Empowered Committee. Thus, it appears that stability and success of VAT will, equally, depend on the States' continued commitment to the interest of all stakeholders. In this regard, it appears desirable to consider having in place an arrangement which ensures stability and continuity of the VAT regime.

8.2 The creation of a truly unified domestic common market is the ultimate objective of the tax reform process. A related and equally important issue is that of a mechanism to eliminate internal barriers to trade and commerce. In this regard it is learnt that the Empowered Committee is contemplating setting up a VAT Council which could continue the work done so far by the Committee itself. In view of the fact that the Empowered Committee has achieved so much it can only be expected that the VAT Council would further consolidate the tremendous work, especially if it also includes representation of the Central Government. An alternate view is to explore the possibility of a consensual agreement taking support of a Constitutional provision, such as Article 307. The Task Force would leave this thought with the Empowered Committee for consideration since it is the body most concerned with the long-term stability of the proposed VAT.

8.3 It is recommended that for the stability and continuity of VAT, a VAT Council or a permanent suitable alternative vested with adequate powers to take steps against discriminatory taxes and practices and eliminate barriers to free flow of trade and commerce across the country should be explored.

10

Service Tax

1. Introduction

The service sector contributes roughly 48.45% of the GDP (2000-01) and, as has been the experience worldwide, its contribution to GDP is expected to grow over the time. Taxation of services in the country was started in July, 1994 in a limited way on three services i.e. stock brokers, telephone services and general insurance. Since then the scope has been considerably enhanced and at present 51 services have been notified for levy of Service Tax. Whereas Service Tax contributed revenue of Rs. 3,227 Crs. in 2001-2002, it is expected that the importance of this tax, as a source of revenue to the exchequer shall increase appreciably over the time.

1.2 Whereas the expansion of Service Tax in the coming days is not debatable certain critical issues need to be addressed at this juncture to ensure smooth administration of this tax. The matter assumes importance considering that the country is progressing towards implementation of VAT and the compensation of revenue to the States (in the case there is revenue loss in the transition period) through revenue from Service Tax is under consideration. At the same time, it is learnt that the Government has already taken a view in the matter of levy of Service Tax in the future. Accordingly, it would not be appropriate at this stage to re-open the issues on which a consensus appears to have been arrived at after much deliberation.

1.3 In the aforestated background, the Task Force has examined the critical issues which, in its opinion, would facilitate the early implementation of a modern Service Tax administration and its integration with central excise and VAT.

2. Comprehensive Service Tax

2.1 Service Tax is currently levied on 51 services. However, there are a large number of services, which are not covered, though in the organized sector. Examples of such services are transport sector, construction activity, legal and tax consultancy services, recreation services, etc. It is of the view that in due course Service Tax should be comprehensive and there should be no selectivity of items. However, it would be in order to identify certain services, which are not to be subjected to Service Tax. Examples of these services are public utilities and social services (health, education, etc.) and activities performed by the Government such as administration, defense, etc. (if these are treated as services in the first place). Needless to state, Service Tax should be levied on services, which are received within the country. In other words, they should be no Service Tax on services, which are exported.

2.2 It is recommended that to the extent possible Service Tax should be levied in a comprehensive manner leaving out only few services by including them in a negative list.

3. Extension of duty credit scheme to service sector

3.1 A beginning has been made in extending the scheme of tax credit to service sector by allowing service providers to take credit of the tax paid on the services received. However, the input service and the output service have to be in the same category. It is necessary to expand this scheme to reduce the cascading effect of taxes. Accordingly, the scheme of tax credit should be extended to include all services. In other words, tax credit of services received should be available to a service provider even if the two are not in the same category (of service). Further, service providers procure excisable goods on payment of central excise duty for use in providing the services. It is logical and desirable that the credit of the duty paid should be allowed. In other words, the Cenvat credit scheme on goods should be amalgamated into the Service Tax legislation.

3.2 In this regard, an important matter for consideration is the proposal for the levy of Service Tax by the Union and its collection and appropriation of the proceeds by both the Union and the States in accordance with a certain laid down principles is under serious consideration. This has implications for the grant of credit of the duty paid on goods and services procured by the service provider. A situation where the credit is availed of duties paid to the Centre but the same is used to discharge duties paid to the States would lead to complexities of record keeping besides going against the principle of equity. Accordingly, the way out is that whereas the credit of duty paid on both goods and services by a service provider would be allowed only that much credit as has been accumulated on account of central taxes (on goods and services) should be used for payment of Service Tax collected and appropriated by the Centre. Likewise, the service provider would utilize credit of the State level duty paid on goods and services to pay the Service Tax collected and appropriated by the State. In other words, they should be a one-to-one correlation between the credit availed and utilized separately for central level taxes and state level taxes.

3.3 It is recommended that the following measures should be taken to allow the credit of duty paid by a service provider on the goods and services procured:

(i) There should be complete integration of the Cenvat credit and Service Tax credit schemes with effect from 1.4.2003.

(ii) Credit of Central duties (on goods and services) should be utilized for payment of Service Tax collected and appropriated by the Central Government.

4. Rate of Service Tax

4.1 At present, Service Tax is levied @ 5% on the value of the service provided. This rate is common to all services. However, the service provider is presently not allowed to pay credit of the duty paid on inputs (goods in services), though a small beginning has been made in this direction by allowing a service provider to take credit of the duty paid on services procured provided both procured service and the service provided are in the same category of service. However, it is the view that a comprehensive Service Tax Law should provide the service provider the facility of taking credit of both goods and services procured for providing the said service. This would enable the service provider to utilize the credit to pay the duty on the services provided thereby reducing the cascading effect of taxes.

4.2 In this regard, it is seen that the mean Cenvat rate of duty on goods is presently 16% ad-valorem. Thus, if a service provider avails credit of 16% and is required to discharge duty on the services provided @ 5% there would be an accumulation of credit. Accordingly, it is necessary that in an integrated scheme of credit of duty paid on goods and services the rate of Service Tax would be required to be enhanced from the present 5%. While doing so the proposed Cenvat rate of 14% should be taken into account. However. It is possible that some service providers do not avail the credit of the duty paid on their input goods and services. Accordingly, the rate structure must also take into account these service providers.

4.3 It is recommended that along with integration of the goods and services credit schemes from 1.4.2003, the rate of Service Tax should be suitably enhanced so as to achieve parity with the Cenvat rate by 2006-2007. However, there should be two rates, one for service providers who avail credit and a lower rate for those who do not.

5. Threshold limit of exemption

5.1 Historically, the Indirect Tax regime in respect of central excise duties has evolved taking into account the fact that manufacturers who have low level of activity in terms of value of output should be kept outside the tax net. This decision is influenced by the fact that the small manufacturers cannot cope up with the procedural requirements of the levy and the cost of compliance would be high. Interestingly this rational has not been applied to Service Tax right from its inception. One reason could be that being the new levy the strategy was to allow time for its acceptance and it was not been strictly administered. Furthermore, it is a fact that the selection of services so far has been such that only big providers are covered by the levy. However, as the scope of Service Tax increases and more and more services enter the net, a decision would be required to be taken as regards providing an exemption limit in like manner as is being done on the central excise side. Administrative convenience and cost of compliance would be on the determining factors. It is also to be considered that an exemption limit has a tendency of inviting pressure groups unless it is applied across the board i.e. to all services. Finally, that an exemption limit may be enhanced from time to time, which would eventually impact revenue collection and smooth administration. Therefore, a considered view has to be taken on the subject.

5.2 In this regard, one view is that all service providers who provide services upto the value of Rs. 10 Lakhs in a financial year should be excluded from payment of Service Tax. However, the proposed exemption limit is subjective, and as aforestated there would be a tendency to enhance it from time to time through use of discretion, which is avoidable. Moreover a exemption results in loss of valuable data which adversely impacts policy formulation in the long run. Hence, it is the view that on grounds of administrative convenience and cost of compliance the small service providers should be exempted from the procedural of levy but consistent with the policy so far they should also discharge their tax liability.

5.3 It is recommended that the service providers who provide services upto a value of Rs. 10 lakhs in a financial year should be subjected to a total tax of 1% on the value of the services on an annual basis on the basis of simple declaration. Such service providers would be exempt from the normal procedures of returns and documentation. This scheme does not envisage availment of the credit of the duty paid on the input goods and services.

6. Separate enactment for Service Tax

6.1 Presently Service Tax is levied through the provisions of the Finance Act, 1994 and Service Tax Rules, 1994. With the progressive expansion of the Service Tax coverage it is necessary to enact a specific legislation to administer the tax. Once this is done there would be increased legal clarity and better administration. Considering the recommendation to allow credit of duties paid on goods to service providers it is necessary to have suitable and similar provisions as are in the Cenvat Credit Rules in the Service Tax Law. This will eventually pave the way to have an integrated goods and Service Tax legislation.

6.2 It is recommended that there should be a separate legislation for levy of Service Tax, which should eventually be integrated with the central excise law.

7. Classification of services

7.1 Service Tax is presently levied on the basis of description of the service. However, as its scope becomes more comprehensive and it is integrated into the central excise and VAT there is possibility of disputes arising on the levy. The absence of scientific classification and categorization of services may also lead to lack of uniformity in its administration. It may so happen that a particular service is taxed in one part of the country and since it is known by another name elsewhere it may escape the levy. In any case it is well established that uniformity of classification ensures better administration and reduces the chances disputes. Accordingly, it is the view that there must be development of a Service Tax classification code. As seen, WTO has come up with such classification.

7.2 It is recommended that the services should be classified on the basis WTO classification, which should be made a part of the Service Tax legislation.

8. Dispute resolution

8.1 Service Tax is relatively new levy and is desirable that steps should be taken at this stage to provide that its administration should not lead to disputes and in the event a dispute arises it should be settled at the earliest. This objective is desirable in all fiscal legislations. In this regard, on the central excise side some recommendations have been made to provide for voluntary deposit of disputed duty on payment of interest and penalty, if warranted. It is the view that a similar provision is required in Service Tax Law. Further, it is the view that as a policy when department detects short levy or payment of duty it should have an open discussion with the assessee before proceeding with the issue of Show Cause Notice, if warranted. This will allow the assessee to exercise the option of voluntary payment of duty thereby saving on time and resource in adjudication proceedings.

8.2 It is recommended that as a measure of early settlement of disputes :

(i) Suitable legal provision should be provided to allow voluntary payment of Service Tax not paid when detected either suo-motto by the service provider or by Department.

(ii) Suitable legal provision should provide for the automatically collapse of a Show Cause Notice if the duty is voluntarily paid along with interest and 25% penalty within a period of 30 days of the issue of the notice in cases involving fraud, suppression of fact etc. In such cases the Notice should also mention in its preamble that there would also be no prosecution proceedings. The provision regarding collapse of the Show Cause Notice should apply to 'other' cases but without the requirement of payment of 25% penalty.

9. Non-recovery of Service Tax in certain situations

9.1 Service Tax is a relatively new tax and as with any new tax it's understanding and correct implementation may take time. This applies equally to the service providers and the tax administrators. Therefore, it may so happen that a practice may develop regarding either the levy or non-levy of the tax on a particular service, which may not be strictly legally correct. For instance, it may so happen that in respect of a particular service the tax may not be levied or be short levied on account of the practice. In this situation there is an apprehension that on discovery of the fact of non-payment or short payment, the service providers would be burdened with duty demands which would adversely impact them. On the other hand, Section 11 C of the Central Excise Act, 1944 takes care of similar problem in the case of central excise duty by empowering the Government to direct that in such situation the duty not paid or short paid shall not be required to be paid. It is the view that like provision in respect of Service Tax would bolster the confidence of the service providers.

9.2 It is recommended that a provision similar to that contained in Section 11C of the Central Excise Act, 1944 should be provide in respect of levy of Service Tax.

10. Service Tax as the first E-tax

10.1 In order to facilitate voluntary tax compliance, reduce cost of compliance, eliminate tax payer inconvenience, and improve administration, Service Tax should be implemented as the first electronic tax (E-tax) with self-assessment and on-line web based connectivity between the department and the tax payers. In this regard it is seen that a number of recommendations have been made regarding the need to increase automation and use of information technology in indirect tax system and procedures. These would apply equally to Service Tax Administration and Procedures.

10.2 It is recommended that there should be a time bound review of the automation needs of the service tax administration and in like manner as proposed for other indirect taxes steps should be taken to automate the processes and allow online filing of returns and payment of Service Tax.

Annexure 'A'

Customs Duty Rate Structure

S.No.	Tariff Chapter	Description of goods	Proposed duty (in %)			
			2003-04	2004-05	2005-06	2006-07
		Commodities Attracting Nil Basic Customs Duty (2002-03)				
1	8	Cashew nuts in shell	*			
2	10	Rye, barley, oats, buck wheat, canary seeds, meslin and other cereals	*			
3	27	Electrical energy	0	0	0	0
4	27	Naphtha, F.O. etc. for fertiliser manufacture	0	0	5	0
5	28	Chemicals used in the manufacture of Centchroman (anti-fertility drug)	0	0	0	0
6	28 or 38	Silicon in all forms for solar cells/panels	0	0	0	0
7	29	Life saving drugs or medicines, bulk drugs used in the manufacture of life saving drugs/medicines	0	0	0	0
8	29	Raw materials, intermediates & consumables supplied by UNICEF for manufacture of DTP vaccines	0	0	0	0
9	29	Maltol, for manufacture of deferiprone	0	0	0	0
10	30	Life saving drugs imported on certification as life saving (for personal use)	0	0	0	0
11	30	Chemical contraceptive preparations based on hormones or spermicides	0	0	0	0
12	30	Japanese Encephalitis vaccine imported by A.P. Government through UNICEF	0	0	0	0
13	31	Sodium Nitrate	0	0	5	8
14	32	Chemicals & Lacquers etc. required for improved finish of export product	0	0	0	0
15	37	Cinematographic film exposed but not developed	0	0	0	0
16	37	Recorded magnetic film use for production of TV serial	0	0	5	8
17	38	Chemical elements doped for use in electronics	0	0	0	0
18	39	Substrated polyester base for medical/ industrial X-ray film, graphic art film	0	0	5	8

19	39	Alatheon for copper T	0	0	0	0
20	39	Nylon gut for mfr. of sports goods	0	0	5	8
21	39	Tags, labels, printed bags, stickers, belts, buttons or hangers, imported by bonafide exporters	0	0	0	0
22	41	(a) Raw hides and skins (fresh, salted, dried, limed, pickled) whether or not split, including sheep skins in wool; (b) Raw hides and skins (otherwise preserved)	0	0	0	0
23	41	Wet blue chrome tanned leather, crust leather, finished leather of all kinds including splits & sides of the aforesaid	0	0	0	0
24	43	Raw furskins and tanned or dressed furskins	0	0	0	0
25	47	Pulp of wood or of other fibrous cellulosic material (except rayon grade wood pulp) intended for manufacture of newsprint	0	0	0	0
26	48	Mould vat made watermarked bank note paper, imported by specified Bank note press/security press	0	0	0	0
27	48	Tags, labels, printed bags, stickers, etc., imported by bonafide exporters	0	0	0	0
28	49	Printed books, printed manuals, maps & charts, UNICEF cards, etc., Commonwealth and International reply Coupons, UNESCO coupons	0	0	0	0
29	49	Periodicals, journals, newspapers, music manuscripts, maps, atlases, globes, hand drawn plans, etc. (excluding topographical plans)	0	0	0	0
30	49	Plans, drawings and designs	0	0	0	0
31	49	Printed Indian Bank notes imported by RBI	0	0	0	0
32	58	Tags, labels, printed bags, stickers, inter-lining material etc., imported by bonafide exporters	0	0	0	0
33	71	Current coins of GOI; Foreign currency coins imported by a scheduled bank	0	0	0	0
34	71	Coin blanks imported by a GOI Mint	0	0	0	0
35	71	Special industrial adhesives, gums and solutions and synthetic diamond powder upto 1% of diamond export value	0	0	0	0
36	71	Silver and gold imported under jewellry export promotion schemes	0	0	0	0
37	71	Platinum imported under jewellry export promotion scheme	0	0	0	0

38	72	HRSS coils for coin blanks	0	0	0	0
39	74	Copper wire for copper T	0	0	0	0
40	84	Specified goods imported for petroleum operations undertaken under specified contracts under the NELP	0	0	0	0
41	84	Specified goods imported in connection with petroleum operations undertaken under petroleum exploration licenses, mining leases, issued or renewed after 1-4-99 and granted by GOI or any State Govt. to ONGC or OIL on nomination basis	0	0	0	0
42	84	Parts & raw materials for manufacture of goods to be supplied in connection with off shore oil exploration or exploitation	0	0	0	0
43	84	CD-Writers	0	0	0	0
44	84	Goods for substitution of ODS and setting up new capacity with non-ODS technology	0	0	0	0
45	84	21 specified machinery for road construction	0	0	5	8
46	84	Engines and parts of Aeroplane, gliders, etc.	0	0	0	0
47	84	Second hand computers donated to schools	0	0	0	0
48	84	Braille printer, braille embosser or braille display specially designed for computer system	0	0	0	0
49	84	Floppy Disk drive, Hard disk drive & CD-ROM drive	0	0	0	0
50	84	Other storage devices	0	0	0	0
51	84	Microprocessors for computers other than mother boards	0	0	0	0
52	84	Deflection components for colour monitors for computers	0	0	0	0
53	84	Personal computers/typewriters/FAX imported by an accredited journalist	0	0	0/5	0/8/10
54	85	Recorded magnetic tapes, CD Rom and micro films by R&D institution,	0	0	0	0
55	85	CD ROMs containing books of educational nature, journals, periodicals	0	0	0	0
56	85	IT software and document/title conveying the right to use IT software	0	0	0	0
57	85	CD-ROMs	0	0	0	0
58	85	TV equipment imported by foreign film unit	0	0	0	0

59	85	Video cassette/Tapes of educational nature	0	0	0	0
60	85	Audio cassettes recorded with materials from books, newspaper or magazines for the blind	0	0	0	0
61	85	Specified items for manufacture of semi-conductors, photovoltaic cells, ICs and micro-assemblies	0	0	0	0
62	85	Stepper Motor for automatic data processing machine	0	0	0	0
63	85	One set of pre-recorded casettes accompanying books for learning languages	0	0	0	0
64	85	Recorded magnetic tape, CD-ROM etc. by UGC	0	0	0	0
65	85	Items for Laser based instrumentation	0	0	0	0
66	85	Photographic, filming, sound recording and radio equipment, raw films, video tapes and sound recorded tapes of foreign origin, if imported into India after having been exported therefrom	0	0	0	0
67	85	Goods imported for being tested in specified test centres	0	0	0	0
68	85	68 specified machinery for semi-conductor manufacture	0	0	0	0
69	85	Data/graphic display tubes	0	0	0	0
70	85	Parts of resistors/semiconductors	0	0	0	0
71	85	Parts of capacitors	0	0	0	0
72	85	Deflection components for use in colour monitors for computers	0	0	0	0
73	85	Electronic integrated circuits and micro assemblies	0	0	0	0
74	87	Certain types of vehicles imported by tourists under Triptyque or carnet de passage, subject to certain conditions	0	0	0	0
75	87	Tanks and other armoured fighting vehicles and parts thereof	0	0	0	0
76	88	Satellites and payloads for launching and ground equipment for testing them	0	0	0	0
77	88	Aeroplanes, Gliders, Helicopters and simulators	0	0	0	0
78	88	Parts of goods of heading 88.01 or 88.03 or 8803.10/20/30- Propellers and rotors and their parts, under carriages and their parts, other parts of aeroplanes/helicopters	0	0	0	0

79	88	All other parts of aeroplanes, gliders, helicopters, simulators of aircrafts (other than rubber tyres and tubes for aeroplanes or gliders)	0	0	0	0
80	88	Raw-materials reqd. for manufacture of aircrafts, parts of aircrafts of heading No. 8802; subject to certain conditions	0	0	0	0
81	89	Cruise/cargo ships and similar vessels for transport of goods/persons, when imported for purposes other than breaking up	0	0	0	0
82	89	Warships, life-boats and vessels other than the above when imported for purposes other than breaking up subject to certain conditions	0	0	0	0
83	89	Barges imported along with ship for unloading of imported goods/loading of export goods; subject to certain conditions	0	0	0	0
84	89	Capital goods and their spares, raw-materials, components, material handling equipment and consumables imported for repairs of ocean going vessels by a ship repair unit, subject to certain conditions	0	0	0	0
85	89	Parts for repair of dredgers	0	0	0	0
86	89	Raw-material and parts used in the manufacture of goods falling under heading Nos. 8901, 8902, 8904, 8906 and 8905.10 and 8905.90; subject to certain conditions	0	0	0	0
87	90	Specified photographic/cinema equipment imported by an accredited press cameraman	0	0	0/5	0/8/10
88	90	Instruments for Pharmaceutical/Bio Technology sector having export turnover of Rs. 20 crore and have R & D wing	0	0	0	0
89	90	Medical, surgical instrument apparatus etc., under govt. to govt. assistance programme	0	0	0	
90	90	Specified goods imported by a handicapped or disabled person for his personal use (Braille printers/writing instruments, electronic & arithmetic aids, orthopedic apparatus, etc.)	0	0	0	0
91	90	LCD and parts thereof	0	0	0	0
92	90	X-ray baggage inspection systems and parts thereof used in anti-smuggling operations, bomb detection/disposal purposes	0	0	0	0

93	91	Braille watches, alarm clocks and parts	0	0	0	0
94	95	Requisites for national/international championships/competitions, cups, trophies & medals won by Indian team etc.	0	0	0	0
95	95	Synthetic tracks, artifical surfaces and specified goods for laying them etc.	0	0	0	0
96	96	Fasteners and poly wadding materials, inlay cards, shoulder parts, buckles, hooks & eyes, rivets, collar stays, laces, badges, velcro tape, embroidery threads, etc. upto 3% of fob value of exports	0	0	0	0
97	97	Postage or revenue stamps	0	0	0	0
98	97	Work of art created by Indian artists abroad	0	0	0	0
99	97	Book of age exceeding 100 years	0	0	0	0
100	97	Archaeological specimens, photographs, plaster casts or antiquities, intended for exhibition for public benefit in a museum managed by the ASI of India or a State Govt.	0	0	0	0
101	97	Works of art and antiques	0	0	0	0
102	98	Specified Life saving drugs or medicines or other life saving drugs or medicines on certification by DGHS, for personal use	0	0	0	0
103	98	Articles intended for personal use imported by post or air as gifts upto a value of Rs. 5000	0	0	0	0
104	98	Used bona fide personal and household effects belonging to a deceased person	0	0	0	0
105	98	Goods imported through postal parcels, packets and letters, the duty payable on which is not more than Rs. 100	0	0	0	0
106	98	Articles imported as baggage other than on transfer of residence upto Rs. 12000	0	0	0	0
107	98	Specified mega power projects and nuclear power projects	0	0	5	5
108	98	Water treatment projects	0	0	0	0
109	All Goods	Imports by UN organisations & UN funded projects	0	0	0	0
110	Miscl.	Blood group sera; artificial kidney; contraceptives, specified works of art; animal or birds imported by zoo; commercial catalogues; specimens and models for instructional purposes; postage stamps, unused; paper money; woolen articles received as gift	0	0	0	0

		Commodities Attracting 3% Basic Customs Duty (2002-03)				
111	40	New or retreaded aircraft tyres	3	3	3	3
		Commodities Attracting 5% Basic Customs Duty (2002-03)				
112	1	Bovine animals, ducklings, rabbits and pureline poultry stock etc.	5	5	5	5
113	5	Pancreas	5	5	5	5
114	5	Animal frozen semen and specified animal frozen semen equipment	5	5	5	5
115	6,7, 8,12	Planting materials such as seed, tubers and bulbs	5	5	5	5
116	6	Bulbs, tubers, Tuberous roots, corms, crowns, chickery plants, trees, shrubs & bushes of all kinds, unrooted cuttings, grafts, mushrooms spawn	5	5	5	5
117	7	Onions	*			
118	22	Angostura bitters	5	5	5	5
119	23	Flours, meals and pellets, of fish or of crustaceans, molluses and other acquatic invertebrates, unfit for human consumption and prawn feed	5	5	5	5
120	25	Crude or unrefined sulphur	5	5	5	5
121	25	Natural calcium phosphate, natural aluminium calcium phosphate and phosphatic chalk	5	5	5	5
122	26	Ores & concentrates, ash & residues (other than Copper)	5	5	5	5
123	26	Copper ore & concentrates	5	5	5	5
124	27	Coking coal of ash content below 12%	5	5	5	5
125	27	Metallurgical coke for bast furnance or COREX technology	5	5	5	5
126	27	LNG	5	5	5	5
127	27	Kerosene for N-Parafine/LAB	5	5	8	8
128	28	Phosphoric acid for fertiliser (end use)	5	5	8	8
129	28	Anhydrous Ammonia, ammonia in aqueous solution	5	5	8	8
130	28,29 or 30	88 specified formulation or bulk drug	5	5	8	8
131	29	DL-2 Aminobutanol, Diethyl Malonate, Triethyl Orthoformate, Acetobutrolactone, Thymidine, Artemisinin	5	5	8	8
132	29	Nine groups of goods used in manufacture of ELISA kits	5	5	5	5
133	29	Giberellic acid	5	5	8	8
134	29	Codeine phosphate and Narcotine imported by Government Opium and Alkaloid Factories	5	5	8	8

135	29,39, 70,90	Specified goods including preform of Silica, reinforced plastic rods for telecom grade optic fibre/cables. Specified raw materials for FRP rods	5	5	5	5
136	31	Ammonium sulphate, mineral or chemical fertilizer containing N,P,K/N,P, Potassum sulphate, Mineral or chemical fertiliser containing N & P	5	5	8	10
137	31	Kyanite salts for manurial purposes, Muriate of potash, ammonium phosphate and ammonium nitrophosphate for use as manure or for production of complex fertilizers, Urea for use as manure, composite fertilizers, pot. Nitrate	5	5	8	10
138	31	Diammonium Phosphate, Ammonium dihydrogenorthophosphate	5	5	8	10
139	32	Silver powder suspension	5	5	10	10
140	35	Hydroxy ethyl starch, for Plasma volume expanders	5	5	10	10
141	37	Instant print film	5	5	10	10
142	37	Color positive, unexposed cinamatographic films in jumbo rolls & color negative unexposed cinematographic film in rolls of 400 ft & 1000 ft.	5	5	8	10
143	38	Reference standard imported by Central Drug Laboratory, Calcutta	5	5	8	10
144	38	Dextran for plasma volume expander	5	5	8	10
145	38	Biopesticides (3 specified ones)	5	5	8	10
146	39	Silicon resins and silicon rubber for Solar cells	5	5	5	5
147	39	Saddle tree	5	5	5	5
148	44	(a) Wood chips (b) Wood in the rough & wood roughly squared or half squared (c) Fuel wood, wood charcoal, etc.	5	5	5	5
149	47	Waste and scrap of paper	5	5	5	5
150	47	Rayon grade wood pulp	5	5	5	5
151	47	Wood pulp (for Paper and paper board)	5	5	5	5
152	48	Newsprint and light weight coated paper weighing upto 70 gms/sq.mtr imported by actual users for printing of magazines	5	5	5	5
153	48	Grape guard paper for packing of grapes	5	5	10	10
154	51	Raw wool for handlooms sector	5	5	5	5
155	51	Raw wool of average fibre diameter 32 microns and above	5	5	5	5
156	53	Raw jute	*			

157	71	Raw pearls and raw cultured pearls (including admixtures), rubies, emeralds and saphires (unset and uncut), rough diamonds, rough semi-precious stones	5	5	5	5
158	72	Melting scrap of iron or steel or of stainless steel for melting; ferro nickel	5	5	5	5
159	75	Nickel oxide sinter and unwrought nickel for manufacture of steel	5	5	5	5
160	84	Plant, machinery, equipment, tools, surveillance systems etc. imported by RBI or currency note press	5	5	8	8
161	84	Capital goods for renovation/ modernisation of fertiliser plant	5	5	8	8
162	84	Specified goods for setting up of crude petroleum refinery	5	5	8	8
163	84	Wind operated electricity generators and battery charges upto 30 KW and specified parts of wind machines	5	5	8	8
164	84	Spares supplied without board motors for maintenance	5	5	8	8
165	84	Parts of outboard motors	5	5	8	8
166	84	Specified Machinery for leather	5	5	8	8
167	84	Iron and steel products, machinery and equipment for renovation or modernisation of a power generation plant (excl. captive power plant)	5	5	8	8
168	84	Fogging machines imported by a municipal committee, district board or other authority legally entitled to, or entrusted by the Govt. with the control or management of a Municipal Fund, for use in combatiting malaria and other mosquito borne diseases	5	5	8	8
169	84	Catalytic converters	5	5	5	5
170	84	Parts and raw materials for manufacture of Catalytic convertors	5	5	5	5
171	84	CNG kits and parts, LPG conversion kits & parts, Propane conversion kits & parts	5	5	5	5
172	84	40 Specified textile machinery	5	5	8	8
173	84	119 specified textile machinery and parts	5	5	8	8
174	84	Specified machinery or equipment for manufacture of ICs and electronic micro assemblies	5	5	5	5
175	84	27 specified machinery for making building materials	5	5	8	8
176	84	Computer parts (excluding PPCB)	5	5	0	0
177	84	Parts of electronic calculators	5	5	0	0

178	84	Ribbon assembly, ribbon gear assembly and ribbon gear carriage for use in printers for computers	5	5	8	8
179	85	Wireless apparatus for HAMs	5	5	8	10
180	85	DC Micromotors for computers	5	5	5	5
181	85	Specified machinery/equipment imported by accredited news agency	5	5	8	8
182	85	Parts of Cellular/pager/trunking hand sets	5	5	0	0
183	85	Parts of telecom equipments	5	5	0	0
184	85	Specified equipment required for basic telephone/cellular mobile telephone/ radio paging and closed user's group 64KBPS domestic data network services and parts thereof	5	5	8	8
185	85	Specified raw materials/inputs for electronic industry	5	5	5	5
186	85	Specified inputs for optical fibres/cables	5	5	5	5
187	89	Fishing and other vessels for processing/ preserving fishery products, when imported for purposes other than breaking up	5	5	8	8
188	89	Tugs and pushercraft when imported for purposes other than breaking up; subject to certain conditions	5	5	5	5
189	89	Dredgers, light vessels, fire floats, floating cranes and other vessels, the navigability of which is subsidiary to their main functions, floating docks when imported for purposes other than breaking up subject to certain conditions	5	5	5	5
190	90	Life saving/sight saving medical equipment and accessories/spare parts and specified medical equipment/parts required for mfr./maintenance of such specified equipments	5	5	5	5
191	90	Specified Medical & surgical instruments, apparatus and appliances including spare parts and accessories thereof	5	5	5	5
192	90	Specified medical equipment and appliances for the blind and deaf subject to conditions	5	5	5	5
193	90	Hospital equipment (equipment, apparatus and appliances, including spare parts and accessories thereof, but excluding consumable items) for use in specified hospitals	5	5	5	5
194	90	Linear accelerator with beam energy 15 Mev or more	5	5	5	5

195	90	Parts and spare parts of hearing aids, hearing aid appliances	5	5	5	5
196	95	Parts of electronic toys for manufacture of electronic toys	5	5	8	8
197	95	Parts of video games for manufacture of video games	5	5	8	8
198	98	Fertilizer projects	5	5	8	8
199	98	Power generation projects	5	5	8	8
200	98	Coal mining projects	5	5	8	8
201		Artificial plasma	5	5	5	5
		Commodities Attracting 10% Basic Customs Duty (2002-03)				
202	7	Dried leguminous vegetables (pulses)	*			
203	27	Crude petroleum	8	5	5	5
204	27	Naphtha	8	5	5	5
205	27	LPG	8	8	8	8
206	27	Petroleum gases (other than LNG); Natural bitumen & asphalt; oil shale; tar sands; asphaltic rocks	8	8	8	8
207	27	SKO (for PDS)	8	8	8	8
208	29	Paraxylene	8	5	5	5
209	52	Raw cotton	*			
210	84	Specified machinery for silk	10	10	8	8
211	84	Specified machinery for development of airports	10	10	8	8
212	84	Specified machinery for development of ports	10	10	8	8
213	85	Cellular Telephones, pagers	8	8	0	0
214	85	Specified loud speakers (other than cone type), line telephone hand sets, telephone answering machines; indicator panels, certain specified parts, etc.	8	8	0	0
215	85	Floppy diskettes	8	8	0	0
216	90	Specified instrument and apparatus for measuring/checking/chemical analysis, drawing and drafting machines	8	8	0	0
		Commodities Attracting 15% Basic Customs Duty (2002-03)				
217	4	Milk powder, of a fat content by weight not exceeding 1.5% or of a fat content exceeding 1.5% by weight but not containing sugar or other sweetening matter (60% is TARIFF rate)	*			
218	8	Miscellaneous Fresh fruits like Pomegranates of bedana variety	*			
219	10	Maize (corn) seed under TRQ	*			
220	12	Beet, seeds, seeds of forage plant, etc.	*			

221	12	Jigat, Jaborandi leaves; plants used in perfumery, pharmacy etc., coca leaves, poppy straw	10	10	10	10
222	13	Vegetable saps & extracts (other than of opium, liquorice, hops and pyrethrum)	10	10	10	10
223	13	Oleopine resins	10	10	10	10
224	13	Pectic substances, pectinates & pectates	10	10	10	10
225	15	Fats of bovine animals, sheep or goat	*			
226	15	Wool grease; lanolin etc.	*			
227	17	Molasses	10	10	8	8
228	18	Cocoa based food preparations for infant use	*			
229	22	Denatured ethyl alcohol and other spirits, denatured	10	10	8	8
230	23	Brans of rice, oil cakes and other solid residues, dietary soya fibre	*			
231	25	Spodumene, strontium ore, natural boron ore	5	5	5	5
232	25	DBM, fused magnesia and sea water magnesia for the mfr. of refractories etc.	8	8	8	8
233	25	Low silica Limestone for goods of Chapter 72	15	10	8	8
234	26	Zinc ash, copper ash	5	5	5	5
235	27	Coking coal of ash content 12% or more	15	10	8	5
236	27	Coke	15	10	8	5
237	28	Zirconium oxide and yttrium oxide, for the manufacture of raw cubic Zirconia	15	10	8	8
238	28	Iodine	15	10	8	8
239	28	Radio active elements and salts, Enriched Uranium and heavy water	15	10	8	8
240	28	Litharge for manufacture of glass shells for CPTs	10	10	8	8
241	29	35 specified veterinary drugs	10	10	8	8
242	29	Acyclic hydrocarbons, Cyclohexane, Benzene, Toluene, Xylenes, Styrene, Ethylbenzene, Cumene, Ethylene dichloride, chloroethyline and acriloritrile	10	10	8	8
243	29	L Lysine, L Lysine monohydrochloride, DL-Methionine or Methionine Hydroxyanalog of animal feedgrade	15	10	8	8
244	29/30	Specified bulk drugs and their formulations (nilutamide, sodium fusidate, low molecular weight heparine and erithropoietin, cyclosporine, doxorubicin HCI, azathioprine, enaxoparin)	15	10	8	8

245	32	Wattle extract, quebracho extract and chestnut extract	15	10	8	8
246	35	Isolated soya protein	15	10	10	10
247	35	Epoxy grade adhesive for manufacture of syringes	15	10	10	10
248	37	Film strips and slides for education, educational film certified by CBFC, microfilms of printed books, maps charts and drawings, exposed and developed film sheets for printing or reproduction of printed books	10	10	10	10
249	37	Exposed cinematograpic films for defence use, film and video cassettes for archival study	10	10	10	10
250	38	Diping oil, Paclobutrazol (cultar)	10	10	10	10
251	38	LAL test kit	10	10	10	10
252	39	LDPE, PP used in mfr. of syringes	15	10	10	10
253	49	Cheque forms including blank travellers cheques	10	10	10	10
254	50	Silk waste	15	10	10	10
255	51	Raw wool, not carded or combed	15	10	10	10
256	51	Waste of wool including yarn waste and garnetted stock	15	10	10	10
257	51	Fine or coarse animal hair, not carded or combed	15	10	10	10
258	52	Cotton waste including yarn waste and garnetted stock	10	10	10	10
259	53	Flax fibre	10	10	8	8
260	60	Pile fabrics for manufacture of toys	15	10	10	10
261	70	Capillary tubes and rods of glass for manufacture of thermometers	15	10	10	10
262	71	Rough Synthetic stones, Non-industrial diamonds (other than rough diamonds), platinum, cut and polished coloured gum stones, ash and residues containing precious metal for recovery of precious metals	10	10	8	8
263	72	Pig iron	15	10	8	8
264	75	Other nickel articles (75.08)	10	10	8	8
265	75	All other nickle and article thereof	10	10	8	8
266	76	Aluminium waste and scrap	15	10	8	8
267	76	Unwrought aluminium	15	10	8	8
268	76	Wrought aluminium products and aluminium articles	15	10	10	10
269	76	All other aluminium and article thereof	15	10	10	10

270	80	Tin and articles thereof	15	10	10	10
271	84	Specified goods for manufacture of ground power units and air jet starters	15	10	8	8
272	84	Specified items for manufcture of solar energy equipment	15	10	8	8
273	84	Specified machinery for wool/flax and VFY and parts	15	10	8	8
274	84	Specified machinery and equipment for setting up of training development project of jewellery production and gemology	15	10	8	8
275	84	PPCB (mother board)	10	10	0	0
276	84	Computers (automatic data processing machines)	15	10	0	0
277	84	Automatic teller machines	15	10	0	0
278	84	Calculating machines, accounting machines, cash registers, etc.	15	10	0	0
279	84	Word processing machines	15	10	0	0
280	84	POS terminals	15	10	0	0
281	85	Ozone generators	10	10	10	10
282	85	Button cells/Raw materials for manufacture of button cells; battery packs for cellular telephones	10	10	10	10
283	85	Membrane electrolysers and parts, membranes and other machinery for caustic soda units	10	10	8	8
284	85	static convertors and other inductors for automatic data processing machines or telecom apparatus and parts thereof	10	10	0	0
285	85	Specified line & wireless telecom equipments (transmission apparatus whether or not with reception apparatus, telephonic switching apparatus, apparatus for current carrier systems etc.)	10	10	0	0
286	85	Router & Modems	10	10	0	0
287	85	Digital still image video cameras	15	10	0	0
288	85	Magnetic disc, magnetic tapes, specified recorded media	10	5	0	0
289	85	Specified electric sound or visual signalling apparatus, specified electronic switches and parts thereof, proximity cards and tags, electrical machines with dictionary functions, specified capacitors and parts thereof, specified insulated conductors	10	10	0	0
290	85	Aerials or antennae of a kind used with apparatus for radio telephony and radio telegraphy	10	5	0	0

291	85	Specified electronic components	10	10	0	0
292	85	Diodes, transistors, similar semi-conductor devices; solar cells & modules	10	10	0	0
293	85	CCTV system for visually handicapped	0	0	0	0
294	85	Optical fibres	10	10	8	8
295	87	Tricycles designed for use by crippled/disabled persons	0	0	0	0
296	89	Vessels and other floating structures for breaking up	15	10	8	8
297	90	Equipment, parts or accessories for setting up of planetarium	15	10	8	8
298	90	Hearing aid appliances and spare parts	10	10	8	8
299	90	Specified medical equipments and parts thereof, external silicon breast prosthesis (generally not produced in India)	10	10	8	8
300	90	Cinematographic cameras, apparatus and equipment for cinematographic labs, etc.	15	10	10	10
301	90	Parts and accessories of photographic cameras for manufacture of photographic cameras	15	10	10	10
302	91	Specified horological raw material	10	10	8	8
303	94	Specified dental furniture	15	10	10	10
304	94	Lamps, light fittings for use in sports or games stadia	15	10	10	10
305	96	Refills for ball point pens, pen nibs and nib points and parts and raw material for pens and pen holders	15	10	10	10
		Commodities Attracting 20% Basic Customs Duty (2002-03)				
306	25	Cement clinkers, ordinary portland cement, other cement	15	10	5	5
307	25	Marble, Granite	15	10	10	10
308	27	MS,	15	10	8	8
309	27	HSD	15	10	8	8
310	27	ATF, FO, LSHS	15	10	8	8
311	27	SKO for parallel marketing	15	10	8	8
312	27	Other petroleum products	15	10	8	8
313	27	N-Paraffin for manufacture of LAB	15	10	8	8
314	28	Soda Ash	15	10	8	8
315	29	DMT, PTA and MEG	15	10	8	8
316	29	Caprolactum	15	10	8	8
317	51	Carded wool, wool tops and other combed wool, coarse or fine animal hair, carded or combed	20	20	15	10
318	51	Yarn of wool or fine or coarse animal hair, not put up for retail sale	20	20	15	10

319	52	Cotton sewing thread	20	20	15	10
320	52	Cotton yarn, not put up for retail sale	20	20	15	10
321	54	Synthetic and Artificial filament yarn (other than sewing thread) not put up for retail sale, Synthetic and Artifical monofilament of less than 67 decitex	20	20	15	10
322	54	Acetate & cuprammonium filament yarn	20	20	15	10
323	54	Sewing thread, monofilaments, strip and the like and filament yarn put up for retail sale	20	20	15	10
324	55	Viscose staple fibre and tow	20	20	15	10
325	55	Synthetic staple fibres and tows	20	20	15	10
326	55	Acetate tow	20	20	15	10
327	55	Sewing thread and spun yarn	20	20	15	10
328	56	Rubber thread and cord, textile covered, metallised yarn, gimped yarn, twine, cordage and cables	20	20	15	10
329	70	Yarn of glass fibre, not coloured	20	20	15	10
		Commodities Attracting 25% Basic Customs Duty (2002-03)				
330	1	Grand Parent poultry stock & Donkey stallions	25	20	15	10
331	8	Fresh plums & sloes	*			
332	17	Lactose and lactose syrup	25	20	15	10
333	21	All goods falling under Chapters 8,12, 13 and 15 to 21 imported by hotel industry	25	20	15	10
334	25	All other goods like Unroasted Iron Pyrites, Quartz, Kaoline, Other clays, Chalk, Natural Barium, Pumice, Emery, Slate, Dolomite, Gypsum, Mica, Natural Steatite, Borates, Felspar, Lime stone, salt, sandstone, pebbles, asbestos	25	20	15	10
335	27	Coal (non coking), Lignite, Peat	20	15	10	5
336	27	Carbon black feedstock	20	15	10	8
337	27	Naphthalene	20	15	10	8
338	27	Phenol	20	15	10	8
339	28	Specified leather chemicals	20	15	10	8
340	29	7-ACA, Pseudoionone, Methyl tertiary butyl either	20	15	10	8
341	29	Acetic acid, adipic acid, epichlorohydrin, tartaric acid and Hydantoin	20	15	10	8
342	29/30	17 Specified bulk drugs or formulations (antibitic/anti-cancer)	20	15	10	8
343	29	Phenol	20	15	10	8

344	29	Specified leather chemicals	20	15	10	8
345	29	Methanol	20	15	10	8
346	30	Homoeopathic medicines	20	15	10	10
347	32	Specified dyes for leather industry (Part of lists)	20	15	10	10
348	33	Extracted oleoresins	20	15	10	10
349	37	All other goods (Photographic goods)	25	20	15	10
350	38	Catalysts	20	15	10	8
351	38	Mixed Alloye Benzenes	20	15	10	8
352	39	Nylon chips for manufacture of nylon filament yarn and Polyester chips for the manufacture of yarns or fibres of polyester, Nylon 6, 12 chips for manufacture of nylon monofilament	20	15	10	10
353	40	Natural rubber in smoked sheets, technically specified natural rubber, natural rubber in forms other than latex	*			
354	41	All other goods (patent leather, composite leather etc.)	20	15	10	10
355	44	Wood sawn or chipped lengthwise, railway sleepers, wood wool, hoop wood, etc.	25	20	15	10
356	49	All other goods (printed matter such as printed or illustrated post cards, calendars, pictures, designs and photographs, trade advertising material, commercial catalogues and the like, etc.)	25	20	15	10
357	52	Cotton yarn (other than sewing thread), contaning 85% or more by weight of cotton, put up for retail sale	25	20	15	10
358	53	Jute waste including yarn waste and garnetted stock	25	20	15	10
359	54	Fabrics of strip and the like and bonded fabrics	25	20	20	20
360	56	Non-wovens, wadding and felt	25	20	20	20
361	58	Terry towelling and similar woven terry fabrics of cotton, unbleached	25	20	20	20
362	58	Labels, badges & similar articles, ornamental trimmings, woven fabrics of metal thread, specified narrow woven fabrics	25	20	15	10
363	59	Textile fabrics coated, covered with plastics, fabrics coated with gum or amylaceous substances, tyre cord fabrics, Textile products & articles for technical uses, transmission/conveyor beltings etc.	25	20	20	20

364	63	Used or new rags, scrap twine, cordage, rope and cables and worn out articles of twine, cordage, rope or cables, of textile materials	25	20	20	20
365	63	Cotton terry towels	25	20	20	20
366	64	Parts of leather footwear	25	20	15	10
367	68	Moulds and dies for electronic parts	15	10	8	5
368	69	Refractory bricks, blocks & tiles (69.02)	15	10	10	8
369	69	Other refractory ceramic goods (69.03) (crucibles, pots, laddles etc.)	20	15	10	10
370	70	Rough ophthalmic blanks for optical lenses	20	15	10	8
371	71	Industrial diamonds	20	15	10	8
372	72	Ingots, Billets, Blooms, Slabs and stainless steel slabs other than seconds and defective	20	15	10	8
373	72	Hot briquetted iron and sponge iron for electric arc furnace or induction furnace unit	20	15	10	8
374	72	Ferro-molybdenum	20	15	10	8
375	72	Other ferro alloys	20	15	10	8
376	72	Rerollable scrap	20	15	10	8
377	72	Iron or non-alloy steel hot rolled coils and hot rolled stainless steel coils, other than seconds and derivatives	20	15	10	8
378	72	TMBP coils for tin plate manufacture other than seconds and defective	20	15	10	8
379	72/73	Steel required for the manufacture of machinery other than seconds & defective	20	15	10	8
380	73, 84 or 85	Agricultural Silos	20	15	10	8
381	74	Unwrought copper and copper waste and scrap	20	15	10	8
382	74	Wrought Copper, semis and articles	20	15	10	8
383	74	Cooking or Heating Apparatus (74.17)	25	20	20	20
384	74	Table Ware, Kitchen Ware (74.18)	25	20	20	20
385	74	All other goods (Copper articles)	25	20	20	20
386	76	Table, kitchen household articles of aluminium	25	20	20	20
387	78	Lead and articles thereof	20	15	10	8
388	79	Zinc and articles thereof	20	15	10	8
389	81	Unwrought magnesium	20	15	10	8
390	81	Graphite synthetic or cobalt alloy for manufacture of diamond tools	20	15	10	8

391	82	Moulds and dies for manufacture of electronic parts	20	15	10	5
392	82	Interchangeable tools for metal working hand tools	20	15	10	8
393	82	Other Interchangeable tools for metal working hand tools	20	15	10	8
394	84	Specified equipment for use in a Green House	20	15	10	8
395	84	All other machinery and parts	20	15	10	8
396	84 or 90	Equipment having multiple function of printing, screening & photocopying	20	15	10	8
397	85	Navigational, communication, air-traffic control and landing equipment and spares for maintenance of such equipment imported by Airports Authority of India	20	15	10	8
398	85	Electrical switching or protecting apparatus for industrial applications	20	15	10	8
399	85	Electrical insulators, insulation fittings and parts	20	15	10	10
400	85	DC Micromotors	20	15	10	8
401	85	CD Mechanism	20	15	10	8
402	85	Other specified machinery and their parts	20	15	10	8
403	85	Glass parts for CPT (excluding neck or reneck tubes)	20	15	10	8
404	85	Glass shells of CPT/Neck or Reneck tubes	20	15	10	8
405	85	Other cathode ray television picture tubes, including video monitor tubes	20	15	10	8
406	84,85, 90,91,94	Goods specified for studio equipment and radio broadcasting	25	20	15	10
407	85	Optical fibre Cables	20	15	10	8
408	85	GPS apparatus	20	15	10	8
409	86	Parts of railway/tramway locomotives or rolling stocks; Railway/tramway track fixtures/fittings; signalling, safety or traffic control equipment for railways/tramways/waterways etc	20	15	10	8
410	90	Medical equipment (general)	20	15	10	10
411	90	Parts of photocopying apparatus, cameras etc.	25	20	15	8
412	90	Instruments and parts (general rate)	25	20	15	8
413	91	Specified clock and watch parts (springs, jewels, dials, plates & bridges, etc.)	25	20	15	8
414	91	Watch & clock movements	25	20	15	8

415	95	Sports goods	25	20	15	8
416	98	Power transmission projects of 66 KV & above	20	15	10	8
417	98	Captive power generation projects	20	15	10	8
418	98	Other industrial projects	20	15	10	8
419	98	Specified articles imported as baggage on transfer of residence	25	20	20	20
		Commodities Attracting Peak Rate (30%) Basic Customs Duty (2002-03)				
420	1	Horses & other animals	*			
421	2	Meat and edible meat officials	*			
422	2	Carcases and half-carcases	*			
423	3	Fish, crustaceans and other acquatic invertebrates	*			
424	4	All other dairy products, eggs and honey	*			
425	4	Cheese/whey/butter	*			
426	4	Bird's egg and yogurt	*			
427	5	All other goods of animal origin (Animal gland, animal organs, ivory etc.)	*			
428	6	Cut flowers, flowers buds, bouquets and foliage etc. for ornamental purposes	*			
429	7	Dried vegetables, whole, cut, sliced, broken or in powder	*			
430	7	All other goods (fresh vegetables etc.)	*			
431	8	Fresh grapes	*			
432	8	Dates	*			
433	8	Strawberries/raspberries/blackberries/ mulberries/apricot/mixture of nuts	*			
434	8	All others (bananas, mangoes, oranges, melons, papays etc.)	*			
435	9	Seeds of caraway, thyme, bay leaves, mate	*			
436	9	All others (Pepper, cinamon, cloves, ginger, spices etc.)	*			
437	11	Products of milling industry; malt; starches; inulin; wheat gluten	*			
438	12	All other goods (soya beans, groundnuts, linseed, rapeseed, other oil seeds, hop cones, sugar beet, sugar cane, swedes, mangolds, etc.)	*			
439	13	All other goods (lac, gums, resins, mucilages and thickeners)	*			
440	14	Vegetable plaiting materials, vegetable products not elsewhere specified	*			
441	15	All other goods (animal fats and oils, vanaspati, industrial grade vegetable oils, glycerine, vegetable waxes etc.)	*			

442	16	Other preparations of meat, of fish, crustaceans, molluses etc.	*			
443	17	All other goods (maple sugar or syrup, glucose & glucose syrup, Confectionery)	*			
444	18	Cocoa beans	*			
445	18	All other goods (Cocoa paste, powder, chocolates and other cocoa preparations)	25	20	15	10
446	19	Preparations for infant use	25	20	15	10
447	19	All other goods (Malt based and other food products such as pasta, noodles, corn flakes, bread, pastry, rusk, biscuits, etc.)	25	20	15	10
448	20	Preparations of vegetables,fruit, nuts or other parts of plants	25	20	20	20
449	21	All other goods (Misc. edible preparations such as instant coffee, instant tea, yeats, sauces, soups and broths, ice cream, protein concentrates, etc.)	25	20	20	20
450	22	Waters incl. mineral waters and aerated waters; vinegar and its substitutes	25	20	20	20
451	22	Wines for sacramental use	25	20	15	10
452	23	All other goods (Residues of waste and food industry, animal feed etc.)	25	20	15	10
453	24	Tobacco and manufactured tobacco substitutes	*			
454	25	Natural graphite	25	20	10	5
455	26	hard zinc spelter, zinc dross and copper mill scale	25	20	10	5
456	27	Coal gas and coal tar distillates, pitch and pitch coke	25	20	10	5
457	28	All other inorganic chemicals	25	20	15	8
458	29	All other organic chemicals	25	20	15	8
459	30	Medicaments containing spirit	25	20	15	10
460	30	All other goods (Medicines)	25	20	15	10
461	31	All other goods (Fertilizers)	25	20	15	10
462	32	All other goods (Dyes, paints, varnishes, etc.)	25	20	15	10
463	33	All other goods (essential oils; Cosmetics & toilet preparations)	25	20	15	10
464	34	Soap, organic surface active agents, washing preparations, lubricating preparations, waxes, polishing or scouring preparations, candles and similar articles, etc.	25	20	15	10
465	35	All other goods (Glues & adhesive)	25	20	15	10
466	36	Explosives; pyrotechnic products, matches	25	20	15	10

467	37	Photographic chemicals	25	20	15	10
468	38	Industrial Fatty acids/alcohol/ Insecticides etc.	25	20	15	10
469	38	All other goods (Misc. chemical products)	25	20	15	10
470	39	Bulk Polymers i.e. LDPE/LLDPE, HDPE, PVC, PP & PS	25	20	15	10
471	39	All engineering plastics/speciality polymers (39.05 to 39.14) waste & scrap (39.15)	25	20	15	10
472	39	Articles of plastics	25	20	15	10
473	40	Tyres	25	20	15	10
474	40	Other rubber products	25	20	15	10
475	42	Articles of leather like saddles, travel goods, hand bags, gloves, belts, articles of leather or of composition leather of a type used in technical applications and other articles of leather	25	20	15	10
476	43	Articles of furskin, artificial fur, etc.	25	20	15	10
477	44	All other goods (plywood and wood articles, fibre board, particle board etc.)	25	20	15	10
478	45	Cork-natural, granulated, agglomerated, waste, roughly squared, articles	25	20	15	10
479	46	Manufactures of straw, etc; basketware and wicker work	25	20	15	10
480	48	Various types of other uncoated and coated paper and paper boards	25	20	15	10
481	48	All other goods (Articles of Paper and Boards, specified variety of paper such as cigarette paper, carbon paper, filter paper etc.)	25	20	15	10
482	50	Silk	*			
483	50	Silk worm cocoons, raw silk, silk yarn and fabrics	*			
484	51	Yarn of wool or of fine animal hair, put up for retail sale & yarn of coarse animal hair, whether or not put up for retail sale	25	20	15	10
485	52	Cotton yarn (other than sewing thread), containing less than 85% by weight of cotton put up for retail sale	25	20	15	10
486	52	Specified varieties of cotton fabrics, unbleached, bleached or dyed	25	20	20	20
487	53	True lemp, sisal, coconut, abaca, ramie and other textile fibres (other than jute), tow and waste of these fibres	25	20	15	10
488	53	Flax yarn, jute yarn, yarn of vegetable fibre, jute fabrics, fabrics of vegetable textile fibres etc.	25	20	15	10

489	53	Woven fabrics of flax	25	20	15	10
490	54	High tenacity fabrics of viscose rayon, unbleached or bleached fabrics of artificial filament, strip or the like	25	20	20	20
491	55	Waste of man-made fibres	25	20	15	10
492	55	Specified varieties of fabrics of man-made fibres (unbleached or bleached fabrics of synthetic fibres, unbleached or dyed fabrics of artificial fibres, etc.	25	20	20	20
493	56	Sanitary towels and tampons, napkins and napkin liners for babies and similar sanitary articles, of wadding	25	20	20	20
494	56	Knotted nettings of twine, fishing nets, articles of yarn strip or the like	25	20	15	10
495	57	Carpets and floor coverings of wool, other animal hair and coconut and other vegetable fibre	25	20	20	20
496	57	Carpets and other textile floor coverings of pile construction of wool or fine animal hair, other textile materials and tiles	25	20	20	20
497	58	Terry towelling fabrics other than of cotton, gauze, handwoven tapestries, narrow woven fabrics other than of man-made fibres, quilted textile products	25	20	20	20
498	58	Gauze, Handwoven tapestries, narrow woven fabrics, braids in the piece, other embroidery and quilted textile products	25	20	20	20
499	59	Bolting cloth, textile fabrics and felts, etc. of a king used in paper making or similar machines	25	20	15	10
500	59	Textile fabrics otherwise coated or impregnated with plastics, painted canvas, textile wicks, incandescent gas manteles and tubular gas mantle fabric, textile hosepiping and similar tubings	25	20	15	10
501	59	Textile wall coverings	25	20	15	10
502	60	All goods other than pile fabrics of man made fibres	25	20	15	10
503	60	Warp knit fabrics of cotton and man-made fibres	25	20	15	10
504	61	Specified apparel such as overcoats, bathrobes suits, etc.	25	20	20	20
505	61	Other apparels and clothing accessories	25	20	20	20
506	62	Babies garments and clothing accessories, gloves, mittens and mitts	25	20	20	20

507	63	Sacks and bags, tarpaulins, awnings and sunblinds, tents, sails for boats etc. other made up articles, including dress patterns; sets of woven fabric and yarn, worn clothing and articles	25	20	15	10
508	63	Other Blankets and travelling rugs, bed linen, table linen, toilet linen and kitchen linen, curtains and interior blinds; curtain or bed valances, bed spreads and other furnishing articles	25	20	20	20
509	64	Footwear, parts etc.	25	20	15	10
510	65	headgear and parts	25	20	15	10
511	66	umbrellas, walking sticks etc.	25	20	15	10
512	67	Prepared feathers, artificial flowers, etc.	25	20	15	10
513	68	All other goods	25	20	15	10
514	69	All other goods (ceramic articles)	25	20	15	10
515	70	All other goods (Glass and glassware)	25	20	15	10
516	71	All other goods (precious metals like iridium, articles of jewellery etc.)	25	20	15	10
517	72	CR coils other than seconds & defective	25	20	15	8
518	72	All other goods (Iron & Steel), other than seconds and defectives	25	20	15	8
519	73	Barbed wires (73.13), Sanitary ware (73.24) tubes, pipes, tracks with chains	25	20	15	10
520	73	Stoves, cookers (73.21), Table ware, kitchen ware (73.23)	25	20	20	20
521	73	All other goods (Articles of Iron & Steel)	25	20	15	10
522	76	Table ware, kitchen ware (76.15), pressure cooker	25	20	20	20
523	81	Tungsten, Molybdenum, Tantalum, Cobalt & other base metal articles	25	20	15	10
524	82	Knives, cutting blades including table knives (82.11), Spoons, Forks (82.15)	25	20	20	20
525	82	Razors, blades (82.18), Scissors (82.13), paper knives, sharpeners (82.14)	25	20	20	20
526	82	All other goods	25	20	20	20
527	83	Miscellaneous articles of base metals	25	20	15	10
528	84	Air conditioning & House hold type refrigerating appliances, household and laundry type washing machines, Dry-cleaning machines, Dishwashing machines, Household type sewing machines, elec. Fans, duplicating machines, etc.	25	20	20	20
529	84	Compressors for refrigerating machines, air-conditioners, etc.	25	20	15	10
530	84	Parts of air conditioning appliances, refrigerators, dish washing machines, etc.	25	20	15	10

531	84	Personal weighing machines, household scales etc.	25	20	15	10
532	84	Typewriters and other office machines	25	20	15	10
533	84	Ball or roller bearings of 60 mm bore diameter or less and Parts thereof	25	20	15	10
534	84	IC Engines for automobiles and parts thereof	25	20	15	10
535	85	Electro-mechanical domestic appliances	25	20	20	20
536	85	Batteries and accumulators	25	20	20	20
537	85	Ignition equipment used with IC engines, lighting or signalling equipment used in motor vehicles	25	20	15	10
538	85	Electrical switching or protecting apparatus for non-industrial applications	25	20	15	10
539	85	Lamps, wires and cables	25	20	15	10
540	85	Programme controller, boards, panels, etc. (85.37)	25	20	15	10
541	85	Connectors	25	20	15	10
542	85	Electro mechanical hand tools	25	20	15	10
543	85	Colour TV picture tube	20	15	10	8
544	85	Colour TVs, Music systems, VCR, VCPs, Two-in-ones etc.	25	20	20	20
545	86	All goods (Railway locomotives, coaches, wagons, containers, etc.)	25	20	15	10
546	87	Motor cars and two wheelers, new or imported in CKD or SKD form	25	20	20	20
547	87	All other goods (Buses, trucks, tractors and automotive parts)	25	20	20	20
548	88	All other goods (Parachutes and parts, balloons etc.)	25	20	15	10
549	89	All other goods (yachts for pleasure or sports, motor boats, sail boats etc.)	25	20	15	10
550	90	Lenses, prisms, mirrors and other optical elements, frames and mountings for spectacles, goggles and the like, binoculars, monoculars, other optical telescopes etc., photographic & projectors	25	20	15	10
551	90	Image projectors, photographic enlargers and reducers, Photocopying apparatus, apparatus and equipment for photographic labs, etc.	25	20	15	10
552	91	Watch straps, bands etc. made of base metals	25	20	15	10
553	91	Watches	25	20	20	20
554	91	Clocks	25	20	20	20

555	92	Musical instruments	25	20	15	10
556	93	Arms and Ammunition	25	20	15	10
557	94	All other goods	25	20	15	10
558	95	Toys	25	20	15	10
559	96	Misc. manufactured goods (Handicrafts, brooms, brushes, snap and slide fasteners, pens, pencils, slates, boards, dealing and numbering stamps, lighters, smoking pipes, coms, hairslides and the like, toilet sprays, vaccum flasks, tailors dummies, etc.)	25	20	15	10
560	97	Collections and Collector's pieces	25	20	15	10
561	97	Original sculptures, engravings, prints and paintings, drawings and pastels executed by hand	25	20	15	10
562	98	Articles intended for personal use imported by post or air other	25	20	15	10
563	98	Lab chemicals	25	20	15	10
564	98	Ship stores	25	20	15	10
		Commodities Attracting 40% Basic Customs Duty (2002-03)				
565	72	Seconds and defectives of Iron & Steel	40	40	40	40
		Commodities Attracting 45% Basic Customs Duty (2002-03)				
566	15	Soyabean oil, crude or refined	*			
567	15	Rapeseed oil, colza or mustard oil, crude or refined upto 150,000 mt in a fin yr.	*			
		Commodities Attracting 50% Basic Customs Duty (2002-03)				
568	10	Wheat, maize(corn) seed, spelt, sorghum, millet	*			
		Commodities Attracting 60% Basic Customs Duty (2002-03)				
569	4	Other Milk powder	*			
570	17	Sugar	*			
571	87	CBUs of Motor cars and two wheelers,	50	50	50	50
572	98	Articles imported as baggage other than on transfer of residence above Rs. 12000	60	50	40	40
		Commodities Attracting 65% Basic Customs Duty (2002-03)				
573	15	Palm oil, ground nut oil, sunflower/safflower oil, coconut oil and other oils, crude	*			
		Commodities Attracting 70% Basic Customs Duty (2002-03)				
574	8	Coconuts	*			
575	9	Pepper, cloves, cardamom	*			
576	10	Semi-milled or wholly milled rice	*			
577	12	Copra	*			
578	40	Natural raw rubber	*			

		Commodities Attracting 75% Basic Customs Duty (2002-03)				
579	15	Rapeseed oil, colza or mustard oil, crude or refined (others)	*			
		Commodities Attracting Nil Basic Customs Duty (2002-03)				
580	10	Rice in the husk (paddy) and husked (brown) rice, broken rice	*			
		Commodities Attracting 85% Basic Customs Duty (2002-03)				
581	15	Palm oil, ground nut oil, sunflower/ safflower oil, coconut oil and other oils, refined	*			
		Commodities Attracting 100% Basic Customs Duty (2002-03)				
582	2	Poultry meat (Chicken leg)	*			
583	8	Areca nuts	*			
584	9	Coffee	*			
585	9	Tea	*			
586	16	Sausages and similar products of meat, meat offal or blood, other prepared meat, meat offal or blood of fowls of the species Gallus domesticus	*			
587	22	Beer, grape must, wines, vermouth, other fermented beverages	*			
		Commodities Attracting 105% Basic Customs Duty (2002-03)				
588	8	Dried grapes	*			
589	87	Motor cars and two wheelers, used	*			
		Commodities Attracting 160% Basic Customs Duty (2002-03)				
590	21	Compound Alcoholic preparations for manufacture of beverages	*			
591	33	Alcoholic preparations of a kind used for the manufacture of beverages	*			
		Commodities Attracting 182% Basic Customs Duty (2002-03)				
592	22	Undenatured ethyl alcohol	*			
593	22	Whiskies, rum, gin, vodka, liquers and cordials, etc.	*			
		Commodities Attracting Composite Basic Customs Duty (25%) or Specific Duty Whichever is more (2002-03)				
594	58	Terry towel!ing and similar woven terry fabrics of cotton, bleached	25	20	20	20
595	58	Woven pile fabrics and chenille fabrics (other than warp cut pile fabrics), tufted textile fabricstulles and other net fabrics, embroidery without visible ground	25	20	20	20
596	58	Wrap cut pile fabrics & upholstery fabrics	25	20	20	20
597	60	Pile fabrics of man-made fibres	25	20	20	20
598	52	Upholstery fabrics of cotton	25	20	20	20

599	54	Upholstery fabrics, fabrics of high tenacity synthetic yarn, specified varieties of man made filament fabrics (unbleached or bleached), polyester filament fabrics of non-textured filaments	25	20	20	20
600	55	Upholstery fabrics of synthetic or artificial staple fibres	25	20	20	20
Commodities Attracting Composic Basic Customs Duty (30%) (2002-03)						
601	61	Specified men's/women's trousers, shirts, blouses, underpants, briefs, panties, T-shirts, jerseys, stocking etc. of cotton or man madc fibrcs	25	20	20	20
602	62	Knitted or crocheted women's, men's or boy's overcoats, raincoats, shirts, trousers, suits, jackets and blazers, skirts, blouses etc.	25	20	20	20
603	63	Blankets and travelling rugs of wool or fine animal hair, bed linen of cotton	25	20	20	20
604	51	Woven fabrics of wool or fine animal hair	25	20	20	20
605	51	Woven fabrics of coarse animal hair or of horsehair			20	20
606	52	Printed cotton fabrics, denim fabrics and specified varieties of cotton fabrics of yarns of different colours	25	20	20	20
607	52	Other specified varieties of cotton fabrics	25	20	20	20
	54	Other specified fabrics of filament yarn	25	20	20	20
608	55	Specified varieties of fabrics of man-made fibres (Dyed printed etc.)	25	20	20	20
609	55	Specified varieties of fabrics of polyester fibres, acrylic fibres and artificial fibres	25	20	20	20
610	57	Carpets and other textile floor coverings of man-made textile material	25	20	20	20
		Note	Specific duty component to be proportionately reduced			
Commodities Attracting Specific Rates of Basic Customs Duty (2002-03)						
611	71	Gold	Specific rates to continue			
612	8	Almonds in shell	*			
613	71	Silver	Specific rates to continue			
614	8	Almonds shelled	*			

* Task force is of the view that an Expert Group should examine and recommend the duty rates of these items

Annexure 'B'

Central Excise Duty Rate Structure
Food Products

Proposed duty (in %)	
2003-04	2004-05
6% with credit	6%

S.No.	Tariff Chapter	Description of goods
1	04.02	Butter, whether pasteurised or processed
2	04.03	Cheese, pasteurised or processed
3	04.04	Other dairy produce; edible products of animal origin, not elsewhere specified or included
4	1103.00	Tapioca Starch
5	1301.00	Compounded asafoetida (hing)
6	1501.00	Animal (including fish) fats and oils, crude, refined or purified
7	1502.00	Fixed vegetable oils, the following, namely, cottonseed oil, neemseed oil, marang oil, silk cotton seed oil, rice bran oil, khakhan oil, palm oil, water melon oil, sal oil, mahua oil, kusum oil, dhupa oil, undi oil, maroti oil, pisa oil, and nahor oil, and their fractions
8	1503.00	Fixed vegetable oils, other than those of heading no. 15.02
9	1504.00	Vegetable fats and oils and their fractions, partly or wholly hydrogenated, inter-esterified, re-esterified or elaidinised, whether or not refined but not further prepared
10	1508.90	Other than linoxyn, -Margarine; edible mixtures or preparations of animal or vegetable fats; animal or vegetable fats and oils boiled, oxidised, dehydrated, sulphurised, blown, polymerised by heat in vaccum or in inert gas or otherwise chemically modified; inedible mixtures or preparations of fats and oils of this chapter
11	1601.90	Preparations of meat, of fish, or of crustaeceans, molluscs or other aquatic invertebrates including sausages and similar products, extracts and juices, prepared or preserved fish and caviar and caviar substitutes, other than those put up in unit containers and bearing a brand name
12	1901.11	Food preparations of flour, meal, starch or malt extract, not elsewhere specified, put up in unit containers for infant use
13	1901.19	Food preparations intended for free distribution to economically weaker sections of the society under a programme duly approved by the Central Government or any State Government
14	1901.99	Food preparations of flour, meal, starch or malt extract, other than those put up in unit containers

15	1902.11	Seviyan (vermicelli)
16	1902.90	Pasta – other than those in unit containers
17	1904.90	Prepared food obtained by the swelling or roasting of cereals – other than those in unit containers
18	1905.19	Biscuits manufactured without the aid of power
19	2001.90	Preparations of vegetables, fruit, nuts or other parts of plants including jams, fruit jellies, marmalades, fruit or nut puree and fruit or nut paste, fruit juices and vegetable juices, whether or not containing added sugar or other sweetening matter other than those put up in unit containers and bearing a brand name
20	2001.90	Preparations of vegetables, fruit, nuts or other parts of plants including jams, fruit jellies, marmalades, fruit or nut puree and fruit or nut paste, fruit juices and vegetable juices, whether or not containing added sugar or other sweetening matter put up in unit containers and bearing a brand name
21	2101.30	Roasted chicory and other roasted coffee substitutes, and extracts, essences and concentrates thereof
22	2103.90	Sauces, ketchup and the like and preparations therefore; mixed condiments and mixed seasoning; mustard flour and meal and prepared mustard other than those put up in unit containers and bearing a brand name
23	2103.90	Sauces, ketchup and the like and preparations therefore; mixed condiments and mixed seasoning; mustard flour and meal and prepared mustard put up in unit containers and bearing a brand name
24	2104.90	Soups and broths and preparations therefor; homogenised composite food preparations other than those put up in unit containers and bearing a brand name
25	2104.90	Soups and broths and preparations therefor; homogenised composite food preparations put up in unit containers and bearing a brand name
26	2108.91	Sterilized or Pasteurized Miltone (Veg. protein toned milk)
27	2108.91	Other edible preparations, not elsewhere specified or included and not bearing a brand name
28	2108.99	Sweetmeats (known as 'misthans' or mithai or by any other name), namkeens, bhujia, mixture, chabena and similar edible preparations in ready for consumption form, and papad
29	2202.30	Soya milk drinks, whether or not sweetened or flavoured
30	2202.40	Fruit pulp or fruit juice based drinks

Commodities Attracting Nil Duty (Cenvat) - (2002-03)

Non-Food Products

Proposed duty (in %)		
2003-04	2004-05	2005-06
6% with credit	14% with credit	14%

S.No.	Tariff Chapter	Description of goods
1	2710.00	Naptha when supplied to 12 specified power projects; for shut down/start up for fertilizer plants; for manufacture of fertilizers and ammonia
2	2710.00	Kerosene received by the factory from the refinery intended for use in the manufacture of linear alkylbenzene or heavy alkylate and returned by the factory to the refinery from where such kerosene is received
3	2713.00	Residues of petroleum oils or of oils obtained from bituminous minerals, including heavy petroleum stock, low sulphur heavy stock and other residual fuel oils falling under heading No. 27.13 of the said Schedule, intended for use as fuel for the generation of electrical energy by electricity undertakings owned by or controlled by the Central Government or any State Government or any State Electricity Board or any local authority
4	27	Residues of petroleum oil, bituminous oil and Furnance Oil for use as feedstock for fertilizer
5	27	Petroleum Gases and other hydrocarbons for manufacture of Poly-Iso-Acetylene or Methyl Ethyl Ketone (MEK)
6	27	LPG for Di-ButylParaCresol
7	28	Sulphuric Acid, oleum, oxygen, ammonia, Ammonium chloride and manganese sulphate intended for use – (a) as fertilisers, fertilizer plants or (b) in the manufacture of fertilisers, whether directly or through the stage of an intermediate product
8	28, 29 or 30	Anaesthetics
9	28.08, 28.09	All goods for manufacture of fertilizers
10	2804.11	Medicinal grade oxygen
11	2804.32	Nitrogen, in liquid form, for use in the processing and storage of semen for artificial insemination of cattle
12	2829.90	Potassium Iodate
13	2847.11	Medicinal grade Hydrogen Peroxide
14	31	Fertilizers other than animal and vegetable fertilizers
15	32	Wattle extract

16	32	Nitrocellulose lacquers produced in Ordinance factories belonging to the Central Government and intended for consumption for defence purpose or for supply to Central Government Departments
17	3204.00 or 3809.00	Finishing agents, dye carriers to accelerate the dyeing or fixing of dye-stuffs, printing paste and other products and preparations of any kind used in the same factory for the manufacture of textiles and textile articles
18	3215.10	Writing ink
19	33	Henna powder, not mixed with any other ingredient
20	3306.00	Toothpowder
21	3401.11, 3401.12 or 3401.19	Soap, if manufactured under a scheme for sale of Janata soap
22	3401.12	Soap, in or in relation to the manufacture of which, no process has been carried on with the aid of power or of steam
23	3401.13	Laundry soaps produced by a factory owned by the KVIC or any organisation approved by the said commission for the purpose of manufacture of such soaps
24	3805.19	Turpentine oil, other than that in the manufacture of which any process is ordinarily carried on with the aid of power
25	3806.19	Rosin, other than that in the manufacture of which any process is ordinarily carried on with the aid of power
26	3824.90	Ready mix concrete
27	39.01 or 39.14	Plastic materials reprocessed in India out of the scrap or the waste of goods falling within Chapter 39, 54, 55, 56, 59, 64, 84, 85, 86, 87, 90, 91, 92, 93, 94, 95 and 96
28	3917.00	Lay flat tubing
29	3920.00	Strips and tapes of polypropylene used in the factory of its production in the manufacture of polypropylene ropes
30	3706.00	Cinematographic films, exposed and developed, whether or not soundtrack
31	3822.00	Chemical reagents
32	39 or 40	Nipples for feeding boottles
33	3904.00	Plastic material commonly known as polyvinyl chloride compounds (PVC compounds), used in the factory of its production for the manufacture of goods which are exempt from the whole of the duty of excise leviable thereon or are chargeable to "Nil" rate of duty
34	3920.39	Products of jute and phenolic resins manufactured by pultrusion process, containing atleast forty per cent by weight of jute
35	4005.10	Plates, sheets or strip of unvulcanised compounded rubber, whether or not combined with any textile material, in relation to the manufacture of which no modvat credit is taken
36	4005.20	Compounded rubber, unvolcanised, in primary form, used within the factory of production for the manufacture of excisable goods falling within the schedule

37	4008.11	Plates, blocks of cellular rubber used in the manufacture of parts of footwear
38	4008.21	Plates, blocks of non-cellular rubber used int he manufacture of parts of footwear
39	4011.90 or 4013.90	Tyres of specified sizes for Animal Drawn Vehicles (ADV)
40	4015.00	Surgical rubber gloves
41	4404.20	Veneer sheets and sheets for plywood manufactured without the aid of power
42	4405.10	Wood, continuously shaped etc., manufactured without the aid of power
43	44.06 or 44.07	100% wood free, plain or pre-laminated particle or fibre-board made from sugarcane bagasse or other agrowaste
44	4404.10	Veneer sheets for matches
45	4404.30	Veneer sheets and sheets for plywood used within the factory of production for the manufacture of goods falling under sub-heading No. 4410.19 or 4410.90
47	46.01	Manufacturers of straw etc. basket ware & meicca ware
48	48	Paper and paperboard or articles manufactured from non conventional raw materials (upto 3500 MT in a Financial Year)
49	4817.00	Envelopes, letter cards, plain postcards and correspondence cards, or paper or paperboard; boxes, pouches, wallets and writing compendiums, of paper or paperboard, containing an assortment of paper stationery
50	4818.10	Sanitary towels, tampons or napkins
51	48.20	Note-books and exercise books
52	4802.10	Writing paper for text books
53	480220	Paper or board in the manufacture of which the lifting of pulp is done by hand and if power driven sheet froming equipment is used, the Cylinder Mould Vat does not exceed 40 inches
54	4819.11	Cartons, Boxes for packing of match sticks
55	4823.90	Paper splints for matches, Ashphaltic roofing sheet
56	68 or 69	Stoneware, which are only salt glazed
57	68	Goods manufactured by Nirma Kendras
58	70	Glassware made by mouth blown processes
59	70	Optical glass manufactured by the Central Glass and Ceramic Research Institute, Calcutta and intended for use by any department of the Central Government
60	7013.10	Glass beads and glass bangles
61	7101.20	Peizo-electric quartz
62	73	Sewing Needles, Castings and forgings for sewing machines and shaft cutter
63	73	Parts of table, kitchen or other household articles (other than pressure cookers); Metal containers

64	74.09	All goods other than trimmed and untrimmed sheets/circles of copper for handicraft/utiensils
65	76	Aluminium unwrought or plates and sheets for utensils
66	7402.00 or 7403.00	Unrefined copper and unwrought cooper for handicrafts and utensils
67	7404.10	Waste and scrap used within the factory of production for the manufacture of unrefined or unwrought copper, copper sheets or circles and handicrafts
68	7408.12 or 7408.22	Coper wire for zari
69	7409.00 or 74.10	Copper strip and foil for manufacture of zari
70	7418.10	Parts of table, Kitchen or other household articles
71	82	Pencil sharpeners and blades
72	8529.00	Television Chassis (Populated printed Circuit Board) used for the manufacture of Broadcast Television receiver Sets Monochrome), other than video monitors video projectors and Projection television sets
73	8601.00 and 86.06	Rail locomotives, Passenger coaches, Goods vans and wagons, etc., under the ownership and use by Indian Railways or the Konkan Railway Corporation
74	87	Motor vehicles for transport of goods, three wheeled motor vehicles and mulity utility motor vehicles manufactured from duty paid chassis by an independent body builder.
75	8705.00	Special purpose motor vehicle like fire fighting vehicles, mobile workshops, mobile radiological units manufactured from duty paid chassis and equipments
76	9017.10	Drawing and mathematical instruments
77	9017.90	Parts of drawing and mathematical instruments, used in the manufacture of such instruments
78	9027.00	Instrument kits manufactured by M/s Hindustan Antibiotics Ltd., for testing narcotics
79	9102.90	Parts of Watches and clocks of retail sale price not exceeding Rs. 500 per piece
80	9404.00	Rubberised coir mattresses
81	9504.10	Playing cards
82	9506.00	Sports goods
83	9603.00	Brooms, brushes and other floor sweepers, and parts thereof, mops, feather dusters; paint pads and rollers
84	9606.10	Buttons and button blanks
85	9608.00 or 9609.00	Parts of pencils including clutch pencils used in the manufacture of such pencils
86	9608.00	Pens and parts thereof of value not exceeding Rs. 100 per piece
87	9608.00	Ball point pens including refills for ball point pens and parts thereof of value not exceeding Rs. 100 per piece

88	9608.00	Pencils
89	Any Chapter	Specified non-conventional energy devices/systems
90	Any Chapter	Parts of aeroplanes or helicopters required for manufacture or servicing of aeroplanes or helicopter (other than rubber tyres and tubes for aeroplanes)
91	Any Chapter	Parts used in the manufacture of locomotives, wagons and coaches covered under 8601 to 86.06, subject to the condition that they are used within the factory of production or in any other factory of the same manufacturer, in the manufacture of goods falling under heading No. 86.01 to 86.06
92	Any Chapter	Goods captively consumed for fabrication on chassis, mounting/fitting of structure or equipment on a chassis of motor vehicles of heading No. 87.02 or 87.04 subject to the condition that they are manufactured from duty paid chassis
93	Any Chapter	Mixture of graphite and clay; Aluminium ferrules used for captive consumption in the manufacture of pencils of chapter heading No. 96.08 or 96.09
94	4901.20	Maps, Globes
95	7204.21	Waste and scrap arising out of the manufacture of cold rolled stainless steel pattis and pattas
96	7219.30	Pattis/pattas when subjected to any process other than cold-rolling
97	7220.30	Pattis/pattas when subjected to any process other than cold-rolling
98	7222.50	S.S. Circles used within the factory of production for the manufacture of utensils
99	7310.00	Metal containers manufactured without power
100	7325.90	Castings and forgings for the manufacture of sewing machines and chaff cutters (toka machines) used for cutting animal fodder
101	76.12	Metal containers in or in relation to the manufacture of which no process is ordinarily carried on with the aid of power
102	7602.10	Waste and scrap used within the factory of production for the manufacture of unwrought aluminium plates and sheets
103	Any Chapter	Goods other than (a) electrical stampings and laminations; (b) bearings; and (c) winding wires if used in the manufacture of power driven pumps for handling water
104	5801.11, 5801.91, 5802.41, 5802.51	Woven pile fabrics of wool and other textile materials (other than cotton, man-made or jute), terry towelling & similar woven terry fabrics of other textile materials, tufted textile fabrics, not subjected to any process (optional duty)
105	60	Knitted/crocheted fabrics of man-made fibres, unprocessed, if no Cenvat credit is availed (optional duty)
106	60	Knitted/crocheted fabrics of cotton & of other textile materials (unprocessed/processed), if no Cenvat credit is availed

107	61.01	Knitted/crocheted articles of apparel, if no Cenvat credit is availed
108	51, 52, 53, 54 or 55	Fabrics woven on handlooms and processed, by a factory owned by a State Government Handloom Development Corporation or an Apex Handloom Co-operative Society approved, in either case, by the Government of India on the recommendation of the Development Commissioner of Handlooms, or by a factory owned by the KVIC or any organisation approved by the KVIC for the purpose of processing such fabrics
109	51, 52, 54 or 55	Multiple (folded) or cabled yarn manufactured in a factory which does not have the facilities (including plant and equipment) for producing single yarn, manufactured out of duty paid yarn of Chapters 51, 52, 54 or 55
110	51, 52	Dyed, printed, bleached or mercerised yarn (other than yarn containing synthetic or artificial staple fibres), whether single, multiple (folded) or cabled, manufactured in a factory which does not have the facilities (including plant and equipment) for producing single yarn, manufactured out of duty paid yarn falling under Chapters 51 or 52
111	5106.00	Yarn of wool purchased by a registered Apex Handloom Co-operative Society, the National Handloom Development Corporation or a State Government Handloom Development Corporation, and the payment for which is made by cheque drawn by such Co-operative Society or Corporation, as the case may be, on its own bank account
112	5106.00	Yarn of wool of counts upto 10 in plain (straight) reel hanks, whether single or multiple (folded) and intended for manufacturing carpets
113	5110.00	Woven fabrics of wool when subjected to any one or more of the following processes, namely:- (a) Calendering with plain rollers; (b) Blowing (steam pressing), not processed in a factory having facilities for bleaching, dyeing, printing or any one or more of these processes with the aid of power or steam
114	5105.10	Carded wool, popularly known as 'lefa' intended for making hand spun yarn of upto 10 counts
115	5105.10	Carded wool used captively in the manufacture of yarn of wool
116	5110.00	Fabrics woven on handlooms, namely processed with the aid of power by a factory owned by a registered handloom co-operative society or any organisation set up or approved by Government for the purpose of development of handlooms, or (d) processed by an independent processor approved in this behalf by the Government of India on the recommendation of the Development Commissioner for Handlooms
117	52, 54, 55	Pleated or embossed fabrics manufactured out of processed fabrics on which the appropriate duty of excise has already been paid

118	52, 54 or 55	Yarn consumed within the factory of production in the manufacture of multiple (folded) or cabled yarn, whether or not dyed, printed, bleached or mercerised, and such multiple (folded) or cabled yarn is purchased by a registered Apex Handloom Co-operative Society, the National Handloom Development Corporation or a State Government Handloom Development Corporation, and the payment for which is made by cheque drawn by such Co-operative Society or Corporation, as the case may be, on its own bank account
119	5205.11	The following goods purchased by a registered Apex Handloom Co-operative Society, the National Handloom Development Corporation or a State Government Handloom Development Corporation, and the payment for which is made by cheque drawn by such Co-operative Society or Corporation, as the case may be, on its own bank account, namely :- (a) Cotton yarn (not containing synthetic staple fibres), supplied in cross reel hanks; or (b) Cotton yarn, containing polyester staple fibre and not containing any other textile material, in which the proportion of polyester staple fibre is more than 40% by weight of the total fibre content
120	5207.00	Woven fabrics of cotton when subjected to any one or more of the following processes, namely :- (1) Calendering (other than calendering with grooved rollers); (2) Flanellete raising; (3) Stentering; (4) Damping on grey and bleached sorts; (5) Back filling on grey and bleached sorts; (6) Singeing, that is to say, burning away of knots and loose ends in the fabrics; (7) Scouring, that is to say, removing yarn size and natural oil found in cotton; (8) Cropping or butta cutting; (9) Curing or heat setting; (10) Padding, that is to say, applying starch or fatty material on one or both sides of the fabric; (11) Expanding; or (12) Hydro-extraction with the aid of power, that is to say, mechanically extracting or mechanically squeezing out water from the fabric not processed in a factory having facilities for bleaching, dyeing, printing or any one or more of these processes with the aid of power or steam
121	5207.00	Cotton fabrics intended for use in the manufacture of cotton absorbent lint
122	5307.11	Sisal and manila twist yarn, thread, ropes and twine, all sorts, if consumed within the factory in which it is produced for the manufacture of sisal and manila products falling under Chapter 53, 56, 57 or 63 of the said Schedule
123	5406.10	Woven fabrics of man made fibres subjected to any one or more of the following processes, namely :- (1) Calendering with plain rollers; (2) Singeing, that is to say, burning away of knots and loose ends in the fabrics; (3) Padding, that is to say, application of natural starch to one or both sides of the fabrics; (4) Back filling, that is to say, application of starch to one side of the fabrics; (5) Cropping, that is to say, cutting away mechanically of loose ends from the fabrics; (6) Hydro-extraction, that is to say, mechanically extracting, or mechanically squeezing out water from the fabric; or (7) The process of blowing (steam pressing) carried on woven

		fabrics of acrylic fibre not processed in a factory having facilities for bleaching, dyeing, printing or any one or more of these processes with the aid of power or steam
124	5402.10	Nylon filament yarn or polypropylene multifilament yarn of 210 deniers with tolerance of 6 per cent
125	5402.31	Dyed, printed, bleached or mercerised yarns, whether single, multiple (folded) or cabled, manufactured in a factory which does not have the facilities (including plant and equipment) for producing single or draw twisted or texturised yarn, manufactured without the aid of power out of duty paid yarn falling under Chapter 54
126	5402.31	Twisted nylon filament yarn manufactured out of nylon filament yarn including crimped or textured nylon filament yarn falling within Chapter 54 of the said Schedule on which the appropriate duty of excise or the additional duty CVD, has already been paid
127	5402.32	Twisted polyester filament yarn manufactured out of textured or draw-twisted polyester filament yarn falling within Chapter 54 of the said Schedule on which the appropriate duty of excise or the additional duty CVD has already been paid
128	5402.39 or 5402.59	Twisted polypropylene filament yarn manufactured out of polypropylene filament yarn on which appropriate duty of excise or the additional duty CVD has already been paid
129	5403.20 or 5403.32	Twisted viscose filament yarn manufactured out of viscose filament yarn including textured viscose filament yarn falling within Chapter 54 of the said Schedule on which the appropriate duty of excise, or the additional duty CVD, has already been paid
130	5404.10	Nylon monofilament yarn, of denierage 210, 330, 420, 630, 840, 1050, 1260 or 1680, with tolerance of 4 per cent
131	5404.10	Monofilament of high density polyethylen or polypropylene, if no credit under the Cenvat Credit Rules, has been availed
132	5406.21	Fabrics of polyester filament yarn containing cotton and polyester staple fibre in which the proportion of polyester staple fibre or filament yarn or both is less than 70% by weight of the total fibre content and processed by a factory owned by a registered handloom co-operative society or any organisation set up or approved by the Government for the purpose of development of handlooms
133	5406.21	Fabrics, woven on handlooms and processed with the aid of power or steam by a factory owned by a registered handloom co-operative society or any organisation set up or approved by Government for the purpose of development of handlooms
134	55.09 or 55.10	The following goods if purchased by a registered Apex Handloom Co-operative Society, the National Handloom Development Corporation or a State Government Handloom Development Corporation, and the payment for which is made by cheque drawn by such Co-operative Society or Corporation, as the case may be, on its own bank account, namely:- (yarn of counts not exceeding 25 of artificial staple

		fibre, not containing synthetic staple fibres and supplied in cross reel hanks; (b) yarn of polyester staple fibre containing cotton (not containing any other textile material) and in which the proportion of polyester staple fibre is less than 70 per cent by weight of the total fibre content; (c) yarn of polyester staple fibre containing cotton, ramie or artificial staple fibre or any on or more of these fibres (not containing any other textile material) and in which the proportion of polyester staple fibre is less than 70 per cent by weight of the total
135	55.11, 55.12, 55.13 or 55.14	Fabrics of man made staple fibres woven on handlooms or fabrics of man made staple fibres woven on handlooms processed with the aid of power or steam by a factory owned by a State Government Handloom Development Corporation or an Apex Handloom Cooperative Society approved by Government of India for the development of Handlooms, other than the following, namely:- (a) fabrics containing only polyester and cotton in which the proportion of polyester staple fibre is less than 70% by weight of total fibre content; and (b) fabrics containing only polyester staple fibre and any one or more of the following fibres, namely, cotton, ramie and artificial fibre in which the proportion of polyester staple fibre is more than 40% but less than 70% by weight of total fibre content
136	5501.20	Polyester tow consumed within the factory of production in the manufacture of polyester staple fibre
137	5607.00	All goods (other than dipped cords falling under sub-heading 5607.90 of the said Schedule) made from yarn, monofilament, tapes or strips on which the appropriate duty of excise leviable or the additional duty CVD has already been paid
138	5608.11	Made up fishing nets of man-made textile materials
139	5703.10	Other carpets and other textile floor coverings, whether or not made up, of coconut fibres (coir)
140	5807.00	Labels, badges and similar articles of textile materials, in the piece, in strips or cut to shape or size, not embroidered
141	5808.10	Braids in the piece, ornamental trimmings in the piece, without embroidery, other than knitted or croacheted, tassels, pompons and similar articles, not subjected to any process
142	5906.91	Knitted or crocheted rubberised textile fabrics
143	5906.99	Rubberised textile fabrics, if no Cenvat credit 1944 has been availed
144	5910.00	Unprocessed cotton belting, woven
145	61 or 62	Raincoats and undergarments
146	6102.00 or 6202.00	Clothing accessories, whether or not knitted or crocheted
147	62.01	Woven articles of apparel made of handloom fabrics
148	6301.10	Made up textile articles made out of handloom fabrics
149	3916.10	Plastic canes
150	4011.10	Tyres for cycles, rickshaws

151	4013.10	Inner tube, of rubber, for tyres, of a kind used on bicycles, cycle rickshaws and three-wheeled powered cycle rickshaws
152	7315.00	Chains of cycle and cycle rickshaws
153	7326.19	Forging of iron & steel for cycles, rickshaws
154	7326.21	Tyre bead rings for cycles, rickshaws
155	8512.00	Dynamos, head lamps, side lamps, tail lamps of cycle and cycle rickshaws
156	8524.32	Audio Cassettes, recorded
157	8714.91	Parts of Bicycles and other cycles, not motorised
158	8413.91	Parts of hand pumps for handling water
159	8414.91	Parts and accessories of bicycle pumps
160	8424.10	Mechanical appliances of a kind used in agriculture or horticulture
161	8424.91	Parts of the above agricultural machinery
162	8432.00	Agricultural, horticultural or forestry machinery for soil preparation or cultivation, lawn or sports ground rollers
163	8433.00	Harvesting or threshing machinery, machines for cleaning, sorting, grading eggs, fruit or other agricultural produce
164	8436.00	Other agricultural, horticultural, poultry keeping or bee-keeping machinery
165	8437.00	Machines for cleaning, sorting, grading seed, grain or dried vegetables, machines used in milling industry
166	8452.11	Hand operated sewing machines
167	8481.20, 8481.92	Bicycle valves and parts thereof

Commodities Attracting 4% Central Excise Duty (Cenvat) (2002-03)

Proposed duty (in %)	
2003-04	2004-05
6% with credit	14%

S.No.	Tariff Chapter	Description of goods
1	30	Unbranded wadding, gauze, bandages
2	44	Articles of wood other than flush doors
3	48	Registers, account books etc. (but excluding notebooks and exercise books), Paper and Paperboard labels, Paper and paper pulp moulded trays
4	56	Metallic yarn (imitation zari)
5	59	Adhesive tape of width less than 20 cm
6	59	Tubular knitted gas mantle fabric, whether or not impregnated, for use in incandescent gas mantles
7	66	Umbrellas & Sun Umbrellas
8	66	Walking sticks, seat sticks, whips, riding-crops and the like

9	68	Articles of mica
10	68	Lightweight (solid or hollow) concrete building blocks
11	68	Mosaic tiles, that is to say, tiles known commercially as 'mosaic tiles'
12	70	Clock or watch glasses, Laboratory, hygenic or pharma glassware
13	73	Table, kitchen articles of iron and steel other than stoves, pressure cookers (other than parts)
14	74	Table, kitchen articles of copper (other than parts)
15	76	Table, kitchen articles of aluminium (other than parts)
16	82	Knives, Spoons, forks, ladles and similar kitchenware/ tableware
17	84	Crankshafts for sewing machines
18	84	Power driven pumps for handling water, Bicycle pumps and hand pumps
19	87	Bicycles and other cycles, not motorised
20	90	Instruments and appliances used in medical, surgical, dental or vetinary sciences, mechano therapy appliances, specified medical equipment and other goods and X ray apparatus for medical, dental, vetinary use, other than parts and accessories thereof
21	94	Kerosene Presure lanterns
22	94	Pre fabricated buildings
23	95	Wheeled toys, Dolls and other toys (other than parts and accessories thereof)

Commoditites Attracting 8% Central Excise Duty (Cenvat) (2002-03)

Proposed duty (in %)			
2003-04	2004-05	2005-06	2006-07
14% with credit	14%	14%	14%

S.No.	Tariff Chapter	Description of goods
1	34	Candles
2	52	Cotton yarn
3	70	Tableware and kitchenware of glass
4	71	Imitation jewellery
5	85	Monochrome television receivers
6	85	Vacuum and gas filled bulbs of retail sale price not exceeding Rs. 20 per bulb
7	90	Sunglasses for correcting vision
8	91	Watches and clocks of retail sale price not exceeding Rs. 500 per piece
9	96	Toothbrushes

Commodities Attracting 12% Central Excise Duty (Cenvat) 2002-03)

Proposed duty (in %)			
2003-04	2004-05	2005-06	2006-07
12%	12%	14%	14%

S.No.	Tariff Chapter	Description of goods
1	61	Textile fabrics
2	61	Textile garments
3	61	Textile made-ups

Commodities Attracting 14% Central Excise Duty (Cenvat) (2002-03)

Proposed duty (in %)			
2003-04	2004-05	2005-06	2006-07
To be converted into specific rates			

S.No.	Tariff Chapter	Description of goods
1	27	High Speed Diesel Oil (An additional duty of Rs. 1/litre is also charged)

Commodities Attracting 30% Central Excise Duty (Cenvat) (2002-03)

Proposed duty (in %)			
2003-04	2004-05	2005-06	2006-07
To be converted into specific rates			

S.No.	Tariff Chapter	Description of goods
	27	Motor Spirit (Petrol) (An additional duty of Rs. 7/litre is also charged)

Commodities Attracting 32% Central Excise Duty (Cenvat) (2002-03)
Category I

Proposed duty (in %)			
2003-04	2004-05	2005-06	2006-07
28%	24%	20%	14%

S.No.	Tariff Chapter	Description of goods
1	40	Tyres for replacement purpose
2	55	Polyester filament yarn

Commodities Attracting 32% Central Excise Duty (Cenvat) 2002-03)
Category II

Proposed duty (in %)			
2003-04	2004-05	2005-06	2006-07
28%	24%	20%	20%

S.No.	Tariff Chapter	Description of goods
1	21	Aerated soft drinks and soft drink concentrates
2	84	Air-conditioners
3	87	Motor cars and multi-utility vehicles and chassis thereof

Commodities Attracting 32% Central Excise Duty (Cenvat) (2002-03)
Category III

Proposed duty (in %)			
2003-04	2004-05	2005-06	2006-07
32%	32%	32%	32%

S.No.	Tariff Chapter	Description of goods
1	21	Pan Masala
2	24	Chewing tobacco and preparations containing chewing tobacco; pan masala containing tobacco

Commodities Attracting Specific Rates of Central Excise Duty (Cenvat)

				Proposed duty (in %)			
S. No.	Tariff Chapter	Description of goods	Present Rate (2002-03)	2003 -04	2004 -05	2005 -06	2006 -07
1	17	Levy Sugar	Rs. 38 per quintal	6%	6%	6%	6%
2	17	Non-levy sugar	Rs. 71 per quintal	6%	6%	6%	6%
3	25	Ordinary Portland cement	Rs. 350 per MT	Specific duty to be retained			
4	25	Cement Clinker	Rs. 200 per MT	Specific duty to be retained			
5	25	Marble slabs and tiles	Rs. 30 per square mt	16%	14%	14%	14%
6	36	Matches (i) machanis cottage sect..	Rs. 0.50 for 100 packs of 50 matches each	6%	6%	6%	6%
7	36	Matches (ii) non-machanised middle sector	Rs. 1.00 for 100 packs of 50 matches each	6%	6%	6%	6%

8	36	Matches (iii) semi-mechanised sector	Rs. 2.00 for 100 packs of 50 matches each	6%	6%	6%	6%
9	36	Matches (iv) mechanised sector	Rs. 3.00 for 100 packs of 50 matches each	6%	6%	6%	6%
10	9	Tea (Bulk)	Re. 1 per kg	Exempt fully			
11	17	Molasses	Rs. 500 per tonne retained	Specific levy to be			
12	24	Biris (a) Hand-made (b) Machine made	(a) Rs. 7 per 1000 biris (b) Rs. 17 per 1000 biris	Specific levy to be retained			
13	24	Cigarettes (a) non-filter (b) filter	(a) Varies from Rs. 135 to Rs. 450 per 1000 cigarettes, based on the length of the cigarettes (b) Varies from Rs. 670 to Rs. 1780 per 1000 cigarettes, based on the length of the cigarettes	Specific levy to be retained			

Central Excise Duty Exemptions which can be Retained

S.No.	Tariff Chapter	Description of goods
1	0201.00	Meat and edible meat offals
2	0301.00	Fish and crustaceans, molluscs and other aquatic invertebrates
3	0401.00	Milk and cream
4	0501.00	Products of animal origin not elsewhere specified
5	0701.00	Dried vegetables, including potatoes, onions and mushrooms, whole, cut, sliced, broken or in powder, but not further prepared; dried leguminous vegetables, including peas and beans, shelled, whether or not skinned or split
6	0702.00	Other edible vegetables, roots and tubers
7	0801.00	Edible fruits and nuts; peel of citrus fruit or melons
8	0901.00	Coffee
9	09.03	Spices
10	0902.00	Green Tea
11	1101.00	Products of the milling industry, including flours, groats, meal and grains of cereals, and flour, meal or flakes of vegetables
12	1104.00	Inulin; wheat gluten, whether or not dried

13	13	Vegetable saps and extracts, used within the factory of their production for the manufacture of medicaments which are exclusively used in Ayurvedic, Unani or Siddha systems
14	1301.90	Lac, gums, resins and other veg. Saps manufactured without the aid of power
15	1401.00	Vegetable plaiting materials; vegetable products, not elsewhere specified or included
16	1701.00	Sugar, in or in relation to the manufacture of which no process is ordinarily carried on with the aid of power
17	1701.20	Khandsari sugar
18	1702.11	Palmyra sugar
19	1703.90	All goods, for use in the manufacture of goods other than alcohol (Khandsari molasses)
20	1905.90	Bread and other baker's wares (other than cakes, pastry and biscuits, waffles and wafers)
21	2108.30	Prasad or Prasadam
22	22.01, 22.02	Water or mineral water not bearing a brand name
23	2201.20 or 2202.20	Aerated waters prepared and dispensed by vending machines
24	2204.90	Ethyl alcohol other than de natured
25	2301.00	Residues and waste from the food industries
26	24.04	Biris, other than paper rolled biris, manufactured without the aid of machines, by a manufacturer by whom or on whose behalf no biris are sold under a brand name (as defined in NOTE 1 to Chapter 24), in respect of first clearances of such biris for home consumption by or on behalf of such manufacturer from one or more factories upto a quantity not exceeding 20 lakhs cleared on or after the 1st day of April in any financial year.
27	2401.10	Unmanufactured tobacco, not bearing a brand name
28	2404.91	Snuff not bearing a brand name
29	2404.99	Tobacco, used for smoking through 'hookah, or 'chillum', commonly known as 'hookah' tobacco or 'gudaku'
30	2501.00	Salt and pure sodium chloride
31	25.03	Asbestos
32	25.04	Marbles in blocks and slabs
33	2505.00	Mineral substances not elsewhere specified (clay, sulphur)
34	26.01 to 26.07	Ores
35	2701.00	Coal, Lignite, peat, coke
36	2705.00	Coal gases, and similar gases other than petroleum gases, and other gaseous hydro carbons
37	2706.00	Tar distilled from coal/lignite/peat and other mineral tars
38	2706.00	Tar distilled from coal/lignite/peat and other mineral tars

39	2709.00	Petroleum oils and oils obtained from bituminous minerals, crude
40	2710.00	Naphtha and Natural Gasoline Liquid intended for use – (i) within the Heavy Water Plant at Baroda or Tuticorin for the manufacture of Synthesis gas or ammonia or both which are to be utilised in the manufacture of Heavy Water in such plants; (ii) by M/s. Gujarat State Fertilizer Corporation, Baroda or M/s. Southern Petro Chemicals Industrial Corporation, Tuticorin, for manufacture of synthesis gas or ammonia or both and if the synthesis gas or ammonia or both so manufactured is supplied respectively to the Heavy Water Plants at Baroda or Tuticorin for the manufacture of Heavy Water in such Plants
41	2710.00	Synthesis gas, if used in the manufacture of Heavy Water
42	2711.00	Bio-gas
43	2711.21	Natural gas in gaseous state
44	28	Steam
45	28	Thorium Oxalate
46	28	Gold potassium cyanide used within the factory of production for manufacture of gold jewellery
47	28	All goods used within the factory of production for manufacture of gold jewellery
48	28 or 29	Specified bulk drugs for NHP
49	28 or 29	Specified goods used for the manufacture of exempted bulk drugs (NHP)
50	28 or 29	All chemicals used in the manufacture of centchroman
51	28 or 38	Silicon in all forms
52	28, 29 or 30	Specified Bulk drugs, or formulation (anti-AIDS)
53	2804.12	Oxygen, for use in the manufacture of heavy water
54	2804.21	Hydrogen, consumed within the factory of production
55	2804.31	Nitrogen, for use in the manufacture of heavy water
56	2804.31	Nitrogen, for use in the manufacture of heavy water
57	2804.33	Nitrogen, consumed within the factory of production
58	2805.11	Potassium metal, for use in a heavy water plant
59	2811.90	Steam
60	2814.10	Ammonia, for use in the manufacture of heavy water
61	2837.00	Gold potassium cyanide solution used within the factory of production for manufacture of zari
62	2844.10	Nuclear fuel
63	2844.20	Thorium Hydroxide
64	2845.10	Nuclear fuel
65	2845.20	Heavy water (Deuterium Oxide)
66	2851.11	Distilled or conductivity water and water of similar purity used within the factory of production

67	2851.21	Liquid air, used within the factory of production
68	2851.30	Compressed air
69	2941.00	2-Cyanopyrazine
70	3002.00	Antisera and other blood fractions; vaccines, toxins, cultures of microorganisms and similar products
71	3003.00	Formulations manufactured from the specified bulk drugs (NHP)
72	3003.00	Desferrioxamine injection or Deferiprone
73	3003.31	Medicaments, including those used in Ayurvedic, Unani, Siddha, Homoeopathic or bio-chemic systems manufactured exclusively in accordance with authoritative books specified in the First Schedule to the Drugs and Cosmetics Act, 1940
74	3003.32	Medicaments (including veterinary) used in bio-chemic system and not bearing a brandname
75	3005.10	Chemical contraceptives
76	3005.30	Oral rehydration salts
77	3005.90	Intravenous fluids
78	3307.41	'Agarbatti', 'Dhoop' & similar preparations in whatever form
79	3307.60	Kumkum (including sticker kumkum), kajal, sindur, alta or mahavar
80	3824.20	Concrete mix manufactured at the site of construction for use in construction work at such site
81	39	Reprocessed plastic made from scrap
82	3903.00	Unexpanded polystyrene beads purchased by the Malaria Research Centre
83	40.11, 40.12 or 40.13	Tyres, flaps and tubes used in power tillers and vehicles for physically handicapped
84	4001.00	Natural Rubber
85	4014.10	Sheath contraceptives
86	4101.00	Leather
87	4401.00	Wood wool, wood flour
88	4403.00	Wood sawn or chipped lengthwise
89	45, 48, 68, 73,85 or 87	Parts of main battle tanks subject to end use condition
90	47.01	Mechanical wood pulp, chemical wood pulp, semi-chemical wood pulp and pulps of other fibrous cellulosic materials
91	4702.10	Recovered paper waste arising in the course of printing of textbooks
92	4801.00	Newsprint
93	4802.00	Security paper
94	4802.30	Maplitho paper supplied to a braille press against an indent placed by the National Institute for Visually Handicapped, Dehradun

95	4804.10	Kraft paper supplied to a braille press against an indent placed by the National Institure for Visually Handicapped, Dehradun
96	4823.10	Braille paper
97	4901.90	Printed books, newspapers, pictures and other products of printing industry
98	5001.00	Silk-worm cocoons suitable for reeling
99	5002.00	Raw silk
100	5003.00	Silk waste (including cocoons unsuitable for reeling, yarn waste and garnetted stock)
101	5101.00	Wool, not carded or combed
102	5102.00	Fine or coarse animal hair, not carded or combed
103	5103.00	Waste of wool or of fine or coarse animal hair, including yarn waste
104	51.04	Garnetted stock
105	5201.00	Cotton, not carded or combed
106	5202.00	Cotton waste (including yarn waste and garnetted stock)
107	5207.00	Khadi, that is to say, any cloth woven on a handloom in India either wholly from cotton yarn or in admixture with silk or woolen yarn, handspun in India and certified as Khadi by an officer duly authorised in this behalf by the KVIC
108	5207.00	Poly Vastra, that is to say, any cloth containing cotton and polyester woven on handloom from yarns hand spun in India and certified as Poly Vastra by an officer duly authorised in this behalf by the KVIC and processed by a factory owned by the KVIC or any organisation approved by the KVIC for the purpose of processing of Poly Vastra
109	5207.10	Fabrics of cotton or man made fibres woven in a prison and subjected to further process outside the prison by an independent processor or a composite mill
110	5301.00	Flax, raw or processed, but not spun; flax tow and waste (inlcuding yarn waste and garnetted stock)
111	5303.00	Jute and other textile bast fibres (excluding jute, true hemp and ramie) raw or processed but not spub; tow and waste of these fibres (including yarn waste and garnetted stock)
112	5305.31	Ramie, raw or processed but not spun; tow, noils and waste of ramie (including yarn waste and garnetted stock)
113	5509.21	Poly Vastra, that is to say, any cloth containing cotton and polyester woven on handloom from yarns hand spun in India and certified as Poly Vastra by an officer duly authorised in this behalf by the KVIC and processed by a factory owned by the KVIC or any organisation approved by the KVIC for the purpose of processing of Poly Vastra
114	6307.10	Indian National Flag
115	64	Footwear of R.S.P less than Rs. 125
116	68 or 69	Sandlime bricks
117	6807.00	Mosaic tiles & articles of mica

118	6807.00	Goods manufactured at construction site for use in construction work at that site
119	6807.10	Goods in which more than 25% by weight of red mud, press mud or blast furnace slag or one or more of these materials, have been used
120	6807.20	All goods
121	6807.90	Goods, in which not less than 25% by weight of fly-ash or phosphogypsum or both have been used
122	6901.10	Clay bricks other than fire clay bricks
123	6901.20	Burnt clay tiles conforming to ISI specification 3367-1975
124	6903.10	Roofing tiles
125	6906.10	Glazed tiles manufactured by a manufacturer exclusively engaged in the process of printing, decorating or ornamenting of the said glazed tiles on job work basis, by whom or on whose behalf no glazed tiles are sold, if no Cenvat credit is taken
126	7101.10	Diamonds, cut or polished or both
127	7101.31	Primary forms of silver, platinum, palladium, rhodium, iridium, osmium and ruthenium
128	7101.31	Silver
129	7101.39	Primary gold converted from any form of gold, with the aid of power
130	7101.39	Articles of ornaments, Waste and scrap of precious metal, dust and powder of semi-precious stones
131	7101.60	Strips, wires, sheets, plates and foils of silver
132	7101.70	Articles of gold, silver, Platinum etc., Ornaments made of gold or silver, Strips, wires etc., of gold used in the manufacture of jewellery and Precious or semi-precious stones, synthetic stones and pearls
133	7222.50	HR/CR sheets and strips cut or slit on job-work
134	7308.50	Fabrications at construction site
135	7608.20	Aluminium extrusions, etc., for manufacture of artificial limbs & specified rehabilitation aids
136	8206.00	Tools put up in sets
137	84 or any other chapter	Specified goods intended to be used for the installation of a cold storage, cold room or refrigerated vehicle, for preservation, stroage or transport of agricultural produce
138	8401.10	Nuclear fuel
139	8442.10	Printing blocks and printing types
140	8442.20	Lithographic plates used within the factory of its production
141	8469.10	Braille typewriters
142	8502.10	Diesel generating sets assembled, at site of installation, from duty paid engine and generator
143	8524.00	Recorded Video Cassettes intended for Television Broadcasting and supplied in formats such as U-matic Betacam or any similar format

144	8524.00	Television and Sound Recording Media Such as video tapes and video discs
145	8524.00	Sound recorded magnetic tapes of width not exceeding 6.5mm, whether in spools, or reels or in other form of packing
146	8524.20	Software
147	8609.00	Marine freight containers manufactured in 100% EOU or EPZ/FTZ, when sold in India for export
148	8713.00	Invalid carriages, whether or not motorised
149	8801.00	Aircraft, spacecraft and parts thereof
150	8901.00	Ships, boats, fishing vessels, factory ships, tugs and pusher crafts. Light-vessels, fire-floats, dredgers, etc.
151	8901.00	Ships, boats and floating structures (other than pleasure yachts, ships for breaking etc.)
152	90	Parts and accessories of specified medical equipment
153	90.18, 90.19 or 9022.10	Parts and accessories
154	9001.10	Spectacle lenses, intraocular lenses and contact lenses other than sunglasses for correcting vision
155	9003.11 9003.19	Frames and mountings for spectacles and goggles of value below Rs. 500 per piece
156	9004.90	Spectacles, googles for correcting vision
157	9021.10	Artificial limbs and rehabilitation aids for the handicapped
158	9021.20	Orthopaedic footwear manufacturede without the aid of power
159	9021.90	Hearing aids and others
160	9101.10	Braille watches, with case of precious metal
161	9102.10	Braille watches of other types, than those of sub-heading no. 9101.10
162	9301.00	Military weapons, other than revolvers, pistols, swords, cutlasses, bayonets etc.
163	9601.00	Goods supplied to foreign diplomatic missions for their official use
164	Any Chapter	Cement bonded particle board, jute particle board, rice husk board, glass-fibre reinforced gypsum board (GRG), sisal-fibre boards and bagasse board
165	Any Chapter	Goods required for - (a) the substitution of ozone depleting substances (ODS; (b) the setting up of new projects with non-ozone depletting substances technologies
166	Any Chapter	Parts of hearing aids captively consumed in the manufacture of hearing aids falling under heading No. 90.21
167	Any Chapter	Water treatment plants
168	Any Chapter	Parts of aeroplanes or helicopters required for manufacture or servicing of aeroplanes or helicopter (other than rubber tyres and tubes for aeroplanes)

Annexure 'C'

F.No. 201/65/2002-CX 6

Government of India

Ministry of Finance & Company Affairs

Department of Revenue

Central Board of Excise & Customs

New Delhi, dated 3rd September 2002

ORDER

Subject : Task Force on Indirect Taxes – Constitution Reg.

Ministry of Finance and Company Affairs has decided to set up a Task Force on Indirect Taxes. The objective is to take advantage of information technology and bring the indirect tax systems and procedures at par with the best international practices and thus, encourage compliance and reduce transaction costs. Accordingly, the Task Force on Indirect Taxes is constituted as under:

1	Dr. V.L. kelkar, Adviser to Minster of Finance and Company Affairs	Chairman
2	Dr. Ashok Lahiri, Delhi	Member
3	Prof. Jayanta Roy, Indian Institute of Management, Kolkata	–do–
4	Shri Sunil Kant Munjal, Hero Cycles, Ludhiana, representing CII	–do–
5	Shri Sanjay Bhatia, Hindustan Tin Works, Ghaziabad, representing PHD Chambers of Commerce and Industry	–do–
6	Shri K.S. Suresh, ITC Limited, Kolkata, representing FICCI	–do–
7	Shri Nihal Kothari, Hindustan Lever Limited, Mumbai representing ASSOCHAM	–do–
8	Shri Y.P. Suri, Rex Enterprises, Delhi, representing FASSI	–do–
9	Shri K.S. Ravishankar, Bangalore, representing NASSCOM	–do–
10	Shri Deepak Puri, Moser Baer, Delhi, representing Electronics and Software Export Promotion Council	–do–
11	Shri Gautam Ray, Joint Secretary, C.B.E.C., New Delhi	–do–
12	Shri S.M. Bhatnagar, Director, C.B.E.C., New Delhi	Member-Secretary

2. The Terms of Reference of the Task Force are as follows :

(i) The review of the Customs and Central Excise law and procedures and recommendations on their simplification, reducing cost of compliance and facilitating voluntary compliance.

(ii) Recommendations relating to increased use of automation for a user friendly and transparent tax administration

(iii) The review of the statutorily prescribed records, documents and returns (including periodicity) and suggestions on their utility and simplification.

(iv) Recommendations to provide for in-built mechanism in the procedures for time bound disposal of matters.

(v) Any other recommendation on different aspects of legal provisions and administration to facilitate the tax payers and improve compliance.

3. The terms and conditions of the Task Force will be as follows :

(i) The Task force should furnish to the Government a Draft Consultation Paper containing its recommendations in 45 days i.e. by 21.10.2002. The same will be made available to the public for feedback and comments by 1.11.2002 which shall be considered by the Task Force and a Final Report submitted to Government by 30.11.2002.

(ii) The Task Force is empowered to interact with departmental officials, trade interests and individuals and visit field formations as it may choose.

(iii) The non-official Task Force members would be entitled to TA/DA as per norms.

(Nisha Malhotra)
Joint Secretary (Admn.)

Chairman and Members of Task Force

Copy to

1. Director (FMO)
2 PS to Adviser to F&CAM
3 PS to MOS (Revenue)
4 PS to Secretary (Revenue)
5 PS to Chairman, CBEC
6 PS to Members, CBEC
7 Financial Adviser, Ministry of Finance & Company Affairs
8 All Directors General/Chief Commissioners of Customs & Central Excise
9 All Commissioners of Customs & Central Excise

(Nisha Malhotra)
Joint Secretary (Admn.)

Dr. Ashok Lahiri resigned from the Task Force on 11.11.2002 upon his taking over the post of Chief Economic Adviser in the Ministry of Finance & Company Affairs.

Report of the Advisory Group on Tax Policy and Tax Administration for the Tenth Plan

2001

Report of the Advisory Group on Tax Policy and Tax Administration for the Tenth Plan

CONTENTS

1 Executive Summary 479

The complete report is on the accompanying CD-ROM as per contents given below

Advisory Group
Preface
Contents
Abstract

1 Introduction
2 A Macro Perspective and Scope of Tax Revenue
3 Tax/GDP Trends and Future Prospects
4 Reform of Direct Taxes
   [A] Personal Income Tax
      [i] Rates
      [ii] Savings incentives
      [iii] External borrowings
      [iv] Income of funds
      [v] Foreign income and remuneration
      [vi] Foreign exchange earnings/exports of goods and services
      [vii] Regional/industrial development
      [viii] Income from salaries
      [ix] Income from self-occupied house property

[x] Charity and Non-Profit Organisations

[B] Corporate Income Tax

[i] Harmonisation of personal and corporate income taxes

[ii] Minimum alternate tax for companies

[C] Direct Tax Administration

5 Reform of Union Excises

[A] Duty Structure

[B] Base of Union Excises

[C] Administration

6 Reform of Customs Duties

[A] Rates and Exemptions

[B] Export Valuation

[C] Treatment of Exports

[D] Administrative Matters

7 Reform of the State Taxes and Introduction of VAT

[A] On Interim Reform of Sales Tax

[B] On an Integrated VAT

[C] On Timing of VAT Introduction

[D] On State VAT Design

[E] On Treatment of Interstate Trade

[F] On VAT Administration

[G] On Taxation of Services

[H] On State Excises on Liquor

[I] On Registration Fees

[J] On Stamp Duties

[K] On Motor Vehicles Tax and Goods and Passengers Tax

[L] On Profession Tax and Entertainment Duty

2 A Macro Perspective and Scope of Tax Revenue: 2000-01 to 2006-07

1 Introduction

2 Sectoral Growth Profiles

3 Regional Profile of Growth

4 Taxing the Growing Output
5 Augmenting Growth: Recasting the Expenditure Priorities
6 Growth Target and Sustainable Debt and Deficit
7 Central and State Fiscal Profiles: Alternative Projections
8 Macro Tax Targets
9 Summary and Conclusions

Appendix 2.1: Sustainability of Public Debt

3 Tax/GDP Trends in the 1990s and Future Prospects

1 Introduction
2 Gross Tax Collections of Centre and States
3 Gross Tax Collection of Centre
4 Gross Tax Collections of States
5 Concluding Observations

4 Reform of Direct Taxes

1 Introduction
2 Rates of Personal Income Tax
3 Tax Base
  [A] Widening of the Tax Base
  [B] Incentives for Investment in Financial Assets
    [i] Section 88
    [ii] Section 80L
    [iii] Savings of capital gains
    [iv] Other savings incentives
    [v] Evaluation
      (a) Impact on efficiency
      (b) Impact on equity
  [C] Incentives for External Borrowings
  [D] Exemption for Income of Funds
  [E] Exemption for Foreign Income and Remuneration
  [F] Incentives for Foreign Exchange Earnings/Export of Goods & Services

[G] Incentive for Regional/Industrial Development

[H] Widening of the Base in Respect of Taxpayers Deriving Income from Salaries

[I] Income from Self-Occupied House Properties

4 Harmonisation of Personal and Corporate Income Taxes

5 Presumptive Tax: A Minimum Alternate Tax (MAT) on Companies

[A] Justification for Presumption

[B] Rationale for MAT

[C] MAT Base: International Experience

[D] Nature and Proposed Changes in the Indian MAT

6 Taxation of Charitable Trusts/Institutions

[A] Rationale for Tax Concessions and Role of NPOs

[B] Modifications Needed in India

7 Issues in Direct Tax Administration

Appendix 4.1 List of incentives under Income Tax Act

Appendix 4.2 Provisions for Incentives for Savings

Appendix 4.3 Incentives for Charitable Trusts

5 Reform of Indirect Taxes

1 Introduction

2 Prevailing Structure of Central Excises

[A] Rates, Base, Valuation and Credit

[B] Structure of Excise Administration

3 Revenue Productivity of Excises

[A] Development of MODVAT Scheme & Restructuring of Duty Rates

[i] MODVAT scheme (Now CENVAT)

[ii] Restructuring of duty rates

[B] Revenue Implications of Excise Duty Reforms

[i] Factors affecting revenue

[ii] Revenue growth

[C] Explanations Based on Administrative Factors

4 Measures to be Undertaken in Excises

[A] Manufacture—Need to Change the Definition

[B] Abolish the Concept of Manufacture from MODVAT

[C] Procedural Reforms for MODVAT

[D] Tariff Reform

[i] Rates of central excise

[ii] Multiplicity of levies

[E] CENVAT and Taxation of Services

[F] SSI Exemption Scheme

[G] Valuation

[H] Dutiability of Complete Plant Erected at Site

[I] Frequency of Tax Payment

[J] Issuance of "Protective Demand"

[K] Exports—Multiplicity of Schemes

5 Reduction of Customs Duty Exemptions

6 Zero Rate Customs Duty

7 Export Valuation

8 Selected Administration Issues

[A] Clearance of Cargo

[B] Modifications Applicable to Both Customs and Excise

[i] Advance ruling on classification

[ii] Stop the flurry of remanding the cases

[iii] Add appropriate explanations in exemptions

[iv] Amend the law prohibiting "Unjust Enrichment"

[v] Preventing Proliferation of Litigation in Customs and Excise

6 A Review of State Taxes

1 Introduction

2 Sales Tax Reform and Advantages of a VAT
- [A] Present Position
- [B] Why a VAT is Needed
  - [i] Eliminates cascading effect
  - [ii] Eases administration
  - [iii] Improves international competitiveness
  - [iv] Imparts transparency
  - [v] Buoyant source of revenue
- [C] Single VAT versus Dual VAT
- [D] Reform of Existing Sales Tax

3 State Level VAT—Design Issues
- [A] Type of VAT—Consumption, Income or Production
- [B] Exemption versus Zero Rating
- [C] Single versus Multiple Rates
- [D] Origin versus Destination Principle
- [E] Method of Computation
- [F] Treatment of Interstate Trade

4 State VAT: Administrative Issues

5 Taxation of Services

6 Other Taxes
- [A] State Excises on Liquor
- [B] Registration Fees
- [C] Stamp Duties
- [D] Motor Vehicles Tax
- [E] Profession Tax and Entertainment Duty

Annexure I : Government Order Setting up Advisory Group

Annexure II: Meetings and Visits of Advisory Group

EXECUTIVE SUMMARY

[1] Introduction

The Planning Commission set up the Advisory Group (henceforth referred to as the Group) in July 2000 (Annexure 1) to study tax policy and tax administration issues and make appropriate recommendations at different levels of government with the purpose of generating adequate resources for the Tenth Five Year Plan (2002-03 to 2006-07).

Two challenges faced the Group. First, the parameters for the Tenth Plan have not been set so far. Thus a 15 per cent nominal growth target was utilised. Second, while various aspects of the tax structure have improved over time, many deficiencies remain that, when corrected, would have a negative revenue impact in the short to medium term. The Group took the option of analysing such aspects and recommending corrective action despite their potential negative impact. This implies that major complementary revenue yielding measures are needed to improve the overall revenue productivity of the tax system, comprising both tax policy and tax administration, and including all levels of government – central, state and local.

[2] A Macro Perspective and Scope of Tax Revenue

Tax policy and tax administration reform measures have to be placed in an appropriate macroeconomic perspective for feasibility of the effort. The questions to address and the results to follow would be the following:

1 How would the growth rates of sectors – agriculture, industry and services – be distributed? Given agricultural and industrial growth rates, the residual growth would have to come from the services sector.

2 Which states/regions would contribute to this growth? Successful states have registered growth more than 3 to 4 percentage points above average, while slower states have

performed almost that much below average. Should the growth strategy need to have a regional focus to achieve the 15 per cent nominal target?

3 What would be the role of government? How much national resources should it draw upon for government expenditure and, of that, how much for capital expenditure, given the persistent decline in capital expenditure over the last 15 years? Which sectors should government investment focus on?

4 How much tax revenue and non-tax revenue should government draw upon? Given the fall in the tax/GDP ratio, the stagnation of non-tax revenue, and their relation to the fiscal deficit and sustainability of public debt, appropriate macroeconomic considerations are essential to receive definitive implications for needed resource mobilisation.

5 Given the tax revenue target as implied, as well as the base year tax/GDP ratio, what is the incremental effort required to be obtained.

6 How should tax revenue effort be divided into centre-state targets and tax-wise targets?

The agricultural sector is characterised by a low and falling share of GDP in the second half of the 1990s (Table 2.1) and a small potential for contributing to the buoyancy of tax revenue. An annual growth rate of 3.5 – 4 per cent may be expected over the next few years, given recent performance of 3.3 per cent growth rate (Table 2.2). Industrial growth may be expected at 8 per cent given recent performance of just over 7 per cent.

Achievement of 15 per cent overall nominal rate of growth – an increase of 2-3 percentage points of real growth rate – would, therefore, imply need for very high growth in the services sector at the beginning of the Plan period – as much as 11 per cent – declining to 10.5 per cent by the end of the Plan period (Table 2.2). Slight variations are of course also possible, as indicated by various simulations carried out (Table 2.3).

A strategy that attempts to increase growth would need to modify the distribution of funds to regions. A services-oriented growth would be focussed on urban centres with strong infrastructure. states with high dependence on agriculture would achieve lower growth. If governance and infrastructure improve, low performing states with unutilised potential could indeed improve performance. Special category states have such small shares in GDP that high growth rates there would make only marginal difference to aggregate GDP growth (Table 2.4). The distribution of development funds (Table 2.5) would need to take these factors into account.

A 15 per cent nominal growth rate would also require fundamental changes in the structure of government expenditure. Capital expenditure, which has been crowded out in both central and state government budgets, has to be restored. Further, such expenditure would have to be in growth augmenting sectors such as power, telecommunications and roads. The composition of revenue expenditure has to shift to education and health. Though interest payments in current periods may be considered exogenous, future payments, working through the fiscal deficit and accumulation of public debt, would depend on the success of collection of tax and non-tax revenue. Table 2.11 projects, for 2006-07, the revenue deficit, fiscal deficit, capital expenditure and public debt compatible with a 9 per cent real growth rate target.

The tax/GDP ratio reached a peak of almost 16 per cent in the late 1980s and has fallen since, to 14 per cent of GDP in 1999-2000. Additional tax effort has to focus heavily on the service sector. First, as GDP share of industry decreases while that of the services sector increases, the tax base becomes narrower, aggregate buoyancy of tax revenue[1] declines, and the tax/GDP ratio falls (Table 2.6). Second, states' own tax revenue is also negatively related to the share of services.

Tax revenue targets are shown in Table 2.12 consistent with expenditure restructuring needed for the 15 per cent nominal growth rate. Total tax/GDP ratio would need to rise from 14.09 per cent in 1999-2000 to 17.78 in 2006-07. Of this, states would need to increase the ratio from 5.29 to 6.90, reflecting rationalisation of the sales tax and smaller taxes, and future replacement of the sales tax by a value added tax (VAT). Much of the Centre's increase comes from direct taxes and from expanding the tax base by including services, and some from central excise duties, while customs duties fall slightly.

[3] Tax/GDP Trends and Future Prospects

Between 1989-90 and 1999-2000, the decline in the tax/GDP ratio has been 1.9 percentage points, mainly reflecting the Centre's revenue loss. As a result, the Centre's share in total tax collection has declined from 66.5 per cent to 62.0 per cent. Likewise, against the total tax buoyancy of 0.90, the Centre's is 0.85.

As against this, given the macroeconomic growth target, the system's tax buoyancy would have to jump from 0.90 to 1.26. The tax/GDP ratio should reach 17.8 per cent in 2006-07, which is 3.7 percentage points above 1999-2000 (Chart 3.1). Of this increase, the Centre would have to achieve 2.1 percentage points (Graph 3.2) and the states 1.6 percentage points (Chart 3.3). Nevertheless, the share of states vis-a-vis the Centre in the gross collection of taxes increases in the terminal year 2006-07[2], implying an intensified tax revenue effort by states in the Tenth Plan period.

Of central taxes, corporation income tax revenue has grown the most between 1989-90 to 1999-2000, from 1 per cent of GDP to 1.6 per cent of GDP. The personal income tax grew from 1.0 per cent to 1.4 per cent. Customs duties and excises recorded declining trends, customs duties from 3.7 per cent to 2.5 per cent, and excises from 4.6 per cent to 3.2 per cent[3]. Given anticipated further reductions in customs tariffs and comprehensive extension of the tax credit system under the MODVAT-governed excises, it would not be prudent to assign significant efforts to indirect taxation for the Tenth Plan.

Thus, customs collections have been assigned a slight decrease in terms of GDP from 1999-2000 through the Plan period, excises a slight increase from 3.2 per cent to 3.5 per cent, corporation income tax a jump from 1.6 per cent to 2.4 per cent, and personal income tax also a significant increase from 1.4 per cent to 1.9 per cent. Thus, the shift in tax composition evident in recent years is expected to continue through the Tenth Plan.

State level taxes have been stable in terms of GDP between 1989-90 and 1999-2000. The sales tax remained at 3.1 – 3.2 per cent which accounts for about 60 per cent of state's tax revenue, and state excises at 0.8 per cent. Together they comprised 74 per cent of states' tax revenue. Stamps and registration increased from 0.5 per cent to 0.6 per cent. Land revenue declined from 0.14 per cent of GDP to 0.08 per cent. The stagnancy of the professional tax at 0.07 per cent of GDP points towards the need for extensive coverage of services under the tax base.

In the projections, inter-se weights of individual state level taxes as obtained in 1999-2000 (historical trends) are maintained for the Plan period[4]. In terms of GDP, state taxes will have to increase by about 1.6 per cent. Sales tax is projected to increase from 3.1 per cent of GDP to 4.1 per cent mainly reflecting the anticipated introduction of the VAT that would go beyond first point taxation. State excises are projected to grow from 0.8 per cent of GDP to 1.0 per cent. The remaining increase would have to come from other taxes. The shares of both central and state taxes for 1989-90, 1999-2000, and 2006-07 are depicted in Charts 3.4a, 3.4b and 3.4c.

[4] Reform of Direct Taxes

Even though there has been a sharp increase in the direct tax-GDP ratio in the 1990's, there continues to be large number of incentives and exemptions in the tax structure, which inhibit the realisation of the full revenue potential of direct taxes. Our recommendation on the direct taxes essentially relate to base expansion and rationalisation in the context of the Income Tax Act as it existed prior to its amendment by the Finance Act, 2001.

[A] Personal Income Tax

[i] Rates

Over the years, while progressivity of rate structure has been scaled back, the exemption limit has, however, been revised to exceed inflation thereby leaving more individuals below the tax net. Further, there has also been some "bracket creep" in that inflation has dragged taxpayers into higher tax brackets.

It was therefore recommended in the Interim Report that the maximum marginal rate of personal income tax rate be retained at 30 percent and the surcharge should be removed. Also, correction must be made to remove bracket creep from the structure by broadbasing the various brackets/slabs as indicated in (Table 4.2) even though it may lead to some revenue loss at existing levels of compliance. However, this should be done along with streamlining base erosion as explained below. While the Union Budget 2001-02 has removed the surcharge, the recommended adjustment in the tax slabs and brackets would still need to be followed up in the next budget.

[ii] Savings Incentives

The base of the personal income tax remains narrow for various reasons. One aspect is tax relief for savings in specified assets. The main provisions appear in Appendix Table 2.1. Tax credit is governed by Section 88, deductions by Section 80L, and exemptions by Sections 10(11) and 10(15) of the Income Tax Act, 1961. Also available are deductions under Section 80CCC, 80D, 80DD, 80DDB and 80E, exemptions from long term capital gains under Sections 54, 54B, 54D, 54EA and 54EB. Assets in incentive schemes are also exempt from wealth tax.

The scope of Section 88 has been expanded during the 1990s and the amount of tax rebate from Rs.10,000 in assessment year 1991-92 to Rs.16,000 in assessment year 2001-02. The rate at which the rebate is calculated is 20 per cent even though the lowest marginal tax rate is 10 per cent. The scope of Section 80L has been likewise increased and the maximum available deduction is Rs.15,000 in assessment year 2001-2002.

Taken together, the schemes do not comprise a rational whole and have built up in an ad hoc manner over time. Such schemes do not necessarily result in additional savings; rather, they encourage substitution. They have negative efficiency effects favouring debt financing, crowding out the private sector, discriminating against selected activities such as home construction out of taxed savings, and de-equalising rates of return on savings that have the same risk or holding period. For example, National Savings Certificates and provident funds enjoy deductibility of investment (Section 88) and of interest earnings (Section 80(L) or 10(11) or 10(12)), leading to inordinately high effective rates of return on these assets.

Overall, the incentives are also iniquitous in that the manner in which they are offered tends to favour the richer tax payers. For example, deductions from income under Sections 10 and 80L and the provisions relating to rollover of capital gains tax favour upper bracket tax payers disproportionately. Given the complexity of the savings incentives structure (Table 4.4), inequity also arises simply from asymmetric information available to the lower income earner.

It is recommended that, ideally, tax incentives under Sections 80CCC, 88, 80L and 10 (15) of the Income Tax Act be abolished, at least in phases as has already been initiated by the Union Budget 2001-02.; that tax concessions under Sections 80D, 80DD, 80DDB and 80E be given in the form of tax credit rather than as deduction from income (to improve equity); and the rollover provision relating to capital gains under Sections 54, 54B, 54D, 54EA and 54EB be removed. This reform should eventually enable further reduction in the overall tax rate structure that should enable improved savings behaviour by all tax payers.

[iii] External Borrowings

Section 10(15) provides for exemption of interest paid on external borrowings at a concessional rate. However, since the lender is subjected to tax in the country of his residence, it is doubtful whether the rates of interest are truly concessional. In effect, the revenue loss on these borrowings is a gain for the foreign countries' treasury. It was therefore recommended in the Interim Report that the exemption for interest on foreign borrowings should be withdrawn. The Union Budget 2001-02 has withdrawn this exemption for interest on ECB in respect of borrowings on or after June 1, 2001.

[iv] Income of Funds

Essentially, funds are in the nature of pass-throughs and therefore income received by them should be exempt, though the beneficiaries of the income should be subjected to tax. Keeping in view the administrative difficulty of collecting tax from millions of small beneficiaries, it is recommended that the income of the Funds should be subjected to tax at the lowest marginal rate of personal income tax, i.e., at 10 per cent.

[v] Foreign Income and Remuneration

There being no economic rationale for exempting remuneration received from international organisations, and reflecting the practice in several western countries, it is recommended that the provisions of Sections 10(8), 10(8A), 10(8B) and 10(9) be deleted.

[vi] Foreign Exchange Earnings/Exports of Goods and Services

The government's decision to phase out the various incentives for foreign exchange earnings/export of goods and services is a step in the right direction. However, the Group finds no justification in the continuation of the incentives under Section 10A and 10B since the international competitiveness of exports covered under Section 10A is greater than exports from outside the special economic zones. Similarly, the incentive under Section 10B is a premium on licensing. It is, therefore, recommended that the provisions of Section 10A and 10B be phased out.

[vii] Regional/Industrial Development

The tax incentives under Sections 80 IA and 80 IB of the Income Tax Act are inefficient and iniquitous. Empirical evidence also suggests that these have not significantly contributed to the industrial development of backward areas. It is, therefore, recommended that the provisions of Sections 80IA and 80IB be deleted.

[viii] Income from Salaries

The Group notes with some alarm that the Union Budget 2001-02 has, contrary to our recommendations in the Interim Report, raised the maximum level of the standard deduction to Rs. 30,000. While it is true that the level has oscillated over time, the level of Rs. 500 in 1974-75 would be equivalent to approximately Rs.5,000 in current terms. However, reflecting the changes in the Union Budget 2001-2002, it is imperative that the ceiling be brought down to Rs.15,000 in the next budget. This reflects the fact that, at present, transport allowance is being given as a separate deduction, which was not the case prior to assessment year 1998-99 and most employers provide at their expense the facilities of books and periodicals. Further, it cannot be overemphasised that the goal of resource mobilisation becomes more difficult to achieve with increasing base erosion.

[ix] Income from Self-occupied House Property

The present provision for allowing of interest deduction on borrowed capital for construction of a self-occupied house property should be discontinued since it is inconsistent with the matching principle for income determination. However, the Group is rather dismayed to note that contrary to its recommendations, the Union Budget 2001-02 has further enhanced the limit from Rs.1,00,000 to Rs.1,50,000.

[x] Charity and Non-profit Organisations

Under the Income Tax Act, donations to non-profit organisations (NPOs) are eligible for deduction under Section 80G and 80GGA from the gross total income. Since these are income-based deductions, these are iniquitous. Further, there has been a proliferation of NPOs in recent years. Numerous income tax exemptions in respect of their incomes are provided to them. Many of them are inefficient such as Sections 10 (23) (i) to (iii a) and (iii ab) to (iii ae) since there is no bar imposed on the distribution of net earnings. They are also anomalous and, possibly, iniquitous in that NPOs enjoying exemptions under Sections 10 (23) (iii ab) to (iii ae) coexist with for-profit organisations in their respective areas of operations. Also, the existing provisions produce tax subsidies that increase with income.

Though Sections 11 to 13 do restrict distribution, they overlap with Sections 10 (23) (iv) to (vi a) which do not restrict distribution. In any event, even if distribution of net earnings were restricted, there would be some inequity vis-a-vis for-profit enterprises because of the exemption itself. Further, no differentiation is made between donative and commercial NPOs.

It is recommended that, first, the income-based deduction for donations under Section 80G and 80GGA should be converted to a tax credit at the lowest marginal tax rate of 10 per cent – for equity reasons – without any limit as a fraction of gross income as set under Section 80G. Second, the exemptions under Section 10 and 11 to 13 of the Income-tax Act in respect of income of charitable trusts and institutions of various categories should be restricted only to donative NPOs, to be defined as those in which 90 per cent of the receipts are through donations. Third, the non-distribution constraint should be made explicit and universal.

[B] Corporate Income Tax

[i] Harmonisation of Personal and Corporate Income Taxes

If the corporate income tax rate is higher than the top personal income tax rate, it tends to lead to tax induced non-corporatisation of the business sector and less organised business activity. It is, therefore, recommended that the present corporate tax rate should not exceed the maximum marginal personal income tax. Hence, the corporate tax rate should be reduced to 30 per cent to bring it in line with the existing level of maximum marginal personal income tax. Further, we also recommend the abolition of the distribution tax on dividends and consequent reduction of the tax rate for foreign companies to the level recommended for domestic companies.

[ii] Minimum Alternate Tax for Companies

Corporate tax legislation all over the world, no matter how streamlined at the outset, becomes subject to a "creeping incrementalism" with respect to special concessions and provisions over time, typically through excessive depreciation allowances. This is because the corporate sector constitutes a focused interest group with financial backing. A group of so-called "zero tax companies" emerges. The result is a higher marginal tax rate for those caught in the tax net.

An indirect attack through presumptive taxation may become more successful than direct attempts to reduce concessions. Such indirect methods also reduce tax evasion. Further, transfer pricing practices by multinationals to optimise on cross-country differences in corporate tax rates become less profitable. A Minimum Alternate Tax (MAT) that targets the average tax liability across taxpayers is a method that allows to keep the marginal tax rate low.

Countries have used various bases for a MAT: Colombia on net worth, Argentina and Mexico on gross assets, Canada and the United States on exclusion of deductions, selected francophone African countries on sales, and so on. It is well known that a minimum tax based on gross assets has proved to be a good revenue earner and equitable across small and big corporations. It is also efficient in terms of reallocation of resources since non-performing companies, that are unable to pay the minimum tax in the medium term, would have to close down and reinvest capital in an area of comparative advantage. In India, however, it might be difficult to introduce given the authorities' restrictive exit policy for businesses.

As the statutory corporate tax rate has declined significantly since 1987, India has developed a history of presumptive taxation—Section 115J through Finance Act, 1987; Section 115JA through Finance Act, 1996; and the present Section 115JB through Finance Act, 2000, which provides for a minimum tax of 7.5 per cent on "book profit" (defined as commercial profit). A major shortcoming of the MAT is the fact that it continues to be on reported income, unmindful of the widely prevalent practice of under-reporting. The effective rate of corporate tax has been estimated to be around 21 per cent as against the statutory rate of 38.5 per cent.

"Book profit" – a flow concept – can be easily manipulated since it is amenable to accounting changes/practices and subject to the existing tax incentives. The base of the MAT could combine a stock and a flow to appropriately reflect a plausible taxable capacity of the company. Thus the Interim Report recommended that the 20 per cent dividend tax should be abolished. Instead, the MAT should be reconstituted as a tax equal to the aggregate of 0.75 per cent of adjusted net worth plus 10 per cent of the dividend distributed. The MAT should be allowed to be carried forward for setoff against future tax liability in excess of the MAT as provided in Section 115JAA. The adjusted net worth for tax purposes would be the average of capital employed as on the first day and the last day of the previous year. The definition of capital employed should be the same as was in the case of Section 80J of the Income Tax Act, 1961. The choice of adjusted net worth reflects administrative ease. Several judicial pronouncements exist on the definition of capital employed that would serve well to both taxpayers and the administration. While the 2001/02 Union Budget brought down the dividend tax rate to 10 per cent, no step was taken to restructure the MAT. This must be attempted in the next budget.

The proposed base would be efficient since, first, it is neutral between retained earnings and dividend distribution. To the extent dividends are distributed, currently they suffer a higher rate of tax in the year of distribution. In the proposed base, if the company chooses to retain its earnings it will be penalised by the capital market and still end up paying tax on it since it would result in an accretion to net worth. Second, the greater is the performance shortfall of a company, the greater is the excess of the implicit tax rate on income actual over the prevailing corporate tax rate.

The proposed base would be equitable since it would remove the bias through depreciation allowances in favour of the manufacturing sector vis-a-vis services. The stock-flow combination also protects base erosion from inflation. When net worth is eroded by inflation, the real tax loss is partly compensated by the capital gains tax paid by shareholders. (Recall the recommendations made to improve capital gains taxation). Further, if assets are revalued periodically, the increase is reflected in an increase in the net worth. If a company chooses otherwise, it will end up paying a substantially larger liability upon liquidation.

[C] Direct Tax Administration

The Department is currently in the process of restructuring to facilitate large scale induction of information technology (IT) and expects to mobilise Rs.10,000 crores from enhanced capability to address tax arrears and stopfilers. Over the last few years, several important steps have been taken to improve administration. They include: (1) expanding the universe of taxpayers from 12 million to 25 million, through a "one by six" scheme that requires any income earner who satisfies any of the six given criteria to register for income tax purposes; (2) extending the scheme of tax deduction at source (TDS) so that an increasing proportion of revenue comes from this source; and (3) a genuine effort towards improvement in the quality of taxpayers' service.

The Group recommends the following immediate reform measures in direct tax administration:

1 extend the pilot voice message system of Calcutta to other centres;

2 make available of forms and returns on floppy diskettes;

3 allow the tax administration to print forms in private presses;

4 develop a long term plan for non-discretionary information gathering;

5 notify the categories of transactions for which the Permanent Account Number (PAN) must be quoted;

6 refuse to accept taxpayer forms by the administration without the PAN;

7 replace the income tax clearance certificate system by the simple requirement of quoting of the PAN;

8 remove the deficiencies from the Taxpayer Master File to enable identification and notification of stopfilers;

9 write off arrears in cases where the identity of the taxpayer is not established beyond doubt;

10 maintain a credible minimum deterrence level by ensuring that a certain minimum percentage of taxpayers are scrutinised annually through a selection pattern that is secret and fair;

11 decentralise selected expenditures to local offices that are currently consolidated at the cost of efficiency at the Ministry of Finance level;

12 identify areas on which resources could be saved with the advent of IT;

13 require banks to furnish information regarding collection of taxes on a magnetic media;

14 provide computers to the staff members;

15 set up an inter-Ministerial Committee to oversee the time bound program for networking of all income tax offices across the country; and

16 specify clearly the rights & obligations of all parties and supporting institutions for greater accountability in the proposed MOU between government and the CBDT.

[5] Reform of Union Excises

The structure of excises levied at the central level has been simplified considerably over the last ten years. The number and level of rates have been reduced with the current central rate at 16 per cent. Credit/offset (referred to as CENVAT) is, in general, given for input tax. Nevertheless, many lacunae do remain in the overall structure, rendering it effectively complex and distorted. First, apart from the 16 per cent rate, there are ancillary rates. Second, the immediate credit for tax on capital goods has been staggered over two years from the current year. Third, exemptions continue to be given on a large scale many of which appear to exist on grounds of populism, and resulting in classification disputes and adverse administration. Thus much room remains for structural reform and improved revenue productivity.

[A] Duty Structure

Most goods are taxed at the main rate of 16 per cent. Higher rates existed until 2000-01: 40 per cent for panmasala, aerated water, chewing tobacco, and motor vehicles for less than six persons; 32 per cent for cosmetics and toiletries, tyres, polyester yarn, air conditioners, and motor vehicles for six-twelve persons; 24 per cent for cement, carpets and floor coverings, tiles, and two wheelers. These rates have now been combined at 32 per cent, a measure in the right direction. Others attract lower rates such as cotton and wool yarn and kerosene. Though the non-16 per cent rates pertain only to a selected number of goods, the administration of multiple rates is not amenable to financial control methods (based on a self removal procedure) that have primarily replaced physical controls. The creation of an additional rate of 4 per cent for selected items with an option to pay 16 per cent with input credit which were exempted earlier, in the 2001-02 budget has added some complexity into the system. A better method would have been to simply tax them at the 16 percent rate with input credit.

It was recommended in the Interim Report that a two-rate structure of 16 per cent together with a higher rate should be introduced. An increasing number of items were to be converged to fall under the 16 per cent rate to minimise classification problems. This would be economically desirable and administratively simple. The rates would have to be adjusted for inclusion of services in the CENVAT. The 2001-02 Union Budget has moved clearly towards a two-rate duty structure of 16 per cent and 32 per cent. However, the lingering lower rates of 4 per cent and 8 per cent should now be merged with 16 per cent in the next budget.

There is also a multiplicity of levies that include, apart from the excise rate structure, additional excise duty (goods of special importance) in lieu of sales tax on sugar, fabrics and tobacco; additional duty on motor spirit (petrol and diesel); additional duty on textiles and textile articles (fibres, yarn and fabric) under a subsidy scheme for "controlled cloth"; and cesses leviable under miscellaneous enactments.

Separate accounts are to be maintained for each of these levies, increasing administrative and compliance costs. It is difficult to work out effective tax rates since CENVAT credit is not given for all of them. There should be a single levy under the Central Excise Act. For example, conceptually there is no reason why a central excise duty could not be charged on textiles and sugar without jeopardising a state level sales tax on these items. This is what happens with all other goods.

[B] Base of Union Excises

The base of excise is manufacture. While many disputes have occurred over the definition of manufacture, the effective twin test is: (a) a new article should come into existence; and (b) it should be marketable. The current definition – that does not include activities that may be deemed to be manufacture such as labelling or printing a brand name – encourages segregation of manufacturing activities to avoid tax. It was recommended in the Interim Report that the definition of manufacture be widened to include the chain of value addition by or on behalf of the manufacturer (undertaken before marketing the product) to be charged to duty. The 2001-02 budget has accepted this principle though only in the case of branded garments. This now needs to be extended to other items like shoes, electrical gadgets etc.

The credit for CENVAT (earlier MODVAT) is given for tax paid on manufacture. In the case of credit/offset for tax paid on capital goods, the concept is goods "used in the factory of the manufacturer". This gives rise to less litigation than the concept "used in manufacture of final products" that is used for credit of tax paid on raw material. It is recommended that both capital goods and other inputs "used in the factory of the manufacturer" should be allowed CENVAT credit. Thus, capital goods and other inputs should not be distinguished for purposes of input tax credit.

While raw materials and capital goods both received input tax credit in the current year until 1999-2000, the credit for capital goods was staggered over two years from 2000-01 for no other than obvious revenue reasons. Therefore, input tax credit on capital goods should be immediately restored by giving the credit in the year of purchase itself.

The excise base is eroded by exemptions, inter alia, for: (a) small scale industry (SSI); (b) village industry marketed with KVIC assistance; (c) specified goods supplied to various types of public institutions; (d) goods produced without power; (e) cooperative society produced tea; (f) goods produced in the North-East[5]; (g) a number of food items including bread, spices, coffee, khandsari sugar, cereals, edible oils and several unbranded food items; (h) fertilisers; (i) unregistered branded garments, clocks, watches upto Rs.500, electric bulbs upto Rs.20; (j) aircraft, ship and boat; etc.

Further, the formulation of exemptions is extremely complex. Of the standard publication of tariffs of 720 pages, 220 pages are devoted to exemptions. There are 90 exemptions for textiles. For small scale industry, there are 5; for exports, there are 20; for job work, there are 5, and so on. Each exemption has many entries, conditions and lists, in turn, containing hundreds of items in each list.

The Interim Report had recommended that an intensive effort is necessary to rationalise exemptions on the same subject through abolition and merger. Conditions for exemptions must be minimised. When an item is covered under the SSI exemption scheme, there should not be any separate exemption except for some very valid reasons. SSI exemption should be extended to textiles also by replacing the individual exemptions. Overall, there has been no significant change in the area of exemptions.[6]

SSI units receive concessional duty as well as full CENVAT credit. SSI units below a turnover of Rs.3 crores should pay a duty of 85-90 per cent of the normal rate if they opt for CENVAT credit. The 3 crores turnover calculation should not exclude exports and exempted goods produced by a SSI unit. SSI units must maintain all records and give a declaration. Only really small units with a turnover of Rs.15-20 lakhs should be exempted from declaration/maintenance of records. The unutilised credit should lapse once the Rs.1 crores exemption limit is reached.

An important issue in expanding the base is the inclusion of services in the tax net through comprehensive taxation of services. It is important to integrate services as early as possible with the CENVAT to arrive at a full fledged VAT at the Centre, perhaps as early as in the Budget of 2002-03, rather than to continue with a separate structure of service taxation that cascades and causes economic distortions. The Centre should also allow states to tax services so that they can integrate services into their VAT base. A mechanism that would make this feasible is elaborated below (see Section 7e).

[C] Administration

While the VAT mechanism reduces tax induced economic distortions by reducing cascading (of "tax on tax"), the aspect of input tax credit tends to pose particular demands on administration. A substantially faster growth in MODVAT credit vis-á-vis growth in gross revenue has caused concern regarding potential misuse of MODVAT credit invoices. A field survey has indicated that, besides procedural and technical offenses, other violations included: (1) undervaluation of goods; (2) non-reversal of credit in respect of returned rejected inputs; (3) misuse of facility of job work; and (4) availing of credit on exempted final products; twice on the same invoice; without payment of duty; by using fraud/fake documents.

It appears that 10 per cent of revenue may be lost from these factors. There is also the perception that the exempted SSI sector exacerbates the misuse of CENVAT credit invoices. As the SSI sector has no interest in CENVAT credit invoices, the invoices relating to their purchases have been misused by the non-exempted sector. Thus rationalisation of SSI exemptions from CENVAT should check evasion over and above improving the excise structure.

While many procedural improvements have been made during the last decade, anomalies continue to bug the system. Some examples should suffice. Union excises are levied on transactions price i.e. the price paid or payable, in reflection of commercial considerations. However, when a good is sent from factory to depot or other places of removal, duty is paid at the factory gate on a value which is the transaction value at the depot/place of removal at or about the time the goods are cleared from the factory, though the goods in question may be sold from the depot at a different price at a later date. Therefore, the depot or other places of removal should be made into duty paying agencies, with accounts-based checks and audits at regular intervals.

The new procedure that has delinked duty payment from clearance is consistent with improved administration. The fortnightly payment requirement reflects the commitment of the authorities to move towards an accounts based system of administration and audit. The fortnightly payment should be replaced by monthly payment to enhance the liquidity of units and to reduce excessively stringent accounting needs.

Despite the move towards financial control, vestiges of physical restrictions remain. When goods are returned by buyer to seller, in certain circumstances, approval is necessary from the Chief Commissioner for re-entry of goods to the factory. This is time consuming and unnecessarily exacerbates the need for tax official – taxpayer contact. Reentry should be allowed on accounts based self declaration or simple intimation to the Department.

Manufacturers may acquire spare parts for use or they may resell them. For such trading activities, approval of the Department is needed which is generally not given. Resale should be allowed on the basis of maintenance of accounts and penalty imposed in case of misuse. On the whole, therefore, excise administration should complete its movement towards financial control from physical control based methods.

[6] Reform of Customs Duties

[A] Rates and Exemptions

The important challenge in customs tariffs is to reduce them to comparable international levels. The average effective rates (customs revenue as a per cent of the value of imports) in East Asia for example, were 5 per cent in Indonesia, 4 per cent in

Malaysia, 14.4 per cent in the Philippines, and 7.4 per cent in Thailand in 1995. In 1999, the average nominal customs tariff rates were 0 per cent in Hong Kong and Singapore, 9.5 per cent in Indonesia, 10.2 per cent in Malaysia, 10.7 per cent in the Philippines, and 17 per cent in Thailand.[7]

The median tariff rate in India is much higher. At 35 per cent, it is still among the highest in the world. This should be brought down to 25 per cent in the 2002-03 budget. Finance Ministers have previously indicated their intention to sequentially bring down the rates further, and of making them comparable to East Asian levels. The objective should now be to bring down the median tariff rate to 20 per cent in 2003-04 and 15 per cent in 2004-05. This would nevertheless be somewhat above the East Asian average (even ignoring the zero rate structures of Hong Kong and Singapore).

Accompanying reductions in exemptions should accommodate any loss in revenue and help meet the revenue objective assigned to customs duties in the Tenth Plan.[8] In any standard publication of the customs tariff structure containing 1150 pages, 400 are devoted to exemptions, further compounded by exemptions of other customs related duties.[9] As many exemptions as possible have to be removed. Relatedly, the countervailing duty (CVD) of 16 per cent should be levied uniformly – without exemptions.

[B] Export Valuation

While in the case of excises and imports transaction value has been introduced, in the case of export, the "deemed value" continues. This lack of uniformity has led to much confusion. Transaction value should be adopted since international prices vary from transaction to transaction. This is also supported by Article 1 of the WTO agreement. The change can be made by adding an explanation to Section 14(1) of the Customs Act.

[C] Treatment of Exports

There are many schemes for export promotion, remission, exemption and entitlement, including Duty Free Replenishment Certificate (DFRC), DEEC, Export Promotion Capital Goods (EPCG), export under bond, drawback, and special scheme for gem/jewellery/diamonds, Export Processing Zone etc. These tend to create problems for administration since they are linked to export obligations over a period of years. Some of them are superfluous when others exist. There is a need to evaluate if the duty foregone (35-40 per cent of export revenue) is compatible with export growth. There is no need for so many export promotion schemes. They need to be rationalised by combining them and removing the overlapping. For this, the authorities should immediately constitute a time-bound Expert Group to examine the schemes and recommend an appropriate scaling back.

[D] Administrative Matters

Many countries are beset with corruption in customs administration. This is worsened by a complex tariff structure since it encourages administrators to summon taxpayers for "explanation" of classification categories sought. Simplification of the tariff structure and computerisation of procedure seeking to reduce the customs official – taxpayer nexus have helped check the problem in many countries. In India, computerisation in customs administration is progressing and improvement is an ongoing process. Thus, as in the case of excises, the number of entries has increased.

Immediate improvements are possible in customs procedures. For example, delay in the clearance of imported cargo in airports and ports was reported by trade and industry. Delay increases cost of production, congestion, under-utilisation of port facility and corruption. Despite computerisation, it was found that, given 300 clearance documents per day, 18 percent were subjected to queries. Thus, of 54 queries in a single day, 42 per cent asked for catalogues, 25 per cent asked for provisional duty bond without indicating reason, and the rest for chemical tests and other documents.

In sum, the Fast Track Clearance Scheme (STCS) is highly restricted and has not produced the desired result on a sufficient scale. While in excise self removal scheme applies to everybody, the STCS is only for those with "unblemished record". To speed up clearance, based on examination of practices in Canada, Holland, the United Kingdom and the United States, and recalling that not many cases of large scale evasion have been detected by physical examination by the Customs over a period of time, only targeted goods should be checked on the basis of intelligence. Thus the intelligence collection machinery should be strengthened, while selective post audit should be based on computerised information. This will modernise customs administration and minimise the source of delay and abuse.

Provision for advance rulings on classification for Non-resident Indians (NRIs) has been enacted but it is fraught with judicial formalities. This could better be done by the Central Board of Excise and Customs (CBEC) which already has a sufficient stock of technical people to do this job. The CBEC should be allowed to give advance rulings. What is important is uniformity and certainty. Further, the advance rulings should be made available to all and not be restricted to NRIs.

Section 115B of the Excise Act and Section 12B of the Customs Act deny "refund in cases of unjust enrichment". Unjust enrichment is considered to be caused by a refund to a manufacturer (or importer) from the tax administration (based on a subsequent claim by the manufacturer) when a higher tax has already been realised by the manufacturer from his customers. The customers may be too numerous for the manufacturer to give refunds to them. This should not be a justification for the tax administration to keep the revenue. Hence, the provision to deny refunds to the manufacturer by the tax administration should be removed, and the law appropriately amended.

Finally, excessive litigation has been a major problem for both customs and excises particularly because a lot of revenue is held up because of it. While slow disposal by judiciary is also responsible for this, the following actions are recommended to stem the occurance of litigation: (a) simplification of MODVAT principles and procedures by allowing MODVAT credit on all goods except those in a negative list; (b) more explanations to be added to notifications to minimise doubts in interpretation; (c) introduce more definitions in the tariff; (d) department should file less appeals to the Tribunal and courts; (e) reduce remanding of cases; (f) exemptions should be reduced in number and conditions simplified; (g) issuing of protective demand should be stopped when assessment has been made under the order of the CBEC; (h) system of advance ruling should be made operative; and (I) the mindset prevailing now to err in favour of revenue should be changed in favour of effective rationalisation.

[7] Reform of the State Taxes and Introduction of VAT

The terms of reference of Group enjoin separate and explicit treatment of central and state level taxes. The Interim Report essentially focused on central taxes with only a brief mention of state taxes in its concluding chapter. We decided that a more detailed treatment of state taxes would be covered in the Final Report after acquiring first hand experience enabled through interaction with various state governments. Based on this and for the detailed reasons indicated in Chapter 6, the Group recommends the following:

[A] On Interim Reform of Sales Tax

1 While awaiting the introduction of a state-level VAT, a beginning should be made by streamlining the existing sales taxes further. Though states recently introduced floor rates for the sales tax, more can be achieved by abolishing the turnover tax and entry tax wherever they continue to exist, and reducing concessions and incentives from the prevailing sales tax structures.

[B] On an Integrated VAT

1 The Group's terms of reference require us to assess a comprehensive VAT whereby the central and state VAT stand integrated. To achieve this end, our proposal of a state level VAT would be for one that could co-exist with the present arrangement of the central VAT (or CENVAT). Thus central jurisdiction would give setoff only for central duties and state jurisdiction for state duties. Such a national integrated centre-state VAT arrangement can easily exist in parallel or dual format. However, respective tax jurisdictions (and administrations) would have to be careful about excluding the taxes paid to the other jurisdiction from the assessment of value bases.

[C] On Timing of VAT Introduction

1 The Group does not recommend VAT introduction by individual states in isolation. Rather, they should act in

unison on the issue.

[D] On State VAT Design

1 The next step on the agenda should be to move over to a state Value Added Tax (state VAT). The Empowered Committee of State Finance Ministers must decide expeditiously on the design of the VAT so that appropriate VAT legislation can be enacted and rules and regulation framed well before April 1, 2002. Similarly, the Committee of Commercial Tax Commissioners that has already been formed must decide on the various administrative issues relating to VAT like manner of registration, establishment of an efficient information system, collection, audit, taxpayer education, a system of penalties and appeal, training and computerisation.

2 Since income tax is already fairly well established in India, we recommend that states should adopt a consumption type VAT i.e. there should be no distinction between raw materials and capital goods in allowing VAT credit. Only this VAT variant is equivalent to a retail sales tax. The consumption base must be as wide as possible and must comprehensively include manufacturers and dealers of all goods indicated in sales tax schedules.

3 A two floor VAT rate structure in addition to the zero rate: one for essential commodities and another for all other items would be best.

4 The states must draw up a common exemption list.

5 Unprocessed food articles, life-saving drugs and commodities with negative externalities whose consumption needs to be checked should be exempted from state VAT.

6 All concessions with regard to the sales tax should be eliminated under the state VAT and benefits if any should be given only in exceptional circumstances through budget based subsidies.

7 Small dealers whose annual turnover does not exceed Rs. 15 lakh should be exempt from the liability of VAT but subjected to a sales tax of one per cent.

8 All international exports should be zero-rated.

9 Commodities with negative externalities whose consumption needs to be checked should, however, be subject to the Special Additional Tax (SAT) against which no input tax credit should be granted. The states must draw up a common list for the purposes of SAT and the number should not, in any case, exceed ten.

10 Luxuries should not be taxed under the SAT. Instead, it would be better to have a common, high, third VAT rate for luxuries.

11 States should refrain from designing SATs with the primary objective of maintaining revenue equivalence with selected commodities under the prevailing sales tax regime as this would defeat the very purpose of a noncascading VAT.

12 The local VAT rates should be close to uniform across states, reflecting the existing consensus on uniform floor rates. The two floor rates should be set with smaller states in mind that may need to have lower floor rates reflecting the particular characteristics of their production and distribution patterns, small size of consumption, geographical distance and lack of access to markets. To accommodate these states, the floor rates should be fixed at lower levels than what larger and economically more powerful states may want. That would enable the smaller states to operate at lower floor rates while the others would be obliged to operate at higher than floor rates, given their revenue needs. This would be better than enacting two sets of floor rates, one for smaller, and the other for larger states.

13 The VAT should be structured on the destination principle.

14 The computation of the VAT liability should be based on the credit method.

[E] On Treatment of Interstate Trade

1 A destination based VAT is recommended for the Indian state level VAT, which must remain the ultimate goal.

This could be achieved through an application of the "Versano method", named after the Brazilian expert who proposed it. In any VAT return, there would be two columns, one for intrastate transactions and one for interstate transactions, the latter to be taxed at a common rate by all states. The net VAT payable on interstate transactions would be remitted by every taxpayer to an overarching all-state administration, or to the central tax administration. The revenue would be distributed at the end of the period according to the consumption size of states. This is one example of the so-called "clearing house" mechanism that could be operated by the states themselves or by the Centre. However, the Group did not find any consensus among states regarding such a mechanism though it is not at all impossible to achieve.

2 The use of "C Forms" should not be a feature of the VAT.

3 The initial arrangement for the interstate segment of the VAT when introduced on April 1, 2002 should be a transitory alternative that eschews the difference between destination and origin states would be to require the granting of credit in a state whenever tax is collected. If an interstate sale took place from state B to state A, state B would collect the VAT on sale and also give the appropriate input credit on it. If, however, the good was sent on consignment from B to A, state A would collect the VAT reflecting that no sale took place in B and that any sale subsequent to the interstate transfer would take place only in A. Thus any applicable credit for input tax paid in state B would have to be given in state A. This would meet two elements of the VAT i.e. it would be a tax on consumption and it would remove cascading. But the revenue would accrue to the state where the sale takes place. Such an arrangement would also reflect international practice such as in the transitory arrangement in the European Union and regular practice in Brazil.

4 Consequently, the Central Sales Tax Act must also be abolished simultaneously.

5 If the Centre were to compensate states, it should not do so according to the origin principle in any event. A lasting solution would be to allow states to tax services and for the Centre to assist in building institutional capacity through modernisation of tax administration in the states.

[F] On VAT Administration

1 The administration of VAT on imports should continue to vest in the Customs and Excise Department under central government.

2 The central VAT should continue to be administered by the central customs and excise under the central government.

3 The state level commercial tax department should administer the VAT, which is proposed to replace the state level Sales tax. The VAT administration should be restructured – from the current sales tax administrative structure – into a functional classification based departmental organisation. The objective should be to enhance administrative efficiency and to minimise the taxpayer – tax administrator nexus. The organisation of the department should be based on return filing, selective audit/assessment, judicial interpretation, collection and investigation, anti-evasion and policy unit/VAT monitoring unit.

4 Since the income tax administration has established a system of Permanent Account Number (PAN), is otherwise engaged in collecting information relating to sale and purchase by taxpayers, and has the largest computerised network amongst the various tax administrations, the state level tax administration must co-ordinate and draw upon the same information to avoid duplication of effort and reduce compliance burden of taxpayers.

5 The entire process of computerisation of the tax administration both at the Center and the state levels should be treated as a separate project for augmenting the institutional capacity and not a mere exercise in office modernisation.

6 The central government must provide full financial assistance to the state level tax administrations, CBDT and the CBEC towards this institutional capacity building through computerisation and training (both domestic and foreign). For this purpose, an adequate provision under the Plan budget must be made.

7 The road map to administrative preparedness for the introduction of VAT in April 2002 is presented in Table 6.1.

[G] On Taxation of Services

1 An interim method that should enable states to tax services with cooperation from the Centre and without the need for a Constitutional amendment could be one where the Centre may levy the service tax on them and authorise the states to administer/collect them. However, the Centre and states must first arrive at a consensus on the list of services that can be administered by the states.

2 The service tax collected by the states would have to first go to the Consolidated Fund of India as per Article 266(2). After that, the Centre would disburse an equivalent amount to the states. This interim method has found favour with the Chief Ministers of states with whom the Group discussed the matter.

3 The states should be given the powers to tax services whose consumption is of an intrastate nature.

4 After the initial introduction, services could be incorporated into the VAT.

5 The rate structure for the VAT on services should be identical to those for goods to obviate distortions in producer and consumer decisions.

6 The state taxes like luxury and entertainment tax on restaurants, hotels and other lodgings, professions tax, motor vehicles tax, goods and passengers tax and electricity duty should be integrated with the state level VAT.

7 Various public utility services that have scope for

corporatisation should be brought within the state level VAT on services.

8 The VAT on services should be fully integrated with the VAT on goods, both in its design and administration, with an appropriate mechanism to setoff service input tax against goods output tax and vice versa. Therefore, a destination based, invoice credit method, dual VAT – one at the central level and another at the level of states – comprising both goods and services could be envisaged by the end of the Tenth Plan.

9 The assignment of the powers to tax services to states must be viewed as adequate compensation for revenue loss on account of abolition of the central sales tax.

[H] On State Excises on Liquor

1 There should be a two-part levy for liquor. The first part should be the excise component, which would be levied at the manufacturing level. This should be ad valorem and the base should be the Maximum Retail Price (MRP) and not the invoice price, which would be the MRP less trade discount. The second component should comprise regulation fee/charges, which could be based on an auction mechanism as has been done in some states.

[I] On Registration Fees

1 The registration fee should not exceed one percent of the value of the property registered.

[J] On Stamp Duties

1 In the transition, stamp duties have to be continued.

2 The existing multiple rates of stamp duty should be replaced by a single rate duty of five percent of the value of the property.

[K] On Motor Vehicles Tax and Goods and Passengers Tax

1 The motor vehicles tax should be merged with the state VAT. The VAT rate for all categories of motor vehicles (both commercial and personal vehicles) should be higher

by eight percentage points than the general commodity VAT rate.

2 To the extent the motor vehicle is used for personal purposes the VAT so paid will be on final consumption and accordingly, no input credit would be available to the owner of the vehicle. If the vehicle is used for commercial purposes, the VAT treatment will be same as in the case of any other capital good, i.e. the owner would be eligible to claim input credit.

3 Similarly, since the transport of goods and passenger results in consumption of services, the goods and passenger tax should be replaced by the service tax on carriage of goods and passengers and integrated into the state VAT.

4 The existing administration for goods and passenger tax should be abolished and merged with the state level VAT.

[L] On Profession Tax and Entertainment Duty

1 The ceiling on profession tax should be increased to Rs.5,000 immediately.

2 The profession tax should be merged with the VAT in the same way as the motor vehicles tax. The same argument holds also for entertainment duty.

Notes

1 Defined as percentage change in tax revenue as a proportion of percentage change in GDP. In practical terms, it may be estimated over a period of time by dividing the average annual growth in tax revenues by the average annual growth in GDP.

2 This is because, notwithstanding a greater effort assigned to the Centre with respect to the base year, the final effort as projected in 2006-07 for the Centre exceeds the 1989-90 levels by a smaller amount as compared to the states.

3 Nevertheless, indirect taxes continue to maintain a higher, though declining, share than direct taxes.

4 Thus, the sales tax maintains its 60 per cent share and so on.

5 Credit is given on inputs manufactured in the North East even though no duty is paid on such inputs. This is said to cause considerable leakage.

6 In the main notification which combines all exemptions for the different chapters (3/2001 Central Excise), there are now 262 entries while in the previous year's notification (6/2000), there were 259 entries. The list has, thus, expanded, though marginally.

7 In Latin American countries also, tariff rates have been slashed in the 1990s. For example, Chile has used a uniform tariff rate that has varied between 10–12 per cent reflecting revenue needs in recent years.

8 Indeed, in the 2001-02 budget, the number of rates has increased from 14 to 18. Above the median rate of 35 per cent, there are nearly ten rates, ranging from 40 per cent to 200 per cent. The recommended reductions in customs tariffs should target these high rates as well, though agriculture may need temporary special consideration.

9 This leads to much complexity in interpretation and to administration

Tax Reforms

Chelliah Committee Report - I

1992

Tax Reforms

Chelliah Committee Report - I

Guiding Principles of Tax Reform

The guiding principles underlying the tax reforms proposed by the Committee are as follows:

(a) The tax system and its burden must be acceptable to the citizens i.e. the potential taxpayers.

(b) Given our past experience and the present totality of circumstances affecting the tax system and its operation, it is better to have moderate rates with broader bases.

(c) While the tax structure should be progressive, it should not be such as to induce the generation of unaccounted income and wealth.

(d) The tax system must be rational from the economic point of view. For this purpose, the structure once established must remain stable unless and until the economic conditions undergo a radical transformation. Ad hoc changes from year to year will undermine rationality and reintroduce complications.

(e) The tax system and law should be as simple as possible; it should have the strictly limited objectives of raising revenues for the government in a fair and efficient manner, achieving redistribution and discouraging some industries and the use or consumption of some products as well as granting a reasonable degree of protection to domestic industries. A simple system will have only a limited number of rates and exemptions or deductions and give the least possible discretionary power to the tax officials

---

Summary of Chelliah Committee report tabled in Parliament on Feb. 29, 1992.

for interpreting the law.

(f) Methods of tax administration should be modernised and tax enforcement should be visibly improved.

(g) The tax reforms suggested should be fully, or at least nearly, revenue neutral in their totality; however, the system should become more income elastic.

Income Tax

Ideally, a single rate income-tax would be the simplest both for compliance and administrative reasons. However, for the present, the following tax rate schedule for different taxable entities is recommended.

(a) In the case of individuals, the exemption limit should be fixed at Rs 28,000. The marginal rates of tax (inclusive of surcharge, if any) should be: (i) 20 per cent for total income in the range of Rs 28,000 to Rs 50,000; (ii) 27.5 per cent for total income in the range of Rs 50,000 to 2,00,000; and (iii) 40 per cent for total income exceeding Rs 2,00,000.

(b) In the case of a Hindu Undivided Family the existing distinction between a "specified HUF" and "non-specified HUF" should continue. The rate schedule for nonspecified HUFs should be the same as recommended in the case of individuals. For specified HUFs, the exemption limit should continue at Rs 12,000. The marginal rates of tax (including surcharge, if any) should be 27.5 per cent for total income in the range of Rs. 12,000 to Rs. 1,00,000 and 40 per cent for total income exceeding Rs 1,00,000.

(c) In the case of local authorities, tax should be levied at a flat rate of 30 per cent.

(d) In the case of domestic companies, the tax rate (inclusive of surcharge) should, in the course of the next three years (i.e., by assessment year 1995-96), be reduced to the same level as the maximum marginal rate of tax (inclusive of surcharge) in the case of individuals i.e. 40 per cent. Further, the existing distinction between companies in which the public are substantially interested and companies in which the public are not substantially interested for the purposes of tax rate, should also be abolished within the next three years.

When the new scheme of taxation of partnership firms, AOP and BOI recommended in this report comes into operation there will be no need for prescribing a separate tax schedule for registered firms.

Complete integration of the incomes of both the spouses or, for that matter, all adult members in the family is not feasible or necessary. However, the existing safeguards in the income tax law for aggregation of incomes in the case of splitting of assets should continue with the modifications that all incomes of a minor other than wage income, should be aggregated with the total income of

(i) the parent having the higher income, where the total income of one parent or of both the parents happen to fall below the exemption limit for individuals.

(ii) any one of the parents at the option of the parents where the income of both the parents exceeds the exemption limit.

(iii) if over time the income of the parents, with whom the income of the minor was aggregated earlier, goes below the exemption limit the parent having the higher income.

(iv) the income of the minor arising from assets transfered to him or her by any one including his grand parents should be aggregated with the income of the parent as recommended above.

The following tax concessions now available under the income-tax Act should be abolished:

(a) exemption under Section 10(15) (ii) (c) in respect of interest on notified Relief Bonds.

(b) exemption under Section 10(15) (iv) (h) in respect of interest received from any public sector company in respect of notified bonds or debenture;

(c) exemption under Section 10(15) (iv) (i) in respect of interest received from Government deposits in notified scheme out of moneys due on account of retirement.

(d) deduction under Section 80-L in respect of income from specified sources.

The tax rebate allowed under section 88 for investment in provident fund, NSCs etc. should continue to be allowed at the entry point rate of tax but only for investment upto a reduced maximum level of Rs. 10,000. Further, the tax concession should be restricted to contributions to provident fund, life insurance policies and repayment of loans taken for purchase or construction of a residential house property.

The tax concession under Section 80-CCA for any investment in the Jeevan Dhara or Jevan Akshay annuity plans of the Life Insurance Corporation of India should be withdrawn. The tax concession under Section 80-CCB for investment in equity linked saving scheme should be abolished.

The existing ceiling of Rs. 40,000 for deposits in the National Savings Scheme under section 80-CCA should be increased to Rs 50,000.

The provisions of Section 35-AC, 35-CCA, 35-CCB and 80-GGA should be amalgamated with Section 80-G. The 100 per cent deduction at present allowable under Sections 35-AC, 35-CCA, 35-CCB and 80-GGA should be restricted to 50 per cent as in the case of deduction for other donations under Section 80-G. Further, deductions should be allowed only in respect of donations to an approved association/institution and not for expenditure incurred on an in-house programme.

The tax incentives under sections 80-HH, 80-HHA, 80-I, 80-IA, 80-JJ, 80-QQ and 80-QQA should be abolished with immediate effect. With the result the taxpayers would not henceforth be eligible for the tax benefits they have been enjoying under the above-mentioned provisions.

The provisions such as sections 80-HHC, 80-HHE, etc. need to be kept under review.

The rules for perquisite valuation of concessional rent accommodation or rent-free accommodation should be modified so as to remove the present distinction in perquisite valuation between employees of the Government, companies in the private sector and public sector and other autonomous bodies. The perquisite value of both the rent-free accommodation and concessional rent accommodation should be taken to be equal to twenty per cent of the salary or the expenditure incurred by the employer in providing housing, whichever is lower. This rule should be made applicable to all employees irrespective of whether the employee is in the private sector or in the public sector or in the Government. However, where the expenditure incurred by the employer in providing housing is fully recovered from the employee, the perquisite value should be taken to be nil. Further, the perquisite value should be taken to be nil in all cases where the annual income under the head Salary (excluding non-monetary benefits or amenities) does not exceed Rs 36,000.

The provision of clause (13A) of Section 10 of the I.T. Act providing for exemption of house-rent-allowance as per rule 2A should be abolished.

All taxpayers, whether enjoying a rent-free accommodation or concessional rent accommodation or in receipt of house rent allowance or receiving no such benefit on account of being self-employed should be entitled to relief under Section 80GG of the Income Tax Act for rent paid. For the purposes of computing relief under Section 80GG, 'rent paid' should mean the rent actually paid as increased by the amount of HRA that would otherwise have been admissible to the taxpayer. The existing provisions of Section 80GG of the I.T. Act should be modified to provide for deduction in respect of rent paid in excess of ten per cent of salary upto a maximum of twenty per cent. The limit of Rs. 1000 under Section 80GG of the I.T. Act should be removed. Further, since the income from a let-out property is taxable and the income from a self-occupied property is deemed to be nil, the benefit under this provision should not be available in any case where the taxpayer or his spouse or minor child or the Hindu Undivided family of which he is the Karta has a self-occupied property anywhere in India.

Where the expenditure incurred by the employer in providing housing to its employee is in excess of twenty per cent of the salary of the employee, such excess which remains uncaptured in the tax assessment of the employees, should be subject to a separate fringe benefit tax in the hands of the employer at the flat rate of 30 per cent. The tax so paid by the employer, however, should not be allowed a deduction in the computation of profits of the employer. The expenditure incurred by employer in providing housing to its employees should be the rent which a similar accommodation would realise in the same locality of actual rent paid if accommodation is hired by the employer or the municipal valuation in respect of the accommodation, whichever is higher.

At least, 80% of the leave travel allowance, home travel allowance, travel allowance on retirement, passage money and such other payments should be subjected to tax.

The allowances paid to legislators should be fully subjected to tax.

The exemption in respect of allowances covered under sub-clause (ii) of clause (14) of section 10 of the Income-Tax Act should not exceed 10 per cent of salary.

All loans given to the employee should be deemed to have been given at the rate of 12 per cent and any concession implicit in the interest actually charged should be treated as a fringe benefit and taxed accordingly. However, where the concessional interest loan is utilized for construction of a house property or any other income generating asset, the perquisite value of the concessional interest should also be allowed as a deduction in the computation of income from such house property or any other income generating asset.

The value of all other perquisites as contained in rule 3 of the Income-tax rule should be revised upward to take account of inflation since the values were last fixed or revised.

For purposes of computation of capital gains arising on the transfer of a capital asset -

(i) A long-term capital asset be defined to mean a capital asset transferred after one year from the end of the financial year in which the asset is acquired. To compute long-term capital gains, all long-term capital assets should be seemed to have been acquired on the last day of the financial year in question and transferred on the first day of the financial year in which the transfer takes place.

(ii) The cost of all assets acquired prior to cut-off date be converted into the value of the asset on the cut-off date. For the present, the existing cut-off date of 1.4.1974 should continue.

(iii) The value of the asset should be indexed for inflation for the subsequent period of holding in a manner described below.

(iv) The cost of acquisition of an asset or the value of the asset, as the case may be, should be increased by a cost-inflation index (CII), which should be equal to 75 per cent of the consumer price index for urban non-manual employees (CPI), for the entire period of holding or for the period reckoned from the specified cut-off date, respectively. Similarly, the cost of any improvement undertaken to the asset should also be inflation indexed using the CII.

(v) In the case of non-corporate taxpayers, long-term capital gains duly indexed will be subject to tax at the marginal rate applicable to the assessee in the concerned year subject to a maximum of 27.5 per cent. If income other than capital gains is below the general exemption limit the tax on long term capital gains will be applied to the excess of the sum of other income and long term capital gains over the exemption level. In the case of corporate assessees the indexed long term capital gains will be subject to a flat rate of 40 per cent. When the rate of tax on corporate profits is reduced to 40 per cent, as per our recommendations, the rate of tax on long-term capital gains for the corporate assessees should be fixed at 30 per cent.

(vi) In the case of firms, the income from capital gains should be apportioned among the partners in the ratio of their share in the partnership. This income should be treated as capital gains in the hands of the partner.

(vii) The roll-over provisions should be retained but the special exemptions granted under Sections 53 and 54E of the Income-Tax Act should be withdrawn. Roll-over relief should, however, be granted uniformly in each roll-over section of the Income-Tax Act in the following manner:

(a) The gain should be computed after adjusting the cost of acquisition and improvement by the cost inflation index as recommended earlier.

(b) The fraction of the capital gain that is allowed "roll-over" relief should be equal to the proportion formed by the cost of the newly purchased asset ("new asset") to the net sale consideration from the sale of existing asset ("old asset"). In the case of a new asset, capital gain should be reckoned as the sale price less the inflation adjusted cost of the old asset. The inflation adjusted cost of the old asset should however, be calculated for the entire period of holding of the new asset and the old asset. Where the old asset is acquired prior to the cut-off date, the cost of acquisition and the period of holding of the old asset should be reckoned to be respectively, the value of the old asset on the cut-off date and the period from the cut-off date.

(viii) The existing Capital Gains Accounts Scheme should be replaced by a simple scheme along the lines of a money-multiplier scheme promoted by some banks in the country.

(ix) The existing method for computing the period for re-investment with reference to the date of transfer should be replaced by a method whereby the period is computed with reference to the financial year in which the asset is transferred. Accordingly, the period specified for reinvestment should be either within the financial year immediately preceding or within two successive financial years immediately after the financial year in which the original asset is transferred.

(x) There is no necessity to make any further change in the existing scheme of allowing set-off of capital losses only against capital gains.

(xi) Capital loss should be computed after adjustment of the cost of the asset by the cost inflation index. Provisions relating to scaling down of long-term capital losses may, consequently, be deleted.

(xii) The existing provisions relating to tax treatment of capital gains from depreciable assets used for business or profession does not merit any change.

The existing provisions seeking to restrict the deductibility of certain expenses in business be reviewed and limits prescribed be revised. The restriction on the deductibility of certain expenses have been rationalised.

The deductions of Rs 3600 in respect of each residential unit forming part of a building for a period of five years from the date of completion of such a building at present allowable under second proviso to sub-section (1) of Section 23 of the Income-Tax Act should be withdrawn. Further, since the proposed lower rates of personal income tax will benefit also tax payers having income from house property, the deduction for construction of new residential units in a building completed prior to the implementation of this recommendation, an amount equal to 1/5th of the "annual value" of the property should be allowed as a statutory standard deduction for the aggregate expense on repair of the house property and collection of rent.

The number of years in which the interest on borrowed capital relating to pre-completion period that is allowed as a deduction in the computation of "income from house property" should be reduced from five to three.

In the case of partnership firms:

(a) The scheme of registration of firms for income tax purposes should be abolished. All firms should be treated alike for income tax.

(b) The existing separate tax on the income of the firm should be abolished. The firm should be required to calculate capital gains and its income other than capital gains separately. The income other than capital gains should be apportioned amongst the partners in the ratio of their share in the profits of the firm, for taxation in their hands at the appropriate income tax rates. In computing the income of the firm, it should be allowed, as against the present practice, to claim as a deduction any payment of interest, salary, bonus, commission or remuneration to any of its partners.

(c) Where new partners are admitted to the benefits of a partnership at any time during the accounting year after the end of the first three months, the share of the new partners in the profits of the firm should be ignored and profits should be apportioned amongst the old partners in the revised ratio of their share in the manner indicated in Chapter 6. However, this should only be in respect of the financial year in which the new partners have been admitted. This however will not apply when a firm is reconstituted on the death of a partner.

(d) Where a firm has any income from capital gains, it will be eligible to claim "roll-over" relief wherever permissible. Any capital gain (after allowing for the "roll-over" relief) or loss incurred by the firm should be apportioned amongst the partners in the ratio of their share in the profits of the firm. However, the partners should not be allowed any "roll-over" relief in respect of such share in the capital gains. The relief for "bunching" of gains should be allowed to be claimed by the partners in their personal assessments.

(e) All association persons and bodies of individuals should be taxed in the same manner as firms.

(f) Where the shares of partners in a firm or of members in the AOP or BOI are not specified, they should be presumed to be equal amongst them and no partner or member should be allowed to claim differently at any time in the future in respect of profits of the year for which such presumption is made.

(g) The firm or AOP or BOI should not be allowed any credit for the tax deducted at source from payments received by it. However, it should be allowed to apportion the same amongst its partners in the ratio of their share in its profits.

(h) The firm should be required to pay advance tax on behalf of partners in respect of the income of the partner from the firm and income from all other sources along the same lines as the facility available under sub-section (2), (2B) and (3) of Section 192, to both the employer and the employee, in respect of deduction of tax at source. The advance-tax paid by the firm on behalf of the partners should be deposited with the Central Government through a single challan. The firm should after the end of the previous year be required to submit separate annual statement regarding advance tax paid on behalf of the partners.

(i) Every firm should be required to issue a certificate to every partner indicating the amount of interest, salary, bonus, commission or remuneration paid by it, the share of the partner in the profits of the firm, the share of the partners in the tax deducted at source on payments received by the firm and the advance tax paid by the firm in respect of income of the partners.

(j) Notwithstanding the fact that there would be no tax liability on the part of the firms, AOPs and BOIs, they should be required to file their returns of income irrespective of their level of income. Where the firm files the return of income voluntarily but after the due date, they should be required to pay one-half per cent of the computed income of the firm subject to a minimum of Rs. 200, as a late fee for every month of default. If the returns is filed in response to a notice issued after the end of the assessment year and the firm has not deposited the deducted tax at source, in the appropriate manner, from payments made to the partners, the firm should be assessed to tax at the maximum marginal rate of tax for individuals and also be required to pay late fee as indicated above. In such a case, distribution of income in the partners' hands would not arise.

(k) In a case where the returned income of the firm is increased as a result of additions or disallowances, the difference between the assessed income and the income declared should be taxed at the maximum marginal rate in the hands of the firm but exempt from any additional tax liability in the hands of the partners. However, in case where loss is returned and where the additions made result in a reduction in the loss or in the computation of a positive income, the income or loss computed should be appropriated amongst the partners and consequential rectifications should be carried out in their tax assessments.

(l) The problem of "benamidar" partners should be tackled only by sustained investigation under the Benami (Prohibition) Act, 1988 without causing undue distortion in the tax structure. Where it is established that a partner in a firm is the benamidar of any other partner of the firm or is an undisclosed benamidar of an outsider and any one or more of the other partners know or had reasons to believe that it was so, the whole of the income of the firm (including any payment income to the partners) should be taxed at the maximum marginal rate.

In the case of co-operative societies:

(a) The deduction, presently available to cooperative societies under Section 80-P, in respect of whole of their profits from business, should be restricted only to 20 per cent of their profits. However, all other deductions under Section 80-P should be abolished.

(b) The income exemption limit for cooperative societies should be increased from the present level of Rs 10,000 to Rs 25,000.

(c) The total income of the cooperative society, in excess of the exemption limit, should be subjected to tax at the flat rate of

30 per cent.

For inducing traders and manufactures operating on a small scale but enjoying taxable income to make some contribution to income-tax, two simple schemes based on the presumptive approach are recommended. The first variant which we call the scheme of presumptive taxation envisages a very simple system under which one is required only to pay a lump-sum tax in lieu of income tax. This scheme will apply only to traders and manufacturers having total business turnover of between Rs 3 lakhs to 5 lakhs. Under the other scheme the net income of the taxpayer will be estimated as a specified percentage of the gross turnover in business (the percentages depending on the type of business activity). This we call the estimated income scheme (EIS). The specifications of the two schemes are outlined below:

(i) Presumptive Tax Scheme

Under this scheme, traders and manufactures deriving income from business should be allowed an option to pay tax in a lump-sum of Rs 1,000/- without filing any return if their total turnover in business happens to fall between Rs 3 lakhs to Rs 5 lakhs as estimated by themselves.

It is possible that even such small traders/producers have income from other sources like brokerage from commission agency, interest, dividend, property etc. The facility of this scheme should not be denied to them so long as income from these sources remains modest. For brokerage income, this limit may be fixed at Rs 25,000. But tax at the rate of 20% may be realised from such income without going through the process of aggregating such income with income from other heads. When the trader/producer has income from other sources, again the scheme would still be open to the trader or producer if the receipts from such other sources do not exceed Rs 10,000. Here receipts from other sources would include interest, dividend, property, salary etc. However, in such cases the tax payer should not be permitted to claim any refund of tax deducted at source on such receipts.

Taxpayers opting for this scheme should not, however, be allowed any deduction on account of savings incentives or any other provision of the Income-Tax Act. As mentioned earlier, no return need to be filed by persons opting for this scheme. Nor should they be required to make any advance payment of tax in instalments. It should suffice if they pay the tax in one lump-sum any time before the 15th of March during the accounting year.

(ii) Estimated Income Scheme (EIS)

Persons having business turnover of more than Rs 5 lakh or brokerage or commission receipts exceeding Rs 25,000 or receipts from other sources above Rs 10,000 should come under the alternative scheme, namely the Estimated Income Scheme (EIS). Under this scheme, net income from business will be presumed to be equal to-

(a) eight per cent of the turnover from trading or manufacturing operations.

(b) fifty per cent of the receipts from brokerage or commission.

(c) ten per cent of receipts from contracts relating to construction of roads, bridges, buildings, other public works and transporting. This is in line with the scheme of estimating income taxation for contractors as outlined.

(d) eighty per cent of receipts from other sources, being in the nature of interest, dividend, rent, export incentive schemes or any other receipt of similar nature.

'Receipts from other sources' for this purpose will not include any receipts falling under the head 'salaries' or income from house property or profits and gains from business or profession'. The income estimated in the aforesaid manner will be aggregated with income from profession and income under the heads like 'salaries' and 'house property', if any to determine the gross total income. Taxpayers opting for the scheme will be eligible for deductions allowed for savings and specified activities as may be available under the Income-Tax Act from time to time. The total income so computed should be subjected to tax at the appropriate rates. Unlike in the case of PTS, tax due under the EIS should be paid in advance in three instalments and the provisions in the Income-Tax Act relating to the payment of advance tax should apply. The EIS should, however, be restricted to persons whose turnover and or receipts do not exceed Rs 25 lakhs.

Further, a simple statement should be furnished by taxpayers coming under these schemes to the nearest income tax office. The challan and statement forms should be made available freely in all bank offices or branches, market committees, office of trade associations, etc.

For the first three years, the statements of turnover may be accepted without any question, unless there is strong evidence to the contrary.

Every attempt should be made to estimate the ratio separately for each separate activity and for different locations as has been done in Israel for the Takshivs. Once these ratios are set up they should be given wide publicity (subject to periodic revisions) so that they can be used for self-assessment by tax-payers having income from business on their own and also by tax officers as a check against gross understatement. In other words, these ratios can be used as benchmarks or guides for estimating business income where verifiable accounts are not maintained. Incomes computed on the basis of the ratios should be accepted without any question. Any variation above or below the norms so set up beyond say 10 per cent should be subjected to scrutiny and approval by the next higher official.

In order that the presumptive income approach suggested above for small enterprises does not come under any legal attack, it would be necessary to make the presumptions rebuttable.

In the case of contractors, 10 per cent of contract receipts from all contracts relating to construction of roads, bridges, buildings, other public works and transporting, should be presumed to be the income in such cases and the same should be formalised in law.

Efforts should be made to introduce the estimated income system on the basis of physical indices. A beginning may be made by prescribing that each truck with an interstate permit could be presumed to yield an income of Rs 4,000 per month. Similarly each truck with a State permit could be presumed to yield an income of Rs 3,000 per month.

Taxation of Wealth

The tax on wealth should be abolished in respect of all items of wealth other than those which can be regarded as unproductive forms of wealth or other items whose possession and use could legitimately be discouraged in the social interest.

The new scheme of net wealth tax should be as follows:

(a) An annual tax on the aggregate capital value, in excess of the specified exemption level, of the following items of wealth will be levied in the hands of individuals, Hindu undivided families, and all companies.

(b) The items on which wealth tax would be levied are: residential houses, motor cars other than those used in the business of running them on hire, bullions and jewellery (other than those used as stock-in-trade), yachts and boats and planes (other than those used for commercial purposes) and urban land.

(c) Residential houses should include all farm houses within 25 Kilometers from the local limits of any municipality or cantonment board.

(d) For the purpose, the valuation of the above items for wealth tax purposes would be according to the procedures now being adopted under the Wealth Tax Act. However, the rules regarding valuation of residential property would be required to be reexamined as there is a general feeling that these rules are a little too liberal. Simultaneously, efforts should be made to suitably adjust the rates of stamp duty on transfers of property and the level of municipal property tax. The objective should be that the total burden of all these taxes on property income should be reasonable.

(e) Any liability specifically incurred for acquiring the assets which are liable to wealth tax and charged against them will be deductible from the computed value of the assets before the tax is applied.

(f) The first Rs 15 lakhs of the net value of the taxable items of wealth will bear nil tax. Any excess of net value over that level will bear tax at one per cent of value.

(g) The existing provisions in the Wealth Tax Act will apply to taxable items of wealth transferred to members of one's family without adequate consideration. However, in line with our recommendation in respect of income of minor children, we recommend that the net value of the taxable items of wealth in the hands of any minor child should be aggregated with the net value of such assets of the parent whose taxable assets have a higher value if one or both of them are not liable to pay wealth tax and with the net value of the taxable assets of either parent if both of them are liable to pay the wealth tax.

(h) Although only items of wealth mentioned in (b) above will be subjected to wealth tax, all income tax payers whose gross total income exceeds Rs 1 lakh should be required to file a net wealth statement in the form indicated in Annexure to this Chapter. For this purpose, all assets should be valued at cost. The statement should form an integral part of the return of income. The statement need not give details of individual items of wealth, but only values of specified categories of wealth, e.g., equity shares and debentures, bank deposits and money invested in partnerships or in own business.

Net wealth tax should also be levied on the specified assets owned by all public and private sector companies. The wealth tax paid should not be allowed to be claimed as expense for income tax purposes.

Restructuring Import Tariff

The main elements of the programme of reform of import tariff should be:

a. Reduction of the general level of tariffs;

b. Reduction of the spread or dispersion of tariff rates;

c. Simplification of the tariff system;

d. Rationalisation of tariff rates, along with the abolition of numerous exemptions and concessions; and

e. Abolition of the practice of making changes in effective rates through notifications.

In the next four years, the general level of import tariff should be reduced by about 50 per cent, so that the import-weighted average rate of protective import duty comes down to about 45 per cent. In subsequent years, further reduction in duty rate should be attempted so that the average is brought down to about 25 per cent by 1998-99. Of the 50 per cent reduction in the average rate of nominal tariff to be achieved in the first phase of tariff reduction, 10 to 15 per cent reduction should be made in the next

Budget for 1992-93 and the remaining part of tariff reduction should be carried out in the years 1993-94 to 1995-96.

There is need to greatly simplify the tariff system. One step in this direction would be to combine the basic and auxiliary rates of customs duty into one protective rate.

Another step towards simplification of the tariff system is to reduce the multiplicity of rates. It should not be difficult to achieve in the coming years a rate structure of protective customs duties with only a small number of rates.

Where the rates are expressed on specific duty basis, or as specific cum ad valorem basis, the combined ad valorem incidence should be reviewed taking into account changes in the international prices.

There is also a case for reducing, and eventually removing end-use exemptions which cause tariff rates for the same product to differ among uses, with a few possible exceptions.

The practice of making changes in effective duty rates of customs through notifications should be done away with if any change in the statutory customs is to be made because of special circumstances such as a drastic change in the international price of imported goods, the change should be made only on the recommendation of the Tariff Commission, into which the BICP is proposed to be converted.

If the loss of customs revenue has to be kept under Rs 2000 crore, the maximum duty rate may be confined to 120 or 110 per cent. Choosing 120 per cent as the peak rate in the Budget for 1992-93 has the advantage that the net loss of customs revenue on account of lowering of the peak will be only about Rs 1000 crore, so that there would be scope for making other changes in the structure of the tariff rates.

A tariff reduction by ten percentage points be made for those items of basic metals, basic industrial chemicals and machinery, which are at present subject to a rate of duty in the range of 80 to 120 per cent.

Even after these changes are made, many commodities (nearly 50 per cent of the items) will be subject to a rate of protective customs duty of 100 per cent or more which is quite high in relation to the levels of tariff rates prevailing in most other developing countries. It should be noted further that a large part of capital goods imports and a number of important raw materials and intermediate goods are at present subject to a rate of duty in the range of 40 to 70 per cent. The tariff changes proposed for the next year will leave the duty rates of such items unchanged. Appropriate changes in the duty rates of those items will have to be made in the years 1993-94 to 1995-96. Substantial reduction in duty rates would be necessary also for items for which the rate of duty is at present 80 per cent or higher.

The average duty rate for capital goods should be reduced to 55 per cent by 1995-96.

The import-weighted average tariff rate for intermediate goods should be brought down to 45 per cent by 1995-96.

By 1995-96, the average tariff rate should be brought down to about 50 per cent and the peak rate to about 80 per cent in the years 1996-97 to 1998-99, tariff rates should be reduced further to bring down the average rate to around 25 per cent and the maximum rate to 50 per cent by 1998-99.

By 1998-99, all end-use exemptions should be removed with a few exceptions.

There are several anomalies in the duty structure and all such cases should be looked into and necessary corrections in duty rates made. In making the corrections, the broad structure of duty rates suggested for 1995-96 should be kept in view.

By 1998-99 a minimum rate of import tariff, say 10 per cent, should become generally applicable. A beginning should be made in this direction in the next budget.

Taxation of Domestically Produced Goods and Services

The indirect tax at the Central level should be broadly neutral in relation to production and consumption and should, in course of time, cover commodities and services. This means we should move towards VAT covering services and commodities. To make the VAT scheme simple and easily administerable, it should be levied at two or three rates, say, at 10, 15 or 20 per cent. The selective excise duty on non-essential consumption could be levied at 30, 40 or 50 per cent (This means that the maximum rate on a commodity will not exceed 50 per cent with a few exceptions like cigarettes).

There is a need to widen the tax base and extend the coverage of excise duties. The Committee has identified a number of commodities which could be brought under the excise net. Except Black & White T.V. sets which should bear duty at the rate of 20 per cent ad valorem, other commodities should be subjected to the minimum duty rate of 10 per cent ad valorem.

In respect of Ayurvedic and other indigenous systems of medicine, articles of plastics and ready-made garments which are recommended to be brought under excise net, the Simplified Assessment Procedure (SAP) scheme should be made applicable.

All end use based exemptions for inputs should be withdrawn and the minimum duty rate of 10 per cent ad valorem should be levied on such inputs. If it is not possible to withdraw all such exemptions immediately, this should be done gradually over a period of time when inputs and finished products will bear duty with the benefit of Modvat credit for inputs.

A new scheme, Simplified Assessment Procedure (SAP), should be introduced for goods covered under the general scheme of excise duty concession in respect of those small scale units whose turnover in the preceding year did not exceed Rs 30 lakh.

The proposed duty structure for small scale sector is as follows:

Slab *Rs. lakh*	*Proposed Duty*
0-15	Nil
15-25	2% of the turnover for units operating under SAP, for others, duty at normal rates minus 10% ad valorem subject to minimum duty of 5% ad valorem.
25-75	Duty at normal rate minus 10% ad valorem subject to a minimum duty rate of 5% ad valorem.
75-200	Duty at normal rate.

The following procedural relaxations should be allowed for

units operating under SAP.

i. No excise license would be required for such assessees.

ii. Duty shall be paid quarterly.

iii. The requirements of the filing of price lists and classification lists and of clearance of goods on gate passes will be waived. Records maintained for sales tax/income tax purposes shall be accepted for the purpose of verification of production figures and turnover in lieu of statutory Central excise records. The returns filed by the assessees shall be production figures and turnover in lieu of statutory Central excise records. The returns filed by the assessees shall be accepted without question with a provision for random audit.

iv. Investigation, enquiry or audit in these units shall be only with the approval of the Assistant Collector of Central Excise.

Since no duty paying documents will be issued for goods cleared under SAP, Modvat credit shall not be available.

The desirability of extending this scheme to other small scale units should be examined in the light of the experience gained while administering this procedure in respect of goods covered under the general scheme.

The subsidy in the form of notional higher credit available to industries using inputs covered under the general scheme should be withdrawn.

The present distinction in regard to the availability of concession, between brand name of trader or organised sector and that of the small-scale sector should be removed. All goods manufactured under the brand name of any person other than the manufacturer should be charged to normal duty. Corresponding amendments regarding branded goods may be made in the special schemes of exemption for the small-scale sector producing cosmetics and toilet preparations, air conditioners and refrigerators.

All exemption notifications should be subjected to a close scrutiny with a view to ascertaining whether these can be withdrawn. Where notifications prescribe effective rates of duty without any condition, such rates can be incorporated in the tariff after adjusting them in line with the proposed rate structure.

The power of granting exemptions from excise duty should be withdrawn. However, Government may retain the power of adjusting the rates of duty under very exceptional circumstances.

In a system of commodity taxation ad valorem duties are preferable to specific duties, particularly under Modvat regime. Switching over to ad valorem rates in respect of a number of commodities is, therefore, recommended. Simultaneously, rationalisation of the existing rates has also been suggested with a view to reducing multiplicity of rates. The ad valorem rates suggested for various items broadly conform to the duty slots in which the tariff is required to be structured in the long run. For administrative considerations, however, some commodities like, petroleum products, tobacco products and textiles, coffee, tea, marble, etc., may continue to have specific rates.

Where specific rates are retained, there should be a system of revising the rates every year to take into account price increases as represented by the relevant sectoral wholesale price index. While fixing ad valorem rates, goods falling within the same class should as far as possible be made to bear the same rate.

In certain cases like, coffee, tea and marble, the specific rates should be revised immediately since these rates have remained practically unchanged for a number of years while prices have gone up considerably.

As the Modvat or the value added tax system gets extended and becomes the main plank for raising revenue from domestically produced goods and services, it would be necessary to move over to a system of assessment on the basis of invoice value. However, for this to be possible and easily administerable it would be desirable to fulfil two conditions. First, there should be extension of value added tax from the manufacturing to the wholesale stage; this would considerably reduce attempts at under-valuation of products. Second, it would be necessary to give up the traditional method of administering excise on the basis of clearance of goods from the factory and move over to a system of assessment on the basis of periodic returns to be submitted by manufacturers. These are important changes and their feasibility would have to be studied in greater detail. The Committee does not, therefore, recommend a changeover to the system of assessment on the basis of invoice value at present. However, it is recommended that a beginning may be made, by way of experiment, with the use of invoice value for assessment of excise in respect of selected commodities which are largely eligible for Modvat in the sense that they are mostly sold to taxable manufacturers. Meanwhile, the question of extending the collection of Modvat to the wholesale stage must be taken up for active consideration.

The Committee recommends introduction of following methods of measurement of value:

(i) Where only a portion of the total produce is sold at the factory gate and the balance from the depots, it could be provided in the law that the assessment of the goods removed from the factory to the depots shall be made on the basis of the price at which the goods are sold from the depots after giving necessary abatement for the freight from the factory gate to the depots.

(ii) In case of goods covered under Standards of Weights and Measures (Package Commodities) Rules, 1977 the maximum retail price can be taken as a basis for devising the measure for levy of excise duty. The rate can be applied on a value worked out after giving an abatement for various taxes and other items which are not to be included in the assessable value. Such abatement by its very nature cannot be very exact and would vary from commodity to commodity. The quantum of abatement could be worked out in a fair manner in consultation with the manufacturers' associations.

A Directorate of Valuation should be created which will be responsible for closely monitoring the movement of prices of goods produced by individual manufacturers especially in those cases where the revenue implications are large. The responsibility of having consultations with the manufacturers' associations in regard to fixation of the quantum of abatement from the retail price, the work of fixation of tariff value, etc, should also be entrusted to this Directorate. On the basis of studies of this Directorate, Government could take a decision in regard to addition to or deletion from the list of commodities which are assessed to duty on the basis of tariff value or retail price.

The valuation method should be simple and fair so that by and large manufacturers are not provoked to take up the issues to the courts and at the same time the unscrupulous elements do not make this as a gateway for evasion. Ultimately, the department will have to adopt invoice value for assessment and carry out the needed changes in procedures.

The Committee envisages that the Union excise on commodities gets gradually transformed into a value added tax at the manufacturing level, the services tax will get woven into that system and, therefore, tax could be levied also on services that enter into the productive processes.

The Committee recommended that a tax be levied for the present on the following services:

(a) Advertising services,

(b) Services of stock brokers,

(c) Services of automobile insurance,

(d) Services of insurance of residential property, personal effect and jewellery and

(e) Residential telephone services.

In all the cases above except for telephone services, the tax will be levied at 10 per cent of the value of the transaction. In the case of telephone services, an annual telephone service tax on every residential telephone connection of Rs 1,000 shall be levied.

The Centre should work out a package measures with the States that would represent a just compromise of the interests of the individual States and those of the Union as a whole. The enactment of the law imposing the consignment tax should be one of the measures.

The harmful effects of the inter-State sales tax-cum-consignment tax can be avoided or minimised in two different ways. The first and the more satisfactory arrangement would be as follows: (a) The inter-State or Central sales tax or the consignment tax imposed by the exporting State will be given credit by the importing State against the sales tax payable to it by the "importer" (b) The exporting State will credit the inter-State sales tax and consignment tax collections to a Central pool. (c) Thus all collections of these two taxes will be deposited in the Central pool and will be then shared among the States on the basis of an agreed formula. The formula should be so devised as to give even treatment to the producing and consuming States. (d) The rate of inter-State sales and consignment taxes would be two per cent. The second best arrangement could be that the consignment tax would be imposed at one per cent after the ceiling rate of the Central sales tax has been reduced to one per cent.

Issues Relating Tax Administration and Procedure

Appeals should be provided against any adjustment made under Section 143(1)(a) of the Income-Tax Act.

A Tariff Guide should be issued giving the classification of all commodities currently manufactured in the country and the classification given therein which would be in line with the established practice should be made on the basis of the decisions of the Board. This arrangement should be brought about simultaneously with the setting up of the computer network among all the Collectorates.

The Committee would urge that the pace of implementation of the computerisation project in the Customs and Excise Department should be accelerated.

Tax Reforms

Chelliah Committee Report - II

1993

Tax Reforms Committee Final Report

(Part II)

Chelliah Committee report on Tax Reforms Part II gives the committee's final recommendations on the changes to be effected in the duty structure relating to specific group of industries and the time period within which changes should be brought about. The report also deals with the restructuring of excise duties and review of exemption notifications in the import tariff. The basic recommendations relating to import duty reduction and the concluding remarks of the report are reproduced below.

BASIC CONSIDERATIONS RELATING TO IMPORT DUTY REDUCTION

The Objectives

In our Interim Report, we had given a fairly detailed description of the very complex and economically irrational import tariff system prevalent in India. The very high or high rates applicable to most commodities, the multiplicity of statutory rates, the wide spread of rates and the continued issue of a large number of exemption or concessional rate notifications not only made the administration of the system extremely complicated, but led to unintended and undesirable effects on the allocation of resources in the economy. All of this was documented in the Interim Report (Paragraphs 4.28 to 4.30 and Paragraphs 8.2 to 8.5). Further, there is general agreement now that the import tariff system should be drastically simplified, the levels and spread of the rates of duty must be reduced significantly, and as early as possible with the re-structuring of the duties, most of the notifications must be eliminated. We will, in this Chapter, discuss some broad aspects that should weigh in shaping the Tariff struture in the next three or four years. The questions that need to be answered are:

a. What should be the guiding principles for initiating and bringing about duty reductions?

b. What should be the structure of rates at the end of the reform period and what economic principles should determine this structure? and,

c. What should be the time period by which the reform should be completed?

In what follows, we attempt to provide answers to these questions. Before we take up these and related matters, we would like to urge that, in accordance with our recommendation in the Interim Report (Para 8.16), basic and auxiliary duties should be combined into one protective duty for a given commodity. It could have been argued earlier that the arrangement for preferential rates of duty with some developing countries stood in the way of such a merger. However, according to the decision already taken by the Government, the preferential rates of duty under the GATT Protocol and the Tripartite Agreement will cease to be applicable after March, 1993. In the case of the remaining preferential trading arrangements, the rate applicable should be the single rate emerging on combining the basic and auxiliary duties.

Degree of Protection in 1992-93 as Compared to That in 1986-87

In the Interim Report (Para 8.5), we had pointed out that between 1980-81 and 1989-90, the trade-weighted real effective exchange rate of the rupee depreciated by about 28 per cent and that the import-weighted average rate of import duty increased from 38 per cent to 87 per cent during the same period. This meant that the level of protection, quite clearly the nominal rate of protection, enjoyed by Indian industries went up substantially. The increase in the same average duty for manufactured products during this period was from 38 per cent to 98 per cent. "Thus, compared to the average level of nominal protection enjoyed by Indian manufacturing in 1980-81 (which was already high), the average level of nominal protection of Indian manufacturing in

1989-90 was higher by about 88 percentage points" (Interim Report, p. 95).[1]

We note that the real effective exchange rate depreciation in the 7-year period between 1985-86 and 1992-93 has been much greater than during the earlier period considered. This means that Indian industry in general is getting, as of 1992-93, a much higher nominal rate of protection than in the early 1980's. We have, for our purposes, gone only as far back as 1985-86. As Table 2.1 shows, the import-weighted real exchange rate appreciation of the basket of four major currencies has been of the order of 135 per cent between 1985-86 and 1992-93. In other words, the real exchange rate of the rupee has depreciated by 57.45 per cent during the period. Hence, the nominal rate of protection, other things remaining the same, would have increased to an undesirably large extent. Even if we take 1986-87 as the base, the appreciation is seen to be to the extent of 105 per cent. However, duty reductions and fall in international prices in respect of particular commodities, increases in input costs higher than the general rate of domestic inflation and any increases in the duty rates on imported inputs of the concerned commodities, would have partially neutralised the increase in the nominal rate of protection. Nevertheless, the increase in the nominal rate of protection due to the depreciation in the external value of the rupee has been so great that the net increase in the nominal rate of protection is bound to be substantial in most cases. And wherever the proportion of the cost of imported inputs to total costs is small, the effective rate of protection would also have risen substantially.

Table 2.2 gives the nominal tariff rates applied to 50 imported items in six different groups of commodities in the years 1986-87[2] and 1992-93. It will be seen that there have been substantial percentage point reductions in rates of duty between the two years in the case of a number of items. However, as the figures under the heading (4) in the table show, because of the depreciation in the external value of the rupee, the nominal rate of protection given, other things remaining the same, has increased in all cases. Thus, for example, in the case of item 3, DMT, the degree of protection has increased by 48 per cent in 1992-93 as compared to 1986-87, if only the depreciation in the external value of the rupee and the change in the import duty rate are taken into account.

Thus although the duty has been reduced from 190 per cent to 110 per cent, it is as though the duty is now 330.5 per cent with unchanged exchange rate.[3] Hence even a duty reduction by 50 percentage points would still leave the commodity well "protected", since the international price of the commodity has not fallen in relation to the price level in 1986-87.[4] If duty reductions are applied to most commodities, then the effective rate of protection will also be maintained at the higher level.

The tables and the inferences drawn from them are merely intended to demonstrate that an across the board duty reduction by a fairly substantial margin would not in general hurt Indian industry. This is more true now than when the Interim Report was written and submitted (December, 1991). Having said this, it must be pointed out that in working out the desirable and feasible extent of import duty reduction in respect of different commodities, we have taken into account the international prices in rupees and have worked out the cif prices or taken the cif prices as furnished to us by the industry. Wherever possible, we have obtained domestic costs and in some cases studied the extent to which these costs are affected by high import duties on imported inputs. We have then worked out "the implicit tariff rate" which would equate the international price and the estimated, or in some cases, prevailing domestic prices.

In arriving at the extent of reduction in the import duty rates, we have taken into account as many relevant factors as possible. As far as domestic industries are concerned, we have tried to ensure that they would not be hurt and would be given adequate time for adjustment. For this purpose we have kept in mind the inherent disadvantages from which varying types of Indian industrial units suffer because of the general inefficiencies in the economy such as higher interest costs, power cuts, lack of efficient infrastructure and cascading types of State and local taxes. All these disadvantages cannot be precisely quantified in monetary terms. Nevertheless, we have attempted to form a broad idea of the extent of cost disadvantage that could be said to arise at the present time. Of course, as the reform process proceeds, these disadvantages would be gradually reduced.

The Structure of Duties

Many economists would argue that it would be best to have only one (ad valorem) rate of import duty. Apart from achieving administrative ease, this would least hinder the allocation of resources for domestic production by the market forces. In addition to the single rate, a surcharge or additional duty could be imposed on the products of a new or infant industry, which might not be able to withstand competition from established foreign producers, until it achieves scale economies and establishes itself firmly with a proper marketing framework, etc. Such a surcharge or additional duty would have to be subject to a "sunset" provision whereby the extra protection will be removed within a period of, say, 5-7 years.

The prescription of a single import duty rate is given on the premise that national economic policy need not really concern itself with the pattern of industrialisation and need not, or should not, discriminate as between final products, capital goods, raw materials and intermediates. But tariff policy should have some relation to the stage of development and in a developing country, while the market should have a large role to play, the structure of import duties should be used to achieve the longer term goals of industrialisation and to further the strategy of dealing with the world market. We note that except for one developing country, namely, Chile, at least a few import duty rates prevail in all other developing countries that we have looked at.

We take as datum the fact that petroleum products and agricultural products are subject to quantitative restrictions and that the imports of non-essential goods are banned except when they come as part of baggage. We shall have to deal with these three classes of goods separately. As for the others, as indicated in the Interim Report (Para 8.22), the basic duty rate structure suggested in the Long Term Fiscal Policy Document (1985) could be taken as providing the guiding principles. Accordingly, we are recommending that essential goods such as inputs for fertiliser and newsprint should be subject to very low rate of 5 per cent, a low rate of 10 to 15 per cent should apply to basic raw materials such as metals, the next higher rung of rates to capital goods and parts and slightly higher rates to chemical intermediates. Final products will attract the highest rate of duty of 30 per cent.

In the Interim Report we had envisaged that the task of restructuring the import duties could be completed by the year 1998-99, when the average rate of duty could be brought down to around 25 per cent (Para 8.47). We had not then anticipated the shift to partial convertibility and the consequent further depreciation in the value of the rupee and the corresponding increase in the cost of most imports. We had, therefore, envisaged a somewhat longer period within which restructuring of import duties should be achieved than what seems called for now. We now feel that the basic reform of the tariff structure could be completed by 1996-97 or latest by 1997-98. By that time the import weighted average rate of duties should have come down to around 25 per cent (excluding any zero rated commodities, but including consumer goods).

While we have ruled out a single duty rate regime, we are clearly in favour of having only a very limited number of rates and of abolishing the zero rate in course of time. A large number of rates not only create administrative problems, but leads to non-transparency in the degrees of effective protection given to different products as well as to distortions in the allocation of resources. By keeping only a limited number of rates, we shall render administration of the tariff a fairly easy task, and by limiting the spread, we shall minimise distortions. The structure of duties will be such as to encourage value addition activities and to ensure that products at later stages are not subjected to negative effective rate of protection. In the Chapters that follow, which deal with different groups of products, we are applying the above-mentioned principles to determine the appropriate rates. We are recommending that by 1997 or 1998 March end, the structure of ad valorem rates of duties in place should be: 5, 10, 15, 20, 25 and 30. In addition, when non-essential consumer goods are allowed to be imported, there should be another "slot" for them, namely, 50 per cent.

In the Interim Report, we had suggested that all goods should be subject at least to a minimum tariff. Even if the goods are essential and/or their imports are restricted, there is no reason why the domestic producers of those goods should not be entitled to any protection. We suggest that the minimum of rate of 5 per cent should be applied to those that are now exempt. It may not be possible, for some reasons, to apply immediately this rate to fertiliser and ammonia and phosphoric acid used in the manufacture of fertilizer. Even these commodities should be made subject to duty at the earliest possible opportunity.

We may, at this stage, point out the necessary consequences of exempting the capital goods and inputs for the fertiliser industry from all import duty. This means that while substantial protection is being extended to most industries, industries producing machinery, parts of machinery and inputs for the fertiliser industry will receive no protection at all. A necessary consequence of this is that domestic production of these goods would be discouraged; and a probable long-term consequence will be that we shall become largely dependent on imports in respect of machinery and inputs for the fertiliser industry. These are not desirable consequences.

Anti-dumping

A number of complaints have been received in recent years from the domestic producers alleging the adoption of the unfair trade practice of dumping by some foreign exporters. In a low tariff regime that we are recommending, it is essential that provision is made to see that the domestic industry does not fall a victim to such unfair practices.

The Indian law relating to anti-dumping has adopted GATT guidelines and would appear to be an adequately powerful weapon. The effectiveness of this weapon, however, is considerably lessened because of the lengthy procedure involved in initiating the proceedings and completing the investigation to arrive at the final findings. No doubt, the Customs Tariff (Identification, Assessment and Collection of Duty or Additional Duty on Dumped Articles and for Determination of Injury) Rules, 1985 provide a time-limit of one year from the date of initiating of an investigation (or within an extended period in exceptional cases) to give the final findings and a time-limit of six months of the publication of final findigs for imposition of duty. We are of the view that these time-limits are too long and could be curtailed, though we do appreciate that by their very nature, such investigations are time-consuming. We would suggest that the time-limit for giving the final findings could be reduced to six months and the time-limit for imposition of duty to three months.

The Rules provide for the imposition of provisional duty at any time, after a preliminary finding that there is dumping in respect of articles which are the subject matter of investigation. This provision should be invariably made use of where the final findings are not likely to be arrived at within a month or two of the preliminary finding.

We also feel that the machinery for dealing with anti-dumping matters needs to be strengthened.

Levy of Surcharge

Where international prices dip steeply (not due to dumping), say, by as much as 25 per cent or so, a regulatory duty may be imposed for a specified period of time so that the domestic industry is given an opportunity to adjust itself. The regulatory duty may be expressed in specific terms and may be withdrawn, once the prices reach the "normal" level. The period in any case should not be more than a year; in other words, if the lower level has come to prevail, Indian industry should adjust itself to it, and the consumer should be allowed to benefit from it.

Additional or special protection can be given for a specified period to a new industry to be established or a new product to be launched through a new technology in strategic area. Such protection could be through an additional duty, say, not exceeding 25 per cent of the basic duty to be in force for a period of 5 to 7 years, as may be determined.

Advance Licensing for Exporters

Because of the inherent disadvantages suffered by Indian industry due to the inefficiencies present in the economy, including those attributable to irrationalities in the tax system, it is not possible to reduce import duty rates to very low levels as in some other developing countries. Hence, the system of advance licensing for exporters should continue. Furthermore, since there is no remission of duty on capital goods for exports, it is necessary that the import duty on capital goods should be brought down according to our recommendations.

As the structural reform process continues, the inefficiencies and cost disadvantages would gradually diminish. We would urge that Government should take steps to remove infrastructural deficiencies quickly. Equally important is the improvement in the movement of goods which are now subject to delays caused by some of the policies of the State Government and local authorities. It is also extremely important that State and local indirect taxes must be reformed so that they do not add to the cost of production, thereby hindering export effort and preventing the lowering of import tariff.

The Nominal Exchange Rate (NER) against any foreign currency is the number of Indian rupees needed to obtain a unit of that foreign currency. In a dual exchange rate system, as prevails in India at present, more than one nominal exchange rate may co-exist. In computations made, market exchange rates have been used as these are the rates relevant to the majority of imports, the focus of this exercise.

The Real Exchange Rate (RER) against any foreign currency is the number of Indian rupees needed to obtain a unit of that foreign currency after correcting for erosion in the value of both currencies due to inflation. If I_i and I_f are, respectively, the (cumulative) Indian an foreign inflation relative to a chosen base year, then RER = NER x $(1+I_f)/(1+I_i)$. The price indices used should ideally be for tradeable goods relevant to the group being studied (in this case importers). Due to data limitations, wholesale or producer price indices have been used.[5]

When the RER (or NER) of any year is divided by the RER of the chosen base year, the *real depreciation of the Indian rupee against the foreign currency*, that has occurred since the chosen base year, is obtained. Similarly, if relative inflation rates are not taken into account, *nominal exchange rate depreciation* is obtained. Table 1A and 1B provide estimates of real and nominal exchange rate depreciation in the value of the Indian rupee against the Pound Sterling, the US Dollar, the Deutsche (German) Mark and the Japanese Yen. Figures show the depreciation that has occurred by 1992-93 since each of the (base) years indicated in the first column.[6]

The weighted average of the RER or the NER across countries gives the *Real Effective Exchange Rate (REER)* and the *Nominal Effective Exchange Rate (NEER)* of the rupee. The weights chosen should be relevant to the group being studied. Clearly, import weights (that is the bilateral import shares of import originating countries) should be taken in this exercise. The weights used are the average import shares (among the four countries considered) for the three year period 1988-89 to 1990-91.[7] Export and trade Weighted indices are also reported in Table 1 for comparison. The percentage weights are given below along with the share of the four countries (the UK, the US, Germany and Japan) in total imports, exports or trade.

Weights	*Pound Sterling*	*US Dollar*	*Deutsche Mark*	*Japanese Yen*	*4-country share in total*
Import	21.69	32.93	22.59	22.80	36.18
Export	15.36	41.90	17.37	25.37	39.18
Trade	18.87	36.91	20.27	23.94	37.47

Concluding Remarks

Table 12.1, brings together our recommendations on the structure of tariff rates to be brought into existence by 1997-98, or if possible, by 1996-97, for the major commodities in the various groups considered in this report. The duty rates on other items which we have not considered specifically in the preceding chapters could be dovetailed with the general pattern of rates indicated in the aforesaid Table. It will be seen that the structure implements the guiding principles with which we started. The rates on finished products are kept distinctly higher than on the basic raw materials, and the rates of duty on components and machinery come in between. This structure is intended to encourage value addition activites at home, while the fairly low rates on the metals and the other basic raw materials will serve to keep the costs of production low throughout the economy. At the same time, we have endeavoured to ensure that the industries producing all the raw materials and components and machinery would be reasonably protected so that backward integration will not be hindered and that India will continue to have a diversified industrial economy.

Table 2.2

Effect of Import Duty and Real Effective Exchange Rate Changes on the Real Landed Cost of Import of Selected Items

Description of Product/Product Category	Nominal tariff rate as a percentage of cif price* 1986-87	Nominal tariff rate as a percentage of cif price* 1992-93	Tariff mark-up in 1992-93 as a %age tarrif mark-up in 1986-87	Real landed cost of imports in 1992-93 as a %age of real landed cost of imports in 1986-87	Tariff rate for 1992-93 giving the same real landed cost of imports in 1986-87
	(1)	(2)	(3)	(4)	(5)
Chemicals and Minerals					
1. Naphtha	0	0	100	205	- 51
2. Propylene	110	80	86	176	2
3. Dimethyl Teraphthalate (DMT)	190	110	72	148	41
4. Monoethyl glycol (MEG)	110	110	100	205	2
5. Caprolactum	90	50	79	162	- 7
Polymers and Plastics					
6. Low Density Polyethylene (LDPE)	120	63	74	152	7
7. High Density Polyethylene (HDPE)	100	64	82	168	-2
8. Polypropylene	100	80	90	184	-2
9. Polyvinyl chloride (PVC)	75	41	81	165	-15
Iron and Steel					
10. Pig Iron	65	35	82	168	-20
11. Iron Bars & Rods	100	105	102	210	-2
12. Iron and Steel Structurals	100	105	102	210	-2
13. Hot Rolled Iron Coils	100	57	78	161	-2

	(1)	(2)	(3)	(4)	(5)
14. Cold Rolled Iron Coils	140	95	81	167	17
15. Galvanised Plain (GP) Sheets	140	110	88	179	17
16. Tinplate	95	85	95	194	-5
17. Tin Mill Black Plate (TMBP) Coils	100	50	75	154	-2
18. Steel Billets	55	45	94	192	-24
19. Steel Melting Scrap	25	10	88	180	-39
20. Specified Alloy Steels	80	90	106	216	-12
Non-Ferrous Metals					
21. Copper Wire Rods and Bars	75	54	88	180	-15
22. Unwrought Nickel	80	60	89	182	-12
23. Unwrought Aluminium Ingots	50	35	90	184	-27
24. Other Unwrought Aluminium	90	105	108	221	-7
25. Unwrought Tin	80	85	103	211	-12
26. Unwrought Zinc	125	53	68	139	10
27. Unwrought Lead	125	85	82	169	10
Machinery and Equipment					
28. Super Heated Water Boilers	75	55	89	182	-15
29. Machine Tools: Peak Rated Items	110	110	100	205	2
30. Machine Tools: General Rate	75	80	103	211	-15
31. Machine Tools: Specified Milling Machines	35	60	119	243	-34
32. Machine Tools: Parts & Accessories	35	35	100	205	-34
33. Moulds and Dies for Plastic Articles	25	50	120	246	-39
34. Tower Cranes	75	55	89	182	-15
35. Self-Propelled Fork Lift Trucks	100	95	97	200	-2

	(1)	(2)	(3)	(4)	(5)
36. Domestic Refrigerators	150	110	84	172	22
37. Generators with Output over 750 Watts	75	55	89	182	-15
38. Transformers with above 1 KVA capacity	75	55	89	182	-15
39. DC Micromotors (upto 13.5 Volts and 20 Watts)	75	75	100	205	-15
40. Electrical Resistors	75	80	103	211	-15
41. Black and White Television Picture Tubes	75	80	103	211	-15
42. Radio Transmitters	140	95	81	167	17
43. Oscilloscopes	100	95	97	200	-2
44. Specified Medical Equipment	40	40	100	205	-32
45. Specified Machinery for the Leather Industry	35	35	100	205	-34
46. Specific Machinery for the Garment Industry	35	40	104	213	-34
47. Specified Food Processing Machinery	50	40	93	191	-27
Other Items					
48. Mechanical Wrist Watches	140	110	88	179	17
49. Parts of Mechanical Wrist Watches	50	70	113	232	-27
50. Project Imports	55	55	100	205	-24
Unweighted Average of 50 Items	86	70	93	190	-10

Notes: (*) Nominal Tariff Rates: Basic Duty plus Auxiliary Duty less the effect of applicable exemption notifications. Unless otherwise indicated end-use based exemption notifications are not taken into account.

(1) Tariff mark-up: 100 plus the (percentage) ad valorem tariff rate.

(2) Real landed cost of imports: Real effective exchange rate x Tariff mark up. Computations assume that all international (cif) prices of imports increase at a uniform rate equal to the rate of inflation in the import originating country: commodity to commodity relative price changes are ignored.

(3) Equivalent ad valorem rates for specific rated items are annual averages, or, where information was available for 1986-87, the lowest rates prevailing in that year.

(4) Naphtha: Raw naphtha imported for manufacture of petrochemicals and fertilisers.

(5) Due to non-availability of comparable cif prices for 1986-87, PVC duty in 1986-87 has been approximated as (Specific duty in 1986-87 x Ad Valorem rate 1988-89).

We have assumed that even by the end of our reference period imports and exports of agricultural products would be subject to restrictions as of now and such products would in general be allowed to be imported only when domestic supplies are felt to be insufficient. We are of the view that agricultural imports when permitted also should be subject to some "protective" import duty. However, in respect of cereals like wheat and rice, the duty free tariff may continue. Other essential agricultural goods such as oil seeds and pulses could be subjected to a duty rate of 10 per cent. Non-essential agricultural products like almonds and cashew nuts are now subject to a very high rate of duty. Duty rates on them should be brought down to 50 per cent.

The domestic prices of petroleum products are under the regime of administered prices. Since we have not considered the question of rationalisation of these prices, we have refrained from making any recommendations on excises and customs on petroleum products. Nevertheless we feel that with the opening up of the petroleum sector to private enterprise and given the wide ramification of any duties on a petroleum product, the customs duty on crude oil, etc., should be such as to fit into the broad structure of the tariff.

In the Interim Report, we had suggested that as and when the non-essential consumer goods (mainly durable consumer goods) are removed from the negative list, they should be subjected to an import duty of 50 per cent. Since these goods will in addition be subject to CVD, the total tax burden on them will be sufficiently high to discourage imports; at the same time the unlimited protection enjoyed by the domestic manufacturers of these goods will be brought under limit. Of course, to the extent that there has been considerable smuggling of many of these goods, the degree of protection has been under some restraint. With the imports of these goods coming in legally, smuggling will go down and government revenue would gain without any additional drain on foreign exchange.

It is difficult to predict what the pattern of imports would be with the much reduced level of duties on many items, which are now highly taxed. If there is no radical change in the pattern and if consumer goods are also allowed to be imported, the import-weighted average rate of duties would be around 25 per cent. This is on the assumption that all imports will be subject to at least a minimum rate of duty.

The structure of duties that we have recommended, while taking care of the needs of industrialisation of the country, is such as to make administration vastly easier than totay. With the reduction in the general level of rates, most of the notifications would become redundant and can be rescinded and the resultant reduction in the number of effective rates of import duty would all but eliminate classification disputes. Moreover, the abolition of end-use exemptions and concessional rates of duty for particularised items will ease the administrative burden and cut out delays and abuse of provisions.

Government should rigidly adhere to one basic principle, namely, while consumers should not be asked to bear undue burnden through unwarrantedly high protection to particular groups of producers, domestic producers should not be exposed to unfair competition in the name of not adding anything to the cost of "essential goods". Hence we recommend that even the so-called essential goods like inputs for fertilisers and newsprint should be subjected to a minimum rate of duty, say 5 per cent, so that domestic manufacturers would get some protection. Similarly, we have suggested levy of import duty of 20 per cent in 1997-98 on medical equipments (electronic and non-electronic) for protecting the domestic manufacturers and encouraging indigenous production of medical equipments. Incidentally, if our recommendation is implemented, much of paper work and delay would be eliminated along with the abuse of existing provisions regarding exemption of equipment acquired by hospitals obtaining the required certificates.

We are aware that the duty rates that we have recommended for some groups of commodities, for example, machinery, are higher than in several other developing as well as developed countries. We feel that low rates would not be appropriate within the medium term context that we have in view. Some of the cost disadvantages from which Indian industry suffers will be removed or scaled down when the import duties on inputs are reduced. However, disadvantages due to the inefficiencies present in the economy will remain. In some cases, scale economies have yet to be fully reaped, and in some other cases adequate time for re-structuring and adjustment must be given. The situation can be reviewed during the next decade. Meanwhile, Government should take urgent action designed to remove all of the important factors creating inefficiencies and leading to higher costs.

It will be difficult to reform the import tariff without hurting the domestic industries if the irrational excise duty regime is allowed to continue. We are of the view that it should be possible to implement the proposed restructuring of excise duties and extend Modvat fully over the period of the next three to four years without losing any revenue.

We would also emphasise the need for strengthening the administrative machinery for collection of indirect taxes on the lines suggested by us in the Final Report, Part I. Needless to say, the thorough reform of the system of domestic indirect taxes should figure high in the agenda of policies for minimising distortions and costs in the Indian economy.

Government of India, Ministry of Finance, Tax Reforms Committee Final Report (Part — II) chaired by Prof. Raja J. Chelliah, January, 1993. Extracts.

Table 12.1

Import Duty Structure Recommended for 1997-98

	Industry	*Import Duty (excluding CVD) (in per cent ad valorem)*
1.	Essential agricultural goods likewheat and rice	0
2.	Other agricultural goods like oilseeds and pulses	10
3.	Non-essential agricultural goods like almond and cashewnut	50
4.	Petrochemical building blocks*	15
5.	Organic and inorganic chemicals*	20
6.	Polymers*	25
7.	Textile fibres and yarn	25
8.	Iron and steel -	
	a. Pig iron	15
	b. Semi and finished steel including stainless steel and other alloy steel	20
9.	Copper	20
10.	Aluminium	15
11.	Nickel	15
12.	Lead and zinc	20
13.	Tin	15
14.	Wastes and scrap and concentrates of ferrous and non-ferrous metals	10
15.	Articles of iron and steel	30
16.	Articles of non-ferrous metals-	
	a. of copper, lead and zinc	30
	b. of aluminium, nickel and tin	25
17.	Machinery including machine tools	20**
18.	Electronics-	
	a. Raw materials	20
	b. Piece parts, components, sub-assembly and equipment	30
19.	Instruments	30
20.	Medical equipment	20

* Example of petrochemical building blocks are ethylene, propylene, butadiene, benzene, ethyl benzene and styrene. Organic chemicals will not include drugs in respect of which we are not making any recommendation but drug intermediates will be covered under this heading. Polymers include LDPE/LLDPE, HDPE, PP, PVC, PS, polyesters, synthetic and natural rubber and the whole range of plastics and synthetic resins.

** At present there is no CVD. We are suggesting 10 per cent CVD which is to be modvated over a period of four years.